# The United States and International Oil

# Robert B. Krueger

The Praeger Special Studies program—utilizing the most modern and efficient book production techniques and a selective worldwide distribution network—makes available to the academic, government, and business communities significant, timely research in U.S. and international economic, social, and political development.

# The United States and International Oil
## A Report for the Federal Energy Administration on U.S. Firms and Government Policy

**Praeger Publishers**   New York   Washington   London

PRAEGER SPECIAL STUDIES IN INTERNATIONAL ECONOMICS AND DEVELOPMENT

Library of Congress Cataloging in Publication Data

Krueger, Robert B
    The United States and international oil.

    (Praeger special studies in international economics
and development)
    Includes bibliographical references.
    1. Petroleum industry and Trade.  2.  Petroleum
industry and Trade—United States.  3.  Energy policy—
United States.  I.  United States.  Federal Energy
Administration.  II.  Title.
HD9566. K78        338. 2'7'282        75-906
ISBN 0-275-05300-8
ISBN 0-275-89340-5 pbk.

PRAEGER PUBLISHERS
111 Fourth Avenue, New York, N.Y. 10003, U.S.A.

Published in the United States of America in 1975
by Praeger Publishers, Inc.

Printed in the United States of America

# FOREWORD

This book was prepared as a report for the Federal Energy Administration under the title, An Evaluation of the Options of the U.S. Government in its Relationship to U.S. Firms in International Petroleum Affairs, under contract by my firm, Nossaman, Waters, Krueger, Marsh & Riordan.

The report, for which I was the Project Director, required extended research into the activities of U.S. and foreign firms in international petroleum affairs. In this respect we were assisted greatly by many U.S. and certain foreign oil companies both through thoughtful responses to the questionnaires which we distributed and interviews. We were also assisted in a similar respect by consumer and environmental associations and the public utility industry.

Our work has also required assistance from a number of Federal agencies and committees of the Congress. All have been helpful. I wish to note, however, the special assistance of the Senate Committee on Interior and Insular Affairs and the Committee on Foreign Relations. I also wish to thank the Department of State for its assistance in arranging foreign interviews and providing substantive assistance as well.

Many in our office assisted in this project; their names are set forth on the last page of this report. Of my firm's professional staff, Bruce G. Merritt, Paul R. Alanis, Thomas J. Weiss and Sarah Giffen were of primary assistance. Walter J. Mead, Professor of Economics of the University of California (Santa Barbara), contributed on certain economic aspects of the Study and was responsible for Appendix A and, largely, Appendix B. I am accountable for substantive content and final editing.

John K. Wilhelm and John E. Treat of the Federal Energy Administration Office of International Energy Affairs served, respectively, as Project Officer and Associate Project Officer for the Study. Their assistance was very important.

Lastly, I would be remiss if I did not point out the patience and devotion of my wife, Virginia, and my children, Lisa, Paula and Robert, during the many absences that this project required.

I gratefully acknowledge the contribution of all.


March 25, 1975
Los Angeles, California                    Robert B. Krueger


v

# TABLE OF CONTENTS

PART I

## INTRODUCTION

A.   [§0.0]   General

The United States, and indeed the free world, have
benefited enormously from the technology, scientific expertise and managerial skills of the U.S. petroleum companies,
both the large, multinational companies and the independents.
With relatively little governmental intervention, they were
the leaders in creating the present global supply system
which until recently operated in a highly efficient and
adaptable manner and historically responded very well to the
demands placed upon it.   In the process these companies
became and remain an important component of the U.S. presence
abroad.

Beginning in the late 1960's and continuing at an
accelerated rate in this decade, however, the bargaining
position of the companies in dealing with foreign governments eroded to the point where today they are virtually the
hostages of the producer countries who unilaterally determine price and supply policies and whose demands the companies are powerless to resist.   The issue, therefore, is
whether and how the presence of the United States Government
should be introduced into international activities of the
United States petroleum companies in order to ensure that
the national interests of this country are appropriately and
adequately protected.

The options available are many and include forms
of national regulation, international arrangements, and
combinations of them.   The issue is very difficult because
it is clear that implementation of a number of the options
could substantially impinge upon the efficiency of the
international logistical system which industry has so
creatively fashioned.   At the same time, the importance of
ensuring that foreign supply arrangements do not conflict
with identified national policy objectives cannot be minimized.

This Study was commissioned by the Federal Energy
Administration ("FEA") in order to provide information and
analyses to assist the political process in the evaluation
of options.   The Study attempts to identify the issues,

marshal relevant data which illuminate them, and objectively explore the consequences of the various options. The Study does not endorse any option. Great care has been taken to assure that all viewpoints were comprehensively and fairly examined.

Several insights have emerged as this Study has progressed. First, the international oil industry is enormously complex. It is a system that has served and continues to serve the modern world well. Care must be taken to assure that changes introduced into the system do not seriously impair its efficiency. On the other hand, it seems clear that controls should be established in the system at critical points so that at a minimum the United States Government has informational access and an ability to assert its presence if it should be deemed to be in the national interest. An appropriate method of regulation of supply arrangements which would permit a Federal agency to review and approve or disapprove those which could significantly impact upon the national interest deserves careful study, as does an expanded program of consumer country cooperation and the initiation of broad-based consumer-producer country discussions.

Second, a confrontation exists between producer and consumer countries in which the companies serve not as a "political buffer" but merely as linkage. The confrontation has resulted in massive trade imbalances and created a perilous fiscal condition for many consumer countries, developed as well as developing. The recycling of petro-dollars by means of virtually any form of loan among the consumer countries is only a temporary device which to some extent ameliorates an increasingly grievous situation. There is, therefore, a clearcut need to eliminate the confrontation and this will require broadscale discussions between the leading consumer and producer nations. Predictably the discussions will involve the relationships between petroleum, other resources, and goods and services. World petroleum is politics and the discussions will be political and difficult, but they must begin, begin soon and continue until a detente has been achieved in the present confrontation and order restored to world trade. Hopefully, from the discussions a set of norms can eventually be negotiated to guide producer-consumer country relationships. For the present it is clear that virtually every mutually acceptable

4.

change that is effected in the existing relationship between producer and consumer nations can only serve to improve it. Experience to date also clearly suggests that the issue of price levels is best raised indirectly and after progress has been made on other issues. It is also clear that a resolution to the Arab-Israeli dispute will be a prerequisite to successful producer-consumer discussions.

Third, there have been many misconceptions regarding international petroleum supplies and the energy situation generally which have been counterproductive in the evaluation and framing of rational responses to deal with the problem. The serious impact of our Middle East foreign policies on the petroleum supply issue is often underestimated or misunderstood. The Outer Continental Shelf sometimes has been made to appear to be simply a target of convenience for the oil companies rather than an indispensable source of primary energy. The massive impact that environmental and political restraints have had upon the development of energy sources, such as nuclear, has not been appropriately understood. The United States imports over six million barrels of oil per day. When the Trans-Alaska Pipeline comes onstream approximately 1.5 million barrels of new oil will be coming into the west coast, with an additional .5 million estimated by 1980. If the Trans-Alaska Pipeline had been onstream and if we had been assiduously developing available sources of energy in this country in the early part of this decade, the positive effects on producer-country negotiations before, during and following the energy crisis would have been inestimable. On the other hand, little attention has been paid to the positive aspects of the energy crisis in terms of social and political attitudes. It is unlikely that the American people who increased their consumption of petroleum and other nonrenewable resources over 50% from 1960 to 1970, while their population was growing approximately 15%, would have been willing to accept the changes in life-style, consumption and controls that will be necessary to bring about needed conservation had they not received the shock of the crisis and the basic education in resource management which followed. These events brought the reality of the finite limits of global resources into focus for many in the consuming nations of the world.

Too little illumination has been shed on any of these matters by the government or the media. It seems

still to be the belief of many Americans that the major oil
companies either caused or in some way conspired in bringing
about the energy crisis and the attendant higher prices.  It
is clear beyond any doubt that the companies benefited from
the higher prices that resulted from a very unstable market
condition, but it serves no purpose to perpetuate the myth
that they brought it about.  They did not and do not have
the power to cause such an event.  The producer countries
have that power and that fact forms a very basic element of
the issue which confronts us.  An informed public will make
the political task of selecting and implementing a particular
option much easier.  The Federal Government bears a burden
in this regard and hopefully this Study will contribute to
that end.

This Study has been particularly challenging
because it has explored options in light of changing and
anticipated world conditions.  The precedental impact that
the current petroleum situation has had upon other resources
and commodities is well known.  There is a commonality of
solutions as well as problems to many resource issues.  In
this respect the utility of this report may transcend its
relevance to international petroleum affairs.

B.    [§0.1]  Study Concept

The Study was based upon an investigation of the
historical, legal, political and economic aspects of the
existing international system of petroleum supply and the
probable effects of other options.

In order to elicit candid views from knowledgeable
observers both in the private and public sectors the Study
contractor conducted a large number of interviews.  The
Project Director and his associates conducted approximately
110 interviews with 217 people in the petroleum and public
utility industries, governmental agencies in the United
States and six foreign countries, and public interest groups.
In addition, extensive use was made of questionnaires which
were sent to foreign and domestic petroleum companies,
public utilities, public interest groups and governmental
agencies.  Forty-two responses were received from petroleum
companies, including six foreign companies, with an aggregate input of approximately 1100 pages.  Nineteen of the 20
largest U.S. petroleum companies responded.  In addition, 20
responses were received from U.S. public utility companies.

6.

All such information was collected and analyzed on a confidential basis. Economic assistance in certain aspects of the Study was provided by Walter J. Mead, Professor of Economics, University of California, Santa Barbara. The Nossaman firm and Dr. Mead also conducted research into existing literature on related aspects of the Study. Research assistance and advice were also generously provided by the staff of the Subcommittee on Multinational Corporations of the Senate Committee on Foreign Relations.

C.  [§0.2]  Summary

[§0.3]  Historical Perspective

In attempting to determine the role which the United States Government should play in the international system of petroleum supply and pricing one must be cautious in looking to history for the answer. In fact, the international petroleum industry has been radically altered since the beginning of this decade and traditional assumptions regarding the power of the multinational oil companies lose their meaning when considered in the context of an effective cartel of petroleum exporting countries. For roughly four decades, with amazing dexterity, the major multinational oil corporations manipulated production in an effort to sustain prices throughout a network of oil producing areas. These efforts became progressively less effective as competition asserted itself.

During this period the U.S. Government saw fit to interject itself into the international petroleum system in only a sporadic and sometimes inconsistent manner, and always on an ad hoc basis. In fact, the Government has never chosen to inform itself or develop its expertise to the point that it possessed the capability of responding to a situation such as that which developed in Libya in the early part of this decade. The blame for this cannot be laid solely on the shoulders of the Government; the companies have sought to perpetuate the independence and secrecy under which they have grown accustomed to performing their essential tasks.

At the very least the history of the last five years demonstrates that the Government must make every effort to fully inform itself and to develop the competence required to evaluate and cope with developments in international petroleum affairs, since the companies standing alone no longer serve as a viable instrument to effect national purposes. The Government cannot do this through the intermittent and inconsistent involvement which it has had in the past. A consistent and rational national energy policy can only be formulated if there is a foundation of accurate information underlying it and if there are reliable methods to implement it nationally and internationally.

Serious misconceptions abound in our society regarding the power and attitude of the major multinational petroleum companies. In fact, these companies have not willingly created the present situation, but with no bargaining leverage left, they have largely acquiesced to it. Accordingly, to attempt to rectify our present predicament by focusing solely on the companies and by taking action which only affects them is to deny existing realities. While constructive legislation to assure that the companies are responsive to the public interest of the people of the United States is desirable, it must be recognized that this alone will not solve the problems of the instability of our foreign supply of crude oil or reverse the sudden and enormous increases in the price of crude oil imposed by OPEC.

Critics of the industry argue that it has until recently been oligopolistic, controlled markets and rigged prices in international petroleum. In support they cite the Red Line and "As Is" Agreements and the Cartel case. The industry claims it has been competitive, citing the entry of Socal into the Persian Gulf and later the entry of the independents on a global scale with the resultant downward pressure on price that ultimately resulted in the formation of OPEC to control price.

Both are true to an extent. The American companies did not form an oligopoly. They came into one and thereafter were always maneuvering with one another for advantage in a not uncompetitive way. It must be observed that the pricing practices of the U.S. majors in international petroleum affairs had the positive aspect of being high enough to cause some conservation of a vital depleting resource and the generation of sufficient capital to develop necessary foreign infrastructure, but low enough to permit

the rapid development of industrial economies.  Their practices brought stability to a then very erratic market, both
domestically and abroad, and the American consumer was
provided with petroleum products at a relatively modest
cost.  In any event, regardless of past practices, it is
also clear that for more than a decade there has been effective
competition among the companies.

The competitive forces which brought a company
like Occidental into Libya, however, undercut the ability of
the established major petroleum companies to influence world
petroleum supplies and prices.  Because they forebode further
cuts in price, it encouraged producer governments to act in
unison to protect their common interests.

With the dramatic price increases imposed by OPEC
in the past eighteen months, it has become painfully clear
that if competition among companies for access to production
in OPEC countries is counterproductive, serious consideration
must be given to whether such competition should be permitted,
much less encouraged, by consumer governments.  Coordination
and cooperation among consumer governments and the many
petroleum companies operating internationally may be difficult,
but recent history seems to indicate that it is desirable.

The power of the major producer countries to date
has been enhanced by the hostage character of the companies
and proposals have been made in the United States that our
companies should be prohibited from having preferred access
to oil in these countries because it perpetuates that fact.
The present trend would indicate that producer countries in
order to effect their goals such as complete nationalization
and an arm's length character to all sales transactions, may
be paying very high economic costs.  If the trend continues,
the producers may accomplish that which the United States
individually cannot:  the elimination of the hostage position
of the oil companies.  The ensuing competition by producer
governments for crude oil contracts could, in the long run,
introduce a great deal of stress upon the cartel's price
structure and cause it to break.  In addition, transparency
in international petroleum transactions from both producer
and consumer nations' standpoints will give viability to the
needed deliberation between the two groups.  Such transparency
will also tend to result in a degree of self-regulation
within the petroleum industry.

[§0.4]  Policy Objectives of the Federal Government

Today, national energy policy can be described as
a set of governmental actions designed to be consistent and
comprehensive in dealing with difficult energy-related
issues that will permanently be with us.  Yet the word
"policy" is a metaphor for a reality whose true nature is
most elusive.  Although the word denotes a settled, definite
course of action, in fact policy only needs to be formulated
where problems and alternatives are so complex that a single
definite course of action is insufficient.

"Energy policy" derives from a variety of objectives including:

(1)  Establishment of an Adequate and Secure Supply
     of Petroleum;

(2)  Maintenance of a Reasonable and Predictable
     Price for Petroleum;

(3)  Maintenance of National Security;

(4)  Maintenance of Viable Foreign Relations;

(5)  Efficiency of Resource Utilization;

(6)  Protection of Environmental Quality;

(7)  Encouragement of Free and Effective Compe-
     tition;

(8)  Encouragement of Private Participation in
     Resource Development; and

(9)  Maximization of Revenue to the Federal Govern-
     ment.

Any policy objective, if pursued single-mindedly,
will conflict with others.  Moreover, changing circumstances bring changes in the means appropriate for
achieving basic policy objectives.  Circumstances relevant
to energy policy were changing rapidly in the early 1970's.
As a result, conflicts among certain of the above objectives became particularly acute and difficult to resolve
within the framework of an overall national energy policy.
Two such conflicts stand out:  first, that between the

10.

goals of adequate and secure supply on the one hand and
a reasonable and predictable price on the other; second,
that between the objective of an adequate, secure supply at
a reasonable price, and the maintenance or improvement of
environmental quality.

These and other conflicts sometimes appear to defy
resolution through the usual political processes of bargaining and compromise to achieve consensus. Even though many
Americans probably would agree as to the elements that constitute the nation's long-term well-being, it is exceedingly
difficult to find a "constituency" for any energy policy
aimed at promoting this objective. The enormous task of
creating and implementing such policy can only be accomplished through extraordinary leadership and political
judgment on the part of Congress and the President.

In the analysis which follows, the maintenance of
an adequate supply of petroleum at a reasonable price is the
primary objective against which each policy option is analyzed. Some consideration is also given to the impact of
these options on many of the other aforementioned objectives.

The recent history of international petroleum
clearly illustrates the need for the U.S. Government to
formulate new policies to cope with changed realities.
Those new policies must reflect both the new emphasis in our
national energy policy and priorities as well as the fundamental changes which have occurred in the international
industry and the producing countries.

Cooperation among consuming nations has already
resulted in the establishment of the International Energy
Agency in Paris. At present, intensive consultations within
IEA are registering daily progress in expanding the awareness of the participating governments. Tentative steps
towards IEA-industry consultations have already been initiated. Less specific, but potentially even more important,
OPEC and the United States have tentatively agreed to the
French proposal for a joint producer-consumer conference
during 1975. Future policies selected by the U.S. Government will inevitably take account of these important new
relationships.

Whatever policy options are selected, there are also certain realities about the international petroleum system which must be reflected in our policies. The establishment of the preeminence of OPEC as a determiner of price in the international petroleum market has radically altered the decision-making criteria for setting price. The highly diffuse and sophisticated incentive structure of the major companies gave them a vested interest in global economic growth and stability as well as the retention of a system which most countries found acceptable. This incentive structure has now been supplanted by the far more narrowly based national interest incentives of the producer countries.

The companies which were once oligopolistic sellers of petroleum and petroleum products are now in the position of competing buyers confronting a cartel. Competition among the companies tends to reinforce the upward tendency in price, particularly so long as OPEC is prepared to continue the curtailment of production.

It is very doubtful that there can be any significant downward market pressure exerted on price by consumer countries at least in the short to medium-term (up to several years). The spread between the cost of production, the price floor (perhaps $2 per barrel) toward which competition among producer countries would tend, and current prices ($11 per barrel) is so great that cooperation among the producers is clearly in the interest of all petroleum exporting countries. Producing countries could increase their aggregate revenue somewhat by cutting prices slightly and selling relatively larger quantities. If many producers did this, however, price would then fall much further. Therefore, as long as each producer can be relatively certain that no or very few members of the cartel are "cheating" by shaving the price, each is strongly motivated to follow the rules and be satisfied with a stable share of the market.

When that assurance is lacking, or if significant new production remains outside the cartel, the motivation is just the opposite: then each producer would have to compete in order to preserve its market share. Consumers would, however, in the foreseeable future find it far too costly in terms of lost employment and GNP to reduce demand sufficiently to break OPEC unity. Thus, assuming that the cartel remains stable, there would be downward pressure on price only if it

appears that a reduction in that price would elicit a more
than proportional increase in aggregate demand, so that a
price reduction would increase aggregate revenues for those
producers who could sufficiently expand production.  We have
not yet reached that point.

For the foreseeable future, long-term considerations
have little chance of influencing OPEC price decisions.
Almost all relevant considerations which would go into a
long-term calculation--the rate of successful exploration,
the export policies of new producers, the rate of development of alternative sources of energy, the impact of conservation in consumer countries--are speculative.  It is,
therefore, extremely unlikely that producers would lower
prices on the basis of such a calculation when revenues at
current levels, assuming they can be invested, are so great
as to swamp any long-term anticipations.

Clearly, the current status is such that the companies in the international petroleum industry are price
takers so long as they continue to compete with one another
for the product of a cartel--OPEC.  There is no cause for
optimism that OPEC will break up.  The fact that producer
governments have become sellers of oil strongly suggests
that governments of crude purchasers must influence the
transaction to protect the interests of the consumer.  At
the same time the companies fill vital roles which government is unequipped to supplant.

U.S. policy, in addition to meeting national
objectives and accommodating new international realities,
must also concern itself with preserving or salvaging the
strengths of the existing structure.  At a minimum, the
unique integrated logistical, technological and managerial
system of the U.S. oil companies constitutes an important
national asset.  Because it is a functioning system, it must
be approached as such, and not altered piecemeal.  Moreover,
recent events clearly indicate that we can no longer assume
that, come what may, the companies can take care of themselves.

In the context of these observations, it is possible to evaluate the range of options available to the U.S.

Government in its relationship with the industry as it pursues certain national objectives. Nine options have been selected for analysis.

1.  Removal or modification of Federally created incentives and disincentives to international petroleum production

Any appraisal of the overall net effect, or of the net effect of altering or abolishing any combination of the principal incentives and disincentives is necessarily highly subjective, in view of their complexity and the many political judgments involved in such appraisal.

The high current price of "new" oil is the dominant element changing the recent sum of incentives in favor of additional investment in U.S. oil production. Such investment is still significantly deterred, however, by two important factors: price controls on "old" oil and their uncertain future duration and scope and uncertainty about the permanence of the current high level of international oil prices. Eliminating both controls and tax incentives would probably result in a significantly increased incentive to invest in domestic production, even though uncertainty over international prices would remain.

The FEA price controls, however, have no direct effect on the profitability of investment in foreign production, since regulations exempt the first sale price for imports into U.S. commerce. Consequently, abolishing those controls would affect the attractiveness of foreign production only by making domestic investments more attractive to available capital.

Tax incentives for foreign operations have declined in importance recently, however, for two main reasons both related to the trend toward increasing nationalization. This trend has increased producer country control over the effective per barrel margin a company can reap from its operations. The size of this margin is the most important factor affecting investment abroad. Second, producing countries have increasingly become sellers of oil at wholesale to the companies and have been moving toward setting a

14.

single price for it.  If this is done, and if the price is denominated exclusively as a price rather than as royalty and income tax, the companies will have no choice but to treat the costs of crude as business expenses.  Under these circumstances tax considerations would cease being significant incentives to foreign oil operations.

One qualification is in order, however.  If per barrel margins in the future stabilize at a level where they are just barely profitable, tax incentives of U.S. law could be significant in tipping the balance for or against foreign investment.  Knowing this, producer country governments may plan their new price and tax structures to take maximum possible advantage of U.S. tax laws and interpretations thereof, in order to enhance the ability of the companies to profit from low margins.  To this extent, the future importance of U.S. tax incentives for foreign operations remains an open question.

In terms of the major U.S. objectives of affecting price and assuring security of supply, the modification of the incentive structure offers limited opportunities. Nevertheless, the current structure has two overall liabilities.

The first is that the current tax structure creates a strong identity of interest between the producer government and the company.  To the extent that it is desirable to weaken this identity, the removal of foreign tax credits resulting from the substitution of income taxes for royalties warrants consideration.  Second, the producer countries have almost total discretion in the determination of the price to be paid for their oil and the fee to be paid to the producing company.  To the extent that the costs of these companies are reduced by U.S. tax benefits, those benefits will tend to accrue to the producer country rather than the companies or the consumer.

If, however, the United States alone were to remove tax incentives, then U.S. firms would tend to be disadvantaged vis-a-vis other foreign competitors. There are two possible remedies for this.  The U.S. could seek through diplomatic means an adjustment in tax structures of the host governments of non-U.S. firms which negate this advantage and result in an accrual of revenues to their treasuries. This could be done either through a series of bilateral negotiaions, or perhaps also through the resulting established International Energy Agency. Second, if the U.S. should find itself unable to secure the cooperation of other consuming governments in equalizing the tax incidence on the companies, the same effect might be achieved by introducing the principle of reciprocity whereby the companies of those countries which did not equalize the tax incidence would not be allowed further access to U.S. resources.

## 2. Regulation of oil companies as public utilities

Comprehensive cost of service/rate-of-return regulation as is used for public utilities, if applied to the oil industry would entail heavy costs and be of very dubious benefit to consumers. Limited forms of price regulation or allocation could be useful to cope with special situations in which there exist possible monopolistic or oligopolistic behavior but where for some reason an antitrust remedy is not feasible or desirable.

The most important point regarding this option is, however, that it can have no positive impact upon the stability or price of international petroleum supplies and could have a number of negative impacts both domestically and abroad. It would establish public control over the oil companies but in a less creative and functional way than a number of other options. The option has little to recommend it.

## 3. Establishment of a national system to limit petroleum imports

Of the kinds of import limitation schemes discussed, the aggregate quantity ceiling would be the most effective means of meeting the oft-repeated goals of reducing imports by a certain number of daily barrels by a certain date. It is a somewhat deceptively high-cost option, however, in two ways. First, significant but unknown output and employment costs are immediately imposed on the nation by the reduction in petroleum supplies. Second, prices will rise to reflect the reduction in supply, but the extent of such price rise is difficult to determine in advance.  Thus, in terms of domestic economic impact, it is an imprecise tool.  To the extent that the price increase of domestic crude stimulated new production, domestic producers would benefit.  At the same time, importers would experience a windfall unless it were taxed away, or unless import allocations were auctioned.  If the domestic price effects should prove to be undesirable, other administrative measures would have to be devised to offset them.

The use of a per unit price ceiling to eliminate expensive imports from the U.S. may be feasible given certain conditions, namely: (1) a continuing significant rate of inflation; (2) a per unit ceiling no lower than present (or then-current) OPEC prices; and (3) the existence of a much larger strategic petroleum reserve stock than the U.S. now possesses.  Its main disadvantage is that it involves a potentially high risk of an interruption of oil to the U.S. It would be vulnerable to evasion, frustrate spot markets and be difficult to administer.

The tariff limitation, on the other hand, has the advantages of simplicity, flexibility, and reasonably predictable costs.  Moreover, because it employs the price mechanism, it retains consumer choice as the criterion for allocation.  It is pervasive in its impact and is consequently most efficient in causing the national energy infrastructure to be adjusted to meet the designated goals of reducing consumption and developing energy independence. If the tariff has a significant impact on consumer prices, it may require a companion program to mitigate those effects deemed undesirable.

Government market operations where the Federal authority is the exclusive importer for the U.S. market would be highly effective as a means of limiting imports. The creation of the necessary agency to competently carry out the desired import policies, however, would involve high initial expenses.  Moreover, any such agency created to implement a long-range import policy seemingly desirable today may become a liability if international market conditions change in the interim.  Most such policies, such as favoring certain import sources, could be effectively implemented more simply, such as by direct subsidies to existing importers or producer countries.

## 4. Regulation of all significant international supply arrangements

At a minimum it appears necessary for the U.S. Government to obtain information regarding international arrangements directly affecting U.S. petroleum supply from companies operating in the United States whether the U.S. or foreign. Functionally, it would seem that this disclosure system would also best encompass all international supply arrangements made or proposed to be made by these companies. It would also appear to be desirable to require disclosure of petroleum-related investments in the United States by foreign governments and corporations, wholly or partially government-owned, which may materially affect U.S. petroleum supply or other considerations of national interest, including national security and foreign relations. Finally, it may be desirable to have greater information regarding certain forms of foreign downstream investments.

There will be a clear need to narrow the quantity of information required to that which is the most relevant and material. There can be little question, however, that this informational base is necessary and desirable in the important area of evaluating and formulating U.S. policy and action in international petroleum affairs.

There is a risk that the disclosure requirements could serve as a springboard for the sort of broadly based administrative action by the reviewing agency which could effectively convert the process to a more cumbersome and time consuming form of regulation, as has been the case with the disclosure requirements of the Securities Act of 1933 and in a sense with the reporting requirements of NEPA. The potential regulatory character of a disclosure statute poses both the issue of how the legislation authorizing it can be limited to the disclosure function and whether practically it should be. If the present situation is one that realistically requires the involvement of the Federal Government, the question goes logically to the best form of that involvement. It serves little to either the President or the Congress to permit a system to grow by accretion through ad hoc administrative actions.

A much more serious question is presented by the review and approval concept of regulation. This system,

18.

unlike disclosure, has a potential for causing severe and immediate dislocations within the international supply system unless used with great care and sensitivity by the responsible agency.  The direct cost of creating an appropriate Executive Branch monitoring capability could be quite significant because of the sophistication that would be required in its personnel and the extensive nature of its regulatory functions.  The indirect costs of the system could be even greater in terms of the potential for disruption of the national and international economy.  If the energy supply to the United States and/or the rest of the world were materially impaired because of the unwise operation of the system, the economic consequences would be severe.

On the other hand, it is very true that events in global petroleum affairs have drastically changed the traditional system of supply, demand and distribution and that the oil companies today are relatively powerless in dealing with producer countries.  The basic question is whether the presence of the U.S. Government should be interjected, even if only indirectly, into international petroleum arrangements affecting U.S. national interests.  The question is a highly political one and this consideration is emphasized by the fact that under prevailing conditions the implementation of this option would have little direct impact on world petroleum prices, at least in the short term.  On the other hand, it does provide both a window and a potential lever for the Federal Government in international petroleum affairs which could prove to be of benefit.  If consumer nation cooperation is increased, if the world petroleum supply base is broadened, if consumer nations develop a strong program of conservation and utilization of alternate energy supplies and if safety net arrangements are established, this regulation by the U.S. and other important consumer governments could provide an instrument through which foreign supply arrangements could be made more responsive to the national interests of consumer countries.

The oil industry generally strongly and with some reason opposes this form of regulation in view of its potential for economic disruption.  The day of laissez faire arrangements in international petroleum affairs, however, has clearly passed and a new role for the U.S. Government is indicated.  This option, particularly in conjunction with selected other options, might establish U.S. Government control points in international petroleum transactions and restore public confidence that such arrangements are consistent with national policy objectives.

5. Creation of a petroleum corporation, fully or partially owned by the Federal Government, to engage in international activities

The option here examined is of establishing a Federal oil company to explore, produce and import oil in international petroleum arrangements. There is no basis for believing that the presence of such a Federal oil corporation would contribute to lower oil prices for consumers. It is also relevant that import controls could probably be handled by existing agencies and that ERDA has already been established to conduct research and development. The presence of a Federal oil corporation in international petroleum would not enhance the security of supply to the United States; it could, in fact, have a counterproductive effect in this regard.

If government corporations are less efficient than their private counterparts, the public corporation holds a profit umbrella over (a price floor under) private firms. There is some evidence that this is the case in France. If this is true, the "yardstick" becomes counterproductive in causing consumer prices to be higher than necessary.

Whether viewed economically, functionally or from the standpoint of the overall public interest, there appears to be no convincing basis under today's conditions upon which to recommend the creation or acquisition of a company of which the U.S. Government would be the whole or partial owner to participate in international petroleum transactions. Undeniably, the U.S. Government must have a greater role in international petroleum affairs than it has had in the past, but this option clearly appears to present an inefficient, and potentially counterproductive, method of asserting the U.S. presence.

6. Coordination of international supply arrangements through an industry-wide association of consumer country companies

This option is not a panacea for the problems of international petroleum supply and price. It does, however,

have the advantage of relative low cost and a basic compatability with other options examined.  If the U.S. companies cooperate, it could maximize their bargaining leverage
in negotiations with producer governments.  Whether or not
this option would, in fact, have any effect upon prices is
indeterminate.

In addition to whatever effect the association
might have, the role of the designated monitoring Federal
agency would give the U.S. Government a better understanding
of the role of the companies in international petroleum
affairs and of their ability and willingness to negotiate
terms consistent with the national interest.  Such knowledge
would, if profitably used by the Congress and the Executive,
provide a basis for future action to eliminate such inconsistencies as may exist between the interests of the companies
and of the United States.  Finally, this option would provide a vehicle by which consuming nations could cooperate to
maximize the market leverage which rigorous conservation and
alternative energy development will hopefully give them and
to do so in a commercial context with less risk of political
confrontation.

It cannot be ignored that this option would constitute a dramatic departure from the United States' traditional antitrust policies, but a greater appreciation of the
costs of such policies to the U.S. consumer is needed if we
are to be sure that our priorities in this vital industry
are correct.  Further, the value of this option, like that
of so many of the available options, depends upon viable and
effective cooperation among consumer nations.  Without the
requisite degree of control over other consumer nation
companies, an association of companies could be expected to
accomplish nothing.

7.  Bilateral arrangements between the United
    States and producer governments

There are three basic objectives which may be
sought by use of bilateral arrangements with producer
countries:  (1) greater security of supply, (2) development of "special relationships," and (3) improvement of
the consuming nations' balance of payments.

A review of past and current bilateral agreements indicates that they may not be any more secure than agreements entered into by private companies. While consumer governments may have a degree of economic and political leverage not possessed by the companies, recent history seems to demonstrate that producer governments have few qualms about unilaterally altering the terms of their agreements with them. Further, the terms of bilateral agreements used to secure a particular supply of petroleum are generally less advantageous than those customarily made by the companies, except in the instance in which a special or long-standing relationship enables the consumer government to obtain a preferential price.

Bilateral arrangements which establish "special relationships" between producer and consumer countries and which do not contain substantive provisions regarding supply, price or specified monetary considerations appear to achieve worthwhile purposes and should probably be encouraged. The working relationships which are sometimes created in this type of arrangement could be very useful in assisting in the elimination of the confrontation which today exists between producers and consumers.

8. <u>Establishment of an international organization to coordinate national petroleum policy with other importing countries</u>

Several policy areas have been discussed in which the IEA and related or similar international organizations may facilitate coordination of U.S. petroleum policy with other consumer nations.

Strong support for the IEA or any similar organization appears on balance to be a relatively low cost option with potentially high benefits. Such benefits are not of such a nature as to be readily quantifiable, but are qualitatively important. From the emergency oil sharing plan, the U.S. may derive security against a selective embargo at a cost of possibly foregoing a share of imported oil to other countries suffering a temporary interruption in supplies. Only in an extreme emergency would the U.S. actually be called upon to export part of its domestic oil production.

The coordinated demand reduction and economic stabilization measures reduce the danger of a breakdown of the international economic system. Their cost to the U.S. is conservation measures that probably would ultimately be undertaken unilaterally in any event, and of possibly having to make high-risk emergency loans to other nations.

The oil market information system of the IEA would help give the U.S. Government monitoring capability which it probably should acquire in any event, at a cost of a possible competitive disadvantage to U.S. companies should sensitive proprietary information become available to foreign companies. This risk to the U.S., however, is probably not proportionately greater than to other major countries such as Great Britain or West Germany.

Finally, the coordination of consumer nation policies in preparing for negotiations with the producer countries appears to have been facilitated by the work of the IEA without impairing the ability of the U.S. to reach agreement with non-member France on some important pre-conference issues, and arguably even making such agreement easier to achieve.

Perhaps the most important function of the IEA is to serve as a public barometer of U.S. commitment to international cooperation among consumer countries in these important areas. Whether the potential benefits of such international cooperation will accrue to all major consumer countries depends to a great extent on both actual and anticipated U.S. policy choices. While the U.S. cannot alone guarantee that an organization such as the IEA will be successful, by not supporting it, the U.S. can drastically reduce the incentive for other nations to support it and thereby virtually assure its failure.

9.  Establishment of multilateral negotiations
    between producing and consuming countries

Price is a very important issue to consumer nations but it cannot be made the focal point of producer-consumer discussions. There are numerous issues including, among others, access to supply, indexation, recycling of petrodollars, sanctity of contract and security of supply.

There are also issues which, while not involving petroleum directly, are of concern to producer nations. These issues involve, among others, the availability and prices of manufactured goods and food. The total mass of this web of interrelated issues is so enormous as to defy any single manageable resolution. The only approach which can expect to handle problems of this magnitude and complexity is a system which can accommodate the entirety of the issues but "chip off" pieces and find solutions to these in smaller manageable packages. In accomplishing this, the producer-consumer dialogue can reasonably be expected to continue for a number of "rounds," spanning many years.

The resolution of the differences between producers and consumers will probably never be fully accomplished. A changing world will continually create new problems and issues, particularly as we move toward the interrelationships between the various resources of the producer and consumer nations. For this reason the search for a continuing "process," rather than a "solution," offers far greater prospects for stable relationships. A mini-conference, such as that currently proposed by Sheikh Yamani and French President Giscard D'Estaing, may serve the important function of beginning the dialogue. The GATT-type procedural mechanism could follow and move on to the important second step of adjusting and resolving specific ongoing issues.

The critical problem which exists today is the highly visible and sensitive state of confrontation between producing and consuming nations. This atmosphere has resulted in the adoption of simplistic positions and impeded the achievement of any real progress toward accommodation of the varying interests. It has also precluded effective progress toward the resolution of the economic problems created by current high prices which threaten even the more affluent of consuming nations. In their efforts to recycle petrodollars and thereby assist the more hard-pressed of their number, consumers are only buying time.

24.

Achieving a solution is very difficult in light of the disunity among consumers and their relative lack of bargaining leverage, even if fully united. Nevertheless, it will be difficult to find a solution without the participation of producers, and accordingly a multilateral dialogue should commence. Since the major purpose of the conference would be to institutionalize a producer-consumer dialogue and to reduce visibility through piecemeal consideration of various interrelated issues, the GATT-type format appears to be a promising vehicle.

Although a producer-consumer dialogue will probably not deal directly with the role of the international petroleum companies, it will probably serve, in the words of one U.S. company, "to provide a stable environment," and to reduce "uncertainties about prices and supplies." At present, both producer and consumer governments are threatening the role of private oil companies in both upstream and downstream operations. To the extent that a producer-consumer dialogue can restore a more cooperative atmosphere, the valuable and efficient logistical structures of the companies can be retained. In the absence of a dialogue, a feeling of distrust may encourage precipitous action by both producer and consumer governments alike in a competitive scramble to seize control of the international petroleum system. Such a development would irrationally sacrifice the proven capabilities of the international oil companies to transport, refine and market petroleum efficiently. In this context, the producer-consumer dialogue would provide an "umbrella" which would preserve the strengths of the existing system.

Any decisions taken in producer-consumer discussions would inevitably require implementation with the assistance of U.S. companies. In fact, if the discussions deal with non-petroleum resources, as they probably will, a wide range of U.S. firms outside the petroleum field might be affected. Looked at broadly, ultimate producer-consumer cooperation should result in a resource management plan, the elements of which will touch on many facets of all nations.

[§0.6]  Conclusion

Developments of the past four years have radically transformed the international petroleum system.  In the past, our domestic petroleum market remained relatively insulated from international pressures; since 1970 foreign developments have come to dominate and profoundly affect the price and security of supplies of energy to the United States.  U.S. dependence on imports has risen sharply, while the security and cost of those imports have increasingly been subjected to unilateral manipulation by foreign producer governments.  The integration of the United States into the international energy market makes it essential that it develop for the first time a coherent and consistent international energy policy.  That in turn cannot be divorced from the need for a comprehensive domestic energy policy which encompasses  conservation and accelerated development of alternate energy sources.

Traditionally, the U.S. Government, with a number of rather isolated and ad hoc exceptions, has relied upon U.S. oil companies to independently establish the terms of international supply arrangements.  Until recently, this policy worked quite well.  It encouraged these companies to acquire resources throughout the world and obtain preeminence in international petroleum affairs.  Because of this policy, however, the U.S. Government developed little information or competence to monitor international petroleum transactions.  Thus, when the Arab oil embargo struck in 1973, there was no Federal agency capable of taking independent action to protect the national interest of the United States with respect to foreign supplies.  The performance of the large U.S. multinational firms during the embargo, moreover, emphasized that the United States cannot rely upon those companies to favor its interests to the detriment of other major consuming nations.  In large part, those companies are held hostage by the producer governments.

The issue thus is whether the U.S. Government should have a greater role in international petroleum affairs and, if so, what type of role. It is difficult to examine the issue without concluding that the existing incentives for the companies do not assure that their behavior will be consistent with the national interests of the United States. Accordingly, there appears to be a need for monitoring and for the establishment of a sufficient number of control points within the system to insure that the national interests are independently protected by the U.S. Government.

Any new role for the U.S. Government will probably draw on a variety of the options discussed in this Study. No single option could solve all of the international petroleum problems the nation faces today. Nor does any combination of these options offer a predictable solution. While this Study endorses no option, at the very least it would seem appropriate that the U.S. Government have access to relevant information regarding present and future significant international petroleum arrangements. It would also seem appropriate for the Federal Government to have the power to review and approve such transactions where they may affect significant aspects of the national interest.

Such massive power could admittedly be used in a fashion that would be detrimental to both the economic well-being of the U.S. companies and of the country. This factor makes it important that any act creating the authority be drawn so as to minimize the possibility of abuse and to carefully define the standards for administrative action. It is readily apparent that under the circumstances an entity with the stature and independence of the Federal Reserve Board, for example, would be necessary.

The establishment of such a scheme of regulation would, of course, be largely domestic in its operation, but its potential benefit could be substantially enhanced by a number of initiatives that are international in thrust. Key among these is the continuation and broadening of consumer-country cooperation under the International Energy Program and the undertaking of broadly based consumer-producer nation discussions. Both of these concepts appear to be established U.S. policy and the analysis made in this Study

27.

has focused largely on the ways in which these approaches
might be effected. The concept of bilateral supply arrangements is less promising, although it appears that agreements
of this type have developed "special relationships" which
may have utility.

Careful consideration should also be given to the
possible benefits of establishing the authority within the
Federal Government to enter into bilateral petroleum arrangements. Although it is questionable whether such authority
should be employed on a routine basis, it may be advantageous
to the national interest for it to exist. Finally, the
concept of establishing an industry-wide association of
companies from consumer countries to coordinate international supply arrangements deserves serious consideration.
The consumer countries and their companies are required to
deal with OPEC, a self-acknowledged cartel, and in the
international area it would seem to serve no purpose for the
U.S. to require the same competitive performance of the
companies that is expected domestically as long as the
interests of the American consumer are not prejudiced.

The potential utility of any or all of these
initiatives is, however, subject to a major qualification.
It is very unlikely that any effective progress can be made
in dealing with the major producer countries until the
ongoing Arab-Israeli dispute has been settled. That dispute
continues to color petroleum policy in the Middle East and,
therefore, the remainder of the world.

The Study has also examined a number of other
concepts such as the removal of Federal incentives and disincentives, the regulation of the companies as public
utilities, the establishment of a national system to limit
imports and the creation of a petroleum corporation fully or
partially owned by the Federal Government. In each case,
the Study focused on the impact of these systems upon international petroleum affairs. It is questionable whether any
of these options alone could have a positive effect upon the
level of world prices under existing conditions. The
public utility option would appear to present a potential
negative impact upon supply and the creation of a Federal
oil corporation presents few attractive features.

The Study has examined the changing realities of international petroleum. This is a period of stress for both the consumer nations and their companies. Hopefully, the United States will provide the leadership to create conditions under which U.S. companies can effectively carry out their essential mission as world suppliers of petroleum. Hopefully, too, in the process a pattern of cooperation rather than confrontation can be created between the producer and consumer nations of the world.

D.   [§0.7]  Glossary*

Barrel - Abbreviated bbl.  A liquid measure of oil, usually crude oil; equal to 42 American gallons, or between 280-380 lbs, depending upon API gravity, and equal to 35 Imperial (British) gallons.

Barrels Per Day - A customary unit of measurement of rates of output of oil fields, and throughput of pipelines, refineries and marketing facilities.  Reference ordinarily is to the average number of barrels per calendar day over a specified period, usually a year.  Abbreviated Bpd or B/D.

Business Review Letter - In the event a business believes that a contemplated foreign transaction could violate U.S. antitrust statutes, the business can apply to the Justice Department for approval in the form of a Business Review Letter.  This approval, however, is not final and a company can later be charged on civil grounds by the Justice Department.

Buy-Back - An agreement whereby the holder of an oil concession agrees to repurchase oil which, under the terms of a participation agreement, belongs to the producing country government.

Concession - An operating right to explore for and develop petroleum fields in consideration for a share of production in kind (equity oil).

---

* Adopted primarily from U.S. Senate Subcommittee on Multi-national Corporations, Hearings on Multinational Corporations and United States Foreign Policy, Part 4, January 30, 1974.

Crude - Oil in its natural state, before refining or processing.

Downstream - Oil is said to flow downstream from well head to gas pump. Refining and marketing are generally considered to be downstream activities.

Embargo - A prohibition against trading a product or many products with one or more countries. In 1973 Saudi Arabia embargoed oil shipments to the United States and the Netherlands.

Equity Oil - The portion of production which a concession owner has the legal and contractual right to retain. Taxes and royalties may be imposed, however, upon this share of the production by the producer government.

Field - An aggregate of overlapping, contiguous, or superimposed pools located on the same geological structure. All fields are not created equal; in the United States, for example, 200-odd fields out of 10,000 account for more than half of total reserves.

Foreign Tax Credit - Assume that, under the "posted price" system, a company calculates its earnings before taxes from its foreign operation as $100. Assume further that the foreign government imposes a 48% income tax on oil earnings. The company would then pay $48 to the foreign governments. The question then becomes how much tax will be paid to the U.S. There are a variety of ways in which the IRS might treat the $48 paid by the company to the foreign government. It could disregard it, imposing the U.S. rate of 48% on the full $100 of earnings. It could treat the foreign tax like it treats U.S. state income taxes and business expenses i.e., as a deduction. This would mean that the $48 of foreign tax would be deducted from the $100 of earnings leaving $52 of earnings after the deduction. Then the U.S. rate of 48% would be applied to the $52 - giving the U.S. about $25 in tax revenue and leaving the company with $27 of after tax earnings.

IRS takes neither of these routes. Instead it imposes a "shadow" U.S. tax on the $100 of pre-foreign government tax earnings. This yields a potential U.S. income tax of $48 (48% of 100). Then the foreign tax is subtracted from the $48 ($48-48=0). This leaves a balance of $0 of taxes for the U.S. and $52 of earnings for the company from its foreign operations.

30.

In actuality the income taxes paid to the Arab countries are about 55% of the posted price of oil. The excess (55%-48%=7%) of the tax over the U.S. "shadow tax" can be carried forward for five years from the date of the original tax year. The major oil companies have built up millions of dollars of excess tax credits.

Intangible Drilling and Development Costs ("IDC") - All expenditures made by an operator for wages, fuel, repairs, hauling, supplies,etc., incident to and necessary for the drilling of wells and the preparation of wells for the production of oil and gas. They include the cost to operators of any drilling or development work (excluding amounts payable only out of production or gross or net proceeds from production, if such amounts are depletable income to the recipient, and amounts properly allocable to cost of depreciable property) done for them by contractors under any form of contract, including turnkey amounts. . . . In general, this option applies only to expenditures for those drilling and developing items which in themselves do not have a salvage value. (Int. Rev. Code of 1954, §1.612-4)

Independents - In international oil, an independent is any company other than one of the international majors. Atlantic Richfield, Union, Getty and Amerada Hess, while very significant in international petroleum affairs would be called "independents." In the United States, an independent is usually one of the smaller nonintegrated companies involved in only one phase of the oil industry, such as, an exploration company, a local chain of gas stations or a fuel oil distributor.

Integrated Company - Oil companies which are involved in all of the steps in processing oil from its crude state to ultimate use, such as exploration, production, transportation, refining, distribution, and retail sales.

London Policy Group ("LPG") - An organization created in 1971 in order to negotiate jointly as an industry with OPEC regarding increases in producer-government "take." It was composed of representatives from approximately twenty-four petroleum companies operating in the Persian Gulf and Libya.

31.

Majors - In international oil circles, the majors are
the seven largest companies which control most of the free
world's oil:  Exxon, British Petroleum, Royal Dutch Shell,
Texaco, Gulf, Mobil, Standard of California.

Maximum Efficient Rate ("MER") - The producing rate
consistent with maximum recovery of reserves (about 1/15
of proven reserves per year in the case of domestic oil fields,
and 1/15 to 1/20 of proven reserves per year for domestic
natural gas).  The MER for any given field may, however, be
significantly greater or less than this approximation.
Production at a rate in excess of the MER for the field
concerned may result in such depressurization or other
reservoir drainage that very large amounts of crude become
unrecoverable.

Natural Gas - A naturally occurring mixture of hydrocarbons and varying quantities of nonhydrocarbons that exist
either in the gaseous phase or in solution with crude oil in
underground reservoirs; primarily methane and ethane.

Naval Petroleum Reserves - Since 1910 certain of the
public lands of the United States have been set aside from
those available for sale or lease for purposes of oil production.  Since 1928 these have been under the jurisdiction of
the Department of the Navy.

There are four Naval Petroleum Reserves:  Reserve
Number One is at Elk Hills, California and contains at
least 1.3 billion barrels of proved reserves.  It may hold
nearly 3 billion barrels of crude.  This reserve is in a
high state of readiness for production, and could begin to
produce at a rate of 250,000 barrels per day within 6-12
months.

Naval Petroleum Reserve Number Two is located at
Buena Vista Hills., California, just south of the Elk Hills
Reserve.  Because of the pattern of ownership in the area, it
is not feasible to keep this reserve shut-in, and it is
therefore presently producing at its maximum efficient rate.
The proven reserves of this area are about 50 million barrels.

Reserve Number Three is at Teapot Dome, Wyoming.
This reserve is shut in except for some minor drilling to
prevent seepage.  Reserves are estimated at 50 million barrels.

Naval Petroleum Reserve Number Four is on the
North Slope of Alaska, just west of the lands to be served
by the Alyeska pipeline.  Estimated recoverable reserves
in this area are 50 billion barrels of crude oil and 80
trillion cubic feet of natural gas.  This does not include
the offshore areas.

Offtake Price - The offtake price is the price that the
parent companies pay the joint producing venture for a barrel
of crude oil.

Offtaker - A parent company which receives petroleum
from a joint venture.

Oil - Crude petroleum oil and other hydrocarbons regardless of gravity which are produced at the wellhead in liquid
form and the liquid hydrocarbons known as distillate or
condensate recovered or extracted from gas, other than gas
produced in association with oil and commonly known as
casinghead gas.

OECD - Organization for Economic Cooperation and Development.  A Paris-based organization whose membership consists
of the major western industrialized nations and Japan.  The
OECD has a special committee for oil, whose purpose is to
coordinate the energy policies of its member nations.  This
committee has, thus far, been largely ineffective.

OPEC - Organization of Petroleum Exporting Countries.
Founded in 1960 to unify and coordinate petroleum policies
of the members.  The members and dates of membership are:
Abu Dhabi (1967); Algeria (1969); Ecuador (1973); Indonesia
(1962); Iran (1960); Iraq (1960); Kuwait (1960); Libya (1962);
Nigeria (1971); Qatar (1961); Saudi Arabia (1960); and
Venezuela (1960).  Gabon was admitted as an associate member
in 1973.  OPEC headquarters is in Vienna, Austria.

Participation - An agreement between a government and
a foreign-owned company for government purchase of part
ownership in the company operation.  An oil producing country
buys into, or participates in the oil company operation.

Petrochemical - Products synthetically manufactured
from petroleum feed stocks; e.g., plastics.

Petroleum - Here it is used to include oil, gas
and any other form of commercial hydrocarbon unless otherwise stated.

Posted Price - An arbitrary value placed on a barrel of
crude oil for the purpose of computing the amount of revenue
the company must pay to the country.  Posted prices may or
may not approximate the market price or market value of the
oil.

A computation of revenues and company costs of a
hypothetical posted price for a barrel of oil would be as
follows:

```
Posted price---------------------------------------- $4.00
       Minus: production cost------------------------   .50
       Minus: royalty (12-1/2 percent of $4)--------   .50

       Equals: tax reference price------------------  3.00

The Government would receive:
       Royalty (12 1/2 percent of $4)---------------   .50
       Plus: tax (50 percent of tax reference price
        of $3)-------------------------------------- 1.50

       Total revenue to Government------------- 2.00

The cost to the company would be:
       Production cost------------------------------   .50
       Plus: revenue to Government---------------- 2.00

       Total cost to company or the tax paid
        cost--------------------------------- 2.50
```

Production Cost - To arrive at the price oil sells for
in the market, we must begin with cost.  Cost includes the
investment required for development (to drill wells and install
gathering, processing and shipping facilities) and operation
(labor and maintenance).  Operating cost, as one would imagine,
is typically small in relation to development cost.  Some
prolific Middle East and North African fields, for example,
are said to operate at costs as low as one cent per barrel.

One of the most striking features of the petroleum industry is the existence of enormous cost differences among different regions of the world. Whereas the average oil well in the United States yields approximately 14 B/D at a cost of about $2.50 per barrel, it is estimated that the average well in the Persian Gulf yields well over 5,000 B/D at a cost as low as ten cents per barrel (including a 20 percent return on investment). In Venezuela, light crudes - which make up about 70% of total output - cost around thirty cents per barrel and heavy crudes around sixty cents per barrel, with an overall country cost average of about forty cents per barrel.

Recycling - Reintroduction of petroleum revenues in excess of a producing country's current account requirements into the financial systems of major consuming nations.

Secondary Recovery - Enhancing the production of oil left in a reservoir by conventional methods, including water or gas injection, water-flooding, heat, or nuclear.

Shut-In - To close valves on a well so that it stops producing; said of a well on which the valves are closed, but which can be put back in production by reopening the valves.

Spot Market - The market for either single purchases of crude oil or "spot" tanker charters. The rates in this market are not necessarily the same as those for long-term or medium-term agreements entered into contemporaneously.

Royalty - Owner's share of product or profit; oil companies pay royalties to governments for the right to explore, for the right to pump oil, or for the right to put the oil on the market. Royalty to producing governments has typically been calculated at 12-1/2% of posted price.

Tar Sands - Sand deposits that contain recoverable hydrocarbons. The most extensive known deposits are the Athabascan tar sands near Ft. McMurray, Alberta, Canada.

Tax Paid Cost - The amount the company has paid for oil at source: the cost of production plus royalties plus taxes.

Tax Rate - The rate of tax a country applies to the tax reference price or company profits for companies operating in its territory; also called the 50-50 split because the prevailing rate from the early 1950's until the 1970's was 50%. The common rate is now 60%.

Tertiary Recovery - The process of flooding an oil reservoir with chemicals to recover reserves remaining after secondary recovery.

Ton - (short ton, long ton, metric ton) - Short ton = 2,000 lbs. Long ton = 2,240 lbs. Metric ton = 2,204.62 lbs. A metric ton is the common foreign measure of quantity of petroleum. Because the common American measure is the barrel (a unit of volume not of weight), no single conversion factor applies to all crude oils: heavier crudes weigh more per barrel than light crudes. The normal range is 6.5 to 8.5 barrels per metric ton. At API gravity of 30, one long ton of crude equals 7.31 barrels. For convenience, a conversion factor of 7.3 barrels per metric ton is frequently used. At this rate, 1 million metric tons per year equals 20,000 barrels per day; or metric tons per year equals 50 X barrels per day.

Transfer Prices - A vertically integrated enterprise must, for tax and internal accounting purposes, set some price on raw materials and intermediate products which various of its affiliates sell to each other. These transfer prices need not bear any relation to cost or to external market forces. In many multinational corporations, therefore, they are set at levels chosen chiefly to reduce overall tax liability. The oil industry has been no exception to this rule.

Upstream - Refers to the production of crude oil, as distinguished from "downstream" operations such as refining and marketing.

PART II

U.S. POLICY PAST AND PRESENT

CHAPTER 1

SHORT HISTORY OF THE SYSTEM

A.    [§1.0]  Introduction

        The history of international petroleum demonstrates
that a free market has probably never prevailed with respect
to international petroleum supplies.  To the contrary, the
large international companies endeavored with diminishing
success to restrict competition and access to supplies and
to control production so as to maintain prices largely for
the same economic reasons that led to prorationing in this
country on grounds of conservation pursuant to the Interstate
Oil Compact. 1/  This is not to suggest that the conservation
which resulted from higher prices was in any respect improper, but rather to point out that it was initiated by the
companies to serve their own economic purposes, higher
profits.  Further it is clear that the United States had
little difficulty in supporting a basically noncompetitive
system abroad because it encouraged U.S. firms to control
substantial interests in foreign resources.

        It was not until the entry of the independents
into international petroleum that serious competition began
to develop among the companies.  It was this competition and
the surplus production that resulted from it during the
1950's and 1960's that made the implications of a free
market clear to the producer countries:  supply surpluses
caused by spirited competition will lead to declining prices
and producer-government revenues.  At this point, seeing the
potential inability of the major oil companies to maintain
prices, the economic logic of the Organization of Petroleum
Exporting Countries ("OPEC") became unassailable to the
producer countries.  From that point on, we have moved
inexorably to the present situation in which the producer
countries by political action protect and maintain the price
of their most valuable depleting asset, petroleum.

B.    [§1.1]  U.S. Entry Into Middle East

        In the early days of the petroleum industry, the
United States was the dominant producer and exporter.

From 1859, the first year of commercial production, through 1883 the United States accounted for over 80% of world production. In fact, with the exception of a few years when Russian production was greater, the United States continued to be the world's largest petroleum producer through the end of World War I. By the end of the War, however, the great demands on the country's petroleum resources caused by the war effort and the advent of the gasoline-powered automobile created fears of an oil shortage in the United States. 2/ In addition, British companies had so effectively tied up valuable concessions in Persia (Iran) and Mesopotamia (Iraq), that a London newspaper boasted:

> "Britain will soon be able to do to
> America what Standard Oil once did
> to the rest of the world--hold it
> up to ransom." 3/

In the early 1920's these concerns synthesized into active U.S. Government support for adherence by all countries to the "Open Door Policy," a policy originally formulated to secure privileges from 19th century China equal to those granted to European concessionaires.

In practice, the Open Door Policy was merely a convenient label for a policy which was essentially aimed at expanding American interests abroad. As described by Dr. George Otis Smith, then Director of the U.S. Geological Survey:

> "The 'open-door' policy is best for
> America and the world; encourage
> American capital to enter foreign
> fields and protect foreign capital
> wherever invested in our country.
> However, the spirit of reciprocity
> does not require that the United
> States shall always keep its own
> door of opportunity open to the
> nationals of all nations, irres-
> pective of their attitude to
> Americans in the other parts of
> the world." 4/

One of the first tests of the application of the Open Door Policy to foreign petroleum concessions came in

Iraq, when the Standard Oil Company of New Jersey ("Exxon") requested State Department assistance in purchasing a portion of the Iraqi concession held by the Turkish Petroleum Company (later Iraq Petroleum Company - "IPC"), a company whose shareholders included Anglo-Persian Oil Company (later British-Petroleum - "BP"), the Royal Dutch Shell Group ("Shell"), the largest French oil company, Compagnie Francaise des Petroles ("CFP", which acquired as a result of World War I reparations the interest held by the Deutsche Bank), and an individual, C. S. Gulbenkian.

The United States took the position that any territory acquired under the Versailles Treaty should be held in such a way as to guarantee equal treatment "in law and in fact to the commerce of all nations" and that U.S. companies were, therefore, entitled to share in IPC. In addition, as evidenced by a telegram from the Department of State to the U.S. Embassy in London dated September 20, 1922, there was strong sentiment that "this Government has contributed to the common victory, and has a right, therefore, to insist that American nationals shall not be excluded from a reasonable share in developing the resources of territories under the mandate." 5/

With the approval of the Department of State, Exxon, therefore, began direct negotiations with the IPC to purchase a share of the concession. The State Department indicated, however, that it would be inappropriate for the U.S. Government to lobby on behalf of a single company. Accordingly, a group of seven U.S. companies, including Gulf, Mobil, Texaco, Sinclair, Standard of Indiana and Atlantic, was assembled, all of which were represented by Exxon in the IPC negotiations. Texaco and Sinclair withdrew from the group as the negotiations with the IPC dragged on for many years. Finally, in 1928, the IPC shareholders acceded to as 23.75% American participation, but subject to very onerous conditions. The shareholders of the IPC had signed an agreement in 1914 stating that they would not compete against one another for future oil concessions within the area of the old Ottoman Empire. As a condition of entry into the IPC, therefore, the participating American companies were required to become signatories to a similar agreement, the 1928 Red Line Agreement. While inconsistent with the principle of the Open Door Policy and the U.S.

antitrust laws, the State Department consented to this
arrangement. 6/

C.    [§1.2]  U.S. Entry Into Indonesia

        Government support was probably more instrumental
in gaining access for U.S. companies to the oil reserves of
the Dutch East Indies (Indonesia) than in "opening the door"
to Iraq.  Prior to 1918, Shell controlled the only significant producing concession in Indonesia and attempts by U.S.
companies, notably Exxon, to develop new sources of production were frustrated by a local law which prohibited the
grant of additional concessions.  In 1918 the law was amended,
but U.S. companies were disappointed when the new concessions
were given only to Shell.  The U.S. Government expressed its
disapproval of this policy to the Dutch Government, but more
importantly, in 1920, the U.S. Congress passed the Mineral
Leasing Act which established the principle of reciprocity,
that is, leases on U.S. public lands would be denied to
companies of any nation which discriminated against U.S.
companies. 7/  Concerned that Shell would lose further access to production in the United States, the Dutch Government assured the United States that in the future leases in
Indonesia would be granted on a non-discriminatory basis.

        Shortly after making this assurance, however, the
Dutch Colonial Government offered a promising area in Southern
Sumatra to Shell without extending an opportunity to participate
to U.S. firms.  The U.S. Government in response denied Shell
leases on Federally owned lands in Utah, Wyoming and Oklahoma and informed the Dutch Government that Shell would only
be granted further leases in the United States if the
discriminatory policies in Indonesia were terminated.  As a
result, in 1928 the barriers to American entry were finally
broken when Exxon was officially awarded a concession in
Indonesia. 8/

D.    [§1.3]  U.S. Entry Into Latin America

        In addition to their entry into Iraq and Indonesia,
after World War I American companies were actively developing
Latin American petroleum resources.  Although production was
begun in Mexico before the War (72,000 barrels per day
were being extracted in 1914), the improved technology

and increased demand resulting from the War stimulated serious exploration interest in the country. By 1922, production had increased to 508,000 barrels per day, with the large majority of it controlled by American companies. 9/ The Mexican Constitution of 1917, however, signified a dramatic change in the relationship of the government to the companies, and led eventually to substantial reductions in the development of Mexican resources. Article 27 of the Constitution states that the direct ownership of certain resources is vested in the nation, such as "petroleum and all solid, liquid, and gaseous hydrocarbons." 10/

During the next twenty years, the companies argued with the Mexican Government over the interpretation of the constitutional provision, contending that it did not apply to previous grants. At times the companies enlisted the aid of the U.S. Government, which employed such tactics as "nonrecognition" in dealing with uncooperative Mexican administrations. In 1920, for instance, the United States broke off diplomatic relations and refused to recognize the tenure of President Obregon until he would give a pledge of security for foreign investments. As a result, the Mexican Government affirmed the mineral rights of certain U.S. landowners. 11/

The Mexican Petroleum Act of 1925, however, created another serious dispute which once again required the attention of the U.S. Government. Although it was settled favorably for the U.S. companies, the taxes being imposed by the Mexican Government were by this time so high and the security of ownership so uncertain that Mexican production continued to plummet sharply from its peak in 1921. Furthermore, petroleum had been discovered in more attractive areas such as Venezuela and Columbia, and capital was being transferred to these areas. Finally, in 1938, the Mexican Government expropriated the properties held by foreign petroleum companies, thus ending American involvement in Mexican petroleum development. 12/

Until the end of World War I, Shell dominated petroleum production in Venezuela. The early 1920's, however, witnessed the entrance of major U.S. companies, such as Exxon and Gulf. Prior to the arrival of the majors, a few U.S. independents, such as the Maracaibo Oil Exploration Company, had obtained large concession areas in Venezuela.

It was, therefore, largely through the purchase of properties held by these small companies that the U.S. majors
made their penetration.  As a result of the infusion of
capital and technology by the majors, Venezuela went from an
insignificant producer in 1922, to the leading exporter and
second leading producer (the United States remaining first)
in 1928. 13/  In addition, the percentage of American-owned
production in Venezuela increased from 31.5% in 1925 to
54.8% by 1929. 14/  Although there was occassional political
uncertainty for the U.S. companies operating in Venezuela,
in general, the investment climate was a favorable one
during this period.

E.    [§1.4]  Oversupply and Prorationing

The "oil scare" which developed after World War I
was quickly dispelled through significantly increased production in the United States, Venezuela, Iran, Iraq and the
Orient.  In 1920 world production was less than two million
barrels per day; by 1929 it had more than doubled.  In the
United States, daily production increased from 1.2 million
barrels to over 2.7 million barrels.  In fact, such concern
was now expressed regarding the problem of overproduction
that in December, 1924, President Coolidge created the
Federal Oil Conservation Board, to investigate and recommend
various methods of petroleum conservation. 15/  At the same
time, the domestic oil industry began to voluntarily proration production.

Nevertheless, by 1929, petroleum surpluses were
causing the industry such problems that the American Petroleum Institute created a committee to examine world production and make appropriate recommendations.  The committee
suggested that average production during 1929 should be held
to 1928 levels and "that so long as serious overproduction
exists in the world, a permanent organization within the
American Petroleum Institute should be formed for study of
the situation, not only in the United States, but throughout
the world." 16/  For the companies to agree to limit production in such a manner, however, would have raised serious
antitrust problems.  Accordingly, they sought the sanction
of the Federal Oil Conservation Board.  Such approval was
denied on the basis that "there were no constitutional
grounds upon which the Federal Government could impose such
a regulation on drilling . . .; the sole legal authority for

such action lies within the State governments themselves." 17/
With the burden thus placed on the individual oil producing
States, a cooperative agreement, the Interstate Oil Compact,
was eventually signed in 1935. 18/  It created a commission
charged with the responsibility of studying the demand for
domestic production, and determining how such demand could
be met without physical waste.  Individual State agencies
were left with the authority to actually proration production
within their respective jurisdictions.  The State prorating
laws which were enacted, together with the Interstate Oil
Compact and the Connally Hot Oil Act formed a rather comprehensive system within the United States, aimed at "conservation" and preventing wasteful practices, but also
clearly intended to maintain petroleum prices by preventing
production surpluses. 19/

F.   [§1.5]  Company Efforts to Restrict Supply

        The oversupply of petroleum during this period
created an additional problem for the major companies with
world markets (notably Exxon, BP and Shell):  how to maintain world petroleum prices and established market shares.
To this end, the "As Is" Agreement of 1928 was negotiated
pursuant to which the companies pledged to avoid overproduction and "destructive competition" in established markets. 20/
Therefore, although the antitrust laws made an agreement of
this type among domestic producers impossible, U.S. companies
continued their international activities largely unimpeded
by antitrust considerations.  Even with such agreements in
force, however, surpluses continued to develop (due in large
part to new discoveries such as the East Texas field) such
that the price of petroleum dropped from $1.30 per barrel in
1930 to $.24 per barrel in 1931. 21/

        By the beginning of the 1930's American companies
had made great headway in obtaining foreign petroleum concessions
in a number of countries, including Iraq, Indonesia, and
Venezuela.  The implications of the 1928 Red Line Agreement,
however, soon hampered the further Middle Eastern expansion
of the new American participants in the IPC.  Prior to
signing the Agreement, Gulf had acquired an option for a
concession on the island of Bahrain.  Since Bahrain was
within the domain of the old Ottoman Empire, the Agreement
required that Gulf offer the concession to the IPC.  When

45.

the British interests in the IPC, represented by BP and Shell (40% owned by British investors) balked at such a purchase and refused to allow Gulf to hold the concession alone, Gulf was left with no alternative but to sell the concession. Its sale brought a newcomer to the Middle East -- the Standard Oil Company of California ("Socal"). 22/ In 1932, Socal struck oil in Bahrain, thus exacerbating the oversupply of world petroleum already existing.

Therefore, when Socal sought to expand its interests by obtaining a concession in Saudi Arabia, IPC intervened to obtain the concession for itself in the interest of "keeping out all competitors." 23/ Because Socal was not a participant in the Red Line Agreement or the "As Is" Agreement its potential access to cheap and abundant Middle Eastern crude presented a threat to the established European and Far Eastern markets of Exxon, BP and Shell. IPC's geologists, however, were pessimitic regarding the potentials of the Saudi Arabian concession. As a result, IPC was outbid by Socal, to which the concession was ultimately granted in 1933. The State Department remained in the background throughout these negotiations. Later it was to claim that this non-intervention had actually benefited the Socal subsidiary formed to develop the Saudi Arabian concession, the California Arabian Standard Oil Company ("CASOC") 24/, as evidenced by the fact that in 1939, when extended concessions were negotiated, CASOC received them even though they offered less than government-controlled Japanese and German companies, "whose diplomats at Jidda were extremely pressing with their offers." 25/

G. [§1.6] Gulf's Entry Into Kuwait

Another example of the U.S. Government's invocation of the Open Door Policy occurred with respect to the acquisition of a one-half interest in the Kuwaiti concession by Gulf in the early 1930's. Unlike Bahrain, one of the desirable features of Kuwait was that it lay beyond the realm of the Red Line Agreement. After Gulf had begun negotiations, however, the British invoked a provision in a previous agreement with Kuwait which stipulated that no oil concession would be awarded without British approval. At that point, BP immediately dispatched a representative to Kuwait to negotiate for the concession. BP's chief interest, however, was in protecting its established markets rather than developing Kuwaiti resources. As the BP negotiator later acknowledged:

> "But we had to get the concession
> so as to protect our huge invest-
> ment in Persia. . . Kuwait is nearer
> markets and, if competitors found
> oil there, the Persian business
> would have been undercut and
> ruined." 26/

Stymied by the British, Gulf turned to the Department of
State for assistance, which again demanded that Britain
recognize the Open Door Policy.

Despite the efforts of the State Department, Gulf
remained stalemated with BP until the Kuwaiti ruler, Sheikh
Ahmad, rejected the bid of both companies in the hope of
creating bidding competition. The companies had just witnessed how petroleum surpluses and serious competition could
drastically reduce world petroleum prices and company profits.
Accordingly, BP and Gulf decided to compromise by splitting
the concession between them. In the process, BP assured
itself that Kuwaiti production would not be used competitively
against it in its existing markets by requiring Gulf to sign
an agreement, similar to the "As Is" Agreement. It provided
that Kuwaiti oil would not be distributed so as to injure
the marketing position of either company and that, at its
discretion, BP could supply Gulf's crude requirements from
production in Iran or Iraq in lieu of maintaining Kuwaiti
production. 27/

By 1934, therefore, most of the promising regions
of the Middle East had been carved up between predominantly
British and American interests and a complex web of interrelationships had been established. Concessions in Iran,
Iraq and Kuwait had all been divided to permit production
decisions that would hopefully prevent another glut of
petroleum on the market and consequent lower prices and
profits. Saudi Arabia remained the potential nemesis.

H.    [§1.7]  The Saudi Arabian Concession

Unhampered by agreements to restrict supply, Socal
possessed the potential to upset the delicately balanced
supply situation in the Middle East. Socal, however, lacked
the capital necessary to adequately develop its vast Saudi
Arabian concession and therefore needed a financial partner.

BP and Exxon were interested, but the Red Line Agreement
came back to haunt them when CFP, which owned 23.75% of IPC,
and Gulbenkian, who owned 5%, vetoed a scheme to amend the
Agreement to exclude Bahrain and Saudi Arabia.  Disagreement
among the IPC shareholders also prevented BP and Exxon from
negotiating with Socal to purchase its anticipated production from Saudi Arabia.  Its discussions with IPC being
unfruitful, in 1936 Socal sold a one-half interest in its
Saudi Arabian concession to Texaco in exchange for $3 million
in cash and $18 million in deferred obligations to be repaid
out of sales of crude oil.  Earlier in the year, Socal had
acquired a one-half interest in Texaco's marketing facilities
east of Suez in exchange for a one-half interest in the
Bahrain concession. 28/  Accordingly, Socal and Texaco were
well prepared to produce and market the Saudi Arabian oil
which they finally struck in 1937.

When the Second World War broke out, however, such
acute financial problems developed for King Ibn Saud that he
continually pressured CASOC to provide him with additional
revenues.  The interruption of transport and supplies resulting
from the War was reducing Saudi oil production.  In addition,
pilgrimages to Mecca were sharply curtailed, thus diminishing
the other major source of the King's revenue.  In an effort
to shore up the Saudi economy, the Company by 1941 had advanced the King approximately $6.8 million against future
royalties.  Asserting that it was unable to make additional
advances, the Company then sought U.S. Government aid for
Saudi Arabia, emphasizing that the King was strongly pro-
Ally, but that the financial stability of his country was
threatened.  It was determined, however, that such assistance
could not be made directly by the U.S. Government under
existing law. 29/ President Roosevelt therefore suggested
that the British advance to the Saudi Arabian Government a
portion of their $400 million Lend Lease Loan received from
the United States.  The British Government thereafter advanced
over $30 million to Saudi Arabia from 1941 through 1943.  Fearing
that the apparent largess of the British would greatly
expand their influence in Saudi Arabia, CASOC also advanced
to the Saudis approximately $5 million during the same
period.  In addition, CASOC began an extensive lobbying
effort to obtain direct U.S. financial aid for the country.
The company achieved success on February 18, 1943 when
President Roosevelt declared the defense of Saudi Arabia

vital to that of the United States, and Saudi Arabia thereby
became eligible to directly receive Lend Lease funds. 30/

    I.    [§1.8]  <u>The Petroleum Reserves Corporation and</u>
                      <u>Its Aftermath</u>

        It was now becoming increasingly apparent that
CASOC's position in Saudi Arabia was largely dependent upon
the diplomatic and financial assistance of the United States.
This condition soon engendered in some the belief that the
U.S. Government should directly take control of the Saudi
Arabian concession.  Foremost among the proponents of
such action was the Secretary of the Interior and Petroleum
Administrator for War, Harold Ickes.  At the same time,
there was mounting concern among various experts as well as
military and political leaders that the fuel requirements of
the War were causing our domestic reserves to fall to
seriously low levels.  This concern was manifested in a
draft letter from William C. Bullitt, Undersecretary of the
Navy, to President Roosevelt in June 1943.  Bullitt wrote
that:

> "The United States faces a shortage of
> crude petroleum.  Our current production
> of 3,900,000 barrels per day barely
> meets present requirements.  Increased
> demands for our armed forces and essen-
> tial industry during the remainder of
> 1943 and 1944 make it certain that
> before the end of 1944 we shall run
> short from 128,000 to 746,000 barrels a
> day." 31/

In that same month, Ickes wrote to President Roosevelt encouraging him to organize a "Petroleum Reserves Corporation" and
recommended that the "first order of business of the Corporation
should be the acquisition of a participating and managerial
interest in the crude oil concessions now held in Saudi Arabia." 32/

        Viewing the British threat to the security of the
American concession in Saudi Arabia as genuine, Ickes came
to the conclusion that the U.S. Government could compete
more effectively against the British Government than the
companies.  As Ickes wrote:

"In short, American private interests
have had to compete with the sovereign
interests of foreign companies, particularly Great Britain. Any realistic
appraisal of the problem of acquiring
foreign petroleum reserves for the benefit of the United States compels the
conclusion that American participation
must be of a sovereign character compatible with the strength of the competitive forces encountered in any such
undertaking." 33/

The State Department was opposed to this proposal,
believing it to be both unnecessary and unacceptable to King
Ibn Saud. Instead, it advocated acceptance of an offer from
CASOC, whereby the U.S. Government would be given an option
to buy significant quantities of petroleum in the ground in
Saudi Arabia at a discount from the market price. The
petroleum would remain underground, and available whenever
the Government requested. The State Department believed
that the concession would thus develop a semi-official
status which would "discourage jealous or unfriendly in-
trigues." 34/ After an extensive bureaucratic debate,
President Roosevelt concurred with Ickes, stating that the
acquisition of the Saudi concession was "the least ambiguous
and most effective way to increase the security of our
future oil supply." 35/

On June 30, 1943, the Petroleum Reserves Corporation
was officially organized within the structure of the Reconstruction Finance Corporation. When negotiations commenced
shortly thereafter, CASOC unequivocally rejected the proposal
that the United States purchase the entire concession. The
Government negotiators then sought agreement on the Government's acquisition of a controlling interest; this, however,
was also unacceptable to the CASOC partners. Ultimately, an
agreement appeared to be reached for the purchase of a one-
third interest, but when Texaco increased its asking price,
negotiations broke down and were terminated. Secretary
Ickes later remarked:

"They (Socal and Texaco) came up here to
the Hill and built a fire under us on

50.

the theory that this was an attempt on
the part of the Government to take over
a private-business enterprise, which of
course, was against the American tradition, as they put it, and perhaps it
was.  But this was more than a business
enterprise, this involved the defense and
safety of the country." 36/  [Emphasis
added]

     After failing to negotiate the purchase of the
Saudi Arabian concession, the Petroleum Reserves Corporation
considered another project which envisioned U.S. construction
of a pipeline from the Persian Gulf to the Eastern Medi-
terranean.  This proposal, however, encountered such bitter
attacks from the industry and certain members of Congress
that it was soon scrapped.  With this second failure, the
Petroleum Reserves Corporation faded into obscurity and was
eventually disbanded.

     Unable to directly interject itself into the
Middle Eastern petroleum industry, the U.S. Government then
turned to the concept of improving the access of American
companies to the petroleum resources of the Persian Gulf
states.  British interests so thoroughly dominated the area
that in 1943 they accounted for 81% of Middle Eastern oil
production compared to a mere 14% produced by U.S. companies.  The efforts of the U.S. Government culminated in
the draft Anglo-American Oil Agreement of 1944.  The Agreement was largely a statement of general principles but also
provided for the creation of an International Petroleum
Commission to oversee international petroleum affairs and
recommend methods by which supply and demand could be
correlated "so as to further the efficient and orderly
conduct of international petroleum trade."  Industry, however, opposed the Agreement and it subsequently was never
ratified by the Senate. 36a/

     The most significant consequence of this series of
unsuccessful forays into international petroleum affairs was
that the U.S. Government thereafter implicitly left the
function of control and supervision over the international
petroleum system to the multinational petroleum companies.

Unlike the British, French and Dutch, with their governmental interests in BP, CFP and Shell, respectively, the
U.S. Government now, for the most part, divorced itself from
the international petroleum industry.  These events signified
as well a virtual cessation of the Government's efforts to
obtain an information base independent of the companies,
which might help it to formulate petroleum policy and take
independent action.

J.    [§1.9]   The Birth of the Arabian American Oil Company
                ("Aramco")

        After the War, Exxon, together with Mobil, renewed
its efforts to purchase a portion of the Saudi Arabian
concession from CASOC.  It was still necessary, however, to
nullify the Red Line Agreement.  A legal technicality provided the answer when English counsel opined that CFP and
Gulbenkian had become "enemies" and therefore broken the
Agreement by virtue of remaining in France during the German
occupation.  The British Government acceded to this approach
when Exxon and Mobil agreed to purchase large quantities of
crude from BP's production in Iran or Kuwait over a twenty-
year period.  37/  The French, represented by CFP, and
Gulbenkian were irate since the Red Line Agreement had
worked to their benefit by tying their fate to that of their
more aggressive partners.  Years of diplomatic haggling
followed, with the State Department supporting the position
of the U.S. companies.  In 1947 Exxon and Mobil finally
negotiated an agreement with CASOC for a 30% and 10% interest, respectively, in the Saudi Arabian concession.  In
November of the following year all barriers to the merger of
these companies into a new company, Aramco, were removed
when an accord was reached ending the Red Line Agreement. 38/

K.    [§1.10]   The 1950 Foreign Tax Credit Decision

        Shortly thereafter, Aramco's position in Saudi
Arabia was threatened by the appearance of J. Paul Getty in
the Middle East.  For many years, Getty had sought a concession in this area, and when in 1949 he saw an opportunity
in the Neutral Zone, jointly controlled by Kuwait and Saudi
Arabia, he seized upon it.  His company, the Pacific Western
Oil Corporation, negotiated for a one-half interest in a
concession in this area and agreed to pay Saudi Arabia a
royalty of fifty-five cents per barrel, whereas Aramco was
paying only twenty-one cents a barrel. 38a/

King Ibn Saud's ministers immediately demanded more money from the Aramco shareholders. Turning to the U.S. Government for assistance, Aramco was advised that, as an alternative, it might relinquish the parts of its concession which it had not developed so that Saudi Arabia could then auction them for additional revenues. There was yet another alternative, however, which Aramco preferred. In 1943 Venezuela had proclaimed a 50% income tax on the difference between the cost and selling price of Venezuelan crude, and this tax had been declared creditable against the United States taxes which would be imposed upon these same revenues. This ruling was in accordance with the foreign tax credit provisions of the Internal Revenue Code which were enacted to avoid double taxation. If Saudi Arabia were to enact an income tax, then all or a portion of the amounts which Aramco was paying to the United States in taxes might be diverted instead into the Saudi Arabian treasury. The Treasury and State Departments were not opposed to this device, and in fact, a Treasury official advised the Saudis of the differing consequences between the imposition of an income tax and an increase in the royalty rate. Accordingly, in November of 1950, King Ibn Saud imposed a 20% income tax on Aramco, which by the end of the year, with Aramco's consent, was increased to 50% in accordance with the Venezuelan precedent. As a result, Aramco's payments to the Saudi Arabian Government increased from $56 million in 1950 to $110 million in 1951, whereas in the same period tax payments to the United States decreased from $50 million to $6 million. 38b/ The precedent was thus set for company acquiescence and accommodation to the continuing demands for higher revenues by the producer governments.

L.   [§1.11]   The Iranian Consortium

The 50-50 tax arrangement in Saudi Arabia was soon imitated by Iraq and Kuwait. In Iran, however, trouble between BP and the Iranian Government had been brewing for some time and the announcement of the 50-50 arrangement in Saudi Arabia simply intensified the dispute. In 1947, the Iranian Parliament had enacted a law which required that the terms of its concession with BP be renegotiated to provide the government with additional revenues. BP, with the active support of the British Government, however, remained intransigent to the Iranian demands, and sentiment for nationalization of BP began to build. Hostilities grew so

intense that in 1951 Premier Razmara was assassinated after
he informed the Iranian Parliament ("Majlis") that his
experts advised against the nationalization of BP.  The
radical Dr. Mohammed Mossadegh, who had led the opposition
against BP in the Majlis, succeeded Razmara.  A bill nation-
alizing the assets of BP was immediately presented to the
Majlis, passed unanimously, and signed by the Shah. 39/

The British considered the actions of the Iranians
to be a clear violation of international law, and accordingly, put the world on notice that they would take legal
action against any company which purchased and tried to
distribute oil produced from their former concession.  While
the U.S. Government was opposed to the use of force, it did
not oppose the British position and brought "influence to
bear in an effort to effect an early settlement of the oil
controversy between Iran and the United Kingdom, making
clear both our recognition of the rights of sovereign states
to control their natural resources and the importance we
attach to international contractual relationships." 40/
President Truman sent an emissary, Averell Harriman, to Iran
in an effort to effectuate a settlement.  Harriman's mission
failed, however, when Mossadegh announced that BP would have
to pay to Iran $140 million before negotiations regarding
BP's reentry could be commenced.

Virtually all international petroleum companies
took BP's warnings seriously and declined to purchase
Iranian oil.  Iran was thus faced with a virtual embargo on
its production, the effects of which impacted upon its
economy to such a degree that by 1953 a $23 million loan
from the United States was required to purchase necessary
food supplies. 41/

Within the U.S. Government concern was mounting
that the state of affairs in Iran would lead to increased
Soviet influence and possibly Soviet domination.  In 1952
the United States, therefore, devised a plan by which a consortium of the major U.S. petroleum companies and BP would
be used to get Iranian production onstream once again.
At the time, however, Exxon, Socal, Texaco, Mobil and Gulf
were under investigation by a Grand Jury for possible
criminal violations of the antitrust laws arising out of
their Middle Eastern operations. 42/  The U.S. Government

faced a dilemma -- it would now be asking these companies to engage in precisely the type of activity for which they were being investigated. Accordingly, the Departments of State, Defense and Interior prepared a report for the National Security Council which recommended that the criminal investigation be terminated, since its continuation "could impair not only the immediate position of the oil companies abroad, but also the broader interest of the United States as a whole." 43/ In the report, it was recognized that: "American oil operations are, for all practical purposes, instruments of our foreign policy toward these [oil producing] countries." 44/ Furthermore, the United States was continually trying to dispel the notion that capitalism is "synonymous with predatory exploitation" 45/ and the notoriety associated with a criminal indictment against the major oil companies ran directly counter to that objective. Accordingly, on January 12, 1953, President Truman instructed the Attorney General to discontinue the criminal investigation against the companies and to substitute a civil suit. By this decision, the President gave his imprimatur to the report's conclusions that the presence of the major U.S. petroleum companies in the Middle East was an important objective of American foreign policy and that national security considerations should be paramount in evaluating their conduct.

Although apprehensive at first that the consortium was merely a convenient scheme for the American companies to move into Iran, by 1954 BP was reconciled to the concept of a consortium in which they would have a 40% interest and receive compensation from their new partners (which included the five U.S. majors, CFP and a small group of U.S. independents). 46/ Moreover, with the assistance of the U.S. Central Intelligence Agency, the Shah had by this time deposed the radical Mossadegh. With the major obstacles removed, an August, 1954, Agreement was consummated with the Consortium. 47/

The Agreement seemed universally attractive. With the Soviets excluded and the access of U.S. independents to Iran's production limited to a token five percent participation, the major petroleum companies were better able to prevent a competitive increase in the supply of petroleum on the world market which would lower prices and profits. The British gained reentry into Iran and were compensated for the reduction in their interest to 40%. The United States

achieved a victory in the "Cold War." The Iranians benefited from a restoration of all oil revenues while retaining
ownership over their own resources. Under the Consortium
Agreement, the production was now owned by the National
Iranian Oil Company ("NIOC") which was to sell the oil to
the various trading companies established by the Consortium
members. In fact, an important precedent had been established since the Consortium received only the right to
purchase the production at a discount from market price
without enjoying an equity interest. 48/

        One of the only individuals unhappy with the
Consortium arrangement was Enrico Mattei, the head of Ente
Nazionale Idrocarburi ("ENI"), the Italian national oil
company. During Mossadegh's reign he had refused to deal in
the oil which Iran had "stolen" from BP and expected to be
rewarded for his loyalty. When he was not given a portion
of the Consortium, however, he retaliated. In 1957 he
negotiated a joint venture with the Egyptians and the
Iranians, under which the countries would share equally with
his exploring company. 49/ Along with the Consortium arrangement, Mattei's joint venture further undermined the
concessionary system.

M.    [§1.12]  The Impact of the Independents

        At this time, smaller "independent" companies were
greatly expanding their role in the international petroleum
system. "In 1953, twenty-eight American firms other than
the five largest companies possessed foreign exploration
rights. Ten had ventures in the Eastern Hemisphere and
twenty in Latin America." 50/ From the standpoint of entry
into new concessionary areas, therefore, after World War II
an increasingly competitive international petroleum system
developed. As demonstrated by the following table, by 1953
independents controlled a relatively small portion of
foreign production; by 1972, however, these companies had
substantially increased their market share in all facets of
the foreign petroleum industry. 51/

56.

|                                | 1953 | | 1972 | |
|--------------------------------|------|------|------|------|
| Division of the Industry | "Seven Largest" Companies Combined (Percent) | All Other Companies Combined (Percent) | "Seven Largest" Companies Combined (Percent) | All Other Companies Combined (Percent) |
| Concession Areas | 64 | 36 | 24 | 76 |
| Proven Reserves | 92 | 8 | 67 | 33 |
| Production | 87 | 13 | 71 | 29 |
| Refining Capacity | 73 | 27 | 49 | 51 |
| Tanker Capacity | 29 | 71 | 19 | 81 |
| Product Marketing | 72 | 28 | 54 | 46 |

52/

One of the clearest examples of the increasing
role of the independents in the international petroleum system was the development of Libya's petroleum resources.
When oil was discovered in Libya in the 1950's, instead of
granting concessions to a restricted group of major companies, as had been done in Saudi Arabia, Kuwait, Iran and
Iraq, Libya favored the independents, awarding seventeen
different companies a total of eighty-four concession areas.
Libya hoped thereby to stimulate the rapid development of
its petroleum resources.

With Iranian production onstream again, Libyan
production beginning to make its impact on European markets
and independents entering new concessionary areas throughout
the world, the intricate supply system of the international
majors began to falter.  The majors found it increasingly
difficult to satisfy the incessant demands of the Shah and
King Ibn Saud for increased production levels, without at

the same time flooding the market with excess petroleum that would force prices down significantly.

In Iraq, the partners in the IPC quite purposely and systematically curtailed known development and slowed production as a consequence of pressures in Iran and Saudi Arabia. 53/  But ultimately trouble developed for IPC. Angered by the British and French attack on Egypt in 1956, the landing of the U.S. Marines in Lebanon and long disturbed over the amount of revenues derived from IPC, a new revolutionary regime in Iraq under General Kassem threatened to nationalize the IPC concession.  In 1961 the Iraqi Government finally took over 99.5% of the concession area, permitting IPC to retain only its producing wells. 54/

Even with decreasing production in Iraq, however, the world petroleum surplus was so great that in 1959 Exxon felt compelled to lower the posted price for Saudi Arabian light crude by 18 cents per barrel.  An additional cut in the posted price occurred in 1960.  The posted price system had previously tended to insulate producer-government "take" from declines in market prices.  These actions, therefore, lowered producer government per barrel revenues and soon prompted a response. 54a/

N.    [§1.13]  The Creation of the Organization of Petroleum
                Exporting Countries

For many years, Venezuela had feared the competitive threat of Middle Eastern crudes.  Prior to World War II, petroleum exports from Venezuela continually surpassed those from the Middle East.  As the demand for petroleum accelerated, however, the major oil companies turned increasingly to the Middle East with its plentiful reserves and low production costs, and by 1950 its production surpassed Venezuelan for the first time.  When the posted price was reduced in 1959, therefore, the Venezuelans were understandably concerned that this would only accentuate the competitive advantage already enjoyed by their Middle Eastern competitors.  Accordingly, the Venezuelans began to advocate unified producer government action to protect their oil revenues and counteract the power of the multinational oil corporations to determine prices and output levels. 55/ When the first Arab Petroleum Congress met in Cairo in April, 1959, Dr. Juan Perez Alfonzo, the Venezuelan Minister

of Mines and Hydrocarbons, attended as an "observer" and
suggested that the various producer governments meet at
least annually to discuss their problems and seek mutually
beneficial solutions.  Realizing that Venezuela's proven
reserves were small compared to those in the Middle East,
Alfonzo also favored a system of regulating production and
thereby maintaining prices.  In effect, the Cairo discussions demonstrated to the producer countries that their
common interests and problems were strong enough to be the
basis for unified action. 56/

        Not surprisingly, therefore, when the posted price
was reduced again in August, 1960, the major producing
countries reacted by convening a September meeting in Baghdad,
out of which developed the Organization of Petroleum Exporting Countries ("OPEC").  The founding members, Venezuela,
Saudi Arabia, Kuwait, Iran and Iraq, collectively represented sixty-seven percent of the world's petroleum reserves, thirty-eight percent of its production and ninety
percent of the oil in international trade. 57/  With this
economic power, OPEC immediately demanded that the petroleum
companies operating in their countries restore former price
levels and agree to consult with the organization before
reducing prices again.

    O.    [§1.14]  Production Sharing in Indonesia

        At the same time as the founding of OPEC, the
status of the major petroleum companies in Indonesia also
began a process of change, which resulted in another precedent leading to complete control by producer government's
over their petroleum resources.  The three major companies
in Indonesia, Shell, Stanvac (a joint venture of Exxon and
Mobil) and Caltex (a joint venture of Socal and Texaco),
controlled virtually all of Indonesia's production.  Numerous
disputes were arising between the companies and the government
over the status of the companies' existing concessions,
marketing price controls and the failure of the government
to grant additional concessions.  This growing disenchantment
between the companies and the Indonesian Government crystalized
in 1960 when Law No. 44 was passed, proclaiming that the
foreign companies would henceforth be contractors instead of
concessionaires.  The companies regarded Law No. 44 with
serious concern, largely because of the possible impact this

might have on their more important concessions in the Middle East. 58/

When the companies refused to accept Law No. 44, negotiations commenced in an effort to reach a settlement. By 1963, the Indonesian Government had grown impatient and decreed that if an agreement were not reached soon the companies would be nationalized. At this point, the U.S. Government became involved since nationalization would result in a cutoff of foreign aid to Indonesia and thereby increase the potential of Communist influence over the country. 59/

A special team of U.S. Government negotiators was assembled, who succeeded in hammering out an agreement between the companies and the Indonesians whereby the companies would continue operating under "Contracts of Work." Under these agreements the companies assumed the new status of "contractors," while retaining management control. The "realized" price of the production was to be divided 60-40 between the Indonesian Government and the companies. 60/ This new arrangement represented, therefore, another gradual step in the changing relationship between the companies and the producer governments.

An even more important precedent, however, was set by Indonesia in 1966 when it established the concept of the "Production Sharing Contract." Under this arrangement, the production is shared between the exploring company and the Indonesian national oil company, Pertamina. When first suggested, the major companies in Indonesia, with the active support of the U.S. Government, vigorously opposed the idea since it would transfer ultimate managerial control to Pertamina and deprive them of the right to market the government's share of the production. 61/ A number of Japanese companies and American independents, however, readily entered into such contracts, thus undercutting the position of the majors. Ultimately, the major companies acceded to this arrangement which has actually resulted in a more stable relationship between the companies and the government. 62/

P.    [§1.15]  The 1960's

During the 1960's OPEC membership expanded and the
dependence of the consuming countries on OPEC oil increased.
The major petroleum companies continued their efforts to
appease the various producer governments with acceptable
growth rates in their respective production levels while at
the same time maintaining current prices.  In addition, the
Iranian Consortium and Aramco, in particular, had to reconcile the conflicting needs of the individual parent
companies.  Although the multinational petroleum companies
were generally able to cope with these problems, their
control over production and pricing decisions was increasingly jeopardized by the nationalistic aspirations of the
producer governments and the proliferation of additional
firms throughout the international petroleum system.  During
this period, the U.S. Government basically remained in the
background and did not attempt to influence or control
international supply arrangements.  In fact, the capacity of
the U.S. Government even to monitor, much less respond to,
changes in this important industry diminished significantly.
Whereas the Department of State had previously made an
effort to stay informed regarding major international petroleum
developments, even this far from comprehensive effort was
now impaired.

"During the 1960's, however, the
resources and expertise of the Department
in this area were subject to steady erosion.
In 1962, just two years after the formation
of OPEC, the office of Regional Petroleum
Officer for the Middle East was abolished.
Then, in January 1968, President Johnson
instructed the Director of the Budget to
help in correcting the U.S. unfavorable
balance of payments position by reducing
the number of American civilians abroad.
In response to this Presidential directive,
the position of petroleum attache in the
various producing countries was also
abolished." 63/

Q.    [§1.16]  Libya 1970:  The Beginning of the End

In 1969, an event occurred which would soon
radically alter the entire shape of the international petroleum system.  In Libya, the reign of King Idris was overthrown

61.

by Colonel Muamer Qaddafi, who immediately demanded that the companies operating in Libya make substantial increases in the posted price. Strongly nationalistic, the Qaddafi regime also successfully demanded that the United States and Great Britain remove their military bases from the country. 64/ When the Qaddafi's regime began negotiations with the companies, it cleverly narrowed them to discussions with two companies, Exxon and the Occidental Petroleum Company. Occidental, a small and relatively unknown company, had surprised many of its competitors when in 1966 it obtained some of the most promising concession areas put up for bid by Libya. By 1970, Occidental had become a large company due primarily to its Libyan output which accounted for practically all of its production outside the United States and the major portion of its revenues. Perceiving Occidental's vulnerability, the Libyans broke off negotiations with Exxon to concentrate solely on Occidental. In an effort to force the companies, and particularly Occidental, into acquiescence to their demands, the Libyans began imposing production cutbacks. Occidental's production was cut from 800,000 to 425,000 barrels per day, while total Libyan production cutbacks totalled approximately 800,000 daily barrels. Realizing that it could not hold out very long against such tactics, Occidental sought Exxon's assistance. Exxon refused, however, to provide Occidental with a "safety net" -- replacement oil in the event further cutbacks were imposed upon it. Seeing no viable alternative, Occidental agreed to a thirty cent increase in the posted price, an additional two cents each year over the succeeding five years, and an increase in the income tax rate from 50% to 58%. 65/ Most of the other independents in Libya now yielded and signed agreements roughly similar to that negotiated with Occidental. After the U.S. Government advised the companies that it could be of minimal help to them, the major companies operating in Libya agreed to similar increases in the income tax rate and posted price. 66/ Libya's success demonstrated to all producers that they could impose unilateral changes upon the companies without being challenged by consumer governments, particularly the United States.

Before the end of the year, most other producer governments had demanded and obtained a 55% tax rate. At the 1970 OPEC conference in Caracas, resolutions were adopted demanding a 55% tax rate for all member states and

establishing a pricing committee of Persian Gulf countries
("Gulf Committee").  The Gulf Committee than called for
immediate negotiations with the petroleum companies in
Teheran to "discuss" increases in government "take." 67/

The meeting at Caracas was a victory for the more
radical members of OPEC.

> "It was apparent from the support at
> Caracas by moderate OPEC states for
> extreme Libyan demands, that either
> those moderate states were deliberately
> setting up the companies and consumers
> for a flim-flam or else they were
> afraid of internal and external poli-
> tical pressures if they were seen to
> be less demanding than the revolu-
> tionary regimes.  In either event,
> the issue was too political for
> Western oil companies to handle
> without the full support of their
> home governments." 68/

The creation of the Gulf Committee, since it
excluded the more radical members of OPEC, such as Libya and
Venezuela, was the harbinger of continued price leapfrogging.
Any agreement negotiated by such Committee would surely
precipitate moves by the other OPEC members to exact even
greater concessions from the companies.  The leapfrogging,
however, resumed even prior to the commencement of negotiations with the Gulf Committee.  On January 3, 1971, the
company representatives in Libya were told that the government was prepared to exert severe economic pressures on the
companies to bring pressure on the U.S. Government to alter
its Middle East policies with respect to the Arab-Israeli
dispute. 69/  Specifically, Libya demanded that the companies invest internally twenty-five cents for each barrel
of oil exported, increase the posted price by six to nine
cents and submit to a new tax rate varying between 59% and
63%. 70/  These latest demands demonstrated to the companies
that their attempts to appease the Libyan Government by submitting to the 1970 price increases had been futile.  In
effect, the companies' former inability or unwillingness to
stand together was now working to their mutual detriment.

The companies then made the decision to present a common front and deal with OPEC as an entity. It was contemporaneously observed:

> "[T]he entire emphasis . . . was upon the need to have OPEC-wide discussions rather than individual country discussions. Producing company solidarity was seen to be entirely reasonable and the only effective response to firm producing country solidarity." 71/

The major companies also realized that the independent producers within Libya would insist upon some form of "insurance" before agreeing to join in the confrontation with OPEC. Therefore, unlike the 1970 price negotiations when Exxon rebuffed Occidental's requests for assistance, this time the companies reached an accord and signed the Libyan Producers Agreement, which guaranteed alternative sources of crude to any company whose production was cut by the Qaddafi regime. 72/ Significantly, Gulf agreed to share part of the burden resulting from a Libyan cutback even though it had no Libyan production.

The companies appreciated that their plan to negotiate jointly with OPEC, as well as the Libyan Producers Agreement, might pose serious problems under the U.S. antitrust laws. Accordingly, clearances were sought from the Department of Justice in the form of Business Review Letters. 73/ On January 13, 1971, the letters were issued to cover both the concept of joint negotiations with OPEC and the Libyan Producers Agreement. Thereafter, the companies delivered a joint message to OPEC:

> "We have concluded that we cannot further negotiate the development of claims by member countries of OPEC on any other basis than one which reaches a settlement simultaneously with all producing governments concerned. It is therefore our proposal that an all-embracing negotiation should be commenced between representatives of ourselves . . . on the one hand, and OPEC as

representing all its Member Countries
on the other hand, under which an overall and durable settlement could be
achieved." 74/

In addition, a London Policy Group ("LPG") composed of representatives from the petroleum companies participating in the joint message to OPEC, was organized.  The
purpose of the group was to assist in the selection of
members of the companies' negotiating team and to consider
and agree upon modifications on the "terms of reference" for
the negotiating team.  An additional group of company representatives was organized in New York, the purpose of which
was to review and comment upon policy decisions proposed in
London and provide additional technical expertise and information as needed. 75/

Unlike the 1970 price negotiations with Libya, the
U.S. Government now became involved in the confrontation
between the companies and OPEC.  The U.S. Government, however,
upset the companies' essential negotiating strategy in a
rather clumsy and uninformed effort to support it.  With
some form of confrontation inevitable, the companies were
understandably anxious to have the support of the United
States, and other consumer governments such as England,
France and the Netherlands.  It was therefore decided that
an emissary of the U.S. Government would be dispatched to
Iran, Saudi Arabia and Kuwait to accomplish the following
objectives:  prevent an imminent impasse in discussions
between the oil producing countries and oil companies from
resulting in an interruption of oil supplies; explain the
reasons why the U.S. Government had taken steps to make it
possible under our antitrust laws for the oil companies to
negotiate jointly, and seek assurances from the Gulf producers
to continue to supply oil at reasonable prices to the free
world. 76/

Upon contacting the Shah, the Department of State
envoy "made it clear that the U.S. Government was not in the
oil business and did not intend to become involved in the
details of producing countries' negotiations." 77/  Ultimately,
having been warned by the Shah that OPEC resented the condition of an OPEC-wide agreement, and assured that Persian
Gulf countries would adhere to an agreement negotiated with
the companies regardless of any more favorable terms negotiated elsewhere, the State Department advised the companies
that:  "they would be well advised to open negotiations with
the Gulf producers and conduct parallel negotiations with
Libya." 78/

With the Gulf Committee negotiations scheduled to begin almost immediately, the companies had to swiftly decide whether to accept the recommendation of the State Department and conduct "parallel negotiations," or maintain their original strategy without the full support of the U.S. Government. The companies were primarily concerned that the Gulf states would not live up to the assurances given to the U.S. State Department. After an initial meeting with the Gulf Committee, it became apparent that OPEC-wide negotiations were no longer feasible. Thereafter, the London Policy Group unanimously agreed to follow the recommendation of the State Department. 79/

The failure of the U.S. policy at this critical juncture reflected the State Department's lack of a comprehensive and coordinated approach to international petroleum issues. In fact, U.S. officials appear to have been preoccupied with more limited objectives, such as maintaining friendly ties with the Shah, assuring that both he and the Saudis had sufficient revenues to continue their roles in the Gulf, and maintaining a steady flow of petroleum from the Gulf. 80/ While it can be questioned whether informed and strong support of the companies by the U.S. Government would have changed the course of events, nevertheless, the course of conduct adopted by the U.S. Government appears to have contributed to the bargaining position of OPEC. 81/

R.    [§1.17]  Persian Gulf-Mediterranean "Leapfrogging"

The Gulf Committee negotiations culminated in the 1970 Teheran Agreement, which gave the Gulf producers, among other things, an immediate thirty cents per barrel increase in government "take." The following year an agreement was reached in Tripoli increasing Libyan revenues by approximately sixty-five cents per barrel. 82/

OPEC immediately renewed its demands upon the companies. This time, the producer governments sought subtle price increases through obtaining "effective participation" in the oil companies' assets and through adjustment of the currency exchange rates applicable to the payments made to producer governments. 83/ In January, 1972, an agreement was reached between the companies and OPEC whereby the official price of gold was fixed as the

standard for oil payments, and the posted price was increased by 8.49% to reflect the decline in the value of the
American dollar relative to gold prices.  Shortly thereafter
negotiations on "participation" began.  Before a settlement
had been reached, however, the Iraqi Government nationalized
the assets of IPC, thus adding an element of credence to the
demands of the producer governments.  In October, 1972, an
agreement was consummated with the Persian Gulf producers
providing them with an immediate 25% interest in their
production, to be followed by progressive increases reaching
51% participation in 1983.  In effect, the participation
agreement was merely a disguised price increase.  Pursuant
to its terms the companies were to have a preferential right
to purchase the government's share of production.  The
companies soon found, however, that the prices which they
would be expected to pay for this buy-back crude were much
higher than originally agreed. 84/

As before, Libya attempted to outdo the Persian
Gulf states by demanding a 50% participation in the assets
of one of the smaller and more vulnerable Libyan producers,
the Bunker-Hunt Oil Company.  When the company refused to
accede to the Libyan demands, in June, 1973, it was nationalized.
The currency parity and participation agreements failed to
solve anything; all Middle Eastern arrangements were in a
state of flux. 85/  The producer governments were incessantly
making greater and greater demands upon the companies and
threatening unilateral action.

Following the nationalization of Bunker-Hunt, the
Libyans demanded and obtained a 51% participation in the
assets of the independent companies operating in Libya, and
subsequently decreed similar terms for the major companies. 86/
Thereafter, the leapfrogging continued with Saudi Arabia and
Kuwait indicating to the companies that the 51% participation
obtained by Libya would not be sufficient to satisfy them. 87/

Before new terms could be negotiated, however, the
1973 Arab-Israeli War erupted.  After the United States
declared that it would supply Israel with military armaments
to replace its losses, the Arab petroleum producing countries
announced that they would cut their crude production by five
percent each month and embargo all shipments to the United
States and the Netherlands, until Israel returned to its

1967 borders and the rights of the Palestinian people were recognized. 88/ When Saudi Arabia announced an initial crude oil production cutback of ten percent, Aramco immediately cut its production by slightly more than the required amount, clearly demonstrating its responsiveness to the wishes of the Saudi Government. 89/

Although the Arab production cutbacks were eventually increased to 25%, the impact of the embargo was ameliorated by increased production in non-Arab countries and by the skillful and evenly balanced distribution of available supplies by the major petroleum companies. In fact, the companies were forced to comply with complex administrative procedures imposed by the Arab producers to enforce their embargo and were also required to make critical political decisions regarding the distribution of their scarce supplies, in view of the total absence of consumer nation guidance. 90/

The outbreak of Middle East hostilities gave an added impetus to OPEC demands for price increases. At the September 1973 meeting of OPEC, the companies offered to increase the posted price by 15%, from $3.00 to $3.45 per barrel. OPEC, on the other hand, indicated that it would be willing to accept a 100% increase in the posted price. Faced with this exorbitant demand, the companies asked for time in which to formulate their response. During this brief hiatus in the "negotiations," the companies consulted their home governments. Nearly all of the consumer governments consulted recommended that the companies hold out for moderate price increases. As a result, OPEC met in Kuwait and imposed a unilateral posted price increase of 70%, raising the posted price of Saudi Arabian light crude from $3.01 per barrel to $5.21 per barrel. All pretense of negotiations was abandoned in December, 1973, when OPEC decreed an additional 130% hike in posted prices, raising the posted price of Saudi Arabian light crude to $11.65 per barrel. 91/ Although there was no direct link between the Arab oil embargo and the price increases, the shortages of oil resulting from the embargo and production cutbacks had sharply escalated spot market prices and thereby encouraged and sustained the posted price increases.

Throughout 1974, posted prices remained stable but OPEC progressively increased effective prices and producer-government revenues by demands for participation, increasing

the price of participation crude by raising the percentage
of posted price demanded and by raising taxes and royalties
on the diminishing share of the companies' "equity" crude.
At the OPEC conference in Quito in June of 1974 royalty
rates were increased 2%; and at the OPEC conference in
Vienna in September, in order to "compensate for .inflation
in the industrialized countries," royalty and tax rates
levied on the companies were adjusted to increase total
producer-governments "take" by 3.5%. 92/  In addition,
during the first half of 1974, the Arab Gulf states negotiated for a 60% participation in the assets of all petroleum
companies operating within their domain. 93/  By December,
Aramco had consented in writing to 100% Saudi Arabian
participation, with only the specific details of such takeover
unresolved.  Accordingly, during 1974, OPEC took great
strides toward abolishing the concession system and reducing
the price advantage historically enjoyed by the major multinational oil companies.

In the fall of 1974, all of the major consuming
governments, except France, entered into an emergency sharing
agreement, to become operative in the event of another
embargo or shortfall in supply.  In addition, the United
States vowed to reduce its dependence on foreign petroleum
by two million barrels per day within the next three years.
The Project Independence report released by the Federal
Energy Administration indicated, however, that it would be
most difficult to obtain any substantial reduction in United
States dependence upon foreign petroleum before 1980. 94/  At
the present time, therefore, the multinational oil companies
continue to perform their traditional role of developing
petroleum resources and bringing them to market.  Control
over production and pricing, however, has been transferred
almost entirely into the hands of the OPEC countries.  The
consumer countries have thus been placed in the posture of
being forced to rely upon the fairness and rationality of
the OPEC powers.

S.    [§1.18]  Conclusions

In attempting to determine the role which the
United States Government should play in the international
system of petroleum supply and pricing one must be cautious
in looking to history for the answer.  In fact, the international petroleum industry has been radically altered since

the beginning of this decade and traditional assumptions
regarding the power of the multinational oil companies lose
their meaning when considered in the context of an effective
cartel of petroleum exporting countries. For roughly four
decades, with amazing dexterity, the major multinational oil
corporations manipulated production in an effort to sustain
prices throughout a network of oil producing areas. These
efforts became progressively less effective as competition
asserted itself.

During this period the U.S. Government saw fit to
interject itself into the international petroleum system in
only a sporadic and sometimes inconsistent manner, and
always on an ad hoc basis. In fact, the Government has
never chosen to inform itself or develop its expertise to
the point that it possessed the capability of responding to
a situation such as that which developed in Libya in the
early part of this decade. The blame for this cannot be
laid solely on the shoulders of the Government; the companies have sought to perpetuate the independence and
secrecy under which they have grown accustomed to performing
their essential tasks. It may be debatable whether the U.S.
Government could have improved the present petroleum situation had it kept more abreast of the changing relationship
between the industry and producer governments. At the same
time, it is difficult to imagine that had the Government
done this, the situation would be any worse than it is
today.

At the very least the history of the last five
years demonstrates that the Government must make every
effort to fully inform itself and to develop the competence
required to evaluate and cope with developments in international petroleum affairs, since the companies standing
alone no longer serve as a viable instrument to effect
national purposes. The Government cannot do this through
the intermittent and inconsistent involvement which it has
had in the past. A consistent and rational national energy
policy can only be formulated if there is a foundation of
accurate information underlying it and if there are reliable
methods to implement it nationally and internationally.

On the infrequent occasions when the U.S. Government has seriously involved itself in international petroleum affairs, limited short-term objectives have generally

taken precedence over assessments of America's longer range
interests.  In particular, a lack of confidence in the
Congressional foreign aid appropriations process has led
policy-makers to favor less conspicuous methods of extending
financial assistance to countries deemed important to our
foreign policy objectives.  Increasing the payments of U.S.
oil companies to producer governments through vehicles such
as the foreign tax credit has, therefore, appeared a seduc-
tive alternative to a more politically controversial direct
foreign assistance program.  In 1970, for example, Washington appears to have ignored the potential long-term costs of
capitulating to Iranian demands for separate negotiations in
a short-term effort to avoid a disruption in supply and
appease the Shah's desire for increased petroleum revenues.

        In retrospect, U.S. policy appears to have been
short-sighted in dealing with the problems of foreign petroleum supply and price.  Nonetheless, it should be recalled
that at the time these decisions were made, the price of
domestic oil far exceeded the cost of foreign production and
any cost increases in foreign crude were largely passed
through to foreign markets rather than U.S. consumers.
Import controls were deemed necessary to protect the domestic industry.  Moreover, in 1970 U.S. dependence on
imported petroleum, restrained by quotas, stood at 22%, a
modest increase from 1960 when the United States imported
18% of its petroleum requirements.  Accordingly, the rapid
acceleration in U.S. dependence upon foreign oil which
developed after 1970 (with the United States importing 35%
of its petroleum needs by the end of 1973), while predictable, was largely unanticipated by American policy-makers.  95/
Viewed in this light, the limited response of the U.S.
Government to international petroleum developments can be
more readily understood.

        Another impression left by this history is that
serious misconceptions abound in our society regarding the
power and attitude of the major multinational petroleum
companies.  In fact, these companies have not willingly
created the present situation, but with no bargaining leverage left, they have largely acquiesced to it.  Accordingly,
to attempt to rectify our present predicament by focusing
solely on the companies and by taking action which only affects them is to deny existing realities.  While constructive legislation to assure that the companies are responsive

to the public interest of the people of the United States is
desirable, it must be recognized that this alone will not
solve the problems of the instability of our foreign supply
of crude oil or reverse the sudden and enormous increases in
the price of crude oil imposed by OPEC.

A further historical observation can be made
regarding the effects of competition in the international
petroleum system. One of the fundamental assumptions of the
capitalistic system is that competition will minimize costs
of production and maximize the welfare of society. Looking
at the recent history of the international petroleum industry, however, one sees that competition in this area has
been at best a two-edged sword.

Critics of the industry argue that it has until
recently been oligopolistic, controlled markets and rigged
prices in international petroleum. In support they cite the
Red Line and "As Is" Agreement and the Cartel case. The
industry claims it has been competitive, citing the entry of
Socal into the Persian Gulf and later the entry of the
independents on a global scale with the resultant downward
pressure on price that ultimately resulted in the formation
of OPEC to control price.

Both are true to an extent. The American companies did not form an oligopoly. They came into one and
thereafter were always maneuvering with one another for
advantage in a not uncompetitive way. On the other hand,
the companies were able to contain supply expansion sufficiently to keep price substantially above cost of production
which is where competition would have placed it. The spread
between cost of production and the downstream sales price of
the majors was sufficient to allow the independents to pay
substantially more for oil to the producer upstream, cut
prices to the consumer downstream and still make a profit.
It must be observed that the pricing practices of the U.S.
majors in international petroleum affairs had the positive
aspect of being high enough to cause some conservation of a
vital depleting resource and to generate sufficient capital
to develop necessary foreign infrastructure, but low enough
to permit the rapid development of industrial economies. In
retrospect it is difficult to assess what pricing structure
might have obtained in the absence of control by the majors

72.

during the formative years of Middle Eastern development.
It is clear, however, that their practices brought stability
to a then very erratic market, both domestically and abroad,
and that the American consumer was provided with petroleum
products at a relatively modest cost.  In any event, regardless of past practices, it is also clear that for more than
a decade there has been effective competition among the
companies.

The competitive forces which brought a company
like Occidental into Libya, however, undercut the ability of
the established major petroleum companies to influence world
petroleum supplies and prices.  These competitive forces
forbode further cuts in price, and thereby encouraged
producer governments to act in unison to protect their
common interests.  The entry of the independents also showed
the various producer governments that others besides the
major multinational companies have the ability and skills to
produce and distribute their petroleum resources and are
willing to pay a much greater price for the opportunity of
doing so.

With the dramatic price increases imposed by OPEC
in the past eighteen months, it has become painfully clear
to all petroleum importing countries that any oligopolist's
profits generated by the major petroleum companies in the
past are miniscule compared to the enormous revenues now
being generated by an effective cartel of producing countries.
Accordingly, consumer nations must now seriously consider
whether competition among their companies for access to
crude serves a useful purpose if the predominant product of
such competition is to increase the bargaining leverage and
ability of OPEC to impose unilateral price increases.

This is not to say that competition among the
petroleum companies of the various consuming nations is the
sole, or even the major, reason why OPEC has been able unilaterally to increase petroleum prices four-fold.  To be
sure, the ever-growing dependence of consumer nations upon
OPEC petroleum is a major cause of our difficulties today.
Nevertheless, if competition for access to production in
OPEC countries is counterproductive from the viewpoint of
the ultimate consumer, serious consideration must be given

to whether such competition should be permitted, much less encouraged, by consumer governments. Coordination and cooperation among consumer governments and the many petroleum companies operating internationally may be difficult, but recent history seems to indicate that it is desirable.

Moreover, the emerging trend in OPEC toward a single price structure, 100% government participation and transparency in transactions could put the oil companies essentially in the position of purchasers of crude, in which case they would be both limited in terms of upstream profits and lose the tax advantages that they have enjoyed in the concession form of arrangement. By the same token the producer countries would clearly identify the huge amount of profit which they are receiving in international petroleum transactions. With due regard to the past ambiguities of international petroleum transactions, it has been difficult to determine in many cases exactly what profits the countries and companies have respectively made, giving rise to the common charge that the companies and the producer countries conspired to raise prices. Once these figures become transparent the oil companies will no longer be able to be portrayed as the only villains and world opinion may shift in its assessment of OPEC.

The power of the major producer countries to date has been enhanced by the hostage character of the companies and proposals have been made in the United States that our companies should be prohibited from having preferred access to oil in these countries because it perpetuates that fact. The present trend would indicate, however, that producer countries in order to effect their goals such as complete nationalization and an arm's length character to all sales transactions, may be paying very high economic costs. If the trend continues, the producers may accomplish that which the United States individually cannot: the elimination of the hostage position of the oil companies. The ensuing competition by producer governments for crude oil contracts could, in the long run, introduce a great deal of stress upon the cartel's price structure and cause it to break. In addition, transparency in international petroleum transactions from both producer and consumer nations' standpoints will give viability to the needed deliberation between the two groups. Such transparency will also tend to result in a degree of self-regulation within the petroleum industry.

CHAPTER 1

FOOTNOTES

1. See S. L. McDonald, Petroleum Conservation in the United States, An Economic Analysis (1971).

2. Hearings on S. Res. 36 Before the Special Committee Investigating Petroleum Resources, American Petroleum Interests in Foreign Countries, 79th Cong., 1st Sess., 298-299 (1945).

3. London Daily News, as quoted in L. Mosley, Power Play, Oil in the Middle East, 45 (1973).

4. Hearings on S. Res. 36, supra note 2, at 299.

5. Id. at 317.

6. H. M. Larson, E. H. Knowlton and C. S. Popple, History of Standard Oil Company (New Jersey), New Horizons, 1927-1950, 44 (1971).

7. Subcommittee on Multinational Corporations of the Senate Committee on Foreign Relations, Multinational Oil Corporations and U.S. Foreign Policy, 33-34 (Comm. Print Jan. 2, 1975).

8. A. Bartlett III, R. Barton, J. Bartlett, G. Fowler, Jr. and C. Hays, Pertamina, Indonesian National Oil, 49 (1972).

9. Hearings on S. Res. 36, supra note 2, at 335.

10. G. Barrows, Petroleum Legislation, Supplement 7, 52 (1973).

11. J. R. Powell, The Mexican Petroleum Industry, 1938-1950, 14 (1956).

12. W. C. Gordon, The Expropriation of Foreign-Owned Property in Mexico, 118 (1941).

13. E. Leuwen, Petroleum in Venezuela, 38 (1954).

14. Hearings on S. Res. 36, supra note 2, at 337.

15. Id. at 308.

16. Id. at 309.

17. Id. at 310.

18. S. L. McDonald, supra note 1, at 39.

19. For a more extensive discussion of the system of prorationing within the United States, see Appendix B, §B.10.

20. L. Mosley, Power Play, Oil in the Middle East, 50 (1973).

21. H. M. Larson, et. al., supra note 6, at 813.

22. S. Longrigg, Oil in the Middle East, 102 (2d ed. 1961).

23. H. St. J. B. Philby, Arabian Oil Ventures, 106 (1964).

24. The California Arabian Standard Oil Company ("CASOC") was the subsidiary to which Socal originally assigned its Saudi Arabian concession. In 1936, this company became jointly owned by Socal and Texaco. In 1947, when a merger with Exxon and Mobil was effected, a new corporation, the Arabian-American Oil Company ("Aramco") was created to operate the concession.

25. Hearings on S. Res. 36, supra note 2, at 319.

26. R. Hewins, The Golden Dream, as quoted in L. Mosley, supra note 20, at 80.

27. G. W. Stocking, Oil in the Middle East, 115 (1970).

28. N. H. Jacoby, Multinational Oil, 36 (1974).

29. L. Mosley, supra note 20, at 145.

30. Id. at 151.

31. Subcommittee on Multinational Corporations of the Senate Committee on Foreign Relations, A Documentary History of the Petroleum Reserves Corporation 1943-1944, 3 (Comm. Print May 1974).

32. Hearings Before the Special Senate Committee Investigating the National Defense Program, Petroleum Arrangements With Saudi Arabia, 80th Cong., 1st Sess., Part 41 at 25237 (1948).

33. Ibid.

34. H. Feis, Seen From E.A., 113 (1947).

35. Id. at 122.

36. Hearings Before the Special Senate Committee Investigating the National Defense Program, supra note 32, at 25240.

36a. Multinational Oil Corporations and U.S. Foreign Policy, supra note 7, at 41-43.

37. L. Mosley, supra note 20, at 167.

38. G. W. Stocking, supra note 27, at 106.

38a. L. Mosley, supra note 20, at 184.

38b. Id. at 195; Multinational Oil Corporations and U.S. Foreign Policy, supra note 7, at 85.

39. C. W. Hamilton, Americans and Oil in the Middle East, 48 (1962).

40. Multinational Oil Corporations and U.S. Foreign Policy, supra note 7, at 58.

41. L. Mosley, supra note 20, at 211.

42. Multinational Oil Corporations and U.S. Foreign Policy, supra note 7, at 61.

43. Departments of State, Defense, Interior and Justice National Security Council Report No. 138/1, National Security Problems Concerning Free World Petroleum Demands and Potential Supplies, 9 (1953).

44. Id. at 5.

45. Id. at 9.

46. L. P. Elwell-Sutton, *Persian Oil, A Study in Power Politics*, 324-325 (1955).

47. *Id*. at 326.

48. G. W. Stocking, *supra* note 27, at 159.

49. P. H. Frankel, *Mattei: Oil and Power Politics*, 116 (1966).

50. N. H. Jacoby, *supra* note 28, at 128.

51. *Id*. at 211.

52. For a rather detailed analysis of competition within the petroleum industry, see N. H. Jacoby, *Multinational Oil* (1974).

53. *Multinational Corporations and U.S. Foreign Policy*, *supra* note 7, at 309.

54. R. Rouhani, *History of OPEC*, 50 (1971).

54a. For an interesting chronological summary of events leading to the creation of OPEC, see *Venezuela and OPEC* (1961) at 87-93.

55. J. Lichtblau, "Arab Oil Weapon More Dangerous Now," *Petroleum Intelligence Weekly*, Oct. 21, 1974 at 8.

56. *Id*. at 76.

57. *Id*. at 77.

58. H. Bartlett III, *et. al*., *supra* note 8, at 186.

59. R. S. Knowles, *Indonesia Today, The Nation That Helps Itself*, 65-66 (1973).

60. *Id*. at 66.

61. H. Bartlett III, *et. al*., *supra* note 8, at 295.

62. In interviews conducted by the Study Contractor with affiliates of U.S. petroleum companies in Indonesia, strong and near unanimous approval was

expressed for the concept of "Production Sharing."
For a list of Production Sharing Contracts entered
into as of September 1, 1972, see Bartlett, et. al.,
supra note 8, at 382.

.63.  Multinational Oil Corporations and U.S. Foreign
      Policy, supra note 7, at 16.

64.   L. Mosley, supra note 20, at 353.

65.   H. Schuler, "The International Oil 'Debacle' Since
      1971," Special Supplement, Petroleum Intelligence
      Weekly, Apr. 22, 1974 at 3.

66.   Multinational Oil Corporations and U.S. Foreign
      Policy, supra note 7, at 125.

67.   Id, at 126.

68.   H. Schuler, supra note 65, at 5.

69.   Ibid.

70.   Ibid.

71.   Id. at 6.

72.   For an excellent description of the negotiations
      between independent and major oil companies leading
      to the Libyan Producer's Agreement, see H. Schuler,
      supra note 65.

73.   Hearings Before the Subcommittee on Multinational
      Corporations of the Senate Foreign Relations Com-
      mittee, supra note 53, pt. 5, at 14.

74.   H. Schuler, supra note 65, at 6.

75.   Multinational Oil Corporations and U.S. Foreign
      Policy, supra note 7, at 129.

76.   Hearings Before the Subcommittee on Multinational
      Corporations of the Senate Foreign Relations Com-
      mittee, supra note 53, pt. 5, at 147.

77.   Id. at 148.

78. H. Schuler, _supra_ note 65, at 9.

79. _Ibid_.

80. For a rather complete description of the U.S. State
    Department's role in the OPEC price negotiations,
    see Hearings Before the Subcommittee on Multi-
    national Corporations of the Senate Foreign Relations
    Committee, _supra_ note 53, pt. 5, at 145.

81. For somewhat differing views regarding the conse-
    quences of the U.S. Government's failure to insist
    on an OPEC-wide negotiation, see Hearings Before
    the Subcommittee on Multinational Corporations of
    the Senate Foreign Relations Committee, _supra_ note 53,
    pt. 5, at 122 (Testimony of H. Schuler) and pt. 5,
    at 221 (Testimony of G. T. Piercy).

82. Report of the Ad Hoc Committee on the Domestic and
    International Monetary Effect of Energy and Other
    Natural Resource Pricing of the Committee on Banking
    and Currency, Oil Imports and Energy Security:  An
    Analysis of the Current Situation and Future Pros-
    pects, 93d Cong., 2d Sess., 50 (Comm. Print Sept. 1974).

83. "Full Text of New Geneva Oil Agreement," Petroleum
    Intelligence Weekly, Jan. 31, 1972 at 5.

84. "Saudis Set and Get High Prices For Participation
    Oil," Petroleum Intelligence Weekly, May 14, 1973
    at 1; "OPEC Nations Act to Up Posted Prices and
    Buy-Back Terms," Petroleum Intelligence Weekly,
    Sept. 17, 1973 at 1.

85. See generally "New Geneva Deal Surpasses Oil Pact
    in Complexity Too," Petroleum Intelligence Weekly,
    June 11, 1973 at 1; "Iran's Sale Suggests the Sky's
    the Limit on Crude Oil Prices," Petroleum Intelli-
    gence Weekly, June 25, 1973 at 1.

86. Multinational Oil Corporations and U.S. Foreign
    Policy, _supra_ note 7, at 138.

87. _Id_. at 139.

88.  "Arab Producers to Cut Output By Minimum of 5 Percent Monthly Until Israel Withdraws From Occupied Lands," Middle East Economic Survey, Oct. 19, 1973 at 1.

89.  "Aramco Is A Lesson in the Management of Chaos," Fortune, Feb. 1974 at 58.

90.  Id. at 64.

91.  "OPEC Ready to Initiate Dialogue With Consuming Countries Following 130 Percent Increase in Gulf Posted Prices," Middle East Economic Survey, Dec. 28, 1973 at 1.

92.  "Full Text of OPEC's Quito Communique," Petroleum Intelligence Weekly, June 24, 1974 at 10; "Here's the Full Text of OPEC's Pricing Communique," Petroleum Intelligence Weekly, Sept. 23, 1974 at 6.

93.  "Kuwait's New Terms Offered to Qatar and Abu Dhabi," Petroleum Intelligence Weekly, Feb. 11, 1974 at 2; "Qatar's New Pact a 'Carbon Copy' of New Kuwait Deal," Petroleum Intelligence Weekly, Feb. 25, 1974 at 2; "Saudis Call Aramco For Early Talks on Kuwait's 60% Deal," Petroleum Intelligence Weekly, May 27, 1974 at 1; "Iran Also Signs Interim Pact Equal to 60% Participation," Petroleum Intelligence Weekly, June 17, 1974 at 1.

94.  Federal Energy Administration, Project Independence Report, 14-15 (Nov. 1974).

95.  Oil Import and Energy Security: An Analysis of the Current Situation and Future Prospects, supra note 82, at 30.

CHAPTER 2

POLICY OBJECTIVES OF THE FEDERAL GOVERNMENT

A.    [§2.0]  Specific Policy Goals

        While the U.S. Government has from time to time in
the past been concerned about particular issues relating to
petroleum and other energy sources, until the early 1970's
there was no consciousness of a need to develop a consistent
and comprehensive national policy regarding energy.  Not
surprisingly, energy policy was the child of the "energy
crisis."  One can speak of national energy policy before
that time only in a de facto sense, as the sum total of the
laws, regulations, ad hoc actions and deliberate inactions
of the Government which affected the flow of energy in our
society and economy.

        Today, national energy policy can be described as
a set of governmental actions designed to be consistent and
comprehensive in dealing with difficult energy-related
issues that will permanently be with us.  Yet the word
"policy" is a metaphor for a reality whose true nature is
most elusive.  Former Under-Secretary of the Interior J.
Cordell Moore made the following remarks in a 1966 speech in
which he attempted to explain the nature of United States
energy policies:

                "Few words so innocently incorporate
        into their basic meaning as much simpli-
        fying illusion as does the word policy.
        It means a settled, definite course of
        action, and yet by its very nature,
        policy only needs to be formulated when
        there are complex, uncertain alternatives
        so difficult to analyze and resolve that
        it is almost impossible to settle on a
        single, definite course.  The illusory
        qualities of the word have merit, however,
        for once the compromising, hedging judg-
        ments have been made, choosing, chances
        are, not one but several somewhat in-
        definite and conflicting courses, it is
        comforting to be able to describe them
        by a word implying such wisdom, certainty,
        and singleness of purpose." 1/

"Energy policy" derives from a variety of objectives or values. However, the most basic objectives or
values are also the broadest and most abstract (e.g.,
"national security" and "the maintenance of viable foreign
relations") and it is often difficult to relate these most
basic objectives to more limited, specific, and frequently
short-term objectives (e.g., lower prices for consumers).

With these caveats, it is possible to describe
the specific energy policy objectives of the Federal government. Not all of the energy policy objectives which the
Federal government pursues are equally important, nor do
all policy-making elements with the Federal government always agree on the priorities among such objectives. Nevertheless, there is general agreement that each of the policy
goals specified below ought to be seriously pursued by the
Federal government.

## [§2.1]  Development of a National Energy Policy

An important element of national energy policy is
the very commitment to developing it. This commitment was
reflected in President Nixon's Message on Energy of June 4,
1971. It proposed a number of steps to increase the supply
of clean energy in America, such as stepped-up research and
development, increasing energy supplies from Federal lands
and a new Federal organization to plan and manage energy
programs.

The Executive Order establishing the Federal
Energy Office ("FEO") on December 4, 1973, declared that
the Administrator of the FEO "shall advise the President
with respect to the establishment and integration of
domestic and foreign policies relating to the production,
conservation, use, control, distribution, and allocation
of energy and with respect to all other energy matters." 2/
On May 7, 1974, the President signed P.L. 93-275, the
Federal Energy Administration Act of 1974, which created
the Federal Energy Administration ("FEA"), successor to
the FEO. 3/  In Section 2(a) of this act, Congress declared:

>". . . the general welfare and the common
>defense and security require positive and
>effective action to conserve scarce energy
>supplies, to insure fair and efficient

distribution of, and the maintenance of
fair and reasonable consumer prices for,
such supplies, to promote the expansion
of readily usable energy sources, and
to assist in developing policies and
plans to meet the energy needs of the
Nation."

The FEA was created to "help achieve these objectives and
to assure a coordinated and effective approach to over-
coming energy shortages." 4/

Both the Presidential and Congressional commitment
to the development of a coordinated energy policy were again
demonstrated in October, 1974, when President Ford declared
his intention to create a new National Energy Board charged
with developing a "single national energy policy and program."
Shortly thereafter, President Ford signed into law the Energy
Reorganization Act of 1974 (P.L. 93-438, October 11, 1974),
which created an Energy Resources Council ("ERC") charged
with functions which, according to President Ford, "are
essentially the same as those I had intended to assign to
the National Energy Board." 5/  The Council, headed by Secretary of the Interior, Rogers Morton, includes the Secretaries
of State, Defense, Treasury, Commerce, Transportation, the
Attorney General, the heads of various other Federal agencies
and other Presidential designees.  The FEA Administrator
serves as the Executive Secretary to the ERC.  The same Act
established the Energy Research and Development Administration
("ERDA") to centralize and expand Federal research and development efforts, as well as the Nuclear Regulatory Commission.

Finally, in recent weeks, an even more explicit
and urgent commitment to the development of a national energy
policy has emerged.  On January 13, 1975, President Ford
proclaimed "we need, within 90 days, the strongest and most
far-reaching energy conservation program we have ever had."
Two days later, in his 1975 State of the Union message, the
President presented a comprehensive and detailed package of
energy proposals to the Congress, setting "national emergency
goals" and promising "energy independence."

[§2.2]  Establishment of an Adequate and Secure
        Supply of Petroleum

        Probably the most pervasive element of national
energy policy during the past 50 years has been the concern
for assuring the United States an adequate and secure supply
of petroleum.  U.S. Government policy-makers have always
given this element of energy policy the highest priority,
and continue to do so today.  Since World War I, the military and economic importance of petroleum has been such that
the Federal Government has always been concerned with acquiring and maintaining access to substantial oil reserves.
Immediately after World War I and again during World War II
fears that the United States was running out of oil impelled
Washington to encourage participation by American oil companies in the international competition for control of major
sources of petroleum outside of North America (See historical
section).  American participation in Indonesian exploration
after World War I, in Saudi Arabia and Kuwait in the 1930's
and 1940's, and in Iran during the 1950's was assisted by
the U.S. Government out of concern for future oil supplies
and the desire to prevent this production from being controlled by Britain, France or the Soviet Union.

        More recently, Federal policy-makers have repeat-
edly asserted that assuring adequate supply is the central
goal of U.S. energy policy.  In 1966, Interior Undersecretary
Moore, summing up the elements of U.S. energy policy, said
that the first element of that policy was:

            "To assure adequate and diverse
        supplies of energy--sufficient for con-
        tinued economic growth, dependable
        under emergency and non-emergency con-
        ditions, and diverse in both source
        and form." 6/

Indeed, in this emphasis all major consuming nations apparently
agree.  Moore's statement of policy was itself drawn from the
description by the Energy Committee of the Organization for
Economic Cooperation and Development ("OECD") of the energy
policies of all OECD member states. 7/

86.

President Nixon, on September 8, 1973, after conferences with various energy policy advisors, reiterated
the same theme:

> ". . . the programs that I have discussed
> here today, for the most part, as you know,
> deal with developing within the United
> States itself, the capability of provid-
> ing for our energy resources. We can
> develop those resources. It can be done
> within a matter of a very few years. I
> am not going to put a timetable on it,
> but it can be done. Because the United
> States, as a great industrial nation,
> the most advanced industrial nation of the
> world, must be in a position and must
> develop the capacity so that no other
> nation in the world that might, for some
> reason or another, take an unfriendly
> attitude toward the United States, has
> us frankly in a position where they can
> cut off our oil, or basically more impor-
> tant, cut off our energy." 8/

President Nixon even more explicitly alluded to the national
objective of self-sufficiency in a statement October 11,
1973, saying:

> "As I indicated in my Press Statement
> on September 8, our goal must be self-
> sufficiency--the capacity to meet our
> energy needs with our own resources.
> I intend to take every step necessary
> to achieve that goal. A great nation
> cannot be dependent upon other nations
> for resources essential to its own social
> and economic progress." 9/

In an address to the nation on the energy emergency, November 7, 1973, Nixon stressed the same theme and
introduced the term "Project Independence":

> "Our ability to meet our own energy
> needs is directly linked to our con-
> tinued ability to act decisively and

independently at home and abroad in the
service of peace, not only for America
but for all the nations of the world." 10/

He compared this effort to the Manhattan Project and said:
"Let us pledge that by 1980, under Project Independence,
we shall be able to meet America's energy needs from
America's own energy resources." In a message to Congress
on March 9, 1974, he once again declared: "We must, above
all else, act to increase our supplies of energy." 11/

Maintenance of an adequate and secure energy
supply is the cornerstone of "Project Independence." In the
pursuit of such supply security, however, the Project Independence Report observes that the United States need not
necessarily seek total self-sufficiency. A significant
reduction of imports could provide a sufficient degree of
energy independence, particularly if the sources of those
imports were unlikely to be interrupted for political
reasons.

In an address to the World Energy Conference in
Detroit on September 23, 1974, President Ford elaborated on
the concept of Project Independence, speaking of the "challenge of formulating Project Interdependence," which he
described as "a comprehensive energy program for the world,
to develop our resources not just for the benefit of a few,
but of all mankind." 12/ The shift in emphasis under the Ford
Administration indicated not a retreat from the primary
policy objective of assuring an adequate and secure supply
of energy, but a deepened appreciation of the fact that it
cannot be pursued to the exclusion of all other considerations. This attitude is reflected by active U.S. participation in the International Energy Agency ("IEA").

Even if achieved, U.S. energy self-sufficiency
would not solve all of the nation's energy-related problems
as long as high oil prices threaten the stability of the
world economy. Moreover, this policy embodied the recognition that energy self-sufficiency may not be desirable if
it inhibits the flow of international commerce, or raises
the price of energy in the U.S. substantially above that in
the rest of the world, thereby rendering many U.S. exports
less competitive.

In his 1975 State of the Union message, President Ford therefore recommended not immediate self-sufficiency, but "a plan to make us invulnerable to cutoffs of foreign oil." He set three policy goals:

> "--First, we must reduce oil imports by 1 million barrels per day by the end of this year and by 2 million barrels per day by the end of 1977.
> --Second, we must end vulnerability to economic disruption by foreign suppliers by 1985.
> --Third, we must develop our energy technology and resources so that the United States has the ability to supply a significant share of the energy needs of the free world by the end of this century."

The current Administration has thus made a firm commitment to achieving energy independence by 1985, planning to reduce petroleum imports to 3-5 million barrels per day and to establish a strategic storage capacity of 1.3 billion barrels.

[§2.3]  Maintenance of a Reasonable and Predictable Price for Petroleum

Before the energy crisis, Federal policy regarding petroleum prices was to try to keep a floor under domestic prices in a situation where cheap imported oil threatened the economic well-being of the domestic oil industry. This was one of the purposes of the oil import quota program which existed from 1959 to 1973. 13/

Currently, Federal policy is chiefly concerned with keeping foreign prices as low as possible, fearing that the existing price level will create an international financial credit crisis, or may lead to transfer of wealth to oil exporters great enough to affect seriously the national standard of living. 14/

Once the embargo had ended and concern for the supply of foreign oil abated somewhat, the price policy issue publicly came to the fore. At the World Energy Conference in Detroit, September 23, 1974, President Ford spoke of the "pulverizing impact of energy price increases on every aspect of the world economy," and made it plain that the U.S. sought to bring those prices down. 15/

Secretary of the Treasury Simon observed in a speech November 18, 1974: "Oil is now over-priced for one reason and one reason only: because a small group of countries have joined together to manipulate the price." 16/

On the same day as Ford's Detroit speech, Secretary of State Kissinger further described the Administration's views in an address to the U.N. General Assembly:

"Despite our best efforts to meet the oil producers' legitimate needs and to channel their resources into constructive uses, the world cannot sustain even the present level of prices, much less continuing increases. The prices of other commodities will inevitably rise in a never-ending inflationary spiral. Nobody will benefit. The oil producers will be forced to spend more for their own imports. Many nations will not be able to withstand the pace and the poorer could be overwhelmed. The complex, fragile structure of global economic cooperation required to sustain national economic growth stands in danger of being shattered." 17/

In the face of the market power of the OPEC cartel, however, it soon became apparent to U.S. officials that there was no practicable policy the U.S. could pursue which held promise of bringing about lower international oil prices in the near future. By the end of 1974, little was being said about bringing down international oil prices and the Administration appeared to have accepted the view that stability of oil prices at or near current levels was the best that could be hoped for in the next several years. In January, 1975, Secretary Kissinger in an interview said:

"The objective conditions depend upon a number of factors: One, a degree of consumer solidarity that makes the con- sumers less vulnerable to the threat of embargo and to the dangers of financial collapse. Second, a systematic effort at energy conservation of sufficient magnitude to impose difficult choices on the producing countries. Third, in- stitutions of financial solidarity so

that individual countries are not so
obsessed by their sense of impotence
that they are prepared to negotiate on
the producers' terms.  Fourth, and most
important, to bring in alternative
sources of energy as rapidly as possible
so that the combination of new discoveries
of oil, new oil-producing countries, and
new sources of energy create a supply
situation in which it will be increasingly
difficult for the cartel to operate.  We
think the beginning of this will occur
within two to three years. 18/

Thus, although there remains general agreement
within the Administration that international prices are "too
high," no policy is believed likely to bring them down in
the near term.  On the Congressional side, no generally
supported initiatives have yet emerged which would achieve
lower international prices.

U.S. consumers have been until now protected from
the full impact of higher international prices through price
controls on domestic production, as authorized under the
Emergency Petroleum Supply and Allocation Act of 1973. 19/
Currently, Federal policy is torn between the desire to keep
prices to the consumer as low as practicable and the need to
promote conservation and stimulate more domestic energy
production in order to reduce the very dependence on imports
which makes OPEC control of prices possible.

[§2.4]  Maintenance of National Security

National security has long been fundamental to
U.S. petroleum policy.  Although it is one of those basic,
abstract goals which energy policy is designed to serve,
national security, when reduced to specifics, has in the
past translated into maintaining adequate and secure energy
supplies for potential military needs.  This was the rationale
for establishing Naval Petroleum Reserves in Alaska and
California as long ago as 1912, and was one of the grounds
for the Mandatory Oil Import Program which existed from 1959
to 1973.  National security considerations were also important in the genesis of Project Independence.  Historically
then, as an energy policy objective national security has
been inseparable from the objective of assuring adequate and
secure supplies.

Recently, however, the awareness has grown that national security is a far more complex and abstract objective, which in large part consists of securing the economic well-being of society. As one Federal official has remarked, "Security and economic policy are, of course, the parents of energy policy." 20/

This broader view of the relationship between national security and petroleum policy was evident in hearings concerning strategic petroleum reserves held in mid-1973 before the Senate Committee on Interior and Insular Affairs. The Committee chairman, Senator Henry Jackson, observed that whereas strategic petroleum reserves were formerly of interest only to "a handful of economists, professors and military specialists," they have now become a matter of vital concern to the entire nation. 21/ Civilian as well as military requirements for petroleum are currently considered essential to our national security. Accordingly, Senator Jackson proposed a bill to create a petroleum reserve equal to a 90-day supply of imports to meet civilian as well as military needs. 22/ Presidential energy messages in 1973 and 1974 reveal a similarly broad view of national security requirements. For instance, on January 23, 1974 President Nixon called on Congress to authorize production from the Elk Hills Naval Petroleum Reserve in order to help achieve energy self-sufficiency, a call reiterated by President Ford a year later. 23/ President Ford has also explicitly emphasized the national security goals of energy policy:

> "Americans are no longer in full control
> of their own national destiny when that
> destiny depends on uncertain foreign
> fuel at high prices fixed by others.
> Higher energy costs compound both in-
> flation and recession. And dependence
> on others for future energy supplies is
> intolerable to our national security." 24/

[§2.5]  Maintenance of Viable Foreign Relations

Foreign policy considerations of a political rather than strictly military nature have often affected U.S. petroleum policies. In the early 1950's the U.S. Government was seriously concerned that Soviet influence might become dominant in Iran due to its faltering economy. Attempts to encourage the development of a strong,

friendly government in Iran took the form of encouraging
American oil companies to participate with British Petroleum
in an international consortium to exploit and market Iranian
oil reserves in a manner that would provide substantial
revenues for the Shah's government without creating an
international oil glut that would disrupt world markets and
hurt other producer governments. Since World War II, the
maintenance of anti-Communist regimes in the Middle East has
been a continuing goal of U.S. foreign policy, and has
frequently taken precedence over economic considerations.
In fact, aside from the Iranian Consortium, there were
elements of this policy objective in the 1950 foreign tax
credit decision, and the 1971 Teheran and Tripoli price
negotiations. 25/

Today there is a new emphasis on the foreign
relations aspect of energy policy. It now includes as an
objective the creation or maintenance of international
organizations or structures, such as the International
Energy Agency, within which the United States and other
consuming nations can coordinate their policies regarding
temporary and long-term plans for dealing with problems of
supply and price of energy. 26/ Such a framework will hopefully, from the viewpoint of U.S. policy, allow consuming
nations to develop a united front in the face of the demands
of producing nations and help create a situation where
producing and consuming countries can bargain with each
other to mutual advantage. As President Ford said, in
September 1974:

>"A cooperative spirit and conduct are
>essential to success in a global energy
>program. Nothing could be more harmful
>than policies directed against other
>nations. If we lapse into confrontation
>of exporters and consumers, or an un-
>seemly scramble of consumers being
>played off one against another, all
>hopes for a global solution will be
>destroyed." 27/

[§2.6]  Efficiency of Resource Utilization

Efficient resource utilization has taken on a new dimension in U.S. energy policy. Only with the onset of actual energy shortages (as distinguished from possible future shortages) was there any significant incentive to adopt a national policy designed in some measure to curb energy consumption or to seek an allocation of the nation's energy supplies consistent with the new price structure of energy. Concern in the past had been largely confined to avoiding waste in oil and gas production by means of state-level prorationing. Even that concern was very limited and soon became more of an instrument for supporting price than for conservation. Prorationing received Federal support in the form of the Connolly Hot Oil Act of 1935, 28/ but it was never adopted as a consistent national policy.

Congress declared in the Federal Energy Adminis-tration Act of 1974 that the general welfare and common defense now require, among other things, "positive and effective action to conserve scarce energy supplies" and "to insure fair and efficient distribution" of such supplies. 29/ The beginnings of a system of end-use controls for petroleum and gas products emerged from the allocation authority given to the President under the Emergency Petroleum Allocation Act of 1973. 30/ This Act authorized and directed the President to deal with the shortages of oil products so as to minimize the "adverse impacts of such shortages or dis-locations on the American people and the domestic economy." 31/ This authority, subsequently delegated to the FEA, was used to impose production quotas for various products on refiners, to order sales to various priority customers, and to specify prices for such products.

The Federal Power Commission ("FPC") has reacted to growing natural gas shortages with adoption of an indirect form of end use controls, and has sought to exercise its powers in such a way as to favor residential and small business use of natural gas and to discourage large-scale industrial use of it. 32/

The Project Independence Report envisioned a mandatory energy conservation program which would require new cars to get 20 miles per gallon of gasoline, provide tax credits for improved insulation of new construction,

94.

create national lighting and thermal standards, and require
all new construction to be heated and cooled by electricity
in order to promote the substitution of coal for oil and
gas by utilities and large industrial users. 33/ It should
also be noted that the Ford Foundation Energy Policy Project
emphasized demand growth restraints in its policy recommendations.

Specific initiatives to improve the efficiency
of petroleum utilization were proposed by President Ford
in his 1975 State of the Union message, including:

"--Legislation to make thermal efficiency
standards mandatory for all new buildings
in the United States. These standards
would be set after appropriate consultation with architects, builders and labor.
--A new tax credit of up to $150 for
those home owners who install insulation
equipment.
--The establishment of an energy conservation program to help low income
families purchase insulation supplies.
--Legislation to modify and defer automotive pollution standards for five years
to enable us to improve new automobile
gas mileage 40 per cent by 1980."

In addition, the President has proposed new incentives to
encourage the development of synthetic fuels, shale oil and
nuclear power, and the expanded use of domestic coal reserves.

[§2.7] Protection of Environmental Quality

National concern for protection of environmental
quality became serious shortly before the energy shortage
became acute, and in fact itself accentuated the severity of
the shortage. Perhaps the most comprehensive statement of
this policy goal is contained in the National Environmental
Policy Act of 1969. 34/ Section 2 of that Act declares:

"The purposes of this Act are:
To declare a national policy which will
encourage productive and enjoyable harmony between man and his environment;
to promote efforts which will prevent

or eliminate damage to the environment
and biosphere and stimulate the health
and welfare of man; to enrich the understanding of the ecological and natural
resources important to the nation; and
to establish a Council on Environmental
Quality."

At the heart of the new policy as advanced by the
NEPA was the requirement that an environmental impact statement be a part of "every recommendation or report on proposals for legislation and other major Federal actions
significantly affecting the quality of the human environment." 35/  The Act further required the President to transmit
to the Congress an annual "Environmental Quality Report."

In 1970, Congress extensively amended the Clean
Air Act in order "to speed up, expand, and intensify the
war against air pollution in the United States with a view
to assuring that the air we breathe throughout the Nation
is wholesome once again." 36/  These amendments mandated,
among other things, a 90 percent reduction in emissions of
hydrocarbons, carbon monoxide and nitrogen oxides from
motor vehicle engines by 1975.  In December, 1970, President
Nixon created the Environmental Protection Agency and transferred to its Administrator a wide range of functions of
various executive officers and agencies concerning the
maintenance and improvement of environmental quality. 37/

The policy reflected in these statutes and orders
directly affected petroleum usage, accelerating the conversion of utilities and other stationary sources from coal to
oil and gas and increasing gasoline consumption by motor
vehicles.  More importantly, as a result of litigation, NEPA
delayed U.S. offshore drilling and the construction of the
Trans-Alaska Pipeline, thus magnifying our dependence on
foreign imports. 38/  Some adjustments between environmental
goals and the basic energy goals must be made if an efficient
exploitation of domestic energy resources is to occur.  The
failure to reduce the uncertainty resulting from an unpre-
dictable environmental policy has materially hampered the
development of energy resources, has materially increased--
because of uncertainty alone--the cost of energy, and will
continue to do so until that policy is stabilized.  Clearly

a mechanism needs to be established within the Federal
Government to resolve conflicts arising from environmental
issues.  The present system is inadequate.

[§2.8]  Encouragement of Free and Effective Competition

        Encouragement of competition in industry has been
a goal of the U.S. Government, although in international
petroleum affairs it has been subordinated at times to other
national policy objectives.  Antitrust activities of the
Federal Government since early in the century have manifested a continuing concern with actual or potential anti-
competitive structures or practices within the industry.  In
fact, antitrust concerns are a major obstacle to constructive consultation among companies, as in the development of
the International Energy Program.

        Probably the most famous, as well as most lengthy,
such antitrust action was initiated in 1951 following a
Federal Trade Commission ("FTC") investigation of the major
international companies for anti-competitive activities
designed to maintain a cartel over world petroleum production. 39/  The case, however, had a complex history of
less than active prosecution and lasted twenty years.  In
his aforementioned 1966 speech, Interior Undersecretary
Moore cited preservation of competition as one of those
fundamental "national goals and philosophies that are the
base from which policy is laid in nearly all fields." 40/
Energy policy is no exception.

        In 1973 this policy objective was evident in
Congressional concern over the fate of independent marketers
of petroleum products in a seller's market.  The major
integrated oil companies, it was feared, would soon eliminate or absorb all the independent marketers since the
latter did not have access to their own supplies of crude
oil.  The FTC in July, 1973 completed a staff report on
competition in the industry which concluded that anti-
competitive actions of the integrated firms had resulted
in a "threat to the continued viability of the independent
sector" in the refining and marketing of petroleum in large
parts of the country. 41/  Within the month, the FTC had
issued a complaint against the major integrated firms
charging them with a variety of anti-competitive practices.
The Senate Committee on Interior and Insular Affairs in
late 1973 also held extensive hearings on the state of
competition in the petroleum industry. 42/

The Emergency Petroleum Allocation Act of 1973 43/
also demonstrated Congressional concern with encouraging
and maintaining competition in the petroleum industry. As
mentioned above, the Act directed the President to promul-
gate a regulation providing for the mandatory allocation
of crude oil, residual fuel oil, and each refined petroleum
product in specified amounts and at specified prices. The
Act spelled out in some detail the ends that such regulation
should be designed to serve, and included among them:

> "preservation of an economically sound
> and competitive petroleum industry;
> including the priority needs to restore
> and foster competition in the producing
> refining, distribution, marketing, and
> petrochemical sectors of such industry,
> and to preserve the competitive viability
> of independent refiners, small refiners,
> nonbranded independent marketers, and
> branded independent marketers." 44/

Most recently, antitrust concerns have proved an
obstacle to constructive consultation among the oil companies in the development of the International Energy
Program ("IEP"). The Justice Department has only reluc-
tantly issued Business Review Letters granting permission
for two industry committees to convene in order to discuss
data requirements and emergency sharing operations of the
new International Energy Agency ("IEA"). 45/

[§2.9]  Encouragement of Private Participation
        in Resource Development

Development of petroleum resources on public
lands, onshore and offshore, has been entirely by private
enterprise under leases from the Federal Government. Such
leases are sold by the Department of the Interior under the
authority provided by the Mineral Leasing Act of 1920, 46/
for onshore areas, and by the Outer Continental Shelf Lands
Act for offshore areas. 47/  Onshore leases are sold on a
first come, first served basis for $1 per acre per year for
10 years and a 12-1/2% royalty, whereas the outer continental
shelf lands leases are sold via competitive bidding, plus a
royalty of at least 12-1/2%. 48/  The only onshore lands
eligible for competitive leasing are those within a known

petroleum-bearing geologic structure. If simultaneous multiple applications are received for onshore leases of lands not within a known petroleum-bearing geologic structure, a lottery is held among the applicants for the leases. 49/

In 1973 and 1974, the Nixon and Ford administrations put heavy emphasis on the need to accelerate the offshore leasing program. Encouraging private participation in re-source development thus remains a high priority objective of Federal energy policy. In his special message to Congress on the energy crisis, January 23, 1974, President Nixon announced that he was directing the Secretary of the Interior to increase the acreage leased on the Outer Continental Shelf to 10 million acres beginning in 1975, "more than tripling what had originally been planned." 50/ In President Ford's 1975 State of the Union message he stated:

> "It is the intention of this Administra-
> tion to move forward with exploration,
> leaving and production on those frontier
> areas of the Outer Continental Shelf where
> environmental risks are acceptable."

Encouraging private participation in resource development thus remains a high priority objective of U.S. energy policy.

[§2.10] Maximization of Revenue to the Federal
Government

Until recently maximization of revenue has not been an important policy objective of the Federal Government. Revenue considerations have become important, however, in the operation of the offshore leasing program, and have affected the size and timing of offshore lease sales. 51/ The offshore lease sales generate large amounts of bonus revenue. Indeed, the rationale for competitive bidding on lease sales is to establish a fair market value for those leases. In lease sales between June, 1967 and June, 1968, for instance, the Federal Government received bonuses of more than $1.7 billion. 52/

The leasing of four 5,120-acre tracts of oil shale lands in 1974 brought total bid prices of more than $445 million (less possible reductions of up to 40 percent under

certain subsidy provisions in the lease). 53/  In October,
1974, bonus bids were accepted totalling $1.43 billion for
136 tracts (635,000 acres) offshore Louisiana. 54/

If Federal plans to sell far more offshore leases
than in the past are pursued vigorously, and assuming oil
prices stay at 1974 levels or higher, maximizing the
potential revenue to the Federal government will very likely
become a more important policy goal.  In testimony before
the Senate Interior Committee in 1972, Harrison Loesch,
then Assistant Secretary of the Interior for Public Land
Management, described as one of three major goals and objectives of the Department of Interior with respect to the
management of publicly owned mineral resources "to insure
the public a fair market value return on the disposition
of its resources." 55/  Loesch observed:

> "The receipt of fair market value
> is one of the principal objectives of all
> leasing or disposal programs.  However,
> the law frustrates this objective in
> certain cases.  Noncompetitive oil and
> gas leases are obtained without a bonus
> bid and at a minimal cost and, if a dis-
> covery is made, fair market value probably
> is not obtained.  The royalty rate, for
> example, is less in most cases for a pro-
> ducing noncompetitive lease." 56/

The onshore leasing system, with minimal rentals
and a system of royalties of 12-1/2 percent appears to
yield to the Federal government less than the fair market
value of those leases. 57/  President Nixon, in his energy
address January 23, 1974, called the Mineral Leasing Act
of 1920 "obsolete" and urged Congress to pass a bill creating
a single Federal leasing system for all Federal lands.  He
did not, however, allude specifically to the objective of
increasing the Federal revenue derived from such leases.
Instead, he stressed that the Federal leasing system should
"assure that the persons who obtain the leases are those
who have an interest in early exploration for oil, gas, and
other minerals," 58/ a goal obviously consistent with Project
Independence.

B.    [§2.11]  Conflicts Among Policy Objectives

Any policy objective, if pursued single-mindedly,
will conflict with others.  Moreover, changing circumstances

bring changes in the means appropriate for achieving basic
policy objectives.  Circumstances relevant to energy policy
were changing rapidly in the early 1970's.  As a result,
conflicts among certain of the above objectives became
particularly acute and difficult to resolve within the
framework of an overall national energy policy.  Two such
conflicts stand out:  first, that between the goals of
adequate and secure supply on the one hand and a reasonable
and predictable price on the other; second, that between the
objective of an adequate, secure supply at a reasonable
price, and the maintenance or improvement of environmental
quality.

[§2.1₂]  Supply versus Price

        As available resources are depleted, the incre-
mental costs of obtaining additional resources will inevitably rise.  Moreover, the costs associated with increasing
the security of resources must also be computed--either as
the cost of an interruption or as the cost of insurance
against interruption (stockpiling or the development of
domestic sources).  In any event, there is an inherent
conflict between the desire for a lower price and the need
for secure and adequate supplies.

        The intense concern over the security of petroleum
imports abated somewhat when the 1973-74 Arab oil embargo
ended and U.S. policy then centered on cost rather than
supply, reflecting fears that high oil prices might damage
both the U.S. and world economies.  The Ford Administration
urged voluntary conservation as a counterweight to high oil
prices and in late 1974 there were suggestions that the
White House was considering a restoration of some form of
import controls, either by volume or total dollar value, in
order to limit American payment outflows to oil producing
nations. 59/  This would require a reduced supply, and
possibly rationing, in order to reduce aggregate national
costs for foreign oil.  (France in 1974 set such a dollar
limit on the total value of oil imports.)  The balance of
payments benefits of reductions in consumption must, however, be weighed against the unemployment and losses in
gross national product which increase dramatically with
successive cuts.  Thus, despite the Adminstration's opposition to rationing and a gasoline tax, it accepted the fact
that very large international payments for oil, even for
adequate and secure supplies, must be traded off against
other costs.  It, therefore, has logically placed increasing
emphasis on the importance of reducing aggregate demand.

101.

A similar dilemma exists with respect to natural gas. Although there is considerable logic in decontrolling the price of natural gas to permit it to rise to the level needed to induce increases in supply, and decreases in demand, there is concern that elasticity of supply may be relatively low. A U.S. Geological Survey study in 1974 concluded that prices would have to rise to at least $2 per Mcf in order to maintain the current level of production to 1985. The study concluded that additions to proven reserves would peak by 1985 and decline thereafter. 60/ The difficult policy judgment is whether a much higher price for gas would be "justified" by the increased supply or decreased demand that would be created. In any event it is clear that the present regulation of interstate sales of natural gas by the FPC has created an artificial dependence on it and has encouraged industry to seek unregulated sources of supply both domestically and abroad. 61/

The price controls on crude oil and petroleum products administered by the FEA under the Emergency Petroleum Allocation Act illustrate the same conflict between price and supply. In order to avoid depressing output the price control structure repeatedly has had to be adjusted upward for a variety of products and producers and new administrative measures devised to deal with the now more complex regulatory system. 62/ Even with these attempts, in most instances price controls both reduce supply somewhat and encourage consumption.

President Ford appears to have determined that the security of supply must prevail over the price of supply. His 1975 State of the Union message clearly calls for substantial rises in the price of oil and natural gas in order to stimulate domestic production, restrain demand and reduce imports. 63/

[§2.13]  Supply and Price versus the Environment

This conflict reflects the fact that protecting or improving the environment increases the cost of producing energy and often increases the demand for it. A national policy commitment to environmental protection became strong only shortly before the impact of the energy shortage began

to be felt throughout the economy.  The requirements for
reduction of motor vehicle exhaust emissions, for instance,
by 1973 had increased gasoline consumption at least by an
estimated 300,000 barrels per day. 64/  President Nixon's
message to Congress January 23, 1974, called for amendments
to the Clean Air Act to extend the deadlines for improved
emission controls in order to "permit auto manufacturers to
concentrate greater attention on improving fuel economy
while retaining a fixed target for lower emissions." 65/

        The Energy Supply and Environmental Coordination
Act of 1974 66/ addresses itself to this conflict.  The Act was
intended to promote the use of coal as a substitute for oil
and natural gas.  Section 2 of the Act requires the Federal
Energy Administrator to prohibit any powerplant, and allows
him to prohibit other major fuel-burning installations, from
burning natural gas or petroleum products as its primary
energy source.  The Administrator is given authority to
temporarily suspend fuel or emission limitations on stationary
sources, if fuel shortages make it impossible to comply
with them or if the Administrator has ordered the source to
convert to coal. 67/  The Act also delays for two years the
motor vehicle exhaust emission standards.  Thus, the "coordination" provided for in the Act constitutes a modification of the environmental priority.

        The House Report on the bill observed that the Act
"permits narrowly defined and limited variances from certain
specified Clean Air requirements so as to effectuate proper
coordination between measures taken with respect to energy
supplies and measures respecting environmental protection
and enhancement." 68/  In this context "coordination" means
that the Congress and the Administration have modified their
earlier commitment to improve the environment.  In October,
1974, only months after the passage of this Act, the Ford
Administration again sought new amendments to the Clean Air
Act that would delay compliance deadlines and permit sulfurous
coal to be burned except when meteorological conditions require low sulfur fuel. 69/

        The question of tapping shale oil deposits on a
major scale also sharply accentuates the conflict of supply
and price with the maintenance of environmental quality.

The development of shale oil and strip mining coal areas
of the West causes serious environmental problems, including
water availability, salinity, disposal, dangers to vegetation
and wildlife, and air pollution. 70/ At the same time they
constitute massive secondary energy sources that if developed, even in part, could have a beneficial limiting effect
upon the price of domestic and foreign oil.

        In his 1975 State of the Union Message President
Ford called for "amendments to the Energy Supply and Environmental Coordination Act which will greatly increase the
number of power plants that can be promptly converted to
coal" and "Clean Air Act amendments which will allow greater
coal use without sacrificing our clean air goal." He also
recommended a less stringent strip mining act and "[l]egis-
lation to modify and defer automotive pollution standards
for 5 years to enable us to improve new automobile gas
mileage 40 percent by 1980." Trade-offs between environmental protection and energy development have been brought
into very sharp focus.

        These and other conflicts sometimes appear to defy
resolution through the usual political processes of bargaining
and compromise to achieve consensus. Even though many
Americans probably would agree as to the elements that would
contribute to the nation's long-term well-being, it is
exceedingly difficult to find a "constituency" for any
particular energy policy aimed at promoting this objective. 71/
The enormous task of creating and implementing such policy
can only be accomplished through extraordinary leadership
and political judgment on the part of the Congress and the
President.

        In the analysis which follows, the maintenance of
an adequate supply of petroleum at a reasonable price is the
primary objective against which each policy option is analyzed.
Consideration is also given to the effect of the options as
to other identified objectives.

    C.    [§2.14] Parameters of U.S. Policy

        The recent history of international petroleum clearly
illustrates the need for the U.S. Government to formulate
new policies to cope with changed conditions. These new

policies must reflect both our changing perceptions of U.S.
interests and the fundamental changes which have occurred
in the international industry and in the producing countries.

Cooperation among consuming nations has already
resulted in the establishment of the International Energy
Agency in Paris.  At present, intensive consultations
within IEA are expanding the awareness of the participating
governments.  IEA-industry consultations have been started. 72/
Less specific, but potentially even more important, the United
States has tentatively agreed to the French proposal for a
joint producer-consumer conference during 1975.  To this end,
IEA members have begun serious attempts to work out common
positions on conservation, development and finance. 73/
Future policies selected by the U.S. Government will inevitably take account of these important new relationships.

Whatever policy options are selected, there are
also certain realities about the international petroleum
system which must be reflected in our policies.  Until
recently, the international petroleum market was characterized
by a group of loosely coordinated firms facing competitive
producer governments.  There is considerable evidence that,
with the exception of Iraq, those governments probably fared
better than they would have under free market conditions.
Yet compared to other forms of energy international oil was
cheap, even with the price supporting practices of the major
oil companies.

The establishment of the preeminence of OPEC as a
determiner of price in the international petroleum market
has radically altered the decision-making criteria for setting price.  The highly diffuse and sophisticated incentive
structure of the major companies gave them a vested interest
in global economic growth and stability as well as the
retention of a system which most countries found acceptable.
This incentive structure has now been supplanted by the far
more narrowly based national interest incentives of the
producer countries.  They often seem to feel little or no
concern or responsibility for the economic well-being of
consumer countries, or even the long-term maintenance of
the international economic system which generates the very
revenues flowing to them.  Appeals to long-run common
economic interests of producer and consumer countries are
answered by statements that in maximizing profit through a
cartel they are redressing past injustices and, indeed,
acting as any rational Western businessman would. 74/

The companies which were once oligopolistic sellers are now competing buyers confronting a cartel. Competition among the companies tends to reinforce the upward tendency in price, particularly so long as OPEC is prepared to continue the curtailment of production. It is very doubtful that there can be any significant downward market pressure exerted on price by consumer countries at least in the short to medium-term (up to several years). The spread between the cost of production, the price floor (perhaps $2 per barrel) toward which competition among producer countries would tend, and current prices ($11 per barrel) is so great that cooperation among the producers is clearly in the interest of all petroleum exporting countries. Producing countries could increase their aggregate revenue somewhat by cutting prices slightly and selling relatively larger quantities. If many producers did this, however, price would then fall much further. Therefore as long as each producer can be relatively certain that no or very few members of the cartel are shaving the price, each is strongly motivated to follow the rules and be satisfied with a stable share of the market.

When that assurance is lacking, or if significant new production remains outside the cartel, the motivation is just the opposite: then each producer would have to compete in order to preserve its market share. Consumers would, however, in the foreseeable future find it far too costly in terms of lost employment and gross national product to reduce demand sufficiently to break OPEC unity. Thus, assuming that the cartel remains stable, there would be downward pressure on price only if it appears that a reduction in that price would elicit a more than proportional increase in aggregate demand, so that a price reduction would increase aggregate revenues for those producers who could sufficiently expand production. We have not yet reached that point.

For the foreseeable future, long-term considerations have little chance of influencing OPEC price decisions. Almost all relevant considerations which would go into a long-term calculation--the rate of successful exploration, the export policies of new producers, the rate of development of alternative sources of energy, the impact of conservation in consumer countries--are speculative. It is, therefore, extremely unlikely that producers would lower prices on the basis of such a calculation when revenues at current levels, assuming they can be invested, are so great as to swamp any long-term anticipations. 75/

Clearly, the current status is such that the companies in the international petroleum industry are price takers so long as they continue to compete with one another for the product of the OPEC cartel. There is no cause for optimism that OPEC will break up. The fact that producer governments have become sellers of oil strongly suggests that governments of crude purchasers should interject their presence into international petroleum transactions to protect the interests of the consumer. At the same time the companies fill vital roles which government is unequipped to supplant, a factor which strongly affects the form of any governmental interruption.

U.S. policy, in addition to meeting national objectives and accommodating new international realities, must also concern itself with preserving or salvaging the strengths of the existing structure. At a minimum, the unique integrated logistical, technological and managerial system of the U.S. oil companies constitutes an important national asset. Because it is a functioning system, it must be approached as such, and not altered piecemeal. Moreover, recent events clearly indicate that we can no longer assume that, come what may, the companies can take care of themselves.76/

In the context of these observations, it is possible to evaluate the range of options available to the U.S. Government in its relationship with the industry as it pursues certain national objectives.

The options selected for analysis are:

A.   National Options

1.   Removal or modification of Federally created incentives and disincentives to international petroleum production;

2.   Regulation of oil companies as public utilities;

3.   Establishment of a national system to limit petroleum imports;

4.   Regulation of all significant international supply arrangements;

5.  Creation of a petroleum corporation, fully or partially owned by the Federal Government, to engage in international activities;

B.  Bilateral/Multilateral Options

6.  Coordination of international supply arrangements through an industry-wide association of consumer country companies;

7.  Bilateral arrangements between the United States and producer governments;

8.  Establishment of an international organization to coordinate national petroleum policy with other importing countries; and

9.  Establishment of multilateral negotiations between producing and consuming countries.

CHAPTER 2

FOOTNOTES

1. "Observations on U.S. Energy Policy," in Senate Committee on Interior and Insular Affairs Considerations in the Formulation of National Energy Policy, Appendix A, 84, 92nd Cong., 1st Sess., Ser. No. 92-4, 1971.

2. Executive Order 11748, December 4, 1973.

3. 88 Stat. 96 (May 7, 1974).

4. Id. at Sec. 2(b).

5. Executive Order 11814, October 11, 1974.

6. "Observations on U.S. Energy Policy" supra, note 1, at 90.

7. OECD Energy Committee, Energy Policy: Problems and Objectives (Paris: OECD, 1966).

8. Senate Committee on Interior and Insular Affairs, Presidential Energy Statements, 71, 93rd Cong., 1st Sess., Ser. No. 93-23, 1973.

9. Id. at 79.

10. Id. at 85.

11. U.S. Code Cong. and Admin. News, 1974, 491.

12. Petroleum Intelligence Weekly, Sept. 30, 1974, 9.

13. See Appendix B, §B.4, infra.

14. The recycling issue dominates much of the current policy debate. See §11.0, infra.

15. Petroleum Intelligence Weekly, Sept. 30, 1974, 9.

16. Dept. of Treasury News Release, Nov. 18, 1974, 5.

17. Dept. of State News Release, Sept. 23, 1974, 6.

18. Petroleum Intelligence Weekly, Supplement, Jan. 13, 1974, 2.

19. 87 Stat. 627 (Nov. 27, 1973).

20. "Observations on U.S. Energy Policy", supra, note 1 at 88.

21. Hearings on S.1586 before the Senate Committee on Interior and Insular Affairs, Strategic Petroleum Reserves, 1, 8, 93d Cong., 1st Sess., May 30 and July 26, 1973, Ser. No. 93-11 (92-46).

22. S.1586, 93d Cong., 1st Sess.

23. U.S. Code Cong. and Admin. News, 31 (1974) and Presidential Speech, January 14, 1975.

24. 1975 State of the Union message.

25. See §§1.16-1.18, supra.

26. Petroleum Intelligence Weekly, Sept. 30, 1974, 9.

27. S. L. McDonald, Petroleum Conservation in the United States, An Economic Analysis (1971).

28. 88 Stat. 96 (May 7, 1974).

29. P.L. 93-159, 87 Stat. 627 (Nov. 27, 1973).

30. Ibid.

31. See 18 C.F.R. §2.78, Order No. 467-C, April 4, 1974.

32. Los Angeles Times, Oct. 23, 1974, 1.

33. P.L. 91-190, 83 Stat. 852 (Jan. 1, 1970).

34. Ibid. at Sec. 102(c).

35. 42 U.S.C. §§1857 et seq.; H.R. 91-1146, U.S. Code Cong. and Admin. News, 1970, 5356.

36. Reorganization Plan No. 3 of 1970, 3 C.F.R. (Compilation of 1970), 199.

37. The Wilderness Society v. Morton, 479 F.2d 842, 847 (D.C. Cir., 1973).

38. See The International Petroleum Cartel, staff report to the FTC submitted to the Subcommittee on Monopoly of the Senate Select Committee on Small Business, Washington:G.P.O., 1952.

39. "Observations on U.S. Energy Policy," supra, note 1 at 85.

40. "Preliminary Federal Trade Commission Staff Report on its Investigation of the Petroleum Industry," transmitted to the Senate Committee on Interior and Insular Affairs, 93rd Cong., 1st Sess., Ser. No. 93-15 (92-50), 1973, 43.

41. See Hearings before the Senate Committee on Interior and Insular Affairs on Market Performance and Competition in the Petroleum Industry, 93rd Cong., 1st Sess., Nov. 28, 29, 1973, pts. 1-4, Ser. No. 93-24 (92-59).

42. 87 Stat. 627 (Nov. 27, 1973).

43. Id. at Sec. 4(b)(1)(D).

44. Platts Oilgram News Service, Nov. 26 and Dec. 20, 1974.

45. 41 Stat. 442 (Feb. 25, 1920).

46. 67 Stat. 467 (Aug. 7, 1953).

47. See Appendix B §§B.8-B.9.

48. 41 Stat. 442 (Feb. 25, 1920). See Appendix B §B.8.

49. U.S. Code Cong. and Admin. News, 1974, 41.

50. See Nossaman, et al., Study of the Outer Continental Shelf Lands of the United States (1968), 661.

51. Krueger, "An Evaluation of the Provisions and Policies of the Outer Continental Shelf Lands Acts," 10 Natural Resources Journal 763, 784 (1970).

52. See Angus McDonald, Shale Oil: An Environmental Critique (Washington, D.C.: Center for Science in the Public Interest, 1974), iv.

53. Los Angeles Times, Oct. 29, 1974, pt. III, 11.

54. Hearings before the Senate Committee on Interior and
    Insular Affairs on Federal Leasing and Disposal Policies,
    92nd Cong., 2nd Sess., June 19, 1972, Ser. No. 92-32,
    p. 17.

55. Id. at 24.

56. John Sprague and Bernadette Julian, "An Analysis of the
    Impact of an All Competitive Leasing System on Onshore
    Oil and Gas Leasing Revenue," 10 Natural Resources
    Journal, 515, 531 (July, 1970).

57. U.S. Code Cong. and Admin. News, 1974, 38.

58. Los Angeles Times, Oct. 24, 1974, 1.

59. Oil and Gas Journal, Sept. 9, 1974, 42

60. Id., Aug. 26, 1974, 58.

61. See, for instance, the difficulties the FEA has had in
    devising regulations controlling international transfer
    prices between affiliated companies. Los Angeles Times,
    Oct. 29, 1974, pt. III, 9.

62. 1975 State of the Union message.

63. Hearings before the Senate Committee on Interior and
    Insular Affairs on a bill to Create a System of Stra-
    tegic Petroleum reserves, 93rd Cong., 1st Sess., May 30
    and July 26, 1973, Ser. No. 93-11 (92-46), pp. 26, 97.

64. U.S. Code Cong. and Admin. News, 1974, 40.

65. P.L. 93-319, 88 Stat. 246 (June 22, 1974).

66. Ibid.

67. H.R. 93-1013, U.S. Code Cong. and Admin. News, 1974,
    1799.

68. Petroleum Intelligence Weekly, Oct. 14, 1974, 5;
    Capital Energy Letter, Oct. 12, 1974, 6.

69. See Angus McDonald, Shale Oil: An Environmental
    Critique (Washington, D.C.: Center for Science in
    the Public Interest, 1974).

70. Since any such policy would require short-run sacri-
    ficies for longer term objectives, it would inevitably
    arouse opposition from affected groups.

71. See §10.0, _infra_.

72. _Petroleum Intelligence Weekly_, Dec. 30, 1974, 3.

73. J. Amuzegar, "The Oil Story: Facts, Fiction and Fair
    Play," 52 _Foreign Affairs_ 676 (1974).

74. See §11.1, _infra_; interviews Government officials.

75. See §§1.15-1.18, _supra_.

PART III

FUTURE POLICY OPTIONS:

NATIONAL OPTIONS

CHAPTER 3

REMOVING OR ALTERING FÉDERALLY CREATED INCENTIVES
AND DISINCENTIVES TO PETROLEUM PRODUCTION

A.    [§3.0]   Introduction

Although the U.S. Government is not directly
engaged in the production, refining and marketing of petroleum, Federally created incentives and disincentives have
historically played an important role in the development of
the U.S. oil industry.  The first option analyzed by this
Study is the modification of the existing system by removing
or altering those incentives and disincentives.

B.    [§3.1]   Tax Incentives

The current Internal Revenue Code includes a
number of provisions which are, in part or whole, subsidies
to the production of oil both domestically and abroad.
Proposals are frequently made to reduce or eliminate completely such tax incentives or subsidies.  The usual justification for these provisions is that they increase the
supply of oil available to U.S. markets. Each of them has
some incremental value as an investment incentive and it can,
therefore, be plausibly contended that its removal would
reduce investment, and thus production, by some amount. 1/
Any measure which increases the expected rate of return
within the industry should increase investment in it.

The usual arguments against these provisions are
that they have some undesirable side effects (such as encouraging consumption or discouraging use of alternate
energy sources) or that they are not cost-effective.  The
first argument is most plausible where these tax incentives
tend to reduce the price of oil.  If a subsidy results in
oil prices so low as to encourage wasteful consumption or
to make energy from other sources, such as shale or solar
energy, uneconomical in comparison, then it creates a misallocation of resources.  Because of the impact of OPEC
pricing policies and the FEA controls this argument appears
inapplicable at present.  On foreign oil OPEC pricing policies
have probably transferred any foreign profits attributable

to U.S. tax incentives to the producing countries themselves. Moreover, at present prices, there are ample incentives to exploration without subsidies. 2/

The cost-effectiveness point is important. Recent international developments have reduced, in effect, existing tax subsidies on oil investment to relative insignificance, or at least made their importance disproportionate to their cost. On the other hand, it must be borne in mind that where it is decided that a given activity, such as investment in oil production, should be subsidized, an evaluation of the cost-effectiveness of exising subsidies to that activity must take into account the indirect but very real costs that would attend their replacement by other, "more efficient" subsidies. For instance, the political costs to the President or the Congress of creating a new form of subsidy may cause them to prefer the continuation of a relatively inefficient existing subsidy.

## [§3.2]  Foreign Tax Credit

The foreign tax credit provisions of the Internal Revenue Code allow a U.S. taxpayer to elect to credit income taxes paid to foreign governments against U.S. income tax liabilities on foreign income. 3/

Such credits are limited to the amount of tax that would be payable if the foreign country taxed at U.S. rates. The taxpayer may elect to compute that limit on either a "per country" or "overall" basis. Under the "per country" rule, the income and taxes from each foreign country are treated separately in determining the allowable credit; under the "overall" method, all foreign net income and all foreign taxes paid are aggregated. Taxpayers may elect either method, but there are restrictions on shifting between methods. 4/

The basic principle of the foreign tax credit is well established in international tax law: income earned by a taxpayer in one country by a citizen, resident or corporation of another country should not be subject to full taxation by both the home country and the host country. Two important controversies exist, however, regarding the use of the foreign tax credit by the oil industry. The most important

118·

question concerns what should constitute foreign income tax, as distinguished from a royalty payment or from the cost of purchased oil. Second, there is a question of the propriety of certain ways of computing the allowable amount of the credit. 5/

Although these two issues are analytically distinct, as a practical matter they are very closely related. If the payments to foreign governments now deemed income taxes were not so large, there would be less concern about the possible manipulation of tax liabilities resulting from different ways of computing the credit. In this area, therefore, any proposal for change in the law must consider both issues, as well as several others that affect the U.S. tax burden on foreign oil income. 6/

[§3.3]  Income Taxes versus Royalties

Probably the most difficult, as well as most important, issue surrounding the foreign tax credit as it relates to oil production is the definition of an income tax. Royalties, excise taxes, and costs of purchased oil would normally be treated as deductible business expenses, but not as credits. Producing countries and companies operating abroad have long had an incentive to characterize as income taxes payments to the host country that are in substance indistinguishable from royalties. As mentioned earlier, the U.S. Government itself to some extent encouraged this practice. 7/

The repeal of the foreign tax credit for international petroleum transactions would subject U.S. corporations to double taxation of foreign income and place them at a great disadvantage relative to foreign competitors. 8/ If, however, the tax credit were restricted to payments that are in fact income taxes and not royalties or a cost of purchasing oil, it would conform to its intended function of preventing double taxation. Taxes would be due to the U.S. Government from profitable operations wherever the effective income tax rates were lower than the U.S. rates, either on a per country or overall basis. Where the rates are the same or higher than in the U.S., there would be no U.S. income tax liability. The present system's broad interpretation of "income taxes" is a factor which has encouraged producer countries with the active support of the U.S. companies to impose higher taxes in lieu of higher royalties, which would merely be deductible business expenses. 9/

The U.S. Treasury in 1974 proposed a plan which would treat pre-tax income, net of royalty payments, from foreign oil-producing operations as equal to an amount which, if taxed at U.S. rates, would leave net after-tax income equal to the net revenue actually realized by the taxpayer. 10/ For instance, assuming the foreign tax rate is 48% or more, if the company realized 52 cents per barrel after foreign taxes, pre-tax income net of royalties would be deemed to be $1, foreign income taxes would be deemed to be 48 cents and 48 cents foreign tax credit allowed. Payments to the producer country above 48 cents would be deemed royalties. 11/ The plan would also eliminate the foreign depletion allowance. Under this plan, foreign oil-producing income could not generate foreign tax credits capable of sheltering any other foreign income. 12/

If Congress takes no action on this issue, it may become moot in many cases because oil-producing companies owned by U.S. firms abroad are increasingly subject to nationalization. U.S. companies are rapidly becoming mere service companies and purchasers of products from producer governments. Under these conditions it may become undeniably clear that the price paid for such oil is a deductible purchase cost and not a creditable income tax. On the other hand, producer governments may try to structure their new tax system to take maximum possible advantage of existing U.S. tax laws, even after complete nationalization. 13/ Very difficult tax issues may arise for the companies and for the U.S. Government if, for instance, the producer countries reduce the companies essentially to suppliers of services and then both pay and tax such service income on a per barrel basis. Evaluating the extent to which such taxes should be deemed income taxes would probably require the Internal Revenue Service in effect to decide what is a "reasonable" per barrel margin for the services rendered in each case. Assume, for instance, that a producer-country government were willing to pay $1 per barrel, net after its own taxes, for lifting oil. The $1 per barrel fee would clearly be more attractive to a U.S. company if it were calculated on the basis of a "gross income" of $5 per barrel and an "income tax" of $4, or 80%, than if it were calculated on the basis of a "gross income" of $1.50 and an "income tax" of 33.3%, or in the extreme, $1 and no income tax. The higher the hypothetical "gross income," the larger the foreign tax credit generated, enabling the company to shelter other foreign income or to carry credit over to future years. 14/ The value of this tax benefit would very likely be discounted and split between the producer-country government and the company when they set the after-tax net. To police this possible abuse, the I.R.S. would likely peg the hypothetical "gross income" at the "reasonable value" of the services provided by the company, limiting the foreign tax credit to the difference between that "reasonable value" and the company's actual after-tax net. There is an economic incentive for producer countries to retain a semblance of the concession system because of the obvious advantage that the ambiguity between the purchase price and tax has given to both the countries and the companies. 15/

[§3.4] Computing the Allowable Credit

The foreign tax credit as now administered has generated tax credits far greater than are needed to eliminate any U.S. tax liability on such income. Under the "overall" rule, part of some companies' allowable tax credits has been used to reduce U.S. tax liabilities on other foreign income, particularly from shipping. 16/ Oil tankers are often registered under foreign flags of countries having relatively low income tax rates. They can absorb some of the otherwise unusable foreign tax credit. In the absence of such tax credits, a U.S. income tax would be due on other foreign income subject to low tax rates. Such opportunities were reduced somewhat by the Tax Reform Act of 1969, which included a provision to the effect that foreign tax credits atributable to the amount of the percentage depletion allowance on mineral income from a foreign country cannot reduce the U.S. tax payable on other foreign income. 17/

Critics of allowing this use of the overall limitation declare that it amounts to an indirect U.S. subsidy for oil companies or for foreign shipping and therefore that it should be ended. 18/ Its defenders, however, point out that if this use of the overall limitation were not allowed, U.S. companies would be more likely to sell their tankers and withdraw from the shipping business. This might be undesirable from the viewpoint of the U.S. national interest because it would tend to give producer countries more opportunity and incentive to extend their control downstream to the transportation of crude produced in their country. At the same time, the U.S. Government might find it awkward to give a direct subsidy to "foreign" shipping, that is, to tankers under foreign flags of convenience. In fact, in 1974 Congress passed (but the President vetoed) a bill requiring a significant percentage of imported oil to be transferred in U.S. flag ships. Since U.S. flag ships are far more costly to operate than foreign, it may be that an indirect tax subsidy to "foreign" shipping is more in the national interest than a direct subsidy to U.S. shipping which would have to be much larger to have a comparable effect.

It appears, however, that most oil companies do not use the overall limitation. From 1968 through 1972, five of the seven largest U.S. oil companies consistently used the per country limitaion, while only one consistently used the overall. The remaining company used the per country for two years and the overall for three. 19/

Use of the per country limitation sometimes raises another controversy. This method allows a company to deduct its foreign losses in one country, including expensed intangible drilling and development costs ("IDC"), from U.S. source income 20/, rather than having such losses offset by income from other foreign countries. If in later years the operations which produced the loss begin to return a profit, there is still no adjustment of the allowable foreign tax credit to take account of the earlier loss deduction against U.S. income. Since the foreign tax rates are usually at least as high as U.S. rates, this means that the U.S. Treasury in effect loses 48% of the loss amount, but can never get any tax revenue out of profits on the same operations. Arguably, that loss ought to be recouped by the Treasury before foreign tax credits are allowed on the profits from such operations. The proposed Oil and Gas Energy Tax Act of 1974 would deal with this problem by prohibiting oil companies from using the per country limitation. 21/

A widely held view among the international oil companies was expressed by one U.S. company as follows:

"Retention of the foreign tax credit
concept is absolutely essential if U.S.
companies are to continue to be economically viable when competing with foreign
owned companies.  If foreign taxes paid
were to be deducted as royalties, our
U.S. companies would be taxed out of
competition and foreign source oil would
be in the full control of foreign owned
companies." 22/

This possibility must be acknowledged, although
its significance is an open question.  It is also possible that
if the U.S. eliminated or reduced its foreign tax credit, other
countries would do likewise.

[§3.5]  Percentage Depletion Allowance

The percentage depletion allowance permits 22% of
the gross well-head value of oil and gas production from a
producing property, whether domestic or foreign, to be
exempt from Federal income tax, up to a limit of 50 percent
of the net income from that property. 23/  The depletion
rates applicable to other energy minerals, excepting uranium,
are lower, 24/ thus favoring oil production relative to other
energy sources, and relative to non-energy investments.

Domestically, percentage depletion has in the past
encouraged more independents to be in the oil business and
has caused the drilling of some wells that would not otherwise have been drilled, some marginal and some not.  It has
increased the after-tax profitability of domestic oil production and thereby the output of U.S. companies.  By causing
output to be higher than otherwise and more importantly by
being an indirect subsidy to the producer and necessarily
the consumer, the depletion allowance has resulted in lower
oil prices.  Thus, this tax incentive has also encouraged
the consumption of petroleum relative to other energy sources
and non-energy consumer items.  A 1973 study based on data
for 1971 estimated that if there had been no depletion
allowance prices would have been nine percent higher, assuming a constant ratio of imports; or production would have

123.

been eleven percent lower, assuming imports had increased
enough to keep prices constant. 25/

Under current price controls it is probable that
the depletion allowance continues to increase the after-tax
profitability of oil production for both royalty owners and
producers above what it would be if there were no percentage
depletion allowance. If price controls are removed as
President Ford recommended in his 1975 State of the Union
message, 26/ U.S. crude oil prices should rise to the level
of foreign prices (including U.S. tariffs, transportation
and other costs). 27/ Thus the depletion allowance should
no longer result in lower crude oil prices. The share of
the increased profits which under past free market conditions was passed along to consumers will be retained by the
companies. This enhanced profitability should encourage
further investment by the companies. 28/

The percentage depletion allowance has had relatively limited impact on foreign exploration and development.
The size of the foreign tax credit in the past has rendered
the foreign depletion allowance superfluous in many cases,
and it does so in most cases today. International oil
companies, therefore, are not strongly opposed to proposals
to eliminate it. 29/ If the foreign tax credit were reduced
or eliminated, however, percentage depletion for foreign
production would be vastly more important. 30/ For instance,
if most of the payments to the producer countries presently
deemed income taxes were regarded as royalties, the percentage depletion might be computed on the value of the foreign
oil either gross or net of such royalties. 31/ If figured
net of royalties, higher taxes could result.

[§3.6] Expensing of Intangible Drilling and
Development Costs

A taxpayer may elect to deduct as a current expense
the intangible drilling and development costs rather than to
amortize them as capital expenditures through periodic
depreciation deductions. Costs eligible for this treatment
include labor, fuel, hauling, supplies, tool rental, and
drilling equipment repairs incident to the drilling of wells
or their preparation for production. 32/

The controversial issue of IDC relates to productive, not dry, wells. There is general agreement that dry holes should be allowed to be expensed. 33/ With productive wells the argument can be made that IDC ought to be considered part of the investment in the producing property, properly recoverable over the productive life of that property by means of depreciation deductions. 34/ But more is at stake than merely the timing of the deductions and a "no interest loan" from the government through tax deferral. The immediate income deductibility of these costs, plus the use of percentage depletion, creates what is arguably a double deduction for productive wells. If capitalization and depreciation are required for productive wells, very likely the result in most cases will be that the companies will be taxed on the full amount of such costs, since under existing law a taxpayer may not simultaneously take advantage of the percentage depletion allowance and also amortize his leasehold and intangible capital investment in the same property. 35/ Thus, where percentage depletion is applicable, the taxpayer either expenses IDC or gets no further deduction at all for such costs.

Requiring capitalization of intangible drilling and development costs would affect the sources of drilling funds. High tax bracket investors, a significant but not essential source of drilling funds, would be less attracted to such investments. 36/ Under current law, approximately 75% of an investment in a drilling venture in effect can be written off against current income. The higher the investor's tax bracket, the greater the advantage. If IDC were required to be capitalized, drilling investments would be judged on their merits in terms of prospective rates of return. Funds could then be expected to flow into drilling ventures only if the expected rate of return was attractive relative to alternative investments. 37/

Foreign drilling investments receive IDC benefits. In a number of cases, large foreign tax credits have rendered the IDC superfluous for foreign exploration. Because of high foreign tax rates, removal of IDC treatment for productive foreign wells would have negligible effects under present

conditions for companies using the overall limitation. 38/
For companies using the per country limitation, however, the
expensing of foreign intangible drilling and development
costs often will have the effect of reducing U.S. taxable
income by that amount. 39/  In such situations, the provision is a significant tax incentive to foreign as well as
domestic exploration and drilling.

        The effect of the three foregoing tax provisions
in their present form is to continue to encourage foreign as
well as domestic oil exploration and development relative to
other energy forms and relative to alternative non-energy
investments.  In addition these provisions also affect the
distribution of income.  Currently, crude oil prices are
controlled in the United States. 40/  If price control is
effective, tax provisions which encourage production and
thereby increase supply have no effect on price.  In this
event, removal of the tax provisions would not cause crude
oil prices or product prices to rise.  Removal of the tax
provisions would reduce oil company after-tax profitability
where the oil company was a lessee of oil lands, and would
reduce rents earned by royalty owners.  Because after-tax
income from oil and gas development would be reduced, bonus
bids for oil and gas properties owned by both governments
and individuals would be lower. 41/

        Where foreign production is concerned, these
income distribution effects are international.  In the
past approximately 90% of the foreign oil production by
U.S. companies has been sold to European and other foreign
markets. 42/  It can be argued, therefore, that U.S. taxpayers through these provisions, have subsidized the taxing
powers of producer-country governments, the taxing powers of
foreign consuming-country governments, and oil consumption
by citizens of foreign importing countries. 43/  On the
other hand, the absence of such benefits might have made
U.S. companies less competitive abroad and would have to
some extent discouraged foreign investments.

        Recent changes in world oil prices, cost conditions,
royalty terms, taxation, and nationalization have been so

important as to reduce greatly the relative significance of
the above discussed tax incentives. The four-fold increase
in world oil prices has made domestic oil exploration and
new production very attractive, regardless of tax incentives.
The attractiveness of investments in foreign exploration and
production now depends mainly on the policies of the producer-
country governments, and particularly upon the per barrel
margin they allow the companies to reap from their operations.
In the early part of 1974, for instance, foreign production
was very profitable for the companies as margins between the
price of their equity oil and world market prices rose to as
much as $3 per barrel. 44/ Subsequently, however, the
producer-country governments began reducing those margins by
various means, in some cases to the point where operations
in a given country could no longer be conducted at a profit.
Moreover, as demand slackened and output increased, competition among the companies intensified and further eroded
profit margins. 45/ Presently such factors are more important
than U.S. tax incentives and may even make such incentives
nugatory. Surveys done in connection with this Study show a
clear shift in exploration emphasis to the U.S. from all
other areas of the world, except the Far East which is still
a small part of the total. 46/ The rate of new exploration
and development in the U.S. appears currently constrained
primarily by the availability of labor and equipment. 47/
Under such conditions, reducing or abolishing existing tax
incentives would probably not significantly affect expected
profitability of either domestic or foreign oil operations,
and consequently not affect the pattern of domestic and
foreign exploration.

[§3.7]  Tax Advantages for Foreign Oil Operations

        The extent to which companies operating abroad
have tax advantages which they would not have if they were
conducting the same operations in the United States is a
matter of considerable controversy. There is the issue of
the distinction between an income tax and a royalty payment.
A royalty payment to a U.S. landowner is a deductible
expense, 48/ whereas a substantially equivalent payment to a
foreign government can be characterized as an income tax and
becomes a credit. 49/

        Even where a true foreign income tax is levied,
however, it appears anomalous that it is a credit but U.S.

state and local income taxes are not. 50/ Even more striking, if an income tax were levied on a U.S. company by, for
example, the Canadian province of Alberta it would be a
credit against U.S. taxes, but the same tax if levied by the
State of Texas would be only a deductible expense. 51/ This
distinction can, of course, be defended by pointing out that
allowing U.S. state and local income taxes as a credit would
give too great an incentive to states and cities to increase
their taxes at Federal expense. Nevertheless, tax neutrality
as between foreign and domestic investment is sacrificed in
this respect.

A few major U.S. oil companies benefit significantly
from the creation of a Western Hemisphere Trade Corporation,
through a special deduction allowed to companies operating
primarily in the Western Hemisphere. 52/ A U.S. corporation
can create a domestic subsidiary doing business solely in
the Western Hemisphere, the income of which will be taxed at
a rate of 34% rather than the usual 48%. Such subsidiaries
may also elect to use percentage depletion. 53/ For the tax
years 1968-1970, subsidiaries of three large oil companies
accounted for over one-third of all the Western Hemisphere
Trade Corporation deductions taken by U.S. corporations. 54/
The provision apparently was originally intended to promote
U.S. investment in Latin America, but in practice it has
become a tax planning tool of dubious rationale. 54a/

Finally, there is the issue of deferral. Earnings
of foreign subsidiaries of U.S. companies operating in the
country of their incorporation are not attributed to the
U.S. parent unless and until such earnings are distributed. 55/
In practice, this means that if such earnings are reinvested
in the country of their origin, and in some cases in other
foreign countries, whether in the same enterprise, another
subsidiary of the parent, or an unrelated business, U.S.
taxes on such earnings are deferred indefinitely. Thus, if
tax rates in the foreign country are lower than U.S. rates,
there is an incentive for U.S. companies to invest abroad
through foreign subsidiaries rather than in the U.S. For
instance, a U.S. company might form a foreign subsidiary to
do refining or to perform exploratory and drilling services
in a low-tax country. By investing the earnings of the
subsidiary in the country of its incorporation, the parent

128.

may continue to increase its subsidiary's earning power with money that would have been subject to further U.S. taxes if repatriated to the U.S. parent. As a practical matter, U.S. taxes on such earnings can often be deferred indefinitely. Defenders of deferral correctly point out that it is consistent with the principle of not taxing shareholders on undistributed corporate earnings. 56/ On the other hand, U.S. tax law does depart from that principle to impute a "constructive dividend" in various circumstances where undistributed earnings are accumulated by a corporation to avoid taxes on controlling shareholders. 57/ Ending deferral of taxation on the earnings of foreign subsidiaries would, therefore, not be unprecedented in the Federal tax system.

## [§3.8]  The Impact of Tax Incentives

The net effect of the foreign tax credit, percentage depletion, the IDC allowance and other lesser U.S. tax incentives in international petroleum affairs clearly has been to encourage U.S. companies to develop foreign supply and marketing arrangements. The United States Government has probably lost some tax revenues thereby, but has benefited to the extent that foreign reserves have been discovered and developed, supplying U.S. needs as well as those of the free world generally. 58/

In assessing any of these incentives a basic issue is whether the global supply network established by the U.S. companies is worth maintaining and, if so, whether the removal or modification of any particular incentive would have a substantial impact upon the system.

Judged in this light it would appear that the large companies would have a substantial interest in developing foreign supplies with or without these incentives, based upon the assumptions that today's higher prices or something relatively close to them will continue and that the margins of the companies will not be squeezed too drastically by the host countries. On the other hand, it is clear that hundreds of billions of dollars will be needed for exploration and development, if we are to supply the energy needs of the future, 59/ and in some cases the elimination or reduction of these tax incentives could have a negative impact. Nevertheless, given the magnitude of other forces now determining the future trends of investment in foreign and domestic production, with the exception of the foreign tax credit it is questionable whether the above tax incentives are important enough to have a significant impact on such investment decisions. To the extent such provisions are in fact subsidies consideration should therefore be given to their elimination. 60/

Most of the oil companies surveyed indicated concern that abolishing these tax incentives would make foreign oil investments unprofitable. 61/ They were chiefly concerned regarding their competitive position vis-a-vis foreign oil companies, particularly the major European ones. 62/ To the U.S. international companies, "tax neutrality" in an international context means primarily that they should not be taxed more heavily by the U.S. Government than their foreign-based competitors are taxed by their home countries. For instance, a number of countries, including the United Kingdom and the Netherlands, 63/ permit companies to expense drilling costs on essentially the same basis as the U.S. now does. If the allowance were removed for foreign operations of U.S. companies, they could be put at a competitive disadvantage with the companies of other countries bidding for arrangements to explore and produce abroad, even though the dollar value of that allowance could be relatively low compared to anticipated profits from such operations.

There is evidence that parent countries of non-U.S. firms structured the taxation of those firms to match the tax advantages of the U.S. firms. 64/ It is possible that if these U.S. tax advantages were removed, the parent countries of non-U.S. firms would follow suit; it is also possible that they would not, in order to assist their companies. If a phased reduction or elimination of these provisions were used, there would be time to coordinate U.S. policy with that of other countries. If other countries showed no inclination to follow the U.S. changes, they could be curtailed or restored and the risk to the competitive position of U.S. companies would be minimized.

In any event, the seriousness of this possible competitive disadvantage to U.S. firms must be evaluated in a broader context than only the interests of the U.S. firms themselves.

[§3.9]   Creation of Tax Disincentives to Investment
in Foreign Oil Production

There have been suggestions in Congress that tax
provisions applicable to companies undertaking foreign oil
operations might be altered or manipulated in order to
discourage foreign operations altogether or to redirect them
to relatively reliable countries. 65/  Use of the foreign
tax credit might be denied for operations in countries which
have imposed an embargo on the United States.  Congress
might give the President or his delegate the authority to
suspend the application of certain international tax provisions either selectively or across the board, in light of
his perception of the national interest. 66/

Such measures would have grave shortcomings,
however, even if it were decided that foreign investment in
certain areas should be discouraged.  First, the only such
tax benefit important enough to make any likely significant
difference in the flow of U.S. international investment is
the foreign tax credit.  Second, if such a change is applicable to existing investments as well as new investments, it
could subject affected overseas operations to drastically
increased taxes where disinvestment may be impracticable or
may take a long period of time.  If, however, distinctions
are made between new and old investments, they will be very
hard to defend as equitable.  Third, to the extent that such
changes inject an element of uncertainty in the tax treatment of foreign investments, they will make tax planning far
more difficult and may thereby discourage desirable foreign
investments. 67/  Fourth, such changes could prevent U.S.
companies from competing effectively with foreign firms and
from maintaining and serving their supply systems. 68/
Finally, while the disadvantages to existing taxpayers would
be immediate and often severe, the benefits from such measures would be speculative and uncertain.

The income tax law is a clumsy and indirect instrument for achieving such policy objectives.  There are far
more direct and effective means available.  Under existing
Federal banking laws, for instance, the President has the
authority to impose foreign direct investment controls, and
has done so in the past. 69/  An office exists within the
Commerce Department, the Office of Foreign Direct Investments,
for the administration of these measures.  Alternatively,

131.

the Congress could impose an outright ban on investments in designated countries for a specified period of time. 70/ Finally, Congress can grant direct subsidies to foreign or domestic investments deemed in the national interest. 71/

C.   Disincentives

[§3.10]   Price Controls

Price controls were instituted by President Nixon effective August 15, 1971 and have been continued on crude oil and petroleum products with minor exceptions through successive phases of price control up to the present time. 72/

Price controls on the wellhead price of natural gas flowing in interstate commerce have been in effect since 1954 and are administered by the Federal Power Commission ("FPC"). They are important because oil and gas are joint products. A price control system which holds the price of natural gas below its competitve equilibrium level has the effect of discouraging exploration for oil as well as gas. 73/

Where price controls hold prices below their equilibrium level, two results follow. First, consumption of such products is stimulated. Historically, the United States has pursued a low energy price policy through its tax subsidy system and its natural gas price control system, and more recently under the crude oil price control system. 74/ This policy is inconsistent with President Ford's requests to the American people to conserve on energy use.

The second effect of price controls is to reduce supply. In the case of natural gas, after twenty years of price controls, the quantity demanded substantially exceeds the quantity supplied and a shortage is created by the price control policy. In the case of crude oil, the supply effect is unclear. We currently have a two-tier price system where price controls are in effect on "old" oil only, currently accounting for 63% of domestic production. "New" oil is defined as oil produced from a property in excess of the output in the same month of 1972. 75/ New oil may be sold for whatever the market will bring. Whereas old oil is price controlled at $5.25 per barrel, free market oil in December of 1974 traded at about $11.00 per barrel.

Crude oil price controls appear to be particularly counterproductive with respect to secondary and tertiary recovery operations. 76/ There is a normal decline rate in production from oil reservoirs which, in general, amounts to about 10% per year. A given oil reservoir in January 1975 would normally be producing at about 73% of its 1972 level of production in the absence of new investments to stimulate production. Investment in such stimulation efforts in this example is penalized by the fact that the first 37% increase in output must be sold as old oil at $5.25 per barrel. 77/ Production beyond this level may be sold as new oil at free market prices. In addition, current regulations permit each barrel of new oil to free one barrel of old oil from controls. 78/ Thus, new oil production from an oil field above the corresponding month of 1972 production receives the added encouragement of the difference between the current free market value of oil and the controlled price. In effect, such new oil production may be sold at about $16.75 per barrel ($11 + $11 - $5.25 = $16.75). The 10% decline rate continues and when production falls to the 1972 level, sales at the free market price cease. Thus, price controls retard investments in a major source of near term incremental domestic production.

Because new oil is not subject to price control, its supply appears to be unconstrained. However, the lessons of price control are learned quickly by people who allocate financial resources, both investors and corporate managers. If oil reserves and production can be classified as old oil and price controlled at prices below equilibrium levels, then new oil reserves may at some future date also be classified as old oil and price controlled. Thus, investments to develop new oil resources may be retarded by the present price control system, even though new oil is exempt.

The FPC price controls create similar disincentives to supply. Because of the very large differential between regulated interstate and unregulated intrastate sales of natural gas, companies are not encouraged to explore for gas that will go into interstate sales and this in turn has led them to seek foreign sources for liquified natural gas ("LNG") in places such as Indonesia and Algeria and at prices that are effectively much in excess of either regulated or unregulated U.S. gas. 79/

133.

Over the short term the United States may be able
to obtain as much drilling for natural gas, even that which
would go into interstate sales, as it could through deregulation because of the hope or expectation that natural gas
will eventually be deregulated.  For the medium or long-term
picture, however, it seems clear that deregulation of
natural gas, at least "new" natural gas, is desirable if
domestic opportunities in this area are to be maximized.
Deregulation of natural gas will immediately cause the cost
of deregulated supplies to rise to that in the market for
unregulated, and such costs will be passed along to the
consumer in higher prices. 80/  This would be particularly
the case if all natural gas were to be deregulated, which
suggests that the concept of deregulating "new" gas and
phasing "old" natural gas into deregulation over a period of
time has considerable merit. 81/  President Ford in his 1975
State of the Union message called for the deregulation of
new natural gas and a natural gas excise tax.  He also
called for the deregulation of oil on April 1, 1975 and a
windfall profits tax. 82/

    The FPC also has an impact upon foreign imports
due to its authority over facilities constructed in connection with LNG projects, 83/ but it is quite questionable,
however, whether the FPC as presently constituted is the
agency which should be concerned with energy imports and
whether the procedures followed in the LNG cases are those
which should be applicable. 84/  The record to date seems
clear that regulation of LNG imports by the FPC has been
counterproductive, in reducing supplies and increasing
costs. 85/

    The benefits of price controls are limited to
their income redistribution effects.  The objective of
instituting a price control system is to enable certain
buyers to obtain products below what their market prices
would be. Therefore, to the extent that a price control
system is effective, income will be reallocated in favor of
those who obtain price controlled products at artificially
low prices and at the expense of sellers of such products
and of other potential buyers who, due to a price control
created shortage, are unable to obtain price controlled
products at any price.

[§3.11]   Crude Oil Allocations

By authority of Congress, recently extended from
February 28 to August 31, 1975, the Federal Energy Administration allocates crude oil among users. 86/  Firms that
have in the past invested heavily in exploration and development and found new oil may now, under the allocation
system, be required to sell oil to their competitiors at
prices specified by the Federal Government, generally at the
average cost of their crude supplies.  The FEA estimates the
nation-wide average ratio of owned crude oil to refinery
needs.  Companies with owned reserves in excess of the
national average are required to sell such excess to other
companies with less than the national average. 87/  The
transaction may create a loss for the seller of crude, where
the seller company's only source of incremental crude supplies is imports at a price higher than the average cost of
its crude.  Although regulations allow the seller to recoup
the loss by raising the retail prices on his remaining
production, competitive pressures may make it impossible to
obtain such a higher price. 88/  In such a situation the net
result is a disincentive to import crude.

[§3.12]   The Entitlements Program

The Crude Oil Entitlements Program is designed to
equalize costs of crude among U.S. refiners and to create a
more competitive climate in the petroleum industry. 89/  A
ratio is estimated of the national average of oil crude runs
to refineries in a base period.  Those refiners with less
than the national average of price-controlled crude oil
receive free entitlements from the Federal Government equal
to the volume necessary to bring such refiners up to the
national average of old crude refinery input.  Refiners with
more than the national average are forced to buy entitlements
in order to process their "excess" old crude from other
refiners having less than the national average. Thus, the
entitlement system requires an income transfer from one
group of refineries to another. 90/

The price of entitlements is to be determined and
promulgated by the FEA and is to be based on the difference
between the average price of imported oil and the average
price of domestic old oil.  This difference would appear to
be around $6 per barrel, but the FEA set the initial price at

$5. Thus, since imported oil sells at approximately $11, the entitlements system requires a money transfer of about $5-6 per barrel for every barrel of old oil that one refinery has in excess of the average, to another refinery in a comparable deficit position. 91/

The Entitlements Program also applies to imported distillates and residual fuel oil. Refiners and other established importers may receive product entitlements. Only refiners are eligible to receive crude oil entitlements. 92/

This system has both resource allocation and income distribution consequences. Income redistribution takes two forms. First, income transfers are likely to take place between refineries. Those refineries selling entitlements given to them by the Federal government will receive a contribution from those refineries having more than the national average of price controlled crude oil, distillate and residual fuel oil.

Refiners selling entitlements are required by FEA price regulations to pass such revenues on to consumers in the form of price reductions. On the other hand, refiners who are required to buy entitlements are permitted to raise their prices in order to pass along additional costs of entitlements. Thus, product prices theoretically will be unaffected in the aggregate. The price control system, however, is imperfect. Some marketing areas may not permit higher prices to be passed on to consumers. Where supply and demand currently determine a price below the price permitted by FEA price regulations the purchasing company will be forced by market conditions to absorb at least part of the cost of this income transfer. On the other hand, due to market conditions the company required to pass its new income on to consumers may already by selling at prices below the FEA price regulations. One must assume that less than 100% of the benefits received and costs incurred by refiners will be passed on to the consumers. Therefore, it is highly probable that income will be redistributed between refiners, but the data is not available to assess the net effect of income transfers among refiners.

Second, there is likely to be a massive income transfer between regions of the United States. The FEA has estimated that the Entitlements Program will transfer $29,293,100 per month to residents of New England. Residents of the Middle Atlantic states are expected to receive benefits of $5,443,700 per month and residents of the South Atlantic states, $7,791,000 per month. On the other hand, such benefits would come at the expense of residents of the upper Middle West who are expected to pay $14,235,200 per month, the lower Middle West, $10,330,200 per month, the Rocky Mountains, $1,954,600 per month and residents of the West Coast are expected to pay $16,102,600 per month. 93/

The resource reallocation effects of the Entitlements Program are hard to foresee, but should become apparent as experience is gained. The Entitlements Program affects profitability of refiners by attempting to equalize the cost of inputs among all refiners. If the Entitlements Program reduces the profitability of refining investments, it is likely to retard the future flow of capital into refineries in the United States. Crude oil must be refined. Therefore, the effect will likely not be to lower the worldwide investment in refineries, but rather to shift it away from the U.S. The policy decision of the U.S. to locate refineries in the U.S. or allow product importation from abroad has far-reaching economic and security implications which bear upon the kind of entitlements program deemed desirable.

Second, present regulations also provide that small refiners, those with a capacity less than 175,000 barrels per day, will receive proportionately greater entitlements, relative to large refiners. 94/ If the optimum size refiner is greater than 175,000 barrels per day, then the government program would have the effect of stimulating inefficient refinery construction in the future.

Third, government programs which arbitrarily create sudden massive income transfers have the effect of introducing an unnecessary degree of uncertainty into business investments. Whenever uncertainty is increased investors will require higher rates of return on capital than would be required under normal conditions of uncertainty. Again, crude oil must be refined in approximately the same volumes, therefore this uncertainty is likely to result in a reallocation of investments, not away from refineries, but rather to refineries in areas of the world where financial uncertainty has not increased.

137.

Fourth, regarding the competitive effect of the Entitlements Program, the large international majors may benefit more from the program than the smaller companies, thus aggravating whatever anti-competitive tendencies exist in the industry. 95/

Fifth, the entitlements given to importers of residual fuel oil and middle distillators create a subsidy of about 60 cents per barrel of imported products at a time when the U.S. is trying to reduce imports. 96/

[§3.13]  Effect of Removing FEA Controls on the Oil Industry

Price controls, allocations and entitlements can be considered together because if price controls are removed then the present allocation system and the new entitlements system become moot. In the absence of price controls, there will be one price of oil of any given grade and that price will be the world price plus tariff and tanker costs to the United States. Under free market conditions, supply will by definition equal demand and there will be no shortage. If there is no shortage, there is no need to allocate by any means other than the price system itself. If there is one price rather than the present two-tier price system, then there is no need for entitlements.

Another effect of eliminating controls and one producing a major benefit for the economy is that oil resources would be allocated among competitive uses in a relatively efficient manner. Business managers would buy and use raw materials to minimize cost and maximize profit. Under a control system, profit maximizing behavior is constrained by the requirement to comply with controls, and to circumvent them where possible. 97/

Another effect of eliminating regulations would be to reduce government expenditures that are incurred to administer the control program. Further, expenses incurred by business in operating under and complying with the control program, and in circumventing it, would be eliminated. These expenditures and expenses are large, probably exceeding several hundred million dollars.

138.

Elimination of the control system would have an income distribution effect. First, refiners that are currently benefiting by the allocation and entitlements program by being able to buy low price-controlled oil are gaining income at the expense of others who are currently being penalized. Second, income shifts between regions of the country would reverse those established by the Entitlements Program. Third, if prices are being artifically held below their competitive levels by the price control program, then its removal would cause a price increase. This would involve a shift in income from consumers of petroleum products to producers and royalty owners. If these income redistribution effects are held to be politically unacceptable, then adjustments can be made directly through either raising the current income supplement program or adjusting tax rates or both. A negative income tax system has also been proposed by President Ford in the 1975 State of the Union message as a means of more comprehensively and rationally transferring income from high to low income groups. 98/

The problem involved in using a price control system to redistribute income is that it mixes two problems under one program. While the system may accomplish desirable income redistribution as determined by the political process, it at the same time interferes with a rational resource allocation program within industries and among consumers. The income distribution problem is most efficiently dealt with separately.

If petroleum product prices are in fact being held down by price controls below the level at which free markets and competition would determine, then consumers are motivated to demand more of such products. If prices are allowed to seek a free market level, consumers would more carefully allocate their incomes and less would be spent on oil and oil products. A program of price controls plus tax subsidies that causes prices to be below their competitive levels and forces producers to meet demands at low prices, leads to excessive consumption. Such a program fundamentally is an anti-conservation device. Finally, the system as currently structured favors the development of offshore refineries rather than domestic facilities. This condition increases the security risks associated with imports substantially. Moreover, stockpiling of refined products is much more complicated and expensive than crude oil. 99/

In sum, the elimination of presently existing regulations in the form of price controls, allocations, and entitlements would increase the efficiency level at which scarce natural resources are used.  If income distribution effects are deemed by the political process to be unacceptable, then adjustments can be made in the nation's welfare or tax program.

[§3.14]  Environmental Protection Law and Regulations

The growing body of environmental protection law and regulations in the past decade or so has significantly aggravated the present imbalance between oil demand and supply.  Two important examples of that trend are the National Environmental Policy Act of 1969 ("NEPA") 100/ and the 1970 amendments to the Clean Air Act.  NEPA's requirement that an Environmental Impact Statement must be prepared for any proposed Federal action "significantly affecting the quality of the human environment" has occasioned much delay and expense for various energy investments.  Further, the impact statements themselves, as was presumably intended by Congress in passing the law, have often raised complex and lengthy disputes in courts and administrative agencies.

The Clean Air Act amendments and regulations promulgated by the Environmental Protection Agency have increased the demand for natural gas and oil products for vehicles, utilities, and businesses.  At the same time, the incentive to new investment in oil and gas production which this increased demand might have created has been blunted by price controls.

Probably the most promising area for political initiatives by Congress and the President in this area is the creation of a better means for resolving energy-environment conflicts.  Under the present system frequently all parties to a given dispute, including the general public, lose more than is necessary.  The prospects of costly and lengthy delays, administrative and judicial proceedings, and uncertain ultimate outcome are often important disincentives to investment in needed energy development. 101/  Environmental opposition to the Trans-Alaska Pipeline, for example created very substantial delays and large costs for quite conjectural benefits. 102/  In those cases in which a proposed project has an unacceptable impact on the environment, everyone would benefit from an expeditious authoritative decision to that effect so that necessary alternative plans could go forward as early as practicable. A decision-making process to determine priorities and resolve conflicts among objectives should be established. 103/

One oil company official interviewed made the following observation:

> "Back in the 'thirties,' we created the alphabet agencies because we couldn't trust the courts. Lately we've gone back to the courts because we can't trust the alphabet agencies. What we need is some competent Federal body which would have the authority to weigh a proposed project on its merits and then make a final binding decision. Why should we have to fight over Storm King [a New York power facility] for years before a decision is made?" 104/

It seems clear that a new and independent body, such as the National Labor Relations Board 105/ or the Federal Reserve Board, 106/ must be created to perform this decision making function. It would seem appropriate to assign this agency the resolution of conflicts pertaining to specific categories of Federally related projects, such as siting of power plants and offshore drilling, with judicial review as restricted as practicable. 107/ In some areas, this may involve Federal preemption of existing state authority over such issues, to prevent disputes in state courts and agencies. 108/

## [§3.15]  Cargo Preference Laws

The Jones Act 109/ requires that all shipments including oil between any two U.S. ports be carried in ships constructed in the United States, owned by American companies, and manned by American crews. This law will increase the cost of transporting oil from Alaska's port of Valdez to ports in the lower 48 states. Since U.S. shipping is far more expensive than foreign flag shipping, the effect of the Jones Act is to raise prices on products within its purview and to misallocate freight from artificially high priced water shipment to rail or truck systems.

The Cargo Preference bill passed by Congress in 1974 and vetoed by President Ford would have required a percentage of imported oil to be carried in U.S. ships. 110/ Adopting such a law would have increased the cost of delivering oil to the United States, and forced the construction of unneeded ships in high-cost U.S. shipyards. Such a law would have a pronounced protectionist impact because it would force importers to favor American ships and would increase the incentive for other countries, including OPEC nations, to adopt similar laws for either their imports or their exports. 111/

D. [§3.16] Conclusion

Only the principal incentives and disincentives have been discussed, less significant factors have been examined in Appendix B. 112/ Any appraisal of their overall net effect, or of the net effect of altering or abolishing any combination of them is necessarily highly subjective, in view of their complexity and the many political judgments involved in such appraisal.

The high current price of "new" oil is the dominant element changing the recent sum of incentives in favor of additional investment in U.S. oil production. Such investment is still significantly deterred, however, by two important factors: price controls on "old" oil and their uncertain future duration and scope, and uncertainty about the permanence of the current high level of international oil prices. Eliminating both controls and tax incentives would probably result in a significantly increased incentive to invest in domestic production, even though uncertainty over international prices would remain. 113/

The FEA price controls, however, have no direct effect on the profitability of investment in foreign production, since regulations exempt the first sale price for imports into U.S. commerce. 114/ Consequently, abolishing those controls would affect the attractiveness of foreign production only by making domestic investments more attractive to available capital.

Tax incentives for foreign operations have declined in importance recently, however, for two main reasons both related to the trend toward increasing nationalization. This trend has increased producer-country control over the effective per barrel margin a company can reap from its operations. The size of this margin is the most important factor affecting investment abroad. Second, producing countries have increasingly become sellers of oil at wholesale to the companies and have been moving toward setting a single price for it. If this is done, and if the price is denominated exclusively as a price rather than as royalty and income tax, the companies will have no choice but to treat the costs of crude as business expenses. 115/ Under these circumstances tax considerations would cease being significant incentives to foreign oil operations. 116/

One qualification is in order, however. If per barrel margins in the future stabilize at a level where they are just barely profitable, tax incentives of U.S. law could be significant in tipping the balance for or against foreign investment. Knowing this, producer-country governments may plan their new price and tax structures to take maximum possible advantage of U.S. tax laws and interpretations thereof, in order to enhance the ability of the companies to profit from low margins. 117/ To this extent, the future importance of U.S. tax incentives for foreign operations remains an open question.

In terms of the major U.S. objectives of affecting price and assuring security of supply, the modification of the incentive structure offers limited opportunities. Nevertheless, the current structure has two overall liabilities.

The first is that the current tax structure creates a strong identity of interest between the producer government and the company. To the extent that it is desirable to weaken this identity, the removal of foreign tax credits resulting from the substitution of income taxes for royalties warrants consideration. 118/ Second, the producer countries have almost total discretion in the determination of the price to be paid for their oil and the fee to be paid to the producing company. To the extent that the costs of these companies are reduced by U.S. tax benefits, those benefits will tend to accrue to the producer country rather than the companies or the consumer.

As has been noted above, however, if the United States alone were to remove tax incentives, then U.S. firms would tend to be disadvantaged vis-a-vis other foreign competitors. There are two possible remedies for this. The U.S. could seek through diplomatic means an adjustment in tax structures of the host governments of non-U.S. firms which negate this advantage and result in an accrual of revenues to their treasuries. This could be done either through a series of bilateral negotiations, or perhaps also through the recently established International Energy Agency. Second, if the U.S. should find itself unable to secure the cooperation of other consuming governments in equalizing the tax incidence on the companies, the same effect might be achieved by introducing the principle of reciprocity whereby the companies of those countries which did not equalize the tax incidence would not be allowed further access to U.S. resources. 119/

CHAPTER 3

FOOTNOTES

1. See, for instance, discussions of various tax
   incentives in G. Fromm, ed., Tax Incentives and
   Capital Spending (1971).

2. Assuming, however, that per barrel margins are not
   kept from being profitable by host country taxes
   and direct oil sales policies.

3. Internal Revenue Code (hereafter cited as "I.R.C.")
   §§901, 904.

4. I.R.C. Regs. §1.904-1(d).

5. See §3.4, infra.

6. Such issues include deferral, Western Hemisphere
   Trade Corporations and expensing of intangible
   drilling expenses, discussed in §3.6, infra.

7. See §1.10, supra.

8. France, for instance, does not tax the income earned
   abroad by a foreign branch of a domestic corporation.
   World Tax Series, Taxation in France 709 (1966).

9. See §1.10, supra.

10. See discussion in Brannon, Energy Taxes and Subsidies
    98-99 (1974).

11. In the example in the text, for instance, if the pre-
    tax cost of the oil were $3 per barrel, $2 would be
    considered a royalty payment, reducing net income to
    $1 before host-country income taxes, deemed to be
    48 cents.

12. If the foreign income tax rate were less than the U.S.
    rate, additional taxes would be due to the U.S.

13. Buy-back oil payments may be so structured, for
    instance. See discussion in Report to the Senate
    Committee on Foreign Relations by the Subcommittee
    on Multinational Corporations, Multinational Oil
    Corporations and U.S. Foreign Policy, 93d Cong.,
    2d Sess., at 12-13 (Comm. Print, Jan. 2, 1975).

14. Often, however, much allowable foreign tax credit
    will still ultimately be unusable.

15. See §1.7, supra et seq.

16. I.R.C. §904(a)(2). Several U.S. companies have
    substantial tanker operations conducted through
    foreign subsidiaries, particularly Panamanian or
    Liberian.

17. I.R.C. §901(e).

18. Brannon, Energy Taxes and Subsidies 98 (1974).

19. Permanent Subcommittee on Investigations of the
    Senate Committee on Government Operations, Analysis
    of the Tax Data of Seven Major Oil Companies, 93d Cong.,
    2d Sess., 12 (Comm. Print, Nov., 1974).

20. I.R.C. Regs. §1.904-1.

21. House Ways and Means Committee, The Oil and Gas
    Energy Tax Act of 1974, H.R. Rep. No. 93-1028,
    93d Cong., 1st Sess. (May 4, 1974).

22. Petroleum company questionnaire response.

23. I.R.C. §613.

24. Ibid.

25. Spann, Erickson and Milsaps study as cited in Senate
    Committee on Interior and Insular Affairs, Analysis
    of The Federal Tax Treatment of Oil and Gas and Some
    Policy Alternatives, 93d Cong., 2d Sess., at 35 (Comm.
    Print, 1974).

26. Los Angeles Times, Jan. 16, 1975, at 21.

27. See §5.3, *infra*.

28. *Supra*, note 1.

29. See Appendix C, §C.1, responses to Question 6.

30. See discussion at Analysis of the Tax Data of Seven Major Oil Companies, *supra*, note 19, at 7-9.

31. An example is analyzed at *ibid*, 8-9.

32. I.R.C. Regs. §1.612-4.

33. See Analysis of the Federal Tax Treatment of Oil and Gas and Some Policy Alternatives, *supra* note 25, at 27.

34. *Ibid*.

35. I.R.C. Regs. §1.611-1(a)(1).

36. Company respondents indicated that some decrease in drilling capital would probably follow repeal of IDC. See Appendix C, §C.1, Question 6.

37. At current prices, domestic drilling ventures appear especially attractive. Petroleum Intelligence Weekly, Aug. 12, 1974, 10.

38. Appendix C, §C.1, Question 6.

39. This is true where the taxpayer has a net loss in the foreign country equal to or greater than the amount of his IDC allowance in that country.

40. Authority for price control is provided by The Emergency Petroleum Allocation Act of 1973, 87 Stat. 627 (Nov. 27, 1973).

41. Brannon, Energy Taxes and Subsidies 38-42 (1974).

42. Some of that production, however, may ultimately reach U.S. markets after refining in Europe.

43. The value of the tax subsidies increases the amount of economic rent from foreign oil production, for which rent producer country Governments, consumer country Governments (and thus indirectly consumers), and the companies will be in contention. See Analysis

in R. Mikesell et al., <u>Foreign Investment in the</u>
<u>Petroleum and Mineral Industries</u> 34-40 (1971).

44. Such margins were largely responsible for record
profits for several major companies in 1974.  See
annual reports of companies interviewed; <u>Los</u>
<u>Angeles Times</u>, Jan. 25, 1975, pt. III, at 8.

45. Fourth quarter 1974 company earnings tended down
sharply.  <u>Ibid</u>.

46. <u>Petroleum Intelligence Weekly</u>, July 15, 1974, 7.

47. Appendix C, §C.1, Question 3.

48. I.R.C. §62(5).

49. I.R.C. §901.

50. State and local income taxes are deductible under
I.R.C. §164(a)(3).

51. <u>Ibid</u>.

52. <u>Analysis of the Tax Data of Seven Major Oil Companies</u>,
<u>supra</u> note 25 at 13.

53. <u>Ibid</u>.

54. <u>Ibid</u>.

54a. See <u>U.S. Gypsum Company v. United States</u>, 304 F. Supp.
627, 642 (N.D. Ill., 1969).

55. The inter-corporate dividend deduction does not apply
to dividends from a foreign subsidiary earning its
income abroad.  I.R.C. §245(a), (b).

56. In the case of a Domestic International Sales Corporation (DISC) this principle is explicitly  used as a
tax incentive.  I.R.C. §§991-997.

57. I.R.C. §§951-954, 531-537, 541-547.

58. In addition, repatriated foreign earnings have a beneficial effect on the U.S. balance of trade.

59. FEA, Project Independence Report 279-294 (Nov., 1974).

60. Brannon, Energy Taxes and Subsidies 101-105 (1974).

61. Appendix C, §C.1, Question 6.

62. Many company interviewees emphasized this point.

63. Corporations of countries, such as France, which do not tax foreign earnings of a separately administered branch, have an even greater competitive tax advantage. See supra, note 8.

64. See, for instance, Arthur Andersen and Co., Tax and Trade Guide: United Kingdom, 106-107 (1964).

65. Such suggestions have been made by members of the Subcommittee on Multinational Corporations of the Senate Committee on Foreign Relations. Los Angeles Times, Jan. 12, 1975, at 1, pt. 1-A, at 10.

66. Such authority is given for the Interest Equalization Tax. I.R.C. §494(b)(2). This provision authorizes the President to vary the tax rate by Executive Order.

67. If tax considerations are important to expected profitability, uncertainty regarding the applicable tax rates will make such investments unattractive.

68. For instance, if a refinery has been built abroad to process crude from another foreign country, a new tax against the foreign crude source may also make the refinery a liability to the company.

69. See, for instance, Executive Order 11387 (Jan. 1, 1968).

70. Administering and enforcing such a ban, however, would be difficult.

71. This could be done through such means as grants, loans, guarantees, or tax credits.

72. See §2.11, supra.

73. Where natural gas is freely available, artificially low prices will increase demand for gas and decrease the demand, and thus the free market price, for oil. This therefore discourages oil production. When gas is in short supply, as at present, this effect is probably negligible, except where oil and gas are joint products. Where oil and gas are expected to be found together, an artificially low price for the gas will reduce the incentive for drilling and thus also has a depressing effect on the supply of oil.

74. 10 C.F.R. §§212.1 et seq.

75. 10 C.F.R. §212.72; 39 F.R. 31622 (Aug. 30, 1974).

76. Wall Street Journal, Aug. 22, 1974, 1, 10.

77. In other words, the 1972 level of output must be reached before "new" is produced.

78. 10 C.F.R. §212.72; 39 F.R. 31622 (Aug. 30, 1974).

79. One public utility official interviewed cited anticipated costs of up to $1.90 per Mcf.

80. One estimate is that the price would have to go to $2 per Mcf to maintain production at current levels through 1985. Oil and Gas Journal, Sept. 9, 1974, 42.

81. P. MacAvoy and R. Pindyck, "Alternative Regulatory Policies for Dealing with the Natural Gas Shortage," 4 The Bell Journal of Economics and Management Sciences 454 (Aut., 1973).

82. Los Angeles Times, Jan. 16, 1975, 21.

83. 15 U.S.C. §§717a, 717f; 18 C.F.R. §§154.1 et seq.

84. State Department, Indonesian Government and industry interviews cited examples in which FPC delay of approval for LNG facilities hampered negotiations with producer-country governments and resulted in higher prices. See §6.3, supra at note 26.

150.

85. Several company interviewees independently made this point. Independent evidence was also furnished by interviews in Indonesia. See §6.3, infra.

86. 10 C.F.R. §§211.1 et seq.

87. Ibid.

88. One company interviewed cited monthly losses on the order of $1 a barrel on quantities in excess of one million barrels per month under these circumstances.

89. See general description at 39 F.R. 39740 (Nov. 11, 1974).

90. Ibid.

91. The first list of entitlement buyers and sellers, for the month of November, 1974, was published at 40 F.R. 2562-2573 (Jan. 13, 1975).

92. Ibid.

93. Oil and Gas Journal, Dec. 9, 1974, 40-41.

94. 39 F.R. 39740 (Nov. 11, 1974).

95. For the first month, for instance, net sellers of entitlements included Mobil, Socal, Texaco, and Arco. 40 F.R. 2562-2573 (Jan. 13, 1975).

96. This subsidy may, however, be useful in offsetting the differential impact of President Ford's proposed import tariffs on various sections of the country. See §5.3, infra.

97. See also discussion of constraints resulting from import quantity controls at §5.1 infra.

98. Los Angeles Times Jan. 16, 1975, 21.

99. See Testimony of John Lichtblan and Walter Mead at Hearings on S.1586 before the Senate Committee on Interior and Insular Affairs, 93d Cong., 1st Sess., at 94, Ser. No. 93-11(92-46).

100. 83 Stat. 852 (Jan. 1, 1970); 42 U.S.C. §§4321 et seq.

101. See, for instance, description of the decade-long disputes over the Storm King N.Y. power facility, in 5 Environmental Reporter 77-78 (May 17, 1974).

102. The Wilderness Society v. Morton, 479 F. 2d 842 (D.C. Cir., 1973) culminated a long legal battle by holding that the pipeline would not comply with the then-existing requirements of The Mineral Leasing Act, 30 U.S.C. §185. Up to that point the companies claimed to have spent $9 million in connection with the preparation of the environmental impact statement. Wilderness Society, at 847. The problem was resolved only with passage of the Trans-Alaska Pipeline Act, 87 Stat. 584 (Nov. 16, 1973) codified at 43 U.S.C. §§1651-1655. See description of the controversy and the legal issues involved at S.R. No. 93-207, 1973 U.S. Code Cong. and Admin. News 2417-2424.

103. The enabling legislation should, however, carefully define the parameters within which the administrators are to make their decisions so that the process is politically acceptable.

104. Oil company interview.

105. 29 U.S.C. §151 et seq.

106. 12 U.S.C. §241 et seq.

107. As is done regarding labor disputes, for instance. 29 U.S.C. §§101-115.

108. Such areas may include, for instance, authority over onshore facilities constructed in connection with offshore drilling. See discussion of this and other state-federal issues re offshore drilling in Nossaman et al, Study on the Outer Continental Shelf Lands of the United States, §3.15-§3.22 (1968).

109. 41 Stat. 988 (June 5, 1920). Codified at 46 U.S.C.passim.

110. Oil and Gas Journal, Dec. 23, 1974, 9-10.

111. This could have the effect of enhancing control of downstream operations by OPEC nations. See §6.1, _infra_.

112. Appendix B, §B.1 _et seq_.

113. Such uncertainty could be removed or reduced, however, by the imposition of an import tariff. See §5.3, _infra_.

114. 10 C.F.R. §212.53.

115. I.R.C. §62(5).

116. Appendix C. §C.1, Question 6.

117. The benefit of the tax incentive would likely be split between the companies and the producer country.

118. Multinational Oil Corporations and U.S. Foreign Policy, _supra_, note 13, at 10-11.

119. This measure was taken against Shell in the 1920's in connection with the dispute over U.S. companies' access to East Indies crude. See §1.2, _supra_.

CHAPTER 4

REGULATING OIL COMPANIES
AS PUBLIC UTILITIES

A.   [§4.0]   General

        Proposals or suggestions are made from time to
time that the production and distribution of petroleum
products ought to be subject to the kind of regulatory
control to which public utilities or common carriers are
subjected.  Regulatory arrangements of many kinds and of
many degrees of complexity are conceivable, but at the core
of most such proposals is the idea that the oil companies
should be required to make their products available at
prices fixed or reviewed by permanent regulatory commissions
at either or both the State and Federal levels. 1/

        Such regulation would very likely be chiefly
directed toward one or more of the following objectives:

        1.   To prevent monopoly or oligopoly prices for
petroleum products;

        2.   To keep the prices of petroleum products
"artificially" low, that is, below what such products would
command in an unregulated, free and competitive market, in
order to benefit or subsidize the consumer; or

        3.   To assure an adequate supply of petroleum
products or to allocate the supply which is available.

        The first objective applies to the classic situa-
tion thought to call for public utility type regulation,
namely, the "natural monopoly."  Where economies of scale
require very large plants and firms relative to the size of
the market, so that a given market can reasonably support
only one supplier and the goods or services in question are
considered vital to society, regulation is appropriate in
order to assure that the supplier will not be able to
extract a monopoly price from the public by restricting
output and raising price.  Regulation here thus serves
chiefly to remedy the market defect of a lack of effective
competition.

        The second objective applies to at least two kinds
of situations where it may appear desirable to regulate an
industry even though effective competition exists within it.

155.

One such situation is where the cost of production is high, and the free market price correspondingly high, but for some reason it is desired to subsidize consumption of the product or service by means of an artificially low price to the consumer, perhaps a price even below the cost of production. Fixing low fares for metropolitan mass transit services through public subsidies is an example of this kind of regulatory measure.

A different kind of situation, more relevant to the oil industry, is where the market price for a product is high relative to the cost of producing it, or certain units of it, such as because of the skill or good fortune of particular producers (e.g., the owners of highly productive reserves that are inexpensive to develop). In such a case, regulatory authorities may want to fix a price below the free market price in order to prevent those producers from gaining high profits, commonly known as "windfall profits" and referred to by economists as "rents." 2/ In effect, the regulatory authority transfers those profits directly to users of the product by enforcing low prices for low-cost units of production.

The third objective may apply to situations in which the market is competitive and no producers are receiving high economic rents, but where for some reason it appears desirable that the products in question be produced in greater or lesser quantities than market forces induce; or, where output cannot be increased, it is desired to ration the products in accordance with government-chosen priorities rather than by means of the market. For instance, the regulatory authority might compel suppliers to meet the needs of public agencies at a price lower than would elicit such sales priority voluntarily, before supplying private consumers. Exports of the product may be prohibited, or producers may be required to enter long-term contracts with preferred users as a condition of doing business within a jurisdiction. In any event, the obligation of rationing supply will necessarily accompany any attempt to fix prices below the free market level, because such low prices stimulate consumption and discourage supply. If the product is traded internationally, low prices lead to diversion to any higher-priced markets which may exist outside the United States. 3/

There are at least four basic kinds of criticism
which are commonly directed at the work of regulatory
agencies generally and which might be applicable to any
permanent, large-scale regulation of oil companies as
public utilities.

1. One common criticism of regulatory agencies
is that they fail to fulfill their intended functions
because of shortcomings in their work, which tends to be
slow, inefficient, bureaucratic, and generally "unbusiness-
like." Huge case backlogs, extended litigation, inadequate
staff work, and lack of expertise on the part of agency
or commission members are points commonly stressed by this
kind of criticism. Often cited as exemplars of such
deficiences are the Interstate Commerce Commission ("ICC") 4/
and the Federal Power Commission ("FPC"). 5/ Indeed, the
backlog of the FPC in 1960 was so great that the Landis
Commission appointed by President Kennedy to study the
regulatory agencies concluded:

> "The FPC without question represents
> the outstanding example in the federal
> government of the breakdown of the
> administrative process." 6/

2. A second kind of criticism commonly made of
regulatory bodies rests on a "capture theory" of government
regulation. In this view there is an inexorable tendency
for regulators, at the Federal as well as the state level,
to become strongly identified with the very interests they
are in theory supposed to regulate and in time, to become
advocates for such interests.

Judge William Campbell reflected this view when
he remarked in a Court of Appeals opinion that "the history
of United States regulatory agencies in general . . .
seems to demonstrate that shortly following the establishment of administrative procedures the regulatory agency
usually becomes dominated by the industry which it was
created to regulate." 7/

The Civil Aeronautics Board ("CAB") 8/, the
Federal Communications Commission 9/, the U.S. Geological
Survey 10/ and, again, the ICC are frequently cited as

exhibiting such tendencies.  Critics with this perspective
point out such facts as that, for example, the CAB is
more likely to be concerned about the impact of a major
airline going bankrupt than about an undramatic, but in
the aggregate equally or more important, excessive cost
burden borne by all airline customers to sustain the troubled
company. 11/  They also point out that many agency or commission
members anticipate future lucrative employment within the
industry they are charged with regulating or have which come
from it may create a "conflict of interest."

3.  A third major kind of criticism is typified
by (but by no means confined to) the "Chicago school" 12/
of economic theory:  that the entire regulatory enterprise
is bound to fail in its objectives because the actions of
the regulators tend inexorably to be at cross-purposes with
what economic theory would dictate.  This view holds, for
instance, that the actions of the Federal Reserve Board in
regulating the rediscount rate and the supply of money
aggrevate rather than ameliorate the nation's economic
problems because the impact of such measures is not felt
within the economy until the conditions or problems which
have inspired them have changed significantly, and often
drastically. 13/  In the case of public utilities, regulation
of prices or rates tends to induce various kinds of economically irrational behavior which in the long run increases
costs, decreases efficiency, and diminishes the quantity or
quality of goods and services provided.  Thus the regulator
in the end usually only manages to offset or blunt what
would otherwise be the beneficial impact of free market
forces.

4.  Regulation is expensive.  It requires two
additional bureaucracies, one in government doing the
regulating, and another in the regulated industry, peti-
tioning regulators, and responding to regulation. 14/

To some extent, each of the above four types of
criticism point up likely dangers and drawbacks of any
comprehensive regulatory scheme for the petroleum industry.
In particular, because of the importance of oil products
to the American economy as a whole, the third type of
criticism above deserves most careful consideration, for
it portends possible serious disruptions in the supply of
these products.  Further, it is this type of criticism to
which the work of the FPC in regulating natural gas producers
appears to be most vulnerable.

If, as appears quite possible or even likely, regulating oil companies as public utilities would reduce the aggregate available supply of domestic crude and products, the net result would be greater U.S. reliance on petroleum imports. 15/

Regulation of the oil industry in order to achieve one or more of the above-mentioned three objectives is far from unprecedented. During 1974, the Federal Energy Administration ("FEA") regulated both price and supply of many petroleum products, under the authority delegated to it by the President, pursuant to various acts of Congress, particularly the Emergency Petroleum Allocation Act of 1973. 16/ Such powers, however, were regarded both by Congress and by the Executive branch as extraordinary in nature and limited to the duration of the then-current emergency. The Emergency Petroleum Allocation Act of 1973 was originally scheduled to expire February 28, 1975, but was extended by Congress to August 31, 1975. 17/

Thus, since the FEA's regulatory authority was deemed temporary, the agency did not have to establish procedures for fixing or reviewing prices of petroleum products in light of their possible long-term impact on oil company revenues, supply, and consumption levels. In essence, prices were merely fixed at the level of May 15, 1973 plus cost increases after that date. 18/ Consequently, although some might argue that the effects of the FEA regulation of price and supply have been beneficial, similar regulation on a permanent basis might well have very different results. The FEA's experience through 1974 in any event offers scant basis for predicting any such long-term results.

The Federal Power Commission has had extensive experience regulating the wellhead price of natural gas on an ostensibly permanent basis, and this experience is perhaps the most suggestive of the possible costs and benefits of full-scale regulation of the oil industry. Since 1954, the FPC has had the power to regulate the wellhead price of all natural gas moving in interstate commerce. 19/ This experience has created very much controversy. It is now widely, though by no means unanimously, believed that such regulation has done the consuming public more harm than good, chiefly because the prices set by the FPC have been too low to encourage new production, and have encouraged

159.

wasteful uses of natural gas, with the result that massive
shortfalls of natural gas began to occur in the early
1970's. 20/ On the other hand, it can be argued that FPC
regulation has saved consumers much money that otherwise
would have gone to gas producers as high economic rents and
has helped prevent producers from diverting interstate
natural gas from residential users to industrial users. At
the same time, others desiring to buy natural gas have not
been able to do so at any price. 21/ However one might choose
to balance these factors, it does seem clear that the FPC
experience illustrates many of the problems that would be
created by a full-scale attempt permanently to regulate the
oil industry as a public utility. Such problems include:
determination of an appropriate rate base and rate of return;
eliminating high rents without discouraging production;
maintaining efficiency in production where a "fair rate of
return" is guaranteed; avoiding irrational allocations of
available supplies; and coping with a massive backlog of
rate determination cases. All of these issues can be expected to arise in an aggravated form if the industry is
subject to comprehensive, permanent regulation.

Below are considered in more detail the possible
objectives of regulating the oil companies as public utilities; the various kinds of objections to such policies; and
the lessons that might be drawn from the regulatory experience
of the FPC.

B.   [§4.1]   Preventing Monopoly or Oligopoly Pricing

Whether or not it would make sense to regulate the
oil industry in order to prevent monopoly or oligopoly pricing
depends, in the first instance, on whether the oil industry
is in fact competitive or not. Various studies have been
done on this question, but the opinions drawn from such
studies vary considerably.

In July, 1973, a Federal Trade Commission ("FTC")
study concluded essentially that effective competition was
lacking in the industry. 22/ The study indicated that the
top 20 oil companies' share of domestic crude oil production
was about 63 percent in 1960 and about 70 percent in 1969.
The eight largest firms in the industry, according to the
report, had 55 percent of the market in gasoline and 58 percent

of crude oil production capacity. 23/ The report also concluded that the major oil companies have been able to stifle
possible competition within the industry by means of their
vertically integrated control over all the functions within
the industry, including crude production, refining, retail
marketing, and transportation. 24/ Referring to the "huge
integrated firms who control the industry," the report
alleged:

> "These major firms, which con-
> sistently appear to cooperate rather
> than compete in all phases of their
> operation, have behaved in a similar
> fashion as would a classical monopolist:
> they have attempted to increase profits
> by restricting output." 25/

Coincident with the release of the study, the FTC commenced
antitrust actions against the leading eight oil companies in
order to force them to dismantle their vertical integration
of industry functions by divesting themslves of control of
one or more such functions. 26/

Shortly after the release of the FTC study, the
Department of the Treasury released a staff analysis of the
FTC report which reached very different conclusions about
the existence or nonexistence of competition within the
industry. 27/ The Treasury analysis disagreed with virtually
every important conclusion drawn by the FTC study. In particular, the Treasury analysis questioned the accuracy of
the FTC figures on market shares and shares of refining
capacity of the oil companies, and concluded there was no
trend toward increased concentration within the industry;
rather, the independents were increasing their market shares
at the expense of the majors. 28/ Furthermore, it concluded
that vigorous competition exists within the industry. Regarding the integrated operations of the eighteen vertically
integrated firms, the FTC report concluded that such operations had made possible oligopoly market behavior, to the
detriment of the consumer, but the Treasury staff analysis
concluded that such vertically integrated operations had
made possible economies of scale which have benefited the
consumer. Thus, for instance, whereas the FTC recommends
divestiture of pipeline ownership by the majors, the Treasury

analysis, while agreeing that there is little competition among pipelines recommends against such divestiture and argues in effect that pipelines are natural monopolies or natural oligopolies. 29/

The different attitude taken in the two reports toward the role of government policies in inducing anti-competitive behavior in the industry is very striking. Both reports agree that government policies on price and allocation over the years have often had anticompetitive results within the oil industry, but the FTC approach tends to view this as evidence that the industry has been strong enough to enlist the complicity of the government in its pursuit of oligopolistic power, while the Treasury approach tends to exonerate the companies from wrongdoing with the argument that they cannot be blamed for obeying the law and going along with the national policies. It appears, then, that much of the disagreement between the two analyses is really over something no appeal to "facts" can settle, namely, how the companies would have behaved if government policy had been different.

Another example of the disagreement between the two studies may indicate the difficulty of evaluating the degree of anticompetitive behavior within the industry. Independent gasoline marketers experienced a severe price and supply squeeze in the early 1970's. The FTC report takes the position that the major oil companies were essentially engaged in predatory pricing in areas where gasoline costs were high, in order to undercut the independents long enough to drive them out of business, and were financing such practices with profits derived from other phases of their operations. 30/ The Treasury analysis claims that the cause of the squeeze on the independents was the government price controls during the period of August, 1971, to January, 1973, when, as part of the general wage-price freeze, no price increases were allowed for gasoline and No. 2 fuel oil. This kept demand in excess of supply so that independent refiners and marketers could no longer obtain crude and products on the spot market. 31/

The guidelines of the Antitrust Division of the Department of Justice strongly indicate that this industry is competitive. The number of firms is large enough and their respective shares of market are small enough that oligopolistic pricing would structurally be very difficult to achieve. 32/ Moreover, most independent studies that have been conducted on the matter have concluded that the industry is competitive both domestically 33/ and abroad. 34/ As noted earlier, irrespective of what may have existed in the past, it is today clear that the petroleum industry has for a substantial period of time had very effective competition. 35/

There is no doubt that at times there have been uncompetitive practices in the industry and there is a responsible difference of opinion as to the extent and significance of these practices. 36/ The industry appears structurally quite competitive, however.

[§4.2] Regulation and Antitrust Policy

If it is decided that the oil industry or some segment thereof is not competitive and that, therefore, public utilities type regulation is called for, such regulation would probably have negative implications with respect to antitrust policies. While comprehensive regulation does not in itself exempt an industry from antitrust laws, the decision to regulate typically creates a disposition to accept the inevitability of the lack of effective competition within the industry and to attempt to replicate its results by controlling prices and outputs. Moreover, the regulatory process itself tends to insulate the regulated firm or industry from price competition and thus to bring about oligopolistic market conditions. The logic of that process turns it not only into a means of setting maximum rates for the product or service involved but also minimum rates. 38/ In the airline industry, for instance, the revenue requirements of the least successful lines tend to set the level of fares, at rates higher than what competition probably would produce. The financially hard-pressed lines will be able to justify fare increases to the CAB which the more prosperous lines could not justify, and subsequently the more prosperous lines can increase their fares in concert in order to maintain "consistency" within the industry. 39/

163.

Often, potential new entrants to a market are required to seek regulatory agency approval, so that the regulatory process becomes a barrier to entry, and sometimes a very effective one. 40/

One can reasonably anticipate, therefore, that comprehensive regulation will carry with it a diminution in antitrust enforcement in the oil industry.

C.    [§4.3]  Determination of Rate Base and Rate of Return

Rates charged by public utilities are regulated on the basis of a "cost of service" concept. The utility is allowed a rate which will produce sufficient revenue to:  (1) cover the cost of labor and materials used in producing and distributing the product; and (2) provide a profit to the utility equal to a "fair" rate of return on its "rate base," that is, on the value of its capital investment.

Ideally, through this approach the regulatory authority is able to replicate the profit and price results that would obtain if there existed a competitive market for the utility's product or service.  A fair rate of return and an appropriate rate base are determined, explicitly or implicitly, by reference to what would obtain under hypo-thetical competitive conditions.  In practice, however, the regulatory process itself so changes the market situation that it is very doubtful whether it ever can in fact artificially simulate the results of a competitive free market.

Determining a reasonable valuation for the rate base is difficult.  The regulatory process attempts to determine the appropriate revenue requirement by reference to the value of the capital assets of the utility, but the true economic value of the assets depends on the revenue they can earn.  Value, in short, is a function of the income-earning potential of the assets.  On the other hand, if, to avoid this dilemma, the value of assets is deemed to be equal to cost, or to cost less depreciation, the share-holders or owners of the assets are locked into unreal-istically low or high values after a few years of inflation, deflation, or changes in technology or market conditions. 41/

Even more serious departures from free market conditions occur when the regulatory effort itself loses credibility or fails to work as it should. When producers and consumers begin to suspect that the regulatory effort will be significantly modified or abandoned in the future, they may anticipate sudden and substantial price changes and behave in a manner that increases the likelihood of such changes. Producers try to hold back supply from the market in anticipation of higher fixed or free market prices, while consumers acting on similar logic try to buy and hoard. 42/ Because of such factors it is usually very difficult to estimate the relationship between the price and quality of a product or service when it is provided under regulation and when it is not provided under regulation.

The regulation of electric utilities is another area that has been studied in an attempt to evaluate the impact of regulation. Such regulation has taken various forms, but the general approach has been to adjust the allowed rates on electricity so that the rate of return on the electricity utilities' investment is "adequate." It seems clear that this form of regulation may prevent rate increases, but is ineffective in reducing rates when utilities encounter technological advances or economies of scale that would allow a decrease in rates. 43/ Different methods of evaluating an electric utility's rate base do not seem to influence the level of electricity rates. Not only does the form of evaluation (original cost or fair value) make little difference, but the rate of return earned by the utility does not seem to have any measurable impact on the level of rates. 44/ Instead, the primary factors (at least during the early 1960's) affecting rates appeared to be the cost of fuel, the scale of operations, and the existence of publicly owned power sources. 45/ This suggests that there is some difference between the stated form of regulation (i.e., based on rate of return) and the actual form of regulation.

Finally, a regulatory agency, either because it tends to be "captured" by the industry it regulates, or because it tends to maintain the status quo, in many cases appears to aid or prolong the existence of a cartel. As one example of this problem, Paul MacAvoy cites the early results of regulations of the railroad industry by the ICC.

165.

Between 1875 and 1887 there was a series of cartel agreements between railroads in the United States but rates tended to decline as each cartel agreement broke down, due to "cheating" by its members. In 1887 the ICC began regulating the railroad industry. The apparent result of this regulation was the stabilizing of rates at the level set by the cartel. The government, in other words, was providing what was needed to make the cartel work. 46/

Aside from these problems inherent within the regulatory process in general, certain problems peculiar to the oil industry are likely to arise. The most intractable of such problems arise from the fact that the nature of the industry is such that there is a wide difference between the companies both domestically and abroad. The ratio of their upstream to downstream assets, the ratio of their foreign to domestic assets and the "mix" of petroleum substances which they produce, process and sell typically vary widely. 47/ This results in a wide dispersion of actual rates of return on investment within the industry, and a similarly wide dispersion in actual costs of production for crude oil. These facts would make it very difficult, if not impossible, to fix a single appropriate "rate of return" for the entire industry which had any logical rationale for a given petroleum product. Drilling for oil and gas is functionally not an "averaging" type of industry: successful wells typically bring relatively high rates of return, while unsuccessful ones incur substantial losses. The concept of an average cost for producing oil or gas in the aggregate is therefore, illogical. Most wells drilled are dry. Dividing their cost by zero output is meaningless. There is also the problem of joint costs, which can be divided between gas and oil (when both are produced simultaneously) only in an arbitrary manner. Marginal producers frequently go out of business, which tends to make the rates of return for the survivors seem very high. In other words, the high risks of drilling, (and, internationally, the high risks of expropriation or other foreign Government intervention) suggest that one component of the appropriate rate of return ought to be the opportunity cost of capital incurred by investing in a relatively high risk venture, rather than a safer venture. 48/ There is no satisfactory way of quantifying such risks. One analysis has observed that in regulating the natural gas producers, to determine the rate of return

166.

needed to cover producers' opportunity costs of capital would require "many highly subjective judgmental decisions about thousands of different producers." 49/

A further difficult problems is to determine how much of the producers' capital investment ought to be part of the rate base. Much of the capital invested within the oil and gas industries constitues reinvested earnings. 50/ Arguably, earnings which exceeded a "fair" rate of return ought not to be considered a part of the rate base, for to do so undercuts the very concept of a fair rate of return. The difficulties which follow in the wake of any attempt to implement this principle are obvious. 51/

Furthermore, the distinction between capital costs and expenses is very elusive in the oil and gas industry. But even if the proper items to be included in the rate base be decided upon, valuation of them is largely an arbitrary process. Justice Robert H. Jackson said in a gas producers' case:

> "The value of the rate base is more
> elusive than that of gas. It consists
> of intangibles--leaseholds and free-
> holds--operated and unoperated--of
> little use in themselves except as rights
> to reach and capture gas. Their value
> lies almost wholly in predictions of
> discovery, and of price of gas when
> captured, and bears little relation to
> costs of tools and supplies and labor to
> develop it." 52/

The basic problem is that the value of the industries capital investments is dependent upon the revenue they can probably earn; it is, therefore, inherently illogical to attempt to fix appropriate total revenue in light of the value of the investment. This basic problem is compounded in the international petroleum industry where the further distinc-tion would have to be made as to which portion of these costs to attribute to the U.S. portion of the trade. In short, any prices fixed for oil products based on the traditional approach to public utilities regulation will be largely arbitrary, or determined by factors other than those ostensibly the proper concern of the regulatory process.

The variations in actual costs of production among different producers of oil products are so great that the regulatory authority might fix individual rates and permit different producers to sell the same product at the same time and place for different prices. 53/ To do so the regulatory authority would probably use multi-tiered rate structure, such as, for example, the price differentials between "new" and "old" domestic oil under the FEA regulations in 1973-1974. 54/ This situation raises a large number of problems. First, where two or more different prices are enforced, another bureaucracy would be required to allocate the low cost crude, and downstream price control and allocation would be required. 55/ All buyers would want to buy the low cost crude. If the price system is not permitted to perform the allocation function, then a regulator must. Downstream users and processors would then be subject to price control or the enforced low prices might not be passed on to consumers. The gains would simply be taken from the crude oil producer and captured by the next processor. 56/ A similar set of price control and allocation problems exists for subsequent stages of production, through final consumption.

Second, if the supply of the low-priced product is relatively great, then the suppliers of the higher-priced product may not be able to clear the market of their product, and thus will not obtain their revenue requirement. In such circumstances, the multi-tiered price structure tends to reduce the supply of the higher cost product, even though under free market conditions the high-cost units of production might well be sold. The FPC has, for instance, attempted to use multi-tiered rate structures, or partial decontrol of gas prices, in order to maintain higher-cost production of natural gas. 57/ In a free market, demand would suffice to clear the market of such high-cost production at prices high enough to give such producers a profit. Controls, however, change the incentive structure; the controlled market might not yield the revenue allowed by the regulators, thus subjecting the high-cost producers to a cost-price squeeze.

Attempting to cope with such difficulties inevitably causes regulatory schemes to become both more complex and more arbitrary. The performance of the FPC is a good example. It successively developed a number of ad hoc devices

168.

in pursuit of the goals of expanding supply while keeping price low.  Such devices include credits against refunds of high rates in accordance with a formula tied to the dedication of new gas to customers to whom refunds are due, bargained moratoria on new rate filings by gas producers, differential rates allowed to producers of different sizes or different geographical areas, and periodic escalation of rates. 58/  In 1971, the Commission decided to deregulate the prices of small natural gas producers, while maintaining "indirect" price regulation over them. 59/ This approach abandoned the traditional cost-of-service method of fixing prices and instead put considerable reliance on the "free market" price of new natural gas as a guide to what the Commission's view was a "just and reasonable" price for such gas. The FPC experience provides probably as strong a reason to avoid regulation of foreign and domestic supplies as any other. 60/

It is probably impracticable for a regulatory authority to successfully control the overall rate of return for both a company's domestic and international operations combined.  To do so might require from time to time drastic increases or decreases in the prices for domestic transactions in order to offset losses or large profits abroad, or else some kind of supplementary payments to or taxes on the company to avoid such large changes in domestic prices. Thus, the regulatory authority may have to be content with regulating the return on domestic operations.  In the case of many significant companies, however, such a distinction would be very difficult to make and it would create very questionable differential impacts on individual companies. 61/ The larger the proportion of a company's activities were domestic, the more the company would lose or gain from regulation.

In determining the portion of international assets to be assigned to the "U.S. portion" of sales as distinguished from those generating oil for the rest of the world, an almost insoluble problem emerges.  There would be a high degree of arbitrariness in the development of such a rate base and the mode of its computation would easily lend itself to abuse.  The tendency would be to assign as much of total assets to the "U.S. base" as possible.

D.   [§4.4]   International Effects of Regulating Prices
              and Supply of Petroleum Products

Numerous international issues and effects arise
out of any effort to adopt a comprehensive utilities-type
regulation of the oil industry.

Probably the most difficult such issue is the
question of whether there is an international rationale for
such regulation.  It can be argued that even if the domestic
oil industry is competitive, the U.S. Government ought still
to regulate the price and supply of oil products to compensate
for the impact of the essentially noncompetitive international oil market on our domestic market.  It is generally
agreed that, whatever the degree of competition within the
domestic petroleum market, the international market is
dominated by the OPEC cartel which has caused foreign crude
prices to be substantially higher than prices which would
have resulted from free market conditions.  These world
prices have driven up the market price of domestically
produced unregulated crude because that market price tends
to rise to the level of the administered price of foreign
crude.  If we do not influence that price, or otherwise
adjust domestic prices, the OPEC governments will dictate
the price of crude oil produced in the United States, and
thereby the amount of economic rent paid to domestic oil
producers. 62/

Regulators might deal with this problem in two
ways.  First, the price of domestic crude can be controlled,
the foreign crude left uncontrolled, and the supply of low-
priced domestic and high-priced foreign crude "equitably"
rationed among the consuming public, so that ideally the
consumer pays a price reflecting a "mix" of the two price
levels.  For this system to function, companies which have
discovered and developed lower cost domestic crude oil to
meet their refining needs, would be forced to relinquish a
portion of this low-cost crude to their less fortunate
competitors in order to achieve a "mix" having the desired
average price.  The FEA system of crude oil "entitlements"
is designed to do this. 63/  A system that penalizes firms
that in the past have invested in exploration, and rewards
those who have not, however, will not lead to stable economic
growth within the industry.

Second, imported as well as domestic crude can be
subject to price ceilings and supply requirements.  If a

price ceiling is set below prevailing world prices, the
outcome is indeterminate. Producers might refuse to sell to
the companies supplying the United States at a price below
the ceiling. Then, if producers maintained a unified position, the United States would, in effect, be imposing an
embargo on itself. If producer unity failed, then at least
some oil would be delivered to the United States. In either
event, particularly in the first, the demand for domestic
crude would be very strong and great difficulty would be
experienced in maintaining price ceilings on crude. Government allocation of crude among buyers would be a necessity.
Further, downstream price control and rationing would also
be necessary, involving heavy administrative and enforcement
costs.

### [§4.5]  The Problem of Diversion

Any price control system which attempts to maintain a domestic price level below the world price of crude
oil is immediately confronted with the diversion problem.
Foreign oil would tend to be diverted to more profitable
markets. Unless prohibited, some U.S. production would be
exported if the delivered price to foreign markets were
significantly higher than the domestic price. 64/  As a
practical matter, however, those international companies
with extensive interests in the United States would probably
attempt to continue deliveries even though other markets
offered a greater per barrel return, rather than risk
unfavorable actions on their interests in the U.S. 65/  If
the U.S. price did not go below cost of oil plus delivery,
the companies would have good reason to continue to supply
the U.S. Where such supply entailed actual losses, they
would soon reduce shipments. 66/  To assure that there are
no diversions, each company might be required to deliver a
certain percentage of its output of various products to
certain designated customers. 67/. Failure to meet contract
supply requirements could subject a company to civil liability, fines, or in the extreme case loss of the right to do
interstate business in one or more lines of commerce within
the United States. 68/  In the alternative the Federal
Government could simply impose mandatory import quotas on
each company by reference to some base period. From the

companies' point of view, such a system would be somewhat
more palatable if the prospective profits to be gained from
some segments of the U.S. market for oil products would at
least partially offset the opportunity costs of marketing
certain products in this country rather than abroad.  However, some oil in international markets is handled by
traders who have neither foreign nor domestic assets of
significance.  The Federal authorities would, therefore,
have difficulty in compelling such traders to comply with
mandatory import quotas.

Several difficulties would arise under such a
system.  In the first place, supply requirements would, as a
practical matter, have to be revised in the event of a world
shortage of petroleum.  It would make no sense to attempt to
compel the companies to make deliveries when it is impossible
for them to do so. 69/  But this implies that the regulatory
authority would have to maintain substantial national and
international monitoring capability in order to evaluate
company claims that conditions beyond their control prevented
them from fulfilling their supply obligations.  If such
capability does not exist--and the experience of the shortages of 1973-74 indicated that it did not exist at that
time--it would have to be created. 70/  Second, this procedure would not necessarily force companies to enter into
contracts with new producers, or renew contracts to replace
those which expire.

Third, oil companies without substantial domestic
production could be forced into a loss position if they were
required to pay the world price for oil, plus shipping
charges to the U.S. markets, and then sell in U.S. markets
below these costs.

Fourth, while price can be controlled, private
firms cannot be forced to make new investments in an industry that is made unprofitable by government controls.
This creates long-run supply problems.

Fifth, there may be adverse reactions from govern-
ments of other importing countries to any requirement by
U.S. regulatory authorities that U.S. companies give the
United States market first priority on their available crude

172.

or other products.  Moreover, in the case of a substantial
temporary shortage, such regulations would have to be suspended in light of the oil-sharing obligations of the U.S.
under the International Energy Agreement. 71/  Such regulations run a substantial risk of encouraging similar "go-
it-alone" measures by other importing countries and would
undoubtedly have an adverse impact upon the foreign markets
of U.S. companies.  Such regulations, moreover, would
constitute a substantial reversal of U.S. foreign economic
and energy policy. 72/

### [§4.6]  Market Role of the U.S. Companies

Where the high prices of imported crude are due
primarily to the actions of the producer-country governments, regulating the price of imported crude is far less
likely to have the desired effect than where such prices are
due primarily to the actions of the oil companies.  If the
price ceilings in this country do not equal or exceed the
prices paid by the companies to producer governments plus
other costs, the companies will eventually stop importing
crude. 73/

Few would disagree that whatever the market power
of the international companies in the past, it has been and
continues to be eroded by the aggressive posture of the
producer governments.  Those governments individually or
through OPEC are eliminating equity oil interests, creating
larger buy-back and auction markets for governmentally owned
crude, restricting output to maintain buy-back and auction
prices, raising producer-country taxes and working toward a
single price for crude that will isolate and limit the
companies' margin of profit.  In the aggregate such policies
are reducing the international companies to the status of
suppliers of technology and managerial skills within the
producing countries, and forcing them to compete more
intensely with independents and governmentally owned companies in international wholesaling, refining and marketing
operations. 74/  Thus, it is now easier than before for
regulation to create a situation in which it is no longer
profitable for the companies to do business on the terms set
by the regulatory authority.

The experience in France illustrates the problems
of maintaining a price ceiling for imported oil products in

the face of high prices fixed by the producing countries. In early 1974, France's CFP estimated that the average cost of Persian Gulf crude to the companies was 85 percent of posted price. But the sales of this crude in France brought only an average of 70-75 percent of posted price. Thus, in effect the importing companies were required to subsidize consumption. In the summer of 1974 the companies were losing 70-80 francs per ton of refined oil. Consequently, the companies warned they would soon cease importing crude into France. 75/ The French Government countered with promises of future retroactive price increases which would allow the companies to recoup at least part of their losses. Similarly, in 1974 when ceiling prices in Belgium for petroleum products failed to rise enough to meet the increased costs of crude, companies ceased imports into that country. 76/

If the United States attempts to impose a price ceiling with mandatory delivery quotas under circumstances where the producer countries are keeping crude prices near that ceiling, the delivery quotas will predictably become unenforceable, except by very drastic means, and the ultimate effect will be a boycott of foreign crude unintentionally enforced by the U.S. Government. 77/

E.    [§4.7]   Conclusion

Comprehensive cost of service/rate-of-return regulation as is used for public utilities, if applied to the oil industry would entail heavy costs and be of very dubious benefit to consumers. Limited forms of price regulation or allocation could be useful to cope with special situations in which there exists possible monopolistic or oligopolistic behavior, but where for some reason an antitrust remedy is not feasible or desirable. 78/

The most important point regarding this option is, however, that it can have no positive impact upon the stability or price of international petroleum supplies and could have a number of negative impacts both domestically and abroad. It would establish public control over the oil companies but in a less creative and functional way than a number of other options. The option has little to recommend it.

CHAPTER 4

FOOTNOTES

1. An example would be the proposed Consumer
   Energy Act sponsored by Senator Adlai Stevenson
   (D., Ill.) (S. 2506, 93d Cong., 2d Sess.)
   which would regulate crude oil prices at the
   wellhead; provide for price regulation of oil
   and gas products in both interstate and intra-
   state markets; make all petroleum pipelines
   public carriers; and restrict the right of
   suppliers to terminate supplies to certain
   wholesalers and retailers.  At the state level,
   California State Senator James Mills (D. San
   Diego) sponsored an initiative in 1974 that
   would subject petroleum companies in the state
   to regulation by the California Public Utilities
   Commission.  See Los Angeles Times, April 30,
   1974.

2. See, for instance, Breyer and MacAvoy, "The
   Natural Gas Shortage and the Regulation of
   Natural Gas Producers," 86 Harv. L.Rev. 941,
   950 (April, 1973).

3. See § 4.5, infra.

4. 49 U.S.C. § 11.

5. 16 U.S.C. § 792.

6. Senate Committee on the Judiciary, Subcommittee
   on Administrative Practice and Procedure,
   Report on the Regulatory Agencies to the
   President-Elect, 86th Cong., 2d Sess., at 54
   (1960).

7. Thill Securities Corp. v. New York Stock Exchange,
   433 F.2d 264, 273 (7th Cir., 1970).

8. 49 U.S.C. § 1321.

9. 47 U.S.C. § 151.

10.  43 U.S.C. § 31.

11.  The current controversy over the future of
     Pan American Airways illustrates this problem.

12.  So named because of several famous economists
     at the University of Chicago who have held
     generally pro-free market views, including
     Freidrich Hayek, Frank H. Knight and Milton
     Friedman.

13.  See, for instance, American Enterprise
     Institute, Fixed versus Floating Exchange Rates
     (1967), which features a debate between Robert
     V. Roosa and Milton Friedman over the merits
     of such government intervention.

14.  Arguably, a fourth staff bureaucracy would be
     created by Congressional oversight of the
     regulatory process.

15.  Industry respondents anticipated higher prices
     and reduced supplies as a result of such a
     regulatory policy.  Appendix C, § C.1,
     question 21.

16.  87 Stat 627 (Nov. 27, 1973); Codified at
     15 U.S.C. §§ 751 et seq.

17.  P.L. 93-511 (H.R. 16757), signed Dec. 5, 1974.

18.  See 10 C.F.R. §§ 210 ff., 212 et seq.

19.  Phillips Petroleum Company v. Wisconsin,
     347 U.S. 672.

20.  See Breyer and MacAvoy, note 2 supra, 965, 967.

21.  Ibid.

22.  Preliminary Federal Trade Commission Staff
     Report on Its Investigation of the Petroleum
     Industry, 93d Cong., 1st Sess. (Comm. Print,
     1973).

23.  Id. at 13, 22.

24. Id. at 25-27, 29. See also E. V. Rostow, A National Policy for the Oil Industry (1948).

25. FTC Report, 38.

26. See Keefe and Tierney, "Those Integrated Oil Companies: Is a Breakup Coming?", 59 Amer. Bar Assoc. J. 1444 (1973). Cf. Ritchie, "Those Integrated Oil Companies: Is a Breakup Desirable?" 60 Amer. Bar Assoc. J. 826 (1974). The FTC complaint itself, however, did not specifically request divestiture of any form of relief.

27. U.S. Dept. of the Treasury, Staff Analysis of the Preliminary Federal Trade Commission Staff Report on Its Investigation of the Petroleum Industry (Washington, D.C.: GPO, 1973).

28. Id. at 11, 37.

29. Id. at 54-55.

30. Ibid.

31. Ibid.

32. See guidelines published in Hearings before the Sub-committee on Special Small Business Problems of the House Select Committee on Small Business, 92d Cong., 2d Sess., June 13, 14, 15, 1972, at A 104, A106.

33. For opinions to the effect that the industry is competi-tive, see testimony of Prof. Edward Mitchell before the Senate Commerce Committee, March 28, 1974; Stewart C. Myers before Senate Special Subcommittee on Integrated Oil Operations, February 20, 1974; for the contrary view, see testimony of Beverly Moore for the Subcommittee on Special Small Business Problems of the House Select Committee on Small Business, June 15, 1972, pp. 127-140. For a relatively balanced view that the industry is structurally competitive although certain anti-competitive practices exist, see testimony of Stephen Breyer before the Senate Committee on Interior and Insular Affairs 93d Cong., 1st Sess., Nov. 28, 29, 1973, 442-449. Cf. Statement of Edward W. Erickson, ibid., 364, 370.

34. Jacoby, Multinational Oil (1975); Mitchell, U.S. Energy Policy: A Primer (1974); Nossaman et al, Study of the

Outer Continental Shelf Lands of the United States §§8.22, 11.24.

35.  See §1.18, supra.

36.  See note 33, supra.

37.  Based on the analyses referenced in notes 33, 34 and 35, supra.

38.  See note 41, infra.

39.  For an example of this process see Los Angeles Times, Sept. 28, 1974, pt. III, 9.

40.  See M. Green and R. Nader, "Uncle Sam The Monopoly Man," 82 Yale L. J. 871 (April, 1973).

41.  See Harvey Averich and L. L. Johnson, "Behavior of the Firm Under Regulatory Constraint," 52 Amer. Econ. Rev. 1053 (Dec., 1962); and comments by W. K. Klevorick, "Input Choices and Rate of Return Regulation: An Overview of the Discussion," 1 The Bell Journal of Economics and Management Service, 162 (Aut., 1970).

42.  Anticipating a rise in rates, for example, a company producing natural gas would naturally delay exploitation of new sources until the new rates were authorized. See P. MacAvoy, "Regulation-Induced Shortage of Natural Gas," 14 J. of Law and Econ. 189 (April, 1971).

43.  R. Jackson, "Regulation and Electric Utility Rates," Land Economics (Aug., 1969), 376.

44.  J. Pike, "Residential Electricity Rates and Regulation," Quarterly Review of Economics and Business (summer, 1972), 88.

45.  Ibid.

46.  P. MacAvoy, The Economic Effects of Regulation (1965), v.

47.  For instance, some companies are integrated both domestically and internationally, some domestically

but not internationally, and others are non-integrated.

48. In other words, the companies should be compensated for the risks they assume by investing overseas.

49. Breyer and MacAvoy, supra note 2, at 957.

50. Companies prefer to use internally-generated capital for investment because it reduces the amount of borrowing they must do in the ordinary capital markets. The current exploration and development requirements are, however, so massive that internally generated income falls far short of providing the necessary funds. The result has been a large increase in the debt to equity ratios which may be expected to grow even larger. See 1973 annual statements of the ten largest U.S. companies; answers to Questions 1 and 2, Appendix C, §C.1; interviews by Study Contractor with industry representatives.

51. Such an attempt would require an analysis of the entire financial history of the company and a determination of "fair" rates of return for different times in the past.

52. FPC v. Hope Natural Gas Co., 320 U.S. 591, 645 (1944).

53. Breyer and MacAvoy, supra note 2, at 951-952.

54. 10 C.F.R. §§212.72 et seq.

55. Thus, for instance, the FEA has recently instituted the entitlements program to equalize access to low-cost "old" crude oil. 39 F.R. 29740 (Nov. 11, 1974).

56. Where the unregulated price would rise to the level of the price for the high cost crude, marketers of the cheap will have no incentive to undercut that price.

57. Note 54, supra.

58. See, for instance, the rate agreements reviewed on certiorari by the Supreme Court in Mobil Oil Corp. v. FPC, ____ U.S. ___, 41 L.Ed. 2d 72, 73 (June 10, 1974).

59. See Order No. 928, 45 FPC 454 (1971).

60. Breyer and MacAvoy, _supra_ note 2, at 987.

61. Probably the tendency would be to set rates or prices high enough to maintain the profits of the least prosperous companies. See note 39, _supra_.

62. That amount is the difference between the domestic producer's cost of production and the U.S. landed price of OPEC oil.

63. 39 F.R. 39740 (Nov. 11, 1974).

64. That is, if the delivered price to foreign markets exceeded the U.S. ceiling price plus transportation costs to the foreign destination.

65. See note 68, _infra_, and accompanying text.

66. See note 75, _infra_.

67. Priority for designated classes of customers is enforced by the FPC in gas curtailment proceedings. See 18 C.F.R. §2.78, Order No. 467-C, April 4, 1974.

68. See §6.3, _infra_.

69. Moreover, it would raise a serious question of "due process" under the 5th Amendment of the U.S. Constitution.

70. Under the International Energy Program, however, such capability may have to be created in any event. See §10.4, _infra_.

71. §10.1, _infra_.

72. §2.4, _supra_.

73. See note 75, _infra_.

74. Report to the Senate Committee on Foreign Relations by the Subcommittee on Multinational Corporations, _Multinational Oil Corporations and U.S. Foreign Policy_, 93d Cong., 2d Sess., 141-163 (Comm. Print, Jan. 2, 1975).

75.  *Petroleum Intelligence Weekly*, Jan. 21, 1974, 10; July 1, 1974, 7; Jan. 6, 1975, 7.

76.  *Petroleum Intelligence Weekly*, July 1, 1974, 7.

77.  See §5.2, *infra*.

78.  Such a case could arise, for instance, where the U.S. and other consumer nation governments promote inter-company cooperation to strengthen their bargaining power vis-a-vis OPEC.  See Chapter 8, *infra*.

CHAPTER 5

ESTABLISHMENT OF A NATIONAL SYSTEM
TO LIMIT PETROLEUM IMPORTS

A.    [§5.0]  Introduction

        After the experience of the embargo in the winter
of 1973-74 and the drastic increases in oil prices which
accompanied and succeeded it, there was general agreement in
the U.S. that the nation should strive to reduce its dependence on foreign oil.  1/  President Ford in his 1975 State
of the Union message suggested a goal of reducing imports by
one million barrels per day by the end of 1975, and by two
million barrels per day by the end of 1977.  2/

        A reduction in imports would likely be an indirect
result of any successful policies which reduced aggregate
consumption, or which stimulated domestic oil production and
production of energy from other sources, such as coal, shale,
or geothermal deposits.  3/  In addition, however, various
proposals have been made for attacking the import problem
directly rather than indirectly, in order to reduce as quickly
as possible the aggregate U.S. payments for foreign oil and
to reduce the vulnerability of the nation to a sudden interruption in the flow of imported oil.  Such proposals differ
in the kinds of limits they would impose on imports and the
means by which those limits would be created or enforced.

        Several kinds of limits, directly or indirectly
created, are possible.  The U.S. might try to limit the
quantities imported, the aggregate value of oil imported, or
the price per unit of oil imported.  4/  Aggregate limits
or limits on specific import sources might be regulated.  5/
The costs and benefits of these kinds of limits vary considerably as do the appropriate means of implementing them.

B.    [§5.1]  Setting Absolute Limits on Quantities
              or Values of Imported Oil

        The most direct way to achieve a reduction in oil
imports is by fiat--to impose by force of law a ceiling on
the absolute quantities or values of crude and products
that may be imported during a given period, such as monthly,
quarterly or annually.  If this absolute ceiling is fixed

below the level of current imports, then an immediate reduction in existing levels of consumption becomes inevitable and the shortfall must be spread among consumers by a concurrent allocation or rationing plan, or through increased prices. If a domestic price increase or tariff on imports is chosen to help reduce consumption, it must be in a form that will not accrue to the benefit of the exporting country.

Neither ceiling will directly prevent oil exporters from raising the unit price and further reducing production to take the slack out of the market. If unit prices rise, an importing country with a quantity ceiling will spend more for imported oil than had been planned, whereas an importing country with an aggregate payments ceiling will obtain less imports than had been planned. The choice between the two depends upon which is judged to be more detrimental: the impact on balance of payments of a higher oil bill or the impact on the economy of a larger quantitative shortfall. In either case, the importing country's immediate objective is to force a limitation or reduction in its foreign payments at current price levels, and its longer-term objectives are to exert downward pressure on the international price and to enhance the security of national energy supplies. The price and quantity limitations can, of course, be combined by denominating a range of acceptable unit values or simply by the use of domestic price controls. The value ceiling approach has been little discussed in the U.S., but France in 1974 imposed such an aggregate payments ceiling for foreign oil. 6/ With a quantity ceiling aggregate payments for imported oil would fluctuate from period to period proportionate to changes in price per unit. With a value ceiling the quantity imported would fluctuate from period to period inversely to changes in the average price per unit of oil. 7/ Such a quantity or value limit requires "cold turkey" conservation or demand reduction measures. Its impact is sudden and inflexible and, therefore, it may be advisable to introduce such a ceiling gradually. For instance, imports could first be frozen at present levels and lower ceilings introduced in stages.

An aggregate value ceiling like that of the French would raise special difficulties in the U.S. This form of limit is essentially a foreign exchange control measure. Countries which do not otherwise allow free export of their currency have a mechanism to administer this kind of limit

through their ordinary national banking channels. 8/  Because
the dollar is a reserve currency, however, Federal authorities
in order to enforce an aggregate value ceiling would have to
devise some system compatible with that status for assigning
and controlling values to the quantities of crude and products
entering U.S. ports. 9/  Importers would have an incentive
to declare the lowest possible values in order to maximize
their quantities.  As with the quantity limitation this
approach is basically a device directed at conserving foreign
exchange.  Given the ease with which these controls could be
evaded, however, even if elaborate auditing schemes were
employed it is questionable whether they would have a
positive effect.  Enforcement problems would be formidable.
A quantity limit, on the other hand, being unambiguous is
less difficult to enforce.

Once a specific quantity or value ceiling has been
fixed by Federal authorities, the major issue would be how
to allocate among importers the rights to import the allowable amounts or values of oil.  Any number of schemes
could be devised for this purpose, but there are two basic
approaches between which Federal authorities would have to
choose or compromise:

1.  Allocation by reference to present market
shares.  This would essentially preserve the present proportionate market shares of oil producers by allowing them
to import quantities or values proportional to what they
imported during some selected base period.

2.  Allocation solely by auction, that is, by
selling the right to import given quantities or values of
oil.

Allocation according to present market shares
would probably evoke the least opposition from the oil
industry, since its impact on any given company is known in
advance for any given import ceiling and since present
importers may be expected to be more concerned about their
present market shares than prospective importers about their
potential ones. 10/  Moreover, the market shares of present
small importers would be protected.  Also, it is arguable
that the risk of disruption to normal channels of supply and
the consequent aggravation of the effects of a shortage
would be minimized if proportionate existing import market shares

were preserved. Federal Energy Administration allocations have generally followed the concept of proportionate historical market shares which is probably the least controversial of those which could be devised. 11/ The system, however, presents potential newcomers to the market with a serious handicap.

Under the auction method of allocation anyone could bid for the right to import fixed quantities or values of oil, and the rights so sold by the Government could be freely transferable. 12/ Obviously, those importers expecting the greatest profit per unit would be willing to bid the most for import rights to a given quantity or value of oil. Thus, those prospective deals in which the importer's margin is the greatest will tend to produce the successful bids. Ideally, competition among bidders will tend to reduce that margin to the minimum necessary to induce imports. Some have expressed the expectation or hope that a system such as this could weaken the connection between particular oil exporting nations and their present shares of the U.S. market. 13/ At the same time, companies might well feel less secure with this system, fearing both the loss of rights to import and possible retaliatory moves by exporting countries.

A variety of auction plans can be designed, but a system of secret, sealed bidding would probably be most likely to induce producing governments to eventually compete for larger shares of the U.S. market. The U.S. Government could offer import tickets to the bidder who offered the most oil for a fixed dollar amount or who offered to pay the highest fee for the right to import a fixed quantity of oil. Initially, the bidders would likely be the private oil companies, but eventually producer governments or their oil companies, attempting to market oil in the United States directly, might bid to avoid being forced either to buy import tickets from other holders or lose their access to the U.S. market. 14/

The system does not, however, assure that the producing country governments themselves, the true price setters, will want to export oil to the U.S. If those governments do not bid, or do not bid competitively, then the allocation system, while it may be a highly efficient and fair way of allocating limited import rights, will have negligible impact on the price of imports. 15/ If such a system were instituted, OPEC could reasonably be expected to attempt to coordinate the policies of its members to avoid competitive bidding.

The essence of such a scheme or strategy for
reducing international prices is an attempt to make U.S.
market demand into a valuable commodity to be sold at
auction, just as an exporting country might auction its
oil supply.  Seen in this light, it is plain that access
to the U.S. market will have significant value only if
there is a market surplus of oil at current prices.  At
present, the OPEC cartel can probably survive without the
need for monitoring and enforcing the behavior of each
member by all of the others because it is so clearly in
the interest of each that the cartel continue.  Breakdown
of the cartel would harm all members.  As long as this is
true, ologopolistic pricing by OPEC members is likely to
continue with only minor exceptions, regardless of whether
their behavior is secret or overt. 16/  Until significant
amounts of production begin to threaten to undercut the
OPEC cartel price in order to gain a foothold in world
markets, this kind of auction scheme is unlikely to induce
competition among the producer countries. 17/  On the other
hand, if such an extreme market surplus of oil existed,
then the cartel would likely break down in any event.  In
such circumstances, however, the auctioning of market shares
could accelerate that breakdown.  Only if the markets outside the U.S. offer less opportunity to profit than does
the U.S. market will this system have any tendency to induce
producer-country competitive bidding.  As long as exporting
countries can obtain today's prices for an acceptable
quantity on the auction market, there is no incentive to
make more than nominal bids for shares of the U.S. market.

As the foregoing discussion suggests, the choice
between allocating import opportunities on the basis of
existing market shares or on an auction basis in part
involves a choice for or against increased upstream competition.  Allocation by auction would treat new entrants
to the industry on a par with existing companies and thus
would help to foster competition for access to foreign
sources of crude.  On the other hand, upstream competition
for sources of foreign crude is substantial and tends to
increase rather than decrease price. 18/

Allocation by reference to present market shares
would tend to dampen upstream competition for access to
foreign crude and thus tend to weaken the market strength
of the producer countries.  In this way it may reinforce

an international policy of promoting inter-company coordination by their governments to bargain more effectively with
the OPEC cartel. 19/  Assuming there were no price controls
on the imports, however, this form of allocation would give
a windfall to the holders of import rights, because the
reduction of imports would cause the market value of the
remaining imports to rise without increasing their cost.
Under the auction system, this windfall would be bid away
to the U.S. Treasury.

C.   [§5.2]   Setting Absolute Limits on Unit Prices

        Another approach to import limitation is to
exclude from the U.S. all crude or products whose unit
price was above a set ceiling.  Various European countries,
including France and Belgium, have such controls on import
prices. 20/

        If more imports could be obtained at a lower
cost, this approach would not exclude larger volumes of
imports.  One disadvantage of this approach is that it
creates an "all-or-nothing" import limit.  Where the unit
price ceiling is below the prevailing world price, there
is no limit on imports; whereas, when it is above the world
price no imports will be allowed, unless importers elect
to continue supply at less than the prevailing world price.
As the experience of France in 1974 indicates, importers
may for a time be willing to import oil at a loss if they
anticipate future adjustments of the ceiling or an imminent
drop in world oil prices. 21/

        This approach attempts to encourage oil exporting
countries to reduce (or stabilize) their price in order to
sell in the American market.  Because of its all-or-nothing
character, the imposition of a price ceiling below the
current OPEC price levels could result in a total boycott of
OPEC production, with consequent severe and sudden economic
disruptions. 22/  More likely, the ceiling would be set at
or near import prices at a given time, and oil exporting
nations would know that if they chose to increase those
prices they would be excluding themselves from the U.S.
market.  If inflation were a significant factor, stable
international oil prices in fact would mean declining oil
prices without the politically difficult act, for producer-
country governments, of actually reducing those prices.  If

the price of oil failed to rise as fast as the rate of
inflation, a real reduction in oil prices would be achieved.
A further difficulty of this approach is that it would
eliminate (or require subterfuge for) spot transactions
above the limit. 23/ If successful, this could result in
serious dislocations and losses and would generally be
counterproductive. Indeed the whole approach would
encourage widespread evasion in the event of a conflict
between U.S. price limits and the world price. The oil
crisis illustrated the potential difficulty of enforcement
of unilaterally imposed price limits. 24/

Assuming coordinated pricing on the part of OPEC
members, the U.S. threat to ban imports completely would
have to be at least reasonably credible in order for this
ceiling to deter OPEC price increases. Therefore the
existence of substantial stored emergency reserves of petroleum, in tanks, salt domes, or production-ready well capacity
would probably be a prerequisite to this kind of import
limitation policy.

D. [§5.3] Tariffs

Another possible means of discouraging imports,
reducing U.S. oil consumption, and encouraging further
domestic production is to impose a substantial tariff on
imported crude and products. President Ford in his 1975
State of the Union message proposed both an immediate administratively imposed tariff rising to $3 per barrel by
April 1, 1975 and a $2 per barrel tariff to replace it
which would be part of a congressionally enacted comprehensive tax program. The program would also include the
deregulation of U.S. crude oil and new natural gas, a
windfall profits tax and a natural gas excise tax.

A tariff causes domestic prices to be higher than
foreign prices by the amount of the tariff wherever imports
are necessary to meet part of domestic demand, assuming that
there is no interference in the market mechanism. At the
present time there is an interference in the market by
governmental regulations administered by the FEA. 25/ Where
foreign prices are lower than domestic the tariff can simply
close the gap. Where the two prices are initially equal,
the tariff will cause domestic prices to rise. Under present
(February, 1975) conditions, the effective price of imports

189.

(including the amount of the tariff) sets the price of free market domestic production (i.e. "new" oil). Thus the rationale of the President's proposed tariff is that it will tend to make new domestic oil production and production of energy from alternate sources (such as shale, coal, or sunlight) more profitable, discourage consumption through higher energy prices, reduce imports and thereby improve the balance of payments and increase security of supply, and possibly help reduce world oil prices by reducing demand for OPEC oil. 26/

The incentive to new production of oil and other energy sources created by the tariff is strongest where the Federal Government undertakes explicitly to provide so-called "downside risk" guarantees to encourage long-term domestic energy investments. Under such a program, Federal authorities would guarantee a domestic price floor for the next 10-20 years, pledging use of tariffs or quota controls to protect U.S. energy prices if world prices fall. 27/ Oil companies would probably feel most secure with a tariff designed specifically to maintain a given price floor for all imported oil.

The costs of imports do not include the cost to the nation as a whole of dependency on foreign sources because oil from secure sources brings no market premium. By levying a tariff equal to the cost of an oil reserve storage system, imports can be used to pay the cost of the storage system. 28/ This is only one of several means by which security stocks could be financed.

Thus, import tariffs could reduce demand for imports, increase domestic production, and finance a reserve storage system.

The costs of the tariff approach to import limitation are different from those of the aggregate ceilings or the unit price ceiling. While the tariff does not create an oil shortage, it does raise prices. A tariff may have a greater economic impact on some regions of the country than on others, a factor noted by President Ford in announcing his intention to "take action to reduce undue hardship on any geographical area." 29/ If, however, old domestic oil were decontrolled and the entitlements

190.

program eliminated, the differential impact of the tariff on consumers in various parts of the country would disappear, although importers would not make as much profit as producers of "old" oil. An excise tax on natural gas, as proposed by President Ford, would also reduce the disparity between prices of oil and natural gas that might otherwise result from a tariff. 30/

As a conservation device, a tariff may be inferior in the short-to-medium term to a tax on specific products, such as gasoline, in which the elasticity of demand may be relatively high. Consumption of fuel oil for residential heating or for utility boilers may not be reduced very much by the tariff. Once a householder has lowered his thermostat by several degrees, for instance, it is questionable whether any significant further fuel savings will be achieved or should be forced. In such situations, significant additional conservation can be achieved only in the long run, as new construction, plant and equipment come into use, designed to use less energy. President Ford's State of the Union message included a ten-year program to effectuate this goal. 31/

On the other hand, a tariff, because it employs the price mechanism, is pervasive in its effect and is, therefore, probably the most efficient means to cause the U.S. economy to reorient itself to recognize the realities of finite energy resources and of developing supply independence. 32/ Such economic reorientation is necessary if energy is to be used efficiently. Moreover, because it relies on the market mechanism, the tariff approach is consistent with the U.S. economic system which basically relies on freedom of choice. Because it is self-administering, once the tariff is collected the tariff approach has no direct additional administrative costs. It requires no administrative regulations or policing. 33/ By way of contrast rationing requires intensive administrative costs, encourages evasion and subterfuge and typically results in a large number of arbitrary allocations. 34/ More importantly it fails to address the basic issues involved. Rationing coupled with price controls would discourage the development of new U.S. energy sources and could fail even to reduce demand. 35/

191.

Because this approach may impact heavily on certain income groups, programs to mitigate that impact may be needed, a factor recognized in the program announced by President Ford in his 1975 State of the Union message. 36/

The response to a U.S. tariff by the oil producing countries could pose a problem. A high tariff could appear to the producer-country governments as a device to raise the market price of "their" oil and divert part of that market price to the U.S. Treasury. It thus may be regarded by the producer country as an attempt to siphon off part of "their" profits. 37/ The same reduction in imports induced by a tariff would also result if the producer countries themselves raised the unit price by the amount of the tariff. Therefore, the producer countries may be tempted to raise the price by that amount and suggest that the U.S. rescind the tariff to allow its citizens to purchase oil at what the U.S. Government in levying the tariff implicitly acknowledged was a "reasonable" price. The U.S. could maintain the tariff if it were content to see consumption drop still further, with the resultant progressively greater cost to the economy which that would entail. In a showdown between the producer and consumer governments, each insisting on its tax, whichever was hurt more by the reduced consumption would likely give in. It is doubtful, however, that OPEC or any of its members would respond thus to a U.S. tariff proposed by President Ford in this fashion. 38/ An across-the-board increase in OPEC oil prices solely in response to the tariff is unlikely because it would affect all importing countries and would significantly disrupt existing markets. Moreover, taxes in Europe on various oil products, especially gasoline, are much higher than in the U.S. Yet, while OPEC members frequently call attention to these high taxes, they have not seriously attempted by pricing tactics to force those taxes down. 39/

E.    [§5.4]  International Market Operations by
              the Federal Government

The fourth possible means of limiting imports is through international market operations by the Federal Government itself. 40/ An agency of the Federal Government could be created to buy and sell petroleum in the international market in order to implement a national policy to maximize national bargaining leverage by aggregating import demand, to limit total imports and the amount spent on imports, or to rearrange import supply patterns.

The Federal Government could make itself the sole importer of crude and products, either negotiating purchases directly with producer governments or buying from companies who have access to foreign supplies. By limiting its purchases it would put an effective ceiling on the quantity or value of imported oil. By discriminating among sources of oil it could affect the pattern of U.S. import sources. Such a policy might be designed to favor certain suppliers over others, such as to assure that declining imports from Canada or Venezuela are replaced by non-Arab sources, in order to reduce the impact of Middle Eastern politics on the international oil market. 41/ However, the implementation of the emergency sharing plan under the International Energy Program would eliminate almost all benefits accruing to geographic source dispersion. 42/

Alternatively, the Federal Government might try to diversify import sources among as many exporting countries as possible on the theory that this will increase the potential for competition among would-be suppliers to the U.S. market and make all such suppliers relatively insecure in their U.S. market shares. Pursuing either policy, the Federal Government would probably have to offer newly emerging oil-exporting countries, such as Mexico, China, Southeast Asian countries or the U.S.S.R., better terms for their production than the present world market offers them. 43/ The aggregate demand of the United States for foreign imports of 6-7 million barrels per day is less than some of the bigger international majors. There is, therefore, no reason to believe that on a commercial basis it could exercise a downside pressure on price where the companies could not. 44/ It is possible that the U.S. Government could exert a positive political pressure on price but as examined in detail in Chapters 7 and 9 this is a very uncertain area. It is equally possible that political considerations could cause the price to be higher. 45/ All other things being equal, then, this approach would probably result in higher prices, at least in the short run. In effect, the Government would be paying a market premium for a national benefit which commercial companies would not pay because they would not directly benefit in proportion to the necessary premium.

In addition, by making itself the exclusive buyer for the American market, the Federal Government would be reducing upstream competition for access to foreign crude supplies. No company could guarantee a producer-country government access to the U.S. market. The Government agency would still have to compete with foreign companies and with U.S. companies competing for supplies for foreign markets. Probably, therefore, the Government's bargaining position in most instances could not be expected to be stronger than that of any given company now dealing with foreign producer governments for access to crude intended for the American market. On the other hand, if this concept were extended to all needs of U.S. companies, or even all companies operating in the United States, for domestic or foreign markets, the demand aggregated would be huge and it could have a significant impact upon bargaining. The complex and far-reaching political and economic impacts of this concept from a regulatory standpoint are examined in Chapter 6. 46/ Here they would be even greater and would involve producer government negotiations. 47/

If the Federal Government's import market operations were done on a nonexclusive basis, the Government would in effect be competing with existing importers. Such an arrangement would not limit imports, but by increasing upstream competition would probably exert upward pressure on price. In 1974, a bill was introduced in the Senate which would have created a Federal agency to import oil to assist independent refiners and nonbranded markets to obtain foreign crude independently of the major companies. 48/ Such schemes are, in effect, similar to government arrangements of the type discussed in Chapter 9 of the Study. The increased upstream competition thereby created would be adverse to U.S. national interests to the extent that it helps to strengthen the market position of oil exporters. Such an agency therefore cannot be expected to lead to lower international oil prices.

Any plan to have the Federal Government actively purchasing oil for importation into the U.S. raises the question of how it should dispose of the oil so imported. Again, the major choices are allocation at fixed prices to marketers on the basis of historical market shares, or sale at auction. 49/ Where the Government's import purchases are

194.

not exclusive, the oil purchased may be auctioned to a restricted bidding class, such as small refiners or marketers
which do not otherwise have direct access to foreign crude.
In this case, the Government would be creating or maintaining
limited spot and future markets for oil and subsidizing the
selected class. 50/ In any case, the Government would be
under considerable pressure to use a form of marketing that
would assure continuity of supplies and price at least
roughly comparable to that provided by ordinary commercial
transactions. This constraint would limit the freedom of
the Government to deal with producer-country governments in
ways that depart significantly from ordinary commercial
practices.

F. [§5.5] Conclusion

Of the kinds of import limitation schemes discussed, the aggregate quantity ceiling would be the most
effective means of meeting the oft-repeated goals of reducing imports by a certain number of daily barrels by a
certain date. It is a somewhat deceptively high-cost option,
however, in two ways. First, significant but unknown output
and employment costs are immediately imposed on the nation
by the reduction in petroleum supplies. Second, prices will
rise to reflect the reduction in supply, but the extent of
such price rise is difficult to determine in advance. Thus,
in terms of domestic economic impact, it is an imprecise
tool. To the extent that the price increase of domestic
crude stimulated new production, domestic producers would
benefit. At the same time, importers would experience a
windfall unless it were taxed away, or unless import
allocations were auctioned. If the domestic price effects
should prove to be undesirable, other administrative measures
would have to be devised to offset them.

The use of a per unit price ceiling to eliminate
expensive imports from the U.S. may be feasible given certain conditions, namely: (1) a continuing significant rate
of inflation; (2) a per unit ceiling no lower than present
(or then-current) OPEC prices; and (3) the existence of a
much larger strategic petroleum reserve stock than the U.S.
now possesses. Its main disadvantage is that it involves a
potentially high risk of an interruption of oil to the U.S.
It would be vulnerable to evasion, frustrate spot markets
and be difficult to administer.

The tariff limitation, on the other hand, has the advantages of simplicity, flexibility, and reasonably predictable costs. Moreover, because it employs the price mechanism, it retains consumer choice as the criterion for allocation. It is pervasive in its impact and is consequently most efficient in causing the national energy infrastructure to be adjusted to meet the designated goals of reducing consumption and developing energy independence. If the tariff has a significant impact on consumer prices, it may require a companion program to mitigate those effects deemed undesirable.

Government market operations where the Federal authority is the exclusive importer for the U.S. market would be highly effective as a means of limiting imports. The creation of the necessary agency to competently carry out the desired import policies, however, would involve high initial expenses. Moreover, any such agency created to implement a long-range import policy seemingly desirable today may become a liability if international market conditions change in the interim. Most such policies, such as favoring certain import sources, could be effectively implemented more simply, such as by direct subsidies to existing importers or producer countries.

CHAPTER 5

FOOTNOTES

1.  See §2.2, *supra*.

2.  *Los Angeles Times*, Jan. 16, 1975, 21.

3.  As consumption is reduced, given the price advantage of domestic production, imports would decline.

4.  For a description of past U.S. oil import quota programs, see Appendix B, §B.4.

5.  For example, an import limitation system could be "targeted" against the most insecure sources. See §6.4.

6.  This ceiling was pegged at 51 billion francs for 1975. Purchases are monitored every two months. See *Petroleum Intelligence Weekly*, Jan. 6, 1975, 3.

7.  Thus, as the unit price rose, the volume of oil would fall.

8.  For example, the Japanese currently administer such foreign exchange controls.

9.  To do otherwise would interfere with the role of the U.S. dollar in the international monetary system.

10. For a sample of industry attitudes, see Appendix C, §C.1.

11. See §3.11, *supra*.

12. This is the method proposed by Professor M. A. Adelman of M.I.T. See his letter of Sept. 27, 1974 to the Editor of *The New York Times*, Oct. 3, 1974, at 42.

13. *Ibid*.

14. This point was made in the Report to the Senate Committee on Foreign Relations by the Subcommittee on Multinational

Corporations, <u>Multinational Oil Corporations</u> and
<u>U.S. Foreign Policy</u>, 93rd Cong., 2d Sess., p. 10
(Comm. Print, Jan. 2, 1975).

15.  It is in fact probable that OPEC governments would
     initially coordinate their responses to such a
     system.

16.  At present prices, the benefits of the cartel to its
     members are so great that important producers will not
     undercut it unless they believe they must to preserve
     their market shares.

17.  Such surplus production seems unlikely to materialize
     in the next 3 - 5 years.

18.  See §1.18, <u>supra</u>.

19.  This concept is further discussed in §8.2, <u>infra</u>.

20.  <u>Petroleum Intelligence Weekly</u>, Jan. 21, 1974, 10;
     July 1, 1974, 7.

21.  <u>Id</u>. Jan. 6, 1975, at 7.

22.  See §§6.6-6-7, <u>infra</u>.

23.  See §6.6, <u>infra</u>.

24.  If FEA regulations did not exempt from price controls
     the first sale of imports into U.S. commerce, the im-
     ports to the U.S. would probably have ceased in 1974.
     10 C.F.R. 212.53(b).

25.  See §§3.11, 3.12, <u>supra</u>.

26.  <u>Los Angeles Times</u>, Jan. 16, 1975, 21.

27.  Statement by Thomas O. Enders, <u>Department of State</u>
     <u>Bulletin</u>, Jan. 13, 1975, 48.

28.  For a complete discussion of storage systems, consult
     <u>Project Independence Report</u> (1974), 377.

29.  1975 State of the Union message, quoted in the
     Los Angeles Times, Jan. 16, 1975, 21.

30.  Ibid.

31.  Ibid.

32.  Ibid.

33.  The U.S. Customs Bureau already exists to collect
     tariffs.

34.  The experience of World War II rationing clearly demons-
     trated these effects.  See Time, Feb. 3, 1975, 15-16.

35.  With rationing, there would be little incentive to ex-
     pand domestic production since the market would be
     "frozen" or tightly controlled.  See Time, Feb. 3,
     1975, 15-16.

36.  Los Angeles Times, Jan. 16, 1975, 21.

37.  OPEC has traditionally paid close attention to the
     balance between producer and consumer government
     "takes" on refined products.  See Time, Jan. 6, 1975,
     11-12.

38.  See note 39, infra.

39.  In his press conference on Nov. 2, 1974, the Shah of
     Iran indicated his indifference to consumer country
     tax policy.  Los Angeles Times, Nov. 11, 1974, 17.
     See also "Arab Oil Experts Express No Alarm Over
     Ford's Plans," The New York Times, Jan. 16, 1975.

40.  This option has been considered by the Subcommittee
     on Multinational Corporations of the Senate Committee
     on Foreign Relations.  Multinational Oil Corporations
     and U.S. Foreign Policy, supra, note 5, at 18-19.

41.  See §9.6, infra.

42.  Under the IEP, the companies would "pool" all their
     available supplies, thus defeating any "targeting"
     attempt.  See §10.1, infra.

43.  Mexico has already made it clear that it will not sell

its oil for less than the OPEC price. <u>Petroleum Intelligence Weekly</u>, Dec. 16, 1974, 7-8.

44. See §8.2, <u>supra</u>.

45. See §7.8, §9.3, <u>infra</u>.

46. See §6.3, <u>infra</u>.

47. Moreover, other consumer governments would likely resent such a U.S. role in determining world prices.

48. S.3553, 93rd Cong., 2d Sess. (May 30, 1974), introduced by Sen. James Abourezk (D, S.D.).

49. See §5.1, <u>supra</u>.

50. This was the intention of Sen. Abourezk's bill, <u>supra</u>, note 48.

CHAPTER 6

## REGULATION OF ALL SIGNIFICANT
## FOREIGN SUPPLY ARRANGEMENTS

A.   [§6.0]  Introduction

        The option of increasing U.S. Government regula-
tion of foreign supply arrangements stems from a recognition
that, except for the former import quota system, 1/ the U.S.
Government has exercised virtually no control over the
purchase of foreign petroleum by U.S. companies, even though
that commodity is America's largest and most essential
import and the economic consequences of its price are of
vital concern to the national economy.  The price of foreign
petroleum consumed in this country has historically been a
matter determined in negotiations between foreign producing
governments and private petroleum companies to which the
U.S. Government has not been privy.  In recent years, however,
it has become clear that the petroleum companies, which have
for so long represented the consuming world in producing
countries, are no longer able to negotiate an advantageous
level of price or guarantee a secure flow of supplies for
consuming nations. 2/

        With the well-being of the U.S. economy increasingly
endangered by instability of supply and soaring price levels,
the interests of the nation seem to require a greater presence
and an active supervisory role by the U.S. Government with
respect to foreign supply arrangements.  In this respect
two types of regulation have been suggested:

        1.  The review of foreign supply arrangements
through greater disclosure; and

        2.  The control of foreign supply arrangements
through a power to review and approve contracts or negotiating
terms. 3/

B.   [§6.1]  Scope of Review

        At the outset the question arises as to the scope
of foreign supply arrangements that are to be regulated.  It
seems clear that at the very least major producer-country
supply or upstream arrangements would be included in light
of their direct impact upon a number of national policy
objectives. 4/  A case can also be made that domestic

investments by foreign governments or corporations owned by
them in U.S. marketing or other downstream operations should
also be included.  An example of how this form of arrangement
could impact upon domestic supply and establish a pattern for
other arrangements is the recently announced proposal that the
National Iranian Oil Company acquire a 50% interest in a large
number of the Shell Oil Company's marketing outlets in the
northeastern United States in consideration for a long-term
purchase arrangement for petroleum products that would be
refined in Iran under a joint venture. 5/  Review might also
be extended to oil companies that are partially owned by
governments, such as British Petroleum and CFP, particularly
where as with CFP their operations are conducted with the
express intent of effectuating governmental petroleum policy. 6/
The key issue here may be whether such companies are subject
to influence by the governments by which they are partially
owned in a manner that could be inconsistent with U.S. public
interests. 7/  At a minimum, the same questions must be asked
about foreign government interests in commercial ventures as
are asked about U.S. Government participation.  The standards
applied to the two should be consistent. 8/

        National security and foreign policy objectives might
make it appropriate to extend the scope of regulation to
significant foreign downstream investments by U.S. companies
in producer countries.  Investments such as refineries or
tankers could form a strategic link in the logistical supply
web and render consumer countries more vulnerable to interruption than the existing system. 9/

        In any case administrative considerations dictate
that regulation should be limited to "major" transactions or
investments, appropriately defined. 9a/  It should also be noted
that the extent of company transactions to be regulated
could vary widely.  If the scheme of regulation extended
only to all international petroleum arrangements which
directly pertain to oil imports into the United States, a
relatively limited number of transactions could be covered.
If the scheme of regulation extended to all international
petroleum arrangements made by U.S. companies without regard
to the destination of the imports, a much broader range of
transactions would be covered.  Thirdly, if the scheme of
regulation extended to all such transactions by U.S. companies,
whether made individually or jointly with foreign companies,

a still greater range would exist. 10/ Lastly, if the scheme of regulation extended to all international petroleum transactions conducted by all companies operating within the jurisdiction of the United States, including foreign, a still greater range of transactions might be covered. 11/

C.  [§6.2]  Disclosure of Foreign Supply Arrangements

The requirement of complete disclosure of foreign supply arrangements is consistent with the recent trend in consuming nations to develop "greater transparency" in the petroleum industry.  This has resulted in broad disclosure requirements in the Federal Energy Administration Act 12/ and the transparency provisions of the recently created International Energy Program ("IEP"). 13/  The European Economic Community ("EEC") has shown an interest in a similar system.  Under the IEP Agreement the participating governments in effect agree to require the disclosure of the "terms of arrangements for access to major sources of crude oil." 14/ In fact, two industry committees, headed by BP and Exxon, are currently working with the IEA to develop a broader data base not only to facilitate emergency sharing arrangements, but also to serve as a reference for broader policy issues. 15/ None of these developments, however, has yet provided a system to establish the broad informational base that will be required for the Federal Government to comprehensively assess the impact of a particular supply arrangement upon U.S. interests.

To implement such a system of disclosure, whether or not in conjunction with a power of review and approval, petroleum companies operating within the jurisdiction of the United States could be required to file an abstract for all appropriate arrangements setting forth essential data, such as the parties, term, price, volume and conditions for interruption.  The reviewing agency could have the authority to request further information or documentation required to assess the impact upon identified policy objectives. 16/

It might also be desirable, particularly if there were no power of review and approval, to require that the abstract be filed not less than a stated, but relatively short, period of time before the effective date of the proposed transaction.  The reviewing agency and other relevant agencies of the United States Government would then have an opportunity to "jawbone" with the company if an

adverse effect were anticipated.  Fears that such a requirement would retard negotiations with producers could be
ameliorated by a summary type of procedure under which
required disclosures regarding the scope of proposed negotiations could be filed before negotiations were seriously
undertaken. 17/  This would constitute little more than a
"flight plan" filing and should not prove to be a major
disruption.

Further transparency would result from requiring
complete disclosure of all documents relating to the negotiations.  This could not only include the contracts themselves but also all drafts, memoranda and other related
documents.  This requirement would be founded on the belief
that the government cannot determine whether the national
interest is being protected unless it is fully acquainted
with all the details of the negotiations.  A disclosure
requirement of this type would essentially be a "fishing
expedition" to determine what factors, apart from the level
of price, are of concern to petroleum companies in their
negotiations with producer governments and to what extent
these factors are inconsistent with U.S. national policy. 18/
While indiscriminate use of this requirement could be burdensome to the industry, if used with discretion it might
provide valuable insight into foreign supply arrangements
and establish a very useful informational base.

Although disclosure requirements might uncover
valuable data, they raise problems.  First, the quantity of
documents disclosed could be very large, depending on the
scope of disclosure required.  Production of all of these
documents would not only constitute a burden to the companies
but would require substantial administrative machinery in
the Government to process and analyze them. 19/

Second, even the disclosure mechanism could bring
about a regulatory delay through expanded bureaucratic activity
and review as happened in the case of the Securities Act of
1933. 20/  The "full disclosure" requirements of that Act
have through the years grown cumulatively into a very pervasive
form of regulation with considerable delays. 21/  To a large
extent this has been true also of the reporting requirements
of the National Environmental Policy Act of 1969 ("NEPA"). 22/
An effective disclosure statute will almost inevitably entail

an element of ambiguity as to the exact data required.  This
ambiguity, together with the existence of sanctions for non-
compliance, can be expected to lead to guarded and time consuming disclosures coupled with prolonged negotiations with
and requests for clearance from the reviewing agency.  Any
legislation requiring disclosure should be tightly drawn to
minimize this problem.

Third, safeguards would have to be established to
maintain the confidentiality of this information.  Its release could be a deterrent to producer governments desiring
to secretly undercut OPEC price levels.  On the other hand,
much of the information required would be common knowledge
to the international oil companies and producer governments;
a great deal of inside "intelligence" becomes industry
knowledge through publications such as Petroleum Intelligence Weekly, Platt's Oilgram News Service, the Middle
East Economic Survey and other sources.  Except in the case
of incomplete transactions, unintended disclosures would
probably have relatively little impact. 23/  In any event,
the confidentiality problems of a U.S. agency should be
minor in comparison to those of the IEA and the EEC. 24/

Although greater Federal Government involvement in
the negotiation of foreign supply contracts may be beneficial, disclosure alone could be a useful half-way step.
It does not involve the political costs of a more intensive
regulatory approach to the problem, while providing public
assurance that a vital industry is being scrutinized.
Disclosure of preexisting and proposed international supply
arrangements would, however, be an effective component of a
review and approval type of process.  In this respect,
however, it should be noted that analysis of the data presented will require a more thorough understanding of the
workings of the international petroleum industry than U.S.
Government agencies have traditionally demonstrated.

D.  [§6.3]  Review and Approval of Supply Arrangements

Conferring upon an agency of the U.S. Government
the power to review and approve or disapprove international
supply arrangements is a more active form of regulation.
The purpose would be to safeguard the national interests by
preventing supply arrangements from being concluded that
conflict with national objectives.

There are a number of problems associated with such a scheme of regulation which should be considered in evaluating its potential effectiveness. One of the most important of these is the effect which any such power of review and approval or disapproval would have upon commercial activities. The petroleum industry has assumed too important a role in the world economy to risk the impairment of its operations through the imposition of a cumbersome bureaucratic process. International petroleum is a fast moving industry. 25/ Time is critical and valuable opportunities may be lost while the wheels of bureaucratic review are turning. The necessity of informing government officials in Washington of the terms of a proposed agreement and awaiting consent thereto will inevitably increase the difficulty of closing agreements. Even where disclosure or approval is not compulsory, the mere existence of regulatory machinery will slow the commercial process due to a cautionary concern to obtain a "clearance." The pre-merger discussions by companies with the Department of Justice regarding possible antitrust implications are a case in point. 26/ It is important to the United States that a regulatory scheme designed to control the level of prices paid for foreign supply will not result in an inability to procure sufficient supplies.

The recent experience of the Pacific Lighting Company in its negotiation of the purchase of LNG from Pertamina, the Indonesian national petroleum company, illustrates the way in which governmental review may work to the detriment of U.S. companies operating abroad. Pacific Lighting and Pertamina had worked out the basic terms of the sale just prior to the imposition of the Arab oil embargo of 1973. The agreement was conditional, however, because Pacific Lighting needed the consent of the Federal Power Commission, 27/ and although Pacific Lighting pushed for such consent at an early date, the requisite approval was not forthcoming for several months during which time occurred the embargo and the subsequent escalation of petroleum prices. Unable to firm up the deal before prices soared in January of 1974, Pacific Lighting has had to renegotiate the contract at a price several times that of its original agreement. 28/

Apart from the delays which may be expected to accompany a system of government review and approval, the commercial activity of U.S. companies may also be inhibited by the effect of the regulatory scheme upon their competitiveness. If U.S. companies are not capable of unconditionally committing themselves in agreements with producing governments, they may find themselves at a disadvantage as against other companies which are not so burdened. 29/ Producing nations, who also value time and opportunity, may be expected to prefer to deal with purchasers who can give commitments when and if they are desired. 30/ This problem would be less significant if the regulatory scheme also encompassed foreign oil companies operating in the United States as well as U.S. companies and there are factors that suggest that they should be. It is difficult to perceive why British Petroleum with its large upstream and downstream operations in the United States should be treated more favorably than U.S. companies. This is also true of CFP and Royal Dutch/Shell with their large U.S. affiliates. 31/ The fact that these corporations are invested with a high degree of governmental interest in their home states makes their international supply arrangements of particular interest to the United States in assessing their impact upon national security.

A question would be raised as to whether the U.S. Government has a sufficient jurisdictional nexus to extend a regulatory scheme of this type to the foreign companies operating here through subsidiaries or affiliates. Predictably the foreign companies, and possibly their home governments, would urge that this constituted extraterritorial regulation. 32/ On the other hand, the elements of control and the national interest seem sufficiently strong to give serious consideration to pursuing the international supply arrangements of the foreign company upstream through their U.S. affiliates or subsidiaries. The concept of regulating the "controlling person" is used in a comparable sense in the Securities Act of 1933. 33/ This Act, however, regulates the activities of such persons, if they are foreign nationals, only when they take place in the United States, i.e., if they make a distribution of securities in this country. To attempt to regulate the activities of foreign companies abroad simply because they have subsidiaries or affiliates operating in the United States obviously raises a much more difficult question. While retaliation could be taken against foreign companies (through their domestic subsidiaries or affiliates) which did not comply with regulatory standards, for example, by excluding them from future leasing on the Outer Continental Shelf or imposing downstream investment restrictions, it would seem clearly preferable to use consumer-nation cooperation to achieve the desired goals in disclosure and regulation. In this regard it is relevant that the recently approved International Energy Program ("IEP") requires each "Participating country . . . to ensure that all oil companies operating within its jurisdiction make . . . information available to it," including that pertaining to "[c]urrent and projected levels of international supply and demand." 34/ This is entirely consistent with a cooperative approach and would require disclosure of international supply arrangements entered into by subsidiaries or affiliaties of foreign companies. In addition the potential regulatory power over their parents' foreign activities should be an incentive for encouraging other consumer nations to adopt forms of regulation complementary to those selected by the U.S. Government. It should also give the U.S. Government a strong negotiating position with such other nations if their companies attempted to take advantage of the regulated status of U.S. companies. 35/

Unless there were a clear statutory exemption, NEPA would probably be applicable and the reviewing authority would be required to prepare an environmental impact statement or assessment regarding all arrangements proposed to be approved that would have a significant impact on the environment; 36/ this could extend to the environment of the producer country involved. 37/ The massive delays that NEPA-related administrative and judicial proceedings have caused in energy projects are well-known. 38/ The possibility of a judicial review of the agency decision on the ground that the agency exceeded its authority, or other grounds, is yet another potential dampener of commercial activity. 39/ The practical effect of any such delays could be to render U.S. companies substantially less competitive in the world market. It would appear entirely appropriate, therefore, to shelter the decision-making process from independent intervention to the maximum extent practicable on the obvious grounds of national security. 40/

Another problem associated with government review of foreign supply contracts concerns the degree of competence which will be required on the part of the responsible Federal agency if its task is to be performed in a beneficial manner. The governmental policies which to date have most substantially affected the petroleum industry in the international sphere have too often been set by government officials without a high degree of experience or expertise in petroleum. 41/ Unlike most other major industrial consuming nations, the U.S. Government has made relatively little use of industry personnel in its policy formulation, largely because of widespread public distrust of such individuals in government, and an inability to pay sufficiently attractive salaries. 42/ The result may or may not have been to produce greater "objectivity" in establishing policy, but it has also resulted in a fragmentary and incomplete understanding of how the international industry and market work. More than a few of the problems which are now plaguing the petroleum industry as well as the world economy are due to government attempts to regulate the industry which went astray. 43/ The capacity for damage by misguided governmental regulation to the intricate web which channels the flow of investment capital and petroleum resources is enormous, and there appears to be an unfortunate underestimation of the need for experience and understanding on the part of government officials to be involved in any new regulatory scheme for international petroleum affairs. 44/

Even assuming sufficient competence can be mustered by the reviewing agency, there remains the problem inherent in decision making by any agency which is ultimately responsive to the ebb and flow of political pressure. There are few decisions which involve greater political risks than one which affects the price which consumers pay for gasoline or heating fuel. 45/ The generally mistrustful attitude of the public toward the oil industry as well as the immense power of the large petroleum companies and their thousands of shareholders are important political elements to be reckoned with. If government review of foreign supply contracts is to work effectively, the agency involved must be able to act with a degree of independence from political pressure which may trade short-term political gain for long-term effective resource management. The reluctance of the Federal Power Commission to raise rates on natural gas to a level which would have encouraged investment in domestic production has been largely attributed to the political factors which any such decision and its expensive repercussions to the American consumer would have generated. 46/ In the end, of course, the American consumer will pay much more for this pragmatic trade-off. The lesson is not one which should be easily forgotten when future schemes of government review are considered.

Some of the risks of undue political pressure or favoritism may be eliminated by the promulgation of "objective standards" in the form of regulations. This would seem

to reduce the likelihood that political prejudice against a
particular company or producing nation would work its way
into the review of foreign contracts.  On the other hand,
the complexity of the industry is such as to defy an easy or
precise definition of what is beneficial or not to the
national interest. 47/  An otherwise acceptable foreign
supply arrangement may not be in the national interest
simply because of its timing or anticipated precedental
impact on world price levels, the nature of the parties
involved, the general circumstances in the international
market or national security. 48/  There will be a need to
judge the acceptability of any arrangement on the particular
facts, rather than according to a system of objective
standards, however detailed.

In reviewing such arrangements, it is inevitable
that a great amount of discretion will have to be given to
the agency involved.  In view of the crippling effect which
the disapproval of a major supply arrangement may have on a
petroleum company, the breadth of discretion allowed the
administrator in whose hands the decision is placed may even
raise questions of constitutional due process and the possibility of time-consuming judicial review. 49/  If an
adverse ruling on a reviewed contract would, in effect, put
a company out of the petroleum business or deal it a severe
financial blow, due process or a general sense of fair play
might dictate that some compensation be made to the injured
company.  In some respects the situation is comparable to
the condemning of private property in order to protect or
promote the public interest. 50/  What may often be at stake
in the contract being reviewed is not only a particular
agreement to purchase crude, but also the continuing role
which the company will play in the producing country.  If
the Government decides that national interest cannot permit
a company to enter into such an agreement, the company may
be effectively deprived of assets and a relationship with
the producing government which have taken years and millions
of dollars to create. 51/  This situation was recognized in
the 1970-71 negotiations in Libya when the companies themselves, through their coordinating organization, the London
Policy Group, set up their own "safety net" under which a
company which lost sources of supply by refusing to agree to
the demands of the Libyan Government would receive alternative sources of supply through the other companies. 52/
This type of compensation was preferable to monetary compensation because the companies are in the business of
selling petroleum and would rather have the crude.  As the
largest owner of oil and gas resources in North America, the
U.S. Government is in a position to provide alternate
supplies.  The "safety net" concept should probably be part
of a scheme of review and approval.

The foregoing problems are not necessarily insurmountable, although they do indicate the costs which this option would necessarily involve. An agency with the independence of, for example, the Federal Reserve Board, 53/ which would be able to make discreet use of retired industry personnel might be able to muster the requisite independence and expertise. The timing question could perhaps be resolved by imposing a relatively short and mandatory time limit for the agency to act if it is to disapprove a contract. 54/ This type of deadline, together with sufficient disclosure requirements on the companies and an adequate agency staff, could make speedy decisions possible. It would also seem desirable to provide for an automatic approval of a proposed arrangement at the expiration of the specified time period, unless it was disapproved by the agency within that period.

The question which must be answered is whether, in light of the identified problems, this option would substantially advance any of the national objectives discussed in Chapter 2 above or otherwise improve the position of the United States in international petroleum affairs.

## [§6.4]  Improvement of Security of Supply

It may be contended that foreign supply arrangements would be more secure against interference or interruption by producing nations if the U.S. Government were more overtly involved in their negotiation. The basis for the contention is the assumption that the political risk to a producing government of breaching a straight business contract with a private company is not as high as the risk of breaking an agreement with a foreign government, especially one as powerful and influential as the U.S. Government. It follows that the presence of the U.S. Government in a contractual arrangement between a company and a producing government could give that company a greater bargaining position when faced with demands for a "renegotiation" than it could itself muster.

As discussed in greater detail in Section 9.4, infra, there is considerable reason to doubt the validity of this contention. The producer countries have shown no high regard for consumer-government interests in supply arrangements. Examples are the nationalization of the French Government-owned ELF-ERAP concessions in Algeria and the unilateral escalation of the negotiated price on the Franco-Iraqi bilateral agreement. 55/ Moreover, the discretionary right to review and, if deemed necessary, disapprove a supply contract is not the type of overt U.S. Government presence which has a substantial impact upon producing governments. Notwithstanding its approval of contractual terms the U.S. Government would still not be directly involved in negotiations. Thus, review and approval does not appear to be the sort of U.S. Government involvement which is likely to give such supply arrangements a greater degree of security. It is clear, however, that in negotiations the company would be less of a "hostage" of the producer government in the sense that it has a "fallback" negotiating position which the producer government knows the company cannot change. 56/

It may further be argued that the indirect presence of the U.S. Government might even make the arrangements less secure by increasing the risk that they will be repudiated by producer governments for political reasons. In recent years, producing governments have shown an increasing willingness to use petroleum supply as an instrument for achieving political ends. The Arab embargoes of 1956, 1967 and 1973-74 are the most notable examples. 57/ If a producer government is hostile to the policies of a consumer government, the latter's presence in the negotiation of petroleum supply arrangements may only increase the temptation to the producer to use those arrangements as a means of protesting the policy. The nationalization of partially British Government-owned BP in Libya in purported retaliation for Britain's policies in the Persian Gulf is an illustration of this risk. 58/

It seems unlikely, however, that the mere right to review and approve foreign supply arrangements would constitute a sufficient presence to incite political retaliation where it would not otherwise have occurred. The risks increase, however, in the event that the power of disapproval is actually employed. In a situation, for example, where political tension between the United States and a particular producing nation is such as to cause a disapproval of a proposed contract in the interests of discouraging reliance on insecure sources, the disapproval might be interpreted by the producing nation as an act of confrontation and it could result in retaliatory action by that producer nation or by a block of nations of which it is a

member.  Nevertheless, that seems insufficient reason to
avoid creating the mechanism of review and approval since
the reviewing agency would obviously consider this risk in
determining whether to exercise its power.  Thus, the presence of the U.S. Government under a review and approval
scheme of regulation would neither substantially increase
nor decrease the security which foreign supply arrangements
negotiated by private companies would otherwise have.

The power of disapproval over foreign supply
contracts might promote greater security of supply by providing a tool by which the U.S. Government can direct U.S.
dependence upon foreign imports toward more "reliable"
producing nations. 59/  As long as there exists the unresolved Arab-Israeli conflict in the Middle East, there will
be the ever present danger of a renewed Arab embargo of the
U.S.  Other OPEC nations have so committed themselves to the
maintenance of existing levels of world petroleum prices 60/
that they may be expected to continue to restrict production,
leaving an ever-decreasing supply of their petroleum for
consumer needs. 61/  Still other producer nations may be
less secure because of a possibility of a change of government to one more hostile to the United States.  It is questionable whether this usage would improve the system, however, because the petroleum companies also stand to suffer
from a sudden embargo or production cut, and their decisions
on where to invest and from whom to purchase reflect their
on-the-spot assessments of the relative stability of the
sources involved.

Further, it is questionable if there are any fully
reliable producer countries.  The United Kingdom with which
the United States has a mutually acknowledged "special
relationship" and whose petroleum company, BP, has very
large interests in the Alaskan North Slope and elsewhere in
the United States, is actively considering proposals for
North Sea participation and severe taxation that would
seriously affect U.S. companies. 62/  The U.K. is also
talking of "conserving" its enormous North Sea reserves by
restricting development and has given indications of a
possible intention of restricting future production to
British markets. 63/  Norway has an announced policy of
restricting its very large anticipated North Sea production
so as to generate only such revenues as its economy will be

213.

able to efficiently absorb and is also considering tax raises that would impact upon U.S. companies. 64/ Canada, our neighbor and largest trading partner, has stated that it intends to curtail all exports to the United States within the next few years. 65/ At the same time, by a combination of federally imposed price controls, severely restrictive federal income tax provisions, and dramatically increased royalty rates by the provincial governments, Canada has abruptly reversed the economic incentives for investment by U.S. companies and has made supply arrangements to the United States more expensive and less secure. 66/ Mexico has indicated that when it soon achieves export capacity from its new discoveries it will follow OPEC pricing practices. 67/ Whether it is the Peoples Republic of China or the Kingdom of Saudi Arabia, there appears to be a universal intention on the part of exporters today to maximize returns. Insofar as reliability is concerned there appears to be very little difference between OPEC members and any other exporting countries. 68/

Lastly, as noted earlier, the forcing of U.S. companies away from traditional supply sources in the interest of security may simply render them uncompetitive in comparison with foreign companies and could result in petroleum being directed elsewhere. Investments (e.g., European refineries and marketing outlets) have been made by U.S. companies predicated on particular foreign supply sources. 69/ To require these companies, many of which serve largely foreign markets in any case, to seek other sources could be very costly to them.

It must be constantly remembered in considering this option that the review and approval powers of the Federal Government could be very easily used in a way that would be punitively damaging to the U.S. companies without in any way improving the stability or cost of international sources of supply. On the other hand, it is clear also that it would effect a very basic political benefit: that of establishing the confidence in the public that international supply arrangements by U.S. companies, and possibly other companies operating in the United States, are being made in a way that will not conflict with U.S. national interests. With due regard to the very political nature of international supply arrangements, this consideration alone could outweigh the very substantial economic costs involved. 70/

## [§6.5]  Control Over Petroleum Price Levels

        Some see the power of review and approval of
foreign supply arrangements as positively affecting the
prices which the United States or, perhaps, consuming
nations generally pay for imported petroleum.  In analyzing
this concept, two basic types of price problems should be
distinguished.  The first problem is the transaction which
will result in an adverse precedent in world price levels.
The effectiveness of the option of review and approval as a
means of correcting this problem is analyzed below in Section 6.6.  The second problem is the current level of world
prices itself, which is widely agreed in the consuming world
to be too high.  The impact which this option would have on
those price levels is examined in Section 6.7.

## [§6.6]  Control of Precedental Transactions

        One of the distinguishing features of the inter-
national petroleum market is that pricing decisions are
political in nature and very often a transaction will have a
much greater effect in the world market than it would if
only commercial forces prevailed.  Perhaps the clearest
example of the precedental nature of petroleum transactions
was the "leap frogging" demands of the Persian Gulf and
North African producers during the early 1970's. 71/  Each
group of producers feared that it was not getting as high a
price from the companies as the other.  Thus, the Persian
Gulf countries used the companies' agreement to pay higher
price levels in Libya as a basis for demanding higher prices
for Persian Gulf crude.  Agreement by the companies to their
demands in turn sparked further demands in North Africa. 72/

        An awareness of the danger of setting precedents
led the large multinational majors to oppose higher prices
and greater producer-government participation wherever demanded for fear that other producing countries in which they
were involved would demand similar concessions.  Therein lay
the majors' principal fear of the Production Sharing Contract in Indonesia. 73/  The independents, who often had no
other foreign sources of supply and were therefore less
concerned about precedental effects, were willing throughout
the 1950's and 1960's to offer producer governments better
terms.  The willingness of the independents to pay higher
prices in order to gain access to new sources of supply had
a major precedental impact on the level which all companies
throughout the world had to pay to producers. 74/  This
situation did not, however, greatly affect the price which
consumers had to pay for petroleum since in order to maintain

competitiveness downstream, the independent companies took the increased payments to producers out of their wide profit margins. Indeed, the independents expanded their downsteam operations by cutting prices to the consumer.

Today's international petroleum market is different from that of the 1950's and the 1960's because pricing decisions are made by producer governments and the companies are now basically price-takers passing on new increases to the consumer. 75/ In this situation, there are basically two types of precedental transactions which are detrimental to consuming nations because of the impact which they may have upon the pricing decisions of producer governments. The first situation involves a company which is willing to pay a higher level of price on one purchase of petroleum in order to protect a preferential position within the producing country which may make other purchases cheaper. This was the situation in Kuwait where Gulf and British Petroleum recently accepted a buy-back price of 94.85% of posted price. This price was the highest that any major had agreed to pay for buy-back crude in the Persian Gulf, but was acceptable to the two companies because of a preferential arrangement which they had with the Kuwaiti Government under which they were not required to purchase and market all of the Kuwaiti participation crude. Under this arrangement, only 40% of the crude which the companies marketed was buy-back and the rest was cheaper equity crude. 76/ Elsewhere in the Gulf, companies were required to market the full participation share and the buy-back price constituted 60% of the average price of their crude. 77/ Because Gulf and BP were able to buy a larger percentage of their Kuwaiti crude at lower equity price levels, they could accept a higher level of price on the buy-back crude and still maintain a competitive average cost.

Although their agreement to pay 94.85% of posting for buy-back was a beneficial one for Gulf and BP, the precedental impact was adverse to other companies operating in the Persian Gulf and, therefore, to the ultimate consumer. Aramco, for example, was thereafter required to pay 94.85% of posting for its Saudi Arabian buy-back crude even though that price constitutes 60% of its average cost per barrel rather than only 40% as was the case for Gulf and BP. 78/ The potential detrimental effect of the Gulf and BP arrangement was fully recognized by the U.S. and

British Governments who attempted to "jawbone" the companies into not agreeing. 79/ In the end, however, the companies responded to their own interest in maintaining a preferential position and the Government agreed.

It is important to stress here that Gulf and BP did not do an improper act in maximizing their companies' economic positions; they are in business to do this. The point is that conditions in the international oil industry are such that the companies can be whipsawed and are in no position to protect themselves. Moreover, these companies have no obligation to their stockholders to avoid losses incurred on political grounds. The price of oil is, in the first instance a political issue since the ascendancy of OPEC. No single company is in a position to effectively address that political issue and it is inappropriate to expect its management to cause its owners losses in an attempt to do so. The example of Gulf and BP in Kuwait is used here, not because it is exceptional, but because it illustrates the problem well.

The second situation in which an individual transaction may have an adverse effect occurs in times of short supply when small purchasers, often utilities and other consumers, find their previous sources of supply insecure and are forced out on the world market seeking supplies at any price. The "bidding up" of prices on spot cargoes and small direct purchases, sometimes as high as $20 per barrel, was a common phenomenon during the recent Arab embargo. 80/ Although the quantities of crude involved in such purchases are often so small as to have little direct effect upon the average price which consuming nations pay for their petroleum, the willingness of these small purchasers to pay high prices is a fact which is not lost on producer governments when setting their prices. 81/

Producing nations have a generalized concept of the "fair value" of their petroleum. This notion affects what they consider to be their minimum acceptable price level. When companies, protecting a preferential position or attempting to secure some source of supply, are willing to pay substantially more than other purchasers, producing

governments often interpret this as an indication that the
current price is too low. 82/ In addition, as has been
learned many times in international petroleum affairs,
if one producer government raises its prices, the others
may be expected to follow suit. As the policies of the
United Kingdom, the Peoples Republic of China and Canada
have illustrated, this is no less true of non-OPEC producers. 83/

Every major supply contract has an effect upon
subsequent contracts both in that country and elsewhere.
Under the "most favored nations" clause found in Persian Gulf
supply contracts, for example, a higher price paid by a
company to one Gulf producer to maintain that company's
access to cheaper equity crude will give other Gulf producers the right to the same price from purchasers of
their crude. 84/ The Gulf and BP agreements in Kuwait had
this very effect. Certain foreign governmental representatives have expressed great concern that Aramco in its
current negotiations with Saudi Arabia resist pressure
to make Saudi participation retroactive to September of
1973 or even January of 1974 85/ because of the precedental impact on their companies in other countries. The
precedental effect of major supply arrangements is of
extreme importance.

A governmental power of review would be unlikely
to have substantial effects upon the bidding up of prices
during an embargo or other short-term supply interruptions.
The quantities involved in most of these purchases are
small and the transactions are too numerous and often too
quickly concluded to allow effective governmental review in each
case. 86/ Although the producing governments often attach
considerable inportance to these transactions, the benefit
derived from regulating them would not justify the enormous
administrative cost. A more efficient form of regulation
would be an across-the-board price ceiling on imports, as
discussed in Section 5.2, supra.

Neither a power of disapproval nor a price ceiling, however, will solve the price problem. The precedental
impact upon a producing government of a U.S. purchaser who
is willing to pay a higher price is not lessened by the fact
that the purchaser's government intervenes to prevent him from

concluding the transaction. The effect upon the producer's
notion of "fair value" will probably remain and affect
future dealings with other non-U.S. purchasers. 87/ If
the interruption of supply is sufficient to drive small,
unregulated, U.S. purchasers onto the world market, it can
be expected to have a similar effect upon purchasers
in other consuming nations. 88/ This was the situation
during the recent Arab embargo in which purchasers from
Europe and Japan displayed perhaps the least ability to
hold any reasonable line on price in times of short supply. 89/
If not restrained by their respective governments, these
purchasers will be queuing up to take the place of any U.S.
purchaser whose contract has been disapproved by the U.S.
Government. 90/ The result would be a self-inflicted
compounding of the short supply in the United States, with
the attendant economic cost, while non-U.S. purchasers
continued to exert the same escalating effect upon world prices.

        A more effective way to control the bidding up
of prices during a period of shortage of supply would be an
import price ceiling imposed in conjunction with other consuming nations, such as through the International Energy
Agency. 91/ If real self-restraint on the part of all such
consuming nations could be exercised, the problem created
by non-U.S. purchasers continuing to bid up prices would be
ameliorated. This option may create problems. In any
period of short supply it is likely that those producing
governments which are selling will raise their prices, as
was the case during the recent Arab embargo. 92/ An import
ceiling which would not allow consuming nations to pay the
increased price would substantially aggravate the existing
shortage at a substantial cost to consumer economies in terms
of unemployment and lost gross national product. 93/ This
would in turn greatly strain the solidarity of the consuming
nations.

        On the other hand, if the price ceilings were
set slightly above the world price level, as adjusted upward by producers, it would not increase the already existing shortage of supply and would only prevent the more extreme forms of competition among purchasers for the available
supplies. 94/ The type of bidding up of prices to three or
five dollars above OPEC price levels that was seen during the
recent Arab embargo simply created a windfall profit for
producing nations. It did not serve to increase the amount
of petroleum available but only to determine its allocation

among consumers according to a ruthless competitive bidding. 95/
An import price ceiling might prevent this bidding-up effect
without aggravating the already existing shortage of supply.

The type of precedental transaction in which a
higher price is paid in order to maintain a preferred position
in a producer country is more susceptible to effective
control under a scheme of governmental review and approval.
These arrangements are, as a rule, much larger and their
precedental impact is accordingly greater. 96/ Negotiations
between any of the multinational majors and their Persian
Gulf host governments will be watched with keen interest by
the entire petroleum world. These transactions, unlike the
bidding up of prices on small purchases during times of
short supply, very often are quite favorable to the companies involved. What is of concern and which ought to be
closely supervised is the effect which these transactions
will have on other transactions and world prices generally.

A preferential position in a producing country is
something to which both the company which has it and the
producer government which has given it properly attach
value. 97/ For instance, Saudi Arabia has repeatedly delayed
the implementation of its announced intention to go to 100%
participation (full nationalization) with Aramco. 98/ This
delay has been beneficial for the current owners, and the
Saudis have repeatedly reavowed their intention to make it
attractive for the Aramco offtakers to remain interested in
Saudi Arabia because they can supply the skills and technology
to operate the Saudi oil complex. 99/ It is doubtful that
this contribution could be easily replaced. It is certain
that the special relationship between Saudi Arabia and
Aramco could not. 100/

The relationship works the other way as well. The
Aramco offtakers (Socal, Texaco, Exxon and Mobil) have built
a worldwide refining and distribution system predicated on
Saudi oil. 101/ Thus, they acquiesced in September of 1973
to new Saudi demands for increased payment on buy-back oil
and the Saudi abrogation of its commitment to a gradual
increase to 51% participation by 1983. 102/ Indeed, 51%, a
precedent achieved by the Libyans with Occidental just one
month previous, was now rejected by the Saudis as insufficient. Sixty percent participation soon followed, and under
the strains of the then existing embargo, the companies
accepted these deals despite their precedental quality. 103/

The preferential position enjoyed by a number of companies in several of the producing countries has usually arisen from a long relationship, often spanning several decades, between the producing government and the company. In fact, producing governments have occasionally used the complex formulae by which the price of crude sold to their former concessionaries is calculated to disguise what are essentially bargain price levels. 104/ On the other hand, it has been argued by some that the special position enjoyed by certain of the majors is in fact detrimental to consumers because it makes the worldwide distribution web of the majors available to producer governments to assist them in maintaining their cartel-like unity. 105/ In any event, the preferential position enjoyed by these companies has effectively made them the "hostages" of the producer governments, since they greatly benefit from their positions. Accordingly, the companies can be expected to agree to whatever demands the producer governments place on their continued access to this preferential treatment, even if such agreement is inconsistent with the interests of consumers. It must further be expected that if the companies are prevented by the U.S. Government from agreeing to such demands, they may lose their position in the producing countries. 106/ If no other companies are willing or able to assume that position, the producing governments will have to sell their crude at a single price to all purchasers. 107/

Determining whether this occurrence would be advantageous to consumers would involve a complex matrix of considerations, including the cost to the company and its shareholders of the lost position, the advantage, if any, to consuming nations to promote a single price system and the benefit from avoiding the adverse precedental effects of the agreement being reviewed. 108/ The case for U.S. Government intervention at this point is based primarily on the realization that the costs and benefits which must be weighed in this decision affect the nation as a whole and, accordingly, the decision is better made by the Government than by the company involved, since the interests of the two may not coincide. 109/

The effectiveness of such U.S. Government review might vary depending upon how such governmental review is structured. If the U.S. Government confined its review to contracts involving imports into the U.S. market, the companies, valuing their preferred position and seeking to maintain it, would adjust their distribution network to avoid bringing themselves within the web of U.S. regulation. 110/ They would, accordingly, seek to sell petroleum purchased under such agreements in non-U.S. markets with the result that the precedental impact of such agreements would have the same escalating effect upon the prices of other crude, some of which would be destined for the U.S. market.

An observation of the conduct of non-U.S. consuming nations during the past 18 months would seem to provide ample basis for assuming that these nations and their companies attach as much value to "secure access" as do the U.S. companies. 111/ Thus, conceivably all that this type of U.S. Government regulation might be expected to accomplish would be the transfer of preferential positions from U.S. to non-U.S. companies with no effect upon the precedental impact of higher prices paid to maintain preferential position. Moreover, the regulation could have the effect of creating a "self-imposed embargo" by which the United States, through its unwillingness to permit its companies to enter into certain agreements, diverts supplies away from its market. The U.S. Government, then, has only a limited ability to unilaterally prevent the adverse precedental effect paid for preference; it can only affect which companies are paying. 112/

If, however, consumer nation cooperation were sufficiently advanced so that other consuming governments could and would prevent their companies from seeking the preferential positions abandoned by U.S. companies and vice versa, the action of the U.S. Government would be much more effective in controlling the price problems attributable to payment for preferential position. Without such cooperation, the U.S. Government is engaged in a questionable activity if it is depriving U.S. firms of their advantages only to have foreign firms assume them. The essential element is the requisite degree of consumer-nation cooperation and not the unilateral action of the U.S. Government. Cooperation under the International Energy Program or otherwise does not appear to have developed to the necessary extent, and the refusal of any major consuming nation to cooperate could seriously undermine the implementation of this scheme of regulation. 113/

If, instead, the U.S. Government chose to impose this regulatory scheme on all supply contracts entered into by U.S. companies abroad, the political consequences would be more complex, but the end result would be very similar. A large portion of Western European petroleum and three-quarters of Japan's are provided by the international supply web of the U.S. companies, of which the U.S. market is a relatively small branch. 114/ To the energy dependent economies of Western Europe and Japan the smooth functioning of this supply network is of critical importance. If the U.S. Government were to attempt to regulate the purchase of Middle Eastern and North African petroleum for consumption outside the United States, by seizing upon the U.S. citizenship of the intermediary company, it could seriously prejudice the ability of those companies to perform their function as an international conduit of energy and have an adverse impact upon U.S. foreign relations. 115/

Although five of the seven majors which deliver most of the petroleum supply to Japan and Europe are incorporated in the United States, they are multinational corporations in the broadest sense of the word. Their home state is the United States, but their business involves them deeply in a number of different countries to each of which they owe legitimate obligations. Their recognition of these obligations was demonstrated by their conduct during the recent Arab embargo in which they rerouted shipments of petroleum so as to spread the burden of the shortage essentially evenly among their many multinational customers. 116/

These companies operate under an international patchwork made up of regulations imposed by each country with which they are involved. This presents no problem as long as one nation does not seek to regulate the companies in a manner inconsistent with regulation by other involved nations. When, however, a single nation attaches decisive significance to the particular connection between it and a company, to the exclusion of other involved nations in order to justify a system of regulation which reaches beyond its territorial boundaries, the viability of the concept of a multinational corporation is threatened. While the recent criticisms of multinational corporations within the United Nations and elsewhere may or may not have merit, a substantial abridgement of their logistical and managerial functions in international petroleum could have a crippling effect upon the world economy. 117/ It is a serious error to assume that these companies can be easily replaced. The reaction of the U.S. companies to any such regulatory scheme would be to seek to avoid the reach of U.S. Government jurisdiction by the use of foreign subsidiaries.

Unless the U.S. Government review of supply arrangements affecting other markets were operated in close coordination with the affected consuming nations, the reaction of these nations would be one of grave concern. While basically in accord with the United States on broad matters of energy policy, most other consuming nations are very aware of their greater vulnerability to the economic weapons of oil producers and are sometimes concerned by the approach to these nations taken by the United States. 118/ Accordingly, they may well be very apprehensive over any action which would link their supply of critically needed energy to the political decisions of the U.S. Government. These nations would quickly begin seeking their own sources of supply free of possible U.S. Government interference. While conceding that the U.S. is often working with the interests of other consuming nations in mind, most such non-U.S. customers would probably believe that the decision whether to pay a high price or do without ought to be made by the country which will have to, in fact, do without. The resulting scramble by European and Japanese companies to open up their own lines of supply would itself have an escalating effect upon prices, since the resulting competition among such companies might give an impression of a net increase in demand.

If, however, this right of review were exercised in close coordination with other consumer nations and consumers most affected were assured of participating in decisions affecting their supply, the result would be more productive. If there is logic in this regulatory concept, it should extend to the maximum number of relevant supply arrangements possible, including those made to supply foreign markets. This would maximize the control exercisable by the U.S. Government by closing the foreign market loophole and would further develop an informational base regarding the relationship between U.S. and foregin markets, entirely supportive of the purposes of the International Energy Program. This would suggest that the International Energy Agency is the appropriate aegis for efforts in this area. 119/

The concept of regulating foreign supply arrangements of all companies operating in the United States through affiliates or subsidiaries might give greater cohesiveness to the scheme of regulation, but it would predictably disrupt consumer-nation cooperation. 120/ A more logical approach would be to maximize the use multilateral approaches, specifically through the IEA. 121/

The control of detrimental precedental transactions by the U.S. Government is, then, closely related to the degree of cooperation among consuming nations which can be achieved. In no event is unilateral action by the U.S. Government likely to achieve effective control over either the bidding up of prices during short supply or the payment of higher prices to maintain preferential position. On the other hand, what cannot be accomplished by the unilateral action of the U.S. Government can be achieved, in some cases, with the close cooperation and self restraint of other consuming nations.

[§6.7] Regulation to Affect World Price Levels

The second possible purpose of a review and approval regulatory scheme would be to achieve a lower level of world petroleum prices. In this case, supply arrangements might be disapproved, not because the price was out of line with current levels, but as part of a consumer strategy for lowering these levels. The strategy would be based upon the theory that denial of access to the U.S. market or markets serviced by U.S. companies would be sufficiently injurious to producing countries to force them to lower price levels. Under existing market conditions, however, such unilateral action by the U.S. Government would be unlikely to have any effect, except to cause a self-imposed embargo on U.S. companies and the U.S. market. 122/ As long as non-U.S. consuming nations and companies are willing to pay existing levels of prices, unsuccessful U.S. purchasers would be replaced by European and Japanese companies. Even if with current worldwide softness of demand other consumers were not forthcoming to purchase the supply refused by U.S. companies, the existing level of prices could be maintained by appropriate production cuts on the part of producing countries. 123/

If the U.S. Government's disapproval of contracts at existing price levels were invoked in conjunction with a

225.

a coordinated policy of consumer cooperation, the chances of producing an impact on price would be greater. 124/ The strategy most calculated to have an effect would be the disapproval of contracts with one or two selected producers whose ambitious programs make a reasonably steady flow of revenue a matter of great importance. If the U.S. Government disallowed further purchases of this country's crude (and other consumers either did likewise or declined to fill the void), the resulting necessity of shutting in production would become very costly to that country. It should be noted, however, that the most vulnerable producer countries (such as Indonesia and Nigeria) are nations which the United States would not wish to isolate. 125/ Nevertheless, the effect of this strategy would be to improve the position of the United States in a confrontation over price levels.

This strategy would have the unfortunate effect of injuring those companies which are heavily dependent upon the petroleum of the affected producing country. There would have to be a "safety net" or other form of compensation for these companies to cushion them from the inevitable effects on their business caused by an inability to purchase any petroleum. 126/ In this respect, the offtakers are equally exposed with the producing government to the impact of such a plan. 127/ An unfortunate side effect of this plan may be that the producer government will hasten the development of its own distribution mechanism so that the marketing of its products will not in the future be dependent upon foreign companies which can in turn be controlled by their governments. Thus, the real loser could be the companies.

Whether this strategy would have an actual effect upon prices depends almost entirely upon political decisions rather than the laws of supply and demand. Whether the U.S. and its cooperating consumer allies could endure a self-imposed embargo of any size is doubtful, considering the political impact of the resulting decline in economic activity and high unemployment. This cost could be avoided if the U.S. and other consumers were able to cover the shortfall with purchases from other producing countries. OPEC would, however, undoubtedly immediately recognize that the strategy constitutes an attempt to "pick off" its most vulnerable members. 128/ As with the companies, the producers learned from the Libyan negotiations that the strength of the group can only be maintained by a willingness on the part of all to protect the weakest of the members. The obvious OPEC response would be to make cuts in production equal to the shortfall caused by consumer refusals to purchase. The United States and other non-purchasing consumers might be able to ease the situation by spreading the shortfall in supply among all cooperating nations, but this strategy could be countered by further production cuts.

The position of the producers could be further strengthened by the establishment of a financial "safety net" under which the residual producers in the Middle East not only cut back production, thus keeping up the pressure on consumers, but also made available loans to the producers being isolated so as to relieve the pressure on them caused by declining revenues. Thus, it is clear that if the Persian Gulf residual suppliers are willing to play their part, they can check any such consumer strategy under current market conditions by converting it into a standoff situation in which consumers, who are more vulnerable, are more likely to lose.

The success of any strategy to reduce world price by disapproving selected contracts--whether by the U.S. Government unilaterally or by consuming nations collectively--depends upon the ability of OPEC to recognize the challenge and the willingness of the residual producers to shoulder their burden in order to maintain OPEC unity. 129/ Since producing nations owe much of their recent economic and political strength to the unity of OPEC, it would be very unlikely that they would fail to respond to a clear political confrontation by consuming nations. The willingness of OPEC producers to unilaterally cut production in order to maintain OPEC unity has already been amply demonstrated by the actions of a number of OPEC members. In fact, the political climate both domestically and internationally would make it virtually impossible for any OPEC member not to vigorously respond to a clear threat. 130/ Thus the success or failure of this approach would depend in large part upon the ability of the U.S. and other consumers to orchestrate and implement their actions in such a fashion as to avoid this being construed as a confrontation of OPEC unity. OPEC techniques for raising prices recently may offer some instruction as to how a problem can be examined and in small ways ameliorated, while maintaining that entirely different goals are being addressed. 131/ In short, this process would require a very sophisticated approach.

E.   [§6.8]  Conclusion

At a minimum it appears necessary for the U.S. Government to obtain information regarding international arrangements directly affecting U.S. petroleum supply from companies operating in the United States, whether U.S. or foreign.  Functionally, it would seem that this disclosure system would also best encompass all international supply arrangements made or proposed to be made by these companies. 132/ It would also appear to be desirable to require disclosure of petroleum-related investments in the United States by foreign governments and corporations, wholly or partially government-owned, which may materially affect U.S. petroleum supply or other considerations of national interest, including national security and foreign relations.  Finally, it may be desirable to have greater information regarding certain forms of foreign downstream investments.

There will be a clear need to narrow the quantity of information required to that which is the most relevant and material.  There can be little question, however, that this informational base is necessary and desirable in the important area of evaluating and formulating U.S. policy and action in international petroleum affairs.

There is a risk that the disclosure requirements could serve as a springboard for the sort of broadly based administrative action by the reviewing agency which could effectively convert the process to a more cumbersome and time consuming form of regulation, as has been the case with the disclosure requirements of the Securities Act of 1933 and in a sense with the reporting requirements of NEPA. 133/  The potential regulatory character of a disclosure statute poses both the issue of how the legislation authorizing it can be limited to the disclosure function and whether practically it should be.  If the present situation is one that realistically requires the involvement of the Federal Government, the question goes logically to the best form of that involvement. It serves little to either the President or the Congress to permit a system to grow by accretion through ad hoc adminis-trative actions. 134/

A much more serious question is presented by the review and approval concept of regulation.  This system, unlike disclosure, has a potential for causing severe and immediate dislocations within the international supply system

228.

unless used with great care and sensitivity by the responsible
agency. The direct cost of creating an appropriate Executive
Branch monitoring capability could be quite significant because
of the sophistication that would be required in its personnel
and the extensive nature of its regulatory functions. 135/  The
indirect costs of the system could be even greater in terms
of the potential for disruption of the national and international
economy. If the energy supply to the United States and/or the
rest of the world were materially impaired because of the unwise
operation of the system, the economic consequences would be
severe.

On the other hand, it is very true that events in
global petroleum affairs have drastically changed the traditional system of supply, demand and distribution and that the
oil companies today are relatively powerless in dealing with
producer countries. The basic question is whether the presence
of the U.S. Government should be interjected, even if only
indirectly, into international petroleum arrangements affecting
U.S. national interests. The question is a highly political
one and this consideration is emphasized by the fact that under
prevailing conditions the implementation of this option would
have little direct impact on world petroleum prices, at least
in the short term. On the other hand, it does provide both
a window and a potential lever for the Federal Government in
international petroleum affairs which could prove to be of
benefit. If consumer nation cooperation is increased, if the
world petroleum supply base is broadened, if consumer nations
develop a strong program of conservation and utilization of
alternate energy supplies and if safety net arrangements are
established, this regulation by the U.S. and other important
consumer governments could provide an instrument through
which foreign supply arrangements could be made more responsive to the national interests of consumer countries. 136/

The oil industry strongly and with some reason
opposes this form of regulation in view of its potential for
economic disruption. The day of laissez-faire arrangements
in international petroleum affairs, however, has clearly
passed and a new role for the U.S. Government is indicated.
This option, particularly in conjunction with selected other
options, might establish U.S. Government control points in
international petroleum transactions and restore public
confidence that such arrangements are consistent with national
policy objectives.

CHAPTER 6

FOOTNOTES

1. See Appendix B, § B.4, _infra_.

2. See §§ 1.16-1.18 and 8.1, _supra_.

3. During August of 1974, the Subcommittee on Multinational Corporations of the Senate Committee on
   Foreign Relations (93rd Cong., 2d Sess.) considered a draft bill which would have provided that
   "certain contracts involving the purchase . . .
   of crude oil and refined petroleum products be
   registered with the Federal Energy Administration
   . . . [and] the Administrator of the Federal
   Energy Administration [be authorized] to disapprove
   certain contracts for the importation of crude
   oil and refined petroleum products into the United
   States. . . ."  No action has been taken on this
   draft bill, although Senator Frank Church, Chairman
   of the Subcommittee, has indicated his approval
   of the concept.  _Oil and Gas Journal_, Jan. 20, 1975
   at 44.

4. With approximately 40% of U.S. petroleum consumption
   supplied by foreign imports, the effect of arrangements for major sources of imports to the U.S.
   market is substantial upon such national objectives
   as the formulation of a national energy policy
   (See § 2.1, _supra_), the establishment of adequate
   and secure sources of petroleum supply (See §§ 2.2,
   _supra_, 6.4, _infra_), the preservation of national
   security (See § 2.3, _supra_), as well as the maintenance of viable foreign relations (See § 2.4,
   _supra_).  Lesser but still ascertainable effects
   may also be seen upon such national objectives
   as efficient resource utilization (See § 2.5,
   _supra_), the protection of environmental quality
   (See § 2.6, _supra_), and the encouragement of
   competition (See § 2.7, _supra_).

5. _Los Angeles Times_, Nov. 28, 1974, at 1; industry interviews by Study Contractor. In a similar type of agreement, Ashland Oil, Inc. and Iran have been discussing the sale to NIOC of a 50% share of Ashland's refining and marketing operations in New York State. _Wall Street Journal_, July 27, 1974. _Cf._ _Wall Street Journal_, Jan. 31, 1975, at 3, "Pan Am Nears Pact With Iran Interests to Save Line." See also § 11.1, _infra_.

6. The French Premier instructed the first CFP president in 1923, "You are to create a vehicle for realizing a national oil policy." _New York Times_, April 21, 1974, at 1. See Appendix § A.15.

7. See Chapter 7 at note 7; Appendix A, §§ A.13-A.17.

8. _Ibid._, Chapter 7, _passim_.

9. A number of OPEC governments have indicated a definite interest in developing their own downstream marketing and refining capabilities. Such projects include, for example, a $150 million refinery in Algeria (_Petroleum Intelligence Weekly_, Jan. 13, 1975, at 10), Saudi Arabian attempts to develop a Saudi tanker fleet (_Petroleum Intelligence Weekly_, Dec. 9, 1974, at 3), a Saudi Arabian-Taiwan venture to establish a joint refinery, methanol plant and fertilizer project (_Petroleum Intelligence Weekly_, Sept. 30, 1974 at 12), a $500 million petrochemical complex to be built in Iran with American technology (_Petroleum Intelligence Weekly_, Aug. 19, 1974, at 11), and a French-Qatar petrochemical venture (_Petroleum Intelligence Weekly_, Aug. 12, 1974, at 7). Some industry interviewees have expressed the fear that the more producing governments are able to diversify their operations downstream the greater control they will have over western economies.

9a. The draft bill discussed in note 3, _supra_, contains an exemption for "any contract for the purchase or procurement of crude oil or refined products . . . which is limited by its terms to a period of six months or less or to a volume of one million United States barrels or less, and which contains no option to renew. . . ."

10. This scope of regulation would include such joint ventures between U.S. and non-U.S. companies as the Kuwait Oil Company Ltd. (jointly owned by subsidiaries of Gulf and British Petroleum), the Iraq Petroleum Company Ltd. (jointly owned by subsidiaries of Shell, CFP, BP, Exxon and Mobil), Abu Dhabi Petroleum Company Ltd. (jointly owned by Shell, CFP, BP, Exxon and Mobil), the Iranian Consortium (including subsidiaries of British Petroleum, Shell, Socal, Exxon, Mobil, Gulf, Texaco, CFP), the Iraq Petroleum Company Ltd. (jointly owned by BP, Shell, CFP, Exxon and Mobil), Qatar Petroleum Company Ltd. (jointly owned by British Petroleum, CFP, Shell, Exxon and Mobil).

11. There are a number of foreign-owned companies with leases on the U.S. Outer Continental Shelf, including British Petroleum (U.K.), Royal Dutch/Shell (U.K./Netherlands), CFP (France), Petrofina (Belgium), ENI (Italy), and Burmah (U.K.).

12. 15 U.S.C. §§ 761-786.

13. See Chapter 10.

14. Ibid. See text of the Agreement on an International Energy Program, Art. 27, in Petroleum Intelligence Weekly, Special Supplement, Oct. 14, 1974.

15. Petroleum Intelligence Weekly, Dec. 2, 1974, at 4-5.

16. Such further information might probe other aspects of the relationship between the company and the producing government such as collateral agreements.

17. A prenegotiation filing would give the Government the advantage of extra time in which to make its assessment of the impact of such negotiations on the national interest.

18. See Chapter 2.

19. An almost universal comment from industry personnel was that increased disclosure was already presenting a taxing burden upon the administrative mechanisms of the companies. Moreover, some industry interviewees cited instances in which different agencies of the U.S. Government had requested duplicate information, which indicated to them that the Government was not fully aware of what information it already had in its possession.

20. 15 U.S.C. §77a.

21. Under the Securities Act of 1933, _supra_ note 20, the
Securities and Exchange Commission has no authority
to approve or disapprove any security, but only to require that disclosures be complete and not misleading.
This power, however, proved to be a mechanism for a very
extensive form of regulation.

22. 42 U.S.C. §4321. For good discussions of the complicated administrative and judicial machinery associated
with complying with NEPA, see R. M. Lynch, "Complying
with NEPA: the Tortuous Path to an Adequate Environmental Impact Statement," 14 _Arizona Law Review_ 717
(1972); "America's Changing Environment--is the NEPA
a Change for the Better?," 40 _Fordham Law Review_ 897
(1972).

23. There are few completed transactions of substantial
size in international petroleum about which the general
terms are not widely known within the international industry.

24. See §10.4, _infra_. The confidentiality problems of a
bureaucracy which is multinational in composition and
which for that reason is less able to guard against
security leaks are formidable.

25. A number of industry interviewees pointed out that
although some negotiations with producer governments
span many months, on other occasions producers have
been known to allow foreign companies only hours to
accept terms. Spot cargoes are often sold in transit
between the producing country and the intended market.
Industry interviewees often emphasized that company
officials in the field had to be given wide decision-
making discretion because it was often not practicable
to seek instructions from the head office.

26. 28 C.F.R. Ch. 1, Part 50 (Antitrust Div. Directive
2-68), 33 Fed. Reg. 2442, as amended is by Antitrust
Div. Directive No. 14-73. See Van Cise, _Understanding
the Antitrust Laws_ 206-208 (1963).

27. [N]o person shall . . . import any natural gas from a
foreign country without first having secured an order
of the [Federal Power] Commission authorizing it to do
so. The Commission shall issue such order upon application, unless, after opportunity for hearing, it finds
that the proposed . . . importation will not be consistent with the public interest." 15 U.S.C. §717b. See
_Oil and Gas Journal_, Jan. 20, 1975 at 41.

28. Interviewees in Indonesia indicated that the renegotiated price which Pertamina will have to pay may be
as high as three times the original agreed price of
63¢ per MMBTU. See note 26, supra.

29. One interviewee, the head of international operations of
a large U.S. company, stated that "the Japanese would
have run us out of the international petroleum business
by now," if their style of concluding contracts did not
require the continuous referring back to the head office
in Tokyo for instructions. This cumbersome necessity
for continually keeping the head office informed has,
in the opinion of this interviewee, rendered them substantially less competitive vis-a-vis enterpreneurs
from other consuming nations.

30. One Indonesian official interviewed indicated considerable annoyance at the uncertainty of the Pacific Lighting
deal over a year after it had originally been negotiated.
He also seemed somewhat amused that the environmental
impact report needed for FPC action might have to cover
the impact of an LNG project upon the environment of
North Sumatra.

31. Prior to 1970 BP owned a very substantial number of
both upstream and downstream interests in the United
States, including a massive oil reserve in the Alaskan
North Slope. In 1970 Standard Oil Company of Ohio
(Sohio) acquired all of the assets of the BP U.S. subsidiary in exchange for 25% of Sohio's stock. BP's
ownership in Sohio may increase to 54% depending upon
the rate of production of Alaskan oil leases by January
1, 1984. When the Trans-Alaskan Pipeline comes on stream
Sohio will be the owner of approximately one-third of the
1.5 million barrels of oil per day which will be arriving
on the west coast. See the statement by Sohio to the
Special Subcommittee on Integrated Oil Operations of the
Senate Committee on Interior and Insular Affairs dated
January 29, 1974; Report of Special Subcommittee on the
"Burmah-Signal Merger," dated October 10, 1974, at 3; Oil
and Gas Journal, December 23, 1974, at 12. The Sohio-BP
transaction gives BP a controlling interest in what will
predictably become one of the largest U.S. integrated
companies. CFP, through its subsidiary Total Petroleum
(North America), has recently extended its exploration
activities in the United States, previously limited to
Michigan and Illinois, with the acquisition of an interest
in an offshore lease in the Gulf of Mexico. Total's marketing operations in the United States are still fairly

restricted. CFP, _Annual Report_, 1973, at 8. Royal
Dutch/Shell and its affiliates are deeply involved
in the United States market through their 70% owned
affiliate, Shell Oil Company; 30% of the stock is
privately held and traded on the New York Stock
Exchange. Shell remains the leading oil producer in
the Gulf of Mexico with a production rate of 268,000
b/d. Shell also has offshore exploration leases in
California and Alaska. Shell operates eight refineries
in the United States and sales in the U.S. market
account for approximately one-fifth of Royal Dutch/Shell's
worldwide sales of oil products and crude oil. The Royal
Dutch/Shell Group of Companies, _Information Handbook_,
_1974-75_, at 69, 77, 115, 132.

32.  Several government and industry interviewees in Europe
were critical of the extraterritorial reach of a
number of United States regulatory systems. The antitrust and securities laws were the two examples most
frequently cited of "American imperialisism."

33.  The Securities Act of 1933, §15, provides that

>       "Every person who, by or through stock ownership,
>       agency, or otherwise, or who, pursuant to or in
>       connection with an agreement or understanding with
>       one or more other persons by or through stock owner-
>       ship, agency, or otherwise, controls any person is
>       liable . . . to the same extent as such controlled
>       person . . .". 15 U.S.C. §77o."

Also see SEC Rule 405 which defines the term "control"
as

>       ". . . the possession, direct or indirect, of
>       the power to direct or cause the direction of
>       the management and policies of a person whether
>       through the ownership of voting securities, by
>       contract, or otherwise."

34.  See text of Agreement on an International Energy Program,
Art. 27, _supra_ note 14.

35.  See Chapter 8; Chapter 10.

36.  NEPA requires that there be included "in every recommendation or report on proposals for legislation and
other major Federal actions significantly affecting
quality of the human environment, a detailed statement

by the responsible official on the environmental impact of the proposed action . . ." 42 U.S.C. §4332. U.S. Government approval or disapproval of a significant foreign supply arrangement would probably be considered such a "major Federal action," particularly where large U.S. coastal or onshore processing and distribution facilities would be involved.

37. NEPA clearly specifies that the "human environment" is involved and in no case has this been construed to extend only to the territorial limits of the United States. See Robinson "Extraterritorial Protection Obligation of the Foreign Affairs Agencies: The Unfulfilled Mandate of NEPA," 7 NYU Journal of International Law and Politics 257 (1974).

38. See note 22, supra.

39. Judicial relief is available to correct a failure on the part of a Federal agency to follow the procedural requirement that an environmental impact statement be filed. See Bradford Township v. Illinois State Toll Highway Authority, 463 F.2d 537 (1972) cert. den. 409 U.S. 1047 (1972). See also Environmental Defense Fund, Inc. v. Froehlke, 477 F.2d 1033 (1973), in respect to the availability of injunctive relief.

40. The decision to subordinate other national objectives in favor of maintaining the vital supply of petroleum needed by this country has many precedents. See Chapter 1; §8.3. See also Chapter 11.

41. "[T]he U.S. Government never attempted to create an in-depth institutional capability to evaluate the international petroleum industry and the developing strength of OPEC." Subcommittee on Multinational Corporations to the Senate Foreign Relations Committee, Multinational Oil Corporations in U.S. Foreign Policy; 15 (Comm.Print., Jan. 1975)

42. A typical example of the suspicious attitude which the American public has toward the industry in its relationship to government can be seen in A Time to Choose, Final Report by the Energy Policy Project of the Ford Foundation, at 238-253 (1974).

43.  Perhaps one of the most significant examples of
     counterproductive regulation has been the regula-
     tion of natural gas by the Federal Power Commission.
     About such regulation President Ford stated, in a
     message to Congress, "... our worsening shortages
     [of natural gas] are directly attributable to more
     than twenty years of unsuccessful Federal regula-
     tion of natural gas." CCH Energy Management, Nov.
     26, 1974 at 1.  Another example of governmental
     mismanagement in the international petroleum area
     involves the role played by the U.S. Government
     during the critical Libya and Teheran negotiations
     of 1970-71.  See Chapter 4; §1.17, supra.

44.  Ibid.

45.  See Note 6, infra.

46.  For an example of the way in which the debate over
     the regulation of natural gas has centered around
     what the consumer will ultimately pay, see J. L.
     Buckley, "Deregulating Natural Gas," Washington Post,
     Nov. 11, 1974 at A14; Hearings Before the Special Sub-
     committee on Integrated Oil Operations of the Senate
     Committee on Interior and Insular Affairs, pursuant
     to S. Res. 45, Market Performance and Competition in
     the Petroleum Industry, 93rd Cong., 1st Sess., pt. 3
     at 1055 et seq. (1974).

47.  For a discussion of the manner in which national
     objectives can conflict, thereby defying easy
     definition, see §2.10 et seq., supra.

48.  See, for example,the recent Gulf/BP Agreement in
     Kuwait discussed in §6.6, infra.

49.  See L. L. Jaffe and N. L. Nathanson, Administrative
     Law, Cases and Materials, Third Ed., 484 et seq.
     (1968).

50.  See 29A  C.J.S. §97.

51.  See Chapter 1.  The access which many of the large
     multinational preferred companies have to sources
     of crude is a built-in competitive advantage of
     enormous value to them.

52.  See §1.16, supra.

53. See 12 U.S.C. 241-262.

54. An analogous example of such a mandatory approval is the provision in §8(a) of the Securities Act of 1933 which provides that a registration statement becomes "effective" the twentieth day after its filing with the S.E.C.

55. See §§9.1, 9.4, infra.

56. In addition to giving the U.S. Government some control over the terms which the company accedes to, it may even provide a degree of protection for the company against retaliation by the producer government since the company can quite legitimately claim that its non-compliance is not of its own doing.

57. L. Mosley, Power Play, Oil in the Middle East, 260-261 (1973); Subcommittee on Multinational Corporations to the Senate Committee on Foreign Relations, supra note 41, at 109, 144 et seq.

58. L. Mosley, supra note 57, at 374; N. H. Jacoby, Multinational Oil, 262 (1974).

59. Security of supply has been a national objective since 1912 when the first Naval Petroleum Reserves were established in Alaska and California. See §2.3 supra. U.S. Government involvement in the promotion of greater security in sources of foreign crude dates from the 1940's when the U.S. Government acted in a way to keep certain Middle Eastern producing nations out of the sphere of influence of first the Germans and then the British. Subcommittee on Multinational Corporations to the Senate Committee on Foreign Relations, Multinational Oil Corporations in U.S. Foreign Policy, supra note 41, at 36-38. N. H. Jacoby, supra note 58, at 37-39. Recognition of the desirability of favoring more "reliable" sources can also be seen in the exception from the import quota (see Appendix B §B.4 infra) for so-called "overland sources" shipments from which would not be exposed to hostile naval action in time of war.

60. Venezuela, Kuwait, Libya, Nigeria, Abu Dhabi and Indonesia are all restricting production substantially below their level of capacity. See §E.1, Petroleum Intelligence Weekly, Dec. 30, 1974 at 8; Wall Street Journal, Aug. 23, 1974.

61.  Policies of conservation on the part of OPEC nations
     may in the long term not be detrimental, if consum-
     ing nations have sufficiently developed alternative
     sources of energy.  See, for example, Project Inde-
     pendent projections of substantial world surpluses
     of petroleum at $6.00 and $9.00 per barrel price
     levels in 1985.  Federal Energy Administration,
     Project Independence Report, 356-358 (November 1974).

62.  The Washington Post, July 12, 1974 at F1; New York
     Times, July 12, 1974; Offshore, Aug. 1974 at 51,
     Petroleum Intelligence Weekly, July 15, 1974 at 1.

63.  Estimates of when the United Kingdom will be self-
     sufficient in petroleum vary.  One report has
     suggested that "there is . . . a very good chance
     that in 1980 [the U.K.] can produce oil equivalent
     to [its] demand."  Department of Energy, Production
     and Reserves of Oil and Gas in the United Kingdom, 2
     (Her Majesty's Stationary Office, May 1974).  See also
     the New York Times, May 22, 1974 at 57.  More recent
     estimates, however, are less optimistic.  See, for
     example, Wall Street Journal, August 16, 1974 at 1.
     Interviewees in the U.K. Government indicated that
     the United Kingdom will probably control the develop-
     ment of its North Sea reserves so as to yield only
     such production as is necessary to meet national demand
     together with prior oil debts incurred.

64.  Petroleum Intelligence Weekly, Feb. 25, 1974 at 5-6.

65.  New York Times, Nov. 23,1974 at 1.  Donald S. Macdonald,
     Canadian Minister of Energy, Mines and Resources, in a
     speech to the National Press Club in Washington, D.C.
     on Feb. 1, 1974 remarked,"I suppose the most substan-
     tial underlying misconception is that Canada has vast
     surplus of low-cost oil and natural gas which we are
     capriciously withholding from the United States at its
     time of need . . . In face of . . . soaring American
     demand, Canadian policy-makers had no choice but to
     put on export controls to make certain that Canadian
     refiners dependent upon Canadian source oil would not
     run out of feed stock by competing export demands."

66.  The Wall Street Journal, Nov. 12, 1974 at 40;  The Oil
     and Gas Journal, June 24, 1974 at 98, and Nov. 4, 1974
     at 40.

67. Petroleum Intelligence Weekly, Oct. 21, 1974 at 5.

68. The Shah of Iran put the proposition rather squarely in an interview with British journalist Ian Colbin on Feb. 5, 1974 (published by the Iranian Government) in which the Shah stated: "How is it when Canada increases the price of oil by $8.00 a barrel all at once, you never even question that decision?  And the price that you British people put on your oil when you extract it from the North Sea, who is going to discuss that?  No one will ask the Norwegians what price they are going to put on their oil, and everybody has accepted the price that the Venezuelans put on theirs. So is there a difference between you blue-eyed people and we dark-eyed people?"

69. Interviews with petroleum companies by Study contractors. See also, however, Hearings Before the Senate Committee on Foreign Relations on the Implications of the Current Energy Problem for United States Foreign Policy, 93rd Cong., 1st Sess., at 89 (1974).

70. As stated in the report of the Subcommittee on Multi-national Corporations to the Senate Committee on Foreign Relations, supra note 41, at 19:

> The "United States Government has never had a coordinated international energy policy.  Due to the heavy reliance of the U.S. on domestic oil, U.S. energy policy was dominated by the needs and interests of the domestic oil industry. Internationally, the major American oil companies were used as instruments of U.S. foreign policy. But their instrumentality resulted from ad hoc responses to a series of specific problems and was never conceptualized as a total international policy.  Once the basis system was in place, the U.S. Government was only tangentially involved in the international oil companies . . . It is unrealistic to think that we can cure twenty years of neglect in the course of a year or two.  Rather we are at the beginning of a process of reconsidering traditional policy assumptions, relationships between companies and governments--consumer and producer--and organization of our own government."

240.

71.  See §1.17, _supra_.

72.  _Ibid_.

73.  See §1.14, _supra_.

74.  See §1.12, _supra_.

75.  See §1.18, _supra_.

76.  See _Petroleum Intelligence Weekly_,
     July 22, 1974 at 1 and Sept. 23, 1974 at 2; _New
     York Times_, July 20, 1974 at 41.

77.  See _Petroleum Intelligence Weekly_, Sept. 23, 1974
     at 1-3.

78.  _Ibid_.

79.  Interviews with governmental representatives by
     the Study contractor.  The British Government was
     apparently able to delay BP's agreement to the
     Kuwaiti demands for several weeks, but not after
     Gulf indicated its intention to accept.  Gulf offi-
     cials interviewed stated that they kept the U.S.
     Government fully informed on the negotiations and
     that they accepted the Kuwaiti terms because it
     constituted a good deal for them and, accordingly,
     for their customers and shareholders.

     The U.S. State Department had the following comment
     after the agreement of Gulf was announced:

     > "We regret very much this development which
     > runs counter to current trade in the world
     > oil market."

     _Oil and Gas Journal_, July 29, 1974 at 110.

80.  See, for example, _Petroleum Intelligence Weekly_,
     Dec. 17, 1973 at 1; Dec. 31, 1973 at 5; Feb. 4,
     1974 at 3.

81.  Interviewees in Venezuela stated that officials
     in the Venezuelan Government had been so impressed
     by the prices which small American purchasers had
     been willing to pay during the winter months of

1973-74 that they genuinely questioned whether
even current price levels were "fair."

82. See, for example, the indirect impact which
Occidental's agreement of September 2, 1970
with the Libyan Government had upon the majors
in Libya and, in turn, upon the demands of the
Persian Gulf producers.  Subcommittee on Multinational Corporations to the Senate Committee
on Foreign Relations, supra note 41, at 124.

83. See notes 62-68, supra.

84. Petroleum Intelligence Weekly, Sept. 23, 1974
at 1-2.

85. Interviewees in the French Government were particularly concerned about the extent of the .
retroactivity of the Saudi participation in
Aramco and the effect which it may have on CFP's
operations in the Persian Gulf, and necessarily
the French balance of payments position.

86. See note 25, supra.

87. See notes 81 and 82, supra.

88. See Petroleum Intelligence Weekly, Dec. 31, 1973
at 5 and Feb. 4, 1974 at 3.

89. It was a Japanese refiner, Mitsubishi, which bid
$22.60 a barrel for Nigerian light crude in that
country's auction of December 21, 1973.  The bid
was matched by two other companies from the United
States, although a number of other U.S. companies
declined to match the bid.  The Japanese also bid
up the price of LNG in Algeria and elsewhere in
early 1974 by entering an agreement with Pertamina,
the Indonesian oil company, at previously unheard
prices.  This created a large part of the Pacific
Lighting problem discussed supra at note 27 and
accompanying text.  Interviews with industry and
governmental representatives by the Study Contractor.  Petroleum Intelligence Weekly, Dec. 31,
1973 at 5.

90. See notes 88 and 89, supra.

91. See §5.2, supra.

92. The two OPEC price hikes which essentially quadru-
    pled the price of world petroleum both occurred during
    the months of the Arab embargo. See §1.17, supra.

93. It should be recalled that the recent Arab embargo
    which reduced total petroleum supply in the United
    States 14% below expected consumption reduced gross
    national product by $10 to $20 billion and was re-
    sponsible for half a million unemployed. Federal
    Energy Administration, supra note 61, at 18.

94. See §5.2, supra.

95. An obviously more equitable and rational system of
    allocation of available supplies would be that
    worked out under the International Energy Program.
    See §10.1, infra. The IEP allocates according to
    a pre-established scheme designed at spreading the
    burden of a shortfall in supply evenly among con-
    suming nations.

96. See supra note 75 and accompanying text.

97. See, for example. Petroleum Intelligence Weekly,
    Dec. 9, 1974 at 1-2.

98. The Wall Street Journal, September 11, 1974, passim.

99. See note 97, supra.

100. Frank Jungers, Chairman of the Board and Chief
     Executive Officer of Aramco, recently stated in an
     interview:

     "Aramco's continued presence as an economic
     entity of major importance to both Saudi Arabia
     and the U.S. has contributed to the good rela-
     tions that have long existed between the two
     countries. Aramco's own relationship with Saudi
     Arabia has been a business relationship--one
     based on enlightened self-interest . . . I expect
     Aramco to remain as the largest oil producing
     company in the world."

     World Oil, June 1974 at 67-69.

101. Aramco's production, in excess of eight million barrels per day, is the largest of any company in the world. <u>Petroleum Intelligence Weekly</u>, Dec. 16, 1974 at 3.

102. <u>Petroleum Intelligence Weekly</u> Sept. 23, 1974 at 1-2.

103. Subcommittee on MultinationalCorporations to the Senate Committee on Foreign Relations, <u>supra</u> note 41, at 163.

104. This was essentially the case with the recent Gulf/BP agreement to pay 94.85% of posting in Kuwait. Notwithstanding the record high buy-back price, the net effect of the agreement was quite favorable to the companies.

105. M. A. Adelman, "Is the oil shortage real?", <u>Foreign Policy</u>, (1972-73) at 105. A similar position has been taken by the Subcommittee on Multinational Corporations to the Senate Committee on Foreign Relations which reported that "the primary concern of the established major oil companies is to maintain their world market shares and their favored position of receiving oil from OPEC nations at costs slightly lower than other companies. To maintain this favored status, the international companies helped prorationed production cut-backs among the OPEC members. Their ability to do this derives from the existence of their diversified production base in OPEC countries." <u>Supra</u> note 41, at 10. The Committee Report further quotes from Saudi Arabian Minister of Petroleum, Sheikh Yamani, that "nationalization of the upstream (production) operations would inevitably deprive the majors of any further interest in maintaining crude oil price levels. They would then become mere offtakers buying the crude oil from producing countries and moving it to their markets in Europe, Japan and the rest of the world. . . Consequently, their interest would be identical with that of the consumers--namely, to buy crude oil at the cheapest possible price." <u>Id</u>. at 11.

106. The "safety net" provisions set up by the various libyan companies during the 1970-71 negotiations obviously reflected a conviction on their part that a refusal to accede to producer-government demands carried with it the inevitable risk of loss of

access or of position in the producer country.
See §§1.16-1.17, supra.

107. It appears that OPEC is moving in the direction
of a "single price." In any event, however, significance should be attached to the various devices by
which certain producers, especially Saudi Arabia,
intend to compensate their offtakers for production and exploration services. Such compensation
may in practice be nothing more than a renamed
equity interest.

108. See note 47, supra.

109. See Subcommittee on Multinational Corporations to
the Senate Committee on Foreign Relations, supra
note 41 at 13-19.

110. The companies, having rather resourcefully rerouted their distribution network so as to avoid
the constraints imposed upon them by Arab producing governments during the recent embargo,
clearly have the capability of performing a
similar rearrangement of their distribution network.

111. Some Japanese interviewees indicated a degree of
concern with respect to the reliability of sources
of petroleum which are derived via the international
major oil companies. The creation of the Japan
Petroleum Development Corporation ("JPDC") was a
creature of that concern. JPDC is essentially an
arm of the Japanese Government which provides both
financial and technical assistance to Japanese
companies seeking to develop new sources of foreign
crude. Although none of the several interviewees
contacted in Japan indicated that the majors had
dealt unfairly with Japan during the recent embargo,
several did express the belief that at least among
the Japanese public there is a strong desire to
have sources of crude independent of the international majors. A similar desire lies at the base
of the creation of ELF-ERAP by the French Government.

112. It is important to continually keep in mind in the evaluation of this option,as well as other options reviewed by this Report, the limits on the ability of the U.S. Government to achieve a substantial improvement of the position of the United States in international petroleum without the close cooperation of other consuming nations.  See Chapter 8.

113. Ibid.

114. Of approximately 20 million barrels per day exported from the Middle East during 1973, less than 1 million barrels per day went to the United States.  The British Petroleum Company Ltd., BP Statistical Review of the World Oil Industry, 10 (1973).

115. See note 118, infra.

116. The conclusions of the special study prepared by the Federal Energy Administration for the Subcommottee on Multinational Corporations of the Senate Foreign Relations Committee transmitted by FEA November 22, 1974 are as follows:

> "(1)  U.S. companies helped to blunt the edge of the Arab oilweapon by redistributing global supplies so that the construction of supplies were fairly evenly allocated.
> (2)  Although varying allocation criteria were adopted by the various companies, the net impact was a fairly even distribution of the reduced supplies when measured against current demand.
> (3)  U.S. companies appear to have been more responsive to their assessment of the long term implications of their allocations rather than to their short term interests.
> (4)  It is difficult to imagine that any allocation play would have achieved a more equitable allocation of reduced supplies.
> (5)  There is considerable flexibility in the distribution system of the U.S. oil companies, permitting them to. redistribute supplies on short notice in spite of a wide variety of technological and transportation difficulties.

(6) There is no evidence that the Arab
nations exerted pressure on U.S. oil companies regarding their allocation of non-Arab
supplies.
(7) Some pressure was exerted on U.S. oil
companies by consuming nation governments, but
it was rarely "excessive". In most cases
governments were satisfied by industry assurances
that supplies were being equitably distributed.
(8) Nevertheless, U.S. companies agree that
they were called upon to make difficult and potentially volatile political decisions during the
embargo -- decisions beyond the realm of normal
corporate concerns."

Also of interest are the remarks of Geoffrey Chandler,
President of the Institute of Petroleum in the United
Kingdom, who stated:

"I do not believe that it is the job of an
industry to administer the distribution of
a vital commodity in a time of shortage:
it is clearly the task of governments. But in
the absence of government action the industry
acted in the only manner open to it. The
allocation of oil as a percentage of demand
to all markets appeared to be the most equitable and practicable course in the circumstances. Indeed it was the only defensible
course if governments were not collectively
to agree on any alternative preferred system
. . . For the companies, even if this seemed
the only way to avoid inviting their own
destruction, it was by no means the most
economically attractive." "The Changing
Shape of the Oil Industry," Petroleum Review
(June 1974).

117. It was repeatedly stated by interviewees, both within
the industry and within the U.S. and other consuming
nation governments, that a breakdown in the productive
and marketing network of the major petroleum companies
would have a catastrophic effect upon the quantity of
petroleum available to meet the needs of consuming
nations. The Japanese particularly were conscious of
the importance of the multinational oil companies to
the functioning of their economy.

118. European governments and especially the Japanese have shown considerable reluctance to wholeheartedly support the "tough" positions periodically taken by the U.S. Government with respect to the OPEC cartel. See Chapter 8 at note 12, _infra_.

119. See Chapter 10.

120. See note 31 _et seq._, _supra_, and accompanying text.

121. _Ibid_.

122. See note 35, _supra_, and accompanying text.

123. The estimated excess capacity within OPEC is estimated at nearly eight million barrels per day. _BNA Energy Users Report_ Nov. 21, 1974 at A-29.

124. See note 112, _supra_.

125. Some of the most vulnerable nations, such as Indonesia and Nigeria, are nations with large populations and large development requirements whose hopes for an improvement in the standard of life is very much tied to petroleum revenues. These nations have also earned a degree of consideration for their production reliability and community of interest with the United States.

126. See notes 51 and 52, _supra_.

127. This is especially true when the producing country involved supplies a major portion of the company's total production.

128. Compare §8.6, _infra_.

129. The most important residual supplier is, of course, Saudi Arabia which may have an export production capacity in 1985 of close to 20 million barrels per day, well over twice the capacity of any other OPEC country. Federal Energy Administration, _supra_ note 61 at 356. This enormous capacity coupled with its relatively small population and potential for economic development give Saudi Arabia the unique ability to, if it so chooses, make or break OPEC price policy by the rate at which it sets its production levels.

130. This is particularly true of the conservative pro-American Saudi Government which not only is seeking to maintain its leadership potential within the Arab world and OAPEC, but also within OPEC which is basically Third World in philosophy.

131. At the most recent OPEC meeting in December, 1974, a single price for the purchase of producer government owned petroleum was created at a lower price than the previous direct purchase price. This was heralded by OPEC as a price reduction. The OPEC Secretary General said "The price of crude oil is going to be less than before." At the same time, however, the royalty and tax rates chargeable to the former concessionnaire companies were increased, creating a net increase in the average cost of OPEC crude. Los Angeles Times, December 14, 1974 at 1.

132. See §6.1, supra

133 See notes 20-22, supra and accompanying text.

134. See note 20, supra.

135. See §6.3, supra.

136. See §§ 11.2-11.3, infra.

CHAPTER 7

CREATION OF A PETROLEUM COMPANY, FULLY OR
PARTIALLY OWNED BY THE FEDERAL GOVERNMENT,
TO ENGAGE IN INTERNATIONAL ACTIVITIES

A.    [§7.0]  Introduction

There have been recent proposals to create a
Federally owned oil and gas corporation to explore for and
develop domestic petroleum resources, particularly those
owned by the Federal Government.  The rationale given for
this concept is that such a corporation could serve as a
"yardstick" by which to measure the performance of U.S.
private corporations and also to facilitate the development
of higher risk areas such as the Outer Continental Shelf. 1/
These are, however, essentially domestic concerns and beyond
the scope of this Study.

In the context of international petroleum arrangements the concept of an oil company wholly or partially
owned by the Federal Government has viability largely as a
means through which the Federal Government might assert its
presence in such arrangements.  This option has been given
impetus by the increasing presence in international petroleum affairs today of both producer and consumer government-
owned companies.

At the outset it should be emphasized that if a
precept of a Federally owned international oil company is
that it is to serve as a "yardstick," it can do so only if
it is in all material respects similar to a private company:
if it has no special advantages and no competitive handicaps
vis-a-vis privately owned companies.  It should also be
noted that if the Federally owned corporation is in fact
comparable to a private company, it may well be in no
better position to perform the various petroleum industry
functions than the private companies are.

B.    [§7.1]  Form

A wide variety of organizational and behavioral
models for a Federal oil corporation can be devised.  Yet

251.

while the ownership, financing, tax status and scope of
operations are of course important policy issues, the net
international effects of various structures does not vary
materially with alternative models.  This section simply
describes the common range of parameters for creation of
such a corporation, drawing both on history and on the
existing foreign consumer government oil companies.

[§7.2]  Creation, Ownership and Control

     A Federal oil corporation could be established
either by acquisition of an existing company or companies or
by the creation of a new corporate entity.  In either event,
the corporation would of necessity draw heavily on the U.S.
oil industry for the requisite managerial and technological
expertise.

     The corporation could be wholly or partially owned
by the Government.  U.S. precedent suggests 100% public
ownership, but several foreign oil companies which have
minority government ownership, including CFP (35% French
Government-owned) 2/ and BP (70% British Government-owned),
3/ are probably the most successful. 4/

     If the Federal Government were to elect to purchase
a substantial interest (for example in excess of 10%) of the
stock of a publicly-held major oil company, it would probably
constitute effective control of the company (unless there
were another large block concentrated in single or related
ownership) and would enable the Government to elect the
Board and appoint officers through the normal corporate
processes. 5/  If, however, the existing management resisted
the "take-over," a proxy battle between the government and
the incumbent directors might ensue.  There is no precedent
for such a contest in this country, but the Government
might be at a greater disadvantage than a private party
attempting the same thing if a large number of shareholders
had strong views with respect to non-involvement of government
in business. 5a/  As a result, it might be necessary for
the government to acquire close to 50% of the voting shares
in order to prevail.

     Even if the government acquired control, the
resulting situation would probably present very severe

conflict of interest questions both with respect to the private and the public sectors. Other shareholders would question whether the company were being operated so as to maximize revenues and achieve other legitimate commercial goals and could bring shareholders' derivative suits if this were felt not to be the case. Members of the public would question, on the other hand, whether governmental control was being used so as to effect public goals. The dilemma involved is most clearly seen in the area of antitrust concerns. If a partially owned Federal oil corporation followed the typical pattern of other oil corporations in international petroleum affairs, it would be difficult to exclude it from the antitrust investigations which are frequently being conducted. 6/ If it were not so excluded, however, there would be presented the quite unusual situation of the Justice Department investigating a governmentally directed institution for civil and criminal offenses arising out of its ordinary course of business.

One possible means of ameliorating the dilemma is to restrict governmental representation on the board of directors to less than that which the Government would otherwise control and to attempt to restrict board members from implementing safely governmental objectives in corporate action. This was done in the case of British Petroleum where the British Government, with 70% ownership, elects only two members of the board and it is express governmental policy not to attempt to use the company to interfere in the commercial management of the company except in the case of, in effect, a national emergency. 7/ If, however, this type of limitation were placed upon U.S. control of a public oil corporation it would be difficult to perceive what public purpose would be implemented by the acquisition. Under its Constitutional powers the United States has essentially the same power over U.S. companies that the British Government has over British Petroleum in times of national emergency. 8/ The United States Government, to be sure, would gain "transparency" as to international oil transactions through such ownership, but this perhaps could be just as efficiently achieved through an appropriate form of regulation. 9/

A different form of issue would be presented if the United States Government were to form an oil corporation

a portion of whose shares would be offered to the public to
undertake ventures which private companies were unwilling to
undertake, for example, drilling in remote portions of the
Outer Continental Shelf and other high-risk areas.  Panarctic
of Canada is such a company. 10/  Communications Satellite
Corporation ("COMSAT") is similar in that there is public
ownership but institutional liaison with the Federal Government and governmental representation on the board of directors. 11/
In this situation the private shareholders know in advance
of the special nature and risk of the company.  Nevertheless,
the special character of the oil business, particularly in
the area of antitrust would raise a number of problems for a
partially owned oil company in the United States.  As will
be examined in greater detail later, a wholly owned oil
corporation also presents a number of problems.  The ambiguity inherent in this type of business organization with
its potential conflicts between private and public interests,
however, makes this proposal a particularly novel one for the
United States.  Also, in this country the distinctions
between business and government have typically been much
more clearcut and formalized than this type of arrangement
would permit.  Moreover, a very basic question is presented:
if this type of arrangement is appropriate for the petroleum
industry, why is it not appropriate for other industries
having strategic value to the United States?

        In addition to the problems presented in the
political process in structuring a federal oil corporation,
the appropriations process essential to its establishment
and the probably necessary public subsidies, would likewise
entail continuous governmental scrutiny and guidance.

        [§7.3]  Financing

        A Federal oil corporation capable of operating in
international areas in the same fashion as the larger U.S.
companies, would probably require an initial equity investment on the order of two billion dollars. 12/  The actual
cost would, of course, depend on the desired percentage of
public ownership.

        If, however, the Federal corporation was conceived
as a rival to the major integrated oil companies, an initial

investment of at least five billion dollars would probably
be required.  Finally, if the U.S. wished to create a corporation which would replace the 20 largest U.S. oil companies with significant international operations, the
initial cost would probably exceed 65 billion dollars. 12a/

### [§7.4]  Tax Status

Another important consideration for a Federal oil
corporation would be its tax status.  If exempted from
Federal and/or State taxation, it would enjoy a competitive
advantage over private companies.  If it were designed to
serve the "yardstick" function, tax exemption would then be
self-defeating. 13/  Tax exemptions or advantages could,
however, enable a Federal oil corporation to bid successfully abroad against private foreign firms not enjoying tax
advantages.

### [§7.5]  Scope of Operations

A Federal oil corporation could be authorized to
enter into a completely integrated operation, from exploration,
development and production through transportation, refining
and retail marketing.  Conversely, it might concentrate on
a limited number of operations (such as exploration, development and production).

The relationships between the corporation and
other government entities, both foreign and domestic, would
be very important.  First, the corporation might be required
to supply U.S. military petroleum demand at cost, possibly
even at a loss.  Second, it might be required to provide all
civilian U.S. Government petroleum needs, again at cost or
less than the market price. 14/  Third, its relations with
foreign producer governments would be of critical importance.
Although a partially owned company might succeed in retaining a more "neutral" commercial identity, it is clear
that a wholly owned governmental corporation would have a
strong political personality. 15/ A fourth factor would be
the corporations relationships with other private firms.
Its competitiveness with the private companies, if artificially enhanced by tax benefits and political overtones,
could adversely modify U.S. Government relations with
industry. 16/

255.

Before proceeding with a discussion of the anticipated benefits or disadvantages of a Federal oil corporation, it would be appropriate to review the economic arguments which might justify its creation.

C.   [§7.6]  Economic Justifications for Government Intervention

There have been a variety of measures by the U.S. Government which intervene in the national economy, including subsidies, taxation, regulation, and in a very few cases, the creation of government corporations to perform specified functions. 17/  These forms of government interference can be substituted for one another in dealing with specific problems in many cases and have common justifications.

First, where monopolies have existed government action has been determined to be needed to (1) enforce competition through antitrust action, 18/ (2) regulate private enterprise as in the case of public utilities, 19/ or (3) interject a new government enterprise to stimulate competition and provide a "yard-stick" by which to judge private industry. 20/

Although the major oil companies at a point in the past exerted a degree of oligopolistic control over the international petroleum market, today there is effective competition among private oil firms in international oil exploration, production, processing and importation of crude oil. 21/  The monopoly which exists in international oil is the OPEC seller monopoly and the entry of another buying firm, even though owned by the U.S. Government, would have no significant procompetitive effect. 22/

A second justification for government intervention in the market is on equitable grounds, i.e., to change the pattern of income distribution.  The welfare system in the U.S. is an example.  Taxes are levied on one group and some of the proceeds are given to another group.  For example, Federal control over the field price of natural gas in interstate commerce is typically supported by the contention that the nonaffluent would be disadvantaged by uncontrolled gas prices. 23/  In this sense, a Federal oil corporation might repatriate to the U.S. Treasury funds which private companies would otherwise retain abroad and shelter from U.S. taxes. 24/ Such an approach rests, however, on the questionable assumption that it would be at least as efficient as its private counterparts. 25/

Third, government intervention may be justified where the market fails to function properly because individuals and firms that make investment decisions either do not bear the costs of their actions or do not capture the benefits which their actions generate. 26/ These "external" costs or benefits may also be described as "spillover effects." Private decisions are normally made on the basis of estimated private costs and private benefits and the expected private rate of return on investments. Where some costs or revenues are external to the firms, the market system may fail to properly allocate resources. 27/

Where significant externalities exist, there may be justification for either government subsidies to compensate for (1) net external benefits, (2) special taxation to penalize companies for their external costs, (3) regulation of private industry to prevent an unwanted side effect, or (4) creation of a government enterprise to perform the desired function. Milton Friedman states:

> "the role of government is to do something that the market cannot do for itself, namely, to determine, arbitrate, and enforce the rules of the game. We may also want to do through government some things that might conceivably be done through the market but that technical or similar conditions render it difficult to do in that way." 28/

Friedman, in becoming somewhat more specific, then states that his general position allows for two classes of interference: (1) where monopoly exists, or (2) where there are spillover effects. 29/

With regard to a Federal oil corporation, the appropriate questions to be asked are: (1) Is competition reasonably effective in this industry? (2) Are there any income distribution problems that are relevant to possible

257.

government intervention in the petroleum industry? (3)
What are the net external benefits or costs that flow from
private operation in the international petroleum industry?

As already discussed, there is effective competition today in the international oil industry and income
distribution is primarily a domestic matter. Accordingly,
the basic rationale for creation of a Federal oil corporation must lie in its ability to capture the external benefits
or avoid the external costs which prevail in the existing
international petroleum market.

D.    [§7.7]  Externalities

There are two major "external" factors relevant to
the current petroleum market situation. First, the price of
crude oil is administered by the OPEC cartel and is un-
responsive to market forces as the term is normally understood. Second, the security of crude oil supplies has been
seriously questioned by the Arab oil embargo of October
1973.

[§7.8]  Price

For a variety of reasons, the establishment of a
Federal oil corporation would be unlikely to have a significant effect on OPEC pricing policies, and runs a substantial
risk of provoking further price rises. Creation of a U.S.
Government international oil company would inject one more
oil company into the business of exploring, developing, and
importing oil as well as possible downstream activities.
There are approximately one hundred such firms currently
operating in the international oil industry. The injection
of a public corporation would bring about a price reduction
only if oil supply was increased as a result of this act.

There is no evidence of any shortage of companies to
search for and develop petroleum supplies. Our questionnaires revealed that world-wide oil exploration has increased significantly within the last year 30/ and that the
operative constraint was of supply of equipment and personnel. 31/ The creation of a U.S. Government corporation
to explore for oil may or may not increase the demand for
such equipment but it would not affect international sup-

258.

plies. 32/  There is no evidence that such a corporation
would cause a reduction in crude oil prices.

If this option would not affect supply or demand,
the question is posed as to whether there is reason for
thinking that oil producing governments would sell to a
U.S. corporation at a price lower than that available from
alternative buyers.  There is not; to the contrary, producer
governments have demonstrated their interest in obtaining
the highest price possible for their oil supplies.  Government participation in BP, CFP, ENI and others does not
appear to have yielded economic advantages.

There is a possibility that a U.S. Government
corporation might increase the supply of oil and thereby
lower price if some oil producing countries have a strong
preference for government-to-government arrangements. 33/
Supply would be increased, however, only if this preference
were so strong that in the absence of a U.S. interest the
country in question would enter into no agreement at all.
This condition seems highly unlikely.  There are already in
existence a number of foreign government corporations that
would present acceptable alternatives.

If there is reason to believe that a government
corporation could more efficiently search for, develop and
import oil to the U.S. market than can private companies, we
would expect savings either to the taxpayer, or to the
consumer if such savings were passed on in the form of lower
prices.  There is, however, no evidence indicating that
government corporations are more efficient than private
corporations. 34/  The record of U.S. Government enterprises,
of foreign partially or wholly owned oil companies, and of
industry in general leads to the opposite conclusion.  The
clear indication is that public corporations are less
efficient than private corporations. 35/  If this generali-
zation applies to a Federal oil company, its activities
would in fact tend to raise the price of crude oil to consumers, or if the inefficiency were hidden, raise the cost
to taxpayers. 36/

There is evidence indicating that a government
corporation might choose to sell oil at two different price
levels, one favoring small refiners. 37/  Under the oil

import quota system, government policy favored small refiners by allocating to them a disproportionate share of valuable import tickets. 38/ Currently through the allocation and entitlements programs the Federal Government is shifting income toward those companies, large or small, which have less than an average amount of price controlled old crude oil. 39/ This practice, however, is unlikely to produce savings for consumers. It is either a transfer of wealth between classes of refiners or it is a subsidy to a certain class of refiner. 40/ In the latter case, the subsidy will be paid for by taxpayers in general.

The trend in the international oil industry is clearly away from the old concession and equity oil positions. Former concession holders receiving equity oil are rapidly being transformed into buyers of oil. 41/ This trend appears to be inexorable and a complete transformation from equity positions to purchaser positions appears likely within a few years. 42/

The large number of oil companies operating internationally, periodically augmented by other buyers, including electric utility companies and municipalities, are attempting to buy at the lowest possible price. It is doubtful that a Federal corporation would have a greater incentive to minimize the price. A Federal oil corporation operating internationally would seem to have no functional qualities which would tend to reduce price. 43/

[§7.9]  Supply Security

It is conceivable that a foreign government might be more reluctant to cut-off U.S. supplies channeled through a U.S. Government corporation than if a private corporation were the operator. On the other hand, while it is clear that the international companies do not act as the "political buffer" that perhaps they once did, 44/ they nevertheless do not present the type of consumer government presence in producer countries that a governmentally owned corporation would. As noted earlier, such countries have not hesitated to use even partial governmental ownership as a basis for attacking a company to protest the policies of its government. 45/

Another potential objective of a Federal oil corporation would be to direct future overseas petroleum development to nations outside OPEC, or in those OPEC nations which are least likely to interrupt supplies, a concept discussed in greater detail in Section 6.4 in the context of national regulation. 45a/ While the same effect might be achieved through modification of the existing incentive structure, this concept is perhaps the most valid argument in favor of a Federal oil corporation. A major question, however, is whether such a policy would be cost-effective. The development of domestic energy sources would probably be a better investment since there are no guarantees that "reliable" nations will remain such. 45b/

[§7.10]   Petroleum Storage

Storing a strategic reserve of crude oil is a possible function for a governmentally owned corporation. The security value to the nation of having a relatively large stored reserve of crude is probably not adequately reflected in the ordinary oil market within a time span short enough to be of interest to a private company. 46/ Thus, there may be inadequate incentives for private companies to store as much as would likely be optimal for the welfare of the nation or for consumer nations generally, as evidenced by the storage requirements of the International Energy Program. 47/ For instance, if an embargo could be expected only every 12 years, private companies would probably not be interested in building up supplies in anticipation of it, even if such supplies could be sold at a substantial profit, free from price controls, when the embargo came. 48/ There are, however, various ways more consistent with the other aspects of the U.S. system, including tax incentives, to provide private companies with the motivation to create storage. 49/ Thus, it is doubtful that the storage rationale alone would justify the creation of such a company.

[§7.11]   Research

Government participation in energy research, in-cluding pilot projects in secondary fuel sources, can be justified. This is the concept underlying the newly created Energy Research and Development Administration ("ERDA") and any assignment of these functions to a Federal oil corporation would seem unnecessary. 50/

261.

[§7.12]  Import Limitation

A Federal oil corporation could administer the
import limitation systems discussed in Chapter 5.  It would
be costly, however, to create it solely for such purpose. 51/

E.    [§7.13]  History of Government-Owned Corporations

Externalities aside, there is yet another important
consideration bearing on this option:  the history of
government-owned industries both within the United States
and abroad. 52/

The research performed in connection with the
Study yielded no evidence that any existing governmental
corporation is more efficient than private enterprise,
although there were suggestions that the Tennessee Valley
Authority ("TVA") may be no less efficient, despite its
clear record of subsidization. 53/  There was a uniform
record of opposition to this concept by the industry and
certain of the public interest groups surveyed. 54/  The
latter expressed the view that governmental corporations are
less accountable to the public than private ones, citing the
TVA posture on environmental matters. 55/  There is a danger
that any such inefficiency could result in upward pressure
on market prices if the government corporation was big
enough to have a significant share of the oil market, unless
the inefficiencies were subsidized by unrelated Federal
revenues.

Moreover, this observation is confirmed by the
experience of foreign government corporations, including
some actively involved in the petroleum business.  A number
of significant fully or partially government-owned corporations have been created by consumer governments for such
special purposes, largely to give them secured access to
foreign petroleum reserves independent of the U.S. companies.
When the French Government acquired a 35% interest in CFP,
now the world's eighth largest oil corporation, it did so
"to create a vehicle for realizing a national oil policy." 56/
Notwithstanding this significant governmental influence (the
Secretary of the board of directors is a designate from the
Foreign Ministry), CFP began to conduct its affairs in the
same manner as privately owned companies. 57/  Because of

262.

this, and the magnitude of its proven Middle Eastern reserves, CFP avoided the exploration and development of a
number of areas, including the French-held Sahara Desert and
France itself.  President DeGaulle in 1966, therefore,
created ELF-ERAP, a wholly owned government corporation, to
develop these areas. 58/  In time even ELF-ERAP, together
with its 51% owned subsidiary Aquitaine, began to drift from
its original mission and today it operates very much in the
manner of a private company and is engaged in exploration
and development in areas of the world, such as Canada, the
United States and Asia, and services markets completely
unrelated to those of France. 59/

        ENI, wholly owned by the Italian Government, also
fits this pattern.  While formed for essentially political
purposes, it operates in most respects as does a private
company. 60/  The interest of the British Government in
British Petroleum (now over 70%), was originally acquired
shortly before World War I in order to provide the British
with secure access to Middle Eastern petroleum supplies,
with the then paramount thought of servicing the Royal Navy
which was just converting to oil-burning engines. 61/
While the British Government has representatives on the
board of directors, the company performs largely in the same
manner as do the other major international oil companies. 62/
BP has worldwide supply and marketing arrangements, including
very substantial ones in the United States.

        These illustrations point up one basic factor.  In
order to create a petroleum corporation, whether privately
or governmentally owned, it is necessary to assemble from
the preexisting industry those with technological and
managerial skills sufficient to fulfill the assignment. 63/
If this is done adequately, the personnel have simply been
acquired from other companies and what has in effect been
created is "just another oil company."  This is perhaps
justified when a consumer nation does not have an industry
capable of entry into international supply arrangements, but
in the case of the United States, private industry has
historically maintained a very broad-based access to foreign
supplies. 64/  The creation of a governmentally owned company would, therefore, seem to be in most respects an act of
redundancy.

263.

In addition, it should be noted that there is in many European countries a tradition of government-owned enterprises, established to accomplish policy objectives which in the United States have historically been pursued by the regulation of private industry, such as antitrust laws. 65/ While the British Government acquired British Petroleum in large part because Winston Churchill, then the First Lord of the Admiralty, feared the monopolistic power of the Standard Oil Trust, the U.S. Government broke it pursuant to our antitrust laws. 66/ There appears to be no logical basis in the United States for creating a Federal oil corporation to engage in international petroleum affairs. It also seem clear that whatever merit there is in the proposal would probably apply with equal force to various other industries (such as automobiles, steel, and airlines) in which the governmentally owned company approach has been rejected, if ever seriously considered.

The governmentally owned oil corporations of producer countries, such as Petromin (Saudi Arabia), National Iranian Oil Company, Pertamina (Indonesia), and CVP (Venezuela), do not serve as useful precedent in evaluating this option. They are in large part simply an extension of the government and with very few exceptions lack the expertise, technological skills and managerial competence that is necessary in order to perform the obligations required in international petroleum arrangements. With few exceptions this type of corporation has also been found to be grossly inefficient when gauged by the standards of private petroleum companies. 67/

The record of inefficiency is not confined to companies of producer countries. This has been the pattern elsewhere (most of the government corporations of consumer countries examined have been heavily subsidized) and it is likely in the case of the United States, perhaps even more so with due regard to our relative lack of familiarity with this type of system. 68/ Government corporations are responsive to political pressures that are wholly unrelated to economic aspects of their mission, and this breeds inefficiency.

Finally, two recent studies offer further evidence that the performance of public corporations is generally inferior to that of private industry, measured by a wide range of accepted indicators of economic efficiency. 69/

Therefore, although there are some limited objectives which might suggest that the Federal Government directly interject itself in the international petroleum industry, there is substantial reason to doubt its justification.

F.   [7.14]  Conclusions

The option here examined is of establishing a Federal oil company to explore, produce and import oil in international petroleum arrangements.  As indicated above, there is no basis for believing that the presence of such a corporation would contribute to lower oil prices for consumers.  It is also relevant that import controls could probably be handled by existing agencies and that ERDA has already been established to conduct research and development. 70/  The presence of a Federal oil corporation in international petroleum would not enhance the security of supply to the United States; it could, in fact, have a counterproductive effect in this regard.

If government corporations are less efficient than their private counterparts, the public corporation holds a profit umbrella over (a price floor under) private firms. There is some evidence that this is the case in France. 71/ If this is true, the "yardstick" becomes counterproductive in causing consumer prices to be higher than necessary.

Whether viewed economically, functionally or from the standpoint of the overall public interest, there appears to be no convincing basis under today's conditions upon which to recommend the creation or acquisition of a company of which the U.S. Government would be the whole or partial owner to participate in international petroleum transactions. Undeniably, the U.S. Government must have a greater role in international petroleum affairs than it has had in the past, but this option clearly appears to present an inefficient, and potentially counterproductive, method of asserting the U.S. presence.

CHAPTER 7

FOOTNOTES

1. Hearings before the U.S. Senate Committee on
   Commerce, 93d Cong., 2d Sess., Pt. 4, April 22-23,
   1974, p. 1409.

2. See Appendix A §A.15, infra.  Before 1975 the British
   Government owned 49% of BP's stock.  In January 1975
   the Bank of England acquired a 21.5% interest in BP
   from Burmah Oil Company which would appear to give
   the British Government effective control of over 70%
   of the company.  See The Wall Street Journal, Jan. 24,
   1975 at 12.

3. See Appendix A §A.13, infra.

4. Ibid.

5. See Sommer, "Who's 'In Control'" - S.E.C., 21 The Business Lawyer 559, 566 (1966); Berle and Means, The
   Modern Corporation and Private Property (1932) at
   69-70.

5a. In the event of such proxy fight the Federal Govern-
    ment would seem to be required to file a proxy state-
    ment with the Securities and Exchange Commission and
    make "full disclosure" about it and its "associates."
    See Section 4 of the Securities Act of 1934; S.E.C.
    Regulation 14A.  For it to claim sovereign immunity
    would not place it in a particularly attractive
    posture to shareholders.  This problem would not be
    present at the outset for a new partially owned
    Federal corporation but could arise at any time
    thereafter if the privately held share was 50% or
    more.

6. Such as the recent FTC investigation of eight major
   U.S. oil companies.  See §4.1, supra.

7. While the Government board members appear to have
   never interfered in the companies' operation (Frankel,
   Mattei - Oil and Power Politics (1966) at 164), to
   many experienced observers BP is "to all intents and

purposes an arm of . . . British strategic policy."
Millspaugh, _Americans in Persia_ (1946) at 162. See
Appendix A §A.13, _infra_.

8. U.S. Constitution, Article 2; _Youngstown Sheet &_
_Tube Co. v. Sawyer_, 103 F. Supp. 978 (D.C.D.C., 1952).

9. See Chapter 6.

10. Panarctic is 45% owned by the Canadian Government.
Panarctic Oils Ltd., 1973 Annual Report, 2.

11. The U.S. Government appoints 1/5 of COMSAT'S
directors but owns no stock. 47 U.S.C. §733.

12. See Appendix A §A.5.

12a. _Ibid_.

13. See §7.0, _supra_.

14. TVA has provided electricity at bargain rates to
all its customers.

15. See Appendix A §§A.13-A.17.

16. Other firms would probably resent any special
privileges granted a Federal oil company and
might therefore be reluctant to cooperate with
the Government on important policy issues.

17. See Appendix A §A.1 for a discussion of two U.S.
Government corporations.

18. For example, see M. Friedman, _Capitalism and_
_Freedom_ (1962) or P. Samuelson, "The Economic
Role of Private Activity" in _Readings in Economics_
(1973).

19. _Ibid_.

20. _Ibid_.

21. See §1.18, _supra_.

22. See §1.18, _supra_.

23. Friedman gives a different example:

> "It can be argued that private charity is insufficient because the benefits from it accrue to people other than those who make the gifts -- again, a neighborhood effect. I am distressed by the sight of poverty; I am benefited by its alleviation; but I am benefited equally whether I or someone else pays for its alleviation; the benefits of other people's charity therefore partly accrue to me. To put it differently, we might all of us be willing to contribute to the relief of poverty, provided someone else did." Friedman, supra note 18, at 191.

24. See §3.2, supra.

25. See Appendix A.

26. Samuelson, supra note 18, at 79.

27. See note 18, supra.

28. Friedman, supra note 18, at 27-28.

29. Ibid.

30. See Appendix C §C.1, Questions 1 and 2.

31. See Appendix C §C.1, Question 3.

32. See §§9.2-9.3, infra.

33. See §§9.3-9.5, infra.

34. See Appendix A §A.18.

35. See Appendix A §A.18.

36. Since the inefficiency would obviously raise the company's costs, higher prices or higher subsidies would be inevitable.

37.  As evidenced by the existing preferences for
     small refiners in current FEA regulations.

38.  See Appendix B §B.4.

39.  See §§3.11 and 3.12, *supra*.

40.  In fact, it may raise costs by promoting less
     efficient sectors of the industry.

41.  Aramco, for example, may soon become 100% Govern-
     ment owned. *Petroleum Intelligence Weekly*,
     Dec. 9, 1974.

42.  See §1.18, *supra*.

43.  A Federal oil company might in fact tend to
     raise the price.

44.  See §1.18, *supra*.

45.  As in the case of Libya's action against BP.
     See Chapter 1.

45a. See §6.4, *supra*.

45b. See §9.1, *infra*, for further discussion of
     this point.

46.  See §1.18, *supra*.

47.  See §10.1, *infra*.

48.  The effect of the oil sharing plan of the IEA
     would also be considered by the companies.
     See §10.1, *infra*.

49.  See also §5.3, *supra*.

50.  Created by the Energy Reorganization Act of
     1974 (PL 93-438), signed on October 11, 1974.

51.  See §5.4, *supra*.

52.  See Appendix A §A.1.

53. See Appendix A §A.1.

54. See Appendix C §§C.1 and C.8.

55. See Appendix C §C.8.

56. See Appendix A §A.15.

57. See Appendix A §A.15.

58. See Appendix A §A.15.

59. See Appendix A §A.15.

60. See Appendix A §A.14.

61. G. W. Stocking, _Middle East Oil_, 17 (1970).

62. See Appendix A §A.13.

63. See Appendix A §A.3.

64. See Chapter 1, especially §1.18.

65. Interview with European petroleum consultant.

66. Stocking, _supra_ note 61.

67. A view widely held by U.S. companies, see Appendix C.

68. See Appendix A §A.1.

69. See Appendix A §A.18.

70. 88 Stat. 1233 (Oct. 11, 1974), codified at 42 U.S.C. §5811 _et seq_.

71. See Appendix A §A.15.

PART IV

FUTURE POLICY OPTIONS:

BILATERAL/MULTILATERAL OPTIONS

CHAPTER 8

COORDINATION OF INTERNATIONAL SUPPLY
ARRANGEMENTS THROUGH AN INDUSTRY-WIDE
ASSOCIATION OF CONSUMER COUNTRY COMPANIES

A.    [§8.0]   Introduction

The creation of an international association of
petroleum companies, in which all consumer nation petroleum
companies playing a substantial role in the international
petroleum industry are represented, would be directed to the
objective of maximizing the bargaining leverage of companies
in their dealings with producer governments and expanding
consumer government understanding of the limits of the companies' bargaining position. 1/  Although it is widely
believed that the companies are no longer able to effectively bargain with producer governments on price, full
consideration has not been given to the potential bargaining
position of the companies if enhanced by government encouraged and coordinated planning and strategy.

B.    [§8.1]   The Bargaining Position of the Companies

For over a half century the companies exercised
extensive control over all aspects of the international
petroleum industry, including pricing and supply decisions.
With their control over the transport and downstream marketing
of better than 80% of OPEC's production, the companies
still have some residue of their former market power.
Although producing governments, either acting directly or
through international oil companies, are attempting to
develop greater participation in the downstream operations,
their involvement to date has been fairly limited.  This is
a function which still has to be performed by the companies
because they alone possess the competence to do so. 2/  Although there is cause to believe that some producing governments do not fully appreciate the extent of their dependence
upon foreign companies to distribute their petroleum,
thoughtful representatives of the producing nations appear to
be aware that the companies perform a needed function. 3/

Some national companies, such as Pertamina, Sonatrach and Pemex, 4/ are demonstrating an ability to find oil and produce it without the assistance of foreign companies, although probably less efficiently. 5/ Nevertheless, the producing countries as a whole are still extremely dependent upon the expertise and technical ability of foreign companies for most of their exploration and production. At least for the foreseeable future, the ability of many producing governments to increase, or even sustain, their present levels of revenue will depend upon the continuing effort of foreign companies to find and produce oil. 6/ This consideration may be less critical for the Arab states of the Persian Gulf who are already experiencing considerable surplus revenues, but for the smaller producers seeking to expand their share of the market or those with large financial requirements, the assistance of foreign companies is essential. 7/

Although the once enormous power of the companies has been eroded by the increased strength of producer governments, some of the conditions which contributed to the rapid deterioration of their bargaining position during the last four years might be countered or ameliorated in future negotiations. One of these factors was the extreme vulnerability of certain companies to threats of production cuts or nationalization which thereby reduced the ability of the companies to maintain a united front. A second important factor was the shortsighted policies of the United States and other consuming governments which not only impeded the ability of the companies to coordinate their 1970-1971 negotiations in Teheran and Tripoli, but actually undermined their position by making concessions to producer governments at the diplomatic level. 8/

These two factors combined to render the companies incapable of bargaining individually and left their attempt at shoring up their position through the London Policy Group ("LPG") fragmented and ineffectual. Although these conditions forever ended the era in which the companies could dictate price levels to producer governments, they have not completely nullified the ability of the companies to negotiate price in times of excess world capacity, provided that consumer governments pursue policies which are supportive of that end.

One thing which was learned from the 1970-1971 debacle is that whatever power the companies have it must be exercised with a high degree of coordination. The individual company, bargaining on its own, is too weak when confronted with a producer government which has the backing and assistance of the entire OPEC cartel. While companies cannot hope to influence the basic price-setting decisions of OPEC, they may be able to exert considerable market leverage via the individual producers on the variety of matters negotiated separately by each country, such as adjustments for qualities of the specific crudes, transportation differentials and terms of payment. 9/

C.   [§8.2]   An Association of Companies

It would appear that the system most likely to produce the requisite degree of company coordination would be an organization of companies along the lines of the London Policy Group, consisting of all consumer-nation petroleum companies with sizable producer-country supply arrangements. 10/ A precept of the organization would be full prior disclosure to the association of all proposed major supply arrangements, an understanding not to compete with other companies for certain categories of supply arrangements and "safety net" agreements to provide some measure of insurance for those companies which might lose sources of supply as a result of complying with joint decisions. For political appearance as well as ease of administration, the obligations of the member companies would be on an informal basis, the good faith performance of which would be left to the companies' respective governments to enforce as they saw fit. 11/ For companies with full or partial governmental ownership this would pose few problems in light of the high degree of cooperation with government which has historically been possible with such companies. Consumer governments would have low profile roles, consisting mainly of requiring that their companies live up to the obligations implicit in association membership. The concept of the review and approval of foreign supply arrangements discussed in Chapter 6 would assist in this respect. In any event, a high degree of cooperation among the major consuming nations would be necessary to maintain the effectiveness of the association and it is unclear whether this degree of cooperation has yet been achieved. 12/

275.

The purpose of the association would be to enhance
the companies' bargaining position by the exchange of information, the reduction of upstream competition and the
formulation of affirmative strategies for maximizing downward market pressure on prices by, for example, shifting
purchasing patterns among the companies to focus softness in
world demand on selected producer countries which are most
in need of stable petroleum revenues.  Such strategies would
seek to maximize the temptation of producing governments to
compete without creating a situation in which a direct
confrontation to OPEC can be perceived. 13/  The association
could also develop strategies for inducing producer countries
to increase the attractiveness of their crude by such non-
price variables as discounts for quality, rebates for
services rendered by the company, credit terms, delayed
payment of purchase price or acceptance of soft currency. 14/
By shifting the forum of consumer pressure for lower prices
from a basically political structure in which OPEC cannot
back down to the individual commercial transactions in which
the producer may feel not only the need but the ability to
give hidden price concessions, a situation may be created in
which worldwide diminution of demand might be translated into
a lower price.

Since the effectiveness of this option could be
offset by the large residual producers setting up a financial
"safety net" for OPEC, it is important that any such strategy
be integrated into the complex web of commercial transactions.
The risk of overt confrontation cannot be eliminated, but it
would appear to be much lower than if this strategy were
pursued directly by consumer governments. 15/  The dangers
inherent in diplomatic confrontation over price levels may
be replaced by the subtler effects of indirect coordination
of supply arrangements so as to maximize the incentive and
opportunity of producer governments to compete.

D.    [§8.3]  Antitrust Problems

While this option might create an environment in
which substantial progress can be achieved by the companies
acting in concert, there are a number of substantial problems
which may diminish the utility of this option to the national
interest.  The most substantial problem is the apparent inconsistency
between government-endorsed industry-wide cooperation and the

276.

United States' traditional policy of encouraging competitiveness through the antitrust laws. There can be little doubt that an association of companies combining for the purpose of reducing competition among them in the acquisition of foreign petroleum supplies would raise very serious problems under Sections 1 and 2 of the Sherman Act 16/ and that, absent an express exemption from the scope of the antitrust laws, company participation would not be forthcoming. The question then is posed how such an association of companies could be exempted from the scope of the antitrust laws and whether it should be.

An abhorrence of anti-competitive combinations is deeply rooted in the American legal system. This reflects a strong belief that free and open competition in the marketplace is the best check upon the abuses attendant to the accumulation of market power. This is not to say, however, that the maintenance of competition has always prevailed over other conflicting national objectives. Hence there are numerous cases where practices which would otherwise violate antitrust policies are condoned by the law. Labor unions, agricultural cooperatives, public utilities and patents are all examples of anti-competitive institutions which are condoned because they advance other objectives which are thought to offset the loss of competition. 17/ As examined in Chapter 1, this was also historically the case with respect to the Middle Eastern operations of the major oil companies.

Whether competition in the upstream acquisition of petroleum supplies is of any value to the U.S. national interest is far from clear. Competition among the companies in their dealings with producer governments has resulted primarily in a lessening of their ability to deal with such governments which are a self-acknowledged cartel. The insurgence of competitive companies into the international market in the 1950's and 1960's materially contributed to the strengthening of the bargaining leverage of producing governments. 18/ Such competition has undeniably diminished the ability of the major petroleum companies to take oligopolistic profits, but it has unfortunately enhanced the ability of producer governments to do so. In neither event does the ultimate consumer get the advantage of real competition. The companies, which have become price takers, simply pass on to consumers the cartel prices demanded by producing governments. The competition among the companies

277.

in their upstream activities has been one of the major forces leading to a cartel of producer governments, many times more oligopolistic than the companies ever were and completely beyond the reach of consumer-nation legal systems. 19/ Thus, the continued application of the antitrust laws to the upstream activities of the companies would seem if anything counter-productive to the national interest, at least in terms of the prices which American consumers will have to pay for petrol-eum.

It may be in the best interest of the nation to subordinate the maintenance of competition in the purchase of international petroleum to more pressing national objectives, primarily the reduction of world petroleum price levels. If possible, the most advantageous accommodation of these two apparently conflicting national objectives would be an exemp-tion from the antitrust laws strictly confined to upstream operations. To create such an exemption would not be an easy task either in theory or in practice. The large number of integrated companies in the petroleum industry has caused the existence of competition upstream to have a direct bearing upon the competitiveness of companies in their down-stream marketing activities. 20/ Thus, it must be expected that even a carefully delineated exemption from the anti-trust laws for the purchasing of international supplies would be expected to have significant impact upon the competitiveness of companies in the U.S. market. This is a fact which must be given serious consideration in the weighing of this option.

There have been a number of instances in which exemption from the antitrust laws has been afforded to com-panies brought together in an association for the purpose of advancing some pressing national objective. During World War II, the Petroleum Industry War Council was organized to assist the Government in the formulation and administration of petroleum policies to assist the war effort. After con-sulation with the Justice Department, immunity from antitrust prosecution was granted to the participating companies pursuant to the Small Business Mobilization Act. 21/ Following the war, the National Petroleum Council ("NPC") was established at the behest of the Secretary of the Interior and antitrust immunity was again granted pursuant to an informal arrange-ment between the Department of the Interior and the Attorney General. 22/ The NPC's voluntary industry-wide program for the allocation of scarce materials and facilities was also given immunity by the Attorney General in 1948 under the authority of the Anti-Inflation Act. 23/

In an attempt to encourage voluntary agreements and programs to benefit the national defense, industry coordination was made immune from antitrust prosecution in 1950 under the Defense Production Act. 24/ One of the most important examples of such programs was the Middle East Emergency Committee which operated an overlift program to Western Europe following the closing of the Suez Canal. The most recent example of antitrust immunity in the petroleum industry was the issuance in 1971 of Business Review Letters by the Justice Department to the London Policy Group to enable companies to coordinate their strategies. 25/ Business Review Letters simply state that the Justice Department "does not presently intend to institute any proceedings under the antitrust laws" for the actions described in the company's request. The LPG Business Review Letter was recently revoked. 26/

It is doubtful that companies would be willing to participate in an industry-wide association without a statutory exemption from the antitrust laws. The Business Review Letter provides very little real security for the companies since it only states the "present intention" of the Justice Department and does not bind or otherwise preclude it from later bringing criminal or civil actions. 27/ Nor does the Business Review Letter affect the rights of private parties to bring civil actions under the antitrust laws. 28/ It is unlikely then that such administrative exemptions would provide the sort of incentive which would gain the cooperation of the companies in a strategy necessarily entailing long-term planning and commitments.

A statutory exemption would not only provide the sort of security which the companies want but would also require a direct Congressional assessment of the relative values of maintaining upstream competition in the industry and seeking lower levels of world petroleum prices. This nation's commitment to free competition is sufficiently strong that it could not be put aside by ad hoc administrative efforts and without express Congressional approval.

The problem could probably be best dealt with by giving an exemption for association activities subject to continuous review by a competent and knowledgeable U.S. Government representative who would be present at all meetings and privy to all communications. 29/ Further, a reviewing agency could be charged with making periodic reports to the Congress on the state of competition in the industry, including downstream activities within the U.S. market. In this way, the Congress would be continually informed of the price which was being paid for greater company coordination in terms of lost competitiveness. If at some point it became clear that the adverse consequences were outweighing any benefit, the exemption could be revoked and the association disbanded.

E. [§8.4] Monitoring the Companies

Another major problem with this option is insuring that once the association is set up, the companies will use it in the public interest. There is suspicion among some observers that the companies are not interested in returning prices to lower levels. 30/ The companies have essentially been able to pass on the impacts of higher prices to consumers and in the process make very high profits. 31/ They contend, however, that their ability to do this has been restricted both by the timing and retroactivity of certain of the price hikes and by price control restrictions in consuming nations. 32/ They also point out that their greater profits are being reinvested in petroleum exploration and development and that future profits will be quite limited. 33/ The countervailing popular belief, however, is that higher petroleum prices have resulted in "windfall" profits to the companies. 34/ In any event, it is evident that as holders of large high-cost inventories, the companies might face very substantial inventory losses if prices fell. While the issue of the true motivations of the companies is far from clear, any proposed plan for industry coordination will have to deal with the possibility that, for whatever reason, the companies may not wish to cooperate.

Some companies might be reluctant to join in the association for other reasons. Companies with good relationships with their producing governments, for example, might feel that participation would have an unsettling impact. 35/

Smaller independents, who are seeking to increase their share of the international market, might regard the noncompetitive aspects of the association as merely an entrenchment of the status quo. To the companies who have expressed a belief that prices can only be settled at the diplomatic level, the association may offer them nothing more for their efforts than an increased risk of antitrust prosecution. 36/

Requesting the companies to join such an association and to discuss their foreign supply arrangements or proposed negotiations would probably not present a major problem; a substantial number of the companies indicated they would favor this option. 37/ Requiring the companies' participation in the association would probably not be feasible in view of its strategic and planning functions.

The success of this option will require developing sufficient monitoring capabilities for the Government to know whether the association is being used to its fullest benefit. Only one intimately involved in the association's meeting and planning could judge whether all opportunities were being vigorously pursued and whether the companies were acting in good faith. Companies within the association would be in an excellent position to identify uncooperative members; however, the self policing of the association would only be an effective mechanism if a substantial number of the companies were committed to the success of the option. It cannot be known whether this is in fact the case. The best entity to supervise the performance of the U.S. companies would be an agency of the U.S. Government, acting alone or preferably in cooperation with other consumer governments, and thoroughly acquainted with the operations of the association. The assignment would logically fall to the agency given regulatory responsibility for international supply arrangements, as discussed in Chapter 6. The agency would have to be fully acquainted with the workings of the international petroleum industry, be independent of political as well as industry pressure and be capable of making decisions on very short notice.

There would also have to be significant incentives to the companies to be cooperative in the eventuality that their own interests did not incline in that direction. The power to disapprove foreign supply arrangements entered into by U.S. companies could be a significant incentive. 38/ This sanction would, however, seem appropriate only in clear cases of noncooperation. 39/ Moreover, the power of dis- approval is basically a negative tool which can only prevent or undo individual transactions. It is not the sort of positive incentive which will motivate the companies to actively work together in developing coordinated strategies for negotiating tough agreements with producers where they are most vulnerable. Such a positive incentive might be provided by the interested consumer nations creating agencies authorized to make direct purchases of national needs from producer nations, as is discussed in Chapter 9. 40/

        Probably the fairest and most credible incentive for cooperation by U.S. or U.S. based companies 41/ would be to mandate the designated Federal agency to evaluate the ability and willingness of the companies to use their best efforts to promote lower levels of price and, after an initial period of two or three years, to report its findings to the President and the Congress. 42/ If it found that the companies were unable or unwilling to act in furtherance of the national interest, the agency could further be required to propose legislation to correct the situation. If, on the other hand, the agency found that the companies were in fact dedi- cated to working for objectives consistent with the national interest, the need for greater governmental intervention and regulation might not be present.

        Thus, with sufficient Congressional and public focus upon the findings of this agency, a situation could be created in which the oil companies, by the existence and degree of their cooperation in making the association effec- tive, could influence the likelihood of further intervention by the U.S. Government. The industry, which is noted for its ability to respond to unusual challenges, would hopefully seek to clear the record by applying its vast resources and expertise to maximizing the benefit to consuming nations of industry-wide cooperation.

    F.    [§8.5]   Providing Leadership

        In addition to providing an incentive to active company cooperation, the designated Federal agency could also provide a leadership role. The association would include many companies of differing sizes, types of ownership and

nationality. Their success in achieving substantial breakthroughs on price would be dependent upon their ability to
work and plan in a coordinated fashion. The agency could
provide a central source of guidance and direction, even if
for political reasons its involvement was confined to working
behind the scenes through a caucus of U.S. companies. The
effectiveness of such indirect leadership would depend upon
the ability of the U.S. Government to secure the cooperation
of other consuming nation governments so necessary to maintain
the cohesiveness of the association.

The success of the association, then, would depend
in large part upon the work of the Federal agency which, by
way of summary, might have the following responsibilities:

(1)  To evaluate the ability and willingness of
the U.S. companies to negotiate lower levels of petroleum
prices;

(2)  To provide positive guidance to the U.S. companies in planning the strategy of the association;

(3)  To coordinate these efforts with relevant
agencies of the U.S. Government;

(4)  To review and approve or disapprove foreign
supply arrangements, if such a power is created; and

(5)  To report to the President and the Congress
after an initial term of two or three years on its findings
with respect to mandate (1) above and, if necessary, to
propose legislation which will make companies operating
in the United States more responsive to U.S. national interests.

G.  [§8.6]  Risk of Confrontation

A risk which should be weighed in the evaluation of
this option is that producer nations will regard it as an
attempt to create a consumer cartel. This risk is increased
by the role which the designated Federal agency would play
in connection with the association. It should be possible,
however, for the agency to act in a sufficiently discreet
manner to reduce the risk of a political confrontation by
emphasizing the fact-finding nature of its mission:  an active
and participating form of transparency. 43/  Producer

countries cannot legitimately object to the desire of consumer governments to investigate and report on the activities and interests of their own petroleum companies. The statutory definition of the agency's role within the association should be discreet and ambiguous, relying upon the agency's investigative function and responsibility to report to the Congress on the true interests of the companies to give it the power which it will need to fulfill its role. 44/ Any attempt to enhance consumer leverage has an inherent risk of confrontation, but this option entails less of a risk because the actual strategy of the association would be obscured in the context of the multitude of commercial transactions which constitute the world petroleum market.

H.  [§8.7]  Conclusion

This option is not a panacea for the problems of international petroleum supply and price. It does, however, have the advantage of relative low cost and a basic compatability with other options examined. 45/ If the U.S. companies cooperate, it could maximize their bargaining leverage in negotiations with producer governments. Whether or not this option would, in fact, have any effect upon prices is indeterminate.

In addition to whatever effect the association might have, the role of the designated Federal agency would give the U.S. Government a better understanding of the role of the companies in international petroleum affairs and of their ability and willingness to negotiate terms consistent with the national interest. Such knowledge would, if profitably used by the Congress and the Executive, provide a basis for future action to eliminate such inconsistencies as may exist between the interests of the companies and of the United States. 46/ Finally, this option would provide a vehicle by which consuming nations could cooperate to maximize the market leverage which rigorous conservation and alternative energy development will hopefully give them and to do so in a commercial context with less risk of political confrontation. 47/

It cannot be ignored that this option would constitute a dramatic departure from the United States' traditional antitrust policies, but a greater appreciation

of the costs of such policies to the U.S. consumer is needed
if we are to be sure that our priorities in this vital
industry are correct.  Further, the value of this option,
like that of so many of the available options, depends
upon viable and effective cooperation among consumer nations.
Without the requisite degree of control over other consumer
nation companies, an association of companies could be
expected to accomplish nothing.

CHAPTER 8

FOOTNOTES

1. The rationale is in some respects similar to that
   which underlay the creation of the original London
   Policy Group ("LPG") during the 1971 OPEC price
   negotiations, that is, to present a united and coordinated front of petroleum companies vis-a-vis
   OPEC. See §1.16, supra. The purpose of the new LPG
   would be somewhat different, however, in that it
   would be an ongoing organization which would coordinate company strategy in price negotiations with
   individual OPEC countries as well.

2. See Appendix E, §E.1.

3. "Interim Saudi Pact Eases Some of the Uncertainty
   For Now," Petroleum Intelligence Weekly, June 17,
   1974 at 4.

4. Pertamina is the Indonesian national oil company;
   Sonatrach is Algeria's; Pemex is Mexico's.

5. For a narrative description of Pertamina's accom-
   plishments, see generally A. Bartlett III, et. al.,
   Pertamina, Indonesian National Oil (1972). Pemex
   has recently made a significant oil find and expects
   to increase its future exports. See "Mexican Oil
   Exports Could Ease U.S. Loss of Canadian Crude,"
   Petroleum Intelligence Weekly, Dec. 16, 1974 at 7-8.
   For a description of Sonatrach's expansion, see
   "Sonatrach Rewrites Its Contracts," Petroleum
   Press Service, Oct. 1973 at 266. See also Appendices
   C and E, §§C.1 and E.1 for evaluations of the ef-
   ficiency of producer government petroleum companies.

6. See comments of Saudi oil consultant, 'abd Allah
   al-Tariki, who formerly advocated nationalization
   of the oil companies but now has cautioned Arab
   countries not to "resort to nationalization of oil
   operations as that would result in unnecessary harm
   to them." Middle East Economic Survey, Dec. 14,
   1973 at 2-3.

7. See generally "Indonesia Says It Needs All the Oil Income It Can Get," _Petroleum Intelligence Weekly_, Nov. 11, 1974 at 5. Interviews by the Study Contractor with representatives of foreign governments.

8. For a description of the State Department's role in the 1971 OPEC price negotiations, see §1.16, _supra_. See also Hearings Before the Subcommittee on Multinational Corporations of the Senate Foreign Relations Committee, _Multinational Corporations and United States Foreign Policy_, 93d Cong., 2d Sess., pt. 5 at 145.

9. There are a number of ways in which a producer government can reduce the actual price of crude to its customers without appearing to run counter to OPEC pricing guidelines. Some of these methods are being employed already with the crude surpluses that have developed during the latter half of 1974. See "Extra Credit Terms Adding a Discount For Crude Buyers," _Petroleum Intelligence Weekly_, Jan. 13, 1975 at 3.

10. The original London Policy Group ("LPG") was composed of representatives of approximately twenty-four petroleum companies operating in Libya and the Persian Gulf. British, Dutch, French, German, Japanese and U.S. firms were represented, making the original LPG international in character. See §1.16, _supra_, for a further description of its operation.

11. The original London Policy Group was this same type of informal organization. Companies were not obligated to participate nor were any stringent rules adopted after its inception. The Libyan Producer's Agreement, however, guaranteed replacement crude to any company whose production was reduced as a result of refusing to accede to demands of the Libyan Government. The issue as to whether such agreement was binding is now being litigated in a suit brought by the Bunker-Hunt Oil Company against Occidental and other Libyan producers.

12. If producing countries viewed such an "association of companies" as creating confrontation, it is likely that most consuming governments would be hesitant to have their companies participate. For example, on September 27, 1974, the Japanese Foreign

287.

Minister, Mr. Toshio Kimura, stated after a two-hour meeting with U.S. Secretary of State Henry Kissinger that "confrontation must be avoided at all costs between the oil producing and oil consuming countries." West Germany's Chancellor, Mr. Helmut Schmidt, echoed similar fears when, in response to a question, he told _Time_ Magazine that "it would be difficult and possibly even dangerous if we would allow a sort of economic war to occur between oil consumers and producers." France's Foreign Minister, Mr. Jean Sauvagnargues, told newsmen on September 25, 1974, that "there is no possible way of forcing the Arabs to lower oil prices except through peaceful dialogue." See "Documentary Rundown on World Reactions to US Compaign For Lower Oil Prices," Middle East Economic Survey, Oct. 4, 1974 at 2.

13. Beyond the problem of creating confrontation, a new London Policy Group designed to encourage competition among producer countries would have to gauge its strategy carefully so as to avoid putting a particular producer government in the position of giving apparent price reductions in violation of OPEC's general pricing guidelines. Most producer governments are extremely sensitive regarding accusations that they are secretly reducing price to increase production. See "Abu Dhabi Denies Incentive Plan to Encourage Companies to Overlift Participation Crude; Says Unsold Volumes Will Be Shut-In," Middle East Economic Survey, Oct. 18, 1974 at 7-8.

14. In an interview conducted by the Study Contractor with an industry consultant in the United States, the point was emphasized that producer governments can reduce prices in very inconspicuous ways, and that it is worthwhile to give these various oil exporting countries the opportunity and incentive to do so.

15. Saudi Arabian Petroleum Minister, Sheikh Yamani, reacting to a proposal to establish a consortium of major consuming countries to negotiate oil prices with producing countries, warned that a move on the part of the consumers to force down prices by collective pressure "would lead to a sharp increase in oil prices based on reduced production," See

"Yamani Warns Against Plan For Oil Purchasing Consortium," Middle East Economic Survey, May 10, 1974 at 1.

16. See 15 U.S.C. §§1 and 2.

17. See P. Areeda, Antitrust Analysis, 11-12, 49-59 (1967).

18. For a description of such com  tition and an analysis of its effects, see §§1.12, 1.16 and 1.18.

19. For a description of the competition which has developed among oil companies for access to crude, see §§1.10, 1.12, 1.15 and 1.18.  See also N. H. Jacoby, Multinational Oil (1974).

20. For an excellent statistical analysis of the reduction in concentration of downstream operations within the petroleum industry during the last twenty years, see N. H. Jacoby, supra note 19, at 172.

21. Report of the Subcommittee on Antitrust and Monopoly of the Senate Judiciary Committee, Petroleum, the Antitrust Laws and Government Policies, 85th Cong. 1st Sess., at 14 (Comm. Print 1957).

22. Id. at 14-15.

23. Id. at 15.

24. Ibid.

25. For a complete text of the correspondence between John J. McCloy, attorney for the London Policy Group ("LPG"), and the Antitrust Division of the Department of Justice regarding the request and issuance of Business Review Letters covering the creation and operation of the LPG, see Hearings Before the Subcommittee on Multinational Corporations of the Senate Foreign Relations Committee, Multinational Corporations and United States Foreign Policy, 93d Cong., 2d Sess., at pt. 6, at 223 (Comm. Print 1974).

26. See "J.S. Firms Lose Clearance For Joint OPEC Bargaining," Petroleum Intelligence Weekly, June 10, 1974 at 3.

27. See 28 C.F.R. §50.6 (1973) (Antitrust Division business review procedure). See also National Association of Manufacturers International Economic Affairs Department, The International Implications of U.S. Antitrust Laws (1974).

28. Ibid.

29. The concept of having a U.S. Government representative present at the meetings of the new LPG would not be unprecedented. For example, U.S. Government representatives have attended sessions of two industry committees recently convened to advise the new International Energy Agency.

30. See generally Hearings Before the Senate Committee on Interior and Insular Affairs pursuant to S. Res. 45, Oil Price Rollback Legislation, 93d Cong., 2d Sess. (Comm. Print 1974). See especially Opening Statement of Sen. Henry M. Jackson at 1 and Statement of Sen. Walter F. Mondale at 14.

31. See "Shell and Union Oil Shatter Profit Marks During Year," Los Angeles Times, Jan. 28, 1975 at 13. (Record profits have been reported for 1974 by, among others, the following petroleum companies: Standard of California, Texaco, Mobil, Exxon, Standard of Indiana, Shell and Union).

32. The retroactive agreement for 60% Saudi participation in Aramco reached in the summer of 1974 could add millions of dollars to Aramco's costs which could not easily be passed on to the consumer because the production against which such retroactive price increase was imposed had already been sold. See generally Petroleum Intelligence Weekly, supra note 3, at 4.

33. "Those Huge Profits Don't Look That Big Against Outlays," Petroleum Intelligence Weekly, Jan. 13, 1975 at 7; "The Spectacular Rise in Profits Is Over, Exxon Results Show," Petroleum Intelligence Weekly, Jan. 27, 1975 at 9.

34. See Oil Price Rollback Legislation, supra note 30, at 1, 14 and 351.

35. The oil exporting countries are sensitive regarding the concept of a consumer cartel which might lead to confrontation, and might therefore be inclined to take punitive actions against companies which it considered to be uniting against it. See "Yamani Warns Against Plan For Oil Purchasing Consortium," supra note 15.

36. See Testimony of Thomas E. Kauper, Assistant Attorney General, Antitrust Division Before the Subcommittee on Multinational Corporations of the Senate Foreign Relations Committee, June 5, 1974 at 12.

37. In fact, the major companies, with an Exxon representative as chairman, are now studying methods by which the information provisions of the new International Energy Agency ("IEA") can best be implemented. In interviews conducted by the Study Contractor many of the companies indicated that just as they are cooperating with the IEA they would also be willing to participate in a type of reconstituted London Policy Group--so long as it did not create antitrust problems for them.

38. For an analysis of the potential advantages and disadvantages of granting the U.S. Government power to review and approve foreign petroleum supply contracts, see §§6.3 through 6.8, supra.

39. There might be various legal problems associated with the exercise of such power by a U.S. Government agency charged with the responsibility of approving or disapproving such contracts. Foremost among these would be due process problems relating to the breadth of administrative discretion and fair compensation for a loss resulting from the disapproval of a contract. See §6.3, supra.

40. See §9.6, supra. Most of the other major consumer countries, other than the United States, already have partially or wholly government-owned oil companies which could serve as direct purchases of crude and thereby fulfill certain national policy objectives.

41.  It would seem that foreign oil corporations with U.S. operations would have a sufficient jurisdictional nexus with the United States so as to come within the regulatory control of a U.S. Government agency of the type discussed in §8.4.  See §6.1, _supra_.

42.  This procedure is utilized frequently with respect to investigative committees and was also used in connection with the 1950 Defense Production Act under which antitrust immunity was granted to petroleum companies to participate in cooperative efforts, such as the Middle East Emergency Committee, formed to supply Western Europe with petroleum after the Suez Canal was shut down by Egypt in 1956.  §708(e) of the Defense Production Act directed the Attorney General:  "to make, or request the Federal Trade Commission to make for him, surveys for the purpose of determining any factors which may tend to eliminate competition, create or strengthen monopolies, injure small business, or otherwise promote undue concentration of economic power in the course of the administration of this act." See Subcommittee on Antitrust and Monopoly of the Senate Judiciary Committee, Petroleum, The Antitrust Laws and Government Policies, 85th Cong., 1st Sess., 69-85 (1957).

43.  For an analysis of the benefits to be derived by greater transparency in transactions within the petroleum industry, see §6.2.

44.  It should be recognized, however, that such enacting legislation cannot be so ambiguous so as to give the U.S. Government agency complete and unfettered discretion with respect to its leadership role in the new London Policy Group.  Such legislation should, nevertheless, attempt to downploy the government's involvement in this new organization so as to avoid unnecessary confrontation with OPEC.

45.  This option could be implemented with minimal financial cost in much the same way as the recent International Energy Agency has been created. Furthermore, it would not foreclose other avenues of approach by the U.S. Government to solving our current energy problems.

46. This option could thereby further the consumer nation
    cooperation which has thus far culminated in an
    International Energy Program providing for an Inter-
    national Energy Agency and an Emergency Energy Sharing
    Plan.  For the full text of the Agreement on an
    International Energy Program, see Petroleum Intelligence
    Weekly, Supplement, Oct. 14, 1974 at 2.  See also
    §6.7, supra, for an analysis of a similar consumer nation
    strategy directed at maximizing consumer leverage.

CHAPTER 9

BILATERAL ARRANGEMENTS BETWEEN THE UNITED STATES
AND PRODUCER GOVERNMENTS

A.    [§9.0]  <u>Introduction</u>

One of the results of the 1973-74 embargo was an increased interest on the part of consuming nations in negotiating bilateral agreements with producer governments. Such arrangements were not unusual prior to the embargo, but the current world situation of uncertain supply and high prices has caused these arrangements to seem even more attractive. There are three primary objectives which consuming nations have sought to accomplish by the use of bilateral agreements:

1.    Obtaining greater security of supply;

2.    Cultivating "special relationships" with particular producer nations; and

3.    Improving the consuming nation's balance of payments position.

To evaluate the effectiveness of bilateral agreements they must be analyzed to determine the extent to which they are successful in accomplishing one or more of these identified objectives.

Insofar as this option pertains to supply, it overlaps to a great extent with that of creating a Federal oil corporation to engage in international petroleum arrangements. As a matter of practical administration, a consuming government might seek to negotiate and perform bilateral arrangements through a governmentally owned oil corporation, much for the same reason that some producer governments choose to deal with foreign purchasers through a national petroleum company. 1/ In terms of analysis, however, the fact that a government chooses to act through a governmentally owned company rather than directly would not appear to materially alter either the benefits or problems which are identified in this section as associated with bilateral government negotiations.

B.  [§9.1]  <u>Securing Sources of Supply</u>

The first objective often sought through a bilateral
agreement with a producer government is the securing of particular sources of petroleum supplies.  Such agreements have
been an appealing option to consumer nations concerned regarding possible shortfalls, particularly those highly dependent upon foreign imports. 2/  One of the major bilateral
agreements to be negotiated to accomplish security of supply
prior to the 1973 oil embargo was the French agreement with
Iraq, under which Compagnie Francaise des Petroles ("CFP")
was permitted to retain for ten years its 23.75% share of
the former production of the Iraq Petroleum Company ("IPC"),
which Iraq had nationalized in 1972.  In addition to
guaranteeing a substantial quantity of Iraqi crude for the
French market, the agreement also provided for a reasonably favorable price.  The Iraqi Government has, however,
recently indicated that it intends to adjust the price to a
level generally comparable to the high prices of buy-back
crude in the Persian Gulf. 3/

A number of other direct bilateral petroleum
supply agreements were consummated prior to the 1973 embargo.
In 1972 Italy's national oil company, Ente Nazionale Idrocarburi ("ENI"), entered into a ten-year goods-for-oil
barter arrangement with Iraq involving approximately 20
million tons of crude which would make ENI Iraq's largest
Western oil customer aside from CFP. 4/  In 1972, West
Germany also entered into a direct bilateral petroleum
purchase with Iran.  The terms of the agreement called for
the West Germans to purchase 73 million barrels of crude
from Iran over a five-year period and to enter into an
arrangement "for the joint development of an integrated
oil industry." 5/  To this end, the German Government indicated to the Iranians that the German oil company,
Veba-Chemie, was prepared to negotiate with Iran for the
sale of a participation in all facets of its operations. 6/

At about the same time, Japan consummated its
first government to government petroleum agreements with
Indonesia.  The agreements called for the Japanese to receive 100,000 daily barrels of petroleum from Indonesia over
a ten-year period.  Although exact price was not disclosed,
the Japanese agreed to make a $100 million prepayment to the

Indonesians.  In addition, the Japanese agreed to extend a credit of approximately $234 million, at the interest rate of three percent, to be used for the development of Indonesia's oil industry. 7/  This has, however, been the only transaction of this type in Indonesia and there are clear indications that Pertamina, the national oil company, would prefer that it not be repeated.  It limited Pertamina's flexibility in the distribution of supply and the development funds received come to it from the Government of Indonesia at close to conventional terms. 8/

During this same period, India also sought long-term supply commitments in government to government negotiations with Iraq and Saudi Arabia.  The agreement with Iraq was to provide India with 60,000 daily barrels of petroleum over a ten-year period.  Iraq also agreed to extend a $50 million credit to India to make such purchases. 9/  The price to be paid for the petroleum was not disclosed.  In a similar agreement negotiated with Saudi Arabia, however, India was faced with paying a much higher price for the crude purchased than for the crude being supplied to it by the multinational oil companies. 10/  Japan has experienced similar conditions; its companies have not been able to deliver crude at a price competitive with the international majors in recent months. 11/

For the most part the bilateral supply arrangements negotiated prior to the embargo involved relatively small quantities of crude.  In general, the cost of the petroleum to the consumer government was high, often higher than the prevailing world price. 12/  In certain instances, such as that of CFP in Iraq, a long-standing relationship enabled the consumer government to obtain a generally favorable price.  In other cases, such as the Japanese agreement with Indonesia, it is difficult to assess whether the bilateral arrangement has worked to the benefit of the consumer country. 13/

C.  [§9.2]  The Recent Increase in Bilateral Arrangements

During the embargo and its aftermath, government to government petroleum agreements proliferated due largely to the quite justified concern of the consumer governments that they could no longer depend upon the multinational oil companies to provide them with an adequate supply of petroleum. In fact, nearly all of the industrialized countries of Western Europe and the Japanese either entered into bilateral supply arrangements or entered into serious negotiations with producer governments. 14/

During the first part of 1974, Italy sought to strengthen its access to crude supplies by engaging in direct negotiations with Saudi Arabia, Libya, Iraq and Iran. An agreement was signed with the Libyans whereby additional quantities of Libyan crude would be delivered to Italy in exchange for "economic, technical and industrial facilities and other products of which Libya might have need." 15/ It was expected that the agreement might bring an additional seven million tons of petroleum to Italy each year at prices "yet to be worked out." 16/ Italy, through ENI, also made overtures to Saudi Arabia which consummated in a "pre-accord" signed in February, 1974, providing for the delivery of 20 to 30 million tons of crude oil to Italy over a three-year period in exchange for an undisclosed amount of Italian goods and services. A 15-year agreement proposed by ENI has not yet been accepted by the Saudis. 17/ In addition, the Italians have sought to expand the scope of their existing bilateral petroleum agreement with the Iraqis in order to increase their supply of Iraqi crude to at least four million tons each year. Recently, Italy's ENI has conducted negotiations to have the Iranians purchase a participation in ENI's refining and marketing operations. 18/ If an agreement is signed, it will probably involve some type of supply commitment from Iran to service these refining and marketing operations, in the same fashion as that being discussed with U.S. Shell. 19/

The Japanese meanwhile signed an agreement whereby they would loan $1 billion to the Iraqis in return for Iraq supplying Japan with 90 million tons of crude oil and 70 million tons of liquified petroleum gas and refined products over the next ten years. 20/

Great Britain also entered the competition seeking bilateral arrangements with Saudi Arabia and Iran. Although there has been no report of a specific agreement with Saudi

Arabia, a deal was consummated with Iran whereby Great Britain would receive 100,000 daily barrels of crude over a one-year period. 21/ The agreement was made at the height of the embargo and, in contrast to Iranian crude which was being auctioned in the spot market at prices exceeding $17.00 per barrel, Great Britain obtained the crude at its approximate tax-paid cost of approximately $7.00 per barrel. 22/ On its face the transaction appeared advantageous for the British. It was, however, a barter arrangement pursuant to which they were required to supply Iran with manufactured goods, many of which were in short supply within Great Britain. By August of 1974 the British had no apparent need for this supply and were experiencing difficulty selling it at desired price levels. 23/

France has been the developed country most active in seeking bilateral petroleum agreements with various producer governments. During the last year, France has either consummated or extended existing petroleum supply agreements with Saudi Arabia, Abu Dhabi, Algeria, Iraq and the Soviet Union. 24/ The agreement with Saudi Arabia calls for CFP and ELF-ERAP, the wholly owned French Government corporation, to buy 27 million tons of Saudi Arabian crude over a three-year period. The price to be paid by France was 93% of the posted price. The French, however, were also required to pay a "scarcity premium" of 87 cents per barrel, until the embargo on the United States was lifted. 25/ The arrangement negotiated with Abu Dhabi provided for the sale of 35 Mirage fighter aircraft by the French Government in exchange for a supply of crude oil covering the value of the aircraft. 26/ In Iraq, the French sought to expand their existing relationship and production arrangements under which the Iraqis allowed them to retain their access rights after nationalization of IPC in 1972. 27/ In Algeria, CFP in 1974 began to renegotiate a June, 1971, supply contract. It is estimated that the renewal of this agreement, together with another negotiated by ELF-ERAP, will bring approximately 13 million tons of Algerian crude to France in 1975. 28/ Although the exact price which the French firms are paying is unknown, it is generally speculated that the price is somewhat less than the $12.50 per barrel which third parties are now paying for Algerian crude. 29/ Two years ago, the French signed a twenty-year supply contract with the Soviet Union, whereby

2.5 billion cubic meters of natural gas would be delivered
to France annually beginning in 1976.  Recently, however,
Franch has agreed to pay a price roughly double that which
was originally negotiated, and as a result, will receive an
additional 1.5 billion cubic meters annually, beginning
in 1980. 30/

D.   [§9.3]  Attitudes Toward Bilateral Agreements

The United States organized the Washington Energy
Conference in February, 1974 in an effort to build consumer
unity. 31/  At the Conference, differing views were expressed
regarding the potential benefit of bilateral agreements
with producer countries.  Michel Jobert, French Minister of
Foreign Affairs, stated that:

> "We consider that it is important to
> initiate a dialogue and to develop co-
> operation between consuming and producing
> countries without distinction.  To this
> effect, all bilateral or multilateral
> contracts seem useful, and I said the
> words 'bilateral contracts.'  . . . One
> should question oneself on the reasons
> why a number of countries are trying to
> reach bilateral agreements.  I would say
> that from the moment a certain quantity
> of oil is freed from the grasp of the
> oil companies, and when a number of
> states have recovered the freedom they
> wanted in the production field, I do not
> see how bilateral agreements could be
> condemmed and might jeopardize I wonder
> what world cohesion." 32/

Stating a somewhat opposite view, Helmut Schmidt,

then West German Minister of Finance, noted that there is the:

> "danger of beggar-my-neighbor policies
> among the oil-consuming countries both
> in the scramble for oil and in the at-
> tempt to maintain balance of payments
> equilibrium.  We must by all means avoid

a relapse into bilateral bartering, individual overbidding, competitive devalu-
ations, or escalating trade restrictions
and subsidies . . . I feel it would be
desirable if our countries again undertook at today's Conference not to pursue
policies which would only exacerbate the
problems of others.  At any rate:  the
German Government will abstain from any
such action as I just have mentioned." 33/

Prior to the Washington Energy Conference, French
Prime Minister Messmer succinctly expressed the concerns
which motivate a country like France to seek direct bilateral
agreements with various producer governments.

"But today . . . the big oil companies
are no longer the ones who decide the
destination of oil; they can no longer
choose their customers, nor set prices.
Under these circumstances, there's no
other way for governments than to seek,
by bilateral or multilateral accords,
solutions to problems the oil companies
are no longer able to solve." 34/

E.   [§9.4]  The Results of Bilateral Agreements

There is a serious question, however, whether the
bilateral agreements which have been consummated thus far
have solved the problems facing particular consumer countries.  In some instances, consuming nation governments have
paid a premium for the apparent security of a direct petroleum purchase.  This premium is found sometimes in the form
of a higher price for the petroleum, but more often, through
less identifiable means such as making payment in goods, and
services, extending loans at low interest rates or making
large advance payments.  Government to government petroleum
agreements probably have not had the strong precedental effect
on price that company transactions have had. 35/  Nevertheless, except for a few limited cases, bilateral arrangements

have not been attractive for consumer governments in terms of price. 36/ Moreover, as exemplified by the French agreements with Iraq and the Soviet Union, there is no certainty that a producer government will permit a consuming government to enjoy the benefit of its bargain if the market goes up and the price previously negotiated becomes a favorable one.

In terms of reliability, it is also questionable whether such arrangements are more secure. The nationalization of BP's concession in Libya and ELF-ERAP's concession in Algeria and other incidents of this type certainly indicate that the direct presence of consumer-nation governments in international petroleum arrangements is not beneficial. 37/ The security of a government to government agreement depends fundamentally upon the continued friendly relations between the countries involved. When such relations are poor, the presence of the consumer government will tend, if anything, to reduce security by inviting the producer government to register its disapproval of the consumer government's policies by dishonoring agreements with it. This is a factor which should be thoroughly considered before a consuming nation with as high a political profile as the United States enters into bilateral arrangements in the interest of greater security. 38/

F.    [§9.5]   The "Buffer" Concept

In the course of extensive interviews with petroleum company executives, both in the United States and abroad, the statement that the companies have historically and continue at the present time to operate as a "buffer" between producer and consumer governments, has been consistently cited as one of the reasons why the United States should avoid interjecting itself directly into the international petroleum system. 39/ Implicit in this "buffer" theory is the assumption that companies can isolate commercial transactions from political constraints and considerations, but government or government-owned companies cannot. The companies argue that their existence has minimized the chance that producing nations will translate antagonism toward consuming nations arising out of nonpetroleum matters into a reduction or embargo of supply.

Viewed historically, this assertion by the companies is basically accurate. Some producer governments, such as Venezuela and Saudi Arabia, have for the most part avoided contact with companies wholly or partially owned by consumer governments because of either legal restrictions against foreign governments' ownership of minerals (Venezuela) or the apprehension that the consumer government would meddle in the political affairs of the producer country (Saudi Arabia). 40/ In addition, the nationalization of French petroleum interests in Algeria and of BP's holdings in Libya are clear examples in which political conflict between producing and consuming nations has been carried over into an otherwise commercial relationship. 41/

At least since the oil embargo of 1973, however, petroleum has become an inherently political commodity and the ability of the international companies to continue their role as "buffers" is questionable. History has demonstrated that producer governments, if given sufficient motivation, will embargo consumer countries regardless of the existence of private petroleum companies as intermediaries. Furthermore, with the recent move toward 100% participation by the producer governments, the multinational companies are becoming purchasers rather than producers of crude in OPEC countries. 42/ If OPEC members, therefore, chose to retaliate for a particular political decision made by a consumer government, they would do so largely only through a reduction or cut-off of supply or an increase in the price. As demonstrated by the 1973 oil embargo, the companies can no longer serve as "buffers" to prevent producer government actions of this type. 43/

There is, nevertheless, one element of the "buffer" theory which probably still has viability. If the United States were to negotiate bilateral supply contracts with the Arab members of OPEC, and perhaps Iran as well, 44/ it would thereby invite those governments to attempt to exact political concessions in our Middle East foreign policy in exchange for a secure supply of petroleum. Accordingly, to the extent that the companies are powerless to alter the established foreign policy of the United States, political considerations may remain detached from the negotiations for access to crude in these areas.

G.   [§9.6]   <u>Possible Utility of Bilateral</u>
             <u>Negotiating Authority</u>

        While government to government transactions gen-
erally have limited utility in dealing with the normal
sources of supply, in certain instances the ability of the
U.S. Government to deal directly with a producer government
regarding petroleum supplies could be advantageous, particularly if selectively used in a tactical sense to counter
particular producer country or company policies. 45/   The
U.S. Government could encourage certain policies of a particular producer government by rewarding it with a substantial and guaranteed share of the U.S. petroleum market.
Consideration should be given to granting the Federal agency
that would have regulatory responsibilities described in
Chapter 6 the power to also enter into short- or long-term
supply contracts where appropriate and consistent with
identified policy objectives. 46/   It could be that the mere
existence of this power would have both a beneficial impact
upon the posture of the companies and the producer governments in making international supply arrangements.   Specifically, this power might be used to negotiate on behalf of
U.S. companies where they are unfairly disadvantaged, or it
could be used to test whether or not company negotiations
are in fact being conducted in a manner consistent with U.S.
interests. 47/   Finally, it would allow the U.S. Government
to avail itself of negotiating targets of opportunity not
available to private companies.   If this power were used
wisely and sparingly by the U.S. Government, it could
produce beneficial results in particular instances.

H.   [§9.7]   <u>"Special Relationships"</u>

        A second objective which is often pursued by means
of bilateral arrangements is the cultivation of "special
relationships" with producers.   A good example of this type
of agreement is the Joint Statement on Cooperation announced
by the United States and Saudi Arabia on June 8, 1974.   The
statement was issued after the visit of Prince Faud of Saudi
Arabia to the United States, and provides that, among other

things, the United States will assist Saudi Arabia in its
economic development programs by joining in the establishment of a Joint Commission on Economic Cooperation.  The
purpose of the Commission "will be to promote programs of
cooperation between the two countries in the fields of industrialization, trade, manpower training, agriculture,
and science and technology." 48/  Another Joint Commission
was established to survey and make recommendations regarding
the modernization of the Saudi Arabian armed forces.  In
general, "It was agreed that Saudi Arabia and the United
States will continue to consult closely on all matters of
mutual interest." 49/

        The United States has consistently criticized
the concept of bilateral arrangements aimed at securing a
specific quantity of petroleum from a particular producer
government.  As U.S. Government spokesmen have testified,
the United States continues "to question the advisability
and viability of bilateral arrangements to tie up specified
amounts of oil in exchange for specific goods and projects . . .  These will tend to sustain higher prices." 50/

        Accordingly, the question arises whether the
United States' recent arrangement with Saudi Arabia is not
somewhat inconsistent with its declared policy opposing
bilateral supply agreements.  Throughout the course of
discussions with the Saudis, however, the United States
denied that its motives were to obtain specific supply
commitments:

            "We are not engaged in discussions with
            the Saudis to gain a preferred position
            with respect to the purchase of Saudi
            Arabian oil . . . The United States
            will continue to press for multilateral
            solutions to the world petroleum prob-
            lem." 51/

        These assertions seem basically accurate.  This
type of arrangement is not in reality an agreement but
simply a means of establishing or maintaining relations
between producer and consumer countries that will present
economic benefits to both.  To the consumer country it
affords an opportunity to support production and supply
practices of the producer country which it deems beneficial,

and also to redress balance of payments problems through the sale of goods and services to the producer country. In addition, to the extent that these elements create stability in the area involved and bring about a more thorough under-- standing of common issues and problems, such factors also contribute to the national security of the United States. 52/

Such arrangements provide to the producer country, equally, an opportunity to maintain contacts with important consumer governments and acquire goods and services, particularly military equipment, on advantageous terms. 53/ Thus, while this type of arrangement typically does not deal directly with petroleum supply, it nevertheless may have a very positive impact upon a number of issues relevant to producer-consumer country relations, including petroleum supply. Such arrangements could not be expected, however, to have any beneficial effect upon the Middle East political situation. 54/

A similar philosophy seems to lie behind the recent U.S.-U.S.S.R. Agreement on Cooperation in the Field of Energy. This agreement, signed on June 28, 1974, establishes a formal "umbrella" under which the two countries can conduct and expand their scientific and technical cooperation on energy matters. Specifically, the agreement provides for joint scientific and technological research and development programs and projects relating to the more efficient use of energy and the development of alternative energy sources, the exchange of relevant information and the establishment of a Joint Committee on Energy. This arrangement, while termed an "agreement," is again purely voluntary, serving only as the future basis for purely cooperative action. 55/ Again, however, it could have a positive overall impact on basic energy matters. A number of U.S. companies have shown interest in Soviet oil and gas projects and have met with a favorable response from Soviet officials. In constituting part of the detente in which the United States and the Soviet Union are engaged, the agreement furthers the U.S. policy objective of national security. 56/

The United States has also recently attempted to develop a "special relationship" with Iran. In November of 1974, Secretary of State Kissinger visited Iran in an effort to strengthen the ties between the two countries and foster more "friendly relations." 57/ At the conclusion of Secretary Kissinger's visit, it was announced that agreement had been reached on the formation of a U.S.-Iran Joint Commission, "designed to increase and intensify the ties of cooperation that already exist between the two countries." 58/ In its first meeting, the Joint Commission mapped out a program of political, economic, cultural, defense, scientific and technological cooperation. Joint working groups are to be formed to further the work of the Commission and utilize the assistance of governmental and private institutions.

The Joint Commission will promote cooperation and joint ventures in such areas as agriculture, petrochemicals, electronics, telecommunications, education and social services. An important element of cooperation will be in the field of nuclear energy and especially power generation. To this end, the United States has contracted to supply enriched fuel for two nuclear reactors, with more contracts expected to be signed in the near future. 59/

Other consumer countries have also sought to develop "special relationships" with producer governments. For the past few years, the Germans and Iranians have discussed improving economic ties between the two countries and have apparently created a rather informal joint economic commission. As a result of this new relationship, a host of German companies have now signed "letters of understanding" with the Iranians for petroleum and other industrial projects, involving a total investment of over $2.2 billion. 60/ Similarly, in June 1974 the French and Iranians signed a ten-year, $4-$5 billion development agreement. While this accord will improve France's balance of payment position, it also constitutes a major step for the French in developing a "special relationship" with the Iranians. 61/

In general, the "special relationship" type of arrangement appears to be more a part of the process of maintaining viable relations between producer and consumer countries. While it does have the result of emphasizing the goods and services of the consumer country in the context of the producer country's purchasing ability, such

arrangements do not appear to encourage unhealthy competition among consumer nations. 62/ They are quite low cost
and can result in considerable benefits to both producer and
consumer nations. It is likely that this type of arrangement will be intricately involved in the more broadly based
consumer-producer negotiations discussed in Chapter 11.

I. [§9.8] The Easing of Balance of Payments Problems

A third objective which may be accomplished through
bilateral arrangements with producers is relief from the
severe impact which current petroleum prices have had on many
consuming nations' balance of payments. Recent price increases have quadrupled what consumers must now pay for
imported petroleum, and for many of them with a high dependence upon imported energy, the effect has been a flow of
billions of dollars into the treasuries of producer countries. With their foreign exchange assets badly depleted,
many consuming countries have turned to bilateral agreements
as a way of stimulating the purchase of their goods by producers and thus retrieving petrodollars which will be needed
to pay future oil bills. 63/

The June, 1974 French agreement with Iran is a good
example. Pursuant to this agreement, the Iranians will purchase from France an assortment of technological goods and
services, including five nuclear reactors, having a total
value of $4-$5 billion. In partial payment of the purchase
price, Iran has agreed to make an advance deposit of $1
billion into the Bank of France. This arrangement will
provide badly needed hard currency for France's acute balance
of payments situation. The agreement does not guarantee
France any specific supply of crude, but it does state that
France will be given "consideration" if additional crude
supplies become available to the Iranian Government. 64/
In this respect, the agreement reflects the reality that,
in today's situation of excess capacity, the problem is
not securing supplies but getting the hard currency to pay
for them.

In another bilateral agreement aimed at alleviating
balance of payments problems, France has recently contracted
with Saudi Arabia to sell $800 million worth of military
equipment. It has now become apparent, however, that substantial purchases by the Saudis of U.S. arms and other
goods and services will come out of the U.S. special relationship. 65/

While these agreements respond to the desire of consuming nations to sell their goods and obtain hard currency needed to pay oil bills, there is a danger that as the impact of high prices on these nations intensifies, there will be increasing competition among them to sell their goods and services. In this respect they are quite different from the "special relationship" type of arrangement discussed above. Bilateral arrangements aimed at rectifying balance of payments problems have a divisive potential for encouraging the sort of "beggar thy neighbor" policies among consumers which could prove to be costly to all. 66/ Nevertheless, this type of bilateral agreement is not to be presumptively disfavored. Some have provided remedy for temporary balance of payments problems. In the long term, however, another solution must be found--either in lower prices or through a mechanism for recycling--or the pressure toward an unacceptable kind of competition among consumers will mount. 67/

J.   [§9.9]   The Desire of Producers to Deal Bilaterally

A fourth and as yet theoretical reason for entering into bilateral agreements would be a situation in which one or more producing governments indicated a strong preference for dealing directly with consumer governments, rather than with private companies. Such a preference might arise from an ideological distaste of private enterprise or, more likely, a desire to deal with purchasers who can pay for petroleum in arms or other goods and services which cannot readily be provided by petroleum companies. Some countries, such as Iraq and Venezuela, have indicated such a preference for direct deals, but in no case has the preference become so strong as to approach a blanket refusal to deal with companies. 68/ This being so, there is no reason for consuming nations to pursue such arrangements in the absence of other advantages.

K.   [§9.10]   Conclusions

There are, then, three basic objectives which may be sought by use of bilateral arrangements with producer countries: (1) greater security of supply, (2) development of "special relationships," and (3) improvement of the consuming nations' balance of payments.

A review of past and current bilateral agreements
indicates that they may not be any more secure than agreements entered into by private companies. 69/ While consumer
governments may have a degree of economic and political
leverage not possessed by the companies, recent history
seems to demonstrate that producer governments have few
qualms about unilaterally altering the terms of their
agreements with them. Further, the terms of bilateral
agreements used to secure a particular supply of petroleum
are generally less advantageous than those customarily made
by the companies, except in the instance in which a special
or long-standing relationship enables the consumer government to obtain a preferential price.

Bilateral arrangements which establish "special
relationships" between producer and consumer countries and
which do not contain substantive provisions regarding supply,
price or specified monetary considerations appear to achieve
worthwhile purposes and should probably be encouraged. The
working relationships which are sometimes created in this
type of arrangement could be very useful in assisting in
the elimination of the confrontation which today exists
between producers and consumers.

CHAPTER 9

FOOTNOTES

1. See Dr. A. H. Taher, "Challenges and Opportunities For National Oil Companies," <u>Middle East Economic Survey</u>, May 3, 1974 at (i).

2. This was particularly the case with countries such as Japan which at the time of the 1973 embargo depended upon Arab oil for over 40% of its import requirements of 4 million daily barrels. See generally <u>Petroleum Intelligence Weekly</u>, Nov. 12, 1973 at 6-7. As of August 1973, 99% of Japan's petroleum was imported. Furthermore, it was estimated that by 1975, 75% of Japan's energy needs would be met by oil. See <u>Energy Demands and Resources of Japan, Volume II</u>, Defense Advanced Research Projects Agency, Aug. 1973 at Appendix C, C-1.

3. "Stronger Oil Tie With Iraq Is Sought By France," <u>Petroleum Intelligence Weekly</u>, Aug. 19, 1974 at 7. For text of original agreement, see <u>Middle East Economic Survey</u>, June 30, 1972 at 1.

4. "Italy Seen Activating Its Oil Barter Deal With Iraq," <u>Petroleum Intelligence Weekly</u>, Feb. 12, 1973 at 1.

5. "West Germany to Buy 73 Million bbl. of Iranian Crude," <u>The Oil and Gas Journal</u>, Mar. 20, 1972 at 41.

6. <u>Ibid</u>.

7. "State-To-State Oil Pacts Set By Japan and Indonesia," <u>Petroleum Intelligence Weekly</u>, May 22, 1972 at 3.

8. This information was confirmed in an interview conducted by the Study Contractor with high-level Indonesian officials. He indicated that Indonesia's policy has been to attempt to separate the management of petroleum from politics and that the agreement with Japan constituted a deviation of this policy, attributable to the fact that at the time Indonesia needed the credit extended by the Japanese.

9. "India and Iraq Forging Long-Term Deals on Oil," <u>Petroleum Intelligence Weekly</u>, Apr. 16, 1973 at 4.

10. "State-To-State Crude Deals Aren't Cheap Now, India Learns," _Petroleum Intelligence Weekly_, May 28, 1973 at 4.

11. Interviews by Study Contractor with representatives of industrial groups and the Government of Japan. There is a universal recognition in Japan of the competence and need for the large multinational oil companies, and of the limitations of their own ability to establish independent access upstream.

12. See note 7, _supra_; note 10, _supra_; note 25, _infra_; M. Adelman, "Is the Oil Shortage Real?," _Foreign Policy_, Winter 1972-1973, at 96.

13. See _Petroleum Intelligence Weekly_, note 7, _supra_. In general, due to low interest loans and cash advances, the exact cost to Japan of the Indonesian petroleum is unclear. Furthermore, the Japanese have committed themselves to purchase for ten years, and therefore, may have locked themselves into high prices for this period of time.

14. "Bilateral Deals: Everybody's Doing It," _Middle East Economic Survey_, Jan. 18, 1974 at 1.

15. "Libya and Italy Cement Ties With Two New Oil Pacts," _Petroleum Intelligence Weekly_, Mar. 4, 1974 at 5.

16. _Ibid_.

17. "Italy Joins European Pilgrimage to Saudi Arabia," _Petroleum Intelligence Weekly_, Feb. 11, 1974 at 5.

18. "Iran Looks Anew At European Market--This Time With ENI," _Petroleum Intelligence Weekly_, Aug. 26, 1974 at 5-6.

19. _Ibid_. See also "Deal May Give Iran a Share in 1,900 Shell Gas Stations in U.S.," _Los Angeles Times_, Nov. 28, 1974 at 1. See §6.0, _supra_.

20. _Middle East Economic Survey_, note 14, _supra_.

21. "Bilateral Oil Pacts Aren't Escalating Crude Prices So Far," _Petroleum Intelligence Weekly_, Feb. 4, 1974 at 9.

22. _Ibid_.

23. "Iran Oil Barter Deal Not So Great For Britain Right Now," _Petroleum Intelligence Weekly_, Aug. 19, 1974 at 3; United Kingdom interviews by Study Contractor.

24. The policy of the French has been to turn increasingly to bilateral supply agreements as an alternative to depending upon the multinational oil corporations. For the full text of the remarks of French Minister of Foreign Affairs, Michel Jobert, at the Washington Conference, at which he emphasized this point, see _Petroleum Intelligence Weekly_, Feb. 18, 1974 at 3-6.

25. "France Wants to See Political Ties Yield Lower Oil Prices," _Petroleum Intelligence Weekly_, Mar. 18, 1974 at 3.

26. "Arms For Oil Deal Between France and Abu Dhabi," _Middle East Economic Survey_, Jan. 4, 1974 at 4.

27. "Consumers Scramble For Mideast Oil," _The Oil and Gas Journal_, Jan. 21, 1974 at 42.

28. "France Getting More Algerian Crude at 'Preferential' Prices," _Petroleum Intelligence Weekly_, Dec. 9, 1974 at 5.

29. _Ibid_.

30. "Soviet-French Deal Shows Europe May Pay More For Gas," _Petroleum Intelligence Weekly_, Dec. 16, 1974 at 9.

31. For the text of the final communique issued after the Washington Conference, and other documents relating to it, see _Middle East Economic Survey_, Feb. 15, 1974 at (i).

32. "Excerpts from Washington Energy Conference, Feb. 11-13," _Petroleum Intelligence Weekly_, Feb. 18, 1974 at 4.

33. _Id_. at 6-7.

34. "French Premier Sees 'No Other Way' But State-To-State Deals," _Petroleum Intelligence Weekly_, Jan. 21, 1974 at 5.

35. Since price is sometimes not disclosed by the countries involved in bilateral supply agreements, and because varying elements of additional consideration, such as advance credits and low-interest loans are frequently involved, these arrangements have not generally set adverse precedents regarding the price of petroleum. They instead tend to reflect the particular needs of the individual consumer and producer country.

36. See note 20, _supra_, note 25, _supra_; M. Adelman, _supra_ note 12, at 96.

37. See L. Mosley, _Power Play, Oil in the Middle East_ 374, 399 (1973).

38. See generally Statement of Secretary of State Kissinger regarding U.S. Middle East policy, at press conference in Washington, Nov. 21, 1974; _Middle East Economic Survey_, Nov. 23, 1974 at 8-11. (Secretary Kissinger indicated that the U.S. would not allow itself to be "pressured" into changing its Middle East policy by Arab oil producers.)

39. A number of petroleum company executives acknowledged in interviews that the companies cannot presently perform the role of "buffers" as effectively as in the past. But most, nevertheless, contended that the companies continue to operate to a significant degree as "political buffers" and that the resolution of the Arab-Israeli conflict would do much to enhance their ability to serve as "buffers."

40. See §1.5.

41. See L. Mosley, _Power Play, Oil in the Middle East_, 374, 391 (1973).

42. See generally "Saudis and Aramco Agree on Principles For Takeover," _Petroleum Intelligence Weekly_, Dec. 9, 1974 at 1.

43. The companies can continue, however, to effectively and evenhandedly distribute available supplies during an embargo. For an excellent discussion of the skillful administration of the 1973 embargo by the major oil companies, see Subcommittee on Multi-national Corporations of the Senate Foreign Relations Committee, U.S. Oil Companies and the Arab Oil Embargo: The International Allocation of Constricted Supplies (Comm. Print Jan. 1975).

44. "Shah Warns Next War 'Will Be Our War'," Middle East Economic Survey, Dec. 13, 1974 at 2.

45. See generally M. Adelman, supra note 12, at 69. Prof. Adelman argues that the preferential position of the major oil companies in various producer governments actually makes them hostages of such governments. If the U.S. Government were to directly purchase crude, however, it would theoretically be more able to select the country from which it wished to purchase crude, and could thereby stimulate com-petition among producers.

46. These policy objectives would include most of those listed in Chapter 2, particularly, security of supply, reasonable price and the maintenance of viable foreign relations.

47. These are more limited objectives than those which might be accomplished by the U.S. Government be-coming the sole importer of petroleum. See §5.4.

48. "Text of Joint Statement on Cooperation, June 8," The Department of State Bulletin, July 1, 1974 at 10.

49. Ibid. at 11.

50. "U.S.-Saudi Agreement Seen Good Omen For Oil," The Oil and Gas Journal, Apr. 15, 1974 at 45.

51. Ibid.

52. See §2.3.

53. "U.S. Financial Institutions Swarm into Mideast," New York Times, Dec. 20, 1974 at 55.

315.

54. For instance, the Saudis have repeatedly expressed their sympathy and cooperation with the Arab cause and it is to be expected that such attitude will continue despite any "special relationship" with the United States. As King Faisal of Saudi Arabia has stated: "If and when a just and peaceful settlement has been achieved, a settlement that will guarantee the Arabs their rights and sanctuaries in their lands and the Palestinians their natural rights, then the Saudi-American relationships in particular would improve as well as those of the Arabs with America in genral." Time, Jan. 6, 1975 at 27.

55. "Joint U.S.-Soviet Communique," The Department of State Bulletin, July 29, 1974 at 185.

56. See §2.3.

57. "Joint Communique Issued at the Conclusion of the Visit to Iran," The Department of State Bulletin, Nov. 25, 1974 at 729.

58. Id. at 730.

59. Ibid.

60. "Germany Moves Toward More Direct State Role in Oil," Petroleum Intelligence Weekly, May 13, 1974 at 2.

51. "France and Iran Sign $4-Billion Accord; Shah Will Receive Five Nuclear Reactors," New York Times, June 28, 1974 at 1.

62. See The Oil and Gas Journal, supra note 50, at 45. The U.S. contends that its "special relationship" with Saudi Arabia gives them "solid incentives . . . to produce at levels consistent with the world's economic well-being."

63. This has one of the express motivations of the French in concluding recent sales to Middle Eastern countries, especially Iran (see note 61, supra) and Saudi Arabia (see note 65, infra).

64. "Iran Skirts Promise to France on Crude But Gas Role Looms," Petroleum Intelligence Weekly, July 1, 1974 at 3.

65. See "French Sell Saudi Arabia $800 Million in Weapons," New York Times, Dec. 5, 1974 at 1.

66. See Senate Committee on Interior and Insular Affairs, Implications of Recent Organization of Petroleum Exporting Countries (OPEC) Oil Price Increases, 34 (Comm. Print 1974).

67. See generally "Excerpts of Ford's Warning to Oil Producers," Petroleum Intelligence Weekly, Sept. 30, 1974 at 9.

68. In interviews conducted by the Study Contractor, U.S. petroleum company officials in Venezuela indicated that the Venezuelans have at times indicated a preference for dealing directly with U.S. Government petroleum corporations. Interviewees in France indicated that the Iraqi Government has expressed the desire to negotiate supply contracts directly with consumer governments rather than private oil companies.

69. See N. H. Jacoby, Multinational Oil, 96 (1973). Jacoby gives a brief description of the most significant expropriations of oil company properties, many of which were levelled against wholly or partially government-owned companies.

CHAPTER 10

ESTABLISHMENT OF AN INTERNATIONAL ORGANIZATION
TO COORDINATE NATIONAL PETROLEUM POLICY
WITH OTHER IMPORTING COUNTRIES

A.    [§10.0]   Introduction

        Secretary of State Kissinger pointed out in 1974
that there then existed no international framework within
which comprehensive long-range decisions could be taken to
cope with the severe problems created by the new developments
in the international petroleum market. 1/  The Ford Administration is strongly committed to promoting an international
organization within which to coordinate our national energy
policies with those of other petroleum importing countries.
This commitment has already borne fruit and both the Congress
and the President now and in years to come will continuously
face important decisions about the form and the extent of that
coordination. 2/  The important petroleum-related issues can
no longer adequately be dealt with unilaterally by one nation.

        After World War II, U.S. foreign policy gave high
priority to creating an Atlantic alliance to promote the
reconstruction of Europe and to insure its military security.
U.S. policy recognized international interdependence after
World War II in both a military context expressed for instance
in the concept of "mutual security," 3/ and the economic
interpendence evidenced by the Marshall Plan. 4/  The economic
interdependence has now become much more complex and important.
The United States must, therefore, coordinate its national
energy policies with those oil importing countries whose
well-being and stability are most closely interdependent
with its own.  These countries are essentially the countries
of the Atlantic alliance and Japan.  The petroleum issue has
risen to the highest priority of foreign policy decisions
here and elsewhere. 5/

        Probably the most important international forum
in which the United States has attempted in the past to deal
with international issues in relation to petroleum is the
Organization for Economic Cooperation and Development ("OECD"),
headquartered in Paris. 6/  Its 23 members are:  Australia,

Austria, Belgium, Canada, Denmark, Finland, France, the
Federal Republic of Germany, Greece, Iceland, Ireland,
Italy, Japan, Luxembourg, the Netherlands, Norway, Portugal,
Spain, Sweden, Switzerland, Turkey, the United Kingdom and
the United States.

The OECD has long been active in the study and
multilateral consideration of energy problems. This work
has been done primarily through various energy-related
committees within OECD: the Oil Committee, the Energy
Committee, the Environment Committee, the Committee for
Scientific and Technological Policy and the Nuclear Energy
Agency. 7/ The Oil Committee regularly keeps the oil policies
of member countries under review and studies supply and
demand prospects for the OECD areas. It is also responsible
for the regular monitoring of the OECD Stockpiling program,
originally set up as a consequence of the 1956 Suez crisis.
Because of major disagreements among leading members, however,
and the unanimity rule of the OECD's governing Council, the
OECD did not adopt internationally coordinated oil policies
in response to the 1973-74 oil embargo. 8/

The U.S. therefore, promoted negotiations among a
smaller group (the Energy Coordinating Group, "ECG") beginning
in February, 1974, looking toward the establishment of a
permanent or ad hoc organization to coordinate the national
petroleum policies of as many important petroleum importing
countries as possible. Ultimately, plans for a new organization, the International Energy Agency ("IEA") were adopted
in Brussels on September 21, 1974, by representatives of 12
nations which consume approximately 80% of the world's petroleum supply: the United States, Japan, Canada, the United
Kingdom, the Federal Republic of Germany, Belgium, the
Netherlands, Luxembourg, Italy, Ireland, Denmark, and Norway. 9/

Support for the IEA and the Agreement which created
it is an important element of our national energy policy.
Given the IEA, it may be anticipated that any broader group
or organization would concern itself primarily with the
problems of the less developed countries, and whatever
policies were formed or implemented would have relatively
little impact either on the world oil market or the international economy of the industrialized nations. 10/ The
Brussels plan, entitled "Agreement on an International
Energy Program," applied provisionally to all signatories

as of November 18, 1974, and is slated to come into final force upon acceptance, on or before May 1, 1975, by six nations, accounting for at least 60% of the weighted votes. By November 18, it appeared that of the 12 original members of the ECG, only Norway would not sign the Agreement. Presently, 16 nations have become provisional members: all of the other ECG nations, together with Spain, Sweden, Switzerland, Turkey and Austria. 11/

The Agreement provides a mechanism by which the participating countries can spread among themselves the burden of a shortfall in supplies affecting an individual nation which is selectively embargoed or subjected to any temporary supply interruption. The plan provides that whenever any signatory country has its base period total petroleum and product supplies reduced by more than seven percent, oil sharing measures will automatically come into operation. The affected country would receive an allocation right equal to the reduction of total energy consumption in excess of seven percent, and the deficiency would be made up by other countries proportionate to their respective consumption levels. Each nation is required to maintain a 60-day (to be increased to 90 day) supply of petroleum reserves and to have a plan for reducing its oil consumption in the event of a supply emergency. Each participating country is further required to prepare and have ready "at all times" a program of "contingent oil demand restraining measures" enabling it to reduce consumption by an amount equal to seven percent of its consumption over the latest reported four quarters. 12/

Besides the oil emergency provisions of the Agreement, there are others designed to promote the international coordination of long-term energy policies to reduce dependence on imported oil. 13/ A Standing Group on Long Term Cooperation, one of four such standing groups, has been created and is required to report to the Management Committee on possible cooperative actions in four major areas: conservation of energy; development of alternative sources of energy; energy research and development; and uranium enrichment. The Management Committee, in turn, will review these reports and recommend proposals to the Governing Board, which must decide on these proposals by July 1, 1975. The Agreement is for a term of ten years and thereafter until a majority of the IEA Governing Board agrees on its termination. Any country may terminate its participation upon one year's notice.

The highest decision-making body within the IEA is
the Governing Board, which consists of ministerial-level
delegates from each country. Below it is the Management
Committee composed of one or more senior representatives
from each country. Besides the above-mentioned Standing
Group on Long Term Cooperation, there are standing groups on
Emergency Questions, the Oil Market, and Relations with
Producer and Other Consumer Countries. Various functions
are assigned to these groups in their respective areas, and
further subjects may be delegated to them by the Governing
Board. 14/

Decisions are made by vote of members according to
a weighted voting scheme under which each country receives
three "general votes" plus a share of 100 "oil votes" weighted
according to the country's oil consumption. The United
States under this system has about one-third of the total
votes, assuming membership of only the 16 present provisional
members. 15/

The creators of the IEA thus attempted to achieve
administrative independence from the OECD's formal decision-
making structure, while at the same time retaining the
logistical and political advantages of being in a larger
sense part of the OECD, making use of its facilities and
sharing in its international political stature.

The most important nonparticipant in the Agreement
is France. France may feel reasonably confident, in light
of past experience, that it will not be the direct target of
another selective embargo occasioned by a Middle East crisis.
France has also shown an interest and ability in obtaining
independent supply commitments through bilateral agreements
with producing countries. 16/ France, however, is more oil
import dependent than either West Germany or Britain and is
very vulnerable to the impact of high prices. High prices
caused the French to reduce drastically the volume of crude
oil purchases it had hoped to make from the U.S.S.R. in
1974. 17/ France suffered a record trade deficit of more
than 3 billion francs (U.S. $670 million) in July, 1974, and
in September imposed a ceiling on the aggregate payments for
imported oil which will be allowable in 1975. 18/ Consequently,
France has a strong interest in promoting any collective
consumer action that might reduce oil prices or slow their
increase, and its refusal to join the IEA may only reflect

the present Administration's reluctance to divert from the policy of a previous Administration. 19/

There are five major areas in which the U.S. will be called upon, chiefly through the IEA or OECD, to support multilateral policies which reflect the interdependence of the major petroleum-importing nations:

1. The emergency oil sharing plan;

2. Coordinated long-term demand reduction;

3. Coordinated measures to maintain international economic stability;

4. Creation of an international oil market information system; and

5. Coordination of negotiations with oil exporting countries.

B.    [§10.1]   The Emergency Oil Sharing Plan

The oil sharing plan is designed to promote quick decisions by the members on questions arising in an oil emergency.  Once a participating country's supplies have fallen more than seven percent below its average daily rate of consumption, the automatic oil-sharing provisions can be stopped only by a vote of ten countries.  If the Secretariat of the IEA makes a finding that an oil emergency has occurred or is about to occur, the Management Committee and Governing Board are required to meet promptly to devise means of dealing with it.  Various provisions of the Agreement specify actions that must be taken by these bodies within 48 or 72 hours. 20/

One of the problems to emerge in the course of negotiations for the oil sharing plan was that in order for the participating countries to be able to rely on the plan, and for it to be credible to producers, the operation of the oil-sharing measures must be essentially automatic.  This means that the ability to respond flexibly to particular supply interruptions must be sacrificed.  If a sudden supply interruption is merely the signal for the participating countries to begin negotiations on appropriate counter-measures, the plan itself has little or no significance

either to consumers or exporters.  On the other hand, as
some critics of the plan have pointed out, 21/ the automatic
feature of the plan could have the effect of forcing the
parties to the Agreement to support one of their number in a
confrontation with producing countries over an issue of
little or no importance to the rest.  The principal concern
of these critics is American foreign policy in the Middle
East.  While other members may have no stake in such U.S.
policy, they at least may derive some security from the oil-
sharing plan.  Austria, Sweden and Switzerland have indicated,
however, that they would withdraw or suspend their participation
if IEA actions should conflict with their "neutrality." 22/
The very existence of the plan, it can be argued, may well
serve the interests of all IEA members by making the results
of an embargo more difficult to predict, and possibly more
costly to some or all of the countries participating in the
embargo.

For the companies, the activation of the oil-
sharing plan could create severe problems.  Producer countries
could order them not to distribute their oil according to
IEA directives, demanding, for instance, a certificate of
final destination for all oil shipments from their ports.
There is also the possibility of a conflict between the
directives of IEA members and those of non-member importing
countries.  In such a situation, the companies could face
loss of production, loss of markets or nationalization of
their assets in either producing or consuming nations.  Accordingly, oil company questionnaire respondents expressed
mixed opinions as to the desirability of such an oil-sharing
plan. 23/  The larger, multinational firms, however, generally
endorsed an internationally sanctioned emergency sharing
plan, as long as they would not be required to pay the extraordinary costs which its implementation might entail.

The emergency oil-sharing plan, besides functioning to assure equal distribution of any shortfall, is also
intended to dampen price increases when a shortage exists or
is threatened.  The plan eliminates the need and the incentive for countries to hoard and bid supplies away from one
another, which behavior in the shortages of 1973-74 aggravated the upward pressure on prices.  Because the plan can
thus mitigate the short-run impact of supply interruptions
on the international financial system as well as on the
balance of payments of individual countries, all members

(and non-members as well) benefit from coordinated allocations. The effect of the plan in time of shortage is very similar to that of a buyers' cartel for most of the world oil market.

C. [§10.2] Coordinated Long-Term Demand Reduction

Demand reduction plans which successfully reduce import dependence of the major consuming countries will reduce the aggregate amount paid for foreign oil by a given country and thereby clearly will help alleviate its international payments problems.

In the long term, however, high prices themselves will depress the demand for oil imports even if the governments of consuming countries do nothing. No international coordination is necessary beyond ordinary international commercial intercourse. One of the most difficult decisions for consumer nation governments, however, is whether intensive demand reduction programs pursued in coordination with those of other consumer nations will put downward pressure on OPEC prices sufficiently to lead to lower unit prices, as well as fewer units consumed. Such intensive demand reduction plans may not always be economically advisable if measured from a purely national perspective. Arguably, once demand has fully adjusted to the higher prices, cutting imports further could cost more in lost production, unemployment and a reduced gross national product than would be saved in foreign payments. 24/ If, however, internationally coordinated intensive demand reduction schemes might weaken the OPEC cartel sufficiently to reduce the price of imported oil, the case for such intensive programs becomes much stronger.

U.S. officials in late 1974 and early 1975 showed considerable uncertainty about the potential price-reducing impact of such intensive demand reduction. 25/ The current trend of opinion, however, has been toward the view that current high price levels will be maintained by OPEC at least for the next several years. 26/ While the extra conservation may possibly have the effect of bringing prices down, too many unknowns exist for anyone to have confidence that internationally coordinated demand reduction can actually achieve such a result.

The recently published OECD report, Energy Prospects to 1985, 27/ provides some estimates of the magnitude of the demand reduction which such intensive government policies would yield. The report indicates that in 1972, OECD countries imported about 25 million barrels per day. By 1980, the impact of current high prices alone will drive imports down to about 22 million barrels per day. With further intensive, internationally coordinated demand reduction policies, imports would be cut to about 18.3 million barrels per day in 1980. Thus, in the case of intensive demand reduction, OPEC would have to absorb a cut of about 6.7 million barrels per day rather than 3 million. Existing OPEC members could easily absorb a 3 million barrel-per-day cut. 28/ 6.7 million barrels per day might, however, be sufficient to weaken substantially or destroy the cartel power of OPEC, depending on such unknowns as the extent of newly discovered reserves and growth in demand outside the OECD areas. 29/ This possibility alone, however, would probably not justify the necessary conservation efforts.

Thus, the important benefit of coordinated demand reduction will be its impact on the financial well-being of each consuming country and indirectly therefore on the economic well-being of all. Government-backed demand reduction is chiefly important in hastening the reduction in demand for imported oil to levels reasonable in light of its current high price.

As a price reducing strategy, then, internationally coordinated reductions in aggregate demand must take second place in importance to the development of reasonably priced substitute energy sources. Internationally coordinated demand reduction is important chiefly as a means of reducing balance of payments deficits before they accumulate to the point of a dramatic international credit crisis. Substantial reductions in demand for OPEC oil, however, sufficient to create significant downward pressure on the price of that oil, are likely only where reasonably priced substitute energy sources are available. Producing countries understand this well. 30/ In this important sense, demand reduction is an integral part of international cooperation to maintain the stability of international trade and credit.

D.   [§10.3]   Coordinated Measures to Maintain Inter-
             national Economic Stability

Measures currently being considered or already
undertaken through the OECD and IEA to maintain international economic stability in the face of the oil-related
payments problems of importing countries bear a very
important relationship to U.S. energy policy.

The first such important measure resulted from
a meeting on May 29-30, 1974, of the Ministerial Council
of the OECD to consider the financial stresses being
caused by high oil prices.  This meeting produced an
agreement that members would avoid taking unilateral
restrictive measures to shift the burden of their balance of payment deficits onto their OECD trading partners. 31/

The OECD and IEA could be very useful as channels
through which to implement multilateral measures for avoiding an international credit crisis.  Recent developments in
this area illustrate the potential utility of these organizations in achieving such U.S.-backed policy objectives.
Secretary of State Kissinger proposed in a speech November 15,
1974, that a common loan and guarantee facility be created
to provide for redistributing up to $25 billion in 1975
and as much in 1976. 32/  The facility would be funded by
contributions from the OECD-area governments.  Secretary
of the Treasury William Simon, in a November 18, 1974
speech remarked that such a fund "should be associated
with the OECD in a manner similar to that of the new
International Energy Agency." 33/

One advantage of such association is that the
international financial assistance the fund renders can
be tied to international efforts to reduce dependence on
imported oil.  Both Simon and Kissinger expressed the
view that access to the fund should be based on an overall judgment of a country's needs taken in conjunction
with its resources, its basic economic policies, and the
actions it is taking to reduce dependence on OPEC oil. 34/
Secretary General Van Lennep described the possible relationship of such a facility to the OECD as follows:

"In relation to the plan presented
by Mr. Kissinger the OECD project opens

327.

various technical possibilities.  Several formulas are possible.  One would consist of creating a fund supplied by the contributions of member states, and this seems to have been the formula envisaged by the U.S. Secretary of State. Another solution would be to entrust to the Bank for International Settlements the task of calling on capital markets, with a collective guarantee given by the OECD countries which participate in the new mechanism.  We are trying to establish a security system to  supplement but not replace existing recycling mechanisms such as the Eurodollar market, bilateral agreements, the IMF, Community loans, etc.  The very fact of its existence should help the market to function." 35/

   Thus the activities of the OECD and IEA in connection with such plans has an indirect but very important relationship to the economic welfare of the U.S. in that it may provide a way of improving the working of such international loan facilities.

   The creation and effective use of such a facility demands extensive international efforts and compromises to resolve complex political issues.  In the case of the U.S. proposal, European leaders feared that accepting the U.S. proposal might increase tension with OPEC nations by seeming to tie them too closely to American policy.  A London newspaper observed editorially:

   "In the nature of things the U.S. would be expected to be the main beneficiary of reverse flows of Arab oil earnings; its correspondingly large role in the facility envisaged by Dr. Kissinger would obviously give it a big say in the channeling of money to other participants, and it is difficult to rule out the idea that Washington might contemplate using its voting power in the Kissinger facility to influence European governments, not merely in terms of their domestic policies, but in the broader

328.

field of foreign policy including that of
the Middle East." 36/

As an alternative to the U.S. plan, Common Market
finance ministers endorsed a plan to loan $10 billion or
more of Arab petrodollars through the International Monetary
Fund, with the IMF itself assuming the risk of non-repay-
ment. 37/ Subsequently, a compromise appeared possible as
European and U.S. officials indicated willingness to allow
the IMF plan to operate while the Kissinger plan provides a
lending safety net for leading industrial countries should
they exhaust their ability to borrow elsewhere. 38/

The benefits to the U.S. of such an arrangement,
though perhaps indirect, are important.  The existence of
these resources helps to assure international creditors and
traders that major countries such as Italy or the United
Kingdom will be able to deal with the financial problems
caused by their high payments for imported oil.

E.    [§10.4]  Creation of an International Oil
               Market Information System

Creation of an information system to improve the
"transparency" of the international oil market is an important
objective of the IEA.  Secretary General Van Lennep remarked
that the long-term objectives of the IEA "are concerned
notably with relations to be established between the states
and the oil companies on the basis of a greater 'transparency.'" 39/  The benefits of such transparency, if achieved,
both to the U.S. and other consumer country governments are
plain.  It would enhance the ability of the Federal Government to monitor developments in the international oil market
with an eye toward the national interest, and also may enhance the ability of the U.S. and other consumer nation
governments to bargain with producer country governments. 40/

Articles 25-43 of the Agreement deal with the
creation of this information system and detail the kinds
of information to be exchanged.  Article 27 calls for
members to make available to the organization the following
information on companies operating within their jurisdiction:

329.

"(a)  Corporate structure;
(b)  Financial structure, including balance sheets, profit and loss accounts, and taxes paid;
(c)  Capital investments realized;
(d)  Terms of arrangements for access to major sources of crude oil;
(e)  Current rates of production and anti-cipated changes therein;
(f)  Allocations of available crude supplies to affiliates and other customers (criteria and realizations);
(g)  Stocks;
(h)  Cost of crude oil and oil products;
(i)  Prices, including transfer prices to affiliates;
(j)  Other subjects, as decided by the Government Board, acting by unanimity."

Article 33 of the Agreement calls for members to make available to the organization information regarding:

"(a)  Consumption and supply;
(b)  Demand restraint measures;
(c)  Levels of emergency supplies;
(d)  Availability and utilization of trans-portation facilities;
(e)  Current and projected levels of inter-national supply and demand; and
(f)  Other subjects as decided by the Governing Board, acting in unanimity."

Information would be gathered through the national authority of the respective members.  In theory, no serious problem need exist with these categories of information.  In practice, it may be doubted whether the U.S. Government now has the capacity to evaluate and monitor the completeness and accuracy of the information provided by the companies in these areas.  Such capacity did not exist during the 1973-74 embargo.  The information gathering functions of the IEA or any similar international organization could, however, create problems in the handling of sensitive proprietary information.  For example, the companies indicated that data on new exploration and reserves, if made public, could harm them competitively, but appear less concerned about data on long-established reserves and downstream operations. 41/

There may be some danger that information of this type would be made available to competitor companies. 42/ On the other hand, possibly more sensitive data on exploration and new reserves appear outside the scope of these categories, and the unanimity rule under (f) above would give the U.S. veto power over any possible information "fishing expedition" aimed at U.S. companies. It must be acknowledged, however, that any data so exchanged could not be expected to remain unavailable to foreign competitor companies and might also be used by foreign consumer countries to regulate the companies' operations there.

The IEA has made it clear that there will be extensive and continuing consultation and cooperation with the oil companies. Thus, industry working groups have recently met in both London (under BP) and New York (under Exxon) to make recommendations on data collection requirements. 43/ The emergency sharing plan equally envisages a close working relationship between IEA and the oil companies. In addition, Article 37 of the Agreement requires that the IEA Standing Group on the Oil Market establish "a permanent framework for consultation" with the industry.

F.  [§10.5]  Coordination of Negotiations with Oil Exporting Countries

A final area of U.S. petroleum policy which may productively be coordinated through the IEA is the preparation of joint positions with other major consuming nations in preparation for negotiations with producer-country governments.

In December, 1974, the U.S. and French presidents agreed to promote a meeting between oil consumers (including some less developed countries) and producers as rapidly as possible, and also to attempt to work out joint positions among the major consumer countries in advance of the producer-consumer meeting. 44/

At the same time, representatives of IEA members agreed in Paris to coordinate the work of that body with the principles of the accord reached by Presidents Ford and

Giscard d'Estaing. 45/  The IEA agenda was to prepare common positions on conservation and alternate energy development and financial guarantees in order to set the parameters of the possible future degree of dependence with
producer countries on OPEC oil.  After a preliminary conference on procedure and agenda, IEA plans were to prepare
common positions among the members. 46/  In this manner,
"low profile" technical work and preparatory negotiations
within the IEA may allow France to remain outside the
organization without destroying consumer nation negotiating
solidarity in important areas.

At a meeting in Algeria in January, 1975, ministers of OPEC nations agreed to participate in an international economic conference along the lines of the French-
U.S. proposal.  There were, however, pressures within that
meeting from Algeria, to denounce the IEA as "a war machine,"
which stands in the way of a cooperative dialogue. 47/

G.    [§10.6]  Conclusion

Several policy areas have been discussed in which
the IEA and related or similar international organizations
may facilitate coordination of U.S. petroleum policy with
other consumer nations.

Strong support for the IEA or any similar organization appears on balance to be a relatively low cost option
with potentially high benefits.  Such benefits are not of
such a nature as to be readily quantifiable, but are
qualitatively important.  From the emergency oil-sharing
plan, the U.S. may derive security against a selective
embargo at a cost of possibly foregoing a share of imported
oil to other countries suffering a temporary interruption
in supplies.  Only in an extreme emergency would the U.S.
actually be called upon to export part of its domestic oil
production. 48/

The coordinated demand reduction and economic
stabilization measures reduce the danger of a breakdown
of the international economic system.  Their cost to the
U.S. is conservation measures that probably would ultimately
be undertaken unilaterally in any event, and of possibly
having to make high-risk emergency loans to other nations.

The oil market information system of the IEA
would help give the U.S. Government monitoring capability
which it probably should acquire in any event, at a cost
of a possible competitive disadvantage to U.S. companies
should sensitive proprietary information become available
to foreign companies.  This risk to the U.S., however, is
probably not proportionately greater than to other major
countries such as Great Britain or West Germany.

Finally, the coordination of consumer nation
policies in preparing for negotiations with the oil exporting countries appears to have been facilitated by the
work of the IEA without impairing the ability of the U.S.
to reach agreement with non-member France on some important
pre-conference issues, and arguably even making such agreement easier to achieve.

Perhaps the most important function of the IEA
is to serve as a public barometer of U.S. commitment to
international cooperation among consumer countries in these
important areas.  Whether the potential benefits of such
international cooperation will accrue to all major consumer
countries depends to a great extent on both actual and
anticipated U.S. policy choices.  While the U.S. cannot
alone guarantee that an organization such as the IEA will
be successful, by not supporting it the U.S. can drastically reduce the incentive for other nations to support
it and thereby virtually assure its failure.

CHAPTER 10

FOOTNOTES

1. 71 Department of State Bulletin 123-124 (Feb. 4, 1974).

2. See remarks of FEA Asst. Administrator Melvin Conant and Dep. Asst. Sec. of State Julius Katz regarding the need for legislation to implement the International Energy Agency programs (discussed below), before the House Foreign Affairs international organizations subcommittee, Dec. 18, 1974, as excerpted in Bureau of National Affairs, Energy Users Report, Dec. 19, 1974, A-26, A-27.

3. "Mutual Security" was the rationale for the creation of the North Atlantic Treaty Organization. Ball, NATO and the European Union Movement, 9-12 (1959).

4. To a lesser extent, the concept of economic interdependence was a rationale for the later creation of the Agency for International Development in 1961. 22 U.S.C. §2151.

5. See also §2.4 this study.

6. For a U.S. description of the arms and purposes of the OECD, see Report of the Senate Committee on Foreign Relations, 107 Cong. Rec. 4150-4152 (1961).

7. OECD, OECD History, Aims and Structure, 1971.

8. Ibid., Appendix, art. 6.

9. Don Cook. "Is International Oil Sharing Plan Too Rigid to Work?" Los Angeles Times, Oct. 3, 1974, pt. III, at 11.

10. This would be particularly true, for instance, of U.N. activities relating to energy.

11. Petroleum Intelligence Weekly, Nov. 11, 1974, 3.

12. Text of the Agreement at Petroleum Intelligence Weekly, Special Supplement, Oct. 14, 1974, arts. 2-5, 7, 9, 10, 11, 17.

13. Ibid., arts. 41-43.

14. Ibid., arts. 49-58.

15. Ibid., art. 62.

16. In the summer of 1974, for instance, such a long-term bilateral arrangement was concluded between France and Iran. The New York Times, June 30, 1974.

17. Petroleum Intelligence Weekly, July 29, 1974, 7.

18. Petroleum Intelligence Weekly, Sept. 30, 1974, 5.

19. The New York Times, July 10, 1974.

20. Agreement (supra, note 12), arts. 19-21.

21. "Is International Oil Sharing Plan Too Rigid to Work?," supra note 9.

22. Petroleum Intelligence Weekly, Nov. 11, 1974, 3.

23. See Appendix C, §C.1. question 22.

24. The Project Independence Report states that a 1 million BPD reduction costs the economy up to $60 billion per year.

25. See §2.3, supra.

26. Remarks of Asst. Sec. of the Treasury Gerald Parsky, Los Angeles Times, Jan. 25, 1974, 4.

27. OECD, Energy Prospects to 1985 (1974), excerpted in Petroleum Intelligence Weekly, Jan. 13, 1975. The figures in the following discussion have been converted from tons per year into barrels per day.

28. See Report to the Senate Committee on Foreign Relations by the Subcommittee on Multinational Corporations, Multinational Oil Corporations at 6-7, 93d Cong., 2nd Sess. (Comm. Print, Jan. 2, 1975).

29. Ibid.

30. See, for instance, Iranian Minister J. Amuzegar, "The Oil Story: Facts, Fiction and Fair Play," 52 Foreign

_Affairs_ 676, 681-684 (July 1974).

31. The importance of this agreement was cited by OECD
    Sec. Gen. E. van Lennep in an interview published in
    _Le Monde_ (Paris) Dec. 10, 1974, excerpted in _Middle
    Eastern Economic Survey_, Dec. 13, 1974, iii-iv.

32. Dept. of State _News Release_ Nov. 14, 1974.

33. 71 _The Department of State Bulletin_ 800 (Dec. 9, 1974).

34. _Ibid._, and _supra_, note 21.

35. Sec. Gen. E. van Lennep, _supra_, note 31.

36. _The Financial Times_ (London), Jan. 7, 1975.

37. _Los Angeles Times_, Jan. 8, 1975, 1.

38. _Los Angeles Times_, Jan. 15, 1975, 1, 15.

39. _Middle Eastern Economic Survey_, Dec. 13, 1974, iii.

40. In June, 1974, for instance, the Common Market Countries
    sent a memorandum to the OPEC meeting in Quito, Ecuador,
    suggesting, among other things, that they might cooperate
    with OPEC in monitoring oil company pricing practices
    to see that the companies "do not abuse their position
    in order to realize profits which would not be justified
    by normal market conditions". _Petroleum Intelligence
    Weekly_, June 24, 1974, 9-10.

41. See Appendix C.

42. Art. 30 of the Agreement provides that procedures be
    worked out to ensure confidentiality of the information.

43. _Platt's Oilgram News Service_, Nov. 26; Dec. 20; Dec. 23,
    1974.

44. _The New York Times_, Dec. 17, 1974, 1.

45. _Petroleum Intelligence Weekly_, Dec. 30, 1974, 3.

46. _Ibid._

47. _Los Angeles Times_, Jan. 27, 1975, 1.

48. Remarks of Julius Katz, Dep. Asst. Sec. of State for economic and business affairs, before the House Foreign Affairs subcommittee on international organizations, Dec. 18, 1974, as reported in Bureau of National Affairs, Energy Users Report, Dec. 19, 1974, A-26, A-27.

CHAPTER 11

ESTABLISHMENT OF MULTILATERAL NEGOTIATIONS
BETWEEN PRODUCING AND CONSUMING COUNTRIES

A.  [§11.0]  Introduction

As noted at the outset, an ongoing state of confrontation between producer and consumer nations exists.
The companies do not act as a political buffer in the
confrontation; they merely serve as linkage.  The situation
is difficult.  Modern trade and the fiscal system have
begun to suffer seriously because of the strains and imbalances placed upon them.  Consuming nations, who for years
had built up an ever-increasing dependence upon imported
petroleum when only a fraction of its present cost, are
now faced with aggregate oil bills to the OPEC nations
in excess of $100 billion per year. 1/  In addition to the
basic transfer of wealth from consuming to producing nations
which these payments affect, they have also had a disturbing
impact upon the world monetary system.  In 1974, OPEC
nations had approximately $60 billion in surplus "petro-
dollars" in need of investment in consuming nations. 2/
By 1980, the accumulated OPEC surpluses may exceed $300
billion. 3/  To date, most of the surplus petrodollars have
been invested in short-term, highly liquid assets such
as bank deposits or the Euro-currency markets. 4/  The
threat which short-term investments of this magnitude
pose to the international monetary system is grave.

In an effort to recycle petrodollars and to
offset balance of trade deficits many consumer countries
which are not an attractive opportunity for foreign investment have been forced into massive borrowing, reborrowing
and an export race which do little more than keep them just
ahead of the juggernaut.  The more affluent of the consumer
countries are attractive sources of investment for petrodollars and do not have severe balance of payment problems. 5/
Their resources, too, are being taxed, however, because of
their efforts to assist the weaker of the consumer nations
in providing sufficient resources for them to purchase adequate petroleum supplies.  They are thus confronted with the
dilemma of being asked to loan increasingly greater funds to
countries which are increasingly less able to repay them.

In almost all consuming nations, the effect of
this financial flow has been to seriously slow economic
activity, deplete foreign exchange reserves and increase
government borrowing. If future oil bills are to be paid,
substantial additional loans will have to be made to many
nations or a fundamental economic realignment in the world
must occur. The foreign exchange to make such loans is
available in the massive surplus petrodollars flowing back
into consuming nations. Unfortunately, the investment
dollars flow to consuming nations according to their attractiveness as sellers of manufactured goods and investments. Thus the United States will receive a much greater
percentage of the petrodollars than nations, such as Italy,
which are not as attractive for investments and which
cannot compete in sales. 6/ The problem, then, is to recycle the money flowing to the United States and other
investment centers back to the needy consuming countries.
More important yet, these petrodollars must eventually be
channeled to longer term and more stable investments.

The International Monetary Fund ("IMF") and some
of the more affluent consuming nations have already taken
steps to channel currency into the more hard-hit consuming
nations. The amounts which will have to be paid over the
next five years are astronomical, however, and there is a
growing awareness that the nations to which these loans will
be made available are unlikely ever to repay them. Recycling,
then, becomes another word for foreign aid on a scale so
massive that only one or two of the consuming nations can
even begin to bear the burden, assuming that they have the
political will to do so. Therefore a special "financial
safety net" has been tentatively planned among the OECD
nations, to be initially funded with $25 billion. 7/ In
spite of these measures a growing number of observers are
coming to the belief that consumer nations will not have the
resources available to solve these problems without the
cooperation of the key producer nations, particularly Saudi
Arabia, in either lowering prices or making other financial
arrangements. 8/

There is a real danger of a financial breakdown on
an international scale, and the U.S. has to date been unable
to unilaterally deal effectively with this situation. The
assertions by high ranking U.S. officials that prices will
fall have only succeeded in lulling many consumers into

believing that the problem will disappear or be minimized in due course. 9/ A year of intensive interaction and repeated visits by cabinet-level American officials to Saudi Arabia, in the attempt to use that country to influence OPEC pricing, has yet to bear fruit. Various plans, sponsored by the United States and other consuming nations, to ease the fiscal impact of high prices upon the less affluent consuming nations have all been attempts to live with the problem rather than solve it. 10/

The solution requires the cooperation of producing nations, yet these nations have not only shown little interest in assisting but have actually continued to aggravate the situation by further increases in price. Nor can we be optimistic that producers will be cooperative with consuming nations in the present atmosphere. For a year, the U.S. Government has sought, totally without success, to push petroleum prices down by every peaceful means available to it. Producers are defensive and view attempts to articulate the consumers' position as intimidation. 11/ This defensiveness has contributed to the unprecedented solidarity of OPEC, and has made it virtually impossible for any individual OPEC member to advocate a reduction in price without risking the appearance, both to its own citizens and to the Third World, of buckling under to U.S. pressure. 12/ There is little doubt that the cooperation of producers is necessary if serious damage to the world economy is to be avoided.

A change in the relationship between producing and consuming nations is needed to permit the development of an atmosphere in which reasonable accommodations for the various needs of these nations can be achieved. A multilateral dialogue, if properly structured, may provide such an arrangement by lowering the visibility of individual participants and presenting issues in a broader context so that a more pragmatic process of adjustment and compromise can be pursued. It cannot be known at present to what extent producing nations will be willing to assist in the solution of the problems plaguing the economies of consuming nations, but it is necessary that a move be made toward a defusing of the situation so that whatever compromise is possible will be forthcoming. As Secretary of State Kissinger recently observed:

"The consumer nations should neither
petition or threaten.  They should be
prepared to discuss the whole range of
issues of interdependence.

"It is this system which is now in
jeopardy and therefore the well-being
of all nations is threatened.  We
must, together in a cooperative spirit,
restore the vitality of the world economy in the interest of all mankind." 13/

The producers likewise have recognized, according to a
January, 1975, OPEC communique, that the current economic
crisis "constitutes a growing threat to world peace and
stability." 14/  Accordingly, OPEC has tentatively accepted
the necessity for a producer-consumer conference to discuss
all "problems of raw materials and development." 15/

In evaluating the ways in which confrontation between producers and consumers can be reduced, due regard
must be given to the Arab-Israeli dispute.  It is becoming
increasingly clear that the successful resolution of this
matter will be a prerequisite to the success of any producer-
consumer dialogue.  The Arab states regard a resolution of
this conflict as a basic element of their foreign policies
and have repeatedly declared their intention to use their
only real sanction, their control over petroleum, as an
instrument for achieving that end. 16/  To assume that the
cooperation of the Arabs can be achieved on such issues as
price levels or recycling when no progress is made on the
Palestinian question is to deny everything which has occurred
in the Middle East since the Yom Kippur War.  This problem
is further complicated by the fact that Iran has indicated
that it may support the Arab position in the event of further
fighting between Israel and the Arab states. 17/  A mutually
acceptable middle ground between the United States' commitment to the continued existence of the Israeli state and the
Arab position on the Palestinians and occupied Arab territory
must be, therefore, found as soon as practicable if any
significant producer country cooperation is to be expected
in the resolution of the dire economic situation developing
in the West.  It should be emphasized, however, that resolution of this difficult issue will not itself guarantee the
success of producer-consumer discussions.

B.    [§11.1]  Consumer Bargaining Leverage

     The major risk for consumers of entering into
negotiations with producers is that they will be able to
capitalize on consumer disunity to obtain the support of
weaker consumers for measures which may be unacceptably
costly to more affluent consumers, such as the U.S.  This
lack of solidarity among consumers has been a major concern
for the United States since the recent embargo. 18/  In an
effort to correct it, the U.S. made a concerted effort to
bring consumers together, beginning at the Washington Energy
Conference and culminating a half a year later in Brussels
with the International Energy Program ("IEP").  Although the
IEP allocation of supply provisions are an important safeguard for the western economy, they still fall short of a
comprehensive agreement among consumers on a number of
issues.  A fundamental difference of opinion among consumers
may exist as to the extent to which the more affluent consuming nations should underwrite the oil deficits of other
consuming nations.  The more affluent consumers would like
to see the major part of that burden fall upon producers,
but there is reason for concern that producers may be able
to enlist the support of the developing and less affluent
consuming nations behind a scheme under which the bulk of
the burden would fall upon the shoulders of the United
States and a few other consumers. 19/

     The second major problem with entering into a
multilateral conference with producers is a basic lack of
bargaining leverage on the part of consumers to secure the
assistance from producing nations which they need.

     Secretary of State Kissinger has been acutely
aware of the potential weakness of the consumer position and
has insisted that steps be taken to improve that position
prior to inaugurating discussions with the producer governments.  The creation of the IEA with its emergency sharing
plan, however, coupled to the recent agreements on recycling
facilities and reduction of consumption, has substantially
improved the consumer position. 20/

     Although there are many strategies which consumers
could pursue to increase their leverage, none of them promises
any immediate relief from the power which producers presently
have as a result of their control over much of the world's

343.

energy.  Consumers can pursue vigorous policies of conservation which may partially mitigate the balance of payments effects of current levels of price.  Such programs,
however, are limited by the substantial cost in terms of
employment and gross national product associated with
reduced energy consumption. 21/  More importantly, however,
as a source of bargaining leverage in negotiations with
producers, conservation has very little short-term utility
since most producing countries can cut back on production
and suffer less economic impact due to the loss of revenues
than consuming nations will feel due to the loss of the
petroleum.  Producers may in fact lose no revenues if they
increase price, as many have done during the past year. 22/

The development of alternative indigenous sources
of energy is another important policy objective and one
which for the United States in the long term will be the
only sure insurance against pressure by producer countries. 23/
In the short term, however, it will be of slight benefit to
consumers in their negotiations.  The lag times involved in
the development of most alternative sources are too long, 24/
in some cases even exceeding the estimated life of a number
of the producers' petroleum reserves.

Nor do consumer nations derive any real leverage
from their status as the predominant source of food, manufactured goods, arms or technological and managerial services.
Most of the major oil exporters do not import large quantities of food and a cartel for manufactured goods is not
practicable.  Even if it were, producers could last much
longer without imports of manufactured goods than consumers
could without petroleum.

Another possible bargaining tool for consumers is
their control over most of the investment opportunities
which producers will increasingly need for revenues received
in excess of their current absorptive capacity.  Surplus
revenues will continue to pile up in Arab producing countries for the foreseeable future.  Even the countries with
high absorptive capacity for internal development, such as
Iran and Venezuela, are experiencing short-term surpluses.
If investment opportunities are not made available to such
producers, they may well reduce production.  Petroleum in the
ground is an available alternative for producers, but its
effects upon consuming nations, who would have to endure the
shortfall in supply, would be severe.

The prospect of massive investment in the U.S. and other consuming economies by foreign governments and companies controlled thereby is an ominous one for some. The economic power created by such investment will not necessarily be exercised solely in accordance with commercial considerations. Nevertheless, realistic governmental regulation should be able to provide transparency and put appropriate limitations upon the use of this economic power. Some even argue that as producers become increasingly involved in the well-being of the western economies, the risk of embargoes and massive price increases will decline. 25/ This point remains to be established.

Producers are concerned that their oil revenues will be eaten up by worldwide inflation, and it could be that agreement to the indexing of petroleum prices with other resources, goods and services would be a concession for which producers might be willing to make a price adjustment. 26/ Consumers, however, are properly apprehensive about indexation of petroleum prices at any, and especially at current, levels. The price is already excessive and to tie it to the price of other commodities and finished goods, many of which require significant usage of energy in processing or manufacturing, would exaggerate the spiral of present world inflation. On the other hand, if indexation is viewed as a vehicle for a process of negotiation, rather than a rigid maintenance of price regardless of other considerations, consumers may be willing to give it more careful consideration. 27/

In the last analysis, it is clear that consuming nations are not in the short run in a strong position vis-a-vis producers whether or not they are involved in broad-based discussions with them. Everything which producing nations want or need, they seem able to coerce from consumers by the use of their ultimate weapon, cutting back exports. With consumer-nation conservation and development of alternative sources, this one-sided situation may be expected to right itself in five or ten years, but in the short term, consumer nations will have difficulty in securing substantial concessions.

The spectre of world depression and its resulting political consequences are possibly the only short-term inhibition on the exercise of OPEC's power. The more unstable of the major consuming nations cannot fail without the great likelihood of touching off a progression which could damage even the strongest. With the anticipation of $60 billion or more each year invested in the assets, securities and currencies of these countries, producers must expect that the injury visited upon these economies will inevitably return to them. The political consequences of economic disintegration should also be of deep concern to producers. The collapse of NATO or the rise of extreme governments in Europe would inevitably affect the stability of the Mediterranean and the Persian Gulf. 28/ The possibility of military confrontation increases with the progressive deterioration of developed consumer-nation economies. 29/

C.    [§11.2]   Organizational Format

Notwithstanding the risks associated with inadequate consumer unity and relative weakness of bargaining position, a multilateral dialogue with producers is still a promising approach to the current political and economic problems facing consuming nations. A promising way to initiate broad scale multilateral talks with producers would be through a "mini-conference" such as that proposed by Sheikh Yamani of Saudi Arabia and French President Giscard D'Estaing. 30/ Such a conference could be small and informal and by bringing together the major influential producer and consumer nations could provide an excellent vehicle for the structuring of the more long-term format for a producer-consumer dialogue. And indeed in late January, 1975, there appeared to be general agreement that such a preparatory meeting would take place. 31/

One possible format for the ongoing producer-consumer dialogue would be a conference under the aegis of the United Nations. As an accepted forum for the discussion of international issues, the United Nations might appear to be the logical place for an issue such as petroleum which affects virtually every country in the world. However, for reasons which have been amply demonstrated recently at the U.N. Special Session on Raw Materials and the Third United Nations Conference on the Law of the Sea, such a forum is not likely to be conducive to a profitable dialogue between producers and consumers. In both the Law of the Sea

Conference and the Raw Materials Session, the large cumbersome mechanism of the United Nations' conferences made little progress on the issues involved. 32/ With the large number of member states, observers and nongovernmental organizations that are typically involved, a U.N. conference has built-in administrative and decision-making problems. Moreover, such large formal conferences tend to be characterized by a great amount of rhetoric and domination by the Third World majority. As was clearly seen at the Third U.N. Law of the Sea Conference, lines were quickly drawn over the major issues and accommodation of conflicting interests was rendered virtually impossible by the extreme and oversimplified positions taken by most nations. Rather than reduce the political visibility, such conferences seem to increase it with the result that individual countries may be forced into more dogmatic positions than their true self-interests might otherwise have indicated. Compromise and accommodation can become virtually impossible not only because of the large numbers and wide diversity of views, but also because of the importance which ideology plays in a more formal setting. Thus it would not appear that the United Nations provides a satisfactory forum for such multilateral talks. 33/

Perhaps the most desirable forum would be an institutionalized one that might sustain the dialogue for many years. It should be multifaceted and capable of accommodating a complex system of subgroups, working committees and bilateral negotiations as well as providing a forum for the multitude of issues which inevitably will arise. It is clear that while OPEC members prize their solidarity highly on petroleum matters, they consider their national interests foremost in trade and development issues. Thus, predictably the discussions will need to take place on bilateral, regional and subregional bases depending upon the interests of states involved. The concurrent negotiation of all of these issues will also create a lower visibility for individual participants and hopefully diminish the confrontation between producers and consumers.

Such a diffuse process is essential if the plethora of interests among and between producers, companies and consumers are all to be adequately addressed. What is needed, then, is not so much a "solution" but a "process" in which the terms of reference are sufficiently numerous and encompassing as to accommodate the various interests involved.

In determining the type of format which will best suit such a process, the General Agreement on Trade and Tariffs ("GATT") presents perhaps a very useful precedent. The GATT is an agreement among 83 countries, conceived in a series of international conferences held between 1946 and 1948. 34/ These conferences intended to create a permanent body known as the International Trade Organization ("ITO") which would have worked to promote international economic cooperation and free trade. The draft of the ITO Charter was completed in August of 1947 and the GATT itself in October of the same year. Disagreement, however, persisted for two years thereafter over the text of the ITO Charter and in December of 1950, the U.S. Government sealed the fate of the ITO Charter by announcing that it would not submit it to Congress for approval. 35/

The drafters of the ITO Charter faced many complex problems, but one central conflict stands out--that between free trade and quantitative restrictions on imports to achieve full employment within a single country. The system of rules within the draft Charter failed to reconcile that conflict, but made the partisans of each side unwilling to be bound by those rules for fear of losing more than they would gain. Thus, ITO was unacceptable to American partisans of free trade and to British partisans of Imperial preference. GATT, which was conceived as purely a provisional arrangement, on the other hand, was less comprehensive. In essence, it incorporated the ITO chapter on "Commercial Policy," but omitted those on "Employment and Economic Activity," "Restrictive Business Practices," and "Intergovernmental Commodity Agreements." 36/ While the GATT text proclaims the central value of free trade, no member is bound to reduce any tariffs, nor to refrain from raising any tariffs, unless and until it binds itself to do so. Finally, non-tariff barriers to trade have remained essentially outside the scope of GATT. This experience points up an important aspect of international organizations: very high political costs are often paid for agreement, even highly qualified agreement, on controversial issues and for an advanced degree of organizational structure, whose costs predictably will present major problems in terms of acceptability. 37/ Another ongoing example exists in the U.N.

Conference on the Law of the Sea. 38/ By the same token the
GATT experience points up the low cost and political acceptability of institutions which require essentially no
relinquishment of sovereignty or even ratification.  Such an
institution by definition is imperfect and subject to
unilateral interpretation.  It is this very quality of
imperfection and ambiguity, however, that suggests this as a
workable precedent in dealing with the many and fragmented
issues which would be presented during producer-consumer
discussions.

Although the ITO never materialized, the GATT has
been fairly effective as a vehicle for the complex negotiation of multilateral tariff reductions.  These negotiations
have occurred in the six "rounds," the most recent of which
was the Kennedy Round during 1964-67.  The rounds provide a
continual process for readjustment and renegotiation of
existing trade barriers by the members of the GATT. 39/  In
addition to this continual process of negotiation, the GATT
includes other functions such as the settlement of individual disputes and grievances. 40/  In a more general
sense, it provides an ongoing dialogue in which the changing
relationships among the different categories of trading
nations can be continually reviewed.

Another advantage of a format like the GATT is
that, within the context of a multilateral discussion,
negotiations and grievances which are essentially of a
bilateral nature can be dealt with.  Any long-range instrument for the resolution of petroleum problems will also have
to be able to accommodate the continuation of bilateral and
regional negotiations reflecting other links among nations
than simply the commonality of being petroleum producers or
consumers.  Such traditional relationships as those between
the U.S. and Saudi Arabia, France and Algeria, as well as
regional forums such as the Euro-Arab dialogue, will continue to play important roles and should properly be integrated into any viable multilateral negotiations. 41/

Price is a very important issue to consumer
nations but it cannot be made the focal point of producer-
consumer discussions.  There are numerous issues including,
among others, access to supply, indexation, recycling of
petrodollars, sanctity of contract and security of supply.

There are also issues which, while not involving petroleum directly, are of concern to producer nations. These issues involve, among others, the availability and prices of manufactured goods and food. The total mass of this web of interrelated issues is so enormous as to defy any single manageable resolution. 42/ The only approach which can be expected to handle problems of this magnitude and complexity is a system which can accommodate the entirety of the issues but "chip off" pieces and find solutions to these in smaller manageable packages. 43/ In accomplishing this, the producer-consumer dialogue can reasonably be expected to continue for a number of "rounds," spanning many years.

A final advantage of this type of format is that the confusion resulting from a large number of nations being brought together to discuss an equally large number of issues has a fortunate side effect in the degree of low political visibility which will be provided for the participants. In the obscure and complex trading off of interests which will generally progress as a joint cooperative effort to achieve common solutions, the identification of conflicts and, accordingly, great concessions or advances will be virtually impossible. With international petroleum as politicized as it is, no concessions will be forthcoming from producing nations unless they can be shown to be part of a more generalized understanding with the industrialized powers.

The resolution of the differences between producers and consumers will probably never be fully accomplished. A changing world will continually create new problems and issues, particularly as we move toward the interrelationships between the various resources of the producer and consumer nations. For this reason the search for a continuing "process," rather than a "solution," offers far greater prospects for stable relationships.

The United Nations through the Economic and Social Council, its Committee on Natural Resources, its Committee on Trade and Development or another associated group might wish to take a broad-based interest in international petroleum supplies. It is also conceivable that a specialized committee or conference on world energy might be organized. It is likely, however, that this type of organization would be largely useful as a forum for this expression of views, particularly by the developing countries. As discussed above, recent experiences in the United Nations point up the very severe limitations which it has in decision-making, particularly when affecting the economic status of developed countries. 44/

D. [§11.3] Conclusion

The critical problem which exists today, then, is the highly visible and sensitive state of confrontation between producing and consuming nations. This atmosphere has resulted in the adoption of simplistic positions and impeded the achievement of any real progress toward accommodation of the varying interests. It has also precluded effective progress toward the resolution of the economic problems created by current high prices which threaten even the more affluent of consuming nations. In their efforts to recycle petrodollars and thereby assist the more hard-pressed of their number, consumers are only buying time.

Achieving a solution is very difficult in light of the disunity among consumers and their relative lack of bargaining leverage, even if fully united. Nevertheless, it will be difficult to find a solution without the participation of producers and, accordingly, a multilateral dialogue should commence. Since the major purpose of the conference would be to institutionalize a producer-consumer dialogue and to reduce visibility through piecemeal consideration of various interrelated issues, the GATT-type format appears to be a promising vehicle.

Although a producer-consumer dialogue will probably not deal directly with the role of the international petroleum companies, it will probably serve, in the words of one U.S. company, "to provide a stable environment," and to reduce "uncertainties about prices and supplies." 45/ At present, both producer and consumer governments are threatening the role of private oil companies in both upsteam and downstream operations. To the extent that a producer-consumer dialogue can restore a more cooperative atmosphere, the valuable and efficient logistical structures of the companies can be retained. In the absence of a dialogue, a feeling of distrust may encourage precipitous action by both producer and consumer governments alike in a competitive scramble to seize control of the international petroleum system. 46/  Such a development would irrationally sacrifice the proven capabilities of the international oil companies to transport, refine and market petroleum efficiently.  In this context, the producer-consumer dialogue would provide an "umbrella" which would preserve the strengths of the existing system.

Any decisions made in producer-consumer discussions would inevitably require implementation with the assistance of U.S. companies.  In fact, if the discussions deal with non-petroleum resources, as they probably will, a wide range of U.S. firms outside the petroleum field might be affected.  Looked at broadly, ultimate producer-consumer cooperation should result in a resource management plan, the elements of which will touch on many facets of all nations.

CHAPTER 11

FOOTNOTES

1. Petroleum Intelligence Weekly, Oct. 21, 1974 at 10.

2. Cong. Rec. S20375 (daily ed. Dec. 3, 1974) (Remarks of Senator Percy).

3. Statement of Thomas O. Enders, Assistant Secretary of State for Economic and Business Affairs, before the Joint Economic Committee (Nov. 29, 1974). See also Los Angeles Times, Nov. 4, 1974 at 1, quoting a World Bank estimate that OPEC reserves will exceed $600 billion by 1980.

4. Note 2, supra.

5. New York Times, Nov. 21, 1974 at 71.

6. Petroleum Intelligence Weekly, Sept. 23, 1974 at 10; New York Times, June 27, 1974 at 65 ("Italians Relying on U.S. Aid in Oil").

7. Statement of Thomas O. Enders, supra note 3, at 11.

8. Walter Levy, "World Oil Cooperation or International Chaos," 52 Foreign Affairs 690 (1974).

9. "Simon: U.S. is not at Mercy of Oil Exporters," Oil and Gas Journal, Nov. 18, 1974 at 35.

10. Petroleum Intelligence Weekly, Supplement, Jan. 13, 1975 at 3; "New Ways to Pay for Oil Imports," Business Week, Sept. 7, 1974 at 22-23.

11. The reactions of producing governments to the "Project Interdependence" speeches of President Ford and Secretary Kissinger is indicative of this atmosphere. "Venezuela, Decrying 'Threats' Calls in U.N. for Oil Dialogue," New York Times, Oct. 9, 1974 at 2; "Shah Rejects Bid by Ford for Cut in Prices of Oil," New York Times, Sept. 27, 1974 at 1 ("No one can dictate to us. No one can wave a finger at us, because we will wave a finger back."); "Arab UN Envoys See Threat in Ford Talk," Los Angeles Times, Sept. 19, 1974 at 12.

12. See §11.3, _infra_.

13. _Los Angeles Times_, Jan. 25, 1975 at 10.

14. _Los Angeles Times_, Jan. 27, 1975 at 1.

15. _Ibid_.

16. "Faisal and Oil: Driving Toward a New World Order," _Time_, Jan. 6, 1975 at 31. See also the remarks of Sheikh Yamani of Saudi Arabia:

> "If there is a circumstance again where we are assured that the Israelis will never withdraw from the occupied territories, and the U.S. will assist the Israelis, as it has in the past, to maintain the occupied territories and to continue their plan of expansion, be assured that what happened in October will happen again." _Middle East Economic Survey_, July 26, 1974 at 1.

17. _Middle East Economic Survey_, Dec. 13, 1974 at 2.

18. Secretary of State, Henry Kissinger recently remarked during an interview:

> "I have always had the most serious doubts that an immediate reduction in oil prices could be achieved because I did not see the incentive for the oil producers to do this in the absence of consumer solidarity. A reduction in energy prices is important. It must be achieved, and we must organize ourselves to bring it about as rapidly as possible. . . . [I]n the absence of consumer solidarity, pressures required to bring oil prices down would create a political crisis of the first magnitude. . . . Economic pressures or incentives . . . take time to organize and cannot be effective without consumer solidarity." He added that "[w]e will not go to a producer-consumer conference without having this program [of consumer unity] well established. If we

don't have consumer solidarity we're better
off conducting bilateral negotiations with
the producers."

See also Henry Kissinger, "The Energy Crisis: Strategy
for Cooperative Action," Dept. of State Bulletin,
Dec. 2, 1974 at 249; Bureau of Public Affairs, Office
of Media Services, The Secretary of State: Interview,
(Reprinted from Business Week, Jan. 13, 1975) at 1.

19.  In a recent interview, supra note 18, Secretary of
     State Kissinger stressed the importance of developing
     sufficient consumer solidarity and institutions of
     financial solidarity "so that individual countries
     are not so obsessed by their sense of impotence that
     they are prepared to negotiate on the producer's terms."

20.  See Chapter 10.

21.  See Chapter 6, note 93, supra.

22.  See Levy, supra note 8, at 710-711.

23.  Secretary of State Kissinger has expressed some serious
     doubts about the ability of OPEC to continue to offset
     declining demand with production cuts:

          "Many producers are dependent on their
          revenues for economic development.
          Countries which can cut production most
          painlessly are those that are simply
          piling up balances.  Countries that need
          oil revenue for their economic develop-
          ment, like Algeria, Iran, and Venezuela
          do not have an unlimited capacity to cut
          their production.  If the production of
          these countries is cut by any significant
          percentage, their whole economic develop-
          ment plan will be in severe jeopardy.
          Therefore the problem of distributing the
          cuts is going to become more and more
          severe. . . .  Other countries will have
          less and less of an economic incentive to cut
          production.  As the number of OPEC
          countries increases and as alternative
          sources come in, I think these cuts will
          grow increasingly difficult to distribute."
          Supra note 18, at 2.

355.

President Ford in his speech before the Ninth World Energy Conference, Sept. 23, 1974, stated that the U.S. "will take tough steps to obtain the degree of self-sufficiency which is necessary to avoid disruption of our economy."

24. See Federal Energy Administration, Project Independence Report, 67-74 (1974). Moreover, apart from the time problems attributable to technological difficulties, there are also institutional delays which are already beginning to take a toll. See BNA Energy Users Report, Nov. 28, 1974, at A3, A10, A18.

25. "Simon Sees Oil-Price Dip," New York Times, July 25, 1974 at 43; "Oil Situation 'Manageable' Advisor to Reserve says," New York Times, June 22, 1974 at 36.

26. See "The Shahanshah's Proposal for a New Oil Pricing System," Los Angeles Times, Nov. 11, 1974 at 17, in which the Shah stated:

> "I think this is the basis of our proposal to link [petroleum prices] later to a basket of prices of say 20 to 30 commodities: if they go up, why should we lose our purchasing power? If they go down, oil should go down also to help the world economy. But what is really interesting to us is to hold our purchasing power intact, because we have been cheated so much in the past that we have got to defend our interest in that sense, that with inflation and erosion of the purchasing power of our money the same old situation is not going to be repeated once more."

27. The French have indicated some willingness to discuss the issue of indexation in their proposal for a 3-sided producer-consumer conference. International Herald Tribune, Oct. 30, 1974 at 1.

28. Producers have now and again acknowledged that a major collapse in the West would be undesirable to them. See, for example, "Shah and Kissinger Hint at Bid to Curb Oil Prices," New York Times, Nov. 13, 1974 at 1 ("If the world collapses, we collapse with it. We are going to collapse with you."); "Shah Offers Oil but Bars U.S. 'Dictation' of Terms," New York Times, Oct. 4, 1974 at 3 ("Our aim is not to destroy the developed world.").

29. Although in very guarded terms, there has recently been an increasing discussion of the possibility of an eventual military confrontation. See, for example, "It's Time to Consider Force Against Arab Oil Nations," Los Angeles Times, Dec. 8, 1974, Part VI, at 3; "Kissinger Sees No Oil Price Cut Soon," Petroleum Intelligence Weekly, Jan. 13, 1975 at 4 ("I am not saying that there is no circumstance where we would not use force."); "What Should U.S. Do About The Oil Cartel," Los Angeles Times, Jan. 26, 1975, Part V, at 3 (Angelo Codevilla: "If economic warfare does not work, the United States should be ready to attack and seize the most productive oil fields in the world." Charles L. Schultze: "Higher oil prices alone . . . pose problems which nowhere appear so drastic or insoluble as to warrant a military solution.").

30. "France Backs Saudi Producer-Consumer Conference Idea," Petroleum Intelligence Weekly, Oct. 28, 1974 at 3; "Arabs Back French Plan For Oil Parley," The New York Times, Dec. 4, 1974 at 14.

31. "Solidarity at Martinique," The New York Times, Dec. 18, 1974 at 67.

32. "The 'Law of the Sea' Is Still Unwritten, But Please Don't Fret," Wall Street Journal, Aug. 27, 1974 at 1; "U.N. Session Makes Little Headway on Raw Materials Issue," Petroleum Intelligence Weekly, Apr. 29, 1974 at 9.

33. Interviewees both in the United States and abroad, both government officials and industry representatives, were unanimous in the belief that the United Nations is not an appropriate forum for the producer-consumer dialogue.

34. See generally G. Curzon, Multilateral Commercial Diplomacy: The General Agreement on Tariffs and Trade and its Impact on National Commercial Policies and Techniques (1965); K. W. Dam, The GATT: Law and International Economic Organization (1970); J. H. Jackson, World Trade and the Law of GATT (1969).

35. See R. Gardner, Sterling-Dollar Diplomacy, 378 (1956).

36. Dam, supra note 34, at 11.

37. See Krueger, "An Evaluation of United States Oceans Policy," 17 McGill Law Journal 603, 649 (1971).

38. See, for example, "Law of the Sea: Enough's Enough," Wall Street Journal, Dec. 17, 1973 at 14, criticizing the supportive position of the U.S. Government in the Law of the Sea Conference, and the reply of Ambassador John R. Stevenson, Wall Street Journal, Jan. 7, 1974 at 10, reiterating that "it is U.S. policy to achieve its resource objectives, not by unilateral action, but rather by generally accepted international agreement."

39. See Dam, supra note 34, at 56 et seq.

40. See Dam, supra note 34, at 351-375; Jackson, supra note 34, at 163 et. seq.

41. Regional agreements have continued to survive and perform a function within the GATT. See Jackson, supra note 34, at 621-623; Dam, supra note 34, at 274 et. seq.

42. Professor Jackson in his book, supra note 34, at 766-767, describes similar difficulties in negotiating complex international issues under the GATT:

> "Another difficulty with the negotiating technique is the complexity of international economic relations. The Kennedy Round negotiations almost reached the limit of what the human mind could cope with in a single effort with a large number of variables. The negotiating technique tends to draw into an otherwise narrow subject a large number of related factors. Some of these factors, however, are only remotely related. It is theoretically advantageous that particular international differences of opinion are seen in the context of the broader relationships involved, but there is a limit to this advantage. At some point the whole business becomes so complex that the human mind can no longer deal with it, and the participants in the negotiation tend to rely upon positions discussed and established within their own governments that

358.

are based on overgeneralizations or erroneous
generalizations as to the importance of
other remotely related factors.  A simple
problem of a breach of a particular GATT
obligation, such as a question of national
treatment in local taxation upon an imported
item, could produce discussion of a number
of other facets of international economic
relations, including inconsistencies with
the GATT norms by the complaining country
itself, other negotiations such as tariff
concession negotiations going on at the same
time between these parties and other parties,
foreign aid promised or proposed between the
parties, the status of third parties who also
produce and ship the same article and the
desire of the importing country to achieve
a determination in the negotiation that
would exclude the third-party imports,
political support in other bodies for proposi-
tions that there proposed by one or the other
of the disputants, monetary imbalance of payments problems between the disputants, and
the like. . . .  What is necessary in international economic relations is the development of procedures and techniques that will
'chip off' bits and pieces of the amorphous
complex totality of commercial relationships
and find solutions to those chipped off pieces
so that they are not an issue in every new
negotiation that occurs in the future."

43.  See note 42, supra.

44.  See text accompanying notes 32 and 33, supra.

45.  See questionnaire response of Continental Oil Company,
Appendix D.

46.  For a discussion of the possible problems which might
arise from a gradual replacing of traditional industry
roles with greater involvement by producer and consumer
governments, see Chapters 7 and 9.

PART V

CONCLUSIONS

CHAPTER 12

## [§12.0]   CONCLUSION

Developments of the past four years have radically transformed the international petroleum system.  In the past, our domestic petroleum market remained relatively insulated from international pressures; since 1970 foreign developments have come to dominate and profoundly affect the price and security of supplies of energy to the United States.  U.S. dependence on imports has risen sharply, while the security and cost of those imports have increasingly been subjected to unilateral manipulation by foreign producer governments.  The integration of the United States into the international energy market makes it essential that it develop for the first time a coherent and consistent international energy policy.  That in turn cannot be divorced from the need for a comprehensive domestic energy policy which encompasses  conservation and accelerated development of alternate energy sources.

Traditionally, the U.S. Government, with a number of rather isolated and ad hoc exceptions, has relied upon U.S. oil companies to independently establish the terms of international supply arrangements.  Until recently, this policy worked quite well.  It encouraged these companies to acquire resources throughout the world and obtain preeminence in international petroleum affairs.  Because of this policy, however, the U.S. Government developed little information or competence to monitor international petroleum transactions.  Thus, when the Arab oil embargo struck in 1973, there was no Federal agency capable of taking independent action to protect the national interest of the United States with respect to foreign supplies.  The performance of the large U.S. multinational firms during the embargo, moreover, emphasized that the United States cannot rely upon those companies to favor its interests to the detriment of other major consuming nations.  In large part, those companies are held hostage by the producer governments.

The issue thus is whether the U.S. Government should have a greater role in international petroleum affairs and, if so, what type of role.  It is difficult to examine the issue without concluding that the existing incentives for the companies do not assure that their behavior will be consistent with the national interests of the United States. Accordingly, there appears to be a need for monitoring and for the establishment of a sufficient number of control points within the system to insure that the national interests are independently protected by the U.S. Government.

Any new role for the U.S. Government will probably draw on a variety of the options discussed in this Study. No single option could solve all of the international petroleum problems the nation faces today. Nor does any combination of these options offer a predictable solution. While this Study endorses no option, at the very least it would seem appropriate that the U.S. Government have access to relevant information regarding present and future significant international petroleum arrangements. It would also seem appropriate for the Federal Government to have the power to review and approve such transactions where they may affect significant aspects of the national interest.

Such massive power could admittedly be used in a fashion that would be detrimental to both the economic well-being of the U.S. companies and of the country. This factor makes it important that any act creating the authority be drawn so as to minimize the possibility of abuse and to carefully define the standards for administrative action. It is readily apparent that under the circumstances an entity with the stature and independence of the Federal Reserve Board, for example, would be necessary.

The establishment of such a scheme of regulation would, of course, be largely domestic in its operation, but its potential benefit could be substantially enhanced by a number of initiatives that are international in thrust. Key among these is the continuation and broadening of consumer-country cooperation under the International Energy Program and the undertaking of broadly based consumer-producer nation discussions. Both of these concepts appear to be established U.S. policy and the analysis made in this Study has focused largely on the ways in which these approaches might be effected. The concept of bilateral supply arrangements is less promising, although it appears that agreements of this type have developed "special relationships" which may have utility.

Careful consideration should also be given to the
possible benefits of establishing the authority within the
Federal Government to enter into bilateral petroleum arrangements.  Although it is questionable whether such authority
should be employed on a routine basis, it may be advantageous
to the national interest for it to exist.  Finally, the
concept of establishing an industry-wide association of
companies from consumer countries to coordinate international
supply arrangements deserves serious consideration.  The
consumer countries and their companies are required to deal
with OPEC, a self-acknowledged cartel, and in the international
area it would seem to serve no purpose for the U.S. to
require the same competitive performance of the companies
that is expected domestically as long as the interests
of the American consumer are not prejudiced.

The potential utility of any or all of these
initiatives is, however, subject to a major qualification.
It is very unlikely that any effective progress can be made
in dealing with the major producer countries until the
ongoing Arab-Israeli dispute has been settled.  That dispute
continues to color petroleum policy in the Middle East and,
therefore, the remainder of the world.

The Study has also examined a number of other
concepts such as the removal of Federal incentives and disincentives, the regulation of the companies as public
utilities, the establishment of a national system to limit
imports and the creation of a petroleum corporation fully or
partially owned by the Federal Government.  In each case,
the Study focused on the impact of these systems upon international petroleum affairs.  It is questionable whether any
of these options alone could have a positive effect upon the
level of world prices under existing conditions.  The
public utility option would appear to present a potential
negative impact upon supply and the creation of a Federal
oil corporation presents few attractive features.

The Study has examined the changing realities of
international petroleum.  This is a period of stress for
both the consumer nations and their companies.  Hopefully,
the United States will provide the leadership to create
conditions under which U.S. companies can effectively carry
out their essential mission as world suppliers of petroleum.

Hopefully, too, in the process a pattern of cooperation rather than confrontation can be created between the producer and consumer nations of the world.

APPENDICES

APPENDIX A

## [§A.0] THE EXPERIENCE OF U.S. AND FOREIGN PUBLIC CORPORATIONS

A.   [§A.1]   Performance of U.S. Government Enterprises

    [§A.2]   Ownership and directors
    [§A.3]   Personnel policies
    [§A.4]   Life-span
    [§A.5]   Financing
    [§A.6]   Taxes
    [§A.7]   Financial success
    [§A.8]   Assistance from Federal agencies
    [§A.9]   Relations with other firms
    [§A.10]  Decision making
    [§A.11]  Other problems

B.   [§A.12]  Performance of Foreign Government Oil Companies

    [§A.13]  British Petroleum Co.
    [§A.14]  Ente Nazionale Idrocarburi
    [§A.15]  Compagnie Francaise des Petroles and
             L'Enterprise de Recherches et d'Activities
             Petrolieres
    [§A.16]  Comparative performance data
    [§A.17]  Summary

C.   [A.18]   Empirical Studies of the Relative Efficiency of
             Public Versus Private Industry

    [§A.19]  The Davis Study of Australian Airlines
    [§A.20]  The Polanyi Study of British Industry

D.   [§A.21]  Suggestions for the Structure and Policy of
             Public Corporations in the Mineral Industry

A-1

Appendix A

[§A.0]  THE EXPERIENCE OF U.S. AND FOREIGN
        PUBLIC CORPORATIONS

A.  [§A.1]  Performance of U.S. Government Enterprise

A substantial number of federal corporations or activities have been created in the past that could provide a "track record" by which government enterprise might be evaluated. Many of these institutions are of a lending or guaranteeing nature, such as the Federal Deposit Insurance Corporation. These will not be discussed on the grounds that they are not production-oriented organizations and hence face different problems from those of an operating oil company. There remain a large number of government corporations or production activities including the Panama Canal Zone, Panama Railroad Company, Alaska Railroad, Merchant Marine (Maritime Commission), Inland Waterways Corporation (Federal Barge Lines), Government Printing Office, Tennessee Valley Authority, Bonneville Power Administration, Boulder Canyon Project, St. Lawrence Waterway, Bureau of Mines production of helium, Federal pilot projects for the production of titanium, zirconium and petroleum from oil shale, Virgin Islands Company, production facilities for synthetic rubber, tin and nickel, Postal Service, National Railroad Passenger Corporation and Communications Satellite Corporation.

Many of these corporations are involved in activities that are monopolistic in nature (such as the Panama Canal Zone) or are in many ways duplicated by other corporations on the list (the several flood control/power projects) and will not be mentioned in the following discussion. Examples will be taken primarily from the history of two corporations, the Inland Waterways Corporation (IWC) and the Tennessee Valley Authority (TVA). These two were chosen because: (1) some research is available on both entities; (2) IWC was involved in a potentially competitive industry and its entire life-span is available for study; and (3) TVA is the most widely acclaimed yardstick corporation established by the Federal government. A brief introduction to both of these corporations is provided below.

During World War I a river barge transportation system under the War Department was established on the Mississippi River to aid in the war effort. Not only were substantial sums spent on real assets but also on improving the navigation channels of the rivers as well. Congress, in 1924, created the Inland Waterways Corporation to make use of those assets. One of the motivations for creating the IWC was to have a yardstick with which to judge the efficiency of the railroads.

The committee reporting out the bill in Congress "believed that the government could dispose of the property in five years at a profit after having established the feasibility of water transport on the Mississippi and Warrior rivers." 1/ A similar evaluation of the goal of the Corporation was put forth by Marshall Dimock in his major study of the IWC in 1935:

> "In other words, the corporation has not been considered heretofore [prior to 1935] a purely competitive transportation enterprise, operating under the duty to reduce its costs and to show its profits and losses in the same form which its competitor, the railway, does. On the other hand, it is Congress' announced policy to prove the economical or un-economical character of inland waterway transportation once and for all, and it therefore follows that if a true economy is to appear, the Inland Waterways Corporation must be operated in as economical and as business-like fashion as possible." 2/

This carried with it the implication that the IWC was intended to be a yardstick for private barge lines. It should be noted that, more specifically, the goal was to prove that a common carrier (such as the IWC) could operate economically on the rivers. There was a substantial volume of traffic on the Mississippi River but most of it was private or contract carriers and not common carriers. For example, in 1933, total volume on the relevant portion of the rivers was 14,705 thousand tons of domestic freight. The two largest common carriers were Federal Barge Lines (run by Inland Waterways Corporation) and Mississippi Valley Barge Line which carried 1,300 thousand tons and 300 thousand tons respectively. 3/ The government line operated until 1953 when it was sold to private industry at a loss of $7 million. 4/

The Tennessee Valley Authority was created in 1933 as a semi-independent, quasi-autonomous government corporation. The creation of the TVA came about as the result of a complicated set of circumstances involving the need for the production of nitrates for military purposes, the availability of Mussel Shoals on the Tennessee River for flood control, navigation and electric generation purposes, and the desire for the economic development of the Tennessee River Valley. The Act creating TVA put forth several primary purposes (flood control, navigation and electric power generation) along with several secondary goals (fertilizer production, soil erosion, and social, cultural and economic development). 5/ During the 1950's certain changes were made in the way TVA was to conduct its financial arrangements but by and large the TVA has existed unaltered since its creation.

[§A.2]  Ownership and directors

Perhaps the first three decisions that have to be made in the creation of a federal international oil corporation are (1) fully or partially government owned, (2) the form of ownership (stock or non-stock), and (3) the appointment of the directors of the corporation.

Both the TVA and the Inland Waterways Corporation were wholly owned by the Federal government. There are apparently few, if any, examples of production type corporations in the United States where capital has been provided partially by the private sector and partially by the Federal government. According to LLoyd Musolf there is currently no unit in the national government that meets this criterion of mixed ownership. 6/

The mere fact of historical total government ownership of public corporations in the U.S. by itself is no real argument in favor of 100% government ownership of a government oil company. It can easily be argued that public ownership and market trading of some portion of the stock would lead to a broader interest in the corporation and provide a valid and current indicator of the performance as well as of the value of the government's equity.

If such a corporation was to be a wholly government owned corporation, there would be little real need for stock. Despite the fact that the Government Corporation

Control Act of 1945 allows for stock ownership, there does
exist a policy favoring "no-stock" government corporations. 7/
Both the TVA and the IWC were no-stock corporations. Precedence, for the United States at least, indicates that a
government oil corporation would most likely be created as
a wholly owned corporation.

The appointment of corporation directors is in
many respects dictated by the method of capitalization. If
the corporation is to be wholly governmentally owned, all
of the directors would most likely be appointed, in some
manner, by the Federal government. The Board of Directors
of the TVA had three members who were appointed by the
President with the advice and consent of the Senate. "The
directors were subject to removal at any time by a concurrent
resolution of the Senate and House of Representatives." 8/
The organization of the Inland Waterways Corporation was
somewhat different. The Secretary of War was charged with
the direct control and immediate supervision of the IWC.
An appointed Advisory Board advised on matters of policy
and an appointed President of the corporation handled administrative matters. In 1935 a Board of Managers was
created for improving administrative and business practices. 9/
By way of comparison, COMSAT, which is a privately owned
corporation, has one-fifth of its directors appointed by
the President of the United States.

There are many possible combinations of ownership and director appointment possibilities. The form
chosen will affect the closeness of the relationship
between the Federal government and the corporation. A
decision must be made as to whether, or how much, it is
to simply be an extension of Federal government policies
(which are sometimes politicized) or whether it is to be
given a non-conflicting set of goals and priorities and
allowed to operate as. a sound, economically efficient,
self-sustaining business firm (with no benefits or restrictions differentiating it from other oil companies)
in order to gain accurate "yardstick" information on the
costs and operation of the petroleum industry.

[§A.3]  Personnel policies

Certain personnel policies can also be specified in an Act creating a Federal Oil and Gas Corporation. Personnel, for example, might be included under Civil Service.  There are many arguments on the merits of Civil Service with respect to political influence and business efficiency but these will not be elaborated here.

Neither TVA nor the IWC were included in Civil Service, however.  There were indications that the IWC's ability to operate efficiently was affected because of political appointments.  According to Dimock:

> "It is freely admitted by informed parties and by officials of the corporation that political appointments and removals have been made during the ten years that the IWC has been in existence. . . .  It is well established . . . that political pressure is found at work from the highest to the lowest positions within the . . . corporation.  For example, the writer was told that the appointment of dock workers in one of the terminals . . . was subject to the pressure of the local party boss. . . ." 10/

Part of this political influence in personnel matters was apparently due to the direct role of the Secretary of War, a position that was a direct political appointment.  As Dimock pointed out, an independent Board of Directors, which the IWC did not have, would be a primary step in lessening such political pressure. 11/

The TVA also did not come under Civil Service. The general assessment of the TVA's personnel policies are favorable and its merit system has apparently operated without much political influence. 12/

If a government international oil corporation was created, its successful operation would depend on the hiring of a substantial number of highly skilled professional personnel, be they of the production or management variety.  They would have to be bid away from the

private petroleum industry and restraints placed by civil
service might adversely affect the hiring of qualified personnel.  And it should be noted that freeing the appointment
or hiring policies from political influence does not automatically free the decision-making process from political
influence.  This point will be discussed below.

[§A.4]  Life-span

Another organizational characteristic that could
be specified in an Act creating a government corporation
would be its life-span, limited or unlimited.  If a limited
life-span is anticipated, some thought should be given to
the process of selling the acquired assets.

Historically, a number of government-created
corporations or production activities have been established
to take care of critical wartime shortages.  Many of these,
including the Inland Waterways Corporation, merchant marine
ship production during both World Wars, aluminum plants and
synthetic rubber production during World War II, were all
undertaken as temporary measures and government ownership
in each was initially viewed as a short run proposition.
The current oil problems do have some characteristics of
an artificially induced shortage (i.e., OPEC limitations
on crude oil production) which might tend to put a government oil corporation on a similar basis.

If the enterprise is to have a limited life-span,
thought must be given to how long it would take to get the
corporation functioning in a manner that would reveal cost
figures of any value or provide significant quantities of
oil.  If it was to engage in a wide range of activities
from the exploration to production, for example, a substantial life-span would have to be authorized in view
of the unknown time period required for exploration, and
the long lead times required to put some oil fields into
production status.  Also, because many natural gas contracts
are of a 20-year duration, any limit on the life-span
might decrease its ability to operate efficiently in this
area.

If a limited life-span is desired, preparation
must be made for the sale of company assets.  In the
Inland Waterways Corporation example, one of the reasons

A-7

sale of the corporation was not completed until 1953 was because no one wanted to buy the Corporation on the terms offered.

[§A.5]  Financing

The financing of a government corporation is a major item to be considered. Before discussing how it might be financed, its probable size should first be discussed.

The potential capital requirements for a U.S. Government corporation operating in international oil has been examined as has the net worth of the largest U.S. private corporations that are involved in the international oil industry, plus the six largest foreign (private and public) international oil companies. The data are shown in Tables 1 and 2.

TABLE 1.--Net worth of twenty largest U.S. international oil companies, 1973

| | | |
|---|---|---|
| 1. | Exxon | $12,567,777,000 |
| 2. | Texaco | 7,992,331,000 |
| 3. | Standard Oil of California | 5,806,435,000 |
| 4. | Mobil | 5,714,772,000 |
| 5. | Gulf | 5,569,000,000 |
| 6. | Standard Oil (Indiana) | 4,125,268,000 |
| 7. | Atlantic Richfield | 3,117,632,000 |
| 8. | Shell Oil | 3,096,075,000 |
| 9. | Phillips Petroleum | 1,963,585,000 |
| 10. | Sun Oil | 1,929,631,000 |
| 11. | Tenneco | 1,922,322,000 |

| 12. | Continental | 1,808,372,000 |
| 13. | Union Oil of California | 1,714,664,000 |
| 14. | Getty Oil | 1,586,600,000 |
| 15. | Cities Service | 1,530,100,000 |
| 16. | Standard Oil (Ohio) | 1,131,999,000 |
| 17. | Occidental Petroleum | 891,037,000 |
| 18. | Marathon Oil | 886,005,000 |
| 19. | Amerada Hess | 773,596,000 |
| 20. | Kerr McGee | 558,583,000 |

Source: Fortune, May 1974, pp. 232-240.


TABLE 2.--Net worth of large foreign private and public international oil companies, 1973 (dollars)

| 1. | Royal Dutch Shell | $10,373,654,000 |
| 2. | British Petroleum | 5,115,080,000 |
| 3. | ENI | 1,851,637,000 |
| 4. | CFP | 1,452,166,000 |
| 5. | Burmah Oil | 1,448,113,000 |
| 6. | ELF Group | 1,203,809,000 |

Source: Fortune, August 1974, p. 176.

The net worth for the U.S. international majors runs all
the way from $12.6 billion for Exxon down to $559 million
for Kerr-McGee, the twentieth largest U.S. international oil
company. The foreign companies run in size from $10.4
billion for Royal Dutch Shell down to $1.2 billion for the
ELF Group.

If a fully integrated government corporation is
desired, then the capital requirements would appear to be
around $5 billion. If some of the downstream functions are
excluded such as retail and wholesale distribution and
refining, then capital requirements would be substantially
less. If the role of a government corporation is limited
to large scale foreign exploration, production, and wholesale distribution of crude oil, and excluding ocean transportation and other downstream functions, then capital
requirements would be minimized. Anything less than about
$1 billion, however, would not be viewed as a serious con-
tender among international oil companies. The newest and
the smallest of the foreign public corporations shown in
Table 2, the ELF Group, has a net worth of $1.2 billion.
Thus, a meaningful U.S. government oil corporation would
probably require close to $2 billion in initial financing
at a minimum.

Once an appropriate size is determined, the form
of financing can be arranged. The Federal Government portion,
if it is to be a mixed ownership corporation or 100%, if
government owned, could be financed by some combination of
Congressional appropriations, borrowing and corporation retained earnings. In the example of TVA and IWC, commercial
revenues were to be used against operating expenses first.
In the case of TVA there was government control over much
of its operation because Congress was required to approve
new construction and its form of financing, the Bureau of
the Budget had to approve its administrative expenses, and
the Treasury had to approve its borrowing.

Historically, appropriations have been the main
source of capital for the TVA. As C. Herman Pritchett,
writing in 1943, noted, "The TVA program has thus been
financed in only a relatively minor degree by borrowing." 13/
This has changed recently because since 1953, Congress has

A-10

made no appropriations to finance new power facilities but since 1956 has allowed reinvestment of earnings and borrowing (since 1959) for this purpose. 14/

A government corporation can also obtain funds through borrowing with or without Federal Government guarantees. Federal guarantees would, of course, lower the interest rate that must be paid on borrowed money. The TVA has borrowed money both on the open market and through Federal channels. The exact breakdown of sources of borrowing is not available, but, again, it is possible to say that historically the borrowing has been made via bonds "fully guaranteed by the United States both as to principal and interest." 15/

The effect of these various forms of financing on claims that a Federal corporation is a yardstick will be discussed below. There is one interesting implication that government guaranteed borrowing would have for any government corporation. A production goal, be it crude oil production, electricity generation or whatever, can be achieved using different combinations of available labor and capital. The precise combination chosen depends not only on technology but on their relative prices. A firm that can get one input at a price below what other firms must pay will use relatively more of that input. TVA or a government oil corporation, with low cost capital available, would therefore tend to be relatively more capital intensive than other firms. This raises the question whether such a corporation so constructed is comparable to the firms for which it is supposed to be a yardstick.

[§A.6]  Taxes

Another organizational characteristic that must be specified would be its tax obligation. Taxes are a substantial burden on corporate activity, be they local, state or federal taxes. Freedom from such burdens would substantially lower the cost of operation but would also make any yardstick comparisons difficult. There is another consideration here also. Pegrum pointed out that funds generated by taxes on utilities provide revenue to government bodies. A customer of a non-taxed publicly owned utility, therefore, contributes less to the cost of government than a customer of a privately owned utility. 16/

The TVA does not pay Federal income taxes.  And because the TVA is a Federal organization, it does not pay state or local taxes, including property taxes.  The TVA does, however, make payments in lieu of taxes to states and counties on a basis of 5% of the revenue received from the sale of electricity.  A TVA publication notes that private power companies in surrounding areas pay taxes to state and local government bodies that equal about 4.5 to 10.6% of the power bills of the customers they serve.  The publication further notes that combining tax payments by the TVA with its distributors (the TVA does almost no retail distribution) results in tax payments totaling about 7.5% of combined revenues.  Therefore, TVA concludes that its tax burden is equivalent to that of private electric utilities.  17/

Several things, however, should be noted about this comparison.  First, since TVA sales are almost totally at the wholesale level, its total revenue for a given level of output would be less than any private firm that had some sales at the retail level.  Second, about one-third of TVA sales are to Federal agencies, and these sales are not included in the revenue total that forms the basis for the 5% in lieu of tax calculations.  Hence the TVA actually pays a rate of taxation on all its power revenue (assuming the rates to Federal users are approximately the same as to other distributors) of about 3-1/3%.  This is substantially below the tax rates cited in the TVA publication for private utilities.  The logic for including the tax payments of TVA's power distributors is not clear because they are totally separate entities and the question here is the direct tax burden of the TVA, not its ability to generate tax revenue from other sources.

On the question of tax burden, because the TVA pays no Federal income tax and because its payments in lieu of taxes as a portion of its total revenue are low relative to private utilities, it would appear that TVA has a smaller tax burden on its electricity generated revenue than privately owned utilities.  It seems entirely possible that, because a government oil company might engage in many phases of oil and gas operations over many geographically widely separated areas but with close complex

financial interactions, that setting up some "in lieu of
a tax" system would be involved, expensive and somewhat
arbitrary.  And because such a system would be very complex,
justifying the corporation as a yardstick would be difficult.  It has been argued that "whether or not the 'yardstick' would be 36", 35" or 37", at least we would have a
beginning of a measuring device." 18/  There are some, on
the other hand, that would argue that such a system would
nullify the yardstick value.

[§A.7]  Financial success

Another item that would have to be specified in
the creation of a federal oil corporation would be requirements
for measuring the success or failure of the corporation.
There are, of course, many possible definitions of success.
An example of this is seen in evaluations of the Inland
Waterways Corporation.

It has been stated that one reason for creating
the IWC was to interest private capital in developing inland
water transportation.  Between the time the IWC was created
and 1953, more than 100 private barge lines were brought
into operation. 19/  Hence if the IWC was viewed as a research
and development project aimed at opening up a new field, it
may have been a success.  However, this result did have a
cost because it is agreed that the IWC was in no way a
financial success.  The only real debate on this matter was
how much money was really lost.

First of all, it should be noted that during the
latter portion of the corporation's life, it did not maintain its relative position in the industry.  Between 1937
and 1949, the tonnage transported by the corporation rose 24
percent but the total tonnage moved on the same portion of
the river system that IWC operated on rose 110%. 20/

In assessing the corporation's losses, it has been
argued that because the Federal Government spent substantial
funds improving the shipping lanes on the rivers, some toll
or charge should be included in barge transportation costs
calculations.  Various figures have been calculated for this
cost and these are relatively low or high depending upon
whether they are calculated by the barge lines or by its
competitor the railroads. 21/  If the suggestion is valid,
it could also be argued that the railroads should include

A-13

some fee for the free land they received from the government. This illustrates that creating a yardstick is a difficult problem.

According to Stuart Daggett, the corporation's books showed annual losses prior to 1930 with the exception of two years. Between 1930 and 1939 the corporation operated profitably, but from 1939 until the corporation was sold at a loss to private industry in the early 1950's, it operated in the red. 22/ There is, however, substantial criticism concerning the omission of certain costs from this government corporation's cost calculations. One main charge is that the IWC was not required to earn interest on its capital investment, was not required to pay corporation taxes, and had other benefits resulting from its association with the Federal Government such as a franking privilege and free offices in Washington, D.C. 23/

One of the sharpest criticisms of the profitability of the Inland Waterways Corporation comes from another source. The Federal Coordinator of Transportation, in a study of public aids to transportation, analyzed the costs of the IWC.

> "He held that if the Corporation was to be used to illustrate the feasibility of private ownership of the barge line, in computing profits certain costs should be considered beyond those accounted for by it; these include more ample depreciation allowances, the cost of capital, taxes, the cost of postage and special governmental allowance on telegrams and purchases, and certain other costs. When these were considered, the co-ordinator found that in the years from 1924 to 1936, instead of the net income of $687,000 shown on the Corporation's books, it actually sustained losses totaling more than $15,500,000. Even if the Corporation was conceived of as a government business entitled to low capital costs and advantages of other low government costs, the co-ordinator computed that it had really lost $9,400,000 between 1924 and 1936." 24/

This analysis brings out several important points that must be considered in the creation of a federal oil corporation. The first point concerns the matter of payments for capital. For private capital to be made available to private industry, dividends or interest on that capital must be paid. The dividends are the "price" of capital and serves as a rationing device ensuring that the projects with the best return, with respect to the risks involved, get the capital. If the corporation is not required to pay for its capital through interest payments to the Federal Government, it is on a different footing than any private firm. It should be noted that until the late 1950's the TVA was not required to pay any return on the capital provided by means of Congressional appropriations.

The second point concerns interest payments on borrowing. If the Federal Government guarantees debt capital as it did of the TVA, lower interest rates will be achieved. This will lower the costs of operation but will also place the enterprise on a footing that makes any comparisons with private industry difficult. These two factors, combined with the possible tax exemption status and other possible advantages that will be discussed shortly, combine to have some serious implications for resource allocation decisions.

Suppose Congress wanted to increase the domestic supply of crude oil in the least cost manner, i.e., in an economically efficient manner. In assessing an enterprise like the IWC as cited above, one might argue as follows: "The enterprise (IWC) is making money; it is therefore efficient. I will apply incentives in a manner so that they will benefit the enterprise most, thereby increasing supply most efficiently." If in fact the enterprise was really the least efficient means, but this fact was hidden by special benefits given to it, Congress would have caused resources to be allocated inefficiently. The argument here is simply that resources are scarce and therefore great care should be taken in how they are managed. If it is possible to create a corporation in which costs can be calculated explicitly, and it is no more difficult to create this corporation than one with many "hidden costs," the former would be preferred on economic grounds because both efficiency and information are desirable.

[§A.8] Assistance from Federal agencies

An extremely important facet of the relationship
between a federal oil corporation and the government that
must be explicitly formulated concerns access to various
forms of assistance from government agencies.  This assistance could come in the form of technical assistance or
information.  If agencies are required to provide assistance free of charge, the corporation's reported costs
would fail to reflect its true costs.  These services will,
of course, be paid for through taxes to support the budgets
of the agencies.  To the degree that this occurs, the
corporation's real costs will be understated by an unknown
amount. 25/  Given that the petroleum industry has been a
successful profit-making industry since its inception, any
actions that would place a federal corporation on a footing
different from that faced by private petroleum firms should
be clearly and explicitly justified.

There are, of course, a myriad of ways in which
a government oil corporation could be assisted by other
federal agencies.  For example, the U.S. Geological Survey
could be requested to make extensive surveys of lands for
potential oil and gas deposits.  The Department of Commerce
could make market studies and transportation cost analysis.
Other agencies could provide information concerning drilling
and production technology.  The State Department could provide information and support useful in bargaining for
exploration, development and production rights.  It would
be possible to tie rights to crude oil reserves to military
or development aid programs.  And in every example cited
none of the costs of the assistance to the corporation
would be included in its expenses.  It would in effect be
subsidized by other agencies of the Federal government and
the full cost of its oil or gas would be unknown and difficult to estimate.  It would be quite possible for the
corporation, as in the Los Angeles water case just cited,
to charge the market price for a barrel of oil when the
total cost of that oil might be much higher.  Price, it
should be remembered, is a rationing mechanism.  And a
factor of production that is "free" to one producer and
costly to other producers will tend to be used relatively
more by that one producer.

[§A.9]  Relations with other firms

Congress, in creating a federal oil corporation
can also specify how the corporation must interact with
other firms within the petroleum industry.  It might be
possible, for example, to legislate one degree of competition with the "majors" and a different degree of
competition with the "independents."  Further, recent
legislation and administration concerning crude oil allocations, the Entitlements Program, and the Oil Import
Quota system included intended partiality toward smaller
firms.  The history of the TVA does not yield many parallels
in this area but the history of the Inland Waterways Corporation does.

The IWC was, it will be recalled, created to
demonstrate the economic feasibility of privately owned
common carrier barge lines in the Mississippi River region.
Such an endeavor necessarily implies that the IWC was to
compete with other barge lines and other forms of transportation, primarily the railroads, for cargo.  Several
Acts passed by Congress, as well as action taken by the
Interstate Commerce Commission, vitally affected how the
IWC functioned.

The Dennison Act of 1928 required that "railroads
should be forced to enter into joint-rate agreements with
the Inland Waterways Corporation." 26/  In the early 1930's
about 60% of the barge line's business came from such agreements with the railroads and it was concluded that the
Inland Waterways Corporation could not possibly succeed
"without the business which comes from joint-rate agreements
with the railroads." 27/  Hence, the government was essentially guaranteeing a certain amount of business for the
IWC, at the expense of the railroads, which in turn shifted
the cost to their customers in the form of higher rates.

On the other hand, some actions of the government
prevented competition with the railroads.  By rate competition (lowering rates) the IWC was able to increase its
cotton tonnage in the early 1930's.  By direction of the
White House, however, its cotton rates were revised upwards
such that during the year 1933 the IWC's cotton volume

A-17

dropped over 95%. 28/ During this period the IWC was
also ordered to curtail its competition with privately
owned barge lines. The Interstate Commerce Commission
was also involved in the relationship between the IWC
and the railroads and as a result of one decision in 1933
concerning storage in transit, the sugar tonnage carried
by the IWC was cut in half. 29/ Hence we have the situation
where the Inland Waterways Corporation was set up either
as a yardstick for the railroads or to demonstrate the
feasibility of common carrier barge transportation and its
effort to compete for cargo were disrupted by various
Federal bodies. It should also be noted that Congress
further interfered with the business operations of the
IWC by requiring it to operate certain barge runs that
were clearly unprofitable. If there were external benefits
equal to or greater than the net loss from such unprofitable
operations, then such a requirement might be justified.
This requirement has been cited as one of the reasons for
the failure of the Inland Waterways Corporation. 30/

The importance of these examples is that requirements by Congress (political interference in economic
decision-making) could force a federal oil corporation to
operate in a manner contrary to that indicated by business
efficiency. Great care should be taken when formulating
specific actions that the corporation must take because
economic inefficiency might be rewarded instead of punished.
Political interference should be supported by evidence of
externalities. As a hypothetical example, suppose one oil
company was becoming increasingly efficient and was expanding
its market share at the expense of another less efficient
company. Requiring that the federal oil corporation deal
with the relatively inefficient company solely in order to
protect its market share is in effect, aiding economic
inefficiency. There is no obvious compensating external
benefit. The state of competition in the oil industry is
not so precarious that aid to inefficient but small firms
can be clearly justified as a measure to promote competition.
Such partiality will result in a higher cost of petroleum when
all costs are included. An example of compounding inefficiencies would be to require that the federal oil corporation's oil imports from its international operations be
transported by U.S. built, U.S. manned, U.S. tankers. Such

A-18

tankers are rarely used in international operations because of their high cost. Requiring the corporation to use such tankers would be to force it to use the highest cost means of transportation as a method of subsidizing two other industries, the merchant marine and the ship construction industry. Such a requirement would be an example of forced inefficiency.

[§A.10]  Decision making

Another area in the relationship between the Federal government and a federal oil corporation that should be considered is the degree of influence the government is to have over the decision-making process of the corporation. Two quick examples will serve to introduce this topic.

In his study of the Inland Waterways Corporation, Dimock came across an over-staffing problem. He concluded that this existed because "management does not wish to remove officials from its payrolls when the country's policy has been to bring about re-employment." 31/ Hence there is the problem of conflicting policies, business economics versus political objectives.

The question of Congressional control over a body that receives its appropriations, or requires approval of its bond obligations from Congress, is illustrated by an example from the TVA. In 1939, the TVA wanted to purchase properties of the Commonwealth and Southern Corporation but approval of Congress was required for such an act. Pritchett noted that:

"The proposal met an unfavorable reception
in the House, which cut the amount and
wrote in a limitation on the territory
to be served by the TVA. There was for
a time serious danger that the TVA agreement with the Commonwealth and Southern
would fall through because of Congressional
failure to make funds available." 32/

Senators (perhaps concerned over location of a new development effort, or refinery location) could cause the appropriation for

A-19

a government enterprise to be held up through a filibuster. The mere possibility of such an event would, of course, temper the decision-making process of the Board of Directors of a Federal oil company. It is also possible to hypothesize conflicts between the corporation directors' desires to develop the most promising low-cost foreign crude oil sources and State Department's desires to improve relations with another country through development of its natural resources. The other side of this argument holds that such a tie-in is an advantage because it increases State Department leverage in negotiations. The important issues concern both cost and interference in company management effectiveness.

There are, of course, other restrictions on the activities of government corporations that should not be ignored. For example, according to the Government Corporation Control Act of 1945, all Federal corporations are required to submit budget proposals and obtain approval for their programs each year. This in itself limits the freedom of the corporation. In effect there are two boards of directors instead of one. This area of conflict between political influence and business efficiency on decision-making is one area that should not be underestimated. More will be said on this topic below.

[§A.11]  Other problems

Two things that must never be lost sight of in discussions of a federal oil corporation, or any other government activity for that matter, are: Why is a particular action being contemplated and are the arguments really sound? The debate over the Merchant Marine Act of 1936 illustrated the first point. This Act formulated the method for calculating subsidies to be received by a substantial portion of the privately owned U.S. flag vessels. The point to be gained from the debate of the Act of 1936 was that the debate centered on the means of providing subsidies and not on the question of whether "America's position required that it be in the shipping business at all, and if so, for what purposes. . ." 33/

The second point, are the arguments used on the pro and con sides of each proposition really meaningful, can be illustrated using the TVA. David Lilienthal argued that the TVA was a yardstick in a "more important sense" than just providing data. He argued that the TVA, by successfully lowering rates by substantial amounts, showed the financial feasibility of low rates. And this demonstration that low rates were possible proved that private utilities were basically holding rates unnecessarily high. To support this contention, he wrote in 1944 that:

> "Rates not markedly higher than those
> announced by the TVA in 1933 and
> vigorously denounced at the time as
> 'impossible' are now being charged
> by private utilities. They are re-
> turning a profit to the private com-
> panies in a period of higher costs.
> And the average residential rate for
> the whole country, which was 5.52 cents
> in 1933, 3.67 cents in 1942, a decrease
> of 33-1/3 percent below 1933 levels.
> The average rate paid for electricity
> by all ultimate consumers in the country
> dropped only 2 percent in the seven
> years from 1926 (the first year for
> which the statistics are reported) to
> 1933, the year TVA was created. In the
> seven years after the creation of TVA
> the average rate paid fell 23 percent." 34/

Lilienthal's argument is that creation of the TVA started rates declining and his evidence is that for the seven years prior to TVA's creation, rates fell only 2% but after its creation they fell 23%.

It is possible to dispute this argument. Lilienthal does not cite a source for his data. However, the Department of Commerce published a data series that shows average prices for all electricity consumption in the U.S.

Large Light and Power
TABLE 3.--Average Price of All Consumption
(cents per kw./hr.)

| | | | | | |
|------|------|------|------|------|------|
| 1921 | 7.39 | 1931 | 5.78 | 1941 | 3.73 |
| 1922 | 7.39 | 1932 | 5.60 | 1942 | 3.67 |
| 1923 | 7.20 | 1933 | 5.52 | 1943 | 3.60 |
| 1924 | 7.20 | 1934 | 5.33 | 1944 | 3.51 |
| 1925 | 7.30 | 1935 | 5.01 | 1945 | 3.41 |
| 1926 | 7.00 | 1936 | 4.67 | 1946 | 3.22 |
| 1927 | 6.82 | 1937 | 4.30 | 1947 | 3.09 |
| 1928 | 6.63 | 1938 | 4.14 | 1948 | 3.01 |
| 1929 | 6.33 | 1939 | 4.00 | 1949 | 2.95 |
| 1950 | 6.03 | 1940 | 3.84 | 1950 | 2.88 |

Source:   U.S. Department of Commerce. Historical Statistics
of the U.S. Colonial Times to 1957, Washington, D.C.,
1961.  Series S70-8, p. 510

This shows the average price in 1933 and 1942 to be 5.52 cents
and 3.67 cents respectively, the same prices that Lilienthal
cited.  According to this series, the prices of power seven
years before and after the creation of the TVA in 1933 were 7
cents and 3.84 cents respectively.  This indicates a price
decrease of 21% for the period before TVA and a decrease of
30% after TVA, a far cry from Lilienthal's figures of 2% and
23% respectively.  Hence it is not clear that the creation of
TVA was "the" cause for rate reductions.

        The relevance of technical matters should not be
ignored, as seen by a discussion of costs and prices of
electric generation.  There were technology advances in the

field of electric generation and transmission during the period in question. It is also known that with larger generators, and by operating at near capacity rates of production, lower costs per generated kw./hr are achieved. The Department of Commerce also provides a data series on "Production per kilowatt of capacity" (in kw./hr.). This will provide a crude measure of efficiency in that an increasing value could indicate either larger generators operating at a lower level of capacity or the same sized generators operating nearer to capacity.

This data series reveals some interesting information. For example, for the period 1925-1929, before TVA but also before the Great Depression, production per kilowatt of capacity (P/kw.c.) averaged 3,133 kw./hr. (with no year below 3,090 kw./hr.) By 1932, the P/kw.c. had fallen to 2,337 kw./hr., the lowest figure since 1912. After 1932, the production per kilowatt of capacity steadily increased and the 1936-40 average was 3,333 kw./hr. 35/

This information, together with the price information discussed above, indicates that private utilities were becoming increasingly efficient and were lowering the prices of electricity prior to the creation of TVA. For these reasons, full credit for "low cost" electricity should not go solely to the TVA. Part was due to the deflation that was caused by the Great Depression.

B.  [§A.12]  Performance of Foreign Government Oil Companies

There is a record of public enterprise performance to draw upon in appraising the probable effectiveness of a U.S. government oil corporation. The principal firms that may be analyzed are British Petroleum, Compagnie Francaise des Petroles, L'Entreprise de Recherches et d'Activites Petrolieres and Ente Nazional Idrocarburi. The West German firms, DEMINEX and Veba Chemie, have existed only since 1968 and hence do not provide an adequate basis for a performance analysis.

Because our primary interest is in consumer nation government enterprise we will not review the performance of the producer nation government oil companies. Not only is the mission entirely different from that under consideration here, but it is generally true that the economic environment is quite different from the United States. The OPEC nations are in an earlier stage of economic development, and development is extremely rapid.

One reason to account for the fact that developed European Governments have utilized the public enterprise form is in response to a felt need to compete with the very large American oil companies with their own national company providing access to foreign petroleum reserves independent of the U.S. companies. Given an attractive profit expectation one might expect private capital to flow and to satisfy this need. However, with the exception of Royal Dutch Shell, no European private competitors appeared on the scene comparable to the five American international oil companies.

Another reason why public enterprise developed in Europe is the absence in Europe of strong antitrust legislation. Paul Frankel wrote "a high-ranking Frenchman once told me that the peculiar system of their public enterprise, especially in the oil sector, was in fact nothing less than a European version of the American antitrust philosophy. . ." 36/ Both of the reasons given above may be valid in a European setting but by their nature are not justifications for American public enterprise. The United States already leads the world with not only the historical five international majors, but approximately twenty other integrated oil companies with international operations.

In the sections to follow, we will first review the individual public enterprises, then examine what little data are available to appraise their performance.

[§A.13]  British Petroleum Company

The Anglo-Persian Oil Company was registered in the United Kingdom on April 14, 1909 to develop newly discovered oil resources in Iran. The name was changed to Anglo-Iranian Oil Company Ltd. in 1934 and then to British Petroleum Company, Ltd. in 1954. Effective January 1, 1955 the company became a holding company. All trading activities were taken over by a new wholly owned subsidiary, BP Trading

Ltd. In addition to important operations in the chemical
and plastics industries BP is a fully integrated international oil company. 37/ Its crude oil production by
source country for 1971 through 1973 is as follows:

| Country | 1964 | 1965 | 1966 | 1967 | 1968 | 1969 | 1970 | 1971 | 1972 | 1973 |
|---------|------|------|------|------|------|------|------|------|------|------|
| | | | | Thousands of barrels per day | | | | | | |
| Iran | 640 | 700 | 760 | 900 | 1,000 | 1,150 | 1,330 | 1,490 | 1,770 | 1,980 |
| Kuwait | 920 | 880 | 980 | 960 | 1,020 | 1,050 | 1,110 | 1,170 | 1,480 | 1,320 |
| Nigeria | 60 | 120 | 160 | 120 | 20 | 180 | 380 | 560 | 580 | 620 |
| Abu Dhabi | 80 | 100 | 120 | 140 | 180 | 200 | 240 | 300 | 420 | 400 |
| Iraq | 300 | 300 | 280 | 260 | 360 | 360 | 380 | 400 | 240 | 220 |
| Qatar | 40 | 40 | 40 | 40 | 40 | 40 | 40 | 40 | 60 | 60 |
| Libya | --- | --- | --- | 80 | 140 | 160 | 200 | 160 | --- | --- |
| Other | 200 | 200 | 200 | 240 | 260 | 260 | 300 | 260 | 280 | 180 |
| | 2,240 | 2,340 | 2,540 | 2,740 | 3,020 | 3,400 | 3,980 | 4,380 | 4,830 | 4,780 |

Source: British Petroleum Co., Annual Report, 1973, p. 36.

Two important conclusions can be drawn from production data.
First, from 1964 through 1973, BP recorded a 8.7% annual
growth rate in crude oil production. Second, and far more
important, BP's crude production is almost entirely from OPEC
countries (All Middle East except Nigeria, and all Arab
except Nigeria and Iran) and is therefore vulnerable and no
longer subject to company control. Further, the equity
positions which BP has enjoyed in these countries is already
subject to substantial erosion and the Company will most
likely become a purchaser of crude oil for downstream processing and sale. In Kuwait, BP has owned a 50% partnership

A-25

with Gulf Oil covering approximately half of this country. This concession was granted to expire in the year 2026. However, recent participation negotiations have transferred a 60% share in the concession to Kuwait and seem certain to result eventually in 100% Kuwait ownership.

In 1965 BP discovered natural gas under the North Sea and delivery to the British Gas Council began in 1967. Reserves of crude oil were discovered at Prudhoe Bay, Alaska during 1968 and in that year BP entered the U.S. retail market by purchasing certain marketing and refining assets formerly owned by Sinclair Oil Company and Atlantic Richfield.

BP entered into an agreement with the Standard Oil Company of Ohio whereby SOHIO will obtain undivided interest in 600,000 barrels per day of oil production from Prudhoe Bay. In turn, British Petroelum will obtain 54% interest in SOHIO stock giving BP control over SOHIO. Thus, BP will obtain a major integrated position in the U.S. oil market and a needed diversification from primary reliance on Middle East oil. Further, BP has a major position in North Sea oil which will be coming on-stream between 1975 and 1980.

A critical item of importance in evaluating the performance of BP as a partially owned government oil corporation is the extent to which the British Government has influenced business decisions and injected politics into company management. Entry of the government into stock ownership of BP occurred in 1914. Thus, there has been a long period of history in which government power arising out of its ownership might have been asserted. British Government ownership currently accounts for 48.2% of "ordinary capital" of the company. The other major stockholder in BP is a private oil company, the Burmah Oil Company, which owns 21.5% of BP's ordinary capital. 37a/

BP's articles of association give the Government the right to nominate two members of the board of directors with veto power over any resolution of the Board. As BP's 1973 Annual Report notes,

"The government, however, pledged itself not to interfere in the company's com- mercial affairs, and undertook not to

exercise the right of veto except in
regard to certain specific matters of
general policy. The right of veto has
in fact never been exercised." 38/

Frankel commented in his book on the political
independence enjoyed by BP. He wrote that:

"The board members nominated by the government have never been known to interfere in
the business of the company -- although there
were some rumblings of mutual discontent
when the Labour Cabinet under Wilson came
to power. The experience of what is now
British Petroleum has, however, only limited
general relevance: firstly, because the
innate discipline of the British made it
possible for the government to rely on the
ordinary directors of their company to
take overall national interests as fully
into account as they knew how; secondly--
and this is infinitely more relevant--that
company, due to its endowment but also to
the continuing and outstanding bouyancy of
the oil industry, never needed any actual
help, to which strings would have been
attached, nor did it ever need government-
borne finance of any kind. The company
generated (or on rarer occasions attracted)
all the funds it could possibly need, and
thus the government as a shareholder was,
at least until 1966, excused from taking
part in the fundamental decisions, i.e.
the planning of investments." 39/

British Government ownership does not appear to have caused
decision-making within BP to be dominated by political
rather than normal business considerations. BP appears to
have been managed like any other well-managed oil company.
Anderson describes British Petroleum in his book East of
Suez as "the greatest British trading enterprise that has
yet existed, the third largest company in the world outside
the United States of America." In terms of proven oil
reserves to which BP has access, it has been cited as the
biggest oil company in the world. In terms of actual production of crude oil, BP ranks third in the world, in terms
of refining capacity, fourth. The Middle East interests of
BP are some of the most significant in the world. 40/

Short of a thorough study of BP's operations around the world there is no conclusive way to evaluate its social performance. The following conclusion is from Anderson's work on British Petroleum:

> "BP is a trading enterprise, out to do its
> best for the shareholders. But BP has
> always accepted that working in other
> people's countries involves social as well
> as directly commercial responsibilities--
> indeed, the company accepted responsibility
> for the social welfare of its employees
> in Persia long before such things were
> commonly accepted by industry in Britian.
> Education, health services, water supplies are
> long-term investments, and they pay no
> direct dividends to an oil company's share-
> holders. But their ultimate value is
> incalculable; they help the world to go on.
> In its early days in Persia BP provided
> all these services itself, and got well
> kicked for its pains." 41/

Unlike ENI which has been dominated by and reflects the strong personality of its initial president "there is no Royal Family in BP. In its sixty years it has had seven chairmen, all unrelated to one another." 42/ Anderson provides a short description of each chief executive. He summarized leadership characteristics as follows:

> "The pattern is extraordinarily similar;
> able young men, and twenty or thirty
> years later they have worked their way
> to the board. Their own colleagues, with
> whom they have spent a working lifetime,
> then elect them to the chair. The same
> pattern is repeated in the careers of BP's
> senior executives; they get their jobs
> because they know their job. . . ." 43/

There are several examples which indicate that BP has acted aggressively in business management. The 360 million pound sterling ($936 million) bank loan negotiated by BP was the largest wholly private bank loan ever arranged and involved some innovative financing on the part of BP. 44/

The company drew on the pattern of "ABC deals" and carve-outs used in the United States for tax advantages available prior to 1969, to develop a system in which the company made a forward sale of oil. The advance was secured by BP's Forties Field in the North Sea. The risk of whether or not there was oil in the ground was assumed by the banks. The responsibility for getting the commercially recoverable oil to the surface and ashore was BP's. The kind of innovative finance is a credit to BP management and does not suggest a kind of lethargy often held to be typical of governmental bodies.

BP is not only the discoverer of North Sea oil, but in addition operates the major Forties Field in the UK sector of the North Sea. Production was originally scheduled to occur in 1974. British Petroleum, however, had setbacks in 1973 due to delays of production platform deliveries and pipeline laying was delayed by bad weather. This field contains an estimated 2 billion barrels reserve and is scheduled to be produced at a rate of 400,000 barrels per day beginning in 1975. 45/

The acquisition by BP of Sinclair and Atlantic Richfield's East Coast U.S. gas stations and controlling interest in Standard of Ohio was described by Fortune Magazine as "remarkable coup." Fortune in turn quotes one of BP's competitors describing the SOHIO acquisition as "the most astute ever." 46/

After introductory data are provided on other existing public international oil corporations, comparative performance data will be given which will provide a basis for comparative performance analysis.

[§A.14]   Ente Nazionale Idrocarburi

Ente Nazionale Idrocarburi (ENI) was formed on February 10, 1953 by the Italian Government for the purpose of promoting and carrying out programs of national interest in the hydrocarbons sector and is 100% owned by the Italian government. It is required to pay 65% of its earnings to the government as dividends. Like BP and other public oil corporations, ENI appears to be operated very much like a private corporation subject to the regulatory constraints imposed by the Italian government.

Mr. Enrico Mattei was appointed president of ENI at its formation and served until his accidental death in October 1962. In 1953 ENI absorbed Azienda Generale Italiana Petroli (AGIP), an Italian Government owned company formed in 1926 to operate as a petroleum company. ENI also absorbed Azienda Nazionale Idrogenazione Combustibili (ANIC) in 1953. This company, also owned by the Italian Government, was primarily engaged in refining and chemical operations. 47/ Currently ENI has approximately one hundred subsidiaries and affiliates to which ENI provides overall policy and direction along with planning, coordination and financial assistance. 48/ ENI operates through three major subsidiaries and affiliates: (1) SNAM, a wholly owned subsidiary engaged in transportation of petroleum products and natural gas by pipelines and tankers; (2) AGIP, engaged in oil exploration, production and marketing; and (3) ANIC, sixty-six percent owned by ENI and active in refining and petrochemical operations.

ENI is an enormous company relative to the Italian economy. Its 1972 sales amounted to $3.8 billion. Its oil, gas, engineering and construction divisions accounted for 82% of total sales. Its consolidated gross sales by sector in 1972 were as follows:

Oil, gas engineering and construction $3,102.5 million U.S. dollars

| | |
|---|---:|
| Chemical | 352.2 |
| Mechanical | 93.9 |
| Textile | 171.1 |
| Miscellaneous | 50.0 |
| Total | $3,769.7 |

Source: ENI Annual Report, 1972, p. 8.

Any comparison of ENI with American companies suffers from the fact Italy is a have-not nation with respect to oil. Its deposits of natural gas in the Po Valley are nearly exhausted and Italy has never been a significant producer of crude oil. In 1973 Italy produced only 20,000 barrels of crude oil per day. This is down from 49,000 barrels per day in 1964. Italy's share of world crude oil production is 0.04%. 49/

Another problem arises in appraising the performance of ENI because the company and its record are inseparable from the dynamic leadership of its presidents. Votaw's book on Enrico Mattei noted that any analysis of ENI as a public corporation has been forced into the background:

> "It was forced there by Mattei's total domination of the scene and by the fact that it is extremely difficult in the case of ENI to separate the form of organization from the man who so completely overshadowed it." 50/

In an attempt to correct for the absence of Mattei's leadership, Votaw speculated that "the weight of the evidence would seem to indicate a much weaker ENI in the years to come and a much higher level of government intervention in the activities of the (company). 51/

Frankel similarly stresses the dominance of Mattei's leadership. Frankel ascribed some of the ENI success as "to some extent due to Mattei's undeniable business acumen." 52/ Frankel described Mattei as "a strong, almost demonic personality, who would have left his mark in any sphere into which he might have been drawn. . . ." 53/

Votaw's analysis of ENI as a public corporation makes three points. First, as a "third form," ENI is a modern public corporation which differs from the large private corporations of the western world and from the socialist commissariat of the Soviet Union. As such its first advantage is of greatest importance to the less developed countries in that it offers "a powerful ideological attraction in many of the new nations and in most of the underdeveloped older nations that are now torn between the extremes of free enterprise capitalism, which they are not advanced enough to employ, and the monolithic Communist state, which they would just as soon avoid if possible." 54/ This is an advantage which has no obvious benefit for the developed world and particularly for the United States where capital readily flows to profitable enterprises and where executive talent is readily available.

Second, the public corporation is in the western democratic tradition and is consistent with principles of freedom and individual choice.

Third, the public corporation is able to duplicate some of the ingenuity and innovation of the private corporation that has been used to penetrate political boundaries and to spread modern technology around the world as well as to engage in other activities from which the political state is barred. 55/

None of these three points are relevant to the U.S. situations. The existing private U.S. oil companies are spreading modern technology at least as fast as any public corporation. They have clearly penetrated political boundaries. And they are part and parcel of the western political tradition.

ENI has been one of the major contributors to the disintegration of the ability of the "seven sisters" to influence the international market. Its contribution to effective competition appears to have benefited the oil producing nations rather than consumers. The ENI position in the international oil industry is well stated in a recent Business Week article as follows:

> "The mere mention of Ente Nazionale Idrocarburi, Italy's state-owned oil company, was once enough to send inter- national oil men into paroxysmas of rage. To get drilling concessions, ENI regu- larly thumbed its nose at the major companies by offering Mid-East oil- producing countries more than the traditional 50% share of profits from the output. Internal problems and management changes have tended to tame the giant Italian company, and circum- stances have forced the international oil majors to make more liberal deals of their own, although they do it grudgingly. But oil men are uneasily keeping close watch on the actions of ENI's new Chair- man, Raffaelle Girotti, a dower, 54- year-old man with maverick inclinations, not unlike those of the company's founder, the late Enrico Mattei." 56/

ENI continues to pursue a rather independent role which would seem to make any future collusive agreement, even one supported by governments, difficult to administer and police. ENI's chairman Girotti said:

> "We will continue to be independent as long as we think it is worth our while. We don't simply fight the majors for the sake of fighting. We fight only when we think we must, when we don't like what they are doing." 57/

Business Week notes that "Girotti is wrankling the majors with a campaign to get European Economic Community govern- ments to bypass the oil companies and negotiate deals directly with oil-producing nations." 58/

Thus ENI has performed a countervailing role in stimulating competition mainly for crude oil reserves. It has assisted the oil-producing nations in breaking the old united front of the seven sisters. While worldwide competition has been improved by ENI, the benefits have accrued more to producer than consumer countries. Where competition is now lacking is not among buyers of crude, but among owners of crude oil resources.

Frankel identifies a split personality problem that he believes to be characteristic of public enterprise. He wrote "the amphibian character of public enterprise, which has to orient itself according to two different, not always compatible, goals, makes it impossible to adequately define its character. 59/ The two characteristics identified are first the public characteristic of ENI, emphasizing its role as "the strong arm of the state" and second, the private characteristic "maintaining that if it was sound in itself it would also be a more effective weapon." 60/

[§A.15]   Compagnie Francaise des Petroles and L'Enterprise de Recherches et d'Activities Petrolieres

The French Government has organized two companies to engage in integrated oil operations. They consist of the TOTAL group with Compagnie Francaise des Petroles (CFP) the parent company created in 1924, and the ELF group created in 1966 under another parent enterprise, Enterprise de Recherches et d'Activities Petrolieres (ERAP). The French Government owns 35% of the stock of CFP and controls 40% of the voting power. The Secretary of the Board of Directors is a designate from the Foreign Ministry. Whereas CFP is majority owned by private investors and was organized to manage and develop the petroleum rights granted to France in the Middle East after World War I and "to create a vehicle for realizing a national oil policy," the ELF group is 100% government owned and was the result of a merger of several national petroleum companies after World War II. Its function was to explore oil and gas provinces in France and in former French territory. 61/  ELF group includes Aquitaine which is the largest producer of natural gas in France. Aquitaine is deeply involved in chemical production. Both CFP and ERAP operate through approximately 200 partially or wholly owned subsidiaries, primarily in petroleum but also extensively in other industries.

The French Government has been critical of its own oil corporations. In a report issued coincident with a CFP release showing its first half of 1974 profits increasing 300% from 321 million francs to 1,216 million francs, the French Government "accused the oil companies of tax-dodging and price rigging while under the sheltering wing of the government and called for a 'complete transformation' of the nation's oil industry." 62/ The report holds that the 1928 law which set up a close relationship between the government and the oil companies is out of date and the state should rethink its role. The report suggests a merger between the two French public corporations, CFP and ELF-ERAP.

Crude oil production by CFP is from the following source countries as of 1973:

| Country | Thousand bbls, per year |
|---|---|
| Iran | 105,112 |
| Iraq | 149,926 |
| Qatar | 19,681 |
| Abu Dhabi | 126,899 |
| Oman | 10,636 |
| Dubar | 20,943 |
| Middle East | 433,197 |
| Algeria | 50,177 |
| Tunisia | 676 |
| North Sea | 370 |
| Canada | 2,435 |
| Total | 486,855 |

Source: Compagnie Francaise des Petroles, Annual Report, 1973, p. 78.

Like BP, CFP production is currently highly concentrated in the Middle East and in OPEC countries, the latter accounting for more than 99% of the total company production.

One major problem of a government corporation, particularly one fully owned by the government and subject to some political rather than exclusively business control, is that the rate of return on capital is likely to be relatively low or even negative. To the extent that the company undertakes unprofitable activities it must either receive special subsidies or it must charge higher than competitive prices for its products. Even if the public corporation undertakes no politically motivated and economically unprofitable enterprises, it may still suffer from inefficiency relative to private enterprise. In this event its rate of return again will be relatively low or negative. If it appeals to government and obtains higher prices through such devices as import quotas, market demand prorationing, or higher prices via price controls, then in effect it holds a profit umbrella over the entire industry. Profit records for private enterprise may be initially stimulated as a result of this umbrella activity.

According to Frankel, France's CFP performed this umbrella function for private firms operating in France. Frankel wrote that "because CFP's position had to be buttressed, all other companies too had to work within a system of safeguards which made it exceedingly dirigiste all round, but also remarkably remunerative for the companies operating within it. When some spokesmen for private oil companies complained that they were living in a cage the reply was that at least it was a gilded one." 63/

Appraisal of the French experience with its public oil companies is complicated by the fact that the French government controls virtually every aspect of oil company operations within France. This control includes quotas specifying the maximum amount of oil that firms may refine and sell at retail in the country. The private international oil companies operating in France are allowed 50% of the French market. Companies not granted entry authorization by the French government are excluded from the market. Government control regulates prices and assures a profit to the operating companies. Unlike the British experience, CFP is controlled by the French government as if it were completely state-owned.

Within these regulatory limits, CFP appears to conduct its affairs in the same manner as privately owned companies. Because of this, it avoided the exploration and development of certain high risk areas, including the French-held Sahara Desert and France itself, because of the magnitude of the proven Middle Eastern reserves to which it had access. President DeGaulle in 1966, therefore, created ELF-ERAP, as a wholly owned French corporation, to develop these areas. In time even ELF-ERAP, together with its 51% owned subsidiary Aquitaine, began to drift from its original mission and today it operates very much in the manner of a private company and is engaged in exploration and development in areas of the world, such as Canada, the United States and Asia and serves markets completely unrelated to those of France.

### [§A.16]  Comparative performance data

Using First National City Bank data, the five largest U.S. international companies' performance may be compared with five large foreign international companies including three public corporations which are of special interest.  Table 4 shows production and income data for 1962 and 1972-73.  Income is shown on the basis of total net income rather than on the basis of income per share.  Total data are faulty in that they are influenced by any merger activity as well as by sales of new common stock.  Table 4 shows that the five U.S. major oil companies expanded net income by 187% from 1962 to 1973.  All three foreign public corporations recorded a net income growth in excess of the average of the U.S. majors.  As indicated earlier, net income performance is not necessarily the best standard by which to judge the performance of public corporations.

As a non-income measure, we may examine trends in crude oil production by company from 1962 to 1972.  Table 4 shows that the five U.S. majors expanded company production of net crude oil and natural gas liquids by 120%.  All three of the public corporations individually expanded output by considerably more.  The weighted average of the three companies shows a 171% expansion.  Only the two private foreign companies show expansion records similar to those of the five U.S. majors.

This record of expanding crude oil and natural gas liquid production establishes that the public corporations have pursued a vigorous program of production growth.  It does not say anything about the cost.  Interpreted in conjunction with the relatively favorable record of the public corporations with respect to net income growth it appears that output

TABLE 3a. -- Comparative production and operating data for U.S. and foreign oil companies, 1962-1973 (Net Income -- $ Million; Oil -- Thousand of Barrels Daily)

| | Net Income | | | Percent Chng. | | U.S. - 1962 | | | Other West. Hemisphere 1962 | | | Eastern Hemisphere 1962 | | | Total 1962 | |
|---|---|---|---|---|---|---|---|---|---|---|---|---|---|---|---|---|
| | 1962 | 1972 | 1973 | 1962 to 1973 | 1972 to 1973 | Net Crude & NGL Prod. | Rep finery Runs | Prod. as % of Runs | Net Crude & NGL Prod. | Re-finery Runs | Prod. as % of Runs | Net Crude & NGL Prod. | Re-finery Runs | Prod. as % of Runs | Net Crude & NGL Prod. | Re-finery Runs |
| Five Largest U.S. International Companies | | | | | | | | | | | | | | | | |
| Exxon | 822 | 1,532 | 2,440 | 197 | 59.3 | 520 | 798 | 65.2 | 1,291 | 1,321 | 97.7 | 852 | 1,164 | 73.2 | 2,663 | 3,283 |
| Texaco | 472 | 889 | 1,292 | 174 | 45.3 | 541 | 695 | 77.8 | 234 | 386 | 60.6 | 718 | 405 | 177.3 | 1,493 | 1,486 |
| Gulf | 340 | 447 | 800 | 135 | 79.0 | 406 | 574 | 70.7 | 195 | 179 | 108.9 | 1,098 | 215 | 510.7 | 1,699 | 968 |
| Calif. Std. | 291 | 547 | 844 | 190 | 54.3 | 370 | 505 | 73.3 | 90 | 44 | 204.5 | 657 | 373 | 176.1 | 1,117 | 922 |
| Mobil | 242 | 574 | 843 | 248 | 46.9 | 239 | 650 | 36.8 | 144 | 64 | 225.0 | 415 | 461 | 90.0 | 798 | 1,175 |
| SUB TOTAL | 2,167 | 3,989 | 6,219 | 187 | 55.9 | 2,076 | 3,222 | 64.4 | 1,954 | 1,994 | 98.0 | 3,740 | 2,618 | 142.9 | 7,770 | 7,834 |
| Five Foreign Large International Companies | | | | | | | | | | | | | | | | |
| British Pet. | 194 | 176 | 760 | 292 | 331.8 | 2 | -- | -- | 43 | 20 | 215.0 | 1,655 | 1,140 | 145.2 | 1,700 | 1,160 |
| Royal Dutch/Shell (ex.U.S.) | 470 | 525 | 1,550 | 230 | 195.2 | -- | -- | -- | 873 | 776 | 112.5 | 711 | 1,490 | 47.7 | 1,584 | 2,266 |
| Cie Francaise des Petroles | 45 | 113 | 155 | 244 | 37.2 | -- | -- | -- | 2 | -- | -- | 483 | 335 | 144.2 | 485 | 334 |
| Ente Nazionale Idrocarburi | 5 | 39 | 64 | 1180 | 64.1 | -- | -- | -- | -- | -- | -- | 83 | 150 | 55.3 | 83 | 150 |
| Petrofina (excl. U.S.) | 17 | 58 | 71 | 318 | 22.4 | -- | -- | -- | 10 | 29 | 34.5 | 10 | 190 | 5.3 | 20 | 219 |
| SUB TOTAL | 731 | 911 | 2,600 | 256 | 185.4 | 2 | -- | -- | 928 | 825 | 112.5 | 2,942 | 3,305 | 89.0 | 3,872 | 4,130 |

Source: First National City Bank, "Emergy Memo" April 1974, p. 2

TABLE 3b. -- Comparative production and operating data for U.S. and foreign oil companies, 1962-1973 (Net Income --$ Million; Oil -- Thousand of Barrels Daily) (Con't.)

| Prod. as % of Runs | U.S. 1972 | | | Other West. Hemisphere 1972 | | | Eastern Hemisphere 1972 | | | Total 1972 | | | % Chng. 1962/1972 | |
|---|---|---|---|---|---|---|---|---|---|---|---|---|---|---|
| | Net Crude & NGL Prod. | Re-finery Runs | Prod. as % of Runs | Net Crude & NGL Prod. | Re-finery Runs | Prod. as % of Runs | Net Crude & NGL Prod. | Re-finery Runs | Prod. as % of Runs | Net Crude & NGL Prod. | Re-finery Runs | Prod. as % of Runs | Net Crude & NGL Prod. | Prod. as % of Runs |
| 81.1 | 970 | 1,029 | 94.3 | 1,489 | 1,399 | 106.4 | 2,550 | 2,718 | 93.8 | 5,009 | 5,146 | 97.3 | 88 | 20 |
| 100.5 | 792 | 1,012 | 78.3 | 360 | 626 | 57.5 | 2,625 | 1,314 | 199.8 | 3,777 | 2,952 | 127.9 | 153 | 27 |
| 175.5 | 561 | 767 | 73.1 | 324 | 466 | 69.5 | 2,329 | 712 | 327.1 | 3,214 | 1,945 | 165.2 | 89 | -6 |
| 121.2 | 462 | 815 | 56.7 | 142 | 208 | 68.3 | 2,555 | 1,024 | 249.5 | 3,159 | 2,047 | 154.3 | 183 | 27 |
| 67.9 | 394 | 856 | 46.0 | 231 | 117 | 197.4 | 1,286 | 1,261 | 102.0 | 1,911 | 2,234 | 85.5 | 139 | 26 |
| 99.2 | 3,179 | 4,479 | 71.0 | 2,546 | 2,816 | 90.4 | 11,345 | 7,029 | 161.4 | 17,070 | 14,324 | 119.2 | 120 | 20 |
| 146.6 | -- | -- | -- | 29 | 80 | 36.3 | 4,561 | 2,320 | 196.6 | 4,590 | 2,400 | 191.3 | 170 | 30 |
| 69.9 | -- | -- | -- | 875 | 1,013 | 86.4 | 2,578 | 3,140 | 82.1 | 3,453 | 4,153 | 83.1 | 118 | 19 |
| 144.8 | -- | 12 | -- | 6 | 3 | 200.0 | 1,250 | 934 | 133.8 | 1,256 | 949 | 132.4 | 159 | -9 |
| 55.3 | -- | -- | -- | -- | -- | -- | 289 | 536 | 53.9 | 289 | 536 | 53.9 | 248 | -3 |
| 9.1 | -- | -- | -- | 19 | 58 | 32.8 | 24 | 282 | 8.5 | 43 | 340 | 12.6 | 115 | 38 |
| 93.8 | -- | 12 | -- | 929 | 1,154 | 80.5 | 8,702 | 7,212 | 120.7 | 9,631 | 8,378 | 115.0 | 149 | 23 |

expansion did not come at the expense of reckless bidding
for crude oil resources.  If this had been the case evidence
would tend to appear in a slow rate of income growth.  There
is no such evidence shown in Table 4.  Costs may have been borne
by the French government.

Another measure of performance by which we may
compare the public corporations with their private counterparts is the ratio of crude oil and natural gas liquid
production to refinery runs, all under company control.  A
word of caution is necessary however in interpreting the
data.  Company production of crude oil in the past has
implied company control of that production.  This is no
longer true.  A variety of arrangements now exists between
operating companies and host governments.  Company production must be interpreted loosely to mean that host
governments have complete control over the volume of output,
but that the operating companies have a high degree of
influence and in some cases control over distribution of
that output.

With these caveats we find that the U.S. majors
increased a safety margin of production in excess of refinery runs by 20% from 1962 through 1972.  Only Gulf Oil
shows a reduction in this ratio.  Prudent management in this
case would appear to call for a move toward a lower ratio of
production to refinery runs inasmuch as the 1962 ratio was
extremely high.  With respect to the three public corporations,
British Petroleum moved from a relatively high self-sufficiency
ratio to an extremely high ratio where company production
exceeded company refinery runs by 91.3% in 1972.  CFP refinery construction led to a decline in its self-sufficiency
ratio.  However, in 1972 it recorded 32.4% excess, hence its
10-year trend was in the direction of improved balance.
ENI, as a vertically-integrated oil company, had a dangerous
crude deficit in 1962 which deteriorated slightly by 1972.
ENI's crude self-sufficiency ratio may be improved by its
new Lybian production as well as new production from the
North Sea, Iran, and Nigeria. 64/

Company performance by structure may also be
evaluated in terms of natural gas production.  Table 5 shows
data for the same companies examined above.  From 1963
through 1973 the five U.S. major international companies
expanded their natural gas production by 172%.  For the
three public corporations under study, there is great

A-38

TABLE 5. — Natural gas production by company, 1963 to 1973

(Millions of cubic feet daily)

| | 1963 | 1964 | 1965 | 1966 | 1967 | 1968 | 1969 | 1970 | 1971 | 1972 | 1973 | % Change 1973/1963 |
|---|---|---|---|---|---|---|---|---|---|---|---|---|
| Five largest U.S. International Companies | | | | | | | | | | | | |
| Exxon | 2,616 | 2,845 | 3,470 | 4,071 | 4,419 | 5,296 | 6,309 | 7,491 | 8,527 | 9,323 | 9,767 | 273 |
| Texaco | 1,863 | 1,998 | 2,074 | 2,560 | 2,887 | 3,262 | 3,661 | 4,026 | 4,181 | 4,685 | 4,516 | 142 |
| Gulf | 1,549 | 1,783 | 2,092 | 2,367 | 2,688 | 2,994 | 3,188 | 3,486 | 3,539 | 3,572 | 3,360 | 117 |
| Mobil | 1,214 | 1,474 | 1,522 | 1,673 | 1,843 | 2,040 | 2,352 | 2,812 | 2,967 | 3,072 | 3,156 | 160 |
| Calif. Std. | 1,024 | 1,129 | 1,172 | 1,329 | 1,398 | 1,496 | 1,550 | 1,658 | 1,674 | 1,748 | 1,706 | 67 |
| SUB TOTAL | 8,266 | 9,229 | 10,330 | 12,000 | 13,235 | 15,088 | 17,060 | 19,473 | 20,888 | 22,400 | 22,505 | 172 |
| Five foreign large International Companies | | | | | | | | | | | | |
| British Pet. | 9 | 15 | 24 | 63 | 141 | 241 | 265 | 251 | 344 | 432 | 407 | 4422 |
| Cie. Francaise des Petroles | 30 | 60 | 100 | 188 | 206 | 226 | 273 | 105 | 125 | 148 | 159 | 430 |
| Ente Nazionale Idrocarburi | 684 | 725 | 739 | 835 | 879 | 969 | 1,087 | 1,171 | 1,199 | 1,342 | 1,413 | 107 |
| Royal Dutch/ Shell (ex.US.) | 357 | 441 | 480 | 550 | 738 | 1,093 | 1,469 | 2,016 | 2,583 | 3,280 | 3,929 | 1001 |
| Petrofina (excl. U.S.) | 60 | 58 | 59 | 64 | 65 | 133 | 152 | 127 | 156 | 189 | 197 | 228 |
| SUB-TOTAL | 1,140 | 1,299 | 1,402 | 1,700 | 2,029 | 2,662 | 3,246 | 3,670 | 4,407 | 5,391 | 6,105 | 436 |

Source: First National City Bank, "Energy Memo" October 1974, p. 4.

diversity in results.  British Petroleum had almost no
production of natural gas in 1963 and was only a very small
gas producer by 1973.  However, the percentage increase is
extremely large.  Similarly, CFP while showing a healthy
percentage increase in output was an unimportant factor in
natural gas production in 1973.  Even ENI production of
natural gas in 1973 was small relative to any of the five
U.S. majors.  Its percentage increase was relatively modest.

Finally, the three public corporations have left
themselves vulnerable due to their very high concentration
of crude oil production in the Eastern Hemisphere.  The
three public companies together derive 99.4% of their total
production from the Eastern Hemisphere.  In contrast the
five American international majors derive 66.5% of their
production from that area.

The foregoing analysis of present status and
trends in oil and gas production leads to the conclusion
that the public companies have been very successful relative
to their private counterparts in expanding crude oil production and, with the exception of ENI, in attaining a high
degree of self sufficiency between company oil production
and refinery runs.  In natural gas production, however, the
public companies have been relatively unsuccessful.  The
public enterprises are dangerously dependent on Eastern
Hemisphere and OPEC sources for their crude.

Another standard by which we may judge the performance of private versus public corporations is in terms
of their ratio of after-tax profitability to net capital
invested in the company by stockholders, whether public or
private.  In one sense this rate of return on equity capital
is an ideal standard of performance.  Society's capital
assets are tied up in the corporations listed regardless of
whether those companies happen to be owned privately or
governmentally.  If scarce capital assets are efficiently
employed in a nation's productive processes, then that
nation's standard of living will be high relative to inefficient employment of such assets.  In a given company, if
assets earn a low and declining rate of return, then the
direct burden is normally first borne by the company's
stockholders.  Assets employed by public corporations must

be forced to meet the same high profit standards as in
private business if a high standard of living is a goal of
society.

In another sense the rate-of-return-on-equity
criterion is a faulty measure of performance. Our accounting
system normally fails to reflect external costs and benefits.
Public corporations are frequently established to accomplish
a variety of public goals that are not reflected in revenues
captured by the company. Where this is true, then reported
rates of return for public corporations might be expected to
be below those of private corporations.

Table 6 shows that the five U.S. international oil
companies in 1973 earned higher rates of return on stockholder equity than either of the two French companies.
British Petroleum in 1973, earning 15.3% rate-of-return-on-
equity capital, performed better than three U.S. companies
and worse than two. BP's 1973 rate of return is approximately equal to the weighted average of all five U.S.
internationals.

In 1972 the five U.S. corporations all out-performed
ELF-ERAP which earned only 0.7% rate of return, ENI which
earned only 1.0%, as well as BP which earned 4.8%. CFP out-
performed only Gulf among the five U.S. majors. In 1971 ENI
recorded a net loss.

Rate-of-return data indicate superior performance
for the private companies relative to all public companies
with the exception of BP performance in 1973. This interpretation must remain ambiguous insofar as we have no data on
social returns that are external to the firms studied (returns
that accrue to society but not to the companies involved).
Further, in international comparisons, performance differences
may be due more to differential taxation, subsidy and regulatory conditions than to differences in the factor of primary
concern--public versus private ownership status. These
differences may be of particular importance beginning in 1971
when price controls were introduced in the United States.
Further, percentage depletion allowance was reduced in the
1969 income tax revision and the crude oil allocation system
negatively affected 1973 earnings of companies operating in
the United States.

TABLE 6. — Rate of return on equity capital.

| | ELF ERAP[1] 1973 1972 (Million francs) (or %) | | BP[2] 1973 1972 (Mil.U.S. $) (or %) | | CFP[3] 1973 1972 (Mill.francs) (or %) | | ENI[4] 1972 only (Mil.U.S.$) (or %) |
|---|---|---|---|---|---|---|---|
| Net Profit | 90,550 | 26,063 | 784 | 181 | 874 | 578 | 17.7 |
| Stockholder equity | 3,999,729 | 3,773,666 | 5,110 | 3,769 | 6,824 | 6,121 | 1,840.9 |
| Rate of return on Stockholder Equity Percentage | 2.3 | 0.7 | 15.3 | 4.8 | 12.8 | 9.4 | 1.0 |

1. ELF, Aquitaine, Annual Report, 1973, p. 2
2. BP, Annual Report, 1973, pp. 20-22.
3. CFP, Annual Report, 1973, pp. 85-86
4. ENI, Annual Report, 1972, pp. 32-33

Inasmuch as British Petroleum is almost indistinguishable from other major international oil companies among the so-called "seven sisters," its performance may be measured in terms of its growth in earnings per share of common stock outstanding over a period of years. This comparison, shown in Table 7 indicates British Petroleum out-performed the other six members of the big-seven group over the 21 years ending with 1973. The compound annual growth rate in earnings per share for BP was an extremely attractive 10.7%.

However, 1973 as the terminal year in this comparison is subject to the criticism that it was a year of great turmoil in oil company earnings. In fact, BP earnings increased more than any other international oil company under the pressure of host governments and rapidly escalating prices. If 1970 is taken as the last normal year for oil company earnings and we compute the compound annual growth rate in earnings per share from 1952 through 1970, British Petroleum was out-performed by two of the big-seven firms and in turn performed better than four of those firms. The conclusion indicated by this analysis of performance by a common financial criterion is that BP management has a good record. If its status as a partially owned government corporation had any effect on its financial performance record, one must conclude on the basis of the earnings record alone that its public corporation status must have been advantageous.

The growth rate for CFP is shown for 1964 through 1973. The CFP compound annual growth rate at 4.1% is lower than any of the firms shown and by a substantial difference. This poor record may be due to the inept bargaining described at length by Adelman whereby CFP obtained "une position privilégiée" in Iraq resulting in high-priced crude oil for France. 65/ Adelman concluded that "the French have again been had, most royally, and by their own strenuous effort." 66/

The existing public corporations organized by oil-importing nations and operating in the oil industry are all complex corporations engaged in not only the narrowly defined oil industry but also in other industries including petrochemicals, textiles, power generation, transportation, and the like. As conglomerate corporations with an oil industry emphasis, evaluation of comparative performance based upon operating results is difficult. The problem was expressed

TABLE 7. -- Earnings per share for major U.S. international
oil companies, plus Shell, CFP and BP, 1952-1973
and estimated 1974.

| | | (Dollars) | | | | Royal Dutch | | (Francs) |
|---|---|---|---|---|---|---|---|---|
| Year | Exxon | Texaco | Gulf | Mobil | SOCAL | Shell | BP | CFP* |
| est.1974 | 13.00 | 6.75 | 5.50 | 11.25 | 6.75 | 11.00 | 3.50 | N.A. |
| 1973 | 10.90 | 4.75 | 4.06 | 8.34 | 4.97 | 7.95 | 1.96 | 25.68 |
| 1972 | 6.83 | 3.27 | 2.15 | 5.65 | 3.22 | 3.12 | .45 | 21.45 |
| 1971 | 6.77 | 3.32 | 2.70 | 5.33 | 3.01 | 4.26 | .99 | 21.18 |
| 1970 | 5.91 | 3.02 | 2.65 | 4.77 | 2.68 | 3.84 | .60 | 21.35 |
| 1969 | 5.78 | 2.83 | 2.94 | 4.50 | 2.67 | 4.25 | .64 | 21.34 |
| 1968 | 5.94 | 3.07 | 3.02 | 4.23 | 2.66 | 3.87 | .68 | 19.81 |
| 1967 | 5.54 | 2.79 | 2.74 | 3.81 | 2.48 | 3.27 | .43 | 17.45 |
| 1966 | 5.06 | 2.56 | 2.44 | 3.51 | 2.48 | 2.97 | .66 | 15.97 |
| 1965 | 4.81 | 2.36 | 2.06 | 3.15 | 2.31 | 2.81 | .72 | 12.95 |
| 1964 | 4.87 | 2.14 | 1.91 | 2.90 | 2.08 | 2.60 | .74 | 17.85 |
| 1963 | 4.74 | 2.04 | 1.78 | 2.72 | 1.94 | 2.68 | .74 | |
| 1962 | 3.88 | 1.80 | 1.64 | 2.49 | 1.89 | 2.56 | .63 | |
| 1961 | 3.50 | 1.66 | 1.61 | 2.18 | 1.77 | 2.33 | .53 | |
| 1960 | 3.18 | 1.51 | 1.57 | 1.88 | 1.65 | 2.22 | .57 | |
| 1959 | 2.91 | 1.37 | 1.38 | 1.69 | 1.57 | 2.19 | .58 | |
| 1958 | 2.62 | 1.21 | 1.57 | 1.62 | 1.60 | 2.22 | .60 | |
| 1957 | 3.96 | 1.36 | 1.69 | 2.28 | 1.78 | 3.47 | .52 | |
| 1966 | 4.11 | 1.24 | 1.35 | 2.85 | 1.62 | 2.97 | .53 | |
| 1965 | 3.61 | 1.07 | 1.10 | 2.37 | 1.43 | 2.56 | .43 | |
| 1964 | 2.98 | .92 | .93 | 2.10 | 1.31 | 2.22 | .15 | |
| 1963 | 3.04 | .78 | .89 | 2.14 | 1.17 | 1.99 | .22 | |
| 1952 | 2.86 | .74 | .72 | 1.96 | 1.07 | 2.15 | .23 | |

Compound annual growth rates 1952-1973

| | Exxon | Texaco | Gulf | Mobil | SOCAL | Shell | BP | |
|---|---|---|---|---|---|---|---|---|
| 1952-1973 | 6.6% | 9.2% | 8.5% | 7.1% | 7.6% | 10.7% | 6.4% | |
| 1952-1970 | 4.1% | 8.1% | 7.5% | 5.1% | 5.3% | 5.5% | 3.3% | |

* Income per share after taxation and depreciation.

Sources:  Moody's Handbook of Common Stocks, and Standard and Poors Stock
Guide, and CFP, Annual Reports.

by a recent Library of Congress, Legislative Reference
Service report as follows:

>"The practice of publishing consolidated
>balance sheets and an early and long
>standing policy of company secrecy, have
>made strict comparisons with private
>companies -- whose costs are also closely
>held secrets -- even more difficult.  A
>final answer must be held in abeyance." 67/

Subject to the limitations of data and comparability problems the performance record of the existing
public corporations indicates only minor differences from
that of leading privately owned companies.  In some respects
the record is significantly worse, in some respects the BP
record in particular is slightly better.  For reasons of
inadequate data, precision comparisons are not feasible.

The fact that for some public corporations, most
notably British Petroleum, the performance record is virtually
indistinguishable from the leading private companies points
up the basic dilemma of the public corporation.  On the one
hand, if the public corporation is well-managed, in accordance
with ordinary business procedures, the company will be
operated efficiently, the public's resources will be used in
such a way that their return is maximized, and the return on
equity investment will be comparable with private business.
In this event it is not clear that anything has been gained
by government participation in ownership.  The evidence
examined provides no reason for believing that a public
corporation will be more efficient than a private corporation.  There is no evidence that suggests that a government corporation will be more efficient than a private
corporation.  The overwhelming concensus among informed
people and the conclusions of empirical studies is that a
government corporation has less incentive to be efficient
and is likely to operate less efficiently, and further that
the greater the government ownership up to 100%, the lesser
the incentives to operate efficiently.

On the other hand, if the management of a government corporation undertakes to make investments which are
not justified on a private profitability standard but may
yield an attractive social rate of return (some benefits of
the investment are external to the firm), then the profitability

A-45

record will appear to be poor by the ordinary standards of
measurement. In this event the public corporation should
be paid a subsidy equal to the net value of its externalities.
But performing functions that are uneconomic from a private
point of view and receiving compensating subsidies confuses
the "yardstick" role that a public corporation, particularly
in the United States, would be expected to perform. To serve
in this "yardstick" role requires that the company be
closely comparable to private corporations. If its record
is closely comparable, then there is no obvious net gain
from its government ownership, except the "yardstick" benefit.

[§A.17]  Summary

        This comparison of existing foreign international
oil company performance with that of private companies has
been necessarily sketchy because of the lack of any existing
performance studies and the differences in subsidies, taxation, and regulations between countries leading to differing
performance results.

        The advantages of a government oil company pertain
mainly to countries in a relatively early stage of development.
If private capital will not flow from investors in a given
country into the international oil business, and if such a
flow is desired by the government, then creation of a government enterprise would appear to be a relatively attractive
solution.  If some private capital is available, then a
partially owned government enterprise would appear to be
preferable to a wholly owned enterprise.  These conditions,
however, do not pertain to the United States where there
are already many existing private international oil companies
and private capital readily flows to international oil investments.

        Comparative analysis produces mixed results.  Over a
twenty-one year period the public enterprises were able to
expand crude oil production faster than the leading private
corporations.  Also, net income growth by the public corporations was greater than that of private corporations.  Analysis
of the trend in the rate of return on equity capital showed
that one partially public corporation, British Petroleum, had
an outstanding record.  However, when the turmoil years 1971
through 1973 are removed from the comparison, then British

Petroleum's record is similar to that of the leading private corporations. The CFP return-on-equity capital is very poor and may reflect some of the questionable purchase arrangements that CFP entered into with Iraq.

Crude oil self-sufficiency with respect to refinery runs shows that ENI has been in a poor and slightly deteriorating position through the year 1972. All other firms examined, public and private, have reasonable self-sufficiency records.

The public firms tend to be highly concentrated in Middle Eastern and OPEC crude oil sources. Private companies have more diversified crude sources. British Petroleum, however, has substantially improved its diversification due to its large discoveries in the North Sea and on the North Slope of Alaska.

All of the public companies show poor records in natural gas production. While there has been a large percentage increase in natural gas output by the public corporations, their 1973 position in gas production is universally low.

British Petroleum seems to have avoided political control of its ordinary business activities. The French companies, on the other hand, have been subject to a high degree of political control. This may be a factor which accounts for their poor performance relative to that of BP.

Overall, the comparative performances analysis provides no basis for concluding that public corporations will be more efficiently operated than private corporations, and evidence is available from this record to suggest the opposite, that public control produces less efficiency.

C.   [§A.18]   Empirical studies of the relative efficiency of public versus private industry

[§A.19]   The Davies Study of Australian Airlines

The opportunities for making an unambiguous performance comparison of public versus private industry are rarely available. One such well-known study compared the efficiency of Australia's two domestic air lines, the Trans Australian Airlines (TAA), which is owned by the government, and the privately owned Ansett Australian National Airways (Ansett ANA). The author wrote, "[e]xcept for type of ownership these two firms have a remarkable number of similar characteristics. The two-airline situation in Australia is probably as near to a laboratory experiment as an economist ever comes." 68/ In this case "government policy is expressly designed to make the two firms similar in most important respects. This policy has been successful." 69/ Thus, the yardstick function seems to be effective.

Davies compared three ratios permitting him to evaluate performance of the two firms. Those ratios are the following: "(1) The tons of freight and mail carried to the number of employees, (2) the number of paying passengers carried to the number of employees, and (3) the revenue earned to the number of employees." 70/

The author found that for all three measures, performance by the privately owned firms was substantially better than the public corporation. He drew the following conclusion: "The data support the contention that the private company is economically more efficient than the public firm." 71/

[§A.20]   The Polanyi Study of British industry.

George and Pricilla Polanyi have conducted a series of studies of relative efficiency between private and nationalized industry in England. One such study researched the question of "whether the existing nationalized industries have shown, in the main aspects of their performance, any marked advantage over that of private industry." 72/ On the basis of this British experience the study reached negative conclusions with the following findings:

"1.   The financial performance of the nationalised industries has been consistently far below the average of private industries. Since 1955 the net return on assets has been in the range 2%-6% compared with 11%-19% in privately owned companies.

2.   Net loss of the six industries nationalised throughout the post-war period (coal, electricity, gas, railways, BEA, BOAC), was ₤1,169 million for the period 1956-1972.

3. Since 1956 the nationalised industries have received £6,500 million in government subsidies.

| 1956-1972: | £million |
|---|---|
| Subsidies on Current Account | 2,249 |
| Capital Grants | 3,123* |
| | ———— |
| | 5,372 |

| 1973 (approx. preliminary estimates) | |
|---|---|
| Subsidies on Current Account | 500 |
| Debt written off | 600 |
| | ———— |
| Total: 1956-1973 | 6,472 |
| | ———— |

4. Over the twenty years from 1948-1968 the price rise of nationalised industry output was about the same as for all goods and services.

5. Per £100 of labour and capital, output of nationalised industries was £67 in 1971 compared with £99 for manufacturing industries.

6. In the twenty years 1948-1968 the nationalised industries' increase in output per £100 of extra capital investment was about £7 (at 1958 prices) compared with an average of £24 for manufacturing industries. This comparison of the yield from extra capital investment is after making allowance for the effect on output of a reduction of 33% in nationalised industries' employment during this period, compared with an increase of 16% in manufacturing employment.

7. Since the investment by nationalised industries has been a major part of the total national investment in fixed assets (about one-fifth during the period 1948-1972) it has tended to depress the productivity of UK investment which has been lower than in other countries.

8.  Nationalised industries paid only
    ₤81 million UK taxes on income in the
    period 1962-1972, while privately owned
    companies paid ₤13,729 million.  As a
    proportion of gross income arising in
    the UK, companies paid 15% in UK taxes,
    compared with 0.6% for the nationalised
    industries.

9.  Excess of capital expenditure over receipts
    on capital account by nationalised indus-
    tries in the period 1962-1972 was ₤5,256
    million (32% of capital expenditure),
    compared with ₤799 million (2% of expendi-
    ture) for privately owned companies.  The
    total amount borrowed by the nationalised
    industries in this period was ₤9,750
    million, of which ₤9,261 million was
    borrowed by the central government.

10. Government grants accounted for 7% of privately
    owned companies' receipts on capital account
    in the period 1962-1972, compared with
    28% for the nationalised industries. 73/

    *of which:  debt written off ₤2,849 million

On the basis of the findings listed above the following
conclusions were drawn:

    CONCLUSION

    On the evidence presented in this study, both
    on the record of nationalised industries
    compared with private enterprise and the
    underlying principles of past and future
    nationalisation, we submit that there can
    be no doubt about the answers to the
    questions originally posed in the Intro-
    duction (Page 9):

    1.  The record of nationalised industries
        compared with that of private industry,
        measured by any of the usually accepted
        indicators of efficiency, shows
        generally inferior performance.

2.  There are no aspects of this per-
    formance which provide evidence of
    the inherent superiority of public
    ownership. 74/

It should be noted that the Polanyi study had
political overtones and its objectivity may be questioned.  The
introduction to the study notes that the Labour Party Pro-
gramme of 1973 called for a "substantial extension of public
ownership in British industry."  The intent of the study is to
consider the merits of this political proposal by evaluating
the past performance of nationalized industries.

One fault of evaluating nationalized industries
relative to non-nationalized industries is that frequently
those indistries which are taken over by a government are those
which either have failed or are failing under private control.

Public enterprise frequently arises both in the
United States and around the world, not as a result of conscious
planning by government, but rather as a result of individual
firm or industry failures.  Frankel wrote "in our era and in
non-socialist countries, the state enters business mainly under
conditions of stress; such decisions are taken either in the
course of war or under political seige conditions.  Otherwise,
it is a case of private enterprise gone wrong, asking to be
bailed out by the government:  hence the old saying, that
the capitalists are always in favor of the nationalization
of their losses." 75/  In the United States this is the path
taken by many municipal transportation systems.

The failure route may currently be under way in
England where Burmah Oil Company "surrendered control over wide
areas of its operations to the British Government in return
for backing from the Bank of England." 76/  Burmah announced
that it was "unable to comply with certain provisions of
the loan agreement covering six hundred million in dollar
borrowings." 77/  Burmah Oil sold to the Bank of England its
unpledged holdings in British Petroleum Company and Shell
Transport and Trading Company, the British arm of the
Royal Dutch Shell group.  Burmah owns 21.5% interest in
British Petroleum and a 2% share in Shell Transport.  The
Wall Street Journal wrote that "by placing as much as a

21.5% interest in British Petroleum with the Bank of England, the Burmah rescue plan seems to solidify the British Government's control over BP. The government already owns 49% of BP's stock." 78/ This process fits into Frankel's description of "private enterprise gone wrong, and asking to be bailed out by the government." 79/

Other studies of public versus private industry performance in rubber production, helium production, and electric power have been made. While the conclusions of such studies almost universally support the hypothesis that private enterprise is more efficient than public enterprise, the conclusions are almost always ambiguous. Comparability is rarely achieved. In the public utility area the picture is clouded by public regulations.

D.   [§A.21]   <u>Suggestions for the Structure and Policy of Public Corporations in the Mineral Industry</u> 80/

Arlan Tussing, Chief Economist of the U.S. Senate Committee on Interior and Insular Affairs and a Professor of Economics at the University of Alaska, has offered the following advice on creation of a public corporation:

"I do, however, have some suggestions for the structure and policy of public corporations in the mineral industry, aimed at combining some of the best features of government and private enterprise rather than their worst.

"<u>First, before establishing a governmental enterprise, be clear what its purpose is to be, what the incentive for the management to accomplish their purpose will be and, quite rigorously, will be the measure of the enterprise's success.</u>

"<u>Second, do not set up a monopoly.</u> There is no surer formula for inefficiency and social irresponsibility. Economies of scale do exist in mining and petroleum exploration, but they are very small compared to some other industries or relative to the opportunities for development in an area the size of British Columbia. In petroleum refining, the minimum efficient size of refinery is probably now about the size of the British Columbia market for petroleum products, but if a new government-owned refinery needs a monopoly or protectionist legislation to be profitable, it will almost certainly be a serious burden on consumers. Industries in which scale economies are narrow and where ingenuity and intuition are still crucial, as in mineral exploration or

onshore oil and gas production, are probably not the most
appropriate candidates for nationalization, but where it is
determined to establish a state enterprise, consideration
might be given to establishment of more than one competing
public enterprise.

"Third, do not clothe the corporation in sovereign
immunities. Such immunity can be and often is a cover for
inefficiency, irresponsibility and even lawlessness. The
corporation should be suable, pay taxes or their equivalent
(federal, provincial and local), and be subject to environmental and safety laws and regulations, and above all to the
bankruptcy laws. Its operations should not be protected by
any version of an official secrets act. There is no good
reason why the directors, officers and employees should be
excused from the same civil and criminal liability for their
actions to which their counterparts in private enterprise
are subject.

"I would urge hesitation even in providing guarantees
for the corporation's debt. A public mining or oil corporation will be pursuing a line of business in which private
enterprise regularly borrows money without such guarantees.
The more intense scrutiny of bankers and underwriters toward
a corporation whose debt must stand on its own merit, might
well save the corporation's owners - the public - more money
than the small interest differential associated with government guarantees.

"Fourth, give the public and the corporation's officers
and staff a material interest in its success and its efficiency.
The government need not hold all the shares but only a controlling interest, not necessarily even a majority. One
block of shares (enough to elect at least one director) can
be held in trust for the company's employees and voted by them.
The remainder of the shares would be offered to the public;
they would be voted by their owners, and publicly traded. Not
only would this provision broaden interest and participation
in management, but the market price of publicly traded shares
would be a continuing indicator of management performance and
of the value of the government's equity. I see no compelling
reason to restrict share ownership to residents; it might
in fact be useful to encourage minority participation by
major oil companies or mining companies. A residence requirement for shareholders, however, would reinforce symbolically

the corporation's identity as a national or provincial instrument, and would, of course, limit remittance of dividends abroad.

"Fifth, the corporation's policies should be responsive to public policy but not bend to every political wind. I would suggest that a minority, but only a minority, of the government directors serve at the pleasure of the Cabinet and be regarded as spokesmen for its policies. The remaining directors representing the government's equity would be chosen indirectly for long and staggered terms.

"Sixth, the corporation should be under pressure to pay dividends. A majority of all the shares (and directors) should represent parties who have a material interest that the corporation not retain, reinvest or dissipate all its earnings: private shareholders, the employees, and the members who serve at the pleasure of the Cabinet (who would presumably be responsive to the fiscal interest of the government). The influence of this group will be a constant corrective to tendencies of management, inside directors and permanent directors toward complacency, empire-building, pyramid-building or gold plating.

"Seventh, maintain a clear distinction between the corporation and the government as landowner. The public enterprise should obtain resource rights on Crown lands only in competition with other prospective operators. The corporation should not receive a concealed (and indeterminate) subsidy by access to resources at no charge or at a lower price than a competitor might offer. If it must have a preference right, let it be at most a right to match the high bidder.

"A preference right on the best offshore leases is a feature of the federal oil and gas corporation (FOGCO) proposed recently in the United States Congress. In view of the prices oil companies have been recently willing to spend in these lease sales, such a preference would guarantee that FOGCO would appear profitable, however incompetent its management, and that the federal treasury would lose billions of dollars in lease revenues.

"Eighth and finally, take advantage of the division of labor and competition. The Corporation should not attempt to do for itself the things that even the greatest oil and mining companies contract out to others, such as seismic surveying, core drilling, well drilling, well logging and construction. There is virtually no chance that a state corporation could improve on the performance of private firms in these exceedingly competitive areas.

"In summary, I am generally skeptical of the case for public enterprise in the minerals industry, but hopeful that such enterprises could be established free of many of their usual shortcomings if some thought is given to their purpose, organization and standards of performance."

# APPENDIX A

## FOOTNOTES

1. H. Koontz, Government Control of Business, 863 (1941).

2. M. Dimock, Developing America's Waterways, 103 (1935).

3. Ibid. at 15.

4. C. Wilcox, Public Policies Toward Business, 502 (1971).

5. D. Pegrum, Public Regulation of Business, 670 (1959).

6. L. Musolf, Mixed Enterprises, 3, 51 (1972).

7. Ibid. at 58-59.

8. C. H. Pritchett, The Tennessee Valley Authority, 147 (1943).

9. M. Dimock, supra note 2, at 42, 112.

10. Ibid. at 85-85.

11. Ibid. at 85.

12. C. H. Pritchett, supra note 8, at 306.

13. Ibid. at 238.

14. C. Wilcox, supra note 4, at 521-522.

15. C. H. Pritchett, supra note 8, at 237.

16. Ibid. at 657.

17. Tennessee Valley Authority, TVA Power and Taxes, 7 (1965).

18. U.S. Senate Commerce Committee, Hearings on the Consumer Energy Act of 1974, 93d Cong., 1st Sess., at Pt. 3, 1059 (1974).

19. C. Wilcox, supra note 4, at 502.

20. Stuart Daggett, Principles of Inland Transportation, 44 (1955).

21. M. Dimock, _supra_ note 2, at 29.

22. _Ibid_. at 44.

23. _Ibid_. at 31-33.

24. H. Koontz, _supra_ note 1, at 863-864.

25. The seriousness of this problem of hidden costs is seen in the following illustration concerning the water supply of Los Angeles. According to Dudley F. Pegrum, 5 per cent of the city's water supply is supplied by the Metropolitan Water District. The water is paid for partly by user charges ($25 per acre-foot) and partly by assessments on property owners of the city. The funds collected by property taxes do not appear in the operating statement of the Water Department and yet it amounts to about 40 per cent of the total costs of the department. Re-calculating the cost of water to include the revenue from property taxes yields a figure of $225 per acre-foot, about nine times the user charge for water. The moral of this example is obvious; Los Angeles pays for its water, either through user charges or taxes. The same will be true for oil and gas provided by a federal oil corporation. See D. Pegrum, _supra_ note 5, at 663-664.

26. M. Dimock, _supra_ note 2, at 18.

27. _Ibid_.

28. Calculated from, M. Dimock, _supra_ note 2, at 17.

29. _Ibid_. at 21-22.

30. C. Wilcox, _supra_ note 4, at 502.

31. _Ibid_. at 87.

32. C. H. Pritchett, _supra_ note 8, at 238.

33. S. A. Lawrence, _United States Merchant Shipping Policies and Politics_ 41-2 (1955).

34. D. Lilienthal, _TVA, Democracy on the March_, 24 (1944).

35. Hearings on the Consumer Energy Act of 1974, _supra_ note 18, at Pt. 4, 1357-1498.

36. P. H. Frankel, _Mattei:  Oil and Power Politics_, 157 (1966).

37. _Moody's Industrial Manual_, 1733 (1973).

37a For a discussion of recent developments concerning Burmah Oil, see Appendix A, at A-51.

38 British Petroleum Company, _Annual Report and Accounts for 1973_, at 2.

39. P. H. Frankel, _supra_ note 36, at 164.

40. J. R. L. Anderson, _East of Suez, A Study of Britain's Greatest Trading Enterprise_, 17 (1969).

41. _Ibid_. at 273.

42. _Ibid_. at 278.

43. _Ibid_. at 280.

44. Q. Morris, "How BP Raised its ₤360 Million," _Euromoney_, Aug. 1972, at 14-17.

45. _International Petroleum Encyclopedia_, 16 (1974).

46. _Fortune_, Feb. 1972, at 45.

47. P. H. Frankel, _supra_ note 36, at 179-181.

48. _Moody's Industrial and Government Manual_, 3521 (1968).

49. American Petroleum Institute, _Annual Statistical Review_, Sept. 1974, at 69.

50. D. Votaw, _The Six-legged Dog_, 154 (1964).

51. _Ibid_. at 148.

52. P. H. Frankel, _supra_ note 36, at 118.

53. _Ibid_. at 175.

54. D. Votaw, supra note 50, at 154.

55. Ibid. at 157.

56. Business Week, March 3, 1973, at 68.

57. Ibid.

58. Ibid.

59. P. H. Frankel, supra note 36, at 175.

60. Ibid. at 163.

61. The ELF Group 1973 Annual Report, at 2.

62. Oil and Gas Journal, Nov. 18, 1974 at 51.

63. Ibid. at 165.

64. Business Week, March 3, 1973, at 69.

65. M. A. Adelman, "Is the Oil Shortage Real?" Foreign Policy, Winter 1972-1973, at 96-99.

66. Ibid. at 99.

67. Ibid. at H-2336.

68. D. G. Davies, "The Efficiency of Public Versus Private Firms, The Case of Australia's Two Airlines," Journal of Law and Economics, April 1971, at 154.

69. Ibid.

70. Ibid. at 161.

71. Ibid. at 165.

72. G. and P. Polanyi, Failing the Nation, The Record of the Nationalised Industries, Sept. 1974, at 5-6.

73. Ibid. at 4-5.

74. Ibid. at 6.

75. Ibid. at 150.

76. Wall Street Journal, Jan. 2, 1975, at 2.

77. Ibid.

78. Ibid.

79. P. H. Frankel, supra note 36, at 150.

80. Excerpted from A. R. Tussing, "The Role of Public Enterprise", paper delivered at the British Columbia Institute of Economic Policy Analysts' Conference on Mineral Leasing, Victoria, B.C., Sept. 18-20, 1974.

APPENDIX B

[§B.0]  FEDERAL PROGRAMS AND
POLICIES AFFECTING THE
PETROLEUM INDUSTRY

A.  [§B.1]  Maritime Subsidy

B.  [§B.2]  Highway Subsidy

C.  [§B.3] ,Import Tariff

D.  [§B.4]  Import Quota

E.  [§B.5]  Export Restrictions

F.  [§B.6]  Foreign Investment Guarantees

G.  [§B.7]  Foreign Investment Restrictions

H.  [§B.8]  U.S. Onshore Leasing System

I.  [§B.9]  U.S. Offshore Leasing System

J.  [§B.10]  State Prorationing Systems

K.  [§B.11]  Environmental Policy

       1.  [§B.12]  Failure to Internalize
                    Environmental Cost

       2.  [§B.13]  Environmental Regulation

A.   [§B.1]   Maritime Subsidy

Oil is moved internationally primarily by means of tankers.  For this reason U.S. maritime subsidies, which might affect the size of the world tanker fleet and hence the cost of transporting oil, are relevant to international petroleum supply.  The various forms of U.S. maritime subsidies include:  Operating Differential Subsidy (ODS), Construction Differential Subsidy (CDS), tax benefits, insurance on loans and mortgages, loans, ship exchanges, cabotage (the Jones Act) and cargo reservation laws.

The first two subsidies, ODS and CDS, are both direct subsidies which take the form of payments by the Federal government to builders and operators to maintain parity of cost between U.S. flag ship construction and operation expenses and those of foreign flag operators. Both subsidies were provided for in the Merchant Marine Act of 1936 but only with the Merchant Marine Act of 1970 did these subsidies become applicable to tanker construction or operation.  Although during the early 1970's several Construction Differential Subsidies were awarded for tankers, there had been no deliveries of subsidized tankers as of June 30, 1973.

One indirect subsidy is tax benefits that accrue to shipowners if they maintain certain statutory reserve and construction funds (via Section 511, of the Merchant Marine Act of 1936, as amended).  This is essentially a tax deferral privilege.  Another form of indirect subsidy is Title XI Guarantees.  Between 1954 and 1972 Title XI consisted mainly of government insurance for private financing of ship, including tanker, construction.  The 1972 Act allows the proceeds of guaranteed obligations to be used for shoreside marine facilities as well as ship construction.

Section 510 of the 1936 Act allows for ship exchanges between private owners and the National Defense Reserve Fleet.  Tankers gained by private owners via Section 510 must, however, be used exclusively on U.S. waters and hence only for domestic oil trade.

The other maritime subsidies take the form of cabotage (the Jones Act) and cargo reservation laws.  The Jones Act requires that all marine cargo shipped between two

U.S. ports be in ships built in the U.S., owned by U.S. companies and manned by American crews. Cargo reservation laws, such as Public Law 480 (Food for Peace), Public Law 664 and Public Resolution 17, require that certain portions of government impelled cargo be shipped on U.S. flag vessels.

The net effect of the U.S. maritime subsidies on the world tanker stock and hence on international petroleum supply has been minimal. Until 1970, the main direct subsidies did not apply to tanker construction and operation. Hence any U.S. built, U.S. flag tanker that existed in the world tanker market did so on a competitive basis. However, it should be noted that with U.S. tanker construction costs more than double that of some foreign competitors and with higher U.S. flag ship operating costs (mainly due to higher wages), the cabotage requirement seems to be a major reason for the existence of any U.S. tanker production at all. About two-thirds of U.S. flag tankers operate on purely domestic oil routes and all recent deliveries from U.S. yards have been for use on domestic routes. Thus, U.S. flag tankers, for the most part, have existed in a market sheltered from international competition.

The recent availability of direct subsidies, through the Merchant Marine Act of 1970, to U.S. flag tanker construction and operation should increase the size of the U.S., but not necessarily the world, tanker fleet. The world fleet will only increase if U.S. production is in addition to and not in lieu of foreign construction. In any case, the impact of these subsidies on the world tanker fleet will most likely be small and slow in coming. First, there is a long lead time for tanker construction. Second, and more importantly, the U.S. tanker shipbuilding industry is small relative to total world production. In 1972, for example, U.S. yards accounted for a total of 13 ships delivered, of which 6 were tankers. Total world production, on the other hand, was 1119 ships of which 216 were tankers. Thus less than 3% of world tanker construction was from U.S. yards in 1972.

B.    [§B.2]  Highway Subsidy

        Highways, to the extent that they are made avail-
able to the user at a "below cost" price, are an indirect
means of increasing the demand for petroleum.. The question
of whether highway and road users are being subsidized involves some very difficult issues, including the proper
accounting methods for government activities and equitable
distribution of costs relating to highway construction,
maintenance, regional economic development, national security, policing and administration.

        In general, however, the question can be answered
by comparing the available data on forms and levels of revenues and expenditures related to road construction and use.
Since the beginning of this century there has been a drastic
change in the financing of roads.  Before World War I most
road funds came from non-user sources such as property tax
and poll taxes.  Since then, there has been a continuing
trend toward reliance on user taxes and by 1960 user taxes
provided revenues approximately equal to direct expenditures
for highway and street purposes for all units of government
combined. 1/

        Looking mainly at federal policy, there has been
a radical change not only in the type of financing but in
the level of financing since World War II.  Before the
Highway Revenue Act of 1956, tax revenue from highway excise
taxes (such as taxes on gasoline, trucks, busses, tires, etc.)
were treated as luxury excise tax revenue and allocated to
the general fund.  Federal expenditures on highways and roads
were made from the general budget and were usually on a 50/50
matching basis with state and local governments for specified
projects.  In the early 1950's the Federal government was
providing as little as 10 percent of total highway expenditures.

        The Highway Revenue Act of 1956 made several major
changes in the financing of roads.  The Federal highway user
taxes were earmarked for highway purposes and segregated into
a special fund; the level of Federal highway expenditures rose
substantially; and the Interstate Highway System was instituted, financed almost entirely from Federal highway trust
funds.

Returning to the question whether road users have been subsidized, and looking only at the Federal level, it appears that the answer is no. Federal aid expenditures on roads and highways during the early 1950's generally ran between 65 percent and 75 percent of Federal highway user tax revenues. And the Federal Highway Trust Fund has generally operated with yearly surpluses (the balance in the fund has never been negative) and during the early 1970's some of the surpluses have approached $1 billion. 2/ Hence it appears that during the last twenty years road and highway construction has been essentially user financed and as such Federal highway programs have not been an effective demand-increasing device for petroleum.

FOOTNOTES

1.  Lyle C. Fitch and Associates, Urban Transportation and
    Public Policy, (San Francisco:  Chandler Publishing Co.,
    1964), 31, 255.

2.  U.S. Congress, House, 16th Annual Report of Highway Trust
    Fund, 92nd Cong., 2nd Sess., 1972.

C.   [§B.3]   Import Tariff

An import tariff, if high enough, can effectively
isolate a domestic economy from supply sources in the international market.  If foreign source oil, plus transportation,
is cheaper than domestic sources, an import tariff can
reduce or even prevent  the importation of oil.  This has
consequences not only for the domestic petroleum market but
for the international petroleum market as well.

In the case of the United States, controls on
imports of crude oil and gasoline have ranged from little or
no control to strict quantity importation restrictions.  The
earliest serious attempts at reducing the importation of oil
occurred in the early 1920's.  Crude oil imports were growing
and in fact reached an amount equal to 26 percent of domestic
production in 1921. 1/  Independent producers attempted to
persuade Congress to enact a tariff on imports but the
combination of resistance by President Harding and decrease
in imports (due to decreased production of Mexican oil
fields, the primary source of imports at the time) defeated
the effort. 2/

The Tariff Act of 1930 placed petroleum on the
Duty Free List.  However, during the chaos of the depression,
which witnessed rapidly falling crude prices and fears of
overproduction, Congress enacted and the President signed
the Revenue Act of 1932 which included a Manufacturers
Excise Tax on imported petroleum products.  The excise tax
levels established were:  crude petroleum, 1/2 cent/gal.;
fuel oil and liquid derivatives of crude (except lubrication
oil and gas), 1/2 cent/gal.; gasoline or other motor fuel,
2-1/2 cents/gal.; lubrication oil, 4 cents/gal.

It is difficult to assess the effect of this
tariff/import  excise tax because of the massive economic
disturbances of the early 1930's.  U.S. crude oil imports
reached over 79 million barrels a year in 1928 and 1929,
fell to about 45 million barrels for both 1931 and 1932 and
then fell to 32 million barrels in 1933, the first full year
after the enactment of the Revenue Act of 1932.  Crude oil
imports remained at this level (plus or minus about 15
percent) until 1940.  U.S. crude oil production during this
period reached over 1 billion barrels in 1929, fell steadily
to 785 million barrels in 1932 and increased after that

date.  Gasoline imports, which received a much larger excise tax, reacted much more strongly.  Gasoline imports quadrupled between 1928 and 1930 (from 4 million barrels to 17 million barrels a year).  In 1931, imports were 13.6 million barrels, 8.2 million barrels in 1932 and decreased to negligible amounts thereafter (never reaching more than 150 thousand barrels a year until 1941). 3/ (Between September 1933 and 1935 there was an import quota limiting imports to their level of the last six months of 1932.) 4/

The remainder of the 1930's yielded little major new legislation.  The Trade Agreements Act of 1934 (and as extended in 1937 and later dates) authorized the President to reduce import tariffs (by not more than 50 percent) to achieve better trade relations.  This prerogative was not exercised until 1939 when the Presidential Proclamation of December 12, 1939, issued pursuant to the Venezuela Reciprocal Trade Agreement of 1939, reduced tariffs by 50 percent on petroleum imports up to 5 percent of the quantity of petroleum processed in the U.S. during the previous year. Imports above the 5 percent level were liable for the full tariff/import excise tax.

Following World War II and the doubling of crude oil imports between 1945 and 1950 (1950 imports were approximately 9 percent of U.S. crude oil production) pressure mounted for additional controls on oil imports. 5/  In 1954 President Eisenhower appointed the Cabinet Committee on Energy Supplies which concluded in its 1954 report that national security would best be served by allowing oil imports into the United States if the quantity was kept in the same ratio to domestic production as during 1954.  The Committee urged flexibility in dealing with the situation and suggested that large oil importers make voluntary import restriction plans.

The Trade Agreement Extension Act of 1955 authorized the President to impose increased restrictions on imports whenever imports were large enough to pose a threat to national security.  The Presidential Proclamation of March 10, 1959 instituted the oil import quota system. Tariffs on allowable imports were maintained at the levels indicated earlier (crude oil above 25° API, 1/4 cent/gal.; gasoline, 1-1/4 cents/gal.).  The import quota system is discussed in §B.4.

The next change in tariff regulations was announced in President Nixon's energy message of April 18, 1973. The tariff on petroleum imports was replaced by an essentially equivalent license fee. License fees are scheduled to increased between 1973 and November 1, 1975 (May 1, 1973 levels are: crude oil, 10-1/2 cents/bbl.; gasoline 52 cents/bbl.; November 1, 1975 levels: crude oil 21 cents/bbl.; gasoline, 63 cents/bbl.). Also, imports up to the 1973 levels were exempt from the license fees (the exemption to be gradually lessened and totally eliminated by 1980), while additional imports must pay the full license fees.

In his 1975 State of the Union message, President Ford indicated he would increase import fees by $3 in three steps during the first half of 1975. The fee structure is thus being utilized as an expedient to raise the price of petroleum products in order to encourage conservation and reduce dependence on interruptible foreign supplies.

The import tariff is, in effect, a form of subsidy. Domestic crude oil producers were the primary beneficiaries of this subsidy. The ability of foreign imported oil to compete for U.S. sales was reduced because the import tariff increased the cost of imports relative to domestic oil. The domestic coal producers also benefited from the tariff because it reduced competition from foreign suppliers of residual fuel oil. In 1956 international oil companies opposed the quota system primarily because they would be adversely affected by decreased U.S. imports.

FOOTNOTES

1.  American Petroleum Institute, Petroleum Facts and Figures
    (Washington, D.C., American Petroleum Institute, 1971),
    288.

2.  Gerald D. Nash, United States Oil Policy 1890-1964
    (Pittsburgh: University of Pittsburgh Press, 1968), 53.

3.  American Petroleum Institute, Petroleum Facts and Figures,
    288, 164.

4.  Edward H. Shaffer, The Oil Import Program of the U.S.
    (New York: Praeger, 1968), 9.

5.  American Petroleum Institute, Petroleum Facts and
    Figures, 288.

D.   [§B.4]   Import Quota

Quotas on the importation of oil into the United
States were first established during the 1930's under the
National Industrial Recovery Act.  Low prices for oil had
developed in the late 1920's and early 1930's because of
production methods (lack of unitization regulation) and the
discovery of substantial domestic oil deposits in East Texas.
Import quotas were established as a means of protecting the
then infant petroleum industry from foreign competition.
Quotas were eliminated in 1935 and there was no increase
in imports prior to 1940. 1/

Following World War II there was expansion in
international oil production as large reserves of low cost
oil were discovered and developed, primarily in the Middle
East.  The result of this was increased importation of crude
oil by the United States.  For example, in 1945 imports of
crude oil totaled 74 million barrels a year.  Imports increased
to 178 million barrels and 285 million barrels per annum
for the years 1950 and 1955 respectively. 2/  The impact of
rapidly increasing imports raised two problems.  According to
the Advisory Committee on Energy Supplies and Resources
Policy:

> "If the imports of crude and residual oils
> should exceed significantly the respective
> proportions that these imports of oil bore
> to the production of domestic crude oil in
> 1954, the domestic fuels situation could be
> so impaired as to endanger the orderly
> industrial growth which assures the military
> and civilian supplies and reserves that are
> necessary to the national defense.  There
> would be an inadequate incentive for explora-
> tion and the discovery of new sources of
> supplies." 3/

A significant degree of dependence on foreign source
oil was held to be undesirable for national security reasons.
Large-scale imports had serious implications for the profitability of the existing domestic industry.  As a result of
these considerations, which will be further discussed below,
voluntary import quotas were introduced in 1955 and 1957
and mandatory import quotas were initiated in 1959.

The implementation and operation of the quota system was a very complex operation and will only be outlined here. Two slightly different programs were used, one for PAD I-IV and one for PAD V. For each district a level of allowable imports was selected for each time period. Once this level was selected the allowable imports had to be allocated among the various crude oil importers. Factors that were considered included: (1) the historic level of imports under the voluntary quota system; (2) special handling of imports from Mexico and Canada; (3) a sliding scale which gave small refining companies a relatively larger quota than large refining companies; and (4) a system of barter exchanges between inland refiners that could not always refine imported crude oil and coastal refiners that usually could refine imported oil. 4/ The system was continually modified while it was in use.

The oil import quota system was ended by proclamation with President Nixon's energy message of April 18, 1973 and was replaced by a fee system. Initially all imports, up to the level allowed under the 1973 quota allocations, were free of any fees or import duty. Imports in excess of this amount would be subject to a fee. This fee was virtually identical to the existing import tariffs. There was also established, however, a sliding schedule for: (1) the portion of 1973 quota allocations that could be imported without fees; and (2) the level of fees. On the first point, the percentage of the 1973 quota allocation exempt from license fees decreases from 100% in 1973 to 0% in 1980. On the second point, the schedule of fees on nonexempt imports calls for fees of 10 1/2 cents per barrel on crude oil as of May 1, 1973 (15 cents per barrel for residual fuel oil and 52 cents per barrel for gasoline) increasing to 21 cents per barrel by November 1, 1975 (63 cents per barrel for residual fuel oil and 63 cents per barrel for gasoline). 5/ The effect of this program is to initially decrease the cost of imported oil but increase the cost over the period in question. The import quota, however, was eliminated.

There has been a substantial debate over the costs and benefits of the import quota program. As stated above, a primary justification for the import quotas was national security. With the U.S. reasonably self-sufficient in terms of oil supplies neither its domestic economy nor its foreign

policy objectives would be endangered by an embargo threat
or military actions.  However, the condition of the domestic
crude oil industry was also a consideration in the decision
to impose import quotas.  The market demand prorationing
system led to the situation where the domestic price of
crude oil was higher than the world market price, excess
capacity existed and production was restricted to that amount
which would maintain the existing domestic price for crude
oil.  A substantial level of imports would threaten the
existence of the prorationing mechanism by forcing the prorationing states to restrict production by increasingly
large amounts in order to maintain the existing price levels.
If imports remained unchecked the size and output of the
domestic crude oil industry would be reduced.  This was true
because in the period in question (1959-1973) imported crude
oil was substantially cheaper than domestic oil.  With import
quotas, the United States was somewhat isolated from the
world market price.  The restriction on imports reduced the
amount of oil products available for final consumption.  The
result of this was relatively higher domestic prices with
the domestic producers of crude oil supplying more than
they otherwise would have.  In other words, one of the desired
effects of the import quota, decreased dependency (between
1959 and 1973) on imported oil, was achieved.  Because oil is
a nonrenewable resource, independence was achieved at the
expense of greater future dependency.

There were substantial costs imposed by the import
quota program however.  These costs can be broken down into
four general categories which are:  (1) income transfers from
consumers to producers; (2) income transfers to small refiners,
from large refiners; (3) income transfers to Canadian producers from U.S. consumers; and (4) inefficient resource
allocation.  The Charles River Associates research study
on the import quota system attempted to estimate the yearly
costs of the import quota to the consumer.  Using 1968 data
and estimates on the price elasticity of demand varying from
"0" to "-1", it was estimated that the quota imposed net costs
on the consumer of between $5.6 billion and $6.9 billion
per year. 6/  Another study declined to place a dollar
value on the cost of the import quota system but stated that
the cost to consumers was large. 7/

In spite of the apparently large magnitude of costs
related to the program, these costs would be acceptable if they

provided some degree of security.  The only test of the
security provided by the import quota system occurred during
the Arab-Israeli War of 1967.  During that war there was a
relatively short period in which there was a substantial
disruption of the flow of crude oil from the Middle East.
The impact of these shortages was decreased and virtually
eliminated because of the following factors:  (1) stocks of
crude oil and products on hand in the U.S.; (2) excess
capacity for crude oil production in the U.S. due to the
market-demand prorationing system; and (3) both the U.S. and
Venezuela increased production.  The existence of import
quotas does not directly affect the amount of oil made
available by items one through three above.  Quotas, however, would reduce the shortfall (that would occur under a
war or embargo situation) and hence reduce the amount that
must be made up from stockpiles or increased production.
For example, imports of crude oil in 1966 were only about
13% of total crude oil available in the United States. 8/
It can be concluded that import quotas on crude oil provided
at least a limited amount of "current" national security in
the form of decreased dependence on imported oil and associated with this benefit were additional costs to consumers in
the form of higher fuel prices which were estimated in 1968
to be approximately $5-6 billion per year.

     While there are currently some discussions on
reinstating import quotas, the situation today is quite different from what it was a few years ago.  For example, today
the price of imported oil is an administratively set high
price while domestic prices are (partially) controlled below
the world market price.  Even under price controls (where
the price for "new" oil is allowed to reach a free market
level) there is a strong incentive to search for domestic
oil reserves that can be produced for less than the OPEC
price for imports.  Secondly, there exists no "excess
capacity" in the United States, as there did a few years
ago.  And thirdly, the increased level of imports, since the
elimination of the import quota in 1973, coupled with the
much higher prices associated with crude oil imports, have
caused balance of trade and balance of payments  problems
for the United States.  For these reasons, current arguments
for import quotas would presumably be based on national
security and balance of trade or payments arguments as
opposed to the previous situation where national security
and maintenance of the profitable domestic crude oil industry
were the primary justifications.

There are two additional factors that must be mentioned in a discussion of import quotas. Implementation of an import quota program is necessarily an administrative procedure which may alter the relationship between firms in the oil and gas industry. The previous program was implemented with due consideration for small refinery profitability. However, the import quota system as administered, seems to have "protected the import position of the internationals." 9/ That is, prior to the program, the major international firms' share of imports was rapidly decreasing (from 74% in 1948 to 45% in 1958) 10/ while after the institution of the program their share remained fairly constant. In other words, the degree of competition in the oil and gas industry today may well be less than what it would have been if the import quota system had not been implemented.

And finally, the impact of an effective import quota system is to increase production from domestic sources. As a result of the program the United States was highly self-sufficient during the 1960's. The problem lies in the fact that oil produced in the 1960's cannot be produced in the 1970's or later. With much of the low cost, readily accessible oil already produced in the United States, it becomes more difficult and more costly to be self-sufficient in the future.

# FOOTNOTES

1.  James C. Burrows and Thomas A. Domencich, An Analysis of the United States Oil Import Quota (Lexington, Mass.: Heath Lexington Books, 1970), 2.

2.  American Petroleum Institute, Petroleum Facts and Figures (Washington, D.C.: American Petroleum Institute, 1971), 288.

3.  U.S. House, Committee on Interior and Insular Affairs, Subcommittee on Mines and Mining. Mandatory Oil Import Control Program, Its Impact Upon the Domestic Minerals Industry and National Security, May 1968, 22.

4.  For a description of the import quota program, see: Edward H. Shaffer, The Oil Import Program of the United States (New York: Praeger, 1968), 159-197.

5.  Statement by William E. Simon, Deputy Secretary of the Treasury on the Oil Import Program, April 18, 1973; "Summary of the Modified Oil Import Program," 3, 4.

6.  Burrows, see note 1 above, 151-154.

7.  Shaffer, see note 4 above, 219.

8.  American Petroleum Institute, see note 2 above, 288.

9.  Shaffer, see note 4 above, 177.

10. Shaffer, see note 4 above, 175.

E.  [§B.5]  Export Restrictions

     U.S. restrictions on exports have many effects.
U.S. businesses are prevented from selling their products in
the market that is willing to pay a price which is, at
the margin, the most profitable.  But on the other hand,
U.S. domestic consumers can, by export restrictions, have
the severity of petroleum shortages lessened, and pay a
(controlled) price below a free market price.

     The United States has had the authority to regulate
the exports of crude oil transported by pipeline over Federal
rights-of-way since the passage of the Mineral Leasing Act
of 1920 (Section 28).  Under this law exports of such crude
are allowed provided:  (1) they do not diminish the total
quantity or quality of petroleum available to the United
States; or (2) are in the national interest.  There is
little indication that exports have been rigorously restricted.
During the decade following the passage of the Act, domestic
production of crude oil doubled, exports doubled and imports
fell by about 40 percent. 1/  Crude exports increased to 77
million barrels per year by 1938 and since that time have
fallen continually, with the exception of periods of conflict
such as the Suez Crisis and the 1967 War.

     The Alaskan Pipeline Act of 1973 (P.L. 93-154)
made more specific the requirements for the implementation
of the Mineral Leasing Act but the thrust of the Act was not
changed.

     On December 13, 1973 (38 Federal Register 34442)
petroleum and its products were put under Short Supply Controls and placed on the Commodity Control List.  The effect
of this was to require a validated export license for the
export of crude and its products.  The purpose of this
action was stated as follows:

     "The critical energy shortage now facing
     the world economy has caused a strong de-
     mand for petroleum and petroleum products.
     In accordance with the program announced
     by the Federal Energy Office, our limited
     domestic energy resources are to be allo-
     cated among competing domestic users.  In

order to be successful, such a domestic
allocation program must be accompanied by
a coordinated program which regulated U.S.
exports of the products subject to allocation." 2/

On January 29, 1974, more details of the export
controls were released.  Petroleum products were divided
into categories and assigned different levels of export restriction.  Crude oil was subject to a virtual embargo
pursuant to the Alaskan Pipeline Act.  Gasoline, distillates
and residual fuel oils were placed under quantitative restrictions.  Jet fuel, carbon black feedstocks, butane,
propane and natural gas liquids were placed under a 100
percent licensing requirement (to provide information as to
the levels of exports of these products) "as long as rate of
export does not exceed prior historic rate." 3/

Exports during the period from January 1971
through June, 1973 were used as a basis for export quotas.
In effect, exporting company-importing country relations
were frozen to that existing during the base period.  A
quota set-aside of 5 percent of each commodity group was
established to allow for "hardship" cases such as new exporters without an historical record of exports.

In February those products which had been under
the 100 percent licensing requirements were placed under
quantitative controls.  This was done because:

"Recent export licensing of these commodities, except kerosene, has exceeded
historic levels.  Quota controls on
kerosene are considered necessary because it is readily substitutable for
jet fuel." 4/

On May 1, 1974 additional rules were established
to eliminate a loophole, or technical deficiency, with
respect to exports of crude oil.  The regulations were
expanded to cover crude that was not transported by pipeline
over Federal rights-of-way (and hence was not subject to the
Alaskan Pipeline Act) and required that exports of crude not
reduce the amount of crude (instead of the indefinite term,
petroleum) available to the U.S.  The definition of hardship
exports was also modified and it was noted that:

"A mere showing that there is an opportunity to sell at a higher price in a
foreign market shall not be deemed, by
itself, to constitute an economic hardship." 5/

The effect of this embargo is somewhat difficult
to estimate because of data problems.  Accurate data is
available for the embargo period covering only the first
four months of 1974.  Moreover, the published categories of
data for the embargo period are not always identical with
the categories of the pre-embargo period.  Department of
Commerce data indicate that exports of all refined petroleum
products, including those not under export restriction,
appeared to be down slightly in 1974.  The average monthly
export was 6.97 million barrels in 1973 while the same data
series shows the monthly average for the first four months
of 1974 to be 6.2 million barrels. 6/  Bureau of Census
data, used by the Office of Export Administration, break the
figures down into energy petroleum products (subject to
export restrictions) and non-energy petroleum exports for
the embargo period.  Energy exports remained relatively
constant during the current year as can be seen from the
following table.

TABLE ___1___ Petroleum Exports in 1974
(in thousands of barrels per month)

| Month | Total | Energy Products | Non-Energy Products |
|---|---|---|---|
| January | 7,025 | 1,954 | 5,071 |
| February | 6,280 | 1,266 | 5,014 |
| March | 6,434 | 1,321 | 5,113 |
| April | 7,832 | 1,254 | 6,578 |
| May | 8,776 | 1,331 | 7,465 |
| June | 8,081 | 1,275 | 6,808 |

Source:  See footnote 7.

Crude exports in recent years have been minimal.
They have not exceeded 2 million barrels a year, with the
exception of 1967 and 1970, since 1961, and for the period
from 1971 through 1973 averaged .47 million barrels a year.

Exports for the first six months of 1974, however, have totaled 1,077 million barrels. Over three-quarters of this occurred in the first two months of the year, which was before the loophole mentioned above was eliminated. 8/ Hence it would appear that export controls have reduced the amount of petroleum exports.

It was stated that export controls were required to make the domestic allocation program work. But there is another underlying reason for controls. Prior to the price controls, oil shortages, and increased Arab oil prices, there was little economic motivation for exporting crude and petroleum products because the domestic petroleum industry was protected by devices previously discussed which raised the domestic price above the corresponding foreign price for oil.

With price controls and the other dislocations of the early 1970's, the domestic prices fell below the going international prices. There existed, therefore, an economic incentive to export crude and products. This would have hampered the allocation and price control effort and so export restrictions were necessary. Their use of an historic base period for quotas can be criticized because it freezes supplier-purchaser relations in an arbitrary manner. But given that quotas were required, any other administrative procedure would have been also open to criticism because of possible favoritism, political pressure or corruption.

APPENDIX B
FOOTNOTES

1.  American Petroleum Institute, Petroleum Facts and
    Figures (Washington, D.C.:  American Petroleum Institute,
    1971), 288.

2.  39 C.F.R. 3671, January 29, 1974.

3.  Ibid.

4.  39 C.F.R. 5311, February 12, 1974.

5.  39 C.F.R. 15113, May 1, 1974.

6.  U.S. Department of Commerce, Survey of Current Business,
    May 1974, table S-35.

7.  U.S. Dept. of Commerce, International Trade Analysis
    Staff, International Economic Policy and Research.
    Data Series:  "U.S. Export of Petroleum and Products,
    Annually from 1970 and by Months, 1974."

8.  Ibid.

F.   [B.6]   Foreign Investment Guarantees

    Direct foreign investment encounters risks in addition to those normally associated with business activity. These risks, which are mainly political in nature, include expropriation, inconvertibility and war. The United States Government historically has attempted to reduce these risks.

    During the late nineteenth and early twentieth centuries, aggressive diplomatic support of American enterprise reflected the "active intervention" doctrine which characterized U.S. policy. 1/ Military intervention in Mexico (1916), Nicaragua and Shanghai (both in 1927) are examples of this approach. Since that time, however, the level of intervention has generally receded to diplomatic intervention or protest by the State Department on behalf of U.S. firms.

    Since World War II, Congress has passed legislation providing for a slightly different approach to reducing the risks of direct foreign investment. Under the authority provided by the Economic Cooperation Act of 1948, the Federal government has provided insurance against risks of a political nature as well as government loans and guarantees for certain types of foreign investments.

    The Investment Guaranty Program (since 1969 called the Investment Insurance Program) initially provided only for guaranties of convertibility but has since been expanded to cover risks due to expropriation as well as war. Eligibility for these programs depends not only on the nature of the project but also on its location. Initially investments in only 13 foreign countries were eligible but the number of countries eligible gradually increased. Since 1959 the insurance has been available only in specified less developed friendly countries. Since the passage of the Foreign Assistance Act of 1969, an Investment Guarantee program has existed which provides for guarantees of loans (generally for terms of longer than seven years) against all risks, political as well as commercial, associated with an investment.

There are many public organizations which provide loans for international private business activities. These organizations include the Export-Import Bank, Agency for International Development, Inter-American Development Bank, International Bank for Reconstruction and Development (World Bank), International Finance Corporation, International Development Association and the Overseas Private Investment Corporation. However, the importance of these aids to direct foreign investment in the petroleum industry appears to be very small. Virtually all of the loans available from the sources cited are used for development type projects, or projects where, for some reason, private capital is not available. For example, by 1970 the International Finance Corporation had commitments of $364 million, none of which was related to the petroleum industry. As of June 30, 1969, the World Bank had loans, credits and investments totaling over $12.6 billion, of which $87 million went for pipelines, some of which was used for the transportation of oil and gas. 2/ And looking at an earlier period, of the $2.4 billion in loans provided by AID by the end of 1961 virtually none was provided for direct use in petroleum projects. 3/

The petroleum industry has participated in the investment insurance programs but overall appears to have made relatively less use of the program than other types of companies. For example, as of December 31, 1958, 36 percent of all U.S. direct foreign investment was in the petroleum industry. But an analysis of the investment insurance (covering the risks of convertibility and expropriation) issued between 1948 and 1959 shows that only about 12 percent of the total contracts of over $431 million were issued to the petroleum industry. 4/ And currently only about 7.7 percent ($251.9 million) of total OPIC investment insurance exposure (OPIC is currently the administering agency for the program) is in the petroleum and gas industry. 5/

There are two facets of petroleum investment insurance that should be noted. First, investment insurance is rarely available for oil exploration activities and is available for only the tangible or removable assets of investment in refining and production facilities. 6/ Second, insurance is available only where there exists an agreement between the host country and the United States concerning the insurance program and where the risks involved are of a level acceptable to the agency administering the insurance

program.  Currently, for example, insurance is not available
in Indonesia (because of the lack of such agreement), nor in
most countries in the Middle East (because of the high level
of risk).  In fact, the only substantial oil-producing
countries in the Middle East and Africa that are or have
been eligible for investment insurance are Iran, Israel,
Turkey, Gabon and Nigeria.  Venezuela, a major area of U.S.
petroleum investment, it should be noted, is eligible for
insurance. 7/

Hence, it can be stated that where these insurance
programs do apply they probably have provided an additional
incentive for U.S. direct foreign petroleum investment.
However, a substantial portion of investment has occurred in
areas where insurance is not available.

APPENDIX B
FOOTNOTES

1.  Maria von Neumann Whitman, The U.S. Investment Guaranty
    Program and Private Foreign Investment (Princeton, N.J.:
    Princeton Univ. Press, 1959), 9.

2.  John Loomis, Public Money Sources for Overseas Trade
    and Investment (Washington, D.C.:  BNA Books, 1963), 170,
    189.

3.  Ibid., 63.

4.  Whitman, note 1 above, 83-88.

5.  OPIC Document, OPIC Expropriation Insurance, Current
    Coverage by Industry, as of January 31, 1974.

6.  OPIC Document, "General Policy and Guidelines, March 8,
    1971."

7.  Whitman, note 1 above, 48.

G.  [§B.7]  Foreign Investment Restrictions

A substantial portion of the international petroleum supply exists as a result of the foreign direct investment by U.S. petroleum companies.  Restrictions on such investment might restrict the ability of U.S. companies to achieve a desired level of plant and equipment expenditures which, in turn, may affect petroleum supplies available on world markets.

Such restrictions were instituted in the 1960's by the United States out of balance of payments considerations. The first control instituted was the interest equalization tax (effective in 1963) which was intended to limit the outflow of private capital for portfolio investment.  This program, as well as the voluntary foreign credit restraint program for financial institutions (instituted in 1965) do not directly relate to petroleum investment.  In 1965 there was also instituted a voluntary program to restrain private capital outflow.  On January 1, 1968 the President announced new mandatory measures to combat the balance of payments deficit.  Included in these measures was the introduction of mandatory controls on foreign investment.  For purposes of the control program, "foreign direct investment . . . is defined as the sum of transfers of U.S. funds to foreign affiliates and earnings retained by those affiliates".  1/

The regulations of the control program are complex and are best described in two parts.  First of all:

> "The amount of investment that a firm
> may make during a year (its 'allowable')
> may be calculated in accordance with a
> number of alternative formulas.  Two
> specify minimum amounts that firms may
> invest; another uses the level of an enter-
> prise's average annual direct investment
> during a given base period; and others are
> based on affiliate earnings during the
> prior year." 2/

These regulations have been liberalized since their inception.  3/

Second, for a firm choosing the "base period" formula, a multinational corporation may:

> "[I]nvest in the less-developed
> countries (Schedule A) 110% of its
> base period average, but only 65% in
> such countries as the United Kingdom,
> Japan and Australia (Schedule B),
> and only 35% in the developed coun-
> tries of Western Europe and South
> Africa (Schedule C)." 4/

It is important to note that a number of the oil-producing countries (Abu Dhabi, Bahrain, Iran, Iraq, Kuwait, Kuwait-Saudi Arabia Neutral Zone, Libya, Qatar and Saudi Arabia) fall in Schedule B. Also of importance is the fact that "the program was not intended to discourage direct invest-ment per se, and few restrictions were placed on borrowing abroad by investors. . . ." 5/

What has been the impact of these restrictions on petroleum direct foreign investment? Unfortunately, much of the analysis of these restrictions is not broken down by industry. The Department of Commerce concludes, however, that, "available data appear to support the contention that multinational firms and other enterprises have not seriously reduced their foreign direct investment activities due to the OFDI (Office of Foreign Direct Investment) controls." 6/ A staff paper for the Brookings Institution concludes similarly that, "little or no evidence exists to suggest that the level of direct investment (as distinct from the way in which it was financed) was materially affected by the controls imposed by the U.S. government." 7/

Another source, however, disagrees with this and argues that the controls tended to reduce direct investment. This argument is based on the fact that "expenditures on plant and equipment rose only four percent during 1966-68 which rate of increase was substantially below the 18 percent average annual increases in 1964-66." 8/ The same source, however, also pointed out that "U.S. companies in the aggre-gate did not make full use of their quotas in 1968 and carried forward to 1969 nearly $2 billion in unused allow-ables." 9/ Furthermore, expenditures on plant and equipment rose an annual average of 17 percent for the years 1969-71 10/ while the regulations were still in effect.

It appears that the experience of the petroleum industry has been the same as the total of all direct foreign investment. And the petroleum industry has felt free to invest relatively more in areas subject to stricter controls (Schedule C as opposed to Schedule B countries). For example, in 1970, virtually "all the rise in capital flows was channeled into affiliates in developed countries" 11/ instead of into developing countries, including the Middle East.

One major effect of the regulations has been to shift the financing of direct investment from U.S. to foreign sources. At the end of 1967 U.S. direct investors had outstanding about $2.1 billion in borrowing while at the end of 1971 there was $13.1 billion outstanding. 12/

Interest rates in Europe, a major source of funds, have at times been higher than in of the U.S., and hence it is possible that some investment plans were cancelled. However, the Department of Commerce concludes that "it is difficult to determine with any degree of certainty the extent to which U.S. foreign direct investment has actually been inhibited as a consequence." 13/ Hence it appears that while restrictions on direct foreign investment have affected the manner in which direct investment is financed, there is little evidence that they have seriously affected the level of investment. It should be noted that the restrictions on U.S. foreign direct investment were removed in early 1974.

FOOTNOTES

1.  U.S. House, Committee on Foreign Affairs, Hearings on House Concurrent Resolutions 85 and 86 (Washington, D.C.:  GPO, 1969), 217.

2.  U.S. Department of Commerce, Bureau of International Commerce, The Multinational Corporation (Washington, D.C.: GPO, 1972 and 1973), Vol. I, 42.

3.  U.S. Department of Commerce, Office of Foreign Direct Investments, 1973 General Bulletin, Interpretive Explanation and Analysis of Foreign Direct Investment Regulations (Washington, D.C.:  GPO, 1973).

4.  U.S. Department of Commerce, The Multinational Corporation, Vol. I, 42.

5.  Ibid.

6.  Ibid., 42-43.

7.  Sir Alec Cairncross, Control of Long-Term International Capital Movements (Washington, D.C.:  The Brookings Institution, 1973), 44.

8.  Karel Holbik, "United States Experience with Direct Investment Controls", Weltwirtschaftliches Archiv, Band 108, Heft 3, 1972, 509.

9.  Ibid., 511.

10.  Based on Table 1, page 19, of U.S. Department of Commerce, Survey of Current Business, September 1972.

11.  Ibid., 33.

12.  U.S. Department of Commerce, Office of Foreign Direct Investments, Foreign Direct Investment Program, Selected Statistics (Washington, D.C.:  GPO, 1972), 1.

13.  U.S. Department of Commerce, The Multinational Corporation, Vol. I, 46.

H.    [§B.8]   The U.S. Onshore Leasing System

Onshore lands of the United States owned by the
Federal Government are leased for oil and gas prospecting
and development pursuant to the Mineral Lands Leasing Act of
1920. 1/ This act authorizes the leasing of all Federal
lands, except for lands acquired under the Appalachian
Forest Act, those in incorporated cities, towns and villages,
those in national parks and monuments, those acquired under
subsequent acts, and lands within naval petroleum and oil
shale reserves. Regulations also exclude Indian reservations
and lands within one mile of naval petroleum and helium
reserves. 2/

The Act creates two leasing systems for oil and
and gas prospecting and development:  a competitive system
for those lands within any known geological structure (KGS)
of a producing oil or gas field, and a noncompetitive system
for lands not within any such known geological structure.
Certain features are common to both systems.  No individual
or corporation may hold more than 246,080 acres in any one
state under leases issued pursuant to the Act, of which no
more than 200,000 acres may be held on option to lease.  In
Alaska, up to 300,000 acres may be held in each of the two
Federal leasing districts in the state; up to 200,000 of
these in each district may be held on option. 3/  Undivided
fractional shares count pro rata toward these limits.

The revenue received by the Federal Government from
these leases is divided as follows:   37.5 percent to the state
in which the leased land is located; 52.5 percent to the
reclamation fund created under the Reclamation Act of 1902
for irrigation projects in the arid or semi-arid states and
Texas 4/ and 10 percent to the U.S. Treasury to be credited
to miscellaneous receipts.  In Alaska, 90 percent of the
lease revenues are paid to the state, and 10 percent to the
Federal Treasury as miscellaneous receipts. 5/

Lands Within a Known Geological Structure

Lands within a known geological structure of an oil
or gas producing area may be leased to the highest responsible
qualified bidder by competitive bidding in units of not more
than 640 acres, upon payment of a bonus acceptable to the Secretary of the Interior and a royalty of at least 12-1/2 percent of
the value of the production removed or sold from the lease. 6/

Prospective lessees must submit sealed bids as to the amount
of the bonus, along with a deposit of 20 percent in cash or
its equivalent of the bonus amount bid. The winning bidder
must pay the rest of the bonus within 30 days after notifica-
tion of acceptance or within 15 days after receiving the
lease, whichever is later. A rental of at least 50 cents
per acre per year is also required, and upon discovery of
oil or gas in paying quantities a minimum royalty of $1 per
acre must be paid in lieu of rental. Such competitive leases
are for an initial term of five years and continue so long
thereafter as oil or gas is produced in paying quantities.

## Lands Not within a Known Geological Structure

Lands not within a known oil or gas producing
geological structure are leased on a noncompetitive basis,
first come first served, in units of not more than 2,560
acres. If there are simultaneous applications for the same
lease, a lottery is held among the simultaneous applicants
to determine the eligible offeror. A flat royalty of 12-1/2
percent is imposed on the value of the oil and gas produced
on the leased land. In addition, a rental of 50 cents per
acre per year is charged, and also a $10 filing fee, non-
refundable even if the offer to lease is rejected. Noncompetitive leases are for an initial term of ten years, and
continue so long thereafter as paying quantities of oil or
gas are produced. 7/

## History

During the 1940's and 1950's there was a steady
increase in the annual total of onshore leases sold and
onshore acreage under lease. Frequently, such leases were
obtained by lease brokers, who often attempted to market
unpromising leases to gullible third parties. 8/

In the early 1960's the annual number of leases
sold and the total acreage newly leased began to decline,
for several reasons. First, by then the most promising onshore
leases had already been exploited, and there was a general
decline of new drilling starts onshore within the lower 48.
Second, new drilling and exploration were increasing in offshore areas as yet relatively unexploited and unexplored.
Third, rentals payable under the onshore leasing program
were increased in 1960, with total rentals for the first
five years being raised from $1 per acre to $2.50 per acre. 9/

The total number of barrels of oil produced from onshore leases, however, continued to rise in the 1960's, and reached a peak of 216.3 million barrels per year in 1969, declining to 196.8 million barrels in 1971. 10/ Natural gas produced from onshore leases hit a plateau of about 1 trillion cubic feet in 1967 and remained at that level through 1971. 11/ This oil and gas production came from a small part of the total leased acreage. In 1971, only about seven percent of total onshore leased acreage was commercially productive. 12/ Total royalties received from onshore production in 1971 were $99.1 million; onshore bonus payments received the same year totalled $1.16 billion. 13/ The latter figure, of course, fluctuates greatly from year to year, whereas the royalty totals showed a steady increase throughout the 1950's and 1960's.

## Lands Bearing Oil Shale

Oil shale lands are leased pursuant to section 21 of the Mineral Lands Leasing Act, which authorizes the Secretary of the Interior to lease such lands under such rules and regulations as he may prescribe. 14/ The specifics of such leases are left very largely to administrative discretion. Leases may be for indeterminate periods, upon such conditions as may be imposed by the Secretary, including covenants relative to permissible methods of mining, prevention of waste, and productive development. The lessee must pay royalties as specified in the lease, plus a rental of 50 cents per acre per year with rents to be credited against any royalties due. Royalties are subject to readjustment by the Secretary at the end of each 20-year period. The Secretary may waive the payment of any royalty and rental during the first five years of the lease. One of the few important restrictions on the Secretary's discretion is that no oil shale lease may exceed 5,120 acres and no person, association or corporation may hold more than one such lease.

The Secretary's authority to sell oil shale leases was not exercised until 1974. On April 15, 1930, President Hoover by Executive Order 15/ withdrew all oil shale lands from availability for lease, under the authority of a statute which provides that the President may "temporarily withdraw from settlement, location, sale, or entry" any of the public lands of the United States. 16/ The continuing force of this Executive Order was affirmed in 1966 in Mecham v. Udall, 369 F. 2d 1 (10th Cir., 1966), which held that the word "temporarily" should be interpreted in light of the time perspective of the Federal Government rather than of an individual citizen.

In 1968 the Secretary of the Interior invited lease bids on three tracts of oil shale land, but rejected the bids submitted as too small. Three years later, in his first energy message, June 4, 1971, President Nixon called for the initiation of an oil shale leasing program. In November, 1973, Secretary of the Interior Rogers Morton announced the approval of a limited shale leasing program and released the text of the lease that would be required. 17/ The Secretary prescribed a competitive bidding system similar to that for the onshore KGS lands, involving payment of an initial bonus payable in five annual installments and a royalty of 16.8 cents per barrel of oil. The term of the leases was set at 20 years and as long thereafter as oil is produced in paying quantities. The fourth and fifth bonus installments may be offset by certain subsidies for operating expenses and extraordinary costs. 18/

In January, 1974, six oil shale tracts were offered for competitive bidding. Four of these were leased to bidders in January through April. The total bonuses of the accepted bids for these four tracts was in excess of $445 million, less the subsidies allowable in years four and five of the lease. 19/

## Selection of Tracts for Lease

Selection of onshore tracts for noncompetitive leasing is in the first instance at the initiative of the lease applicant. An offer to lease, however, will be rejected "unless it is found that the land is prospectively valuable for oil or gas." 20/ Moreover, the more desirable lands not within a KGS are usually already under lease. Therefore, in practice the initiative of the Secretary or his delegate is important. Lands for which outstanding leases have been cancelled, relinquished, or terminated by operation of law are made available for new lease offers by the Bureau of Land Management. Lists of available tracts are posted monthly in the office of the BLM. All offers to lease such lands received within five days after posting are deemed simultaneous offers and are included in the lottery to determine the eligible offeror. 21/ A total of about 500,000 lease offers are made annually for some 5,000 available parcels, a 100-1 ratio. 22/

Tracts within a KGS are selected for competitive leasing by the Secretary or his delegate. Notice is published for five consecutive weeks before the lease competition in a newspaper of general circulation in the county where the land is located, or in other suitable publications. The notice specifies the rental and royalty rate, and the method of bidding. The royalty must be at least 12-1/2 percent and generally is on a sliding scale from 12-1/2 to 25 percent, depending on average monthly production. Bonus bid competition may be by auction or sealed bids, but in practice sealed bids are always used. 23/

The shale tracts offered for competitive leasing in 1974 were selected by the Department of the Interior in consultation with prospective bidders. In November, 1971, the Department called for oil companies to select tracts on which they would like to bid. By January 31, 1972, 18 tracts had been nominated, of which the Department selected six. An environmental impact statement, as required by the NEPA, was then prepared by the Department for each tract. On November 26, 1973, Executive Order 5327 of April 15, 1930, was modified to permit the leasing of the six tracts. 24/

## Elements of Current Onshore Leasing Policy

The current onshore petroleum leasing policy of the Federal Government is affected by three important objectives:

First, to encourage prompt and orderly development of oil and gas deposits on Federal lands;

Second, to preserve and enhance the environment; and

Third, to secure to the Federal Government "fair market value" for the petroleum resources on Federal lands.

President Nixon in his energy address January 23, 1974, dubbed the Mineral Lands Leasing Act "obsolete" and called for a single new Federal leasing system for all Federal lands. He suggested what the primary objective of such a new leasing program would be by stressing that it should "assure that the persons who obtain the leases are those who have an interest in early exploration for oil, gas, and other minerals."

In 1972 Assistant Secretary of the Interior for Public Land Management Harrison Loesch had made similar observations before the Senate Interior Committee:

"Additional onshore oil and gas leases are needed, but it is even more important

that the leases be issued under conditions
which will promote orderly development.  It
is believed that a system of all competitive
leasing with appropriate requirements for
exploration and development, instead of the
present noncompetitive leasing system, would
be more responsible to supply and demand and
would lead to less holding of leases primarily
for speculation.

The Administration's proposed bill to reform
the mineral leasing laws would provide that,
with minor exceptions, all leases would
be issued competitively." 25/

As of October, 1974, the Congress had taken no
action on the Administration's proposed reform of the Mineral
Lands Leasing Act.  Reform of the onshore leasing system has
not in fact been an urgent matter for attention either in
Congress or in the Executive branch because it is generally
believed that, apart from oil shale deposits, there is very
limited potential for further new production from onshore
leases.  The government is therefore far more concerned
with the offshore leasing program, and secondly, with the
onshore leasing programs for coal and oil shale. 26/

Environmental Controls

Exploration and drilling activities by onshore
lessees are subject to a variety of environmental controls.
The National Environmental Policy Act, besides requiring an
environmental impact statement wherever Federal programs may
have an adverse impact on the environment, specifies that
all other statutes and regulations must be administered and
interpreted "to the fullest extent possible" in accordance
with its policies.  The Mineral Lands Leasing Act itself
states as a general principle that leases shall contain
provisions for exercising care in the operation of properties
and for safeguarding the public. 27/

Regulations of the Bureau of Land Management
specify that permits for exploratory activity are to be
conditioned on the results of an examination of the environmental impact of such activity.  A BLM manual, No. 3109/3509,
prescribes that the same type of procedures followed for
other minerals under 43 C.F.R. part 23 shall be followed
before the issuance of oil and gas leases.  Under 43 C.F.R.

§23.5(a)(1), before a permit for exploratory activity is
issued, a technical examination must be made to determine
the probable effect of prospecting activity on the environment.  The examination takes into consideration the need
for:

> "[P]reservation and protection of other
> resources, including recreational, scenic,
> historic, and ecological values; the control
> of erosion, flooding and pollution of water;
> the isolation of toxic materials; the preven-
> tion of air pollution; the reclamation by
> revegetation, replacement of soil, or by
> other means, of lands affected by the explo-
> ration or mining operations; the prevention
> of slides; the protection of fish and wild-
> life and their habitat; and the prevention
> of hazards to public health and safety." 28/

Based on this examination the district manager is directed
to formulate the general requirements which the applicant
must meet during the conduct of exploration and extraction
and for the reclamation of affected land or waters.  These
requirements are to be incorporated into the permit, lease
or contract. 29/  Further regulations spell out procedures for
the approval and supervision by the Bureau of the actual
conduct of the lessee's operations. 30/

The oil shale lease also contains extensive environmental protection provisions.  Lessees are required to submit
certain environmental baseline data on the quality of the
water, air, and vegetation, to be collected for at least one
year before submitting a detailed development plan and one
additional year before commercial operations.  Lessee must
also provide annual environmental monitoring data.  Public
hearings are conducted concerning the development plan, and
lessees are responsible for rehabilitation of affected areas.
An environmental bond is required in the amount of $2,000
per acre for mine and disposal areas and $500 per acre for
all other affected lands. 31/

Finally, the Mining and Minerals Policy Act of 1970 32/
declares that it is the policy of the Federal Government to
encourage private enterprise in, among other things, "the
study and development of methods for the disposal, control,
and reclamation of mineral waste products, and the reclamation

of mined land, so as to lessen any adverse impact of mineral
extraction and processing upon the physical environment
that may result from mining or mineral activities." The
Act specifically includes oil, gas, coal, oil shale and
uranium within its scope.

The adequacy of these environmental controls is
a matter of intense controversy, particularly where the
potential environmental damage is great and expensive to
avoid, such as in oil shale operations. Interpretation
and enforcement of the regulations leaves much to administrative discretion of the Department of the Interior. In
the case of the oil shale lease, critics have contended
that the environmental requirements therein cannot possibly
be complied with, given existing technology. 33/

## Maximizing Federal Government Revenue

It is generally believed that the noncompetitive
onshore leasing program has not maximized the revenue obtained
by the Federal Government, that is, has not given the government
"market value" for the oil and gas resources on public
lands. The magnitude of this revenue gap, however, cannot
be estimated satisfactorily. One unofficial estimate, for
instance, is that in 1967 an all competitive leasing system
would have increased Government revenues by anywhere from
$10 million to $100 million. 34/ Assistant Secretary Loesch,
in his 1972 testimony before the Senate Interior Committee
voiced his belief that the leasing law frustrates the receipt
of fair market value for noncompetitive leases: "Noncompetitive
oil and gas leases are obtained without a bonus bid and at a
minimal cost and, if a discovery is made, fair market value
probably is not obtained." 35/

Opposing the government's preference for the bonus
bid system to assure fair market values, spokesmen for the
independent oil companies support the present noncompetitive
system, fearing that they would be consistently outbid by
the richer major oil companies in a bonus system. They
argue that the economic benefits to the government are
maximized, in the long run, not by high bonuses but by
prompt development of production on leased land, and that
this is more likely if independent wildcatters rather than
major oil companies hold the leases. 36/ This argument appears
weak, however, in that it assumes that the majors would be

willing to pay substantial sums just to keep the leased land
out of production, which is very questionable in these times
of shortage.  Moreover, the cost under the present system is
quite low to the lease broker who wishes merely to hold the
leased land for future speculation.

Thus, despite the substantial agreement that the
present noncompetitive system does not give the Federal
Government market value for its resources, it is retained
partly because of its low priority on the Congressional and
Executive energy agenda, and partly because it does encourage
participation by independent companies which perhaps could
not meet the capital requirements of bonus bidding. 37/
Also, the Federal Government may fear that an onshore bonus
system would unduly strain the industry's capital structure.
The Government hopes to lease 10 million acres of offshore
lands in 1975, and the bonus requirements for these leases
will be very substantial.  Changing the onshore leases
as well to competitive bonus bidding may oversaturate the
lease market and thus fail to gain the Government any increase in aggregate leasing revenues. 38/

# FOOTNOTES

1. 41 Stat. 445 (Feb. 26, 1920), codified at 30 U.S.C.A. §§181-287.

2. 43 C.F.R. §3101.1-1.

3. 30 U.S.C.A §184(d).

4. 32 Stat. 388 (June 17, 1902), codified at 43 U.S.C.A. §391.

5. 30 U.S.C.A §191.

6. 30 U.S.C.A. §226(b).

7. See 30 U.S.C.A §226 and 43 C.F.R. part 3100.

8. John Sprague and Bernadette Julian, "An Analysis of the Impact of an All Competitive Leasing System on Onshore Oil and Gas Leasing Revenue", 10 National Resources Journal 515, 517.

9. Ibid., 518-522.

10. Submission of Department of the Interior to Hearing on Federal Leasing and Disposal Policies before the Senate Committee on Interior and Insular Affairs, 92d Cong., 2d Sess., June 19, 1972, Ser. No. 92-32, p.210.

11. Ibid., 211.

12. Ibid., 86.

13. Ibid., 222.

14. 30 U.S.C.A. §241.

15. Executive Order 5327, April 15, 1930.

16. 36 Stat. 847 (June 25, 1910), codified at 43 U.S.C.A. §141.

17. See text of lease at 38 F.R. 3188 (Nov. 30, 1973).

18. See lease text and "Fact Sheet on Shale Oil Leasing",
    Dept. of Interior news release Nov. 28, 1973.

19. Angus McDonald, Shale Oil:  An Environmental Critique
    (Washington, D.C.:  Center for Science in the Public
    Interest, 1974), iv.

20. 43 C.F.R. §3101.1-2.

21. 43 C.F.R. §§3112.1-1--3112.5-2.

22. Dept. of the Interior, B.L.M. news release Aug. 20, 1973.

23. 43 C.F.R. §§3120.2-1--3120.4-2.

24. 38 F.R. 3186 (Nov. 30, 1974).

25. Hearing on Federal Leasing and Disposal Policies before
    the Senate Committee on Interior and Insular Affairs,
    92d Cong., 2d Sess., June 19, 1972, Ser. No. 92-32,
    p. 19.

26. See for instance the Hearing cited in note 25, above,
    in which the emphasis was on coal and oil shale lands
    leasing.

27. 30 U.S.C.A. §187.

28. 43 C.F.R. §23.5(a)(1).

29. 43 C.F.R. §23.5(b).

30. 43 C.F.R. §23.6--23.13.

31. See Fact Sheet on Shale Oil Leasing, Dept. of the
    Interior news release Nov. 28, 1973.

32. P.L. 91-631; 84 Stat. 1876 (Dec. 31, 1970).

33. See the analysis in McDonald, Oil Shale:  An Environmental
    Critique (Washington, D.C.:  Center for Science in The
    Public Interest, 1974), esp. 29-35.

34. Sprague and Julian, note 8 above, 531.

35. Hearing, note 25 above, 24.

36. See, for example, the submission of the Rocky Mountain
    Oil and Gas Association at hearing, note 25 above, 640,
    644; cf. the views of the major oil companies favoring
    a competitive bonus bid system, as exemplified by sub-
    mission of Texaco, at ibid, 633.

37. Arguably independents could submit joint bids as is
    often done (though not often successfully) by indepen-
    dents competing for offshore leases. See Nossaman
    et al., Study of Outer Continental Shelf Lands of the
    United States (Los Angeles: Nossaman et al., 1968)
    §8.17.

38. Factors affecting bid levels for competitive leases are
    complex and very imperfectly understood; see Keith
    Brown, Bidding for Offshore Oil: Toward an Optimal
    Strategy (Dallas: S.M.U. Press, 1969), esp. 61-63;
    Walter Mead, "Natural Resources Disposal Policy--Oral
    action versus Sealed Bids", 7 Natural Resources Journal
    194. (April, 1967).

I.    [§B.9]  U.S. Offshore Leasing System

        The U.S. offshore leasing system is presently em-
bodied in the Outer Continental Shelf Lands Act of 1953. 1/
This Act was passed as a companion measure to the Submerged
Lands Act of 1953 2/ which quitclaimed to each coastal state
the submerged lands lying within three geographical miles
of a state's coastline, with the exception of historic
boundaries in the Gulf of Mexico extending three marine
leagues (9 miles).  Outside of the area quitclaimed to the
states the Outer Continental Shelf Lands Act grants the
Federal Government exclusive authority over lands which
are properly claimed by the U.S. under international law,
whether as continental shelf, continental slope, or otherwise.  By not asserting jurisdiction over any particular
offshore area, this Act constitutes a legislative implementation of the 1945 Truman Proclamation, which claimed U.S.
jurisdiction and control over the natural resources of the
geologic continental shelf contiguous to the U.S. coast. 3/

        The Outer Continental Shelf Lands Act authorizes
the leasing of offshore lands and creates a comprehensive
system governing oil and gas operations in that area.  In
Section 4 the Act extends U.S. jurisdiction and law to the
outer continental shelf and preserves preexisting state
leases.  After setting forth a few procedural, housekeeping
and enforcement provisions, the Act then provides the basic
skeleton for an oil and gas leasing system in Section 8, but
grants the Secretary of the Interior, in broad terms, the
authority to prescribe such rules and regulations as he deter-
mines necessary to administer the Act, prevent waste, conserve natural resources, and protect correlative rights under
Section 5(a)(1).

        Section 8 authorizes leasing on the basis of com-
petitive bidding for the purpose of mineral development.  With
respect to minerals other than oil and gas competitive bidding for leases must be on the basis of the highest cash
bonus and provide for such royalty rental and other terms
as the Secretary may fix.  Biddings on oil and gas are permitted to be either on the basis of (1) a cash bonus with the
royalty, minimum royalty and rental fixed, or (2) a royalty
bid at the discretion of the Secretary of the Interior
with royalty to be not less than 12-1/2% in any case.  Oil and
gas leases may not cover more than 5,760 acres and shall be for
"a period of 5 years and as long thereafter as oil or gas may be

produced from the area in paying quantities, or drilling or well reworking operations as approved by the Secretary are conducted thereon [and] certain such rental provisions and such other terms and provisions as the Secretary may prescribe at the time of offering the area for lease." As a matter of practice, the Secretary has always chosen to use cash bonus bidding for oil and gas leases, fixing in addition a required royalty of 16-2/3% of the value of production. 4/ Each submitted bid must be sealed and accompanied by a deposit in cash or its equivalent of 20% of the bid. Sealed biddings protects the identity of the bidder and induces true estimates of value of a tract. The winning bidder must submit the remaining 80% within 30 days after his name is announced. 5/

No priorities or guidelines by which the Secretary is to select areas for lease are set forth in the Act. As to petroleum and sulphur, the Department of the Interior and industry cooperate in the selection of areas to be leased, with industry conducting all requisite pre-bidding exploratory work and upon request, nominating areas of interest to the Department's Bureau of Land Management ("BLM"). BLM has then, with the assistance of U.S. Geological Survey ("USGS") selected those tracts to be offered for lease sale. 6/ The Federal Government normally has had very little, and at times literally no information with which to evaluate the potentiality of areas nominated before and during the bidding process. While requiring the disclosure of geological data by persons obtaining permits for offshore exploratory work, the regulations do not require the disclosure of geophysical data. Because geophysical data is the most commonly used and reliable means of evaluating potential offshore petroleum and sulfur prospects, industry has had a better knowledge than the Federal Government of tracts with the highest potential yield of oil and gas. 7/

Typically the large independent American oil companies are not independent competitors, but are partners in a multitude of joint ventures and joint bidding arrangements. Because bidders are few in number, the secret competitive bidding system often produces a wide span between the highest and second highest bids, as well as between the highest and lowest bids. 8/

After the Santa Barbara spill in 1969, the regulations were revised to include stricter standards with respect to pollution prevention and control. 9/ In leasing, the Director of BLM is required to "develop special leasing stipulations and conditions when necessary to protect the environment and all other resources", and the regulations with respect to operations were considerably tightened with authority for "major departures" from specified standards being revested in the Washington office of the USGS.

In addition, the Federal Water Pollution Control Act Amendments of 1972 created a comprehensive water management code, providing that "it is the policy of the U.S. that there should be no discharges of oil or hazardous substances" in navigable waters of the U.S., adjoining shoreline or of its contiguous zone. And the National Environmental Policy Act of 1969 requires environment impact reports in all agency decisions, adding an effective new layer of review to the Department actions under the Outer Continental Shelf Lands Act.

Commentators generally agree that the basic mineral leasing system of the Outer Continental Shelf Lands Act is a sound one and has operated well in practice. Its success in fostering oil and gas development is denoted by a dramatic increase in total income from offshore leases under the Act. 10/ The prime reason for the success of the Act may be attributed to its simplicity. The only leasing specifics contained in the Act are (1) competitive biddings, (2) minimum royalty, (3) maximum area to be leased, and (4) set lease term, leaving to the Secretary the authority to implement the leasing system by issuing regulations on a large number of specified matters. This flexible leasing system can readily be adapted to changing conditions, to advances in technology, and to public demand for environmental concern. Nevertheless, various revisions to the Act have been suggested:

Tract Selection 11/

The failure of the Secretary to require the disclosure of geophysical information as a condition to the issuance of an exploratory permit has been cited as one loophole in the leasing system. Apparently this failure of action is motivated by a fear of industry and USGS that

USGS could not maintain the confidentiality of such information and by a concern that it would be unfair for the
Federal Government to have access to such "proprietory"
information. The counterargument is that the Federal Government, as the resource owner, should be entitled to the same
amount of information about the resources as its bidders,
if it keeps the information in confidence. Since other
Federal and state agencies successfully handle confidential
data, there is no reason why the USGS cannot adopt the same
safeguards.

Alternatively, the Federal Government could itself
conduct a survey and make the results known to all bidders,
thereby eliminating the duplication of pre-bidding exploratory work by industry groups. This may not substantially reduce
the number of surveys, however, given the preference of industry
to conduct such work with their own specifications either independently or in groups. Nor may this alternative substantially
increase the number and character of bidders or the amount of
the bid, given the prohibitive cost of entry into offshore oil
and gas development, exclusive of pre-bidding exploratory work,
for small firms. When small firms act jointly, however, either
among themselves or in concert with large firms, their pre-bidding
attitudes and procedures are very similar to major oil companies.

Lease Sales Bonus Bidding 12/

Within either the bonus or royalty bidding arrangement, the Secretary has room for innovation and discretion,
but the existing system of a fixed 16-2/3% royalty combined
with a bonus bid places a growing amount of stress on the
industry. This stress is reflected in a rapid growth of the ratios
of indebtedness to equity among the major oil companies, which
will predictably grow greater with the effort to vastly expand
outer continental shelf production. As a result, the Federal
Government could receive less for the sale of its resources
than it would receive if the sales were smaller and less frequent.

On the other hand, competitive bonus bidding is
the most simple and efficient means of lease sales and
does attract the company that is most economically motivated
toward early development. Those firms most likely to conduct
an ambitious exploratory program are generally those who are

most optimistic about finding oil, who expect a high value of profits, and who will accordingly place a high bid.

Even if the bonuses received may be smaller where sales are large and frequent, the funds that would have been spent on the bonus will instead go into exploration and development. In fact, rapid promotion and development of the outer continental shelf could be achieved by requiring bidders to commit themselves to an exploratory program in advance. However, this latter proposal would be administratively difficult and possibly inefficient, save for remote areas or areas with adverse conditions where exploration must be encouraged.

Other suggestions for altering the existing bonus bidding system include a delayed payment schedule spread out over ten years with the first payment delayed five years after issuance of the lease, and a refusal price based on the calculation of future net income below which bids should be rejected by the government. 13/ Neither of these alternatives would require an amendment to the Act.

## Joint Bidding 14/

A pattern of joint bidding in lease sales had led to the charge that such combinations may have lessened competition and the entry into outer continental shelf sales by smaller companies. Notwithstanding extensive joint bidding, however, effective competition exists due to the need for combinations to share the risk. 15/ If the major oil companies are prohibited from joint bidding, they will predictably have less rather than greater competitive interest in a large number of tracts. It must again be emphasized that the only way small companies have been able to effectively enter the market has been through joint bidding with each other or with the majors. Alternatively, joint bidding could be restricted to those firms unable, due to a capital limitation, to enter the market as a single bidder.

## Alternative Forms of Bidding 16/

The language of the Act is sufficiently broad to permit experimentation with alternate forms of bidding, including bidding on the basis of flat royalty, sliding scale royalty and net profits. But there is a basic defect to any

form of royalty bidding in that any royalty increases the
fixed costs of operations and diminishes an operator's
incentive as such costs approach the value of production.
A flat royalty provides a greater incentive to prematurely
abandon, whereas a sliding scale royalty induces the operator
to produce at the lowest permissible rate in order to reduce
royalty.  In addition, the costs of entry are too high for
royalty bidding to cause greater participation by small companies.  As the resource depletes, however, royalty must be
reduced to effect the maximum recovery of the resource.

        Bidding on the basis of the highest net profits
offered to the Federal Government, coupled with a bonus
and stated minimum royalty, could encourage exploration and
the development of new techniques by permitting the operator
to deduct all cost of exploration and operation before any
payment to the government.  Its one defect is that the larger
the reserve net profits interest, the less incentive the
operator has to be efficient.  But if a lack of competitive
interest is shown in offshore areas where it is particularly
expensive to operate, it would be desirable to amend the
Act to authorize a net profits bidding without any minimum
royalty or bonus requirement.

Drilling Term 17/

        If all the available acreage in the Outer Continental
Self having petroleum potential is leased in the near future,
the five-year drilling term could put unreasonable stress on
the abilities of industry to properly test the many newly
leased areas.  A better alternative would be to amend the
Act and let the Secretary set the term in his discretion.

Operating Procedures 18/

        One significant defect in the Department's control
of operating procedures is the absence of a requirement or
public hearing prior to leasing to explore the impact of the
proposed leasing program on total environment.  The lack of
USGS staff to effectively police enforcement of regulations
and lease terms, particularly in the area of pollution and
pollution control devices, will also create a problem when
new leases in new areas are issued.  Moreoever, the Secretary's
power to regulate pollution under the Act only applies to the

continental shelf and not to the removal of pollutants from
the sea and adjacent beaches. 19/ And unless reasonable limits
are placed on the liability of offshore operators for pollution,
the petroleum industry may be compelled to abandon offshore
drilling altogether.

## Other Uses of the Continental Shelf 20/

The Act presently does not permit the leasing of
areas for the construction of offshore islands, supports,
and oil terminals not used in connection with the development of outer continental shelf resources. Nor does it
authorize the leasing or use of geothermal resources and
fresh water, which has been found to upwell beyond limits
of state jurisdiction. The Act further does not provide
for salvage and treasure trove and ignores the contingency
of the ambulatory boundary between state and federal jurisdictions and resultant "split" leases.

## Conclusion

Despire these specific criticisms, the present
offshore leasing system has effectively promoted development of our offshore mineral reserves through the competitive
allocation of leases and should continue to work well in
the future.

FOOTNOTES

1. 43 U.S.C. §1331 et seq.

2. 43 U.S.C. §1301 et. seq.

3. Robert B. Krueger, "The Background of the Doctrine of the Continental Shelf and the Outer Continental Shelf Lands Act", 10 Natural Resources Journal, 442, 467 (July, 1970).

4. George Miron, "The Outer Continental Shelf--Managing or Mismanaging the Resources", 2 Journal of Maritime Law and Commerce 267, 278 (Jan., 1971).

5. Id.

6. Robert B. Krueger, "An Evaluation of the Provisions and Policies of the Outer Continental Shelf Lands Act", 10 Natural Resources Journal 763, 766 (Oct. 1970).

7. Id.

8. Walter J. Mead, "The Structure of the Buyer Market for Oil Shale Resources", 8 Natural Resources Journal 604, 620-625 (Oct. 1968).

9. 30 C.F.R. §250.43

10. Raymond C. Coulter, "The Outer Continental Shelf Lands Act - Its Adequacies and Limitations", 4 Natural Resources Lawyer 725, (1971).

11. The following discussion is condensed from the Statement of Robert B. Krueger to the U.S. Senate Committee on Interior and Insular Affairs, May 7, 1974, pp. 2-4.

12. Id. at 4-5

13. Mead, supra, note 8 at 629.

14. Id. at 5-7.

15. Nossaman, et al., Study of the Outer Continental Shelf Lands of the U.S., §8.17 (1968).

16. Krueger, _supra_ note 11, 7-11.

17. _Id_. at 10-11.

18. _Id_. at 11-13.

19. John B. Connally, "Governmental Regulation of Operations on Submerged Lands", 21 _Institute on Oil and Gas Law and Taxation_ 31, 40 (1970).

20. Krueger, _supra_, note 11 at 13-14.

J.   [§B.10]   State Prorationing Systems

Prorationing is a state implemented system whereby:  (1) Maximum efficient or basis allowable rates of production are set for each oil reservoir and each well; and (2)
in eight states, state-wide maximum levels of production are
set month by month and this production is allocated among the
reservoirs and wells within the state. 1/  Historically, most
U.S. oil production has occurred in those states with prorationing and as a result there have been, since the mid-1930's,
controls on the amount of crude oil produced in this nation.
Controls on output have an impact not only on oil prices within the United States but also on the international petroleum
market.

Prorationing came into existence as a result of the
chaotic conditions that existed during the early 1930's.  All
oil producing states had "law of capture" statutes in one form
or another which entitled a landowner to all the oil that could
be produced from his acreage despite the fact that "his" oil
might in fact come from a reservoir that extended under the
property of other landowners.  Hence there was an incentive
for overdrilling and overproduction.  It soon became apparent
that:

> "[R]apid and indiscriminate production
> often 'wasted' reservoir energy, caused
> irregular, nonuniform migration of fluids
> and by-passing of large deposits, and
> resulted in 'premature' abandonment of
> the field and reduced ultimate recovery. 2/

Improved technical knowledge led to the concept of
maximum effective rate (MER) of production.  The MER, which is
an engineering concept, is the rate of production "which if
exceeded would lead to avoidable underground waste through
loss of ultimate oil recovery." 3/  Using the concept of MER,
cooperative action in the oil producing states was undertaken
to eliminate wasteful practices and these efforts resulted in
the Interstate Oil Compact Commissions (IOCC) in 1935.

The IOCC is made up of representatives of the oil
producing states.  The duties of the IOCC include:

> "[T]he conduct of studies regarding
> the demand for domestic production and the

recommendation to each state of its
relative part of the total demand for
domestic production that could be produced without physical waste." 4/

The actual burden of regulation is with the individual states.
It should be noted that the regulation is done with the con-
sent of Congress beginning with Section 9(c) of the National
Industrial Recovery Act of 1933 and continued by the Connally
"Hot Oil" Act of 1935.

Prorationing regulations vary from state to state
but all have as a common stated goal the prevention of "waste",
such as the operation of any oil well with an inefficient
gas-oil ratio or permitting any natural gas well to burn
wastefully.   These statutory requirements of themselves have
important implications for production.   As Lovejoy and Homan
point out:

"It is important to the commission to
keep the allocated production closely
in balance with forthcoming demand.
Otherwise, it loses control over its
most important function - that of allocating production back to individual
wells and pools.  If it chronically
authorized production in excess of the
amount demanded, the purchasers could
pick and choose among the available
sources, thus defeating the allocation
purposes of the commission.  The initiative in the proration system would
pass from the commission to the purchasers, into what is known as
'purchasers proration.'  Since one of
the primary purposes of proration is
precisely to prevent purchaser discrimination among sources of supply,
any large and continuing deficiency of
this sort would undermine the system." 5/

As of 1964, however, twelve of the oil producing
states, including five of the seven largest producing states,
"have 'market-demand' statutes that allow or require the
regulatory body to limit production to reasonable market

demand." 6/  The Texas statute, for example, includes in the
definition of "waste" the production of crude petroleum oil
in excess of transportation or market facilities or reasonable
market demand.

The month to month decisions on production are
announced in terms of a percent of state production capacity
(which the commission also affects by other regulations, discussed below).  When setting the state allowable production,
the regulating body will take into consideration the nomina-
tions (purchase estimates) of purchasers (who are usually
also sellers of crude oil), crude and products in storage,
crude and products needed, pipeline capabilities, production
and storage in other states and estimates of consumption
(provided by the state and the U.S. Bureau of Mines).  From
this data the allowable level of production for the state
is set.  This figure must then be allocated to each reservoir
and well.

Under prorationing regulations existing in market-
demand states there is a "basic allowable" rate of production
for each well in the state.  While the method of calculating
the basic allowable differs between states, the method in
general is as follows:

> "Every pool is produced at some particular
> depth.  According to its depth, each well
> in a pool is assigned a 'top' or 'schedule'
> allowable that represents a hypothetical
> 100 percent rate of production if it were
> not restricted, the amount increasing with
> the depth of the pool." 7/

This top basic allowable rate is usually less than
the MER and is also affected by well spacing.  Hence these
regulations provide incentives, which vary between states,
affecting how deep wells are drilled and how well spacing is
planned.  With these maximum rates of production available
it is only necessary for states to choose a monthly "market
demand factor" which when multiplied by total top basic
allowable capacity yields the selected level of total production for the entire state for the month.  Note that some
states, such as Texas, have wells that are exempt from prorationing and hence have a slightly more complicated procedure
to follow in calculating their market demand factor.

There has been a great deal of criticism leveled
against the market-demand prorationing system in general as
well as against the methods used to select the top allowable
well output.  These points are summarized in the Study of the
Outer Continental Shelf Lands of the United States. 8/  The MER-
type calculations are criticized on four main grounds.  First,
the maximum allowable production from hypothetically identical wells varies greatly from state to state.  For instance,
a well in Louisiana is allowed to produce as much as 150
percent more than a similar well in Oklahoma. 9/  Second, deeper
wells are assigned higher allowables despite the fact that
there is neither a solid geological justification nor a clear
economic rationale for this.  Third, spacing incentives
can lead to overinvestment in wells too closely spaced.
Fourth, some states have a system of exemptions, for marginal
or stripper wells, so that "only the high daily output wells
are subject to prorationing restriction." 10/  Adelman comments
that the "basic allowable is not producing capacity, it is
determined in a slapdash manner with the general object of
compensating wells for their higher cost, e.g., depth." 11/  There
are also indications that the MER calculations are not good indicators of current sustainable efficient capacity.  For
instance, during 1963 Texas was operating at an average 28 percent allowable level with production from allowable wells
totaling 1,605 thousand barrels daily (TBD).  This implies a
maximum level of production of 5,730 TBD.  And yet at the time
Texas authorities estimated that "wells in the prorated catagory
had an efficient sustainable capacity of around 3,700 TBD." 12/
It is generally agreed, however, that with common pool ownership
and the absence of unitization, MER type regulation is needed
to prevent overinvestment and inefficient utilization of an
oil reservoir. 13/

State regulatory agencies, by controlling production,
necessarily influence price.  Lovejoy and Homan conclude that:

> "The severe restrictions on output in states
> like Texas, Kansas and Oklahoma in the 1930's
> were designed to have an immediate effect
> in changing the level of prices.  This is
> not, however, true today; the present system
> supports prices, but does not actively
> attempt to revise them." 14/

The resulting conditions of relatively high prices and restricted
output also required the existence of constraints on the importation of oil.

The broad economic effects of market-demand prorationing are: (1) supply is artificially restricted; (2) price is forced above what it would be in the absence of regulation; (3) overcapacity develops. The last point is demonstrated by the fact that the market-demand factor for Louisiana offshore wells for the entire decade of the 1960's averaged 35.3 percent (see table). 15/

The net effect of these regulations is a subsidy to the crude oil producers. Not only has production been limited but in some states (such as Texas) wells with low productivity (stripper wells) are not included in prorationing while highly productive wells produce at a restricted rate. This results in an incentive for including high-cost sources of production in the limited supply of crude oil. The overcapacity has been defended on grounds of national security. But Adelman places an extremely high price on this excess capacity. 16/ It has also been argued that the crude producers are forced, as an uncompensated service, to provide standby capacity. McDonald concludes, however, that "the price reductions of 1957-60 suggest the existence of a critical level of excess capacity which if exceeded triggers price reductions." 1' This implies that, up to a point, any excess capacity is in effect "paid for" by higher prices on allowed production.

However, the importance of market-demand prorationing, as seen in the light of recent monthly market-demand factors, may not have the impact on output in the future that it has had in the past, because the market demand factors for both Texas and Louisiana have been at or near 100 percent since early in 1972 (as late as 1969 both were approximately 50 percent.) 18/

TABLE 2    Annual Average of Monthly Market Demand Factors

| Year | Texas | Louisiana (offshore) |
|------|-------|----------------------|
| 1950 | 63% | a |
| 1951 | 76 | a |
| 1952 | 71 | a |
| 1953 | 65 | 90% |
| 1954 | 53 | 61 |
| 1955 | 53 | 48 |
| 1956 | 52 | 42 |
| 1957 | 47 | 43 |
| 1958 | 33 | 33 |
| 1959 | 34 | 34 |
| 1960 | 28 | 34 |
| 1961 | 28 | 32 |
| 1962 | 27 | 33 |
| 1963 | 28b | 32 |
| 1964 | 28 | 32 |
| 1965 | 29c | 33 |
| 1966 | 34 | 35 |
| 1967 | 41 | 38d |
| 1968 | 45 | 42 |
| 1969 | 52 | 44 |
| 1970 | 72 | 56 |
| 1971 | 73 | 73 |
| 1972 | 94 | 91 |
| 1973 | 100 | 100 |

Sources:  respective state conservation commissions
a.  no fixed allowable schedule
b.  prior to 1963, Texas production was limited by the number
    of days per month that wells were allowed to produce.
c.  introduction of 1965 Texas Yardstock for new drilling.
d.  introduction of new allowable schedule which increased
    base to which market factor applied.

Footnotes

1. McDonald, <u>Petroleum Conservation in the United States;</u> <u>An Economic Analysis</u> 50 (1971).

2. Lovejoy & Homan, <u>Economic Aspects of Oil Conservation Regulation</u> 202 (1967).

3. Buckely, (ed.), <u>Petroleum Conservation</u> 152 (1951).

4. Nossaman, <u>et al</u>., <u>Study of Outer Continental Shelf Lands of the United States</u>, 557 (1968).

5. Lovejoy, <u>op</u>. <u>cit</u>., 139-140.

6. <u>Ibid</u>., 129.

7. <u>Ibid</u>., 142.

8. Nossaman, et al., <u>op</u>. <u>cit</u>., 568-70.

9. <u>Ibid</u>., 569.

10. <u>Ibid</u>., 570.

11. Adelman, <u>The World Petroleum Market</u>, 148 (1972).

12. Lovejoy, <u>op</u>. <u>cit</u>., 165.

13. Mead, "Government Subsidies to the Oil Industry," <u>Natural Resources Journal</u>, January 1970, 116-7.

14. Lovejoy, <u>op</u>. <u>cit</u>., 239.

15. Texas Railroad Commission, <u>Monthly Producing Days and Years in Texas</u>.

16. Adelman, "Efficiency of Resources Use in Crude Petroleum," Southern Journal of Economics, October, 1964, 101-22.

17. McDonald, op. cit., 195.

18. Texas Railroad Commission, op. cit.

K.   [§B.11]   Environmental Policy

　　1.   [§B.12]   Failure to Internalize Environmental Cost

　　　　The environment has become a subject of increasing
concern in recent years.  This concern is in large part
caused by the use of the rivers, land and the atmosphere as
a waste receptacle.  Historically, there have been relatively
few constraints on the use of the environment in this manner,
and the availability of this low cost residuals discharge
point has had effects on the level of production and consumption in many industries.  The petroleum industry, which
creates waste products not only in production but through
the use of its products as well, is no exception.

　　　　The phrase, failure to internalize environmental
costs, refers to third party effects, or externalities.
Freeman, in The Economics of Environmental Policy, explains
these effects:

> "If third parties are adversely affected
> by the production activity, they bear costs
> that are not included in the private cost
> calculation of the producer.  Social cost
> (including third party costs) exceeds
> private cost.  The result is excessive
> production and consumption of the good." 1/

In other words, the producer is willing to provide, at any
given price, more of the good than he would if he himself
had to pay the entire cost of production.  The same analysis
applies to a good (such as gasoline) that has third party
effects in consumption (such as air pollution).  In both
cases, in effect, "consumers are being subsidized since the
price they pay is less than social cost, and the subsidy is
paid by the downstream users who bear the external cost." 2/
As Freeman points out, third party effects arise when property rights are not enforceable or are not clearly defined.
This is clearly the case with the environment, and as a
result the environment is used excessively for waste discharge.

　　　　There have been many ways in which the petroleum
industry has contributed to the use of the environment as a
waste disposal point.  The Environmental Conservation report
of the National Petroleum Council provides a comprehensive

listing of these, and they include air pollution (from sulfur oxides, nitrogen oxides, hydrocarbons, and others), water pollution (by oil, drilling mud, brine spent caustics and others), and land pollution (by oil waste water, trash and litter). This pollution occurs at all levels of industry operations (drilling, production, gas treatment, refining, transportation, storage and marketing) as well as from use of products (stationary combustion sources, vehicles or industrial use). 3/

The internalization of environmental costs can be expensive. For example, it has been estimated that between 1972 and 1976 the petroleum refining industry, alone, would have to make capital expenditures of between $634 million to $1155 million, along with additional annual costs (up to $21 million in 1976), "to meet the air and water pollution abatement requirements that apply to the refining of petroleum." 4/

It is in any event very difficult on either a theoretical or a policy level to effectively regulate externalities. As one source declares, "virtually every author points out that we do not know how to calculate the ideal Pigouvian tax or subsidy levels in practice. . . ." 5/ And as the Council on Environmental Quality concludes, in the study of incentives in the existing and possible future regulations on control of automobile air pollution:

> "Although this strategy may reduce damage
> costs, it may not be the most cost-
> effective strategy in terms of total
> societal costs. This example, related
> to the Clean Air Act, is typical of the
> often perverse incentives created by
> regulations." 6/

In conclusion, it can be stated that the absence of full disposal costs in cost of production and the cost of use of petroleum products has been an unplanned subsidy which has promoted production and use of petroleum products. The current emphasis on environmental quality forces the inclusion of third party costs or externalities in cost calculations. To the degree that regulation provides the proper incentives, petroleum production and use will become more expensive, and this will tend to reduce demand for such products.

FOOTNOTES

1.  A. Myrick Freeman, III, et al., The Economics of
    Environmental Policy (New York:  John Wiley and Sons,
    Inc., 1973), 75.

2.  Ibid.

3.  National Petroleum Council, Environmental Conserva-
    tion (Washington, D.C.: 1971 and 1972), Vol. 1,
    28.

4.  Council on Environmental Quality, Department of Com-
    merce.  The Economic Impact of Pollution Control,
    A Summary of Recent Studies (Washington, D.C.:
    GPO, 1972), 39.

5.  William J. Baumol and Wallace E. Oates, "The Use of
    Standards and Prices for Protection of the Environ-
    ment," Swedish Journal of Economics (March, 1971),
    42.

6.  Council on Environmental Quality, Fourth Annual Report
    (Washington, D.C.:  GPO, 1973), 113.

## 2. [§B.13] Environmental Regulation

Concern over the impact of certain forms of production and consumption on the environment has been increasing in recent years. This concern has manifest itself in several forms. First, there have been delays or cancellations of energy resource development projects as environmental activist organizations have instituted legal action. Second, governments, federal, state and local, have introduced new regulations in an attempt to avoid environmental damage. Third, there is growing interest in using fees or taxes to impose a charge on the polluter to, in effect, make pollution expensive. The impact of environmental regulation on the petroleum and gas industries can be divided into direct and indirect effects. These effects, which in many cases are domestic in nature, will be very briefly summarized and then their implications for the international petroleum industry will be discussed.

### Direct Effects

Direct effects would include only those things which specifically affect the way in which the oil and gas industries operate. Refineries, for example, have been required to operate with less air pollution. Flue gas desulfurization systems, cooling towers (to eliminate thermal discharges), fume afterburners, storage tank modifications and other changes in production methods are or will be required. The EPA has estimated that between 1972 and 1976 the capital costs of such modifications could run to about $845 million and would require an increase in operating costs of about $21 million a year by 1976. 1/

There have been other regulations that directly affect operating costs in the petroleum industry. Regulations concerning the operation of tankers on the open sea have affected the capital cost of tankers and their operating cost. Company liability for spills has also increased costs. Other regulations have influenced not only the type of crude oil that is used by refineries (low sulfur) and the methods of refining (added steps to remove sulfur) but also what products the refineries must make from the crude oil. For example, refiners must increase production of no-lead gasoline. One respondent to the questionnaire pointed out that "With the present projected no-lead gasoline consumption and octaine requirements, gasoline yield per barrel of crude is expected to be reduced by 10 to 11%, which means either lower gasoline output or higher crude consumption."

Another form of direct costs imposed on oil companies can be seen in the form of delays. The difficulties in obtaining local approval for new refinery sites is well documented. Another form of delay is characterized by the situation in Santa Barbara. New offshore drilling has been delayed since the major blow-out in 1969. Recent approval to drill on existing Federal leases has been granted (after lengthy and costly environmental studies) but there are still delays and uncertainty because of state and local reservations about pipelines and the desirability of on-shore facilities. A final example of the impact of environmental concern is the Alaskan pipeline. Several respondents cited the "4-5 year delay in development of the Alaskan North Slope crude oil reserves" which has been caused by the lack of an acceptable means to transport oil and gas to the lower 48 states. These delays have caused increased costs to the companies involved because they have been unable to produce from deposits on which leases have been paid, and have not received any return on the real capital investments that have been made on the North Slope. These delays have had implications for the international petroleum industry.

Indirect Effects

Environmental regulation has had numerous indirect effects on the oil and gas industry. The cost of pollution control devices on automobiles has raised the price of automobiles, and caused a relative shift in demand for automobiles toward relatively high mileage cars. In the long run this might tend to decrease the demand for gasoline slightly. On the other hand, the installation of control devices on cars initially caused a decrease in mileage, which has increased the consumption of gasoline. There are other effects as well. One respondent cited the impact of the Clean Air Act on the production of coal. "As much as 200 million tons per year of coal could be forced off the market by July 1975, the deadline for meeting primary standards. The largest burden from this loss of supply can be expected to fall on petroleum." The strip mining bill, which was vetoed by President Ford in 1974, might further have aggravated a possible shortage of coal, with acceptable amounts of sulfur, and further increased the demand for oil products. Environmental concern over the impact of oil production from oil shale would delay such production and this in turn would increase the demand for oil from non-shale sources. It is clear from the point of view of the petroleum industry

that there are both positive effects (those which increase
the demand for their product) and negative effects (those
which increase the costs of operation) of environmental
regulation.

There is one other type of effect that must be
mentioned. The United States is not the only nation that is
concerned about the environment. As pointed out in a recent study by the Organization for Economic Cooperation and
Development, many member nations of the OECD have enacted and
are in the process of enacting regulations in many respects
similar to the U.S. regulations. 2/ Although little data is
currently available with which to evaluate these foreign
environmental protection programs it is clear that they will
have many of the same effects on oil and gas demand.

International Implications

From the U.S. point of view, perhaps the primary
impact of environmental protection regulations has been an
increased reliance on imports to supply domestic needs.
In response to a question concerning the impact of environmental regulation company after company cited the delays in
getting known reserves to the market as a primary impact. These
delays have kept substantial quantities of domestic oil from
being produced. Development of the rich fields off-shore from
Southern California was stopped in 1969 because of environmental
considerations. The delays on the Alaskan pipeline will delay
the delivery of oil until around 1977. The volume of production
that has been delayed is substantial. A recent Oil and Gas
Journal article quoted current estimates of north slope production for 1980 that ranged from 2.5 to 3.2 million barrels
per day. One of the oil companies has even predicted a District
5 surplus of crude oil of 600,000-800,000 barrels per day by
1982. 3/ The important consideration here is that in the absence
of these delays, the U.S. would currently be producing a larger
proportion of its domestic demand and imports would be less.
This by itself has important international implications. As
one respondent pointed out, "The U.S. was the primary target
of the Arab oil embargo and access to Alaskan crude oil would
have reduced the effectiveness of the embargo."

The requirement on the sulfur content of coal has
lead to the use of oil in power generation plants and has further
increased the demand for oil, and hence the demand for oil
imports. Also, one respondent estimated that the pollution

control devices required on automobiles "will increase U.S. crude oil demand by 450,000 barrels a day by 1975 over that required for uncontrolled 1968 cars. This penalty will be further increased as 1975 and later model cars displace the uncontrolled cars now on the road." It is clear that one of the primary impacts of environmental protection regulations has been to increase the current demand for imported oil.

The presence of environmental protection regulations also introduces certain locational considerations that have implications for the international petroleum industry. Requirements on the sulfur content of crude oil increases the relative value of low-sulfur oil reserves. Hence more international activity will take place in those countries with low-sulfur oil. Further, their selling prices will reflect sulfur content. Libyan oil prices are high due to low sulfur characteristics as well as location.

The additional costs that new domestic refineries must bear in the form of higher capital costs, operating costs, and delays due to siting problems, may also have locational effects. If some countries have fewer restrictions on refineries than does the United States, it is entirely possible that new refineries will be built outside the United States and in the Caribbean area, in Indonesia or elsewhere. This would have two primary implications on the international level. First, the balance of payments and balance of trade figures for the U.S. would worsen because it would be more expensive to import refined products than unrefined crude oil. Second, the U.S. would lose some of its energy independence. If the United States has sufficient refinery capacity to handle all its domestic needs, it is free to change its sources of crude oil imports (subject only to refinery-crude oil compatability). If only refined products are imported, some of this flexibility is eliminated. Having access to crude oil is meaningless unless the oil can be refined into usable products.

The importance of these locational effects depends entirely on the relative impact of the environmental protection regulations in each country. If U.S. regulations are strict relative to those of other countries, the locational implications will be adverse. At present it appears that environmental protection regulation, combined with the impact of state and local restrictions, in the United States imposes more constraints and costs than in many other nations. The relative impact in the future is of course uncertain.

There is one final environmental regulation issue that will undoubtedly become increasingly important in the future. Under international law the ownership of resources on or under the ocean floor is not always clearly defined. Where ownership is unclear there is a tendency to deplete such resources faster than they otherwise would be used (the common property problem). The problem is not yet critical for the petroleum industry because the technology to produce oil and gas in deep water (in excess of about 1,000 feet) is not yet economically profitable. But the problems of the future can be seen in current disputes over fishing rights. Iceland has claimed an exclusive fisheries jurisdiction of 50 nautical miles around the island. But the United Kingdom and West Germany have challenged this claim. The important point here is how arguments concerning this action are being phrased. It has been argued that the extension of such zones "might protect large areas of the seas from resource depletion in addition to protecting the interests of less economically advanced states which cannot yet effectively compete for their 'share' of the shareable resources." 4/ Unless the property rights over such resources are more clearly defined it is quite possible that countries may attempt to control such resources through "environmental protection" type regulation.

## Summary

The primary international implication of environmental regulation has been the effect of such regulation on the quantity of imports of oil and gas. As was stated by one respondent to the questionnaire, "[E]nvironmental regulations and considerations have served to increase U.S. oil imports by about 4 million barrels per day in 1974 versus what would have been imported in the absence of these controls and regulations. This increase is split roughly on a 50/50 basis between increased oil demand from environmental regulations and decreased domestic oil production due to environmental considerations." It has also been pointed out that there are implications for both the source of imported oil and refinery location. And all of these factors carry with them national security implications.

## Footnotes

1. Council on Environment Quality, Department of Commerce and Environmental Protection Agency, The Economic impact of Pollution Control, 269 (1972).

2. Organization for Economic Cooperation and Development, Economic Implications of Pollution Control, 9 (1974).

3. Oil and Gas Journal, December 23, 1974. 12.

4. Note, "New Perspectives on International Environmental Law," 82 Yale Law Journal 1659 (1973).

APPENDIX C

[§C.0]  SELECTED INDUSTRY QUESTIONNAIRE DATA

A.  [§C.1]  Domestic Petroleum Companies

B.  [§C.2]  Foreign Petroleum Companies

C.  [§C.3]  Public Utilities

D.  [§C.4]  ·State Agencies

E.  [§C.5]  U.S. Government Agencies

F.  [§C.6]  Congressional Committees

G.  [§C.7]  Trade Associations

H.  [§C.8]  Consumer and Other Interested Groups

APPENDIX C

## [§C.0]  SELECTED INDUSTRY QUESTIONNAIRE DATA

In order to collect information and to maximize opportunities for constructive comments, this Study sent 171 confidential questionnaires to a comprehensive list of domestic and foreign oil companies, public utilities, federal and state agencies as well as to consumer and other interested groups.

By far the most interesting responses came from the domestic U.S. oil companies, followed closely by the public utilities and foreign oil companies. For the purposes of this appendix, only the responses of the domestic oil companies have been summarized. Valuable information from other respondents were frequently consulted, but did not lend themselves to aggregation.

A.  [§C.1]  Domestic Petroleum Company Questionnaire and Responses

On July 15, 1974, a questionnaire was mailed to the following sixty-eight U.S. oil companies:

     1.  Amerada Hess Corp.

(R)  2.  American Independent Oil Co.

     3.  American Overseas Petroleum Ltd.

     4.  American Petrofina, Inc.

(R)  5.  APCO Oil Corp.

(R)  6.  Apexco, Inc.

(R)  7.  ARAMCO

     8.  ARGO Petroleum Corp.

(R)  9.  Ashland Oil Inc.

(R) 10.  Atlantic Richfield Company

(R) 11.  Belco Petroleum Corporation

12.  Buttes Gas & Oil Co.

13.  Burmah Oil Development, Inc.

14.  Cayman Corporation

(R) 15.  Champlin Petroleum Co.

16.  Charter Oil Company

(R) 17.  Cities Service Company

(R) 18.  Clinton Oil Company

19.  Colorado Interstate Corp.

(R) 20.  Continental Oil Co.

21.  Crown Central Petroleum Corp.

22.  Diamond Shamrock Oil and Gas Co.

(R) 23.  Exxon Corp.

(R) 24.  Farmland Industries, Inc.

(R) 25.  General American Oil Co. of Texas

(R) 26.  General Crude Oil Co.

(R) 27.  Getty Oil Co.

(R) 28.  Gulf Oil Corp.

29.  Hamilton Bros. Oil Company

30.  Hunt Oil Co.

31.  Inexco Oil Co.

32.  Jenney Oil Co., Inc.

33. Kerr-McGee Corp.

34. Kewanee Oil Co.

35. Lone Star Gas Company

(R) 36. Marathon Oil Company

(R) 37. McCulloch Oil Corp.

38. Mesa Petroleum

(R) 39. Mobil Oil Corporation

40. Murphy Oil Corporation

41. Natomas Co.

(R) 42. Occidental Petroleum Corp.

43. Oceanic Exploration Co.

(R) 44. Pennzoil Company

(R) 45. Petroleum Corporation of Texas

(R) 46. Phillips Petroleum Co.

47. Quintana Petroleum Corp.

48. Reserve Oil and Gas Co.

49. Shell Oil Co.

50. Shenandoah Oil Corporation

(R) 51. Skelly Oil Company

(R) 52. Sun Oil Company

(R) 53. Sundance Oil Co.

(R) 54. Standard Oil Company of California

(R) 55. Standard Oil Co. (Indiana)

(R) 56.  Tenneco Inc.

(R) 57.  Texaco, Inc.

    58.  Tesoro Petroleum Corp.

    59.  Texas American Oil Corp.

(R) 60.  Texas Eastern Transmission Corporation

    61.  Texas International Co.

(R) 62.  Texas Oil and Gas Corp.

(R) 63.  Texas Pacific Oil Co., Inc.

(R) 64.  The Standard Oil Company (Ohio)

    65.  The Superior Oil Co.

    66.  THUMS Long Beach Co.

    67.  Transocean Oil, Inc.

    68.  Triton Oil and Gas Corp.

(R) 69.  Union Oil Company of California

       By January 15, 1975, thirty-six responses had been received [responding companies are identified by an (R) on the above list].  Of these responses, thirty-three were utilized to prepare the summary which follows.  The following three companies were not included in the summary since they are not typical domestic oil companies:

       American Independent Oil Company

       Arabian-American Oil Company

       Farmland Industries,

Their completed questionnaires were, however, carefully reviewed.

Following are selected direct quotations from the petroleum company questionnaire responses. In order to elicit candid and thoughtful responses, the Study Contractor assured the companies that all information supplied in response to the Questionnaire "will be used without revealing the name of [the] company and that data will be grouped to avoid any unintended or indirect disclosure." This was also the policy employed by the Study Contractor in conducting extensive interviews with petroleum company officers and governmental officials in the United States and abroad. Accordingly, the responses which follow have been edited only to delete references to particular companies and have been listed alphabetically rather than by company name. Such lettering has been used only to separate the various company responses, and therefore, a particular letter of the alphabet should not be associated with a specific company response. In addition, the answers to Questions 1, 2 and 16 have been aggregated to avoid identifying the response of a particular company.

In a number of cases, companies did not respond specifically to all of the questions. Accordingly, some of the aggregate responses have been compiled on a base of less than thirty-three answers.

The responses are set forth in the same categories set forth in the questionnaire, the form of which also follows.

FEDERAL ENERGY ADMINISTRATION STUDY OF
THE OPTIONS OF THE U.S. GOVERNMENT IN ITS
RELATIONSHIP TO THE U.S. PETROLEUM INDUSTRY
IN INTERNATIONAL PETROLEUM AFFAIRS

July 15, 1974

QUESTIONNAIRE FOR PETROLEUM COMPANIES

Please complete this questionnaire and return it
to the law firm of Nossaman, Waters, Scott, Krueger & Riordan,
445 South Figueroa Street, Los Angeles, California 90017,
Attention: Robert B. Krueger, no later than September 1,
1974. In answering the questions, please state as thoroughly
and precisely as practicable the reasons upon which your
answers are based. In those instances in which a question
is inapplicable to your company, please so indicate. If you
need additional space for your answers, please type them on
additional sheets and attach them to the end of this questionnaire.

"United States," as used herein, includes the
outer continental shelf lands of the United States. "Petroleum," as used herein, includes oil, natural gas, distillates
and any other marketable wellhead products. "Your company,"
as used herein, includes all wholly-owned subsidiaries and
your percentage of ownership of all other partially or
jointly-owned companies.

1. Indicate in the following table the total dollar amount
of your company's expenditures on U.S. and foreign exploration for petroleum:

| Response: (000) | U.S. | Middle East | Latin America |
|---|---|---|---|
| 1960 | $1,123,021 (69.8%) | $ 61,100 | $ 97,954 |
| 1965 | $1,401,703 (68.5%) | $ 94,289 | $ 39,424 |
| 1970 | $2,122,863 (67.3%) | $ 89,458 | $130,711 |
| 1973 | $4,441,946 (72.7%) | $138,371 | $153,392 |

| Response:<br>(000) | Far East | Other or Unidentified<br>Foreign Countries | TOTAL |
|---|---|---|---|
| 1960 | $ 8,270 | $ 318,371 | $1,608,716 |
| 1965 | $ 20,754 | $ 488,904 | $2,045,074 |
| 1970 | $ 59,623 | $ 752,788 | $3,155,443 |
| 1973 | $165,405 | $1,213,717 | $6,112,831 |

2. Indicate in the following table the total dollar amount of your company's anticipated expenditures on U.S. and foreign exploration for petroleum:

| Response:<br>(000) | U.S. | Middle East | Latin America |
|---|---|---|---|
| 1974 | $6,431,576 (70.0%) | $265,051 | $289,450 |
| 1975* | $2,155,718 (76.8%) | $ 35,241 | $ 82,612 |
| 1976* | $2,062,757 (80.1%) | $ 19,380 | $ 43,965 |
| 1980* | $1,136,100 (83.9%) | $ 7,300 | $ 18,500 |

| Response:<br>(000) | Far East | Other or Unidentified<br>Foreign Countries | North Sea |
|---|---|---|---|
| 1974 | $182,171 | $1,749,638 | $266,045 |
| 1975* | $ 83,458 | $ 415,314 | $ 36,000 |
| 1976* | $ 34,100 | $ 405,896 | $ 8,400 |
| 1980* | $ 12,800 | $ 182,600 | $ 9,300 |

```
                    TOTAL
1974          $9,183,931
1975*         $2,808,343
1976*         $2,574,498
1980*         $1,366,600
```

\*    Many of the respondents did not provide estimates for
     post-1974 expenditures.  Accordingly, the 1975-1980
     figures are of value only in terms of percentage dis-
     tribution among geographic areas.


3.  Have you experienced any difficulty in the period from
1972 to the present in obtaining any of the following materials for your company's exploration program:

| Response: | YES | NO |
|-----------|-----|-----|
| Drilling rigs | 30 | 2 |
| Tubular steel | 30 | 2 |
| Other (specify) | 18 | 14 |


If so, indicate the extent to which shortages have affected
U.S. or foreign exploration for petroleum and what steps, if
any, the U.S. Government should take to improve this situation.

SELECTED COMMENTS:

     A.  We have experienced shortages in oil country
tubular goods in recent months.  As a consequence, we have
had to postpone the drilling of a number of wells in the
United States.  With respect to our foreign operations, we
have had difficulties in obtaining a drilling rig and well
casing for our operation in Pakistan, but we have managed to
overcome these difficulties.  Our development program in the
Celtic Sea is in its early stages, but we anticipate long
delivery time for both platforms and pipelines.

Our experience appears to be characteristic of operators within the industry whether they be small or large. The problem of material shortages arose with some suddenness and apparently impacted on a broad front.

The sharp increase in value for petroleum since mid-1973 has caused a corresponding upsurge in domestic drilling activity. Prior to this readjustment, many manufacturers of tubular goods actually questioned whether government policies on price, offshore leasing, environmental regulation and the like warranted their staying in the business. When prices for oil started to increase, oil country tubular goods remained under price controls, and economic incentives to expand the productive capacity for them was delayed. The modification and removal of these price controls has helped the shortage situation, but the lead times for supply expansion within the market have been extended considerably.

We believe that there is a shortage of basic steel in world markets; within this shortage, however, we think that allocation of resources by market forces to the production of tubular goods would improve with adoption of firm policies to encourage petroleum exploration and production. The long-term disincentives to domestic production of oil and natural gas, exemplified in wellhead price regulation of natural gas, have decreased U.S. demand for oil country tubular goods, and consequently, the productive capacity for those goods.

On a worldwide basis, the emphasis on development of the prolific reserves of the Middle East and North Africa required relatively little oil country tubular goods for the production obtained. Worldwide tubular steel capacity adjusted itself to this demand. With political imperatives and economic incentives to explore and develop elsewhere, the demand for tubular goods and rigs has jumped sharply. This expanded demand should bring about a rational response within the world steel industry and elicit increased supplies of needed goods unless governmental policies inhibit the free interaction of market forces (for example, through artificial allocation schemes) or unless governmental policies discourage petroleum exploration and development in the U.S. and elsewhere.

B.  A shortage of offshore drilling rigs and oil
country tubular goods which began in late 1973 has delayed
our plans for drilling about forty exploratory wells and
thirty-one development wells in 1974.  Shortages of other
materials have been relatively minor.  Most of the shortages
of oil country tubular goods are in the higher grades (N, S
and P) of pipe needed for deeper drilling below depths of
about 10,000 feet.  Since we do not attempt to contract for
a drilling rig until the tubular goods needed for drilling a
specific well are available, it is not possible to accurately
assess the effect that the drilling rig shortage would have
on our exploration program in the absence of a tubular goods
shortage.  However, a shortage of drilling rigs is being
experienced, particularly for offshore and deep onshore
drilling.  This shortage would certainly be more severe if
adequate supplies of tubular goods were available.  We
recommend that the U.S. Government take no action to attempt
to improve either rig or tubular goods availability.  The
recent removal of price controls from steel products should
lead to a rapid return of normal supply conditions for
tubular goods.  The shortage of drilling rigs being experienced is caused by the transfer of rigs overseas during
the decline in domestic activities of the past several
years coupled with recent increased industry activity in
the U.S. brought about by higher U.S. prices for oil and
gas and accelerated offshore leasing.  An adequate supply
of rigs will become available given reasonable time, continued demand and the expectation of a good long term
domestic economic climate.  In fact, accelerated construction of new rigs is already taking place.


4.  Do you believe that there has been inadequate petroleum
refinery capacity in the U.S. or elsewhere in the period
from 1972 to the present?  If so, indicate where and what
impact this has had upon petroleum supplies.  In addition,
specify what steps, if any, the U.S. Government should take
to improve this situation.

Response:          YES        NO        NO OPINION

                    18         7             8

SELECTED COMMENTS:

A. With regard to gasoline, U.S. refining capacity has been adequate to meet consumer demands in the United States during the above period. Prior to April 1973, imports of finished gasoline into the U.S. were greatly restricted. The import restrictions were then replaced with a fee system that penalized product imports, especially gasoline. Thus the combination of restrictions of gasoline imports followed by higher fees on gasoline imports (as compared to crude oil) has served to ensure that sufficient gasoline-making capacity is in place in the U.S.

With regard to distillate fuel oils, U.S. refining capacity would have been adequate except for heavy new demands caused by fuel switching due to shortages of natural gas and environmental restrictions imposed on the burning of coal and on residual fuels; that is, the growing use of distillate-burning turbines to generate electricity and the blending of distillates into heavier oils to help meet increasingly severe sulfur limitations. As a result, U.S. refineries were unable to meet U.S. demands for distillate fuels during the winter of 1972-73. With spare refining capacity in Europe and in the Caribbean, the U.S. was able to import sufficient volumes of distillates to supplement domestic production.

In fact, in late 1972, many in the U.S. petroleum industry urged that restrictions on distillate imports be eased in order to better utilize world refining capacity. Under U.S. price controls there was no incentive to expand domestic capacity and due to existing import controls, there was no long-term assurance of access to foreign crude supplies (U.S. crude supplies were inadequate for expansion purposes). U.S. prices as presently controlled still do not provide for recovery of capital of new or expanded capacity.

With regard to residual fuel, U.S. refining capacity had not been adequate for many years. There were two contributing factors; by nature, U.S. crudes have had a very low residual fuel content and by economics, U.S. refiners found it more desirable to produce gasolines and distillates than resids. However, there was a surplus of world-wide capacity for making residual fuel. Imports of residual fuel oil on the East Coast have been exempt from formal U.S. quota limitations since 1966. Caribbean refiners processing cheap Venezuelan crudes were able to produce a very low-cost residual fuel which sold at a much lower price on the East Coast than U.S.-produced resid or U.S. coal. Thus, domestic resid was a low-net back item and very unprofitable for U.S. refiners. As long as crude oil is readily available on world markets, there will be adequate supplies of residual fuel for U.S. markets.

In 1972 the National Petroleum Council undertook a survey of the factors-economic, governmental, technological and environmental-which affect the ability of domestic refining capacity to respond to demands for essential petroleum products. The Council reported formally its conclusions to the Secretary of the Interior on May 10, 1973. [We] participated in and fully support the conclusions and recommendations of that study.

Since that report was issued, several new events have transpired that also serve to inhibit refinery construction:

1. Actions of Arab oil producers who embargoed oil shipments to the U.S. for a five-month period beginning in October 1973 and who raised the world oil prices from $2.50/bbl. to over $10/bbl. and who now set prices and production limits on Arab oil output. It is they who can well determine where and when future refineries will be built.

2. Creation of the FEO, and its successor FEA, with enormous powers to regulate the U.S. petroleum industry. These were staffed with people with negligible petroleum experience and who promulgated thousands of directives that created havoc with existing market and supplier-customer relations. The prospect of continued governmental control retards refinery expansion.

3. The mood of the Congress and the American people to pass punitive legislation with regard to oil companies. This pending legislation can greatly impact the cash flow of a corporation and thus its money available for reinvestment.

Thus, the degree of uncertainty over an investment decision to expand refining capacity is immense. If the U.S. Government wants more U.S. capacity built, it must take positive steps to improve rates of return and reduce uncertainty. Without an assured crude supply, without an expectation of financial reward for the risks involved, without a return to the free market place for product, few refineries will be built or expanded in the U.S.

B.  A rigid standard with which to judge the adequacy or inadequacy of petroleum refining capacity in the U.S. does not exist. Hence, any such judgment must be made in relation to the normal demand for such capacity and the specific demands which existed at a given time.

In the past ten years or so a gap has grown between average annual demand for petroleum products in the U.S. and the operable capacity of petroleum refining facilities in the U.S., after allowance for domestic NGL production and the volumetric gain resulting from processing. This gap resulted primarily from the growing dependency of the East Coast on low-priced residual fuel imports, and the inability of the U.S. refining industry to compete with these low-priced imports. New capacity was not built to "cover" the segment of product demand supplied by such imports, and "normal" adequacy became the capacity to essentially supply product demand less residual fuel imports.

The U.S. refining industry normally has met seasonal peak demand for specific products, e.g., gasoline in summer and distillate in winter, by building inventories in the off season and drawing from them during periods of peak demand. In recent years, U.S. refinery capacity plus seasonal storage has not been sufficient and increasing imports have been required to meet demand.

With respect to the period from 1972, we believe that petroleum refinery capacity in the U.S. was inadequate to meet the demand situation that existed during much of the first quarter of 1973. The early onset of cold weather in the fourth quarter of 1972 combined with sustained high gasoline consumption, a large increase in demand for distillate by utilities to meet environmental standards, and an uncertain crude oil import program placed the U.S. refining industry in a situation with which it could not cope. Consequently the industry began 1973 with depleted stocks and was unable to manufacture products at a rate equal to consumption during this period of peak demand. As a result, imports of distillate were at unprecedented high levels early in 1973.

We believe that U.S. refining capacity rose from barely adequate in mid-1973 to more than adequate at present. This improvement resulted from a large total addition to refining capacity during 1973 and from the restrained demand effected by conservation and higher prices. With regard to refining capacity elsewhere, we believe a surplus of capacity exists in the Western Hemisphere and in the world as a whole, and that such surplus is expected to persist for several years or more.

The well publicized fact that no new refinery was under construction in 1973 tended to overshadow the 800,000 barrels per day of new capacity that the industry added during the year through reactivations, expansions and operating improvements. The industry has invested heavily in debottlenecking and other additions to existing facilities. Although the industry will continue to expand capacity of existing facilities by such means, new refineries need to be built to meet future requirements and to meet what may be a new standard of adequacy as the goals of "Project Independence" are approached.

Uncertainties which contributed to the situation of no new refinery under construction in the U.S. in 1973 still remain and several new ones have been added. With the lead time between decision to build and the on stream date of a new refinery now lengthened to 5 years, it is becoming unlikely that few if any new grass roots refineries not currently under construction will come on stream before 1980.

Uncertainties and hindrances created by the U.S. Government which contribute to the dearth of refinery construction in the U.S. must be solved to provide an environment in which the industry can plan, attract investment and build new capacity. The uncertainties and hindrances are:

(1) Regulation of prices, refiners' margins, crude supply and product distribution, stocks, and refinery crude runs and product yields.

(2) The difference between crude oil cost and product price has been frozen since 1971 and recovery of increased labor and other operating costs have not been permitted.

(3) Threatening punitive tax legislation.

(4) Uncertainties regarding VLCC terminal construction and energy facility siting.

(5) Threatened entry of the government into competition with the private oil industry.

(6) Uncertainties regarding environmental constraints and corresponding fuel sulfur specifications.

(7) Uncertainties regarding government coal and nuclear policy and the corresponding effect on future petroleum product demand.

(8) Requirements that a portion of oil imports be transported in U.S. Flag vessels.

5. Give your opinion as to the present and potential future ability of the OPEC nations to control world prices for petroleum.

Response: All of the companies responding (31) believe that OPEC will control prices in the short term. Eleven companies also expect OPEC to control prices in the long term while 16 did not.

SELECTED COMMENTS:

A. The incremental source of petroleum rests with OPEC-- particularly Saudi Arabia. Within limits, this power over worldwide petroleum supplies gives OPEC the ability to set prices. The limits are, of course, price levels that would depress worldwide economic activity in the short term; and price levels that would cause OPEC petroleum to be uncompetitive with substitute fuels, e.g., shale oil, over the longer term.

OPEC members have vastly differing objectives and circumstances that affect their desires for petroleum revenues. Pressures brought about by these differences could lead to over production and, thus, some reduction of petroleum prices. In our opinion, if such a price reduction should occur it would be of short duration as OPEC members would quickly come to grips with production-sharing policies.

The major key to OPEC's survival, we feel, rests mainly with Saudi Arabia. Their capability as the world's largest potential petroleum producer and their ability to quickly raise or lower production provides them with a power to dictate interim worldwide petroleum prices.

B. The present and near-term ability of the OPEC nations to control world oil prices is probably greater than their potential future ability for such control. In the first place such control in the near term is more a matter of political decision and political will than it is a matter of economics, whereas over time the economic supply and demand factors will start to exert a stronger impact on oil prices. Furthermore, in the long term there may be meaningful volumes of alternative sources of energy which will not only impact on prices through supply, but which will also enable the major consuming countries to exert a stronger political position vis-a-vis OPEC nations. On balance, short of a breakup of OPEC's present cohesion (which is not anticipated as very likely), the OPEC nations will probably have extensive near-term control over prices through their willingness to accept a relatively small (or no) growth rate in their production.

C. OPEC's present ability unilaterally to control prices has been demonstrated beyond dispute by recent events. This power reasonably can be expected to continue until either the internal cohesiveness of the cartel is broken or viable energy supply alternatives external to the cartel sources are developed. Despite indications of some recent fissures and a history of perennial political dissension, there is no solid evidence to suggest that the essential internal cohesiveness among OPEC nations cannot or will not be maintained over the near and medium term. The evidence to date, on the contrary, suggests that the common economic imperative of the group and the consequent political influence enjoyed in the aggregate dominate all

other individual disputes and difficulties.  Voluntary production curtailments by some members lately attest to the
individual "statesmanship" being employed to maintain the
solidarity of the cartel.  Couple these considerations with
the added facts that the medium term holds no real prospect
of alternate crude and other energy sources sufficient to
nullify the cartel's strength nor any promise of conservation savings large enough to be beyond OPEC's ability to
compensate for by managed production, and we conclude OPEC's
cartel strength will be maintained over at least the medium
term.

        Time is the enemy of any cartel, and it is at
least doubtful that the OPEC cartel can control prices over
the long run.  We distinguish between the ability to control
and the power to influence prices.  Perpetuation of the
ability to control prices over the long term involves several added complexities for OPEC.

        First of all, the international companies have
been the primary producers, distributors and marketers of
petroleum.  If equity arrangements are eliminated and the
companies no longer have preferential price or supply
arrangements, the OPEC countries could find their control
of production much more difficult to manage in response to
market conditions.  It is not unlikely in such circumstances
that both supplies and prices for crude and products would
be subject to severe cyclical fluctuations.

        Secondly, the economic and political objectives
of the OPEC nations probably will tend to diverge in the
longer term.  Some producing countries, notably Saudi Arabia
and Kuwait, will accumulate financial reserves of nearly
unprecedented size which many experts expect to threaten
the stability of the world's financial structure.  More
importantly, however, the higher prices also create the
potential for economic dislocation and national bankruptcy
which, if widespread enough, would clearly peril the vital
interests of at least some producer countries.  The question
then is whether the producer countries, particularly those
with large surpluses, will take cognizance of this and increase production and lower prices in order to achieve
world stability.

Thirdly, a similar dilemma for Saudi Arabia and Kuwait can be conceived even absent a financial crisis. Several important producer nations such as Iran and Iraq are only in the formative stage of economic development, have large populations and can easily absorb all revenues even at the current high prices. If some forecasts of demand are accurate, it may be necessary for production to be curtailed below the level OPEC collectively desires. In such circumstances, Saudi Arabia and other surplus countries may not be willing to absorb the cutback in production and revenue while their neighbors reap the advantage of their sacrifices.

Perhaps the most important factor in the equation comes under the heading of the reactive policies of the consuming countries. Intelligent policies can alleviate the consequences -- and hence the threat -- of temporary supply interruptions, and can accelerate the time when energy supplies external to the OPEC cartel will neutralize its economic stranglehold.

The intervention of the U.S. Government into direct negotiation of medium and long-term foreign supply contracts is not, however, a reactive policy which we would endorse. Such intervention is frought with grave political risks and serious potential economic disadvantages. So long as oil trading remains in the commercial arena, only economic concessions can be exacted by the OPEC nations at the bargaining tables. Admittedly, their superior bargaining position enables them to impose drastically inflated economic costs. But a policy of government nonintervention in supply contract negotiations does not preclude government-to-government consultations through normal diplomatic and other channels to moderate the demands made in commercial transactions. On the other hand, direct U.S Government participation in commercial transactions would elevate the negotiations to the political arena with attendant exposure where (i) political confrontation could occur, and (ii) both political and economic concessions could be exacted by those in the dominant bargaining position. U.S. Government participation in supply contract negotiations, in short, would lessen our government's flexibility and reduce its options in responding to commercially overreaching or intolerable situations while at

the same time increasing political risks substantially.
U.S. government direct involvement in bilateral supply
negotiations also would promote multinational dissension
the dimensions of which are not entirely predictable, but
which at least are incompatible with the recent accord
among consuming nations to cooperate in sharing future
shortages.

Government participation in the form of oversight
approval of individual supply contracts would entail delays,
introduce uncertainties sufficient to preclude normal commercial
negotiations and could place U.S. companies at a severe competitive disadvantage relative to foreign buyers. Furthermore,
under government approval requirements, it is difficult to
foresee what type of a just and workable solution could be
accomplished where two or more U.S. firms were competing for
the same supplies. However, the most compelling argument
against direct government intervention is revealed by the
events surrounding the 1971 Teheran negotiations. The U.S.
Government and other OECD nations both before and after this
costly settlement assured OPEC that consuming countries were
more interested in supply stability than price. These government assurances are widely believed to have fostered OPEC's
later demands for larger increases in price and to have provided the impetus for OPEC's eventual unilateral price actions.

The status and functions of the international
petroleum companies are obviously undergoing significant
changes. Since the OPEC countries are in a position to control crude prices, the end of equity oil (100% reversion)
would almost certainly signal an increase in prices to whatever higher level OPEC desired to establish. The end of
preferential supply arrangements would mean less supply
security for the U.S. in our opinion. The end of the primary
role in global petroleum distribution by international
petroleum companies would introduce a rigidity in supply
patterns which would preclude rapid response to market changes
or crises. Only the flexibility provided by these international companies to shift cargo destinations in mid-voyage
and to alter supply patterns to accommodate embargo restrictions prevented the Arab embargo from approaching a disaster
in this country. The role of the major companies has contributed importantly to low petroleum prices through the
economies of scale in transportation, refining and marketing
operations. The efficiencies gained from these huge investments were to a large extent made possible only because these

companies had an assured continuity to their crude supplies. Until 1973, this structure produced a stable price environment and ample supplies even when political events disrupted important supply centers such as in Iran in the early 1950's and in the Middle East in the 1967 war. An historical review of the profits and performance of the international petroleum companies will provide convincing evidence that their vital functions have been discharged in accordance with socially and economically acceptable standards of responsibility and have redounded to the benefit of all affected thereby.

To the extent that the emerging uncertainties regarding equity crude rights and preferential supply arrangements reduce the forward planning ability of the industry and impair its ability to respond promptly and in a flexible manner to market forces and investment opportunities, we would expect periodic shortages to occur more frequently and consumers ultimately to pay more for petroleum.

D. In view of the current strains within OPEC, this question will be answered in terms of any group of significant crude oil exporting countries acting in concert.

Short Term

Recent Saudi Arabian intentions to increase production in order to reduce prices have been met by proposals by other producers to cut production. Over the next two or three years, Saudi potential to increase production over the current 7.5 - 8.0 million barrels per day is perhaps 4 or 5 million barrels per day. This order of increase could easily be countered by cuts in other exporting countries which in no way would jeopardize their short range economic plans. In spite of the potential for industrialization in Iran there are significant difficulties with short term revenue employment. Similar problems prevail in Venezuela and Nigeria. Other countries such as Kuwait and Libya are limited in terms of internal investment opportunities.

Until recently it was felt that cuts to counter Saudi Arabian increases and the then 2 million barrels per day crude oil surplus would cause difficulties between producers because it was felt that each country would expect others to forego revenues. However, recent cutbacks in

Venezuela, Libya, Kuwait and Saudi Arabia would indicate that concerted action is not necessary.

In the short term, therefore, the oil exporting countries have the flexibility to control production and thereby control petroleum and energy prices. In addition, it is not likely that Saudi Arabia will isolate herself from the other Arab states.

## Long Term

The current OPEC group produces 65 percent of the free world crude oil and 85 percent of the oil moved in international trade; estimated production for 1974 is around 30 million barrels per day.

Sufficient reserves exist in the OPEC countries to ensure their ability to supply a significant portion of the world's energy requirements over the next twenty years. This ability carries with it the potential to control energy prices and worldwide development of alternate energy sources. This potential for control could be physically reduced by discovery and development of significant energy sources in the consuming areas.

However, as the producing nations increase their commitment to international commerce in attempts to broaden their economic bases, their business philosophies developed over the past volatile three years will be forced to mature. This change will be necessary because continued energy pricing uncertainty will eventually impinge on their own economic well being.

## Conclusion

The exporting nations will have almost absolute power to control world energy prices over the next twenty years at least. In the future this power will be more moderately used out of commercial and economic necessity than it has been to date. The ability to control prices could be reduced by increased energy production in the consuming areas, reduced worldwide energy consumption and possible internal political difficulties undermining the solidarity of the producing cartel. However, the member nations of OPEC would be loathe to see political difficulties tear the organization apart. Considering the agony undergone during the formation of OPEC, and the fact that the current income of Saudi Arabia, Iran, and Kuwait is in excess of these countries social requirements, it must be concluded that the OPEC nations wll devise some method of controlling production in order to maintain the effectiveness of the organization.

E. Some important background deserves mention here. Until 1970 the function of the international oil companies in providing abundant supplies of oil at moderate prices was carried out on a predominantly commercial basis, although the OPEC countries were becoming increasingly aggressive in their demands for increased benefits and control. The turning point in this regard was reached in 1970. Demands of the OPEC countries greatly escalated and serious political overtones began emerging from the Arab states over the continuing Arab-Israeli conflict. Intensive OPEC-industry negotiations commenced on several important issues but the industry was nevertheless able to negotiate and operate on a commercial basis until the outbreak of the Arab-Israeli War in October, 1973. It was at this time that political actions completely displaced commercial considerations. Overnight the Free World found itself in a serious energy crisis. Led by united and unilateral actions by the Middle Eastern producing countries, posted prices were increased by an astounding 70% (and by another 100% in January, 1974) and the Arab states imposed embargoes (aimed chiefly at the United States for its policies with respect to Israel) and substantial cutbacks in crude production. Oil was finally being used as a political weapon, as the Arab states had warned, and virtually every importing country in the Free World was affected.

Currently, the OPEC countries' ability, acting jointly and in concert, to control crude prices is nearly absolute through control of production levels and the cost of oil to the offtakers and users. There are no alternate sources of crude or other non-oil sources of energy readily available to meet forecasted requirements even with the most stringent conservation measures. Most OPEC countries, with the possible exception of Iran, Venezuela and Indonesia, have enough excess income that they can afford to restrict production to maintain prices, and this is what they are expected to do. Kuwait, Libya and Venezuela have already

made sizable cutbacks in crude production. The oil companies
and most consuming countries will be in a weak position until
consuming governments can get together and carry out determined actions to reach political reconciliations with the
OPEC nations to share available supplies and persuade or pressure OPEC countries to moderate demands.

In the longer term, the ability of the OPEC countries to control world crude prices is more questionable.
With the prospect of crude prices being maintained at or
near current levels through manipulation of production
levels, the following is a possible chain of events:

1. Conservation measures will be stepped up in
the importing countries at all levels of consumption in an
effort to reduce costs and the staggering impact on the
balance of payments situation for many countries. Overall
demand will grow significantly less than that projected
prior to October, 1973.

2. Exploration and production in more secure
areas will continue at an accelerated pace to reduce dependence on imported crude. This will be especially true within
the United States, and will also include significant production via secondary recovery projects that were uneconomic
at pre-October, 1973 prices. These "new oil" discoveries
are apt to be increasingly costly, and it is an economic
fact of life that incentives must not be removed or diluted
if the necessary growth in supply is to be maintained. The
decline in proven natural gas reserves in the United States
under the present pricing policy is a prime example of how
supply can dwindle for lack of eonomic incentive.

3. Alternate sources of energy will be developed
and used to reduce the consuming countries' dependence on
crude from the OPEC countries. Coal and nuclear energy
appear to be the most promising alternates now, but potentially
serious environmental problems must be resolved. Other alternates being evaluated include shale, tar sands, geothermal
and solar, and although progress is being made, it will take
time and a great amount of capital before these alternate
energy sources will be sufficient to bridge the gap between
our total requirements and that supplied from domestic oil and
gas production as well as that from relatively secure areas.

As the above developments proceed, the OPEC countries will feel the effect of the upsets they are causing in world economics and politics. The balance of payments problem will put a very severe strain on the consuming countries of the Free World, and could well bring about a worldwide depression. If this occurs, the producing countries would suffer as well, and some of them are not unaware of this possibility.

There is also the possibility, although remote and very unlikely, that the present unity among the OPEC countries will not last. After becoming accustomed to large revenues, they may be unwilling to cut back production on a concerted and prorated basis. As the consuming countries develop alternates to imported crude, as they surely will in time, each OPEC country may again seek incremental sales of its crude.

6. Do you believe that petroleum prices paid by the American consumer will change if (1) the depletion allowance is repealed with respect to foreign production only; (2) the depletion allowance is repealed with respect to U.S. production only; (3) the depletion allowance is repealed with respect to both U.S. and foreign production; (4) foreign concessions are modified to eliminate a concessionaire's right to equity production; (5) the expensing of intangible drilling costs on foreign operations is restricted to unproductive wells (capitalized for productive wells); (6) expensing of intangible drilling costs on U.S. operations is restricted to unproductive wells (capitalized for productive wells); (7) expensing of intangible drilling costs on both U.S. and foreign operations is restricted to unproductive wells (capitalized for productive wells); (8) the foreign tax credit is modified to become a deductible business expense rather than a credit for amounts deemed to be royalty payments or deemed to be expended for the purchase of oil? If so, state separately in what manner and to what extent each of the foregoing changes will affect consumer prices and your company's after-tax profits. Please be specific (e.g. use a base year such as 1972 to show effects upon your company's after-tax profits).

| Response: | | YES | NO | DON'T KNOW/<br>NO OPINION |
|---|---|---|---|---|
| | (1) | 14 | 16 | 3 |
| | (2) | 30 | 1 | 2 |
| | (3) | 29 | 1 | 3 |
| | (4) | 22 | 1 | 10 |
| | (5) | 23 | 5 | 5 |
| | (6) | 30 | 1 | 2 |
| | (7) | 30 | 1 | 2 |
| | (8) | 23 | 3 | 7 |

SELECTED COMMENTS:

A.   Repeal of Foreign Depletion

Petroleum prices paid by the American consumer will probably not change if the depletion allowance on foreign production is repealed.  This is because the market price for foreign crude oil is not related to cost at the present time.

Even if the market price of foreign crude becomes related to cost in the future, the U.S. tax benefit from foreign depletion is not a significant enough factor to materially affect this price.  This is due to the fact that high foreign tax rates generally result in the foreign tax exceeding the U.S. tax and because of the U.S. tax credit system, no U.S. tax is paid on this income.  However, if the U.S. foreign tax credit system were repealed or changed, then foreign depletion would be a significant factor.

Repeal of Domestic Depletion

There is no question that if the market is not controlled, petroleum prices will increase if the depletion allowance is repealed with respect to U.S. production.  The amount of the price increase cannot be accurately predicted. For example, a taxpayer in a 50 percent tax bracket must earn

$2.00 in additional revenue to replace a $1.00 loss in depletion while a 70 percent bracket taxpayer must earn $3.33
to replace $1.00 of depletion. However, the critical economic
effect of percentage depletion is not found in its average
impact on all oil production, but in the economic incentive
it provides on marginal production. Full restoration of
incentives would require price increases of at least 5 cents
per gallon. However, the marketplace would not respond
directly in this manner.

The value of the depletion allowance to the industry as an incentive cannot be translated into the price
of petroleum in the marketplace. The elimination of the
cash flow available from depletion for investment in exploration and development will obviously reduce the amount of
domestic oil available to the consumer and cause greater
reliance on foreign oil. In our opinion, the depletion
allowance has been an effective incentive for providng the
American consumer with lower priced products than would have
otherwise been available. Its elimination will increase
those prices, and probably in an amount in excess of the
additional tax revenues generated by its repeal.

## Repeal of Domestic and Foreign Depletion

For the reasons set forth in the above paragraphs,
repealing depletion as to both foreign and domestic production will increase consumer petroleum prices.

## Elimination of Equity Interests

Eliminating the equity interests of U.S. oil companies will increase U.S. petroleum prices since it will
eliminate any cost advantage which U.S. companies have had
in the past which may have been passed on to the consumer.

## Capitalize Foreign IDC on Productive Wells

If the current deduction for IDC were disallowed,
this would make foreign oil and gas operations more costly
for U.S. companies, with the likely result that they would
not be able to compete successfully for foreign oil and
gas opportunities. It is important from a national security
and balance of payments point of view that U.S. companies
have control over the widely dispersed source of crude oil

and gas supply. Since the U.S. will continue to depend, for the foreseeable future, upon foreign oil and gas production for a portion of the nation's energy requirements, it is in the nations's best interest to have U.S. companies control reserves that can meet that requirement. The alternative is that such requirements may become dependent upon reserves controlled by companies outside the U.S., particularly companies owned by foreign governments. To the extent the national interest or supply requirements of such countries may be inconsistent with the requirements of the United States, the supplies may become interruptible and thus less secure. Moreover, to the extent that U.S. oil and gas requirements may be supplied from foreign sources, the cost in terms of balance of payments outflow is increased by the amount of the profit which would then flow to a foreign country. Under existing conditions, the profits from U.S. controlled foreign oil and gas flow to the U.S. as they are repatriated by the U.S. petroleum companies. As a result, the U.S. balance of payments position is improved to the extent of the profits on the international oil and gas sales.

Furthermore, the disallowance of IDC on foreign ventures would reduce the after-tax profits of U.S. companies and, therefore, the amount of internally generated funds available for exploration and development in domestic and foreign areas. Such a proposal would appear to represent a move completely in the wrong direction in the face of the country's present energy crises.

## Capitalize IDC on Domestic Productive Wells

The proposal would affect most of the costs of drilling productive oil and gas wells. (The current deduction of dry hole expenses would be continued.) IDC costs related to productive wells would, presumably, be capitalized and depreciated in the same manner as physical equipment.

The right to deduct IDC expenditures is an incentive of vital importance to the economic health of the oil and gas industry. Its repeal or limitation would cause the withdrawal of billions of dollars of capital which would otherwise go into the search for sorely needed oil and gas over the next several years. Many investors would be forced to withdraw from the industry. The oil well drilling industry would be struck a serious blow, and the loss of that technical capacity would be virtually irreplaceable.

The tax revenue to be realized from repeal of the right to expense IDC expenditures would be elusive. First, to the extent that IDC expenditures continue to be made, deductions would be reduced temporarily until annual depreciation deductions increased to an amount equal to the annual IDC expenditures. Thereafter, the tax revenues would not be affected. Second, to the extent that IDC expenditures are reduced, tax deductions would be reduced and tax revenues would increase in the short term. But a reduction in IDC expenditures would reduce discoveries, and in the long term, would reduce profits and tax revenues.

Contrary to accusations of critics, IDC when coupled with percentage depletion does not constitute a double deduction. The current deduction of IDC is a method of cost recovery. If the expenses are not deducted as incurred, they should be depreciated. However recovered, the deduction would be limited to actual costs. The percentage depletion deduction is related to the value of the minerals produced. The two deductions are clearly separate and no "double" deduction is available on the same expense.

## Capitalize IDC on Domestic and Foreign Productive Wells

For the reasons set forth above, capitalizing IDC on both foreign and domestic producing wells would increase petroleum prices paid by the consumer.

## Foreign Tax Credit

If the tax law were changed to treat foreign taxes as a deduction or as a royalty (the same effect as a deduction), the U.S.companies would no longer participate in foreign exploration and producing operations. The current profit margin on foreign production is now somewhere between 30 cents and 50 cents per barrel. If the U.S. attempted to tax 50 percent of this profit, then U.S. oil companies would not be able to compete with their foreign counterparts who would not pay this additional tax.

With reduced profitability, U.S. companies could not compete with foreign companies in bidding for the purchase of participation crude from oil producing governments.

As a result, they would lose much of their position in the supply and distribution of crude in world markets.

Clearly, if the U.S. consumer is forced to rely on foreign owned oil companies or foreign governments for foreign crude oil to supplement U.S. production, this can only cost the consumer more than he is now paying.

B.  All of the items except No. 4 would result in an increase in the taxes paid by a U.S. oil company.  Item No. 4 deals with the appropriation of concession rights by foreign countries and will be dealt with separately.

The possible actions (other than No. 4) posed in the question, each of which would increase taxes paid by the U.S. oil industry, would constitute an increase in the cost of doing business and, as is true in the case of all such increases, would likely end up increasing the price of oil products to U.S. consumers.  This effect would not stand alone - cost for goods, services, and government would also increase.  In those cases where the increased taxes would be related to total foreign production, then the effect on the U.S. consumer would be related to the amount of oil imported into the U.S.  In the case of increased taxes on U.S. operations, there might be two different time periods where the effects could be thought of differently:  (1) the period during which the U.S. needs to increase all of its energy sources at the most rapid, practical rate to avoid excessive oil imports, (2) the period beyond that time when there would be an economic equilibrium between several energy sources in a manner that an increase in one could mean a decrease in the volume of use of another.  This, of course, is not true today because each of the domestic energy sources is supply limited.

First, speaking to the domestic situation in the short-term, the overall oil industry is being called upon for tremendous additional new investments in the U.S., both for the finding and production of oil as well as for the refining of oil.  Under the highly competitive conditions for capital that exist, the return on investment in oil must be sufficient to attract the necessary capital if these national needs are to be met.  Over the past

decade or more, that return has been far too low. For
the future, an increase in the taxes paid by the oil
industry would inevitably result in higher product prices
if the return is going to be high enough to attract the
capital required.

Second, speaking on the effect of increasing
taxes on U.S. operations in the longer term. Hopefully,
after fifteen or twenty years, the U.S. energy industries
of all sorts will have advanced their production capability
so that each can be quickly responsive to new needs by
adding capacity. Under these conditions, a specific change
in the taxes paid by one of the energy industries, such as
the oil industry, would destroy the equilibrium between the
various energy supplying industries. With higher tax costs,
the effect would be to cause less new oil to be found and
used and thereby require additional energy of other sources
to be used. The time when this situation will be operating
is too remote to be of significant consideration at this
time.

Third, speaking about the effect of the U.S. tax
changes on the foreign operations of U.S. companies. The
effect here is to change the equilibrium between U.S. companies operating in foreign areas and companies whose
domicile is in another country. As tax payments to the U.S.
Government on foreign operations are increased, the cost of
oil imported into the U.S. would be increased and drive up
prices of products in the U.S. The great bulk of the foreign
oil, however, is used in other countries. An increase in
taxes paid by U.S. companies to the U.S. Government makes
the competitive position of the U.S. companies weaker relative to their foreign based competitors. Over time, the
result would be that less oil would be supplied by U.S.
companies and more oil would be supplied by non-U.S. companies to the foreign world. As a result, the positive
receipts of income into the U.S. from U.S. oil company
investments abroad would be reduced. Further, U.S. influence on foreign oil production would be diminished.

The calculation of the effect on prices, supply,
demand, etc. of any one tax change is literally impossible,
as it is certain that the effects would cascade through
several following years. It must be accepted as economic
necessity that the industry will require sufficient return

on investment to attract capital. Thus, tax increases which
decrease profits and lower the return on investment will force
an upward price movement to restore profit margins and make
investment returns competitive in attracting financing.
We use as a basis for analysis the provisions affecting the
oil industry contained in H.R. 14462 the tax reform bill
which was before the last session of Congress. Our best
estimate of the effects of such legislation are:

1. The repeal of depletion allowance on foreign
production for U.S. companies is estimated from 1974 onward
to increase industry taxes by $40,000,000 per year.

2. The repeal of the depletion allowance on U.S.
production only is estimated to increase industry taxes in
the years and amounts shown below:

| 1974 | $  600 million |
| 1975 | $  900 million |
| 1976 | $1,600 million |
| 1977 | $1,900 million |
| 1978 | $2,300 million |
| 1979 | $3,300 million |

3. If the depletion allowance on both foreign and
domestic production is repealed, each of the foregoing
domestic amounts would be increased by $40,000,000.

4. This item does not deal with tax policy and
is dealt with elsewhere.

5. If the expensing of intangible drilling costs
on foreign operations is restricted to unproductive wells
(capitalized for productive wells), the increased tax is
estimated at $10,000,000 in 1977 and $20,000,000 per year
thereafter.

6. We are unable to furnish an estimate as to the
increase in taxes that would result from restricting the expensing of intangible drilling costs in the U.S. to unproductive wells and capitalizing these costs on productive wells.
There are too many variables involved and assumptions required.

7. We are unable to furnish an estimate as to the increase in taxes that would result from restricting expensing of intangible drilling costs on nonproductive wells and capitalizing these costs on productive wells in both the U.S. and foreign areas. Again, there are too many variables involved and assumptions required.

8. Modifying the foreign tax credit to become a deductible item would increase industry taxes. Quantitative estimates are impractical because of the many variables and assumptions required.

The fourth item in this question reads: "Foreign concessions are modified to eliminate a concessionaire's right to equity production." Actually, this simply asks what the effect will be if the foreign government nationalizes the reserves discovered by the concessionaire. Historically, these moves have resulted in higher costs and prices. Certainly the strength of OPEC is such that every step toward nationalization gives them more complete control over both production and price. In this connection, it should be noted that increased uncertainty in supply which would result from some of the assumed changes will increase the business risk associated with investments in the petroleum industry. This increased risk should likely result in a further increase in required return on investment.

7. What is your opinion as to the effect of the following upon the supply of petroleum, the incentive to undertake new exploration, and the international operations of your company: (1) U.S. price controls, (2) U.S. crude oil allocation rules and (3) U.S. antitrust laws. In answering this question consider how the distribution of petroleum between U.S. and foreign markets was affected by the aforementioned policies. Please be specific and quantify your answer whenever possible.

Response:

Although the petroleum company responses indicate that generally, price controls are counter-productive, and decrease supply and uncertainty, it was felt that present price controls did present an incentive to find "new" oil but discouraged any secondary recovery projects. Price controls have also contributed to the creation of an uncertain investment climate and if continued could substantially reduce the incentive to develop supplies from existing fields. All of the responses relating to price controls mentioned the FPC regulation of natural gas as a prime example and major factor in not encouraging development while stimulating demand for an energy resource. Most of the oil companies felt that the general effect of U.S. crude oil allocations has discouraged crude oil imports as well as being counter-productive. Most of the oil companies felt U.S. antitrust laws can adversely affect supply and incentives to undertake new explorations if they prohibit projects that require joint capitalization from companies.

SELECTED COMMENTS:

A. We have interpreted this question as requesting an opinion on the effect of (1) U.S. price controls, (2) U.S. crude oil allocation rules and (3) U.S. antitrust laws on the industry supply of petroleum, the industry incentive to undertake new exploration, and [our] international operations.

The question has been answered primarily from the standpoint of the manner in which rules and controls are administered today. Changes have been proposed in the Crude Allocation Program but are not firm. There is a specific proposal and four alternates on crude cost equalization. The basic proposal and the most supported alternate would be reasonably effective in eliminating the problem of uneconomic incremental crude imports. However, they do not solve the problem of excessive demand which results from the artificially low price of old domestic crude oil.

The request to consider how distribution of petroleum between U.S. and foreign markets was affected by the subject policies does not mention what time period should be covered. U.S. antitrust laws have been in effect for many years, price controls for several years and allocation rules for less than a year. What the distribution of petroleum would have been without these rules is purely speculative. There have been many factors that have had considerably more effect on distribution (such as the Arab oil embargo) than these policies.

The request to be specific and quantify the answer on a question of opinion is simply impossible of accomplishment.

It is assumed that "Petroleum" refers to crude oil and its products - not to synthetic fuels.

With the above qualifications, the answers to the question are:

(1)  Effect of U.S. price controls

    a.  Supply of petroleum

The effect on U.S. supply depends on the relative restrictiveness of U.S. price controls compared to those in foreign countries. Government price controls that are most restrictive will tend to diminish supply in that country when availability of petroleum supplies is limited. Controls further tend to increase demand, having a double effect on the supply/demand gap.

The price control system affects each product and each company differently. Hence, the resulting artificial market price structure may radically affect the incentive to supply incremental products.

Secondary recovery projects designed to maintain crude production are discouraged because of the "old" price applied to oil not in excess of previous production levels and not qualifying as stripper well production.

    b.  Incentive to undertake new exploration

Price controls limit cash generation and, hence, industry's ability to explore for new crude even though such crude is not itself under control. The incentive to explore may not be reduced by present controls on old crude prices but the funds required for the large capital outlays required are limited. The general uncertainty on recovery of full crude costs is also an inhibiting factor.

    c.  International operations

Directionally, in the absence of other factors, U.S. price controls are an incentive to expand in areas

with less restrictive price controls. Price controls
inevitably reduce competition and cannot in the long run
reduce costs and prices. Price controls have not helped
find sources of foreign products.

### (2) Effect of U.S. crude oil allocation rules

#### a. Supply of petroleum

The replacement of crude oil allocated to others
may not be possible in time of shortage or, if available,
may be economically unattractive. While passthrough of
costs is permissible under present rules, the allocation
of low cost crude to crude deficit companies may so depress
the market that supply from high cost foreign replacement
crude is unprofitable. This economic disincentive tends
to discourage imports of foreign crude. The proposed Crude
Cost Equalization Program (39 FR 32309, September 5, 1974)
would be a major step toward eliminating the latter problem
by effectively pricing (the sum of the crude oil price plus
entitlement value) crude oil purchased under the program at
close to incremental prices. Many of the alternate plans
would, however, dilute this effect.

Under any circumstances the allocation scheme
tends to cause inefficiency by causing crude to go to the
wrong locations from a transportation standpoint, to be
refined in refineries designed for different crudes and
to be converted to a non-optimum product mix.

#### b. Incentive to undertake new exploration

The integrated crude deficit companies buying
crude under the allocation rules lose the incentive to
undertake exploration risks since they are assured of a
crude supply generally at or below the national average
cost under current rules. For the crude long companies
selling crude under allocation, the uncertainty in the
ability to use one's own developed production (or to sell
it at reasonable prices) reduces the incentive to allocate
funds to this activity. The general uncertainty on the
future changes in the allocation rules brings another
degree of risk into exploration ventures.

c.  International operations

     Because of effects mentioned above, the economic
incentive is to keep foreign crudes in foreign markets.
Notwithstanding this incentive, [we have] attempted to meet
all commitments and to treat all customers equitably.  Of
course, under embargo conditions even meeting commitments
may be impossible.

     (3)  This part of the questionnaire inquires into the
effect of the antitrust laws on (a) the supply of petroleum
(b) the incentives to undertake new exploration and (c) our
international operations.

     The antitrust laws were designed, of course, to
protect the free market place from the adverse effects of
agreements among competitors to lessen the vigor of their
competition.  To the extent that enforcement of these laws
is consistent with their purpose for being, they are appropriately hailed as the watch-dog of our economic freedom.

     On the other hand, when antitrust enforcement is
politicized, when the antitrust laws are seized upon as a
means of attacking and reconstituting the structure of
American business, when they are construed so as to preserve
the small business enterprise no matter what its economic
or social cost, when they are used recklessly to further the
ambitions of politicians, they are then seriously crippling
the very system they were designed to protect.  The evidence
is overwhelming that this is what is happening today - particularly in respect to the oil industry.  The shortage of
crude oil supplies, the lack of adequate refining capacity -
even the Arab embargo - were widely publicized to be the
result of sinister plots of the oil companies.  Accusations
of antitrust violation came from the highest quarters of
government.  Indeed, a hastily contrived complaint against
eight large oil companies was actually filed by the Federal
Trade Commission under severe political pressures (the law
judge in charge of the case has now suggested that the FTC
withdraw its complaint and proceed in the normal way of
first investigating before complaining).  Nevertheless, the
case was filed and it seeks a divestiture order which would
dismantle the only effective tool we have to solve the energy
problem in this country.  Adding fuel to this destructive
fire are those who, again in the highest echelons of government, decry the profits which oil companies have made in the

last year, calling them greedy, excessive and even "obscene". While the most cursory investigation would reveal that the return on investment for oil companies has been severely depressed for years and only now has reached a level consistent with other industries, the charges of the politicians are accepted at face value as further evidence of antitrust violation. The danger here is that punitive tax legislation will be forthcoming which will drain away the resources so badly needed to find and develop new domestic energy sources.

Aside from this general appeal to restore antitrust to a concept of law serving the cause of competition in a free market we point out two areas where responsible enforcement is particularly important in facing up to our energy crisis.

First, [our] effectiveness in obtaining and retaining access to foreign reserves of crude oil and in participating in coordinated consumer country activities may increasingly depend upon its obtaining antitrust clearance to act in concert with other oil companies in dealing with foreign governments. In these circumstances, it is critical to obtain from the Department of Justice a quick and realistic appraisal of the problem at hand and an approval appropriate to the circumstances. The frequency of the confrontations with foreign governments (singly and in combination) over their unilateral abrogation of contracts and concessions has underscored the need for joint company action backed by enlightened cooperation of the home government. An excellent in-depth study of the impact of the antitrust laws on U.S. business firms abroad was recently published by the International Economics Affairs Department of the N.A.M.

Second, the same responsible governmental approach must be made in evaluating joint efforts by oil companies to find and bring into production new reserves of oil and gas. The tremendous capital investments involved in such operations in the areas still unexplored (arctic, deep water, etc.) and the liklihood of failure make it virtually imperitive that companies join together to share the cost and the risk. So long as effective competition is present in ventures of high risk, the Federal Government should not question the existence of joint bids or other types of cooperative undertakings.

In sum, we do not believe in the relaxation of
the antitrust laws or of their enforcement against restraints on the domestic or foreign commerce of the United
States.  What we do ask for is that they not be used as
political, social or economic weapons and that the administration now give public confirmation that those laws
do not apply to the type of joint undertakings - foreign
and domestic - described above.

B.   A.   U. S. Price Controls

These have served to reduce the supply of petroleum,
cut expenditures for new exploration and caused us to shift
capital expenditures overseas where profit potentials are
more promising.  Conversely, controls have encouraged the
wasteful consumption of U.S. mineral resources.

Price controls on natural gas since 1954 have had a
most damaging impact on U.S. exploration for both oil and
gas.  Where price controls did not exist, (intra-state gas)
exploration flourished.

Price controls on crude oil have also discouraged
the drilling for oil.  Currently controls on old oil (about
60% of U.S. production) tend to discourage the higher-cost
secondary and tertiary recovery operations and thus reduce
the potential production of oil.  Price controls (formal
and informal) also have delayed the start of a synthetic
fuels industry from shale oil, coal and tar sands.

U.S. price controls on crude and products are
subsidizing higher-cost imports, and are thus keeping
foreign prices higher than desired.  With U.S. markets at
price-clearing levels, we can only afford these higher
prices by averaging them with artificially lower-priced
domestic oils.

Price controls on products have, (1) greatly discouraged production of distillate fuel oils (1972 and early
1973) because prices were frozen at seasonal lows; (2) discouraged expansion of refineries because prices were not
permitted to rise sufficiently above incremental costs as
to justify new capital investments; (3) in the period before
we were permitted to roll in the cost of higher-cost foreign

oils, the U.S. market under price controls did not offer any incentive to import products.

Finally, price control regulations coupled with crude allocation regulations have at times created great disparities in raw material costs for various refiners. This in turn means great differences in product prices in the market place. Rather than taking steps to eliminate price controls, and thus eliminate all disturbances, federal agencies instead write more and more regulations designed to make the original controls workable.

B. U.S. Crude Oil Allocation Rules

The Rules in Effect from February to May 1974

These rules provided for a sharing of the shortages of oil during the Arab embargo. However, because any increase in imports had to be shared with other companies at a large economic loss, these rules greatly discouraged imports during this period. For every 100 barrels of additional imports, [we] would have been permitted to keep only four barrels. The other 96 barrels had to be sold to our competitors at a several $/bbl. loss to [our company.] An attempt was made by the FEO to soften the impact for the month of May by exempting additional imports from the requirement to share.

A second bad effect of these rules was to create regional shortages of gasoline and shortages of jet fuels as crude was shifted away from the more efficient coastal refineries to the small inland refineries. The severe gasoline shortages in February were primarily due to this.

Because product imports were not shared during this period, it was better for an oil company to import products than crude oil. If these rules had remained in effect, our incentives to undertake new exploration either domestically or internationally would have been greatly reduced.

The Rules for June to November 1974

The effect of the revised allocation system is merely to shift around massed amounts of crude oil from 15

C-40

large refiners to other companies without any attempt to
balance supply-to-capacity ratios as the February to May
program had done.

These rules imposed a requirement that these 15
large oil companies sell crude oil to smaller companies
regardless of each company's own supply of oil. Volumes
were determined by the FEA and apportioned based on refinery
capacity. Thus in the case of [our company,] a crude-short
company, but one of the top 15, we were required to sell oil
to smaller companies, some of which had a greater supply-to-
capacity ratio than we did. Sales were to be made at average
cost even though replacement of lost barrels had to be made
at a much higher cost to the sellers. Losses by individual
sellers of $4/bbl. were common.

These rules had a great impact on domestic oil
supply as it shifted 83 million barrels of crude during June
to August from the supply of the larger refiners to smaller
refiners.

While these rules greatly affected domestic
supplies, they had little impact on plans for domestic or
foreign oil exploration. They do however discourage expansion of refineries by the large companies because selling
obligation increases with refinery capacity.

C.  Antitrust Laws

The current antitrust laws have a dampening effect
on petroleum supply and on international operations in two
instances, (a) regulations that prevent joint operation of
refineries, and (b) rulings that do not allow joint action
by U.S. oil companies dealing with foreign producing countries.

As long as refinery sizes were limited by technology to under 100,000 B/D, U.S. refinery sites readily
available and oil imports at low levels, the prohibition of
joint refinery operation was not a great hindrance on product supply.

However, refineries of 500,000 B/D or larger are
now technically feasible which is beyond the individual
financial ability of most U.S. companies. Refinery sites in

the U.S. are very few and locations nearby in Canada and in
the Caribbean or in the producing countries are more abundant
and often more desirable, i.e., less environmental obligations are required, deepwater ports can be constructed,
natural gas is available, etc.  The need to treat and handle
very large volumes of high sulfer crudes suggests that economies are to be gained by very large refineries.  If U.S.
companies are to compete effectively in the future, joint
operation of refineries is a must.

The success of OPEC nations in operating like a
cartel strongly suggests that joint dealings by U.S. oil
companies is a necessary offset.

Proposed changes to U.S. antitrust laws would
require integrated oil companies to divest themselves of
pipelines or their marketing operations or to split crude
production from refining-marketing.  [We] are opposed to such
proposals and believe they are uneconomic and will increase
the cost of products to the consumer and they are anticompetitive and will tend to reduce the number of companies
operating within a given business segment.  There are many
strong competitors in the U.S. petroleum industry and ease
of entry is indicated by the fact that there have been several recent entrants into the U.S. markets:  Fina, Total,
British Petroleum and Koch Brothers.

Divorcement of any segment of the petroleum
industry will impair an integrated oil company's efforts to
raise capital in financial markets for use in finding and
developing new sources of energy.  This will seriously impair our country's goal of self-sufficiency.  A corollary to
this is that after breakup, U.S. oil companies would be less
able to compete in foreign markets against the foreign
integrated and nationally-owned companies, thereby further
aggravating our balance of payments problem.

Rather than reducing the cost to the consumer by
increasing competition, divorcement would create a large
number of new companies, all of which must earn a profit to
stay in business.  So, the total profit taken out of the
economy would increase.  Divorcement would eliminate the
economics of scale and the operating efficiencies inherent
in integrated companies and would increase total overhead
costs.  The smaller companies created by divorcement would

have difficulty in raising the huge capital investments required for new pipelines or refineries. Many of these smaller companies operating in a given segment, i.e., marketing, would have to combine into larger units in order to survive.

C. (1) Generally, price controls imposed on competitive economic activities are counter-productive. While the effects may appear to be favorable in terms of temporarily holding prices below an uncontrolled level, the benefits of controls are illusionary over the longer term. Absent price controls, competitive enterprises quickly respond to the problems and opportunities indicated by price variations, and tend towards a condition of socially optimized equilibrium. Conversely, attempts to control prices almost invariably introduce artificial and counterproductive stimuli, which depress total investment in new production facilities and impair the most effective application of investments made -- thus, price controls increase the real cost of goods and services over the longer term.

Existing crude pricing regulations tend to distort traditional competitive E&P decisions. While de-control of "new" and "stripper" production is effective in encouraging new exploration and in avoiding premature well abandonments, the existence of a dual-price system tends to promote socially sub-optimal actions in many instances. For example, production increments from properties having established production prior to 1972 may frequently be penalized relative to prospects on new acreage. That is, production from the new acreage would be allowed to sell for about $10 while the production gain from an established producing property may be constrained to about $5. Of course, that portion of the established property's production gain that exceeded 1972 levels would be allowed the higher price; however, normal production declines frequently would preclude the expected production increase from attaining 1972 rates. Thus, production increments of equal social value could vary in allowed price anywhere in the $5 to $10 range, depending on the circumstantial application of crude pricing regulations. An E&P operator faced with an array of project choices therefore might well be motivated to select other than least-cost options due to the economic distortions arising from crude price controls. Note: This problem

C-43

could be minimized by a re-definition of new crude to include updating of the base period to the first half of 1974 for properties then producing at less than 1972 rates, and possibly to qualify all tertiary recovery output as new.

Regarding the regulations on stripper properties, properties averaging less than 10 b/d per well are exempt from controls, and production therefrom can be sold at market prices of about $10. Output from properties averaging more than 10 b/d per well are subject to crude price ceilings of about $5 (excepting volumes qualified as new crude). This regulation is obviously counter-productive at the margin. For example, the owner of a one-well property would be as well off to produce at 10 b/d (10 b/d at $10 uncontrolled price equals $100/revenue) as he would be to produce at 20 b/d (20 b/d at $5 controlled price also equals $100/d revenue). Thus, unless increased production well beyond 20 b/d per well could be effected, operators would be motivated to maintain stripper status in many instances. This problem would be minimized by exempting the first 10 b/d from all wells, thus avoiding any penalty for boosting production beyond the defined "stripper" limit.

Product price regulations now allow refiners to recover only crude cost increases, and ignore the impact of other costs. The key upshot of this restraint is the discouragement of refinery capacity expansion. The cost of adding capacity has increased dramatically, and regulations restricting the recovery of such higher costs would frequently preclude otherwise justifiable expansion. It also appears that product price controls result in greater imports at the expense of domestic refining capacity which is underutilized. This occurs because there are no restrictions placed on the full passthrough of imported product costs, whereas domestic refiners must absorb a substantial fraction of rising raw material and processing costs.

Moreover, the combination of crude and product price controls has caused widely divergent product prices. That is, because of differing proportions of price controlled/uncontrolled crudes in their supply, refiners' crude costs have advanced at varying rates. The crude cost passthrough provisions of product price regulations have thus caused the prices of identical products in the same location to differ widely, depending on the individual refiners' particular crude costs. Of course, the customer of a refiner/marketer having relatively high crude costs suffers unduly because of regulatory provisions.

Absent crude and product price regulations, the crude supply, transportation, refining, and marketing functions very likely would have quickly reoptimized in response to the new high-cost, limited import environment in a manner more equitable to both oil companies and to consumers.

Regarding the impact of price controls on international operations, the tendency is that domestic operations are penalized relative to non-domestic activities. That is, to the extent that price controls restrain unit revenues from domestic crude and product output below world markets, the economic tendency would be toward foreign operations, for both E&P and refining.

(2) Existing crude allocation rules are grossly counter-productive and inequitable. That is, major refiners, who are required to sell crude to others at their average acquisition cost certainly will be discouraged from acquiring additional supplies at higher marginal unit costs. Although passthrough rules allow the recovery of crude cost increases, the differing application of passthrough rules among companies results in a situation in which full passthrough credits cannot be utilized at market clearing prices. Thus, those refiners who have aggressively acquired additional higher-cost imports are now being unduly penalized since their product prices are necessarily higher than those of their competitors, to whom they have been required to sell crude at prices less than marginal cost. Under such conditions, acquisition of additional supply increments, i.e. imported crude, is certainly discouraged, which also tends to cause under-utilization of domestic refining capacity.

Of course, optimal crude allocation would be best achieved by free markets. That is, under free markets, competitive activities quickly respond to market conditions such that least-cost options are soon effected. Alternatively, under control conditions, simply providing refiners equal access to low-cost old crude in proportion to their runs would be adequate. No other control procedures would be needed, and indeed they would be counter-productive.

(3) It would be inappropriate to comment on specific matters that may currently or prospectively be the subject of litigation. The petroleum industry is aggressively competitive at all levels and we expect that it will

remain so. We feel that fair and informed enforcement of
existing U.S. antitrust laws does not pose a significant
threat to our company's operations, foreign or domestic.

    We view with grave concern moves in Congress and
elsewhere to declare the existence of monopoly or anti-
competitive practices by simple fiat where the factual
evidence clearly shows that no such situation exists. By
threatening the petroleum industry with prosecution for
fantasy rather than fact, these actions inject significant
new political uncertainties into the long-range planning
environment. Through their impact on the risk-return
tradeoff, such proposals lower the incentive to undertake
domestic exploration and other risky new ventures, thus
worsening the outlook for future dependence on imported
energy supplies.


8. To what foreign countries or companies and in what
amounts has your company distributed its world-wide
petroleum production during each of the last five years?
Specify only those countries or companies which account
for more than 5% of your petroleum production, and in
each instance, indicate the country or countries to which
such production was ultimately shipped for consumption.

| | Countries or Companies to Which Petroleum Was Distributed | Country in Which Petroleum Was Consumed | Amounts |
|---|---|---|---|
| 1969 | _____ | _____ | _____ |
| | _____ | _____ | _____ |
| | _____ | _____ | _____ |
| | _____ | _____ | _____ |
| 1970 | _____ | _____ | _____ |

|  | Countries or Companies to Which Petroleum Was Distributed | Country in Which Petroleum Was Consumed | Amounts |
|---|---|---|---|
| 1971 | | | |
| | | | |
| | | | |
| | | | |
| | | | |
| 1972 | | | |
| | | | |
| | | | |
| | | | |
| | | | |
| 1973 | | | |
| | | | |
| | | | |
| | | | |
| | | | |

Response:      Company responses to this question were too
              incompatible to permit aggregation.

9.  Describe the type of supply arrangements which currently
exist between your company and any foreign company or country
listed above in the answer to Question 8.

Response:      Company responses to this question were too
              incompatible to permit aggregation.

10.  What is your opinion as to the strengths and weaknesses
of a government-owned and operated oil company such as
Petromin, National Iranian Oil Company, Pertamina and
C.V.P.?  Please be specific.

Response:

              The majority of oil companies responding to this
question felt that government-owned and operated oil companies

are not as efficient as private enterprises, in that lack of
a profit motive prevents this kind of organization from
attracting top management and technical skill.  Several oil
companies also indicated that the support of a national
government can result in the politicalization of the
industry.

SELECTED COMMENTS:

    A.  The strength of government-owned and operated
oil companies such as Petromin, National Iranian Oil Company, Pertamina, and C.V.P. is based almost entirely on
their anticipated role as the main sellers and suppliers
of crude which is produced in their country; this role
tends to assure such upstream companies that outside
interests (either private international oil companies or
national interests in the major consuming areas) will stand
ready to assist the upstream companies in exploration,
development, and production of their fields.

    The weaknesses of the upstream companies listed
are in the areas of project management and technical expertise in the exploration, development, production, transportation, refining, marketing, and overall logistics of the oil
business.  Thus, all will need outside "service contractors"
to perform many of the technical functions in order to work
effectively.

    Another area of weakness relates to the fact that
government-owned upstream companies are neither administratively nor temperamentally geared to the process of large-
scale "risk taking"; it is simply quite difficult for such
entities to risk large sums of public funds, knowing they
must regularly justify their expenditures to governmental
bodies.  Also, the absence of divergent views on the
prospectivity of a venture is another weakness related to
the risk-taking process; whereas a large number of different
(and competitive) views characterizes the private enterprise
approach to risk-taking, the "single view" of the public
entity lacks the innovative spirit deemed necessary to
undertake new exploration ventures.

    Among the companies listed, Petromin has at present
little technical expertise and mainly engages in "selling

crude oil" and participating in minor refinery operations
in Saudi Arabia. National Iranian Oil Company has relatively
more experience, partly because it has been in operation the
longest and has participated in some joint ventures both in
Iran and overseas; Pertamina is much in the same position
as Petromin; and C.V.P. has attempted to do some exploration
on its own but has so far shown little capability for success.

B.   The major strength of government-owned oil companies is that they can assure continuity of operations
regardless of commercial success or failure. Thus, they
are in a position to undertake far greater risks than private companies. In addition, government oil companies in
nations without a strong private industry can serve as a
vehicle for building a core of technical expertise and
diversifying the economy. Occasionally they promote social
goals, and can control development of national resources.

The partially government-owned public corporations
do not have any major inherent strengths but generally receive favorable financial treatment from national financial
institutions, receive preferential treatment in obtaining
prime exploration acreage, and in general have a better
working relationship with governmental authorities. They
also occasionally receive direct subsidies for carrying
out high-risk operations.

Government-owned oil companies are generally
overstaffed and underproductive, have no competitive
stimulus and are not acutely responsive to consumer needs.
Also, most government companies are of recent enough vintage
that they have yet to prove their willingness to undertake
high-risk investments. In general, because government
companies are gauged by artificial yardsticks, their managements prefer investments in refineries, pipelines and marketing facilities, rather than exploration. Government companies
also have a tendency to become extensions of their governments
and become political as well as economic instruments.

Partial government ownership generally lessens the
pressure for efficient operations. Also public ownership
injects a political element into the corporation which can
lead to hostile reactions in foreign areas such as the BP
nationalization in Libya. A further drawback is that the

government faction usually has the potential to thwart the
decision-making process.  In BP, for example, the government's
two board members have veto power over any resolution.  While
this reportedly has never been used, it remains a clear threat
to decisive management.

These companies are generally prone to government
pressures to promote national industries and resources which
can postpone unduly the development of important projects.
Nearly a one-year delay in the development of the "Forties
Field" is attributed to the inability of British Steel to
provide deliveries as promised.

## C.  Strengths

The question presumably relates only to the
national oil companies of significant crude oil exporting
countries.  The objective of these companies is to optimize
commercial activities under the political direction of
the government of the country in question.  The only
significant commercial activity is oil; and therefore, the
greatest strength of these companies is their access to the
oil.  Recent events have also underlined their immunity to
normal business constraints which began and continued during
a period in which the producing exporting countries were in
positions of enormous strength.  Their almost monopolistic
position with respect to the sale of crude oil enables these
companies to be very selective about their methods of
diversification and their access to the consuming nation's
technical and material resources.  Within the individual
countries, these companies have a monopoly in all phases
of the oil business, including petrochemicals.

## Weaknesses

The distinction between the national oil companies
and the governments is often confused.  The link is strong
but the main difference is that the companies themselves do
not generate policy.  This separation of power weakens the
companies commercial credibility since all agreements with
them are currently subject to political volatility.  As a
consequence, most business arrangements with these companies
are considered to be with the countries themselves.

Another weakness relates to the fact that the
companies have difficulty in ensuring that every arrangement finalized is in the nation's best interests.

The national oil companies are not integrated to
any appreciable degree, except in their own countries, and
are still deficient in technical and commercial expertise.
Such expertise can be purchased, but use of alien personnel
is often difficult, especially the eventual phasing out
which is required as indigenous skills increase.

Conclusion

The national oil companies cited in this question
are currently in positions of great strength only because
of their control over the majority of the free world's crude
oil supply, much of which was found and developed by private
companies.  Crude oil production represents the overwhelmingly
predominant economic activity in each of these countries.
It is the central crux of the economy and the political
system and serves as the source of the total wealth of
these nations.  For these reaons, a government owned and
operated oil company is probably required to maintain these
OPEC nations as political entities.

A national oil company is not only unnecessary but
would not be effective in a widely diversified economy such
as that of the United States.  The petroleum industry in the
U.S. is just one of many large industries and, therefore,
does not have the impact upon the total economy as in the
OPEC nations cited.  Furthermore, in the U.S. the petroleum
industry is just one part of the total energy base which is
not the case in these OPEC nations.

Direct government ownership and operation of the
U.S. oil industry would quickly make the industry subserviant
to the conflicting and continually changing special interests
groups which comprise the rest of the economy.  Policies
would undoubtedly be formulated by the political expediencies
of the moment, rather than in an attempt to attain long range
objectives, including maximum efficiency.  Generally speaking,
governmental companies would not necessarily have the same
purposes or disciplines as private companies.

Finally, if there is active participation by a government in the management of a company, exploration and development investment opportunities or other commercial ventures which would be normal for private companies could be inhibited.

D. In general, the four companies mentioned above are not representative of government owned and operated oil companies. They are the top four in terms of revenues and financial strength. If one includes such others as ELF, AFIP, PEMEX, CEPE, PETROPERU, MYANMA, JPDC, ONGC, ENAP, EGPC, NNOC, SOEKOR, PETROBRAS, INA, INI, etc., one gets a much more representative picture of such companies. Only a few of these companies are self-supporting. Most of them are poorly staffed technically and all of them are subject to the political whims of their governments.

E. The strengths and weaknesses of government operated and owned oil companies varies between countries. Petromin in Saudi Arabia is a well organized and efficiently operated company. Its major drawback is its lack of qualified people which will be required in order to carry out the very large task being assigned to it. Decisions are sometimes slow in forthcoming due to this lack of staff. It is structured in such a way that it has some degree of freedom to make decisions within guidelines provided by the central government. On the other hand, the National Iranian Oil Company is closely controlled by the central government and, therefore, is influenced to a greater extent by political decisions. CVP demonstrates a high degree of inefficiency which is attributable to its top people being politically appointed rather than selected from a civil servant category. On the technical level they are inefficient due to being overstaffed with people who are technically trained but demonstrate a very bureaucratic attitude. It is questionable that with a total takeover of the oil industry, an adequate number of technically competent people would be available to efficiently carry out the task at hand. Sonatrach, the Algerian national oil company, demonstrates a fairly high degree of efficiency in that its people at the top are very technically qualified and have learned the basic elements of the international oil business. The operation of this company was quite good until political factors over-rode the commercial aspects of the

operation during the recent crisis.  In general, national
oil companies are subject to political considerations to such
an extent that they never will be able to satisfy the commercial requirements of the international oil business.

F.  The experience of the management of this company
with government-owned and operated oil companies has been
primarily with those of the non-industrialized, less-
developed nations, primarily Petromin, the National Iranian
Oil Company, Pertamina, Petroperu, and the National Oil
Company of Venezuela.  These companies are not commercial
enterprises directed to making a profit for the owners in
the sense of a private-capital company operating in one
of the world's commercial-industrial nations or competing
in the free-world market.  These companies are directed
to achieving the goals determined by the ruling sovereign
and cost-benefit evaluations are determined on a political-
emotional basis rather than an economic basis. In those
rare instances where any indications have been given as to
the economic results of the companies mentioned, it is
our opinion that the costs have been materially understated
and the profits and other benefits materially overstated.  To
the extent that we have been afforded a view of the business
process of such companies, their accounting systems and
methods of reporting and accounting for capital, cost and
income do not correspond even remotely to those of a private
commercial enterprise.

It has been our experience that the national oil
companies have a few brilliant, well-educated, dedicated,
but essentially politically-oriented, key men at the top
administrative level.  For the most part, these men, though
brilliant, have not had experience in commercial enterprises
and do not have the judgment or breadth of outlook that such
experience would bring.  It is our observation that these
organizations lack depth in key personnel and that the
equivalent of the middle-management level present in most
private capital commercial enterprises is completely miss-
ing.  Though these companies often have a cadre of technical
personnel or access to technical services in the geological
and engineering phases of the petroleum business, they do
not have, and do not secure, comparable talent in the
administrative and business areas.  This would appear to be
in keeping with their primary direction and concern as an
adjunct of the sovereign's power in the achievement of

predetermined national goals of the sovereign rather than the achievement of a profit. Thus, efficiency in the use of manpower may receive little, if any, consideration while affording employment to nationals may be of primary concern. Nepotism is prevalent.

Due to their nature and purpose, we do not believe that companies of this type can be compared with private commercial enterprises, and their strengths and weaknesses can only be evaluated on the degree to which they achieve the national goals assigned to them. From the standpoint of a commercial enterprise, the sovereign is paying a substantial price to accomplish a non-commercial goal that the sovereign deems to be important. It is our opinion that these companies could not compete in the free-world market as commercial enterprises, absent the subsidization, support and protection of their national sovereign.

We recognize that the foregoing statements are essentially broad generalizations, but the differences in concept and result, particularly when there are no comparable financial results available for comparison, makes specific analysis extremely difficult.

G. In answering this question, we have described the strengths and weaknesses in terms of economic power and as they pertain to the government-owned company in a producing country and where applicable to the sponsoring government. From the standpoint of consuming countries or international oil companies based in consuming countries, we know of no benefits from government-controlled oil companies in producing countries. The relationship between the strengths and weaknesses of the Petromin in Saudi Arabia, for example, and the purposes of the FEA study is not readily apparent to us.

Strengths

1. Has absolute assurance as to its sources of supply within its boundaries and priority access to the best or most promising sources.

2. Is backed by the power of government and is thus able to compel changes in its agreements with others, abrogate agreements, promote laws and regulations which

inhibit its private counterparts, strongly influence or even control prices, etc., while the company itself is generally free from legal attack, as a practical matter.

3. May have access to technical data and reports prepared by individual private companies but not generally available to the industry as a whole.

4. Usually enjoys a monopoly position in the local market.

5. Is usually not required to show a profit, and generally has preferential tax position compared to private companies.

6. From the sponsoring governments' standpoint - provides an obvious involvement in this key revenue-producing industry, a politically acceptable alternative to foreign participation in the industry, and a vehicle for barter or bilateral trade arrangements with other governments.

Weaknesses

1. Management tends very much to be politically oriented and must implement decisions motivated by political rather than business considerations.

2. Managements often change with changes in government administration, and staffing not always optimum due to political factors in making appointments.

3. Involvement with government bureaucracy can lead to multi-layered and generally inefficient organization which consumes valuable manpower but inhibits decision-making at all but the highest levels.

4. Involvement in selected areas often results in an unnecessary "layering" of the national oil company between private operators and other government agencies which leads to duplication of management/technical functions, additional delay in decision making process, etc.

5. Normally, does not contribute additional expertise to the industry, but instead relies heavily on services of private industry and the commercial sources

normally available to private industry. This is perhaps due to being newcomers in the business rather than government control.

    6. Does not have the strong profit motive which is so important in creating organizational and operational efficiency and in perpetuating the high level of technical development, expertise and innovation which is available today. This will be even more important in the future.

    7. Frequently pay scales are not competitive so organizations may be staffed in part with sub-standard technicians.


11. What is your opinion as to the strengths and weaknesses of public oil corporations partially owned by a government, such as C.F.P., British Petroleum and Veba Chemie? Please be specific.

Response:

    Oil company responses indicated that public oil corporations can be susceptible to political influences and government interference which can be considered either a strength or a weakness depending upon the general efficiency of the particular company.

SELECTED COMMENTS:

    A. Before commenting on the strengths and weaknesses of the "public oil corporations" listed, it may be worth noting that two of the three companies (i.e., British Petroleum and C.F.P.) are generally reckoned among the "major internationals," not only for reasons of size in the international sphere, but also because their policies and behaviour have conformed closely to the pattern of the "major internationals." In this sense it may be somewhat of a misnomer to include them as "public oil corporations" with an enterprise like Veba. Specifically, in the case of British Petroleum it has for many years been standard public U.K. policy not to impose government views on this U.K. company, despite the government's equity position; a fairly similar public policy applies in the case of C.F.P.,

for which reason a second major French company has come
into existence (ERAP/ELF) to undertake ventures more directly
consistent with French government policy.

For these reasons, the strengths and weaknesses
perceived for British Petroleum and C.F.P. are much like
those which tend to apply to most of the largest "major
internationals"; i.e., strengths in the broad diversity of
assets, management, and technical expertise, and weaknesses related to the difficulties in dealing with sovereign
governments on an equal basis, which weakness would in-
cidently also pertain to the dealings of real "public
corporations." With regard to Veba Chemie, this is a
relatively small national group primarily engaged in chemicals and manufacturing in Germany, mainly recognized as
a purchaser of Russian oils; it is not an integrated company
and has not shown any particular efficiencies in its operations.

B. There are two basic conclusions which can be generalized from the experiences of foreign governments with fully
or partially owned oil companies. In the first place, foreign
environments in which such companies were founded and operate
are for the most part completely different from circumstances
in the U.S. Secondly, government owned oil companies have
a tendency to take on tasks other than the oil business as a
result of political pressures; thus such companies often take
on the role of a social welfare agency and it becomes very
hard to judge the efficiency of such a company.

The government oil companies in most major oil
producing countries have as their main objective the control
and exploitation of what is often the only major national
natural resource. This role has expanded greatly in recent
years as producing countries have moved to take control of
local petroleum operations away from private foreign (often
U.S.) concession holding companies which risked their capital to discover and develop these resources. Distinguishing
features of these companies are: (1) that to a major extent
they are involved solely with domestic operations, (2) that
for the conduct of operations they are still very much
dependent upon foreign personnel and contractors, and (3) that
in many of these countries the oil industry has had to build
the whole infra-structure of roads, houses, schools, power

supplies, etc. needed to support operations. The situation in the U.S. is very different. Oil is only one of many natural resources. Also in the U.S. oil resources have been almost exclusively under the control of nationals and there are plenty of skilled U.S. people to conduct all operations. The experience therefore of wholly Government owned producing country companies does not appear relevant to the U.S.

Companies such as BP and CFP with partial government ownership also had their origins in circumstances quite different from the U.S. situation. Both companies were founded to control a source of overseas oil when home country production was negligible. In the case of BP the initial motivation was to provide a controlled source of fuel oil for the British Navy, and in the case of CFP to administer a share of a concession obtained after World War I.

A very important feature of overseas government companies is that they frequently take on the job of providing additional employment in countries where there is massive unemployment. Through political pressures, these companies are made to take on a social role by employing more people than they or private enterprise would need for efficient operations. YPF (Argentina) and ENI (Italy) are good examples of this extension of role. In addition to running oil operations, ENI, for example, has been used as a means of industrializing Southern Italy. It has also been used as a vehicle for salvaging other Italian industries. Experience has shown that once a government company is established it is never liquidated or sold no matter how poor or how good the performance.

Generally, wholly owned government companies have not been successful in finding new reserves of oil outside their own borders. Instead, they have relied upon purchasing into existing producing areas as a means of securing supplies.

The companies with government shareholding which have been most successful appear to be those in which the government has taken a passive role and not involved itself in management, and private shareholding in the company has provided the stimulus to management. BP is the best example of this. The U.K. government, for example, permitted BP to

buy large tankers from Japanese yards rather than force BP
to build the tankers it needed in inefficient and high-cost
U.K. yards which were requiring government subsidy.

In summary, therefore, we see nothing in the
experience of foreign governments with wholly or partially
owned oil companies which suggests that the U.S. would
benefit by having one.  Given the particular circumstances
of the U.S. a government oil company is not needed, and if
one existed it would duplicate at added cost the activities
of private industry.


12.  What do you believe your company's competitive position would be vis-a-vis foreign oil companies if the major
tax incentives (i.e., oil depletion allowance, foreign tax
credits for royalty payments or purchased oil, and expensing
of intangible drilling costs for productive wells) for
U.S. oil companies were immediately eliminated?  Please
be specific.  In addition, consider any tax benefits or
subsidies which your foreign competitors receive from their
governments and for which there is no U.S. counterpart.

Response:

All of the petroleum company responses indicate
that the elimination of major tax incentives would place
U.S.-based oil companies at a serious competitive disadvantage with foreign companies.  The U.S. oil companies,
they believe, could not compete effectively, particularly
with government-owned companies that receive strong
financial support from their governments.  The elimination
of tax incentives would seriously curtail their ability
to compete for foreign exploration opportunities against
foreign companies whose taxes did not change in a similar
manner.

SELECTED COMMENTS:

A.  We would not be competitive at all and would probably get out of foreign oil exploration and redeploy our
company foreign capitol assets.

B.  We believe that the elimination of major tax incentives such as oil depletion allowance and expensing of
intangible drilling costs for U.S. companies would virtually
eliminate on-shore drilling.  The inevitable result will be
further dependence upon oil produced by foreign companies
and countries.

C.  Elimination of the tax incentives noted above would
put any U.S.-based oil company at a serious competitive disadvantage with respect to its European-based or Japanese-
based competitors for foreign oil operations, and these
foreign-based and controlled companies would inevitably
displace the U.S. companies.  At a time when the United
States faces a period in which it will be a substantial
importer of oil, elimination of tax incentives would
clearly not be in the best interests of the United States.

For existing production, such action would immediately create a cost disadvantage for the U.S.-based
companies, and therefore a tendency toward higher prices,
worldwide.  Of far greater importance, however, elimination
of the existing tax incentives would hamper or possibly
eliminate the ability of U.S.-based companies to compete
in the all-important race for new concessions.  Because
of the effect of home-country taxes, the economics of
any U.S. company would be such that it could not afford
to offer as favorable terms to the host country as could
its European or Japanese-based competitors, because they
will continue to enjoy the full benefit of a foreign tax
credit.  If our government enacts legislation to eliminate
the credit for foreign income taxes, the taxes of the U.S.
companies will increase, and their cost of doing business
will increase very substantially and U.S. companies will
tend to disappear from the international scene.

We must point out a conceptual error in the above
question with respect to foreign tax credits and their
applicability to royalty payments and to purchased oil.
U.S. tax law does not permit a foreign tax credit for
royalties paid foreign governments or for oil purchased
from foreign entities.  This misconception has been
responsible for much of the misunderstanding surrounding
the tax liabilities of U.S. petroleum companies.  U.S.
petroleum companies are taxed under the Internal Revenue

Code in the same manner as other U.S. businesses.  When the
United States taxes the world-wide income of its citizens
or corporations, it is faced with the problem of international double taxation.  Most foreign governments avoid
such a double tax by exempting from tax the foreign source
income of its citizens and corporations.  Others, including
the United States, tax the foreign source income of their
citizens and corporations but allow credit against that tax
for foreign income taxes paid, thereby recognizing the prior
claim of the country of source to tax the income arising
within its borders. No credit is allowed for payments other
than foreign income taxes.  If the U.S. oil industry is
taxed in a manner different from other U.S. industries,
such discriminatory treatment and additional tax burden
will have a direct effect upon the abilities of U.S.-based
oil companies to compete with foreign oil companies domiciled
in countries that either allow foreign tax credits or do
not tax foreign source income.  The related economic effects
of such proposals would certainly increase the price of
petroleum products in the U.S. and longer range would
seriously hamper the U.S.-based companies' ability to
provide for our future petroleum needs.  On this general
subject, it has also been suggested that the result of
the existing foreign tax credit provisions is that taxes
paid to host producing governments can somehow reduce U.S.
income taxes to be paid on income attributable to operations
in the United States.  This has never been the case.  The
foreign tax credit has never reduced U.S. income tax on
income derived from operations in the United States.

    Similarly, a repeal of the option to expense
intangible drilling and development costs would cause a
severe competitive disadvantage to be sustained by U.S.-
based companies compared to foreign-based petroleum companies.  Briefly, this option which has been part of our
tax law for 57 years, permits a U.S. taxpayer to expense
labor, services, fuel and repairs expended in the drilling
and development of oil and gas properties.  It provides
the advantage of a more immediate tax deduction as opposed
to a slower recovery of investment costs through capitalization and depreciation.  Considering the time value of money,
this means lower after tax costs to the oil industry, and
therefore more projects and more oil and gas production.
The repeal or limitation of the election to expense intangible drilling and development costs would cause the

withdrawal of large sums of capital from the oil industry
and seriously affect the ability of the U.S. oil industry
to compete with foreign interests.

The curtailment of percentage depletion on foreign
production would have a limited effect on our company due to
the interaction of the percentage depletion limitations and
[our] foreign income tax liabilities.  [We are] subject to
U.S. tax on its income earned throughout the world.  In
order to avoid double taxation, the U.S. presently allows
a tax credit for income taxes paid foreign governments.
Since the income taxes now levied by most of the foreign
producing countries are in excess of the U.S. tax liability,
the percentage depletion allowance on foreign production is
of limited benefit to [us].  However, the overall effect of
percentage depletion as an inducement to explore for new
oil, particularly in the case of smaller companies, should
be carefully considered before enacting legislation which
would eliminate it and increase the cost burdens of the U.S.
petroleum industry.

In comparing the tax laws of different countries,
it is hard to determine if the provision of one country's
tax law has, or has not, a "counterpart" in another country's law.  Usually, there are dissimilarities of varying
degrees either in rates or in application which will result
in some disparity of treatment.  Therefore, in the context
of this question we have listed those countries that offer
incentives to the petroleum industry in one form or another.
Accordingly, we understand that the following foreign
governments grant incentives in regard to the domestic
production of oil and gas under their respective laws at
the present time, or did so within the very recent past.

ARGENTINA

Argentina allows a double deduction for depreciation of fixed assets and exploration expenses in
determining taxable profit for the first exploration
period.  Resulting tax losses may be carried forward ten
years.  Exploration expenses and normal depreciation on
capital assets are allowed a deduction applicable against
non-petroleum activities.

## AUSTRALIA

A taxpayer may recover capital expenditures in regard to exploration and development activities before production income becomes subject to income tax. Expenditures for the formation, exploration, development, and production are accumulated as deductions against future income from the sale of petroleum production. Income tax is thus postponed until the deductions have been fully offset against producing sales. An oil exploration company may transfer the tax reduction for any production or exploration expenditures from itself to its shareholders. The shareholder may then claim the deduction for the stock investment in the oil exploration company against current taxable income, and the deferred deduction of the exploration company is correspondingly reduced.

Subsidies are available to create favorable conditions for petroleum exploration activities.

A deduction for one-third of the calls on shares to the stockholders investing in the exploration venture is allowed. Since the exploration company may claim a tax deduction for its expenditures, the result is an aggregate deduction of 133-1/3% between the company and its shareholders.

## BELGIUM

Allows producers a tax-free reserve limited to 50% of the taxable profits from reserves. Such reserves must be reinvested within five years.

## BELIZE (BRITISH HONDURAS)

Allows percentage depletion of 27-1/2% of gross income limited to 50% of net after royalties but before depletion. Intangible drilling costs are deductible when incurred limited to 50% of net petroleum income after royalties but before depletion.

## CANADA

Allows percentage depletion of 33-1/3% of net profits. Exploration and drilling costs including the cost of acquiring petroleum and natural gas rights may be deducted as incurred to the extent of taxable income and the balance carried forward indefinitely. However, the 1974 fall budget proposes extensive changes in the taxation of resource industries. The proposed changes reduce the incentive to put capital into Canadian resource industries and widespread cutbacks have already taken place in petroleum exploration in Canada as a result of the proposed changes.

## COLOMBIA

Allows percentage depletion of 10% of gross value of the production less royalties or participations limited to 35% of net income before depletion. An additional special depletion allowance of 18% in the East and Southeast Region and 15% in the rest of the country is also allowed. The total of normal and special depletion is limited to 50% of net taxable income in the East and Southeast Region and 45% in the rest of the country. Amounts allowed as special depletion must be reinvested within three years in petroleum-related facilities. Failure to reinvest will result in restoration to taxable income but over-investment may be carried forward to apply against reinvestment obligations.

## DENMARK

For exploration and development under Greenland's mining law, investors in Greenland are permitted to recover 100% of their investment prior to being subject to Greenland income tax.

## FRANCE

Producers are allowed a reserve equal to 27-1/2% of gross value at the wellhead of the crude oil extracted. This reserve is limited to 50% of the net profit from production and from the first stage of processing in the producer's own refineries. To retain the tax exemption, such amounts must be reinvested within five years either in the way of fixed assets or research for new discoveries or by investments by certain companies approved by the government. If not reinvested within this time, the reserve is required to be restored to the taxable profits of the fiscal year during which such five-year period expires and is taxed as ordinary income.

The French Government company ERAP resulted from a merger in 1965 of several French Government oil companies. The French Government has been notably instrumental in encouraging the production of French companies. Favored tax treatment has been extended in domestic and refining activities. France helped its government-owned companies to obtain concessions in Algeria, Saudi Arabia and Iran.

GERMANY

German oil companies operating outside of Germany could obtain through December 31, 1968, low interest loans up to 75% of exploratory costs. They were repayable only when commercial production was obtained. Exploration during the years 1959 to 1962 was a prerequisite to entitlement. A new government incentive for foreign operations effective for the years 1969 through 1974 provides that a total of DM 575 million will be allocated to the loan scheme. Loans will be granted up to 75% of exploratory expenditures and no repayment is required if there is no discovery. Even with discovery, up to 50% of the loan can be waived under certain circumstances. If the financial situation warrants it, a non-repayable contribution of up to 30% of the cost of acquiring a productive field or share in a producing country may be applicable. To be eligible, the company must be domiciled in Germany and must have been producing petroleum in Germany or have been processing petroleum in Germany prior to January 1, 1969.

GUATEMALA

Allows percentage depletion of 27-1/2% of gross income limited to 50% of net income. Exploration and intangible drilling costs can be expensed. Losses can be carried forward indefinitely.

GUYANA

Allows percentage depletion and deduction of intangible drilling costs at a reasonable level as established by the Commissioner.

## HONDURAS

Allows percentage depletion of 25% of gross production limited to 50% of net taxable profits. Exploration expenses, as well as intangible drilling costs, can be expensed. Losses can be carried forward for ten years.

## ISRAEL

Allows percentage depletion of 27-1/2% of gross income limited to 50% net income.

## ITALY

Italy has a national company, which the Italian Government has endowed with one-half billion dollars. The Italian Government helped ENI to obtain concessions in Iran and Saudi Arabia.

## JAPAN

Allows percentage depletion for companies conducting petroleum operations subject to a recapture to the extent that within a three-year period an amount equivalent to the deduction has not been invested in further exploration. The amount is 15% of sales revenue limited to 50% of net income. A current deduction of intangible drilling and development costs for unsuccessful wells is also provided. These incentives apply to both domestic and overseas exploration. The Government has organized the Petroleum Development Public Corporation (PDPC) as a government-owned entity for the purpose of channeling government funds into exploration and production in order to promote the development of petroleum resources and to ensure stabilized supplies of petroleum. PDPC will make investments and loans necessary for petroleum exploration overseas, guarantee debts resulting from loans necessary for overseas operations, lease equipment required for oil exploration, and give technological advice on oil exploration and production. The loans may be extended on favorable terms and repayment is required only if the venture is successful. Loans may be as high as 50% of costs, and joint ventures in which Japanese interests own at least 50% of the enterprise may qualify. The Japanese Government is developing policies to actively encourage domestic oil and gas production. The Japanese Government has required all refiners in Japan to purchase a pro-rated share of the entire production of the Arabian Oil Company (a company owned by the Japanese and assisted by the Japanese Government).

## NICARAGUA

Allows percentage depletion of 27-1/2% of wellhead value less royalties limited to 50% of net income. Intangible drilling costs and dry hole costs are deductible once production is obtained. Losses may be carried forward 10 years.

## NIGERIA

Exploration losses, intangible drilling costs and dry holes can be expensed. Losses can be carried forward indefinitely.

## NORWAY

The government may grant companies in the exploration and exploitation of offshore oil and gas deposits the right to carry losses forward over a 15-year period rather than the usual 10-year period.

## PAKISTAN

Allows percentage depletion at the rate of 15% of the wellhead value, subject to a maximum of 50% of net income.

## PERU

Allows percentage depletion from 15% to 27-1/2% of the gross value of production depending upon whether a national or a foreign company is involved and the geographical region. A foreign company with production in the Coastal Region is limited to 50% of net profit after deducting depletion and the 20% minimum advance payment of income tax. All others are limited to 50% of net profit before deduction of depletion and the advance payment of income tax. Intangible drilling costs are also deductible.

## PHILIPPINES

Percentage depletion of 27-1/2% is allowed based on gross income after rents or royalties are deducted.

## SABAH

Allows percentage depletion at rates deemed reasonable by the Commissioner.

## SPAIN

Allows percentage depletion of 25% of the field value of the production lease royalties but limited to 40% of the net profit before deducting depletion.

## ST. MAARTEN

Allows percentage depletion at rates deemed reasonable by the Commissioner.

## TRINIDAD AND TOBAGO

Allows percentage depletion of 20% of the gross value of production of submarine wells limited to 40% of the income without the deduction of certain specified allowances.

## TURKEY

Allows percentage depletion of 27-1/2% of the gross income from production after deducting rents and royalties limited to 50% of net.

## UNITED KINGDOM

Gives cash grants of 20% (40% in certain onshore areas) for oil and gas operations onshore and offshore available generally as follows:

(1) Geological and geophysical expenses are usually eligible for grant except for the cost of general surveys to determine whether or not to begin exploration.

(2) Lease acquisition costs are ineligible.

(3)  Exploration, evaluation and production drilling costs qualify.

(4)  Production equipment, certain pipelines and drilling platforms, including overheads, qualify.

In effect, all exploration and drilling expenses not in excess of investment grants incurred prior to proving reserves may be expensed.  Thereafter, until production is achieved, both tangible and intangible costs are capitalized and amortized on a unit of production basis.  After production is achieved, tangible costs are still capitalized and amortized but intangible costs are expensed.  Losses may be carried forward for an unlimited number of years.  All items requiring capitalization must be so treated because only an item that is capitalized is eligible for an investment grant. If, for any reason, an investment grant is not received, such items may be expensed.

13.  What do you believe would be the consequences to world petroleum supply of (1) the end of equity oil (100% reversion) in OPEC nations, (2) the end of preferential supply arrangements in favor of certain major petroleum companies (such as Exxon, Mobil, Texaco, Shell, Gulf and British Petroleum) in OPEC nations, or (3) in general, the end of the primary role in global petroleum distribution played by such major petroleum companies?

Response:

The majority of oil company responses indicate that the loss of equity oil could result in a single, higher price for crude oil than the present average of equity oil prices.  It could also result in a disruption of supply in that access to equity oil is an incentive for risk-taking. Several oil companies indicated that the loss of equity oil would limit any new investments in new facilities due to the uncertainty of supply.  The end of preferential supply arrangements could also result in higher crude prices and a less efficient method of distribution.  Most of the oil companies felt that the loss of the role played by the majors in global petroleum distribution would eliminate

the apolitical "buffer" role between producer and consumer
countries could lead to increased direct producer-consumer
confrontations.  Further, if oil distribution was taken over
by OPEC nations, it would replace an already efficient system
of marketing and technology and would probably lead to an
increase in price as well as an end to flexibility of distribution.

SELECTED COMMENTS:

    A.  (1)  The end of equity oil will mean increasing
pressures on oil prices as major oil companies will now
have to earn their profits solely from downstream operations.  The international oil companies will in effect
become either very large petroleum purchasers or service
companies.  Because of the oil companies efficient distribution systems, orderly marketing of petroleum would favor
preferential (service company) treatment.

        (2)  Should the major's lose direct preferential
supply arrangements in OPEC nations their distribution
services would likely be utilized by crude purchasers, who-
ever they may be.  However, to consuming countries such an
action puts the continued operation of their countries
refining and marketing of petroleum under the indirect
control of producing countries who could determine individually or jointly the volumes of oil that would be made
available to any consumer.

        Whether the majors would continue to expand
consuming-country downstream operations is uncertain.  If
their loss of preferential supplies reduces downstream incentives, petroleum importing capabilities may suffer.

        (3)  Major international oil companies own large
segments of the worldwide distribution system including
tankers, port facilities, refineries and marketing systems.
The end of the primary distribution role of the majors would
be detrimental to consuming nation's supply flexibility and
distribution efficiency.

    B.  (1)  The ending of equity oil in the OPEC nations
would resolve a major bone of contention for those countries;
the issue of ownership of their natural resources.  It would

also serve to clarify the role and strengths of the major oil companies in the exploration, production, distribution and marketing of global petroleum supplies.

The major economic impact of ending equity oil in OPEC nations would be to increase revenue flows to the producing nations, thus increasing their economic strength and enhancing their ability to wage economic warfare. To the extent that their financial reserves would be increased, they would be able to lengthen the time span of future production curtailments or oil embargoes against consuming nations. The ending of equity oil could also increase access to oil supplies for other oil companies, including non-U.S. companies.

The end of equity participation would not impact physical supply capacity. The major companies would still be there to run oil operations as contractors. Host countries would be able to provide the financial resources required for continuing exploration and development.

(2) The end of preferential supply arrangements for the major petroleum companies could create dislocation in the existing logistics system for world petroleum supplies and require realignment of some traditional supply patterns. Since this could permit the entry of other foreign oil companies into influential positions, it could create the loss of profit flows to the United States and reduce the United States presence in foreign countries with which the United States desires to maintain positive relations.

(3) The end of the primary role of the major petroleum companies in global distribution of petroleum would cause the United States to lose significant profit flows and reduce the level of economic activity of American companies. Additionally, it would reduce the flexibility and influence available to U.S. companies in crisis situations. Control of the petroleum logistics systems by the major petroleum companies made possible the reallocation of available petroleum supplies among the consuming nations during the 1973-1974 oil embargo, ameliorating the potentially more serious effects of the embargo on the United States.

C.  The end of equity oil (100% reversion) in OPEC nations.

    The end of equity oil arrangements with the extinguish-
ment of the existing concessions is already in sight.  In
fact, it is nominally true of the new agreement in Iran
(although the latter does provide the companies with some
of the advantages of the old system).  Saudi Arabia has
announced its intention to take over completely Aramco's
production operations, and the resulting arrangements will
undoubtedly be imitated elsewhere.  While certain features
of the existing concessions system (posted prices, equity
vs. buyback oil) will thus disappear, the former concession
holder is likely, in many cases, to continue to handle
operations on a contract basis, at least for a time, and
be paid for its services either in cash or in the form of
an agreed discount off market price.  It will also be in
an advantageous position, by virtue of its downstream distribution system, to contract for large volumes on a
long-term basis and should be able to obtain some price
consideration in return.  Moreover, the price it pays may
also reflect to some extent the loss of equity rights.  With
the loss of equity rights by the concession holder, however,
the price the former concessionaire would pay under contract
terms would be a single one (perhaps with some discount off
the market price), rather than a combination of equity any
buyback prices.  This single contract price probably will
not provide the same margin of profit as most companies
presently enjoy under standard 40-60 participation terms.
Another difference will be that sales to third parties are
likely to accrue increasingly to the producing country's
natural oil company.

    The end of preferential supply arrangements in
favor of certain major petroleum companies (such as Exxon,
Mobil, Texaco, Shell, Gulf, and British Petroleum in OPEC
nations.

        The end of all preferential supply arrangements
in favor of major petroleum companies would mean that the
majors would cease to have an established position in any
one or more producing countries and would have to compete
for the oil with all other buyers.  This would probably
be the case only at some point in the future when the producing countries have rid themselves of the need for the

companies' technical assistance, even on a contractural
basis, have satisfied or disposed of any claims relating
to previous equity rights, and have minimized the difficulties of disposing of their oil.  Even in such a case, the
major international oil companies would still enjoy the
advantages afforded by their worldwide marketing and transportation networks and would, therefore, be in a strong
position to acquire the oil on a competitive basis.  In
neither case (1) nor (2) would there likely be strong competition among crude oil selling nations sufficient to bring
about a marked reduction in prices.

     In general, the end of the primary role in
global petroleum distribution played by such major petroleum companies.

          The end of the major companies' primary role
in global petroleum distribution is a hypothetical situation
that would result from the loss of the marketing and transportation advantages mentioned above under (2).  Presumably,
their position would then be comparable to the present
position of the larger U. S. independent oil companies or
the various medium-sized European private and national oil
companies.  The oil industry would then be split into two
groups:  1) the producing countries' national oil companies,
which would have a near monopoly on production and, in addition, have acquired some share of the refining and distribution market; and 2) a number of medium and smaller
companies, both public and private, specializing in refining
and marketing, with some producing facilities in the consuming countries or in non-OPEC countries.  The worldwide
system would presumably be characterized by the absence of
highly integrated systems handling large volumes of oil in
favor of a multiplicity of smaller companies, with a consequent increase in the number of intermediaries between the
producer and the ultimate consumer, and hence an increase
in the cost of doing business with resulting increases in
commodity prices.  It would also be characterized by a considerable loss of flexibility and efficiency.  The producing
countries' share of the world industry would have increased
to the point that they would own not only the major producing operations but also some part of the distribution systems
in the consuming countries as well.  Their resulting bargaining leverage and control over prices would, therefore, most

likely be greater than what it is at present. Under circumstances of a wartime embargo, their leverage would be far greater than it was in the fall of 1973.

The problem of supply under any of the scenarios suggested by this question is, however, less one of short-term interruptions than of the inhibition over the long term of the development of future supplies. The international oil companies would lack the monetary incentive to continue doing this in the absence of an equity profit or its equivalent, and the producing countries' national oil companies would probably be too narrowly-based to take over that function on a worldwide basis. Thus, there would be a real danger of a fall-off in the rate of discovery of new reserves and, hence, of a major crisis in supply.

D. (We note that this question is limited to supply and does not encompass costs. Our reply includes what we believe would be consequences to world petroleum supply and costs, since one cannot be separated from the other.)

Subquestions (1), (2) and (3) are really degrees of the same thing, i.e. loss of the international oil companies' historical and current role in world-wide petroleum distribution. Also, we consider that "distribution" includes not just moving crude oil from producing to refining centers, but also the ultimate distribution of the required products to all levels of trade.

Subquestion (1). The end of equity oil to the companies would cause a world-wide increase in the price of crude and products. For example, using rounded figures for illustration only:

During the first half of 1974, the cost of equity and buyback oil was approximately $7 and $11 respectively. On this basis, if participation had stabilized at 60% to the producing countries, 40% to the companies, the average cost to the companies with foreign production would have been 40% x $7 plus 60% x $11 = $9.40 per barrel. On this same basis, 100% producing country participation (i.e., no equity crude) would have raised the companies' average cost to $11, or an increase of $1.60 which would ultimately have to be recovered in the marketplace if the companies are to stay in business.

However, the recent increases in tax and royalty
rates by the producing countries have increased significantly the cost of equity oil from about $7 to
roughly $10. A small reduction in buyback price, which
is currently about $10.70 results in a current average
cost (still assuming 60%/40% participation) of about
$10.40 per barrel. In the present situation 100%
participation by the producing country (no equity oil)
would raise the cost of crude to about $10.70, or an
increase of about $0.30 per barrel. While not so great
as the previously illustrated effect of $1.60 per
barrel, this still represents a significant increase
in costs which would have to be recovered in the
marketplace.

From a supply standpoint the immediate short-term
effects from the loss of equity oil would probably be indirect
and diluted so long as existing contracts, including cost recovery, remain in force. The companies' ships, terminals,
refineries, etc. would still be available to physically get
products to consumers. Longer term, as existing contracts
expire, the supply consequences are an entirely different
matter. The overriding questions are how much of the increased cost can be recovered and how these costs are distributed. If the costs cannot be recovered, individual
companies, whether large or small, cannot stay in business.
The question of who decides how revenues should be split
among companies, producing countries and consuming countries
hopefully will lead to compromises acceptable to all involved. Also, to the extent that access to equity crude
is an incentive for risk-taking, elimination of this incentive would dampen the enthusiasm of the industry for risk-
taking, thereby reducing petroleum supply.

Subquestion (2). The term "preferential supply
arrangements" improperly implies that a favored position is
given to the companies with producing operations in the OPEC
countries. What these companies have in effect is the contractual right to buy specified quantities of the governments' participation oil. These rights represent a modification of exclusive rights to production under the original
concession agreements and were effected under the takeover
by the OPEC nations.

In a supply-short situation, which is likely to prevail under these circumstances, this first right to produced oil not lifted by the governments enables the companies involved in foreign producing operations to meet their existing downstream commitments, most of which are long term. If the non-equity (or buyback) crude was not available to the companies, the only alternative would be for the OPEC countries to sell it to all takers for whatever price the market would bear just as they do with their own "participation" crude (which constitutes a very large and increasing volume). The net effect would certainly be an increase in world-wide crude costs to majors and non-majors alike, as well as to those consuming country governments who have bilateral deals with the producing countries. Experience has shown that the producing countries often consider the highest price obtained from any single bidder, no matter how small the volume, is applicable to all sales, and may even be retroactive. The effect on world-wide supply would be very disruptive within a short period of time.

The major companies have made huge investments in producing, transportation, refining and distributive facilities worldwide, all of which were made with the expectation of reasonable profits from foreign producing operations. If these companies do not have assured access to sufficient crude to utilize these facilities efficiently and economically, who will perform these necessary functions? It is unlikely that smaller companies would be willing to assume the risks involved or could generate the enormous amounts of capital required. Consuming government subsidies would surely be required, with a predictable increase in the real cost of oil products. Even then, stability of supply and price would be very tenuous indeed. The producing countries are not apt to commit their crude for more than a year at a time, with continuation dependent upon the political "good behavior" of each consuming country government. This would hardly be a climate which would encourage newcomers to make long-term investments in tankers, refineries and the like. However, if such a policy were adopted to subsidize new-comers, duplication of facilities would surely result, and this would be a shameful waste of resources.

Subquestion (3). Elimination of the major petroleum companies' present role in world-wide oil distribution

would result in chaos and in the long term could influence
them to cut back on exploration, new refinery construction,
etc.  The cost of oil would certainly increase.  The proven
ability of the private oil companies, especially the international majors, to acquire and maintain access to indispensable foreign energy source through all but the most severe
political crises is well established.  Additionally, the international majors have the indispensable operational flexibility
that results from diverse sources of supply, efficient
tanker fleets, and widespread refining and marketing operations in many different countries.  The problems of matching
available supply of crudes with a multitude of different
product demand patterns in different countries are enormously
complex.  Without the flexibility currently provided by
these major companies in the areas of planning, transportation, crude substitution and exchanges, swings in demand
or production, etc., efficient supply logistics would be
virtually impossible.

        Elimination of the international major companies'
present role, based on commercial interest, would inevitably lead to government-to-government arrangements.  It is
conceptually possible to visualize each consuming country
being solely responsible for its own movements and needs,
but the cost of such a system would quickly be seen to be
unacceptably high while at the same time it would be in-
tolerably rigid and vulnerable to external events.  Implementation would require resolution of exceedingly complex
problems from the acquisition of crude to the ultimate
distribution and sales of products to the public.  Security
of supply and price stability would virtually disappear (as
discussed under Subquestion (2) above).  The companies and
the consuming countries would be faced with a dilemma --
on one hand requiring increasing energy to fuel growing
economies while on the other the hazards of making new
shipping, refining and marketing investments due to in-
security of supply.  The developing countries would be
especially hard hit since they would not be able to compete
with the industrialized countries in the bidding for available oil supplies.

        On this general subject, we believe some additional
comments are appropriate.

During and after the recent embargo and cutbacks, many bilateral government-to-government oil deals have been proposed by importing countries as preferable to continued reliance on the international companies for oil supplies. The motive, of course, is presumably security of supply and such deals usually involve exchange of specified quantities of oil for manufactured goods (and to a lesser extent services). The dangers of such bilateral deals are many and varied. For example, a portion of the importing country's oil trade is tied to one exporting country on the assumption that the latter will honor its obligation in all circumstances, and that the oil-importing country will be able to always deliver the specified goods on time. Valuation of the oil vs. the goods over an extended period to preserve the "fairness" of the original deal would be a very difficult problem (as it is in any barter arrangement). Bilateral deals would severely limit the diplomatic freedom of the importing government and as previously discussed could not be counted on to increase security of supplies or fairness of oil price. The international oil companies could not prevent the producing countries from restricting production, but neither would government-to-government deals, since it was against governments that the recent embargoes and cutbacks were directed. Also, so long as importing governments continue to press for bilateral agreements, the producing countries will have no incentive whatever to lower oil prices from their current unreasonably high levels, which are now approximately four times what they were in September, 1973. If oil supply is handled on a government-to-government basis, commercial problems will inevitably become political problems.

Experience has shown that private oil companies tend to insulate the oil business from day-to-day political problems. Aramco, an American company, continued to operate effectively in Saudi Arabia during the embargo even though the Arab's "oil weapon" was aimed primarily at the United States. Other examples of countries where the U.S.-based international oil companies were able to continue commercial operations when our government was not permitted to conduct a political policy are Libya (from 1970 to 1973), Indonesia (under Sukharno), Egypt and Iraq (after the 1967 war).

We believe the case for strengthening rather than weakening the U.S.-based international oil companies is very

strong and in the best interests of the United States and
our allies.

14.   What would be your company's attitude toward a system
or agreement whereby the various petroleum consuming nations
agreed to immediately establish mandatory stored petroleum
reserves and to share petroleum supplies and, in addition,
reduce consumption in the event of an embargo imposed by
petroleum exporting countries or a petroleum shortage caused
by any other reason?  To what extent do you believe your
company would be willing and able to cooperate in such
agreement by, for example, selling petroleum products to
designated countries, in designated quantities and at a
designated price.

Response:

        The responses to this question were almost evenly
distributed between a negative and a positive attitude with
respect to establishing mandatory stored petroleum reserves.
Many of the companies that rejected the idea did so on the
basis of the impracticality and rigidity of the scheme as
well as the high cost to the consumer.  The companies that
agreed with the idea did so because it could possibly break
the OPEC cartel but most insisted on the protection of
private enterprise and a guarantee of profit or the ability
to sell the product at the market price.  Also several companies expressed a desire that the burden imposed by such a
program should be shared equitably by all parties involved.
A majority of the companies replied that they would cooperate,
particularly if it involved the issuance of government regulations.

SELECTED COMMENTS:

     A.  In order to combat the OPEC cartel, we strongly
favor cooperation among the various petroleum consumer
nations, including establishing mandatory stored petroleum
reserves, sharing supplies and reducing consumption.  Since
all the oil we produce is consumed within the country produced, we are not in a position to sell oil in the export
market.

B.  Our attitude would be that the American taxpayer
and consumer would be hurt -- we carry too much of the world's
burdens as it is.  We would only "give up" value in such an
event.  Cost of crude oil storage would be extremely high.
Excess producing capacity is the only feasible answer --
brought about by truly excessive controlled prices --
artifically stimulating supply and curtailing demand.  At
this time our company would be virtually powerless to influence the destination of its oil.

C.  We believe that OPEC power would be reduced considerably if the major oil consuming nations could work out
a program to store, share and ration petroleum in the event
of an embargo.  Our company as well as all petroleum companies are likely to be willing and able to cooperate under
such agreements if the burden imposed by such a program
could be shared equitably by all the parties involved and
incurred costs are allowed to be flowed through to price.
However, we do not believe that a large mandatory stored
petroleum reserve constitutes a practical solution to an
embargo.  The extremely high cost of the storage and of
carrying the inventory would prohibit storing sufficient
petroleum to constitute a meaningful supply.  The only
effective course in the event of embargo is reduction in
consumption.  The United States will be more self-sufficient
than most of the other large consumer countries so we would
have more to lose than gain in a sharing program.  Nevertheless, some plan for sharing supplies is probably in order
due to the interdependence of the economies of the large
petroleum consuming nations.

D.  Regarding the first question [a], we would support
the principle of establishing petroleum reserves in consuming countries, and it should be relatively easy to obtain
agreements by the countries on this overall objective,
especially those who rely heavily on imports.  There is
really no alternative in the near term to protect against
unexpected or politically motivated supply disruptions.

However, implementing and administering an agreement to share supplies on a mandatory basis is another matter.
To make such a system work it would have to be uniformly and
fairly applied, without favoritism to any country or to any
specific segment of the industry.  The problem is getting

agreement on what is fair. Diverse national interests would
be almost insurmountable when the crunch came. This was
painfully evident during the recent embargo by the Arab
states. Self-interest will inevitably prevail when the
supply shortage becomes severe enough. Also, the differences
in the situations of the various consumer countries are too
large to facilitate agreement to any mandatory sharing plan.
There are a few countries, like the United States, with high
consumption and relatively high domestic production. There
are many more like the majority of those in western Europe
and Japan with high consumption and relatively little or no
domestic production. Finally, there are the countries in
the most difficult situation of all, such as the developing
countries, with shaky economies and no significant indigenous
energy. The problems in obtaining an effective international
agreement for mandatory sharing are very formidable. To a
degree, each nation would be giving up some of its sovereignty
to some international body. It is likely that internal pressures within consuming countries would prevail during significant shortages and such supply-sharing agreements could
not be fully executed even if they could be negotiated. The
recent problems with the French concerning the U.S.-sponsored
meetings of consumer nations illustrates the difficulty.

Mandatory reductions in consumption via artificial
limits would also be very difficult. Who would set and
measure these reductions? Would the same percentage reduction apply to the developed and underdeveloped countries?
For the industrialized nations, it would be better to let
prices find their proper level in a free market. Recent
events have demonstrated that the oil market is more elastic
than it was thought to be, at least in developed countries.
Since the price increases, consumption has been significantly
below what was expected. On the other hand, some underdeveloped countries have a "base load" demand which could
hardly be reduced. A consumption limit on them would be a
terrible and possibly unmanageable burden.

The costs for the additional storage facilities
and the other effects of building up mandatory stock must
be considered. This requires an enormous investment most
of which will go into inventory. Recent studies by the
National Petroleum Council indicate that for the United

States only, increasing emergency standby supplies by 500 million barrels would cost in the order of 6 to 9 billion dollars for facilities and inventory. Also in a supply-short or balanced situation the material to be stockpiled would have to be made available by under-supplying normal demands for a fairly extended period.

Another important aspect of any collective agreement among consuming countries deserves mention. Aside from the practical difficulties of establishing a multinational program, it should be recognized that this approach could be self-defeating, to some extent at least. In the event of an embargo by one or more of the producing countries, a cooperative storage program with reciprocal drawing rights could subject all members of the cooperative group to embargo even if only one or two were regarded by the embargoing country as "unfriendly." To the degree this occurs, a multinational cooperative storage and sharing arrangement would aggravate rather than alleviate an embargo-caused shortage for the consuming group as a whole. Further, the OPEC countries may decide to discriminate price-wise among consuming countries.

Also, for the next several years at least, given the dependence of the consuming countries (including the United States) on imported petroleum supplies, the major exporting countries have it within their power to seriously hamper a stockpiling effort, without imposing an embargo, simply by further increasing prices and/or curtailing production. Whether they would take such measures depends largely on the extent to which they regard the proposed reserve pool as a threat to the effectiveness of their "oil weapon." Assuming the material to be stockpiled would have to be withheld from normal supplies to consumers in any event, the implications for the United States and our allies of further price increases or production curtailment by the exporting countries warrants serious consideration. If national policy considerations dictate establishment of a mandatory storage program, we believe an independent U.S. program - at least initially - would be the preferred route. Cooperative arrangements with other nations having or desiring to establish similar programs should be attempted as the next step, but the difficulties inherent in establishing a multinational program at the outset seem to us so formidable that we question whether such a program could be negotiated and implemented within a reasonable period.

Regarding the second question [b], our company would, of course, cooperate fully in any regulations that our government may issue, up to our ability to do so without unfair economic harm. The difficulties of allocating products to individual countries are discussed above. The problem of supplying these products at "a designated price" poses an entirely different problem. Who is going to pay the cost of this desirable program for sharing supplies during unexpected cutbacks or embargoes? The industry cannot pay for it unless these costs are recovered in the marketplace or through government subsidy. If the government pays the costs, taxes will rise and/or other programs will have to be curtailed. Someone has to pay these costs; we can't "have our cake and eat it too." Further, these costs must be realistically assessed against the likely benefits. We assume that such a program would be set up to ensure that all companies and segments within the industry would be treated equitably -- but this also will require very careful and knowledgeable consideration of the many and complex factors involved. We sincerely believe that a workable program could not and should not be set up by governments alone. It would take the combined and extensive efforts of the most capable people in the oil industry.

As a matter of interest, several consuming countries in which our affiliates operate already have independent reserve storage programs in which our affiliates participate.

E. Our company already cooperates with nations which have established mandatory petroleum reserves. During the recent oil supply crisis caused by OPEC embargoes in the fourth quarter of 1973 and first quarter of 1974, our company effected an equitable distribution of available petroleum supplies throughout our worldwide system of minimized shortages in any one area. Our response to a mandatory program is that we would, of course, comply, but would expect that the additional economic burden created by such a program would be recognized by the governmental agency. During the recent crisis our company did comply with official requests to supply various petroleum products to designated countries and in designated quantities and would see no difficulty with doing so in any future crisis. However, we would expect to sell products at a market price and not a price designated by regulations.

F.  It is assumed that the petroleum reserves referred to in this question are physical reserves of petroleum that have been produced and that they are not in-place reserves awaiting production.

In the opinion of the management of this company the only consuming nations, either in a comparable or potentially comparable position to the United States, where there is a possibility of both mutuality of contribution and benefit, are Canada, Great Britain and Norway. We believe that the remaining consuming nations for the large part either have such a disparity of supply that (i) there is no potential benefit and much detriment to the United States in participating in such program; (ii) they are financially unable to carry out the program unless financed by the United States; or (iii) that physical problems related to storage of the quantity of oil that would be involved would be a substantial deterrent to the program. Insofar as actually consummating an arrangement of the broad scope that appears to be contemplated by the question, we think that it has no more chance of success than programs that have been designed in the past to meet the even more urgent need of food redistribution.

To have any chance of success, we believe that a program of sharing of supply in time of need should be directed initially to obtaining an agreement with one other country which is believed to be similarly situated, for example, Canada. If this could be accomplished, we believe that it would then be worthwhile to endeavor to expand the group.

We do not believe that it is realistic to seek cooperation of private capital, free enterprise companies on a voluntary basis in a sharing program. If there is to be a sharing program, the cost of such a program should be borne by the citizens of the country as a whole through increased taxes or other levies. We believe it unfair to segregate or discriminate against investors in petroleum companies and force them to bear the entire financial burden of any such sharing program.

G.  Stored petroleum reserves, to be useful, must be
readily accessible.  This suggests the creation of additional
stored reserves close to major consumption centers rather
than shut-in production reserves in less accessible locations.
a desirable mechanism for creating stored petroleum reserves
would be a federal requirement for an assured emergency supply
for each domestic refiner, in proportion to that refiners runs
of imported petroleum.  This would enable the stored reserves
to be technically consistent with the input needs and logistical system associated with each refinery.

    The establishment of stored petroleum reserves and
the related logistics systems in sufficient quantities to
offset a prolonged embargo would involve very high costs.
Since these reserves are intended to supply consumers in
emergency situations, the incremental cost of establishing
and storing reserves should be passed through to petroleum
product consumers by a tax that ensures the equitable distribution of costs.  By having the ultimate user bear the
incremental cost of emergency reserves, some of these costs
might be passed back to the petroleum exporting countries
to the extent the market is influenced by price elasticities,
reducing demand and adding pressure for producing country
price cuts.  Further, the consumption reduction could somewhat
ease the supply protection level needed by the U.S. and the
associated costs.

    An agreement to share petroleum supplies among
consuming nations would be of particular interest to the
United States because of the likelihood of an oil embargo
directed solely against the United States.  The United States
has already indicated a willingness to include production
sharing, which is of interest to consuming nations without
significant crude production, as a quid pro quo for the
sharing of imports by other nations.  The cooperative establishment of stored reserves should be undertaken by each
nation in relation to its own needs, so that each party
bears its own costs.  Shared supplies would be provided out
of production and/or imports.

    To be effective, any oil sharing agreements among
consuming nations must also establish equitable and measurable
programs for the conservation of energy and reduction of

petroleum demand by all participants.  Otherwise the risk
is that those nations most conscientious in reducing demand
would, in effect, subsidize those nations that do not or
will not promote energy conservation, since non-conserving
nations would gain supply protection as well as any price-
reducing benefits of lower worldwide consumption.

Our company will obey all lawful orders and directives of the United States government, although the ability
of this Company to respond to directives to sell petroleum
products at designated places could be impractical or impossible due to lack of facilities.  If an emergency required
product or crude allocation, we do not believe such a program
should include price controls since they reduce the economic
incentive for pre-crisis expenditures on supply protection.

15.  Give your opinion as to the effect which specific U.S.
Government environmental regulations have had upon the
supply and price of petroleum products within the U.S.
Whenever possible, cite relevant environmental regulations
and quantify their supply and price effects.

Response:

All of the petroleum company responses indicate
that U.S. Government environmental regulations have resulted
in increased expenditures that, like all other costs, are
passed on to the consumer.  Environmental regulations have
also decreased the domestic supply of petroleum with the
delay of the Alaskan pipeline, and slowed rate of offshore
drilling.  Simultaneously, the demand for petroleum has
increased with the implementation of automobile antipollution
devices that have reduced gasoline mileage efficiency, the
conversion from coal to oil by thermal power plants and the
decrease in refinery construction.  Several of the oil
companies cited The National Environmental Policy Act and the
Environmental Protection Agency as well as other governmental
regulations as being responsible for unnecessary delays.

SELECTED COMMENTS:

A.  The U.S.G.S. environmental regulations, in the case
of older Louisiana OCS operations, are particularly onerous
and expensive.  For example, we have an offshore platform,
which was built in 1951 and which has produced for 23 years

without pollution problems. Now, that it is reaching the end of its economic-life, we find the life being shortened because of the expense of complying with the environmental regulations. By the same token the recent Spill Prevention Control and Countermeasure Plans that must be implemented by January 10, 1975, probably will be too expensive for some of our stripper production, again causing premature abandonment.

B. (1) Many well-meaning anti-polution efforts contribute very little to reducing polution, while substantially increasing costs and operational problems. In some cases, loss of production and reserves has occurred.

(2) OSHA regulations require capital expenditures which can result in abandonment of operations. They can be unreasonable. The costs caused by these frequently arbitrary requirements will just have to be passed on to the consumer eventually.

(3) Strip coal mining operations have been greatly hampered by environmental restrictions. These must be relaxed or the costs will be excessive. Sometimes reclamation costs are many times the value of the land surface.

C. Effect of specific environmental regulations on the supply and price of petroleum products.

Clean Air Act Amendments of 1970

Title 1 - State Implementation Plans

Compliance with SO2 and particulate regulations created an increased demand for natural gas and low sulfur liquid fuels and a corresponding decrease in the use of coal.

To meet the increased demand for low-sulfur liquid fuels the supply either had to come from naturally occurring low-sulfur stocks or from desulfurized finished products, both of which demanded a premium price.

The East Coast utilities became dependent on imported residual fuel which remained in fairly good supply in areas where regulations stayed at the 1% (or higher) sulfur level.

In areas requiring 0.3 to 0.5% sulfur material the supply was tighter and prices higher. To meet these very low sulfur levels, refiners were blending distillate (home heating) oils into resid fuel. This had some negative effect on the supply of home heating oil and was eventually banned by FEO Regulation 2.

In general, nearly all air pollution control devices needed to comply with the 1970 Act require some form of energy to operate, thus this energy usage reduces the overall pool available to the nation. Examples are:

Flue gas desulfurization systems require 3-6% of the power plant's output to operate the system;

Cooling towers, used to eliminate thermal discharges from power plants, require 1% of the plant's power supply;

Fume afterburners must operate on natural gas.

Certain transportation control plans directionally reduce vehicle miles travelled and hence help to alleviate a tight supply situation. The use of retrofit devices could, however, increase fuel usage through inefficiency.

### Title II - Vehicle Emissions

In order to meet statutory CO, HC and $NO_x$ standards the private automobile has shown a 10-13% decrease in economy for the years 1970-1974.

The use of catalysts will allow more efficient engine designs during 1975-76 and, will result in a regaining of some fuel economy.

If statutory $NO_x$ standards are implemented in 1978-79 we can expect another drop in fuel economy.

The use of catalysts has also created the need for unleaded fuel which requires about 0.5% more energy to produce than conventional leaded fuel.

The lead phase-down schedule will also require an undetermined amount of additional energy to produce complying fuel.

## The Energy & Environmental Coordination Act of 1974

This Act was supposed to bring relief to those regions which were faced with tight timetables and the unavailability of complying fuels due to strict enforcement of State Implementation Plan regulations. Some suspension of regulations and the use of interim controls will be allowed providing primary air standards are met, so that generally available high sulfur fuels (primarily coal) can be utilized. Oil to coal conversions can be applied for or ordered, but it turns out that only a limited number of power plants will be considered environmentally acceptable for conversion. For all practical purposes, this Act appears to fall short of granting sufficient time for compliance after control technology is demonstrated and thus continues to put a strain on the supply of low sulfur fuels. In addition, the mechanism by which FEA can order conversion to coal, with EPA concurrence, but over state objections is not entirely clear.

## The National Environmental Policy Act (NEPA)

Has delayed nearly all energy related projects including:

Alaska pipeline (2-3 million bbls. per day)

Nuclear power plants

Coal and shale development on federal lands

## State NEPA's and Coastal Zoning Regulations

Contributed to delays or discontinuance of projects that would have helped the nation's supply picture such as:

drilling in Santa Barbara

Delaware, Maryland & Maine refinery construction

Geothermal development (CA-SEQA)

These types of regulations along with additional
land use regulations will make it more difficult to site
energy facilities and hence perpetuate the energy-environmental
dilemma.

## Environmental Costs

Figure 3 from API Publication No. 4176 shows that
total environmental expenditures on a cents/barrel of crude
processed were about 34¢/bbl. in 1972. More recent figures
for 1973-74 are not yet available from API.

The financial impact of pollution control regulations
on the petroleum industry falls primarily into four categories:

1) unleaded fuel requirements for catalytically-
equipped post-1975 automobiles;

2) desulfurization of fuel oils for usage in
non-petroleum industry stationary sources;

3) stationary source air pollution control;

4) water pollution control.

[We estimate] the total capital requirements from now
until 1985 from these categories may be as high as $23 billion,
$2.5 billion for unleaded fuel manufacture, $6.0 billion for
water pollution control based on the national goal of elimination of discharge of pollutants, $1.4 billion from stationary
source air pollution control, and $13 billion for desulfuriza-
tion. In return for this huge expenditure, it is expected
that 90 to 95% control of pollution in these categories will
be achieved.

On a yearly capital outlay of $2.3 billion, the
total yearly environmental expenditure would be estimated at
$3.9 billion, assuming the same basis for operating, maintenance,
administrative and R&D costs as used in API Publication 4176.
This total expenditure would amount of 53¢/barrel of crude
processed in 1980.

Specific environmental costs for low sulfur residual fuel range from $1.25 to $2.00/barrel of fuel; and, for
unleaded, low sulfur (100 PPM) gasoline 1¢ to 3¢/gallon,
depending on octane level requirements.

FIGURE 1

Environmental Expenditures per
Barrel of Crude Processed Annually

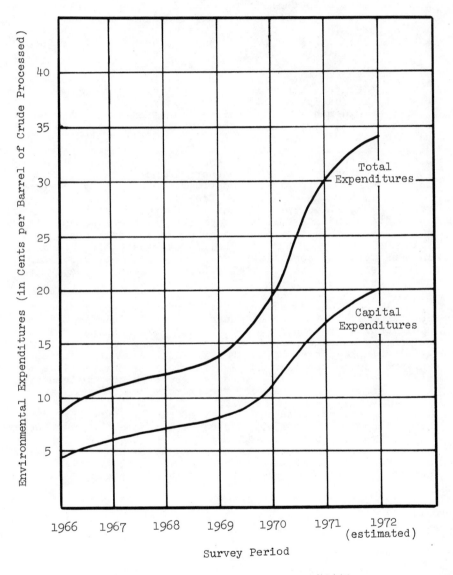

We cannot preduct how much of the added environmental costs will be passed on to the consumer as increased prices.

D. Environmental constraints and considerations have had major effects on petroleum supply and demand. If prices had not been frozen, environmental effects also would have resulted in increases in oil and product prices. Environmental costs have not been fully reflected as yet. We do not have information with which to quantify the effects of specific regulations.

Conversions from coal to oil by thermal power plants to meet air quality standards have caused most of the massive increase in demand for fuel oil encountered during the past few years. In addition, demand for distillate fuel by utilities has increased from an insignificant amount in 1967 to about 200,000 barrels per day in 1973. This resulted from increased use of gas-turbine generating equipment, originally intended for "peak-shaving", while new thermal and nuclear capacity is delayed by environmental considerations, and by blending of distillate with high sulfur fuel oil to reduce sulfur content. Also, a lack of coordination between Federal standards and state standards further complicated matters. Many states moved to adopt highly rigorous standards more quickly than the ability of the industry to make requisite changes in manufacturing specifications. In some cases, state air quality standards substantially exceeded federally approved standards.

Automotive emission standards have been met through engine modifications which reduce engine efficiency. These modifications together with the lower compression ratios required for consumption of unleaded gasoline appear to increase gasoline consumption by about 12%. Although catalytic converters to be installed in 1975 automobiles may permit a portion of lost efficiency to be recouped, use of higher priced unleaded gasoline is mandatory for these cars.

Regarding supply, delay of the Alaskan pipeline by environmental roadblocks acted to increase U.S. dependency on foreign oil at a critical time. It seems likely that without these roadblocks the pipeline would have begun delivering a substantial amount of oil by mid-1973. The U.S. was the primary target of the Arab oil embargo and access to Alaskan crude oil would have reduced the effectiveness of the embargo. Also, environmental considerations slowed the rate of offshore lease sales for several years, restricted further development in much of the Santa Barbara Channel and stopped all activity in 35 Channel leases. With a lead time of at least four years to attain significant production from an offshore lease, the effect on domestic supply of these actions will be encountered in the late 1970's.

E.  The Clean Air Act Amendments of 1970.

These statutes resulted in a number of regulations promulgated by the Environmental Protection Agency, which in several cases have had an adverse effect on the supply and prices of petroleum products. Of particular importance are the Vehicle Emission Regulations and the Fossil Fuel Sulfur Regulations.

The Vehicle Emission Regulations set very restrictive standards for 1975-76. When it became apparent that these standards could not be met in the designated time period, an extension of two years was granted by the EPA and Congress. It is estimated that emission control devices on vehicles will increase U.S. crude oil demand by 450,000 barrels a day by 1975 over that required for uncontrolled 1968 cars. This penalty will be further increased as 1975 and later model cars displace the uncontrolled cars now on the road.

The production of unleaded gasoline required by law starting July 1, 1974, and the required step-wise reduction of lead in regular and premium grades starting in 1975 will further increase the demand for crude oil. This is because the production of unleaded fuel results in less gasoline yield per barrel of crude.

While the requirement for the marketing of an unleaded gasoline is now a fait accompli, the lead phase-down for the remainder of the gasoline supply will occur during the period 1975-79. The phase-down regulation will do very little for clean air, but it will have an immediate and pronounced additional interim effect on the supply and cost of petroleum products. As required by regulation, lead in the total refinery gasoline pool must be reduced to 0.5 gram a gallon by 1979.

In our case, by the time we have achieved a lead-free gasoline regime, the yield of motor fuel will have decreased by 8.6 per cent over 1974 conditions. The decrease in yield could be even worse if our assumed 92 Research Octane Number fails to satisfy the cars on the road in the 1980's. In any case, the result will be more expensive gasoline.

In addition to the gasoline yield losses engendered by the lead regulations, the demands on capital must eventually be reflected in higher gasoline prices. We have committed $47 million to cover the costs of manufacturing, distributing, and marketing of unleaded gasoline. Additionally, we will have to invest $115 million (1974 dollars) between now and 1980 to upgrade the octane number of our gasoline pool to recover the quality lost by the curtailment of lead usage.

The effect on fuel oil supplies and price of the clean air regulations with respect to sulfur content is well known. It is now being suggested in regulatory circles that the sulfur content of unleaded gasoline should be reduced from the present average of about 0.03 per cent to 0.01 per cent or less. If such a requirement should materialize, new and severe catalytic hydrodesulfurization processes would have to be installed with a consequent loss in gasoline yield. Furthermore, additional reforming with additional loss in yield would be required to recover the octane numbers lost in the desulfurization operation. We estimate that the loss in gasoline yield, over and above the loss from lead reduction, would be 2.5 per cent. The capital required to reduce the sulfur content of unleaded gasoline in our U.S. refineries (404,000 B/D of crude oil) is estimated at $120 million (1974 dollars). Thus, each new regulation results in less fuel at higher prices to the consumer.

As required by the 1970 Clean Air Act, the Environmental Protection Agency established ambient air standards for sulfur dioxide as well as other air pollutants. These standards effectively eliminated high-sulfur fuel oil and coal as fuels for industrial and electric generating plants, especially in metropolitan areas. The resulting switch to environmentally acceptable fuels,

natural gas, propane and low-sulfur fuel oils, exerted
a demand pressure which was only partially relieved by higher
prices. We estimate that in 1975 the incremental demand for
petroleum will amount to 935,000 barrels a day to take care
of replacement of coal by oil and the delay in nuclear plant
construction.

## The National Environmental Policy Act of 1969

The provisions of NEPA have often been used as a
means of harassment and delay of projects designed to increase
the supply of petroleum products. In general, the legal
approach used to thwart energy projects is to challenge the
adequacy of environmental impact statements after approval
by appropriate government agencies. Another delaying tactic
is to attack fuel projects on the basis of the "non-
degradation doctrine" which has been upheld by the Supreme
Court as a principle of the Clean Air Act. Following are
examples of successful court actions that have contributed
to the shortage and increased cost of energy:

- The Alaskan pipeline
- Siting and construction of nuclear power plants
- Leasing of Outer Continental Shelf drilling sites
- Siting of coal-fired generating plants.

## The Water Pollution Control Act of 1972

The Water Pollution Control Act of 1972 has
spawned a number of regulations and proposed regulations
that will adversely affect the supply and increase the
cost of petroleum products. Cases in point are the guidelines for water treating in refineries: 1977 - the best
practical control technology currently available, and
1983 - the best available technology economically achievable. Estimated costs for meeting the 1977 and 1983
requirements along with the 1985 goal of "zero discharge"
for existing and new refineries are:

|                                          | 1977  | 1983  | 1985  |
|------------------------------------------|-------|-------|-------|
| Investment Cost, billion $               | 1.832 | 3.394 | 4.841 |
| Contribution to product cost, ¢/bbl      | 7.1   | 12.8  | 17.7  |

## Proposed Toxic Pollutant Effluent Standards

Proposed effluent regulations have been issued for the first list of toxic substances as authorized by the Water Pollution Control Act of 1972. Toxic substances applicable to waste water discharge in the petroleum industry involve mercury, cadmium, and cyanide. The proposed regulations are so restrictive that they would exclude any discharge of these substances into a stream with a 10-year low-flow of 10 cubic feet per second or less. Technology for meeting these standards is non-existent, hence it is not possible to quantify what appears to be a very serious financial problem to U.S. refineries. The "zero discharge" goal could well result in closing some refining operations.

F. A recent issue of the Conference Board Record discussed the results of a survey of industrial pollution control expenditures among manufacturing industries. The report stated in part ". . . the petroleum companies continue to report the largest outlays of funds for capital and operating purposes in pollution control, both as a total industry and on a per-company basis. In the latter case the mean capital expenditure per company in the petroleum industry was $32.4 million in 1973 and is estimated to be $43.9 million in the current year." The report further showed that annual operating expenditures for pollution control in the petroleum industry totaled $184.8 million in 1972 and $209.6 million in 1973. Total capital expenditures for pollution control in the petroleum industry were $272 million in 1972, $421.4 million in 1973, and are anticipated to total $483.6 million in 1974.

Obviously, expenditures in any industry that approach three-quarters of a billion dollars a year are bound to have an effect on the cash flow generated from the products that are produced, manufactured, and marketed by that industry. The petroleum industry is no exception and the monies devoted to environmental control throughout the industry prior to, during and after the energy supply gap of 1973 did little for the country's energy needs.

Environmental regulations are not all bad nor all good. Every company in every industry has a responsibility to not endanger the health of the public. However, when

inconsistent regulations are promulgated by a whole host of
bureaus, offices, commissions and agencies at every level
of government, the result is to overkill with frequently conflicting and irrational regulations.  The expense in time,
effectiveness and money occasioned by this massive conflicting bureaucracy cannot be measured.  Every environmental
regulation should be made to withstand the test of the end
result being worth the price of obtaining the end result,
particularly in areas where esthetic taste, as contrasted
with health, are concerned.  Maybe the result will be worth
the price, but all should be made aware of what to expect
and what impact will take place in other areas of concern
such as our nation's energy supply position.

Lead-free gasoline, moratoriums on offshore
leases, delay of the Alaska pipeline, superport bans, and
zoning restrictions against refinery construction are all
examples of environmental regulations impacting on the
petroleum industry.  A specific example of how conflicting
environmental regulations can materially affect the industry can be found at one of our refineries on the East
Coast where the Clean Air Act and a regulation published
by the then Energy Policy Office are in conflict.

The State in which the refinery is located had
approved by the EPA an implementation plan for attainment
and maintenance of national ambient air quality standards
that required the use of 1.0% sulfur fuel in power generators.  The refinery was burning 3.5% sulfur fuel and was
meeting, per readings at air monitoring stations, the required air quality standards.  Also, Energy Policy Office
Regulation No. 2, dated December 7, 1973, required that no
petroleum product having a lower specified sulfur content
by weight than was in use one month prior to the effective
date of the regulation could be used in a power generator.
Based on the EPO regulation, a variance was requested from
the state to continue burning 3.5% sulfur.

No response to the variance request was made by the
state for ten months, when recently the request was denied
and virtually immediate compliance with the 1.0% sulfur fuel
limitation was demanded.  The state had not coordinated with
the FEA their denial of the variance and the refinery was
caught between two governmental bodies with the problem of
which authority to follow.

The cost to the refinery for moving from 3.5% to 1.0% sulfur fuel is estimated at $33,000 per day, a significant sum. In addition, coke now manufactured by the refinery as a by-product and used as a blend material for generator fuel will have to be stockpiled at a rate equivalent to 130,200 gallons of fuel oil per day. This 47.5 million gallons of fuel oil that would be burned for power generation is capable of heating 32,000 homes in the state, or over 30% of the homes in the state dependent on fuel oil for home heating.

16. Indicate in the following table the total dollar amount of your company's expenditures on research, development and exploration of energy resources other than petroleum.

Response:

| | | Oil Shale | Coal | Geothermal | Solar | Other (Includes Tar Sands, Uranium & Nuclear) |
|---|---|---|---|---|---|---|
| 1970 | Research and Development | 4,333,500 | 9,273,770 | 1,131,000 | -0- | 100,176,000 |
| | Exploration | 2,425,500 | 1,921,000 | -0- | -0- | 12,243,000 |
| 1971 | Research and Development | 4,382,000 | 14,081,430 | 3,156,000 | 400,000 | 100,125,000 |
| | Exploration | 2,665,500 | 3,372,500 | 184,000 | -0- | 14,854,000 |
| 1972 | Research and Development | 4,420,900 | 15,325,960 | 5,525,000 | 600,000 | 78,698,000 |
| | Exploration | 2,758,975 | 6,053,754 | 1,476,000 | -0- | 12,045,000 |
| 1973 | Research and Development | 7,522,800 | 30,901,619 | 8,549,000 | 620,000 | 95,927,000 |
| | Exploration | 2,771,183 | 6,123,731 | 3,036,000 | -0- | 19,377,000 |

State your company's plans with regard to the future development of energy resources other than petroleum.

17.  What role, if any, does your company believe the U.S. Government should play in the development of U.S. oil shale and outer continental shelf petroleum resources?  In the latter case, focus in particular on those resources which can only be obtained under adverse conditions or which would require deep water drilling.

Response:

All of the petroleum company responses indicate that the U.S. Government's role in the development of U.S. oil shale and Outer Continental Shelf petroleum resources should not involve direct participation.  The U.S. Government should make more acreage available for leasing and generally provide an atmosphere, through tax incentives or a guaranteed price-floor for oil shale, to attract the necessary private capital. The U.S. Government should encourage and fund research and development programs as well as maintain a minimum standard of regulation.  Many of the oil companies feel that the present system of bonus bidding should be eliminated in favor of a royalty system.

SELECTED COMMENTS:

A.  We believe the Government should offer a guaranteed price for a small number of specific projects for oil shale as well as for the results of exploration on certain outer continental shelf deep water prospects.

In addition, regarding the continental outer shelf, the U.S. Government should consider following the example of England, in the North Sea, where leases are awarded not on a bidding basis but on royalty offered and on exploration programs submitted.

B.  Outer-Continental Shelf Petroleum

Government should continue leasing oil and gas mineral rights under federal domain to private enterprise at regularly scheduled intervals and allow economic incentives to attract the necessary private capital to develop these resources.

For several years prior to 1972, there has been a period of infrequent and irregular Federal offshore sales. Since then, the industry has had the benefit of an accelerated program. During the years of infrequent and irregular offshore sales, many mobile drilling rigs left the U.S. for foreign work. Skilled drilling crews, as well as service personnel, left the industry for other, more dependable employment. Equipment and personnel are being attracted back to the U.S. industry, but this process takes time. The government could aid to the greatest extent by developing and following a long-range leasing schedule. Such a schedule would not only make exploration acreage available, but allow companies within the industry and the infrastructure time to plan for its orderly development and to provide for the necessary men and materials. The U.S. oil industry has quite successfully developed offshore technology for worldwide use and has demonstrated its ability to find, develop, and produce offshore oil.

Oil Shale

With respect to oil shale, we believe that the U.S. Government should take the following steps to further its development.

Process research, particularly in-situ methods, should be encouraged and supported by both government funds and use of government shale lands, if necessary.

Some consideration should be given to offering larger Federal tracts and allowing larger holdings per company.

A stronger commitment to the stated goals of project independence than has thus far been evidenced is badly needed.

The government should assume a lead role in expediting the processing of necessary permits associated with specific shale ventures, as opposed to some of its agencies being the major cause of current delays.

C.  Oil Shale

Deterrents to rapid development of oil shale, which Federal action might alleviate are:

1. The huge investment required in a time of tight money and competing lower-risk investment opportunities.

2. The risk of inadequate return on investment due to:

    a. dumping of low cost crude in the United States by exporters.

    b. overruns and loss of return on capital due to delays (e.g., Alaska pipeline).

    c. accelerated use of new synthetic fuels technology on a commercial scale.

Possible Federal Actions:

1. a. no-recourse guarantees for loans up to, say, 67% of the capital cost. These should be available to first generatives or proto type commercial-scale plants to encourage establishment at an early date of proven technology, costs and effective environmental program.

    b. full tax credit for interest paid on loans invested in a shale oil or synthetic fuels project.

    c. flexible depreciation for tax purposes.

        1. allow company to take percent of investment desired in year desired.

        2. increase (decrease) depreciation of oil shale mine and plant each year in accordance with construction index so that depreciation reflects current replacement cost.

        3. double depreciation.

        4. increased investment tax credits.

    d. increased percentage depletion allowance.

2. a. Presidential power to impose tariffs on imports promptly and without prolonged administrative delays within government or in response to pressure groups.

## Outer Continental Shelf

It is generally agreed that it is absolutely essential that the resources of the outer continental shelf be developed at a more rapid pace if the nation's energy problems are to be solved. Government and Industry should have a common goal in working out programs fair to all concerned for developing these resources as quickly and responsibly as is economically feasible. Unfortunately, a great number of the bills under consideration in the Federal Congress would impose so many restrictions and burdens on the Petroleum Industry that it would hamper efforts to effectively develop these valuable offshore resources. The trend underlying these bills indicates an anti-private enterprise mood in the U.S. Congress today. The Federal Oil Company, advocated by a small group of U.S. Senators, would further stymie the efforts so badly needed to achieve the goal set forth in Project Independence. Such a company would have, by law, advantages not available to private industry, thus reducing their competitiveness and ability to raise needed capital.

We see as a laudable objective the Department of the Interior's stated purpose to expand development of the OCS. However, we believe that legislation already enacted will accomplish this purpose in an expeditious, orderly, and safe manner, with resultant advantages to the American people. The oil companies have shown a great measure of responsibility in developing the OCS, so if the objective of Congressional legislation is to expedite development we suggest progressive legislation such as amending the National Environmental Policy Act of 1969. This Act as it presently stands has caused unnecessary delays and should be made more realistic. In our opinion, the Department of the Interior, with the cooperation of private industry, is doing a fine job in developing the OCS, and much of the presently proposed legislation now in the hopper would only inhibit and delay the needed additional development.

[We have] three major concerns about [pending] legislation. First, it placed many unnecessary and burdensome restrictions on the oil industry. Second, it would inhibit, not help, in the development of the OCS resources, and third, it would push the Industry into nationalization. Also, various pending legislation had some portions that were constructive, particularly those provisions dealing with Research and Development regarding technology for Environmental Protection and Exploration and Production in deeper waters. [We encourage] such research and development programs.

Furthermore, we would like to see the Department of the Interior given the freedom to lease more of the Federal waters and to modify these offerings by enlarging the tract size from 5,000 to 10,000 acres per tract. This would greatly enhance the probability of assuring the bidding companies the chances of securing a greater portion of a geological prospect initially without having the exposure or need for later drainage sales.

Finally, there are two proposed regulations under consideration by the Department of the Interior which, if implemented, would seriously affect Industry's ability to develop expeditiously and properly the offshore regions. One regulation proposes to limit the right of certain companies to bid jointly on Outer Continental Shelf Lands. The other regulation would require the public disclosure of confidential geological and geophysical information obtained by companies who have conducted exploration and development activities on the OCS.

[We] raised serious objections to both regulations during public hearings conducted before the Department of the Interior. During the testimony, the Department was advised by both independents and major oil companies that any limitation on joint bidding would impede the further development of the offshore areas, while substantially reducing the amount of income received by the Department from cash bonuses.

Independent and major oil companies likewise testified against the proposed regulation requiring public disclosure of geological and geophysical information since such disclosure would discourage exploratory activity and result in the chilling of the competitive atmosphere at future OCS lease sales. Also, the testimony indicated the regulation would result in the curtailment of present exploratory technology so essential to the continued development of the deeper offshore regions.

18. What is your opinion with respect to the existing system of world petroleum supply? What are its advantages and disadvantages? What favorable or unfavorable effects would the continuation of this system have in the next five years?

Response:

Most companies emphasized the efficiency of the pre-1973 world system of petroleum supply. A majority of the respondents expressed concern for the power and disruptive potential of OPEC, but some companies expressed complete satisfaction with the existing system.

SELECTED COMMENTS:

A. It is a viable system developed under competitive conditions of the market place. It cannot be improved on for its feedback mechanism. The advantages are its responsiveness to need. It has no disadvantages. Discontinuation of this system into unilateral national distribution would destroy the orderly economy of the world.

B. At the present time, OPEC controls the world petroleum supply situation. There is no apparent advantage to this, and the disadvantage is that one closely knit group of nations has an excessive amount of power in controlling the energy supplies of the world. The unfavorable effect of a continuation of this over the next 5 years is readily apparent from the position OPEC has taken regarding oil pricing. The control via OPEC almost surely will lead to a severe balance of payment problem to the non-Communist world.

C. The existing system of world petroleum supply, with its large number of participants, is beneficial to petroleum consuming nations. The major oil companies integrated operations gave them significant flexibility and control to efficiently dispose of production all over the world. Such downstream strength was derived historically from their unique resource position. As participation dissolves this unique position an erosion of the existing world supply system is foreseen. As national oil companies become major suppliers in many of the importing countries, effective competition that currently exists between international oil companies may be restricted.

The loss of resource position will likely mean increased margins for downstream services. The prospects for more profitable downstream operations should result in increased opportunities for refining and marketing in oil-consuming countries. However, with participation is likely to come movements by producing countries into downstream activities. Thus, consuming countries may be forced to allow producing countries into downstream areas--as opposed to domestic expansion--to secure foreign oil availability.

D. The major oil companies have been responsible for the establishment of whatever system exists in the area of world petroleum supply, although the role of these companies within the system has been diminished recently by the actions of the governments of many producing nations. It is [our] opinion that the existing system is functioning as well as can be expected, given the pressures on the system exerted by the policies of producing nations' governments. We anticipate the continuing ability of the major oil companies to conduct their supply operations as efficiently as possible during the next five years. We feel that any substantial government intervention in their international operations could only be counterproductive. Most future changes in the world petroleum supply system will be inspired by decisions of producing nations' governments, not those of our government or of the management of major oil companies.

H. The "existing" system of world petroleum supply is in a period of transition as OPEC countries establish a new role in ownership of petroleum reserves and in the reinvestment of earnings from sale of petroleum.

We assume, however, that the question is aimed at the proper role of the United States Government relative to the role of international private companies.

Much of our answer to this question has already been presented in answer to Question number 13. In that answer, we discussed the role of multinational companies and the need for their continued contribution.

Two supplemental points will be made here. These concern first the danger of further politicizing oil and second the importance of developing a cooperative international climate for re-investment of "petro-dollars."

The international petroleum industry has, over the long term, done an excellent job in meeting the Free World's petroleum needs with abundant supplies at stable

and moderate prices.  During the period in which the
industry was in a position to deal with matters of exploration, production, transportation and price on a
predominantly commercial, as distinguished from a political,
basis, supply was plentiful, prices moderate, (and in the
decade of the Sixties indeed declined) and demand never exceeded supply.

The industry carried on this international business on a commercial basis and achieved the record described
through the Korean War, and the Vietnam War and three wars
in the Middle East.

In 1970, certain members of OPEC, and the OPEC
itself, became more aggressive in their demands for alteration in the terms of existing arrangements.  These negotiations were conducted in an atmosphere of threats of
unilateral action if the companies did not submit to their
demands.  In addition, the demands of certain OPEC countries
began to have definite political overtones.  Even in this
period, however, the industry in the various negotiations
starting in 1971 demonstrated an ability to negotiate and
operate on a commercial basis.  It was only in the fall of
1973, coincident with the outbreak of the fourth Arab-Israeli
war, that the Middle Eastern producing countries took united
and unilateral action which brought on the first unmanageable
crisis of supply in the Free World since World War II.

This record is instructive for the future.  The
only time the international petroleum industry has been
unable to perform its function since World War II was that
period which followed the political decisions to which we
have referred.  These decisions to restrict the supply of
oil were made for reasons which had little or nothing to
do with the oil industry or its performance.  It was political, rather than commercial actions which intervened in
the relations between the producing countries and their
customers.  These political decisions eventually induced the
unprecedented unilateral, nearly four-fold, increase in the
cost of oil.

As one thinks about the future of international
petroleum supply these basic facts are worth pondering.
Considering this record, the private oil company approach

has much to recommend it over the alternative of government-to-government confrontation. If oil supply becomes a government-to-government matter, commercial problems inevitably become political problems. Private oil companies tend to insulate consumers from political problems; they are highly competitive and their relations with the producing countries have been based on commercial and economic functions. For example, in 1970 the then new government of Libya could not tolerate a U.S. Government presence in the form of Wheelus Air Force Base, but Libya has to this day tolerated the presence of U.S.-based oil companies. Diplomatic relations with the United States were severed by Egypt in 1967 but this did not interfere with the subsequent entry and operation of private U.S. petroleum interests in Egypt. Private oil companies managed to hang on in Indonesia during the Sukarno regime so that when a change came in 1966 they were well established and ready to expand their operations. Iraq severed diplomatic relations with the United States in 1967 and has maintained a militant anti-U.S. stand ever since. Nevertheless, it permitted two U.S.-based oil companies to continue in certain producing areas until 1973 when political considerations, accented by the October war, intervened.

That private oil companies can operate under many circumstances where governments may not has apparently been the judgment of those responsible officials of our Government who have given thought to this matter over a period of almost half a century. We say this because every administration since that of Woodrow Wilson has, apparently as an incident of its foreign policy, fostered and encouraged the presence of U.S. private companies in the large oil producing areas of the world. This policy has consistently been in the interest of the United States, the consumer, and the Free World.

The second part of our answer to this question concerns the role of the U.S. Government in helping develop an international climate for reinvestment of "petro-dollars."

The United States Government should play a positive role in creating the atmosphere necessary to ensure the stability of commerical arrangements in world trade. It must be emphasized to the producing countries that their emergence as major forces in international monetary and trade channels carries with it a share of the responsibility for the stability of these international systems. The producing countries will expect that the major consuming countries will assist them in the orderly investment of their foreign exchange reserves, and in the development of their international trade. As they proceed to realize this goal, they will become aware of the need for fiscal stability to protect the value of their trade and investments.

In short, the international trade in oil badly needs stability. Since the producing country governments are sovereign and not subject to a superior law, it is necessary for the consuming countries to persuade them that their best interests will be served through the maintenance of stable conditions in which commercial commitments can be freely made and relied upon. Producing countries must be persuaded as to the interdependency of nations and the powerful impact they will have on world economics through the setting of petroleum prices and the handling of petrodollars. In a stable framework, the oil industry is clearly capable of meeting the needs of the consuming nations of the world; and the record of the industry gives us confidence to make that forecast. If we do not have stable conditions, neither the companies nor the consuming countries will enjoy reliable supplies at reasonable prices.

E. The existing system has been effective in providing ample supplies from domestic and foreign sources with very little interruption. Competition among private companies has served to keep prices reasonable. This sytem is capable of adapting to changing requirements imposed by producing nations.

The failures of the existing system can be traced in almost every case to government restrictions that occurred over the last 20 years. These include regulation of natural gas prices at the wellhead, gaps in the Mandatory Oil Import Program that drove refining construction abroad, and excessive efforts to protect the environment. For the future, we think that this system should operate much as it has in the past. Companies will still seek profits by supplying the world's oil requirements as efficiently as possible. By changing the rules governments will either help or hinder that process.

F. Surely no one outside of the OPEC countries could be truly happy with the existing system of world petroleum supply. Production levels, prices, distribution patterns, etc. are all subject to the whims and vagaries of foreign governments, some openly hostile. Thus, instead of obeying the normal laws of supply and demand, decisions are made politically. Prices can be set at such a level as to ruin economies or governments of particular consuming nations singled out as being hostile. Surely continuation of such a system will result in a polarization of the earth's "have" and "have not" nations, with perhaps disastrous results. The concentration of power and wealth possible from such a system are enormous.

G. From an independent refiner's standpoint, the major disadvantage is the control of crude by the major oil companies. Another disadvantage of this system is that an integrated crude sufficient refiner is content to earn his profit off the crude oil which gives him an unfair competitive advantage in the downstream end of the business (refinery and marketing). However, one advantage of the existing system is the national security aspect of a great deal of the world's petroleum supply being controlled by U. S. companies.

Other than the national security aspect, the continuation of this system will act as a deterrant for independent refiners to add capacity.

H. In our response to Question 13 we have reviewed the changes taking place in the international oil industry. What the result of the major changes now taking place will be is hard to forecast. For purposes of this response to Question 18 we have interpreted "existing system" to mean that system of world petroleum supply which existed when private (as opposed to producer-government) companies operated within a competitive market system in all phases of the oil business. The market mechanisms provided the economic basis for decisions subject to various import and price controls imposed by some governments and subject to incentives generated by various forms of taxation. Most national energy policies were loosely defined and resolution of energy problems was left by individual country governments mainly to individual members of the energy industry to resolve. There are, however, three features of the international oil industry demonstrated over many years of performance which we feel should be retained in any system that evolves out of the present unsettled situation.

1.  Flexibility Through Multiple Sources of Supply. Each consuming country's petroleum needs have been supplied by a number of companies drawing crude oil from a number of sources with the supply patterns established by the economics of the choices available, but with recognition of the presence of various political constraints. Thus, no consuming country has been tied solely to any one producing country for its petroleum supplies. Likewise, no producer country has been tied solely to any one consumer country for its crude oil outlet. The risk has been small (as demonstrated through many disturbances) that problems of a single oil company or disruptions in a single producer country would be felt by oil consumers. This has been a direct result of many oil companies with access to multiple supply sources which could be distributed in response to a multiplicity of factors. The benefits of multiple supply sources for consuming countries can continue with reliance on the private, competitive oil companies. Such flexibility would be greatly reduced if not lost with government-to-government supply agreements.

2.  Economics of Supply. A significant factor in the overall supply network has been the economic motivation to minimize logistical costs as far as political constraints permit. Crude qualities have been paired with consumer country requirements to minimize individual companies refining investments while allowing for total transportation costs. As mentioned in our response to Question 13 each company's logistical systems involve more than facilities. Accumulated experience, technology, managerial know-how and planning competence are needed to carry out the logistics function efficiently. The operations and decisions are international in scope and of such complexity that they cannot be assumed by the inexperienced. If future supply arrangements are entered into for non-commercial reasons, they will decrease the ability to operate with "minimum-cost" supply patterns by fixing elements in the supply chain.

3. <u>Investment Planning</u>. Up to now the investment planning by the individual petroleum companies has proved remarkably effective in providing sufficient capacity to meet all demands in normal conditions. The changes now occurring in crude supply sources may have their most significant impact on would-be investors because they will have no assurance of feedstock supplies at reasonable and stable costs for new facilities.

While there seem to be temptations to move away from a "free" market orientation, we feel it is important that the major features, discussed above, of such a market be continued. Market mechanisms provide the best means to allocate the critical resources of capital, manpower, and raw materials necessary for development of various sectors of the economy. In particular, it seems inconceivable that the present complex but effective logistical systems now in place and operated by international oil companies can have an effective substitute.

I. Our company feels that the existing system of world petroleum supply is probably the most efficient attainable and results in the lowest cost to the consumer. The major advantage of the current system is the great degree of flexibility that most international oil companies have within their own world-wide distribution system. Where possible, there is cooperation between the oil companies in adjusting lifting schedules and ship allocations which tends to minimize the overall distribution cost. If this system were discontinued during the next five years, the unfavorable effects would be the total loss of logistics flexibility and a significant increase in transportation cost.


19. What is your opinion with respect to intervention by the U. S. Government into the negotiation of medium (five years or more) or long-range (ten years or more) foreign petroleum supply contracts? What are the advantages and disadvantages of such intervention? When answering this question, clearly specify the type and degree of intervention that you are assuming.

Response:

The overwhelming majority of petroleum company responses indicate that the oil companies do not favor direct government intervention in the negotiation of medium or long-range foreign petroleum supply contracts. If there is government intervention it should be to provide "a political climate in which nations can trade freely" and in an advisory capacity. The majority of the oil companies feel that direct government intervention would only elevate negotiations to the political level, create an institutional bureaucracy that would only complicate matters and reduce the competitive strength of U.S. companies abroad.

SELECTED COMMENTS:

A. Government could be of assistance since foreign oil is now under such great political control. There is leverage which only government could bring to bear. However, the job must be a teamwork effort with the oil companies retaining substantial control. We visualize government functioning as a friendly advisor and intermediary with foreign countries.

B. The government should stay out -- no advantages. The only function of the government is diplomatic support of the U.S. businessmen, and a country that believes enough in free enterprise to let the world know it. We have not had either of these conditions in 20 years.

C.  
## A DRAFT BILL

### FOREIGN OIL CONTRACTS ACT OF 1974

The proposed bill would:

1. Require that all contracts for the purchase or procurement of crude oil or refined petroleum products between corporations and major oil exporting nations be registered with the Federal Energy Administration twenty days prior to the effective date thereof and be made available for public inspection; and

2. Require FEA approval of all such contracts on the basis of criteria set forth in the bill, including such factors as price level, duraation, access to crude oil supply, and degree the Federal Energy Administration was consulted during the negotiation.

Although we recognize the very serious implications of the unilateral price actions taken by OPEC and share the concerns expressed by Congress, we nevertheless submit that this proposed legislation would be contrary to the best interests of the U.S. Government, the American consumer, and the oil industry, and would defeat the purpose for which it is intended. Specifically:

1. This bill ignores the realities of the world oil market. If the FEA were to disapprove future contracts between U.S. oil companies and the oil-exporting countries, foreign companies would be in a better position to contract for the volume being produced. American companies could be effectively forced out of international competition. Imports into the United States from OPEC sources presently account for about 15 percent of the total production of crude oil in the OPEC areas. Some or all of this volume could, over the long run, be absorbed by foreign companies and/or shut-in if necessary. Denial of access to U.S. markets by government action due to this proposed legislation would have little economic impact on the OPEC nations. Lessened access by U.S. companies to major world oil sources could, however, have a severe adverse impact on U.S. national and economic security since the U.S. will, for some time to come, be dependent on imports from such sources.

2. This bill would directly involve the U.S. Government in international crude pricing negotiations without strengthening American bargaining interests.

3. The provision that all agreements covered by the bill shall be available for public inspection is highly undesirable and anti-competitive, and could result in ever-increasing prices. Further, it would establish a price floor from which all other contracts would spiral upward. Producing countries would insist on "favored nation" treatment that would be "triggered" with each contract approved by the U.S. Government, thereby increasing prices of petroleum so affected.

4. The bill proposes a number of criteria in establishing procedures for approval of contracts. Among these is "the degree to which such contract unduly concentrates access to the oil production of any country or area in the hands of one or a small number of corporations or other business entities." This implies that the legislation could be used to discriminate against and undermine long-established crude supply relationships developed by various American oil companies at considerable financial risk. Furthermore, it implies that some contracts at a certain price level might be approved if made by one company, but a contract in the same area at the same price or at a lower price could be disapproved if made by another company. It is difficult to see how this criterion would serve to lower prices.

5. The bill provides the FEA authority to approve or disapprove such contracts even when they may not involve imports into the United States. This extends U.S. Government jurisdiction beyond U.S. territorial limits, and is contrary to general principles of international law. It would create serious difficulties for U.S. corporations in their foreign business activities. Foreign governments would undoubtedly resent such U.S. interference, and would more than likely impose restrictions to protect their fundamental sovereign activities. The injection of the FEA into international oil transactions could seriously impinge upon U.S. foreign relations.

6. Agreements with producing countries for new concessions would be exceedingly difficult to negotiate under the conditions proposed by this bill. Producing countries undoubtedly would prefer to negotiate with foreign companies whose governments do not impose the burdensome procedures and restrictions in the proposed bill. Furthermore, such foreign companies would have an enormous competitive advantage in obtaining concessions.

7. The risks, burdens, uncertainties, and delays created by such legislation could only serve to further reduce incentives to commit the massive amounts of capital which must be expended in the international search for new and diversified sources of petroleum and in the construction of additional domestic refining facilities dependent upon foreign-sourced crude supply.

8.   The proposed FEA review and approval procedure is strikingly analogous to the procedures under the Natural Gas Act.   FPC regulation of natural gas prices is confined to a portion of the U.S. market, while the price regulations contemplated by this bill would be confined to a portion of the world market.   Experience has shown the handicaps which confront consumers in the regulated sector seeking to obtain adequate supplies when a producer has the option of selling to a significant unregulated market.   It could be expected that the price control provisions of this bill would drive the crude oil from the major oil exporting countries to the unregulated markets, where most of it is now sold.

In the long-term the real solution to the problem of escalating oil prices is the exploration for and development of more domestic and geographically diversified foreign petroleum supplies and alternative energy sources.   Whatever assistance the U.S. Government may provide in achieving these objectives would be much more constructive than the proposed legislation.

D.   The bill proposed by the Senate Committee on Foreign Relations is particularly objectionable in that (a) it affords no improvement in the major problem area of enforcement; (b) it places government bureaucracy, without responsibility for results, in the position of substituting its judgment on an after-the-fact basis for the judgment of the business enterprises incurring all the financial risks; (c) it would extend to the participation of U.S. business enterprises in international trade, exclusive of trade with the United States; (d) is so inherently cumbersome in its approach that the delays involved would effectively take U.S. companies out of competitive participation for energy resources outside the jurisdiction of the United States.

Government participation through the medium of a government-buying cartel for foreign crude oil purchases which would, in turn, resell for oil importation for use by domestic refiners, would involve the government in a function for which it is ill equipped to efficiently handle and necessitate governmental determination of the type, quality, quantity, timing and means of delivery of crude oil to each refiner.   The United States companies' operating fields in many of the foreign countries supply a service that the country itself cannot supply on a comparable basis.   There is thus some incentive to sell crude oil to the company performing a valuable service that would not be present in negotiating sales with a government purchasing agent.   A

U.S. Government buying cartel would in all probability drive
U.S. oil companies out of the international oil market where
they have conducted a profitable business.

At the present time, and for the foreseeable
future, we believe term contracts will call for market price
and not a fixed price. Bargaining will be limited to amount
of supply.

In our opinion the U.S. Government has nothing to
offer at this time through intervention in the negotiation
of foreign supply contracts with OPEC members. The U.S.
Government we assume is unwilling to utilize military pressures and in our opinion has no economic sanctions available
that would effectively penalize any OPEC member to the point
of inducing a change in its bargaining position.

E.  Direct government involvement in the prior negotiation or even subsequent approval of supply contracts will
not result in reduced oil costs.  In fact, it could result
in increased costs as the price paid for political considerations.  Government would perform a far more useful role by
providing diplomatic and legal support for the enforcement
of contracts negotiated by private companies whether those
be supply contracts or production licenses.  It is time to
recognize that every derogation from a company's rights
results in an increase in consumer costs.  The United States
and the consuming world can no longer afford to shy away
from the need for countervailing power whether through
embargoes on expropriated oil and the products derived
therefrom or through threatened retaliation against foreign
interests in the U.S. As BP is very much aware, U.K. companies
have about as many reserves on the North Slope of Alaska as
U.S. companies have in the North Sea.  Given the existence
of this leverage, it is difficult to understand why the U.S.
Government is unwilling to take a firm public position
against the Labour Party's threat to "renegotiate" prior
U.K. licenses when such "renegotiation" will damage the
interest of American consumers as well as investors.

F.  The intervention by the U.S. Government into the
negotiations of foreign petroleum supply contracts should
be entirely unnecessary and would also be undesirable.  Some
observers have predicted the early demise of oil companies
as a channel between consuming and producing countries.

It is also suggested that oil producers will negotiate
bilateral and multilateral agreements with oil consumers
and so bypass the oil companies. This, in our view, would
be dangerous as well as an inefficient course of action for
both the consuming nations and probably producing nations
too. Firstly this event would cause the transaction to be
extremely vlunerable to short-term political altercations.
Secondly, the benefit of diversity of supply and distribution found in multi-national oil companies would not be
possible. Thirdly, it removes an efficient fully competitive transportation, manufacturing and marketing system
that fully meets the needs of consumers within the restraints imposed upon oil companies. The U.S. Government
alternatively could make the maximum contribution through
bilateral or multilateral economic agreements with the
producing countries in cooperation with industrial companies
which would provide the best vehicle to implement such agreements.

G.  Basically, this question raises the same issues posed
by the proposed Foreign Oil Contracts Act of 1974 drafted by
the Senate Foreign Relations Subcommittee on Multinational
Corporations.

The expressed purpose of this Act is to require
registration of all foreign crude and refined products purchase contracts with the Federal Energy Administration, to
publicize the details of such contracts in advance of their
execution by United States oil companies, and to give the
Administrator of the FEA authority to approve or disapprove
such contracts prior to performance.

This bill would adversely affect the competitive
position of U.S. international oil companies. It also
appears to contravene certain principles enunciated by the
United States in trade negotiations.

Several problems with regard to the competitive
position of U.S. companies and certain practical difficulties
are noted below.

1.  First, the time required for the Administration
to review these contracts would delay or extend contract
negotiations and a foreign competitor willing to close
promptly would be at an advantage.

2.  To the extent that contract terms were disclosed, foreign competitors would be in a position to improve their offer and gain a competitive edge.

3.  Producing governments would likely object to publication of contract terms and would probably seek to negotiate with non-U.S. companies in order to avoid disclosure.

4.  A number of new exploration and producing contracts abroad provide terms under which oil can be purchased.  Negotiations still underway with producing governments in a number of old concession areas involve this same point.  Making such contracts subject to this Act would inhibit the ability of U.S. concerns to compete for new reserves and, in addition, could hold up ongoing negotiations for procedural reasons.

5.  The Act gives the FEA the right to approve or disapprove contracts involving oil supply from one foreign country to another.  For example, a U.S. company contract with Indonesia for the purchase of crude or products to be shipped to Japan would be covered.  Even if Japan was satisfied with the contract, the United States would be assuming a right to veto.  Both the importer and the exporter would, under these circumstances, presumably prefer to deal with non-U.S. oil companies.

Other practical problems involved with such a system include:

6.  Foreign oil companies with residence in the United States are made subject to the Act -- even as to supplies not intended for the United States.  For example, BP or Petrofina would need prior U.S. approval for their crude or product contracts.  Thus, the U.S. is presuming that other governments will cede to the United States the right to regulate their international oil companies.

7.  The Act covers any contract for more than six months or one million barrels of crude or product.  For all practical purposes, this makes almost all significant transactions subject to U.S. approval.  It is difficult to believe that the FEA staff could review the large number of contracts involved, in the manner and scope contemplated by the Act, within the timeframe permitted.

8. Market prices for petroleum are sensitive to changes in supply and demand. The procedure for pre-approval would require the U.S. Administrator to be virtually prescient with respect to all market trends. It is unreasonable to anticipate that such knowledge could be developed and there is risk of blocking procurement of supplies in a changing market.

The following comments consider how this act would relate to principles enunciated by the United States in trade negotiations.

1. In a summary of U.S. foreign policy for 1972, Secretary of State Rogers said: "...the long-term objective of the U.S. international economic policy will remain what it has been: an open-world economy in which trade and investment flows among countries are not distorted by national barriers to free exchange." (Dept. of State Publication 8699, "United States Foreign Policy - 1972," April 1973.) The Foreign Oil Contracts Act is inconsistent with this statement.

2. The "Foreign Oil Contracts Act of 1974" offends several provisions of GATT. They include Article III, (most favored nations clause); Article XI, (No prohibitions or restrictions other than duties, taxes or other charges, whether made effective through quotas, import or export licenses or other measures, shall be instituted or maintained by a contracting party on the importation of any product of the territory of any other contracting party or on the exportation or sale of any product destined for the territory of any other contracting party.); Article XIII, (prohibits discriminatory quantitative restrictions) and Article XX, (which reiterates the basic denial of "arbitrary or unjustifiable discrimination" in the trade process).

3. The U.S. is currently negotiating with other countries on emergency sharing of supply and on establishing a data system through which member countries could be apprised of petroleum cost and supply trends. These negotiations envisage international cooperation on the development and conservation of energy. It is difficult to see how the U.S. can negotiate a multinational pact calling for broad cooperation, while simultaneously contemplating legislation giving the United States the right to dictate terms of international oil transactions.

In summary, this Act would reduce the competitive strength of U.S. companies abroad, and reduce these companies' ability to compete for oil supplies for the United States.

It appears to place certain transactions made by non-U.S. countries under U.S. regulatory authority. It is difficult to see how the U.S. can take this action unilaterally.

It has broad implications with respect to ongoing U.S. trade and energy negotiations.

Finally, any proposals such as those in this Act would introduce a substantial political element into any negotiation with a producing country. This follows from the fact that the purpose of the legislation is to add U.S. Government's "leverage" to petroleum supply negotiations. This being the case, the producing countries will recognize the U.S. Government's role and respond to it as one government to another. The effect will be that the negotiations will be increasingly concluded on political considerations rather than on economic.


20. What is your opinion with respect to the establishment of a petroleum corporation, fully or partially owned by the U.S. Government, to engage in national and international activities such as (1) resource acquisition within the U.S. (including the outer continental shelf); (2) exploration; (3) development; (4) production; (5) purchase of production of other petroleum companies (primarily foreign) for storage, refining or resale; (6) transportation; (7) refining and processing; or (8) distribution? What are the advantages and disadvantages of each? Consider each of the above functions separately and make specific comments.

Response:

All the respondents vigorously opposed the creation of a Government-owned petroleum company. Several smaller companies, however, voiced limited support for (5) emergency storage and (6) pipeline ownership.

SELECTED COMMENTS:

A. The entrance by Government into areas that can be or are effectively served by private enterprise results in inefficient utilization of resources. First, private capital that could be channeled into private enterprise must find other and possibly less desirable opportunities. Second, public revenues that could be used for public goods are required for such an enterprise. A third impact is the price of the product not reflecting competitive values as public corporations have neither tax burdens, profit incentives nor typical financial constraints faced by the private sector. Moreover, fiscal resources (taxes) are generally lost by the creation of public corporations. Experience has shown that Government enterprise has rarely been successful in terms of economics and operating efficiency when compared with private industry.

The following questions and statements indicate opinions on the pluses and minuses of specific activities such as Federal Oil Company (FOC) might enjoy:

(1) Resource Acquisition - Would this acquisition be free while private companies have to bid for acreage? What method of choosing the acreage would be employed and by whom? Will acreage revert (to whom) if no exploration is carried out within five years?

(2,3,4) Exploration, Development, and Production - How will the Government obtain the manpower and equipment? A shortage already exists in labor and materials required in exploration. Will economic criteria determine production? Who will production be sold to and at what price? Would natural gas be sold intra or interstate?

(5) Purchase of Petroleum - Will the FOC purchase petroleum from all foreign producers? Will the FOC directly negotiate with foreign governments?

(6) Transportation - Would the Government acquire transportation facilities from private enterprise? Would all taxpayers share the burden? How would the services be priced? Would they be regulated by the FPC or ICC?

(7) Refining - Would a FOC get locational advantages for new refineries? How would the manpower shortages be overcome? Would products be sold to independents or in integrated channels and would the prices be the same to each?

(8) <u>Distribution</u> - Would a FOC purchase existing market outlets or would they be newcomers? Would they market nationwide or locally? Gasoline? Fuel oils?

B. The establishment of a petroleum corporation fully or partially owned by the U. S. Government to engage in any or all of the listed activities would clearly be economically wasteful and therefore contrary to the public interest.

All world petroleum reserves, both discovered and undiscovered, are subject to eventual recovery, processing and marketing, given funds sufficient to perform the recovery, processing and marketing operations, whether such funds are derived from corporate income or from tax revenues. The capital expenditure required for start-up of a petroleum corporation, even one engaged in fewer than all of the listed activities, would be staggering (some governments have avoided the high start-up cost by expropriating without just compensation already existing privately held capital goods, although hopefully the U. S. Government would not consider this alternative to be viable). The start-up costs would be reflected in product prices or would be funded from tax revenues. In our opinion, based on experience in the private sector and some exposure to the cost efficiency records of government owned and operated enterprises, the operating costs of a government owned petroleum corporation once established would be markedly higher than those of a corporation required to operate at a profit. The higher costs would be covered by increased product prices or by tax revenues. In the case of either start-up costs or operating costs, it is unlikely that the federal corporation would select the option of charging a product price higher than that of the private sector in order to cover its costs. In that event, part of the costs would be passed along to the consumer, not directly but as an increased tax bill or a decrease in federal services. The only advantage to be gained from this situation would be psychological--the consumer-taxpayer would be unaware of his increased energy bill.

The American petroleum industry has always had the world's most advanced petroleum technology and has been responsible for the discoveries that have led to most of the petroleum production in the world today. The successes of the industry have resulted from a competitive free enterprise setting, not the presence of a risk-proof government corporation.

The federal government is the country's largest single lessor and has a strong interest in carefully overseeing the operation of its properties. This function is excellently performed by the highly capable geologists, geophysicists and engineers of the United States Geological Survey and the United States Army Corps of Engineers. The government does not presently possess, however, nor could it be expected to acquire, the expertise necessary to conduct operations from exploration to distribution.

The federal government has demonstrated with the Apollo Program that given sufficient funding from tax revenues it can create an agency to perform just about any physical task. It has demonstrated with its postal and military operations that its enterprises are wholly incapable of performing their functions with cost efficiency. Just as no private industry would have considered putting a man on the moon, the federal government should decline further intrusion into the private sector.

C. Recent Congressional proposals to create a national oil company have, we believe, been triggered by two factors. First, the world-wide shortage of petroleum that occurred last winter. Second, the sudden realization by some Congressmen that United States energy self-sufficiency has been steadily eroding for several years. This erosion, of course, has now left the United States dependent upon imported oil -- a condition which will continue at least into the next decade. Project Independence is one reaction to these factors. Proposals for a national oil company are a second.

It is instructive, therefore, to examine whether a national oil company could help solve either of these problems.

Considering first the shortage that occurred last winter, it is clear that these shortages were the result of unilateral Arab Government actions to curtail production and embargo certain countries including the United States. There was then and there is now ample producing capacity installed by oil companies around the world to meet demand. Even today, there is probably 3-4 million barrels per day of production capacity in countries such as Libya, Kuwait, Saudi Arabia, and Abu Dhabi that is denied to world markets due to unilateral producing government production controls. The

quantity of crude oil that will be made available to world
buyers is entirely in the hands of these producing governments.  There is absolutely nothing that another United
States oil company -- either private or national -- can do
about this fact.  With regard to additional exploration in
foreign areas, the private companies are searching wherever
opportunities exist.  There is no reason to think that a new
national U.S. company could do better.  Indeed, there are
four reasons to believe it would do worse.

First, it would have no expertise or experience
such as is possessed by existing private companies.

Second, government companies have little incentive to be efficient since they are assured either of
sufficient revenue to cover costs or subsidies to offset
losses.

Third, exploration is a technologically complex
and high risk business often requiring large investments
over a number of years before results are achieved.  The
most favorable foreign areas in which to explore are, additionally, widely spread around the world and involve political
systems of all types.  A company operating abroad must be
prepared to dedicate continuing investments even in areas
where United States foreign relations may be strained.  We
consider it unlikely that a national oil company would be
given this freedom.  Indeed, even if the U.S. Government
provided such freedom, foreign governments would tend to
view the national oil company as an extension of the U.S.
Government.  The national oil company would be unaccepted
in some foreign areas and politically vulnerable in others.

Fourth, successful operation of an oil company requires a flexible and responsive management able to adjust
promptly to changing economic condition.  National oil companies, subject to broad government direction, have been
less successful than private enterprise in developing sound
management.

This is not to say that the U.S. Government cannot
help in the international oil area.  Indeed there are positive and necessary roles to play.  Turning now to the possible
role of a national oil company within the United States,

there is no reason to believe that such a company would help produce more domestic energy. To start with, many of the drawbacks mentioned above for the foreign area would also apply at home.

Perhaps more important domestically, however, is the impact a national oil company would have on existing private companies. First, there is no idle pool of manpower or equipment waiting to be used. Lead times for steel are up to two-three years. There is a shortage of qualified personnel. A national oil company would not add to industry's capabilities, but would have to draw qualified people and supplies of equipment away from existing private companies and existing exploration and construction programs.

If the national oil company is given economic advantages denied to private companies, the impact will be even greater. Consider the pending legislation that would create FOGCO. This legislation would provide FOGCO with the most promising 20% of the acreage held by the federal government onshore and offshore. FOGCO would pay no bonus and no rentals on its acreage; no royalties, no taxes. It would be able to borrow at lower rates than private companies, since the government would guarantee the loans. It would have access to all geological and geophysical data collected by the federal government, including data from private industry-access that private companies do not have. Subsidies of this magnitude would force private companies to hesitate before they exposed risk capital against this kind of competition.

The proponents of FOGCO also argue that this national oil company would provide a yardstick for measuring the costs and profits of private oil companies and would make private companies more competitive.

The question of being a yardstick was really answered above. A national oil company with the subsidies proposed for FOGCO could never be a yardstick for a private company. The ground rules for operation and financing would be too different to permit comparison.

The argument that competition would be increased implies that competition today is somehow inadequate. This,

in turn, implies an excessive concentration in the oil industry.  There is no evidence that this is true and there
is much that it is not.  The oil industry is, for instance,
much less concentrated than autos, steel, computers and many
other industries.  The single largest oil refiner has less
than 10% of total U.S. refining capacity.  A January, 1974
FTC staff report stated that "energy concentration and concentration in each of the three fossil fuels is relatively
low."

        One indication of the competitive structure of the
oil industry is the success of the independent sector over
the years.

        The independent producers are a strong, aggressive
group, benefitting from recent crude price increases and
demonstrably successful in Outer Continental Shelf lease
sales.  Statistics show that non-major companies 1/ participated in over 80% of all winning Outer Continental Shelf bids
awarded between June, 1967 and March, 1974.

        The independent refiners have increased in number
and strength over the years.  In 1951, there were 20 companies
with 50,000 barrels per day or more of capacity each.  These
were classified as "majors" by the Department of Interior.
The total refining capacity of these companies in 1951 was
5.6 million barrels per day or 81% of total U.S. refining
capacity.  By 1974 this same group of companies (reduced to
17 since Sinclair, Pure & Richfield merged with others in
the top 20) had increased refining capacity to 11.1 million
barrels per day but their percentage had declined to 74% of
total U.S. capacity.  There are today an additional 18 companies with 50,000 barrels per day of refining capacity
apiece, and 11 of these were not even in the refining
business in 1951.

        The independent marketers have increased market
share in recent years -- particularly since the mid to late
1960's.  Publicly available data show that independents moved
from 22.5% of the United States market in 1967 to 30.6% in
the first quarter of 1974.  It also appears that the independents held market share through 1973 and through the first
quarter of 1974.  The independent marketer has more than
held his own in recent years.

In summary, we consider that a national oil company operating domestically would have no positive benefits and, conversely, would retard efforts to develop domestic energy resources.

Just as in the foreign area, however, there is a positive and necessary role for the Government to play in encouraging development of indigenous energy resources. This role is one of reconciling conflicting national objectives (e.g., energy and environment), making public lands available for exploration and development (coal as well as petroleum), creating an encouraging economic climate and removing the uncertainties that hang over the energy industries today.

D. The establishment of a federal oil and gas corporation would almost certainly lead to slower development of the nation's energy resources. Under the concepts publicized, such a corporation would not be an equal competitor with industry, but rather would have cost-free access to 20 percent of the federal lands, lower taxes and no royalty payments, capital budget subsidized from tax funds, and free access to confidential data belonging to all competing private companies. Its conceived operation would tend to "skim the cream" of potential exploration areas and greatly reduce the economic incentive for private investment in high risk areas. Such competition would be basically unfair and ultimately destructive, leading to the elimination of some independents and integrated company activities.

One of the serious disadvantages of a federal corporation would be its isolation from market economics and lack of profit motivation. There would be no competitive incentive for efficiency or economic allocation of the firm's (taxpayers') resources. This could result in uneconomic investments, inefficiency and development of a bureaucratic style with associated hidden costs.

While a federal corporation would be able to undertake uneconomic projects contributing to energy independence for the United States, it would tend to delay development of natural resources rather than provide increased supplies. It would take perhaps several years to organize and staff an operational corporation, during which time it would draw investment funds, manpower and equipment

from the private sector.  This would, of course, interfere
with the private sector's operations, reduce its efficiency,
and delay its development of new production.  Once the
federal corporation was operational, it would not provide
more supplies than would otherwise be expected, unless its
activities were limited to projects beyond the scope of
private investment and its prices maintained at a sufficient
level to avoid reducing incentives for private investment.
However, the likely use of "political" pricing as proposed
by some proponents of a federal oil and gas corporation would
not only reduce incentives for private investment, but also
stimulate wasteful consumption and inefficient energy use.
This would be inimical to established energy conservation
and independence goals.  It would increase pressures for
the government corporation to increase supplies while holding
down prices at ever-increasing cost to the Treasury.

The operating and cost data provided by such a
corporation would be a misleading guide to private section
performance due to the built-in cost advantages, probable
inefficiencies and artificial pricing policies of a national
corporation.

E.  The establishment of a government petroleum corporation would be counterproductive.  There is nothing inherent in a government corporation that enables it to operate
with any greater efficiency or to provide products or services to the consumer at a lower price than can be achieved
by private industry.  This has been amply demonstrated in
those foreign countries where government petroleum companies
have been established.  In the area of exploration and production, where significant risks are involved and where the
failure ratio is high, government companies are particularly
ineffective.  This results from the fact that it is extremely
difficult from a political standpoint to justify continuing
expenditures with no or marginal results in the discovery of
new petroleum resources.

In order to obscure the expenses and lack of results incumbent in exploration and production, government
companies universally gravitate into the refining and marketing fields in an attempt to generate revenue-producing
operations.

Government companies pay no income taxes, pay a
relatively low rate of state and local taxes, and have

access to essentially unlimited federal funds at rates far more attractive than those available to private industry. In the face of such dramatic advantages, private industry would not be able to compete. This is particularly true when recognizing that the petroleum industry is capital intensive and that the Federal Government owns most of the potentially productive lands.

Thus the establishment of a national petroleum corporation can only be viewed as the first in an irreversible series of steps leading to socialization or nationalization of the entire industry.

Such a move would be counter to the professed reasons used to justify the establishment of a national petroleum company. Obviously it would take years to develop such a company to where it is as large as any of the present major U.S. oil companies. ($5 to $10 billion worth of assets, and 25 to 40,000 employees, with sales approaching $10 billion) Even at that point this company would be able to provide only approximately 5 to 8% of the total demand for petroleum, assuming it could become as successful as its private counterparts. Obviously, the nation must continue to rely upon the private industry. The existence of the federal oil company would, however, seriously and adversely affect the ability of private industry to generate the capital needed for its activities. Thus the mere existence of a federal oil company would be seriously contrary to our needs to develop adequate domestic petroleum supplies.

This is particularly true, because one reason often given for the establishment of a federal petroleum company is that it could be used as a measure of performance against which to evaluate private companies. In practice, the converse is true. Any federal activity is much less subject to the scrutiny of the press, effectively resists government regulation to a degree unavailable to private industry, and has unlimited ways in which to obscure inefficiency. Its tax, financing and other legislated advantages totally invalidates any comparison between a government owned company and private industry.

A specific and recent example relates to the TVA which is often referred to by proponents of the national

petroleum company as an ideal case. In 1960, provisions
were established to make the TVA self-financing. It was
required to pay back over a 50-year period the capital
originally provided by the government and to generate
additional needed funds through bonds or through rate increases. Earlier this year the TVA requested and received
Congressional approval to default on the repayment of $400
million under this schedule. These funds were to be used
for establishing facilities required to meet the environmental regulations. Thus in effect the TVA defaulted on
its dividends to its shareholder because the political
pressures were such that it was unable or unwilling to increase its rates, and its financial structure would not
accommodate a bond issue. This move received almost no
notice in the press. By comparison, the Consolidated Edison
default on its dividends has been the subject of innumerable
editorials and has been carried on the media throughout every
state and at every level. In effect, the voter and the public
lose a significant amount of their ability to influence industry when it is taken over by the government.

A government-operated industry has the inherent
weakness of having no motivation to cut costs or increase
efficiency in order to increase profits. It is subject to
irresistible political pressure to engage in projects which
are economically undesirable, merely because they create
additional jobs or provide additional income in areas of
interest to influential government officials. Because many
of the decisions would be unduly influenced by political
considerations, needed programs would be further retarded
in an industry which is already besieged by long lead times
and undue delays.

Private industry has continually shown that in
periods when it is not unduly fettered by government regulations it can effectively develop needed capacity. This
is the only sure means for maintaining competition and
providing efficient operations and minimum costs.

F. Traditionally, the U.S. has relied upon the private
sector to provide petroleum supplies. The record with
regard to this reliance has been quite good despite the
interference of government in the free market pricing system,
such as in natural gas, which forced shifts in demand and

supply.  In fact, the private sector energy industries, in
general, deserve credit for a good record of providing ample
energy supplies at efficient economics.

The private sector petroleum companies and other
energy industries can and stand ready to continue to provide
such a service to the American consumer.  These are indeed
complicated industries which operate efficiently in a competitive climate and require skilled employees and management.
The petroleum industry has developed skills in operation, both
in the U.S. and in foreign countries, and this expertise exists
in all phases of operations to the extent that a high degree
of efficiency (and minimum costs) are involved.

Government involvement in the business would not
only be duplicative, but subject to a gross misuse of resources and the tendency to achieve political expediency
at the expense of business efficiency.  Possible distortions
in economics would be a threat to the future continuing supply
of oil.

The establishment of a new petroleum corporation,
fully or partially owned by the U.S. Government, would
represent a sharp reversal of U.S. economic policy with an
immediate and detrimental effect on all privately owned
petroleum businesses.  Without knowing the full terms and
conditions under which such a corporation would be established, it is impossible to enumerate completely the
ramifications of such a move on each of the eight functions
specified in the question.


21.  What is your opinion with respect to the regulation of
U.S. petroleum companies as public utilities?  What are the
advantages and disadvantages?  What would be the effect
upon the U.S. and world petroleum markets?  Please assess
separately.

Response:

Companies unanimously opposed public utilities
regulation of the U.S. petroleum industry.

SELECTED COMMENTS:

A.  The purpose of establishing public utilities is to
supply an indispensable service under monopoly conditions
with government regulations of prices, profits and service
quality segments of the petroleum industry such as the interstate natural gas industry are already under governmental
control.  However, history clearly shows that public utility
regulation in the petroleum sector has actually provided a
disservice to the public by following economically inconsistant
policies.  Public utilities have fallen short of their goal
because cost based regulation cannot effectively allocate
scarce resources such as petroleum.  Free market pricing is
required to allocate most resources in an effective and
efficient manner.

Public utility regulation is unworkable in a highly
complex industry where many products compete with each other,
and that is now made up of a large number of entrants.  In
the petroleum industry, the risk involved in exploring for
hydrocarbons cannot be adequately accounted for by cost of
service regulations.  The use of public utility criteria in
the establishment of natural gas rates has been an ineffective
proxy for supply and demand--creating the present shortage.
Similar arguments preclude both marketing and refining from
effective public utility regulation.

With respect to world petroleum markets, we believe
that U.S. petroleum companies operating as public utilities
would have an anti-competitive affect.

B.  The oil and gas industry does not possess the
essential characteristics of a public utility.  Therefore,
it would make no sense to attempt to regulate U.S. oil and
gas producers as public utilities, and to do so would be
contrary to the public interest and to the objectives of
Project Independence.

The domestic petroleum industry, operating under the
free enterprise system, has efficiently and effectively served
this nation in peace and at war, with adequate oil and gas
supplies at reasonable prices.  The industry supplies about
75% of all U.S. energy and its performance is unmatched anywhere in the world.  Most of the world's oil and gas has been

found and developed by the U.S. petroleum industry or through use of its technology.

The characteristics of this industry fundamentally distinguish it from public utilities. Utilities are not prime producers of energy but, because duplicate facilities or services are unwarranted, they are given monopoly status in the geographic areas served. The thousands of competing oil and gas producers are engaged in risky, high cost ventures and are given no such monopolistic advantages by government. Public utilities are normally characterized by clearly defined costs, high debt-equity ratios, replaceable equipment as basic assets, and exclusive franchise areas of service with an obligation to continue to serve the public. Unlike public utilities, the petroleum industry has no obligation to search for oil or gas, no franchised territories, and traditionally has obtained the capital necessary to continue in business largely from internally generated funds. The high risk and cost of exploration makes it difficult to borrow for such purposes except upon a pledge of its general assets and producing properties.

Experience has already proven that federal utility-type regulation is unworkable for the petroleum industry. The Federal Power Commission's (FPC) effort over the past 20 years to use utility type regulation to fix well head prices for natural gas is primarily the cause of the present critical natural gas shortage.

The FPC first attempted to set wellhead prices for producers by using a company-by-company, public-utility type cost of service regulation. This method proved unworkable and in fact led to a breakdown in the administrative process. Then the FPC turned to its area rate approach to achieve procedured efficiency, but each method of setting prices was still based on utility type costing. It, therefore, failed to establish prices at levels which would provide the incentive for the industry to find and develop adequate gas supplies for the nation.

Artificially low prices and environmental concerns have unduly stimulated demand and depressed domestic drilling for new natural gas supplies. Users of fuel quickly turned to the cheap clean-burning natural gas, preventing development

of alternatives badly needed today to alleviate the energy
shortage.  In light of this experience with utility type
regulation recognized by most experts as the primary cause
of the critical natural gas shortage, it is incomprehensible
that public utility type regulation would be proposed for
crude oil and refined petroleum products.  If 20 years of
failure in efforts to regulate the natural gas prices using
a public utility approach teaches us anything, it is the
clear lesson that public utility regulation will not result
in increased supplies but quite to the contrary will only
exacerbate the energy shortage in this nation.

Domestic supplies of oil and gas can be found and
brought to the market more quickly and at lower cost by
freeing the industry from its regulatory shackles and permitting the free market place to operate.  Only if price
and related incentives are sufficient will the difficult and
costly exploration and development offshore and in Alaska
be pursued rapidly enough for domestic supplies to make a
meaningful contribution to alleviating the energy shortage.

As a consequence of recently improved prices for
natural gas and crude oil, there has been a substantial increase in the exploration and development activity.  The
competitive free enterprise system is still the best regulation of both price and supply.  Therefore, the only real
solution to the energy shortage is to permit this system to
provide the incentives which will encourage the further expansion of exploration and development activities needed to
bring forth the supplies required to meet the ever-growing
demand.  More government regulations is not the answer.

The oil and gas industry must meet tremendous capital
requirements to achieve a turn around in declining supply and
a higher degree of domestic energy sufficiency by 1985.  Even
with increasing profits the domestic petroleum industry will
not be able to internally generate all of the capital needs
essential to do the job.  Therefore, governmental policies
to encourage, not discourage, greatly expanded domestic exploration and development activity are needed to reduce dependence upon insecure foreign supplies with all of the attendant
economic, diplomatic and military risk.

The availability of more energy supplies in the market place is dependent upon the domestic petroleum industry's responses to the incentives offered and the available prospects. Business management confidence is a key motivating factor in exploration and development investments and surely would be destroyed by imposing public utility regulation. Investment decision making by the domestic petroleum industry looks to anticipated costs, not past costs. Oil and gas producers limit the scale of future investments to what is warranted by the prices allowed.

Public utility regulation of the domestic petroleum industry would be highly detrimental to the needed expansion of exploration and development activity domestically. Utility rates are generally set looking to past cost rather than to the future requirements or anticipated cost. In the petroleum industry, perhaps more than any other, unit supply costs tend to increase with an increase in the quantity to be found and developed. This is because the remaining prospects are often at greater depths, less accessible (e.g., in deeper water offshore), and located in hostile environments such as in Alaska where the risk and cost are substantially and progressively greater.

The quantity of oil or gas found or produced in a given year cannot be accurately related to the costs incurred in that year. Patently, this makes utility type costing a complex, inexact and futile exercise. Production in 1974 comes from leases acquired and wells drilled in prior years and 1974 exploratory costs are functionally related to reserves which will be added to available supplies over many years in the future. The characteristics of the oil and gas industry and the realities of the situation simply do not permit the forcing of that industry into the public utility mold.

The public utility approach of using past cost as the determinant of price is hopelessly circular. Prices tend to be cost determining. Thus, past costs based on inadequate past prices cannot be expected to elicit a supply equal to prospective requirements.

The free enterprise competitive market clearing standard, not public utility regulation, is the only way to timely assure optimum development of domestic oil and gas

reserves in conformance with the policy objective of Project
Independence. Public utility regulation would be wasteful
and counter-productive. It would substantially increase the
ultimate cost of the energy shortage borne by consumers and
would force them to turn to the much more insecure and
expensive alternates or to foreign supplies. This could
dangerously increase the nation's dependence upon foreign
sources of supply, adversely affect the balance of international payments and national security and clearly would be
contrary to the national economic objectives of increasing
productivity, achieving full employment, and improving the
environment.

There are no advantages of federal regulation of
U.S. petroleum companies as public utilities but only the
numerous serious disadvantages hereinabove set forth.

C. A utility is a public regulated monopoly aimed at
providing a specific service in a specific geographic area.
Its application has been wisely limited to public services
where the need for standardization and universality of service
outweigh the savings offered by more efficient free market
alternatives.

With the possible exception of pipelines (which are
already highly regulated), the oil industry does not meet
these criteria. The oil industry is dynamic, diversified,
complex, highly competitive and involves high risk investments. Bureaucratic decisions would be unable to keep up
with the complexities of the marketplace and administered
prices would either be too high or too low resulting in excess
profits or insufficient supply. Rate bases would need to be
compiled and administered for a multitude of producers,
refiners and marketers, all with different costs. Lower costs
supplies would need to be somehow rationed between competing
companies and regions. Realizations would tend to reflect
"cost plus" accounting, thus diminishing incentives for
efficient performance.

Federal Power Commission natural gas regulation
presents a clear example of the impact of government controls
on this industry. Since 1954 when controls were instituted,
the FPC has vainly sought a suitable regulatory method. The
artificially low prices imposed by the FPC have greatly

stimulated demand while at the same time diminishing both the incentive and the means to find new supplies. The inevitable result is that our country now has a serious shortage of natural gas that will take years to correct.

D. Public utility regulation is based on geographic monopolies which are franchised to perform public service. The economic criteria for this type of regulation follow two common indicators: the existence of a high concentration ratio of a few firms and a tendency in these firms toward excessive profits. These indicators combine with the desirability to effect economies of scale through nonduplication of facilities to characterize what should be a public utility.

The U.S. petroleum industry does not fit into this mold. This was amply demonstrated when utility wellhead price regulation of natural gas was attempted. The FPC found that it was dealing with monopsonies rather than monopolies, and a commodity rather than a service. Moreover, the rate bases and costs of service were not geographically nor economically related to the points of sale; and costs could not be realistically determined.

Utility regulation of other segments of the industry would encounter similar difficulties. The petroleum industry is not characterized by a high level of concentration. As Professor Mitchell observes in U.S. Energy Policy: A Primer, published in 1974 by the American Enterprise Institute for Public Policy Research, on page 96:

> "Consider the issue of concentration:
> In the first place, after an enormous
> amount of statistical research, there
> appears to be little, if any, correla-
> tion between concentration and monopoly
> profits across industries. Thus con-
> centration does not offer even a pre-
> sumption of monopoly. Second, the
> petroleum industry is not highly
> concentrated: The average market share
> of the four largest firms for all U.S.
> manufacturing industries in 1966 was 39
> percent. In 1972 the four largest do-
> mestic refiners had less than 33 percent

C-137

of the market, and the four largest
domestic crude oil producers had 31 percent of the market.  In 1968 the four
largest natural gas producers had 25 percent of the interstate market.  Most
manufacturing industries are more concentrated than the petroleum industry."

With respect to refining alone, government statistics
indicate that in 1951, 21 companies with refining capacities of
over 50,000 barrels per day made up 80.7% of the total U.S.
capacity; while in 1973, their percentage had declined to
76.8% and there were 16 additional companies in the 50,000
barrel-per-day category -- 10 of them new to the industry
since 1951.

The profitability in the petroleum industry has
not been excessive when compared to other industries and
this, too, suggests the lack of monopoly or oligopoly power.
We recognize that the many economic distortions that followed
the Arab embargo have increased petroelum industry profits.
However, the major portion of these profits is due to inventory
gains and currency adjustments; and it probably is temporary
in nature.  Based on return on net worth, the petroleum industry was, on the average, less profitable than total U.S.
manufacturing.  Professor Mitchell states the following
conclusions on page 93 of U.S. Energy Policy:  A Primer:

"American petroleum companies were significantly less profitable than the S&P
500 over the 1953 to 1972 period.  Indeed,
not one of the twenty-one American petroleum companies equalled the S&P 500's
rate of return!

"The eight companies charged by the
Federal Trade Commission with monopoliz-
ing the industry earned an average rate
of return of 12.1 percent, more than 20
percent below the S&P norm for the 1953
to 1972 period."

While it lacks the concentration and excessive profit
criteria, the petroleum industry also cannot be organized to
perform unique and relatively homogenous functions such as
those performed by public utilities.  It is impossible to
see how the monopolies would be organized.  If they are to
consist of a few integrated companies, they would have no
workable geographical territories and no market monopolies.
They would simply compete at each level with smaller, non-
regulated companies and the independents who abound in each
functional part of the business.  The resulting "competition"
is difficult to imagine -- but surely it could not be dictated
by free market forces.

If the total industry -- large, small, integrated
and independent alike -- were to fall under public utility
regulation, there would be no definition for the term "public
utility".  If regional and functional monopolies were to be
organized, definition would return, but thousands of independent
businessmen would be forced to leave the field and the competition which has characterized the industry would cease.

The industry is a complex one, and the substitution
of regulation for markets would require highly complex and
ultimately unworkable regulation.  One of the complexities
would be the handling of the high-risk side of the business.
Utility rates of return are based on the low risks of regional
and functional monopolies; but in the business of exploration
either the returns must be very high or all cost must be
covered by the regulated rates.  If the second course is
followed, there would be a disincentive for efficient exploration for hydrocarbons.  The relative success of an
individual company in its exploration efforts would have a
direct effect on its price and, therefore, pockets of high
or low prices could exist from monopoly to monopoly.

In addition, public utilities are highly leveraged,
while the petroleum industry generally has a low level of
debt capital.  The public utility's ability to attract capital
for projects with relatively low rates of return is a function
of this leverage; and it has provided adequately attractive
returns on the shareholders' investment.  However, the
regulatory lag in responding to the higher costs which are of
epidemic proportions today has made utility rates of return
inadequate and the raising of capital has become difficult.

This problem would be elevated by exponential proportions when applied to regulated petroleum companies whose expenses for unsuccessful exploration would have to be covered by their prices or their rates of return. If the regulatory authority, in its judgment, were not to allow sufficient prices or returns to cover exploration, a firm could lose out in the "competition" for exploratory acreage. The risk judgments of the regulators would supplant those of boards of directors.

For these reasons, we think that any attempt to regulate the U.S. oil companies as public utilities would result in gross inefficiencies and misallocations of resources, and would impose a heavy burden on U.S. consumers.

A domestic industry burdened by this type of regulation either would be placed at a fatal competitive disadvantage with foreign competition and reliance on imports would increase; or the law would be such as to drive incentive capital outside the U.S. In either event, the nation and its consumers would be the losers. The tragedy of the utility approach would be that it would not be based on sound facts or rationale, but on misinformation, faulty assumptions and political passions.

E.  The current financing difficulties which face many public utility companies today are in part due to their regulation by government agencies which points out a strong disadvantage of this type of regulation. With respect to petroleum companies, regulation could result in sharply decreased exploration as many small independent producers would be unable to compete under the burden of regulation and to some extent major oil company capital commitments would be channeled out of exploration into more profitable ventures outside the petroleum industry.

F.  Public utility regulation substitutes regulation for competition. This is often desirable in the case of an area monopoly where a single company can provide the most efficient and lowest cost service (such as telephones and electric utilities). However, in situations where naturally competitive forces exist, utility regulation can cause severe competitive distortions. Because of the existing competitive environment for U.S. petroleum companies, there are no advantages for utility regulation, and such regulation would be next to impossible to apply without eliminating all but one entity in any single location.

An excellent example of utility regulation distortion is railroad regulation. Utility regulation has prevented the industry from effectively responding to the changing competitive situation resulting from the growth of the trucking industry. This has contributed to the severe financial difficulties of many railroads, and the need for substantial government subsidies. The fault lies not with the regulatory intent but with the failure to recognize that competition and the free market are the most effective regulators.

Another example of distortion is the financial plight of many electric utilities today. Because of the lag resulting from the inherent structure of utility regulation, these companies have been unable to respond competitively to changing basic energy prices and electrical demand patterns. As a result, financing and construction of badly needed facilities have been postponed. The FEA itself has appealed to the states for rate relief and the SEC has had to relax certain financial regulations.

Within the petroleum industry the misallocation of resources resulting from the FPC attempts at utility regulation of gas prices constitutes a prima facie example of the inadequacy and counter-productive nature of this approach.

In contrast to so-called monopolies, the petroleum industry environment in the U.S. is highly competitive by any recognized standard. The industry is composed of thousands of large and small companies which produce, manufacture, and sell a wide variety of products over wide geographic areas and bear no resemblance to a natural monopoly. This competitive structure of the petroleum industry has permitted it to respond positively to the dynamic U.S. energy situation. In response to improved market prices and the national goal of increased energy self-sufficiency, most petroleum companies have announced sharply increased domestic capital spending programs beginning in 1974.

The diverse and competitive structure of the petroleum industry also would make it almost impossible to apply utility regulation to existing individual companies. Since many firms compete in each geographic area and in each segment of the business, nothing resembling a natural monopoly exists. Establishing utility regulation, either in the form of uniform product prices or rates of return, would not be practical since neither test could be consistently applied to the many widely varying sectors and firms in the petroleum industry. On the other hand, the simpler solution of applying cost of service regulation to each company would result in a multi-tiered price structure which could not be sustained in the marketplace.

It should be pointed out that the U.S. petroleum companies are currently under price control and mandatory allocations regulations that approach that of a utility status. Our experience to date with these controls indicates that it is impossible to substitute regulation for the dictates of the free market. The FEA finds that many new regulations require adjustment to undo unwanted or unanticipated side effects. A number of these regulations seem to have a compounding effect of creating distortions, causing unexpected shortages, and inhibiting planning, efficiency, and, of course, competition.

In summary, utility regulation of the petroleum industry is not warranted by its structure, or by any lack of competition. Also, it is difficult, based on experience, to see how utility regulation could be implemented, or could improve the petroleum industry's ability to provide supplies or respond to changing competitive conditions.

G. Under the combined influences of the Arabian embargo on oil shipments to the United States and the unprecedently high prices unilaterally and arbitrarily established by the OPEC governments for crude oil exported from their lands, all in late 1973 and early 1974, prices for petroleum products rose sharply throughout the world, including the U.S. and there were some spot shortages. Also there was much fear, until the end of the embargoes, that the shortages would become more general and more serious. Such price increases, shortages and fears stimulated complaints from the U.S. public along with a variety of suggestions which, however stated, were directed to the wishful objective of somehow getting back to, or near, the former status quo under which there was a plentiful supply of petroleum products at all times at low prices. It is believed the idea of regulating U.S. petroleum companies as public utilities was put forth as one such suggestion with the idea that it would somehow control prices at attractively low levels but without giving thought to the complexities and unsuitable features that public utility regulation would entail.

Fundamental to the whole idea of "public utility" regulation of the U.S. petroleum companies is that the oil industry is totally unlike industries regulated as public utilities.

It is characteristic of public utility regulation to require that one obtain a "Certificate of Convenience and Necessity" upon a showing there is a need for additional service not furnished by others. The utility normally is given some form of monopoly for serving an area and is protected against the entry of competition in its area. Ordinarily, rates or prices are set or approved for the commodity or service furnished. Such rates or prices are reasonably determinable for the utilities because the regulating agency closely observes all costs and ordinarily exercises tight control over investments for capital installations and major contracts. Thus it can calculate prices or rates estimated to give a fair return on the "rate base" -- a valuation of the property owned by the utility which is useful and is used in its public utility business.

The public utility concept works well for the telephone and the electricity services of an area. In each case it avoids uneconomic duplication of capital facilities and, in telephones, avoids the inconveniences and delays that competing systems in the same area would cause. In consideration of the monopoly they obtain, the public's interest is safeguarded by the governmental regulating agency which requires that the quantity and quality of service meet appropriate standards and which closely controls and/or observes costs and sets or approves prices or rates that are fair to the public.

22. What is your opinion with respect to the establishment of a multi-national organization for the allocation of global petroleum supplies, both under normal supply conditions and under emergency conditions only? What are the advantages and disadvantages? What consequences do you believe this system would entail for international petroleum supply and price?

Response:

Companies overwhelmingly opposed such a multi-national organization under "normal" conditions. More than one-third of the respondents, however, expressed support for a multinational allocation system in the event of supply "crises".

SELECTED COMMENTS:

A. The Embargo of November, 1973 proved to the world that an abundant source of energy is a powerful weapon for any country to possess.

Each country has now either formulated its own plan for the preservation of its energy resources or is in the process of doing so and it is inconceivable to this company that any of the major producing countries would agree to commit their reserves to a multi-national organization for allocating global petroleum supplies.

The structuring of such an organization, while admirable, would be a monumental if not impossible task in itself.

B. The free market place is the most efficient allocator of petroleum products and during normal supply conditions. During emergency conditions, the international major oil companies are in the best position to allocate supplies equitable to their customers on a world-wide basis.

Since the OPEC countries currently are in a position to control world supply and prices, neither a multinational company, nor a confederation of international majors, or any individual oil company will likely have any impact on world supply or price.

The best response to OPEC control is not allocation of supply but rather the maintenance of downward pressure against demand for oil in Persian Gulf markets.

C. In theory any multi-national organization binding oil-importing countries to consistant and rational petroleum policies would be a counter force to the oil producing cartel. However, the possibility of forming an effective organization to carry out these activities is remote since many of the countries involved have varying political and economic considerations.

Questions of how such an organization will operate are crucial. Will the organization purchase petroleum? How will the mechanics of allocation be determined? What will be the function of the major international oil companies with their worldwide distribution capabilities? Will this single organization be an "Organization of Oil Importing Countries" that will act as a uniform oil negotiating body? Will it also arrange for stockpiling?

If an effective multi-national organization could be formed some of its other advantages might be:

1. To remove some of the monopoly profits OPEC has gained since the embargo;

2. Preventing the bidding war among countries and companies that had and could in the future raise petroleum prices above postings during an embargo type of confrontation;

3. Avoid importing countries being played against each other with ever escalating political and economic demands;

4. Coordinate and/or become involved in joint programs for the conservation of energy;

5. The joint efforts to find solutions to the trade and balance-of-payment problems resulting from the prospects of significantly high oil prices than had been experience in recent years. Such efforts could result in joint export policies to OPEC nations, a channeling of funds to prevent disruption of the world's financial mechanism; and

6. For the U.S. it could be cheaper than Project Independence.

During an emergency an effective organization might have already set up an emergency storage system which could be used to prevent a significant economic deterioration during a short-term embargo. Rationing plans, the sharing of non-petroleum and other cooperative efforts, could make the consequence of an embargo easier to withstand than a go-it-alone policy. Furthermore, the knowledge by OPEC that such cooperative efforts can be put into effect should reduce the probability of future embargoes.

For the U.S. the disadvantage of the multi-national organization route is national security. If the U.S. alone does not possess the ability to carry out the required integrated petroleum functions--transporting, refining, and distributing--it could be "blackmailed" by one or more dissident nations.

D. We firmly believe that interests of both consumers and producers are best served when market forces are allowed to operate freely. The terms "normal supply conditions" and "emergency conditions" are devoid of meaning unless they are specifically defined. We would define a supply condition as normal if only the laws of economics are operative in any given situation; an emergency condition is one in which forces other than economic are in such preponderance as to destroy the market mechanism. Neither one has ever existed in its pure form. Thus the difference between normal and emergency conditions is one of degree, not of kind.

We do not believe that sovereign states can get together and, by confining themselves solely to economic considerations, devise a truly objective yardstick which they can use in determining whether a supply situation has ceased to be normal.

E. [We do] not believe that a multi-national organization for the allocation of global petroleum supplies would be a workable solution to the petroleum supply problems in either normal or emergency conditions. Such an institutional allocation of petroleum would eliminate the many small and diverse negotiations in the free market system that provide the opportunity for price competition and the process by which prices regulate supply and demand. The relative power to establish a price ceiling of a multi-national organization on the consuming side of the world petroleum market would not be sufficient to compensate for the ability of the producing countries to maintain a price floor. In emergency conditions, sharing agreements among nations should be, and in practice would be, admin-istered by national governments. An international logistics structure through which such agreements could be effectuated already exists in the form of the world petroleum distribu-tion system consisting of international petroleum companies.

Historically, multinational organizations have shown a tendency to introduce irrelevant issues and to operate in the political rather than economic area. Member nations are generally not willing to allow such organizations to make independent decisions, and to the extent some sovereignty would have to accrue for the organization to be effective, it would likely fail. On the other hand, multi-lateral emergency allocation agreements, arrived at jointly by the countries most affected by possible embar-goes, is a concept we strongly support.

F. Under "normal" conditions, i.e., no embargoes, but production levels controlled by the OPEC countries, such an organization for allocation of global supplies would be of questionable value. For the same reasons discussed in our response to Question 14 (re mandatory stored reserves and consumption cutbacks) agreement among the consuming nations as to what was fair and equitable would be very difficult to achieve or administer. Under emergency conditions, i.e., embargoes and/or severe production cutbacks by one or more exporting countries, the incentives for the consuming coun-tries to reach agreement are far greater, but the problems still remain and effective and enforceable agreements under crisis conditions would be reached with great difficulty (however, this does not imply that we shouldn't keep trying to work these problems out).

The recent embargoes and cutbacks imposed by the Arab states provide an excellent example. The immediate scramble among consuming nations for what supplies were available created an atmosphere of near panic, and hopes of cooperation and sharing between countries vanished. Bilateral proposals by the consuming countries to the exporting countries proliferated, in the hopes of getting an assured supply of oil at almost any price. We believe this over-reaction by the consuming nations, in late 1973, had a great deal to do with OPEC's subsequent "doubling" of crude prices on January 1, 1974, in spite of the 70% price increase made on October 16, 1973.

In retrospect, the recent crisis could have been much more severe than it actually was. The final report of the Emergency Petroleum Supply Committee (composed of U.S. Government and industry representatives) concluded that during the first quarter of 1974 the Free World deficit relative to normal total energy demand was 4%, distributed as follows: U.S. 6%; Europe 4%; Japan and South Korea 8%; Other 1%.

This relatively even spreading of the shortfall was a truly remarkable feat under the circumstances, and could not have been accomplished without the efforts, expertise, management, facilities and the widespread operations of the international oil companies, each acting independently from the other in an effort to supply its worldwide outlets and customers as fairly and equitably as possible. Little, if any, assistance or guidance came from governments. The embargo rules imposed by the Arab states were complex and changeable, and even those countries accorded "friendly" status by the Arab nations encountered dislocations of supply.

The point to be made is that even with the relatively small overall energy shortfall (per the findings of Emergency Petroleum Supply Committee) during the recent crisis, self-interest prevailed among virtually all of the consuming nations, and well-intentioned agreements in principle for mutual assistance were quickly forgotten when the pinch began to be felt.

The desirability of an effective multinational organization to allocate petroleum supplies equitably on a worldwide basis under emergency conditions is unquestioned. However the problems associated with determining what is fair to each consuming country (no matter how different their situations may be), and voluntary or mandatory compliance must be resolved before such a program can succeed.

Basically, it would involve the consuming countries giving up some degree of their sovereignty to a supernational organization. The last time this happened was when the Allies banded together in World War II under the threat of almost certain victory by the Nazis in Europe if each had attempted to go it alone.

For the reasons discussed at some length in our responses to Questions 13, 14, 18 and 19, the best and most practical approach is to leave this problem with the oil companies, each operating independently and according to its commercial interests, <u>but with increased support, not restrictions, from their home governments</u>.

Any system that would even out supply disruptions among consuming countries so that none suffered unduly with respect to another might possibly forestall further increases in prices, but any decrease in prices would be unlikely. From the standpoint of the producing countries, the more effective any sharing or distribution plan is among the consuming countries, the more incentive the producers have to further increase prices and/or reduce production. Also, so long as the OPEC countries remain unified on price matters and are willing to restrict production on a concerted basis, there may not be much the importing countries can do about it for the next five or ten years.

The answer, of course, is to seek and develop indigenous oil and gas as rapidly as possible, as well as accelerated and resolute development of alternate energy sources such as coal and nuclear power. Until these things are done, the consuming nations of the Free World will have no leverage on the exporting countries with respect to supply or price. The oil industry can probably contribute more than any other agency, including governments, toward accomplishing these objectives providing adequate economic incentives exist. Current well-intentioned but misguided and ill-informed legislative proposals to restrict oil companies' activities and profits would in fact by very much against the interests of the United States as well as its Allies in the Free World.

23. What is your opinion with respect to the establishment of a multi-national organization to coordinate national petroleum policy with other petroleum importing countries? What are the advantages and disadvantages? What would be the effect upon world petroleum supply and price?

Response:

A majority of the companies expressed support for a policy coordinating international organizations, but many were skeptical of its ability to achieve de facto coordination of policies among consuming nations of divergent national interests. Companies which opposed this option most frequently cited the impossibility of coordination as their rationale.

SELECTED COMMENTS:

A. A consultative organization could be of some help in discouraging leapfrogging in bidding contests between importing countries. However, its effectiveness would be limited to the limited effectiveness inherent in any "jawboning" type inflation control program. Again, the same problems with polarization exist. There is also the risk that a consumer's cartel would merely strengthen the hand of the producer's cartel.

B. A multinational organization to coordinate energy policies will require extensive preparatory consultation and development. As a first step we favor the establishment, either formally or informally, of an overall international framework between consuming and producing countries defining and providing for international terms of trade and cooperation within which private enterprise can then conduct their business and assume their entrepreneurial roles. Such arrangements would include various channels of communication to exchange ideas on such matters as energy conservation, technological improvements and new energy development.

We believe that within such a framework a more cooperative environment would be created which could over time increase trade, provide more optimum allocation and use of energy resources and thereby have a positive effect on the energy supply and price situation.

As a second step but consistent with the overall international objectives that such an arrangement would be predicated upon, we would encourage the establishment of broad, stable national energy policies and goals by <u>individual countries</u> within which business and government can cooperate to mobilize sustained efforts. At present, these policies are generally loosely defined. At such time as they are developed further, then we believe there is some merit and benefit to coordinate national petroleum policies with other countries. However, achieving any level of coordination will be difficult to attain because of the many interests involved. Success of such an effort is beyond our ability to speculate. We refer to our answers to Question 19 and elsewhere for further comments on the subject.

C. The establishment of a multi-national organization to coordinate national petroleum policy with other importing countries has disadvantages similar to that of a multi-national supply organization. The complexities involved in satisfying the diverse objectives of the participating nations are much greater than those faced by the organization of exporting nations. No doubt, self-interest on the part of individual nations would continually disrupt the objective of this effort. It is very doubtful that the organization could effect changes in world petroleum supply or price of any consequence.

D. We believe that importing countries and producing countries need to agree on broad principles which are in the interests of both. These agreements should recognize the desire for assured supplies at realistic and predictable prices and should reflect the wish of exporting countries to maximize the value of their oil and gas over the long run. These could include the optimum development of alternative energy sources in the importing countries as well as in certain exporting countries which may wish to extend the life of their oil and gas exports.

Given such a framework of governmental agreements, the world petroleum industry can then continue to operate both nationally and internationally in a free market, competitively oriented to insure maximum efficiency in utilization of manpower, money, and materials.

This proposed framework of governmental agreements, with a free market, competitively oriented world oil industry operating within them, obviously will reasonably protect the best interests of each country and provide a more stable world economic climate in which all nations can pursue their individual economic planning and development.

E.  A multi-national organization to coordinate national petroleum policy with other petroleum importing countries would have significant advantages.  It could increase the negotiating strength of the major consuming nations through a common strategy for counterbalancing the influence of OPEC.  It could reduce the ability of the producing national to play the consuming nations off against each other.  A multi-national organization could also assist in planning for cooperative activities like emergency reserves, shared petroleum supplies in an emergency, and effective programs for reducing energy demands.  It would be a useful form for the alignment of national policies and could provide guidance to policy implementation.  However, such an organization would have to include a significant portion of the major importing nations to be effective in offsetting the impact of an embargo against all or some of the members.

F.  We believe that a multi-national organization which gathers information and acts as a channel for communication among oil importing nations is highly desirable.  Directionally, this could give more stability to world petroleum supply and prices.

G.  If a fully cooperative multi-national organization could be established, and if that organization held a monopoly of vital goods or services that the producing countries could not do without or get elsewhere, then such an organization would have the clout to force a fair-price and supply of petroleum.  The risks of failure are high and the probability of agreement is low.  The rapport developed between the free world and the non-free world would be further strained.

H.  Bring out the troops and the guns after world supplies decline below basic needs.


24.  What is your opinion with respect to the establishment of a national or cooperatively multi-national system to reduce petroleum demand?  What other consequences could it have?

Response:

Half of the respondents favored a coordinated international demand restraint policy. As in the answers to question 23, most of the companies expressed skepticism on the feasibility of multi-national coordination. The majority of the petroleum companies felt that price, rather than a multi-national system, should be allowed to reduce demand. The size and diversity of a program would be too complicated; thus, volunteerism was recommended. Companies thought that a multi-national system could be effective primarily in the area of conservation information and technical knowledge exchanges.

SELECTED COMMENTS:

A. Any organized system to encourage or require such objective should be on a national, rather than a multinational, basis because of the widely different positions of each nation and the impracticality of multinational enforcement. It must be recognized by all nations that any controls which artificially hold down the real economic value of petroleum will be counter-productive to the objective of reduced demand and will increase the problem of developing new supply. If permitted, the market place will take care of demand reduction.

B. [We support] efforts to conserve energy by trying to find more efficient and less wasteful ways to use energy. We cannot, however, support the idea of a national or multi-national system to reduce petroleum demand for two reasons.

A. The question should be not one of reducing petroleum demand but rather reducing total energy demand. Petroleum products, natural gas, coal, nuclear power can be substituted for one another in many uses. Therefore, all energy forms should be considered as a package and the degree of substitution can best be determined in markets free of price controls and allocation schemes.

B. The word "system" is so broad a concept that it can mean anything from the free exchange of ideas among nations on conservation to rigid allocation and price control schemes. We believe that increases in the price of energy, which must come about to pay for higher costs of exploration, development, production, supplies, labor, and

capital, will provide a compelling incentive for the voluntary conservation of energy and will help promote the
replacement of inefficient machines with more efficient
ones.  It is better to permit free market forces to function
to the maximum possible extent.  In the long run, these
forces are the most efficient way to allocate supplies and
call for new supplies.

We could support the proposed system if it included
all energy forms and were defined soley as the cooperative
exchange within and among nations of information about products, processes, techniques, and practices for the common
purpose of reducing energy demand.

There is an important leadership and contributing
role governments can play in energy conservation.  A recent
study by the National Academy of Engineering suggested the
following:

"Life-Cycle Costing."  Government purchasing
policy, such as on automobiles, could take life-cycle
costs, including energy and appropriate time values for
money, into account, instead of only lowest initial cost.
Similarly, regulations such as FHA housing insulation requirements could embody such life-cycle energy costs.  The
FHA financing basis could be expanded to include, as acceptable appraisal items, storm windows and doors, extra insulation, heat pumps, etc.

"Transportation Systems."  In grants and financial
assistance to transportation systems, preference could be
given to those plans that appear to be energy efficient and
can use more abundant domestic funds.  For instance, coal
and nuclear power can be used to power electrified railroads
and transit systems.

"Information Program."  Government could continue
to encourage voluntary actions to conserve energy.  Specific
suggestions on how to save energy or substitute more abundant
energy forms for oil and gas could be widely disseminated.
The public must be made aware of the long-term nature of our
current energy problem, the economic and political implications of not regaining our oil and gas self-sufficiency,
and the need to adapt to higher energy costs in the future.

As to other consequences, a reduction in petroleum
demand, which reduces the volume of energy purchases, helps

consuming nations with their balance-of-payments problems and lessens the inflationary pressures caused by higher energy prices. In addition, such a system could enlarge the export markets for countries having a high technological capability in the energy conservation field and should promote cooperation among nations in other areas of common concern.

C. A national or cooperatively multi-national system to reduce petroleum demand could be helpful in promoting the sharing of knowledge and data on opportunities for energy conservation. Open sharing of technical data will help overcome the information lags that currently exist between the recognition of a conservation opportunity and the implementation of explicit programs to exploit that opportunity. It could promote projects which use existing technology and have economic and conservation benefits. Government incentives like tax credits to stimulate economically marginal energy conservation could also be explored.

A multi-national program would require mechanisms to encourage energy conservation and cooperative efforts by all countries. This could involve targeted energy demand reductions by all consuming nations to prevent those who actively participate from bearing the costs of the benefits enjoyed by all.

D. We do not believe that a multi-national system to reduce petroleum demand would work due to the size and diversity of the problem. We believe that each nation should study its own situation and develop its own program for reducing petroleum demand.

We do favor a national program which should include such things as alternate energy sources, mass transit systems and other energy-conservation considerations such as standards for insulation and new construction, etc.

E. The establishment of a national or cooperatively multi-national system to reduce petroleum demand should be in the interest of the entire world with respect to conservation of natural resources and would be well worth pursuing. However, the consequences resulting from reduced consumption could more than be offset by equal actions on the part of producing nations restricting the availability of petroleum

supply.  OPEC, which is made up of a smaller number of countries with more similar interest, should have much greater
ability to control supply than the consuming nations will
have in controlling demand.


25.  What is your opinion with respect to the establishment
of a comprehensive system of U.S. Government insurance coverage for foreign investment by U.S. petroleum companies and/or
the establishment of a system of U.S. Government low-interest
loans to encourage such investments?  Assume that such insurance would cover losses suffered as a result of expropriation or other similar governmental action and the low-interest
loans would provide for reduction or cancellation, as appropriate, in the event of such action.  What are the advantages
and disadvantages of such a system?  What would be the effect
upon U.S. and world petroleum supply?

Response:

        Oil company responses were fairly evenly divided on
the establishment of U.S. Government insurance coverage for
foreign investment by U.S. companies and/or low-interest
loans to encourage such investments.  Many companies feared
that the administration of such a program would increase
Government intervention in petroleum affairs.  Several companies thought low-interest loans would stimulate foreign
activity by enabling smaller companies to increase their
foreign exploration.  Several oil companies felt that an
insurance program would not really protect against expropriation, as this can be accomplished through taxation.
Many felt that the low-interest loans could increase the
foreign petroleum supply but would have minimal effect on
the domestic supply.

SELECTED COMMENTS:


    A.  Insurance coverage and the establishment of a system
of U.S. Government low interest loans would definitely encourage foreign investment and would be in the nation's best
interest.  The effect in time would be to increase world wide
petroleum supply.

    B.  Perhaps, an insurance system to cover expropriation
might be feasible, but a country can expropriate by taxation
also, and we see no way to prevent this.  We are opposed to

low-interest loans to encourage foreign exploration. U.S.
companies are adequately exploring abroad now if the U.S.
Government would leave them alone instead of dreaming-up
ways to hamper them.

C. This would be an area of assistance which would
be justified. It would allow government influence in an
appropriate way to bring about some of its foreign policy
objectives, supply distribution objectives and still keep
operations in the hands of private enterprise. It would
be important that government not follow its usual practice,
however, of setting wage and labor policy, safety and
otherwise interfering at the operational level. I'm not
sure government is capable of such restraint. Government
and politicians also seem to have an aversion to having
practical experienced men from industry in key administrative or advisory roles in government. This is bad because
the scholars and bureaucrats which do fill these jobs
cannot weigh properly the decisions which they must make
in the course of setting policy and making regulations
affecting the industry.

D. 1. The advantages are:

A. This would stimulate U.S. domestic petroleum
companies (and possibly other companies), which presently
do not have international investments, to join existing or
create new international groups for exploration and ultimate
development of petroleum reserves.

B. Stimulate some U.S. international petroleum
companies, which have restricted exploration in certain
areas because of expropriation fears, to review the situation and possibly develop new interest.

C. The program probably would result in bilateral
agreements between governments which would promote more
receptive investment atmosphere for related trade and development.

2. The disadvantages are:

A. That the comprehensive insurance would probably
not cover expropriation through taxation, although it may
cover expropriation through other restrictive governmental
action.

B.  Disallocation of limited resources--this would promote investments in selected areas (areas covered by insurance, while in risk areas not covered, the investment probably would decline (not increase at the same rate) due to resources available.

C.  Companies generally, when "expropriated", receive some compensation from the expropriating country (however inadequate) for tangible assets.  Thus, insurance which does not cover costs for intangibles is of limited economic benefit.

D.  If this insurance is viewed as a governmental "subsidy", this program will probably stimulate additional political pressure for more governmental controls of foreign petroleum acitivites.  Examples of these activities are: approval of projects; production rates; pricing, and use of and movement of product.

E.  Since this program would probably cover only tangible assets and not potential profits, most petroleum companies would probably select areas of low to moderate expropriation risk for investment, as opposed to selecting high-risk areas where there might be more potential petroleum reserves.  Thus insurance per se will not stimulate investment in high-risk areas unless other investment opportunities do not exist.

What are the advantages and disadvantages of the establishment of a system of U.S. Governmental low-interest loans for foreign investments by U.S. petroleum companies which provide for reduction or cancellation as appropriate in the event of expropriation or similar governmental action?

1.  The advantages are:

A.  The same advantages as for insurance (see 1A thru 1C).

B.  It could stimulate, to a large degree, international competition by bringing in smaller companies (oil and other) which will now be acceptable to host countries because of the assurance of availability of financing.

C.  Stimulate additional exploration (to the extent of availability of other resources by major petroleum companies).

D.   Maximize the use of available resources utilized in development.

E.   Initial stimulation of petroleum-related industries (i.e., service groups and suppliers).

F.   Accelerate development programs on marginal fields which would not have been developed as quickly because of financing difficulties.

2.   The disadvantages are:

A.   The same as insurance (see 2A, 2B, 2D, 2E, and 2F).

The advantages and disadvantages of a combination of insurance and low-interest loans are basically the same as the advantages and disadvantages of the individual components, assuming that it would be an either/or situation because both cover the same basic situation.  What would be the effect upon U.S. and world petroleum supply?

1.   The initial effect (say five years) would be an increase in world petroleum reserves due to increased foreign activity.

2.   The increase in the world reserves will not necessarily result in additional petroleum dedicated to the U.S. market.  Just because U.S. companies receive incentives to develop foreign reserves does not necessarily mean that petroleum will automatically return to the U.S. if the local countries should require shipments to other areas of the world.

E.   [We do] not believe that a system of U.S. government insurance coverage or U.S. government low interest loans is necessary nor appropriate to encourage foreign investments by U.S. petroleum companies.  Insurance for foreign investors would be too expensive if self-liquidating and paid for by users on a voluntary basis; only the highest risk investors would be interested in buying such insurance.  If the costs and risks are borne by government, the public treasury could be subject to enormous potential claims.  There is no evidence of a real need for such incentives to stimulate foreign investments by U.S. petroleum companies.  Additionally, such incentives could be inimical to the goals of Project Independence, since they would encourage U.S. companies to increase their investments of limited capital resources outside the United States by reducing the relative costs and risks of such investments.

F.  We see no necessity for the establishment of such and insurance system or for such loans.  We believe that the private enterprise system should take the associated risks with their investments.  Those who take the risks should profit in return, unhampered by government regulations and their influence on the marketplace.  Furthermore, we believe that many suggestions of insurance or low cost loans is absolutely counter to the coming self-sufficiency, which is what we thought Project Independence was all about.  It would probably help to decrease the oil supply in the U.S. while it would probably stimulate oil supply in foreign countries since the risks of U.S. companies operating in these areas would be cut down.  Furthermore, we believe that such insurance and loans would leave no incentive for companies to resist take-overs by foreign countries.  In fact, such insurance might encourage such take-overs.

G.  Both insurance and low interest loans would stimulate foreign activity particularly by enabling the smaller companies to increase their foreign exploration and by permitting all companies to accept somewhat higher risk in their foreign programs.  No increases in domestic supply would be generated by this approach, however.  Also, in the event of expropriation the foreign country maintains full control of production, and as a result the insurance or loans would not provide any assurance that supplies could not be disrupted by foreign governments.

H.  The system is costly, unnecessary and politically impossible.  The only insurance worth having is the assurance that the U.S. Government will put its full diplomatic, political and economic weight behind American companies.  Much of what has transpired over the last few years is the result of our government's lack of resolve and abdication of leadership. The electorate and Congress must be enlightened to the fact that we are in a very serious situation from which we will not be extracted by our so-called "friends" or new methods of "recycling money" but only by our own resolve.  The public needs to be educated to the fact that the stakes are much greater than oil company profits and assets.

I.  The principal advantage of either system suggested
would be the protection afforded to capital investment.  The
disadvantage would seem to be the extremely high premium
cost which we believe would have to be incurred by the industry to cover this peril adequately on a continuous basis.
We also believe there would be important administrative and
claims-handling difficulties because confiscation can take
several forms, such as punitive taxation, and the insured may
have considerable difficulty proving a claim.  Under the
current expropriation and currency convertibility program,
we do not believe the coverage extended justifies the premium charged and it has been our policy therefore not to
take such insurance.

It is our opinion that the existence of such a
system would have no appreciable effect upon either U.S.
or world petroleum supply if the oil industry is to absorb
the cost.


26.  What is your opinion with respect to a restriction upon
the distribution of the lessee's (equity) share of petroleum
extracted from public lands owned by the U.S. Government to
the U.S. market only?  What would be the impact upon outer
continental shelf leasing by the U.S. and upon the U.S. and
world petroleum markets?

Response:

Respondents were equally divided.  Most believed
that such an export restriction would have little or no
impact on the exploration and development of the OCS.  Many
companies however fear that the policy would have an undesirable precedental effect, encouraging other nations
to adopt similar policies.

SELECTED COMMENTS:

A.  Any such program encourages expansion of such
restraints by other producing countries.  The U.S. has more
to lose than it is likely to gain under such a program.
Actually, logistics and economics alone would likely dictate that any petroleum found on U.S. lands would be utilized
in the U.S. market, without any need for an official decree
to that effect.  The only likely exception would be a possible

case of sharing with foreign countries in times of shortage, a decision which would be made by the U.S. government rather than private industry.

B.  To restrict petroleum production from offshore Federal leases to the U.S. market would be a meaningless effort.  A lessee could simply utilize such oil for his domestic outlets and use oil from private leases for export. In addition, such a program really does not solve the problem at which it is directed.  There is little question that in cases of emergency the government will restrict or prohibit the exportation of all petroleum, regardless of whether it comes from a publicly owned or privately owned lease.  The Congress can simply and with full effectiveness enable the President to limit or prohibit such exports in times of an emergency.  To encumber any lease provisions with such restrictions would be redundant.

Because of the above factors, the imposition of such a restriction would have little real effect on Outer Continental Shelf Leasing and on the world petroleum markets. It would only serve to increase the bureaucratic red tape, frustrations and costs in an already high-cost operation.

C.  Presumably the objective of "restricting distribution to the U.S. market only" is to prevent export of crude produced from Federal lands.  It is further presumed that such an objective would be subject to appropriate modification in times of emergency if a program such as the Integrated Emergency Program were implemented (see response to Question 14).

Introducing distribution restrictions into Federal lease covenants is not really necessary to accomplish this objective.  Such restrictions would duplicate elements of an existing U.S. Department of Commerce export licensing program which limits product exports to historical levels and prohibits crude exports completely, unless at least an equal volume of crude is imported in exchange.  Historically, the U.S. has exported little crude and is unlikely to be in a position to do so for many years.  Thus, this restriction on Federal leases would at most limit the export of only a fraction of total U.S. production.

The impact of distribution restrictions in Federal lease covenants should be minimal with regard to out continental shelf leasing.  As a practical matter, however,

such unneeded additional restrictions can only create uncertainty and add to administrative burdens.  Administrative
problems would arise due to the very nature of petroleum
transportation and logistics systems.  Because of the
necessity for efficient utilization of high cost offshore
pipeline facilities, crude produced from OCS leases is
often commingled with production from State leases before
reaching shore.  Onshore, it may be further commingled
with oil from privately owned leases in a crude trunkline
system connected to a refinery complex, with crude sales
from the system perhaps being made enroute.  Thus, it would
be a formidable task to trace and account for OCS oil with
distribution restrictions separately from other commingled
oil which has no such restrictions.

In the final analysis a U.S. restriction upon the
distribution of petroleum extracted from public lands owned
by the government could establish a dangerous precedent for
other governments.  Consideration has been given in the U.K.,
for example, to restricting North Sea petroleum production
to domestic requirements.  This would have a quality impact
on European tributary refiners who might otherwise have
access to these supplies.  Wide spread adoption of such
policies would have a disruptive effect on world petroleum
markets by creating inefficient supply patterns.

D.  This is unnecessary interference in world commerce
and we are opposed to such a restriction except during true
emergencies such as occurred during the five-month period of
the recent embargo.

At the present time, such a restriction would have
little or no impact of OCS leasing or upon U.S. and world
petroleum markets.  However, in the 1980's, Alaska and OCS
oils will be produced at much higher rates and will become
a significant portion of U.S. oil production.  It could
then be in the best interest of the U.S. to market such
oil overseas as to:

a.  Improve our balance of trade (burn coal
instead)

b.  Save transportation costs, i.e., ship some of
the Alaskan oil to Japan and receive in return oil from
Africa into the U.S. East and Gulf Coasts.

c. Swap oil with friendly neighbors, i.e., oil found off North Eastern U.S. would be given to Canadian companies for refining in the East. In return the U.S. would receive Canadian crude into the Upper Mid-West.

E. We can see no significant impact to the U.S. market if a restriction is placed on the distribution of a lessee's share of petroleum extracted from public lands.

Because of a geographic anomoly petroleum production in Alaska may have a transportation advantage to certain Far East markets. If worldwide petroleum were priced in a consistent manner such production should be exported as other production displaced from the Far East and subsequent markets is shipped to the U.S.--with transportation costs minimized to both markets.

Although we are a firm believer in free trade being the best way to optimize global resources, we know that petroleum is not priced on a consistent basis. Therefore, the impact of displacing exported Alaskan crude with other foreign petroleum sources may be negative with respect to domestic balance of payments. Furthermore, the revenue differences to the lessee of directing petroleum supplies to the U.S. market as opposed to Far East markets is likely to be minimal. Thus, incentives to OCS leasing by U.S. companies should not diminish significantly by an export restriction.

Should the above restriction be effected there are potential negative affects. First, incentives to consistent pricing by petroleum exporting countries will be diminished. Secondly, a precedent is set that could be detrimental to the U.S. if adopted by other countries. North Sea petroleum, for instance, could be competitive in U.S. markets, but precluded from being importing by similar restrictions on North Sea production.

In any case, U.S. refinery configuration and domestic supply commitments would tend to insure a majority of Alaskan crude for the U.S. market.

F. Enacting such a restriction into law would only result in relatlatory actions on the part of developed countries with exportable supplies and could cause significant dislocations in world trade of other goods and services.

Such a law would not add to total U.S. supplies since crude oil produced from OCS would be expected to flow to U.S. refineries even in the absence of such a law. The U.S. will be dependent on crude imports for many years to come and restrictions by potential exporters to the U.S. in response to this law could only be detrimental.

G. As a practical matter, petroleum extracted from U.S. public lands moves to U.S. markets almost exclusively because of the simple logistics involved. An absolute restriction appears to be unnecessary, and it could cause complications in movements which could result in higher costs to consumers. Moreover, exports of domestic crude, whether produced on private or public lands, might be controlled within the broad purposes of export laws so that the overall flexibility of national purposes can be served.

A statutory restriction could result in small and irritating absurdities involving restricted flow across our broad borders with Canada and Mexico.

It could be, however, that if price controls on domestic crude oil are maintained, an incentive to export old domestic crude at prices slightly below world prices would be attractive. However, this would be a further layering of regulation on a situation which cries for return to free market mechanisms.

B. [§C.2] Foreign Petroleum Company Questionnaire

Questionnaires were sent to the following twenty-three foreign petroleum companies [(R) designates respondents]:

|      | 1.  | Arabian Oil Co., Ltd. |
|------|-----|-----------------------|
|      | 2.  | British Petroleum Co. Ltd. |
| (R)  | 3.  | The Burmah Oil Company, Ltd. |
|      | 4.  | Compagnie Francaise des Petroles |
|      | 5.  | Deminex |
| (R)  | 6.  | E.N.I. (Ente Naziolale Idrocarburi) |
|      | 7.  | Enterprise de Recherches et D'Activities Petrolieres - ELF |
| (R)  | 8.  | Gelsenberg AG |
|      | 9.  | Idemitsu Kosan Co., Ltd. |
|      | 10. | Imperial Oil Limited |

```
       11.  Maruzen Oil Co., Ltd.
       12.  Mitsubishi Oil Co., Ltd.
       13.  Nippon Oil Co., Ltd.
(R)    14.  Oesterreichische Mineraloelverwaltung AG
            (O.M.V.)
(R)    15.  Panarctic Oils Ltd.
(R)    16.  Petrofina S.A.
       17.  PREUSSAG Aktiengesellschaft
       18.  Preussag AG Wasser
(R)    19.  Royal Dutch/Shell Group of Companies
       20.  Shell Oil Co.
       21.  The Shell Transport & Trading Co. Ltd.
       22.  Toa Nenryo Kogyo K.K.
       23.  Veba-Chemie AG
```

The following sample questionnaire is reproduced for reference:

FEDERAL ENERGY ADMINISTRATION STUDY OF
THE OPTIONS OF THE U.S. GOVERNMENT IN ITS
RELATIONSHIP TO THE U.S. PETROLEUM INDUSTRY
IN INTERNATIONAL PETROLEUM AFFAIRS

July 22, 1974

QUESTIONNAIRE FOR PETROLEUM COMPANIES

Please complete this Questionnaire and return it to the law firm of Nossaman, Waters, Scott, Krueger & Riordan, 445 South Figueroa Street, Los Angeles, California 90017, Attention: Robert B. Krueger, no later than October 1, 1974. In answering the questions, please state as thoroughly and precisely as practicable the reasons upon which your answers are based. In those instances in which a question is inapplicable to your company, please so indicate. If you need additional space for your answers, please type them on additional sheets and attach them to the end of this Questionnaire.

"United States," as used herein, includes the outer continental shelf lands of the United States. "Petroleum," as used herein, includes oil, natural gas, distillates and any other marketable wellhead products. "Your company," as used herein, includes all wholly-owned subsidiaires and your percentage of ownership of all other partially or jointly-owned companies.

1. Describe the general petroleum supply and distribution system through which your company receives and distributes its petroleum supplies. Indicate from what countries and in what approximate amounts your company receives its petroleum supplies and to what countries and in what approximate amounts your petroleum supplies are distributed. If your supplies or sales of petroleum are received or distributed through the vehicle of one or more other petroleum companies, please indicate the company or companies and the approximate amounts of petroleum involved.

2. Indicate on the following table the total amount of your company's expenditures on research, development and exploration of energy resources other than petroleum.

| | Oil Shale Tar Sands | Coal | Geothermal | Solar | Nuclear |
|---|---|---|---|---|---|
| 1970 Research | _____ | _____ | _____ | _____ | _____ |
| Development | _____ | _____ | _____ | _____ | _____ |
| Exploration | _____ | _____ | _____ | _____ | _____ |
| 1971 Research | _____ | _____ | _____ | _____ | _____ |
| Development | _____ | _____ | _____ | _____ | _____ |
| Exploration | _____ | _____ | _____ | _____ | _____ |
| 1972 Research | _____ | _____ | _____ | _____ | _____ |
| Development | _____ | _____ | _____ | _____ | _____ |
| Exploration | _____ | _____ | _____ | _____ | _____ |
| 1973 Research | _____ | _____ | _____ | _____ | _____ |
| Development | _____ | _____ | _____ | _____ | _____ |
| Exploration | _____ | _____ | _____ | _____ | _____ |
| 1974 [Projected] Research | _____ | _____ | _____ | _____ | _____ |
| Development | _____ | _____ | _____ | _____ | _____ |
| Exploration | _____ | _____ | _____ | _____ | _____ |

State your company's plans with regard to the future development of energy resources other than petroleum.

3. What are the advantages and disadvantages of the existing system of world petroleum supply? What favorable or unfavorable effects would the continuation of this system have in the next five years?

4.  What do you believe would be the consequences to world petroleum supply of the elimination of equity oil in the major petroleum producing nations?  What would be the role of the large multi-national integrated petroleum companies in world petroleum if this occurred?  How would your company and its customers be affected?

5.  What do you believe would be the consequences to world petroleum supply of the elimination in the major petroleum producing nations of preferential supply arrangements existing in favor of the large multi-national integrated petroleum companies?  What would be the role of these companies in world petroleum if this occurred?  How would your company and its customers be affected?

6.  Give your opinion as to the present and potential future ability of the exporting nations to control world prices for petroleum.

7.  What do you expect to be the future role of OPEC in world petroleum?

8.  What is your opinion with respect to the establishment of a milti-national organization to coordinate the national petroleum policies of petroleum importing countries?  What are the advantages and disadvantages?  What would be the effect upon world petroleum supply and price?

9.  What would be your company's attitude toward a system or agreement whereby the various petroleum consuming nations agreed to establish stored petroleum reserves and to share petroleum supplies and, in addition, reduce consumption in the event of an interruption in supply?  To what extent do you believe your company would be willing and able to co-operate in such an agreement by, for example, selling petroleum products to designated countries, in designated quantities and at a designated price?

10.  What is your opinion as to the strengths and weaknesses of a government-owned and operated petroleum company?  What are the advantages and disadvantages of such a government-owned petroleum company in a developed petroleum consuming nation?  Please be specific.

11. What is your opinion as to the strengths and weaknesses of public oil companies partially owned by a government? If your company is partially owned by a government, what do you consider to be the advantages and disadvantages of such ownership? Please be specific.

12. What is your opinion with respect to the establishment of a petroleum corporation, fully or partially owned by the U.S. Government, to engage in national and international activities such as (1) resource acquisition within the U.S. (including the Outer Continental Shelf); (2) exploration; (3) development; (4) production; (5) purchase of production from other petroleum companies for storage, refining or resale; (6) transportation; (7) refining and processing; or (8) distribution? What are the advantages and disadvantages of each? Consider each of the above functions separately and make specific comments.

13. Describe the role which your government plays in assisting your company to obtain petroleum supplies? Does it do the same for other petroleum companies in your country? Are its actions successful in assisting your company to obtain petroleum supplies? Do they ever work to your disadvantage? How? Please be specific.

14. What government policies do you believe would be most effective in obtaining access to foreign petroleum supplies? Please be specific.

Company Name:_____

Responding Officer:_____

Position with Company:_____

Date:_____

C. [§C.3] Public Utility Questionnaire

Questionnaires were sent to the following twenty-eight public utilities [(R) indicates respondents]:

(R)  1.  American Electic Power Company, Inc.
(R)  2.  American Electric Power Company, Inc.

```
(R)   3.  American Natural Gas Company
      4.  Baltimore Gas and Electric Company
      5.  Columbia Gas System, Incorporated
      6.  Commonwealth Edison Company
(R)   7.  Consolidated Edison
      8.  Consumers Power Company
(R)   9.  Department of Water & Power, City of Los Angeles
     10.  Detroit Edison
     11.  Duke Power Company
(R)  12.  El Paso Natural Gas Company
(R)  13.  Florida Power and Light Company
(R)  14.  General Public Utilities Corporation
(R)  15.  Hawaiian Electric Co., Inc.
(R)  16.  Middle South Utilities, Inc.
(R)  17.  Niagara Mohawk Power Corporation
(R)  18.  Northeast Utilities
     19.  Pacific Gas & Electric
(R)  20.  Philadelphia Electric Company
(R)  21.  Portland General Electric Company
(R)  22.  Public Service Electric & Gas Company
     23.  San Diego Gas and Electric Company
(R)  24.  Southern California Edison Company
(R)  25.  The Southern California Gas Company
     26.  Texas Utilities Company
(R)  27.  Union Electric Company
(R)  28.  Virginia Electric and Power Company
```

A sample of the Public Utilities Questionnaire is reproduced for reference:

FEDERAL ENERGY ADMINISTRATION - STUDY
OF THE OPTIONS OF THE UNITED STATES GOVERNMENT
IN ITS RELATIONSHIP TO THE U.S. PETROLEUM INDUSTRY
IN INTERNATIONAL PETROLEUM AFFAIRS

July 15, 1974

## PUBLIC UTILITY QUESTIONNAIRE

Please complete this Questionnaire and return it to the law firm of Nossaman, Waters, Scott, Krueger & Riordan, 445 South Figueroa Street, Los Angeles, California

90017, Attention:  Robert B. Krueger, no later than September 1, 1974.  In answering the questions contained herein, please state as thoroughly and precisely as possible the reasons upon which your answers are based.  In those instances in which a question is inapplicable, please so indicate.  If you need additional space for your answers, please type them on additional sheets and attach them to the end of this Questionnaire.

"United States," as used herein, includes the outer continental shelf lands of the United States.  "Petroleum," as used herein, includes oil, natural gas, distillates and any other marketable wellhead products.  "Your company," as used herein, includes all wholly-owned subsidiaries and your percentage of ownership of all other partially or jointly-owned companies.

1.  What do you project your company's requirements of oil, natural gas and coal to be in 1973, 1975, 1980 and 1985?

|  | 1973 | 1975 | 1980 | 1985 |
|---|---|---|---|---|
| OIL (barrels) | _____ | _____ | _____ | _____ |
| NATURAL GAS (thousands of cubic feet) | _____ | _____ | _____ | _____ |
| COAL (tons) | _____ | _____ | _____ | _____ |

2.  What type of petroleum supply agreements, if any, does your company have with foreign companies or governments?  Please  indicate the following:

(a)  The names of the petroleum companies or foreign governments;

(b)  The type of agreement with each such company or country (Include the length of agreement and supply commitments);

(c)  The amount and price of petroleum provided for in each agreement; and

(d) Your company's attitude toward the security of such agreements and its ability to enforce such agreements.

3. Has your company suffered any interruptions in service to its customers due to an inability to obtain its petroleum requirements during any of the last 10 years? If so, describe the extent of interruption and the resulting action taken by your company.

4. What steps, if any, has your company taken during the last 10 years (or more) to more efficiently utilize its petroleum resources? Include the introduction of new technology and/or operating procedures which help to reduce your company's consumption of petroleum. In addition, indicate the measures which your company is in the process of adopting or anticipates adopting in the future in order to reduce its consumption of petroleum.

5. Give your opinion as to the effect which specific U.S. Govermnent environmental regulations have had upon the supply and price of petroleum products within the U.S. and the operations of your company. Whenever possible, cite relative environmental regulations and quantify their effects.

6. What is your opinion as to the effect of the following upon the supply of petroleum within the U.S. and the incentive to undertake new exploration: (1) U.S. price controls, (2) U.S. crude oil allocation rules and (3) U.S. antitrust laws. In answering this question, consider how the distribution of petroleum between U.S. and foreign markets was affected by the aforementioned policies. Please be specific and quantify your answer whenever possible. In addition, if there are other U.S. government policies affecting the supply of petroleum and upon which you would like to comment, please do so.

7. Indicate future areas of development or planning within the public utility industry which, in your company's opinion, would most greatly reduce the industry's use of petroleum. (If government participation would be desirable in such future developmental planning, please so indicate.)

8.  What direct governmental action would most effectively assist your company in obtaining adequate petroleum supplies?  (Indicate whether you would favor such governmental action and consider all of its consequences. In addition, indicate any alternatives to direct governmental action which you might recommend.)

9.  What agreements, if any, do you have with other public utility companies to share petroleum supplies? Indicate the following:  (1) whether you believe such agreements are useful; (2) whether you would be willing to enter into such agreements if you are not a party to any already; and (3) on what basis and to what extent petroleum supplies should be shared under such agreements.

10.  What is your opinion with respect to the existing system of world petroleum supply?  What are its advantages and disadvantages?  What favorable or unfavorable effects upon the operations of your company and the U.S. economy in general would the continuation of this system have in the next five years?

11.  What role, if any, does your company believe the U.S. Government should play in the development of U.S. oil shale, Outer Continental Shelf petroleum resources, coal reserves and other non-petroleum energy resources, such as solar and geothermal energy?

12.  What is your opinion with respect to intervention by the U.S. Government into the negotiation of medium (five years or more) or long-range (ten years or more) foreign petroleum supply contracts?  What are the advantages and disadvantages of such intervention and what effects do you believe it might have upon your company's ability to obtain adequate petroleum supplies?  When answering this question, clearly specify the type and degree of intervention that you are assuming.

13.  What is your opinion with respect to the establishment of a petroleum corporation, fully or partially owned by the U.S. Government, to engage in national and international activities such as (1) resource acquisition within the U.S. (including the Outer Continental Shelf); (2) exploration; (3) development; (4) production; (5) purchase of production

C-173

of others (primarily foreign) for storage, refining or resale; (6) transportation; (7) refining and processing; or (8) distribution? What are the advantages and disadvantages of each? Consider each of the above functions separately and make specific comments.

14. What is your opinion with respect to the regulation of U.S. petroleum companies as public utilities? What are the advantages and disadvantages? What would be the effect upon the U.S. and foreign petroleum markets? Please assess separately.

15. What is your opinion with respect to a restriction upon the distribution of the lessee's (equity) share of petroleum extracted from public lands owned by the U.S. Government to the U.S. market only? What would be the impact upon Outer Continental Shelf leasing by the U.S., the U.S. and world petroleum markets and your company's operations?

NOTE: Any additional comments which you might have with regard to issues raised by the Study Outline and Petroleum Company Questionnaire, and not specifically identified by the Public Utilities Questionnaire, would be greatly appreciated.

Company Name:_____

Responding Officer:_____

Position with Company:_____

Date:_____

D.  [§C.4]  State Agency Questionnaire

Questionnaires identical to those sent to the domestic petroleum companies were submitted to the following seventeen State Agencies for comment:

1. Alabama State Oil and Gas Board
2. Alaska Oil and Gas Conservation Committee
3. California Department of Conservation
4. California State Lands Commission, State Lands Division
5. Florida Department of Natural Resources

6. Georgia Department of Mines, Mining and Geology
7. Louisiana Department of Conservation
8. Mississippi State Oil and Gas Board
9. Montana Oil and Gas Conservation Commission
10. New York Department of Environmental Conservation
11. North Carolina Department of Conservation and Development
12. Oklahoma Corporation Commission
13. Oregon Department of Geology and Mineral Industries
14. South Carolina Division of Geology, Division of Geology, State Development Board
15. Texas Railroad Commission
16. Washington Oil and Gas Conservation Committee
17. Wyoming Oil and Gas Conservation Commission

E. [§C.5] U.S. Government Agency Questionnaire

Questionnaires identical to those sent to the domestic petroleum companies, were submitted to the following Federal Government Agencies for comments:

1. Council of Economic Advisors
2. Department of Commerce
3. Department of Defense
4. Department of the Interior
5. Department of Justice
6. Department of the Treasury
7. Environmental Protection Agency
8. Federal Power Commission
9. Office of Management and Budget

F. [§C.6] Congressional Committees

Questionnaires identical to those sent to the domestic petroleum companies were submitted to the following Congressional Committees for comment:

1. House Committee on Foreign Affairs
2. House Committee on Interior and Insular Affairs
3. House Committee on Interstate and Foreign Commerce
4. Senate Commerce Committee
5. Senate Committee on Foreign Relations
6. Senate Committee on Interior and Insular Affairs

G.  [§C.7]  Trade Associations

Questionnaires identical to those sent to the domestic petroleum companies were submitted to the following petroleum industry trade associations:

1.   American Petroleum Institute·
2.   American Petroleum Refiners Association
3.   California Independent Producers Association
4.   Independent Petroleum Association of America
5.   Mid-Continent Oil & Gas
6.   National Petroleum Council
7.   National Petroleum Refiners Association
8.   Rocky Mountain Oil and Gas Association
9.   Texas Independent Producers and Royalty
        Owners Association
10.  Western Oil and Gas Association

H.  [§C.8]  Consumer and Other Interested Groups

Questionnaires identical to those sent to the domestic petroleum companies were submitted to the following groups for comment:

1.   Bank of America
2.   Center for Law and Social Policy
3.   Center for Law in the Public Interest
4.   Center for Science in the Public Interest
5.   Center for Study of Responsive Law
6.   Chase Manhattan Bank
7.   City of Long Beach
8.   Common Cause
9.   COMSAT
10.  Environmental Defense Fund
11.  National Academy of Engineering
12.  National Academy of Sciences
13.  Natural Resources Defense Council
14.  Sierra Club
15.  Tennessee Valley Authority

APPENDIX D


[§D.0] CONTINENTAL OIL COMPANY QUESTIONNAIRE RESPONSE:
"ISSUES IN THE INTERNATIONAL OIL INDUSTRY"


## Introductory Note

In response to our Questionnaire, Continental Oil
Company chose to utilize the format of an essay, and accordingly, it was impracticable to include excerpts from such
reply within the Selected Comments sections of Appendix C.
Because it was one of the more thoughtful and interesting
responses received with Continental Oil Company's permission, it has been reproduced, unedited, as Appendix D.
Continental's response was prepared in November of 1974 and,
therefore, reflects assumptions and developments as of that
date.

[§D.0]  CONTINENTAL OIL COMPANY:

ISSUES IN THE INTERNATIONAL OIL INDUSTRY

International oil now occupies a central role in world economic and political affairs.  Oil's current importance is the result of developments that occurred largely in the quarter of a century following World War II.  During that period, the foundation was laid for the recent upheaval in the oil industry and the current apprehension in the United States and other oil importing countries about the future availability and prices of oil, factors which are crucial to the economic and political health of the international community.

In addition to the broader international problems, the dramatic changes in international oil have created uncertainties about the position in oil affairs of both private oil companies and the United States government.

In this position paper, Continental Oil Company examines the background of the current oil crisis and the issues involved in (1) an assessment of the outlook for the oil industry (2) an evaluation of the future role of private companies in international oil and (3) a consideration of the appropriate role of the U.S. government in international and domestic oil activities.

THE POST WAR PERIOD:  A UNIQUE ERA

In the twenty-five year period after World War II, international oil emerged as a major factor in the world's economic political scene.  Led in large measure by American oil companies, this development was mainly the outgrowth of a unique circumstance:  falling oil prices based on low cost Middle East oil.

Normally, declining prices would not be expected to persist over a long time period because oil as a natural resource, extractive industry tends to have rising long term costs. Typically, richer resources are developed first and lower-grade resources must be resorted to subsequently. Geologists believe that it is unlikely that large, low cost reserves similar to those in the Middle East will be found in other parts of the world. Thus, the unique occurrence of massive amounts of low cost oil coming on the market fairly rapidly is unlikely to be duplicated in the future.

The increasing economic importance of oil plus the concentration of crude oil reserves in a few countries located in the politically volatile Middle East inevitably generated a close interrelationship between economic and political forces. The increasing power of producing countries led to the sudden collapse in the early 1970's of the system based on low cost oil.

## Attractiveness of Cheap Oil

In retrospect, the penetration of cheap Middle East oil into world energy markets was one of the most important economic developments of the post war period. This penetration was based initially on low cost reserves in Saudi Arabia, Iran, and Iraq. Later discoveries in Libya, other Persian Gulf countries, and Nigeria augmented the supply of exportable oil.

U.S. companies were in the forefront of this big expansion in international oil. Before World War II, major U.S. companies already had production in Iraq, Saudi Arabia and Bahrain. The formation of the Iranian consortium in 1954 brought American companies into Iran.

Possibilities of using already developed technology and available capital to find large cheap reserves attracted numerous other U.S. companies into international oil exploration in the 1950's and 1960's. Other factors encouraging U.S. oil companies to go overseas included (1) the willingness on the part of these companies to undertake risky exploration ventures (2) fast growth in foreign oil demand (3) declining geological opportunities in the U.S. onshore plus a very restrictive Federal policy on leasing offshore areas and rising domestic crude costs and (4) defensive moves by some companies to develop oil for importation for the domestic market in order to remain competitive with other importers of low cost foreign oil.

There was strong governmental support to the entry of U.S. companies into international operations. Investments were concentrated in largely underdeveloped countries, who welcomed the stimulus to their economies.

The big infusion of capital, largely American, resulted in rapid, efficient development of oil production. The basic low cost of finding reserves, the efficiency with which private companies developed them, lowering of transportation and refining costs by the use of larger tankers and refineries, and competition among an expanding number of oil companies all contributed to a lowering of oil prices.

Low prices expanded demand for oil in two respects: (1) more expensive, less desirable coal was displaced in many markets and (2) the cheapness of oil contributed to a fast growth in overall energy use. In 1950, coal accounted for 61% of the world's energy supply; by 1970 this share had slipped to 34%. Oil, on the other hand, increased its market share from 27% in 1950 to 43% in 1970. Overall world energy consumption was growing at a 5% rate in the 1950-1970 period.

Low cost oil benefited from and contributed to the rapid economic growth and rising standards of living in Western Europe and Japan. This widespread prosperity was linked to an unprecedented expansion in world trade, with oil as a principal trading commodity.

With these economic benefits, a system that provided low cost oil was not seriously questioned in industrial nations. Economic forces were allowed to shape events; interference by consuming country governments was minimal. Cheap oil was taken for granted; it was the norm. This view of oil still conditions the thinking in oil importing countries.

By the late 1960's, oil prices were stable at low levels or declining. Economic growth was rapid in the industrial nations. In many respects it was the best of all possible worlds for these consuming countries, at least from an economic standpoint. But gradually and largely unnoticed, the locus of power was shifting from the western oil companies and consuming countries to the producing countries.

## Consequence of Energy Dependence

The most significant measure of this shift of
power was the increasing dependence of oil importing countries on energy supplies from a relatively few exporting
countries.  By 1973 Middle East and North African countries
were supplying about half of the non-Communist world oil
supply, up from about one-fourth in 1960.  This is illustrated in the following table.

### Non-Communist World Oil Supply

| | 1960 | | 1973 | |
|---|---|---|---|---|
| | Million BD | % | Million BD | % |
| OPEC | | | | |
|     Middle East and | | | | |
|       North Africa | 4.8 | 24 | 24.1 | 50 |
|     Other | 2.9 | 15 | 7.0 | 14 |
|     Total OPEC | 7.7 | 39 | 31.1 | 64 |
| Non OPEC | 12.0 | 61 | 17.7 | 36 |
|     Total | 19.7 | 100 | 48.8 | 100 |

Several developments were responsible for this rising
dependence on Middle East and African oil:

1.  The coal industry, particulary in Europe, had
been allowed to languish.  As oil and gas rose to primacy,
energy shifted from a national to an international activity.

2.  Non-Communist world energy demand growth had
been rapid (5.6% per year in the 1960's).

3.  The reserve cushion of unused U.S. oil productive
capacity, which had supplied Europe in earlier cutoffs of
Middle East oil supplies, had disappeared.  Drilling in the
U.S. had accelerated through the mid 1950's and considerable
reserve producing capacity developed.  The reserve capacity
peaked at about 3.5 million BD in 1957, the time of the first

Suez crisis. As U.S. spare capacity slowly dwindled, the vulnerability of the West increased commensurately.

4. Discoveries in new areas were not large enough to be effective in disciplining the market. As a result, the finite nature of existing oil reserves became apparent. Even the prolific, low-cost oil discoveries of the Persian Gulf would have been largely depleted by the end of the century if demand had continued to grow as it did from 1965 to 1973; namely at the annual rate of 5% in the U.S. and 10% in the Eastern Hemisphere.

At the same time these economic factors were strengthening the position of producing countries, political developments were also moving in the same direction.

1. Governments in several Arab producing states had fallen into the hands of radical, nationalistic elements.

2. The Arab-Israeli conflict was giving the Arab world an element of cohesiveness formerly lacking.

3. The organizational structure for exercising the producing countries' power was already in place. OPEC had been formed in 1960 in response to price cuts by oil companies.

The coming together of these economic and political forces in the 1970's gave an opportunity to the producing nations to seize the upper hand. Their power was demonstrated by the recent quadrupling of oil prices and their takeover through participation of varying degrees of ownership in producing properties. In Saudi Arabia, for example, the market price of Arabian Light crude has increased from about $2.30 per barrel in the summer of 1973 to a current level of about $10 per barrel and that country's ownership of producing properties is now 60% with the possibility of rising to 100% in fairly short order. These developments led to massive increases in oil revenues by oil producing countries. In some cases, the producing nation's population and economy are too small to absorb the big inflow of revenue.

The system that originally gave ample supplies of low cost oil to industrial nations now has made these nations vulnerable to oil supply interruptions, arbitrary oil price hikes and serious balance of payments problems. Between 1973 and 1974, for example, payments for oil imports are expected to increase from $9 billion to $25 billion for the U.S. and from $21 billion to $75 billion for other major importers. In addition to economic woes, the diplomatic freedom of many oil importing countries has been limited by the dependence on OPEC oil.

The primacy of international oil companies arising from their know-how and capital availability has been seriously eroded. Control of prices and producing rates has shifted to producing nations. Companies retain basic technical skills and demonstrated considerable logistical capability in 1973 and 1974 during the production curtailment and oil embargo by some producing nations. Nevertheless, the recent upheaval has left the international oil industry in a state of confusion and uncertainty.

OUTLOOK FOR THE INTERNATIONAL OIL INDUSTRY

In exploring the issues involved in an assessment of the outlook for the international oil industry, it would be appropriate to (1) ascertain where we are today (2) define and evaluate available policy options and (3) recommend a course of action.

Present Situation

The big increase in crude oil prices occurred during the period in which Arab producing countries cutback crude oil production and instituted an embargo on oil shipments to the U.S. and certain other countries. Concern at that time was focused on obtaining oil supplies; prices were a secondary consideration.

With the lifting of the embargo and increasing crude oil production by the Arab producing nations, attention shifted to the massive price increases. Questions about the ability of importing countries to absorb the higher costs and the strain this was placing on the international monetary system were widely explored. Optimists expressed the view the enormous increase in OPEC oil revenues could be recycled into investments in consuming countries and that oil importing countries could adjust to the new situation. Others, more pessimistic, voiced alarm that the international monetary and trade system would collapse.

So far, the results are mixed. The international economic mechanism is still functioning, but some countries are in a serious position (such as Italy and India).

## Basic Policy Options

There is considerable uncertainty about the interpretation of recent developments, which is reflected in the debates about the available policy options. Essentially, two points of view have emerged:

1. Confrontation Thesis - The OPEC countries are engaged in a unjust and inequitable use of monopoly power for political ends. Their actions threaten the basic prosperity and well-being of the western industrialized nations. Most western political leaders seem to hold this view and insist prices should be reduced substantially by the OPEC bloc.

This interpretation of developments suggests a policy of economic and political confrontation may be appropriate and necessary. The success of this approach would depend upon mobilizing sufficient countervailing power in consuming countries.

2. Accommodation Thesis - A second interpretation of developments contends that what has occurred is an inherent, inevitable trend toward higher raw material costs. The dynamics for change were inherent in the international petroleum situation. OPEC's cataclysmic actions in 1973 and 1974 greatly compressed the time frame and enormously magnified the impact but trends in this general direction were inevitable. This interpretation suggests a policy of accommodation in order to make an effective adjustment from the old to the new era.

## Outlook for Significant Crude Price Reduction

An assessment of future crude oil prices is a necessary point of departure in deciding on policy options.
What are the chances of securing a substantial reduction in
crude oil prices, which would bolster the confrontation
approach?  Many government analyses apparently conclude that
there is a good possibility, as evidenced by scenarios based
on $7 per barrel crude oil prices.

Continental concludes that the possibilities are
remote for substantial reductions, say from the current market
price of about $10 per barrel to $7 or $8 per barrel.  This
conclusion is based on an assessment of (1) the outlook for
OPEC solidarity (2) possibilities of a major change in
world oil supply/demand through either drastic oil conservation or discoveries of large, low cost reserves (3) the
ceiling that synthetic fuels could place over oil prices and
(4) the possibilities that OPEC countries will voluntarily
reduce prices substantially out of concern about the international economic and political order.

OPEC Solidarity - Despite some internal division,
OPEC solidarity will likely continue.  Their past success and
a realistic assessment of the consequences of a break up will
probably keep OPEC countries together in the important area
of controlling prices.  Formerly, it was expected that OPEC,
like other cartels, would flounder when it became necessary
to allocate production among the cartel members.  Since several
large producers (Saudi Arabia, Libya, and Kuwait) are unable
to absorb increased revenues, these countries may be accommodating in adjusting their output to support agreed upon price
levels.  The threat of cheap alternative energy supplies from
either new discoveries or low cost synthetics appears to be
minimal.

Changes in Supply-Demand  The supply-demand picture
could be altered (a) if large, low cost reserves were found
or (b) if energy conservation proved so successful that OPEC
production would be driven down to levels unacceptable to the
member nations.  Neither possibility looks promising.

Geologists conclude that it is unlikely large deposits
of low cost oil similar to Middle East reserves will be found.
There is a widespread search for oil going on now.  But the

size of discoveries has been small by Middle East standards.
Also areas of sizeable discoveries (North Sea and the Arctic) and
potential discoveries (Atlantic offshore and the Gulf of Alaska)
are high cost regions.  New producers will probably join OPEC or
at least support that organization's pricing policies.  Mexico,
for example, has announced it will not attempt to undermine OPEC
prices as a result of the recent Mexican discovery.

Energy conservation, although highly desirable for
other reasons, is unlikely to undermine OPEC.  Cutbacks directed
against producing nations are likely to hurt the consuming
nations more than the intended victims.  For example, a cutback
of 20% in non-Communist world demand in 1975 and in 1980, if
applied entirely to OPEC production, would reduce production in
OPEC countries to 22 million BD in 1975 and 24.9 million BD in
1980.  This compares with estimated OPEC production of about 31
million BD in 1974.  This assessment is illustrated by the
following tabulation.

## Non Communist World Oil Supply-Demand
### (Million BD)

| | ------------1975------------ | | ------------1980------------ | |
| | Continental's Forecast | 20% Reduction in Demand | Continental's Forecast | 20% Reduction in Demand |
|---|---|---|---|---|
| Demand | 50.2 | 40.2 | 63.2 | 50.6 |
| Supply | | | | |
| OPEC | 32.0 | 22.0 | 37.5 | 24.9 |
| U.S. | 11.2 | 11.2 | 14.0 | 14.0 |
| Other | 8.0 | 8.0 | 12.7 | 12.7 |
| Total* | 51.2 | 41.2 | 64.2 | 51.6 |

*Historically, total crude supply has exceeded demand by about
one million BD (due to stock changes, etc.)

With several countries unable to absorb increased revenues,
the OPEC countries could probably adjust to a cutback of this
magnitude.  Saudi Arabia with production of some 8.5 billion BD
and a relatively small population could play a major role in such
a cutback.  But a demand reduction of 20% would likely have
serious repercussions on consuming countries.

Synethetic Fuels.  A popular thesis in current energy
analyses is that synthetic fuels will provide a ceiling to
OPEC prices.  There are two reservations to this thesis.
First, the costs of these alternative fuels are likely to be
higher than earlier expected.  While there is considerable
uncertainty in cost estimates, it does not appear likely
that these fuels can be produced in the $7 to $8 per barrel
range.  Second, there are long lead times and enormous
capital commitments needed to bring on enough synthetic fuels
to act as a discipline to crude oil prices.

OPEC Concern About Impact of High Prices.  There has
been considerable discussion about OPEC voluntarily reducing
oil prices substantially in order to stave off a collapse
of the international economic order.  Such a collapse, it
is reasoned, would cause an economic depression and development of authoritarian regimes in western industrialized
countries as occurred during the unstable times of the 1920's
and 1930's.  Under such circumstances the impact on the OPEC
countries might be considerable.  The specter of such developments is unlikely to motivate OPEC to reduce prices, however.
As a quid pro quo for technical assistance, OPEC countries
may make modest reductions in crude prices which would help
some to alleviate the balance of payments problems, but
large scale price reductions seem unlikely.  This evaluation
is based on the premise that while the international order
may be threatened, it will survive without OPEC making a large
reduction in crude prices.

Learning to Live with High Oil Prices - Soundest Policy
Available

In the foregoing discussion it was concluded that, at best,
stability or only a modest reduction in world oil prices can
be expected.  A significant reduction appears unlikely.  This
conclusion indicates a policy of accommodation--learning to
live with high oil prices--is the soundest policy available.
Success along this route is not certain.  Some bridging
mechanism to handle the critical balance of payments problem
is vitally needed or this could force the consuming countries
into a confrontation posture.  But balancing all factors, it
appears accommodation is the preferred approach.

Although undesirable in other respects, high energy
prices have the beneficial effect of promoting energy

efficiency and conservation.  This both fosters environmental
quality improvement and may conserve scarce capital because of a
reduction in energy consumption.

A continued use of imported energy would be called for in
the accommodation approach.  In terms of resources used (capital,
labor etc.) foreign oil costs are much below domestic energy
sources.  Middle East and North African oil can be produced at a
resource cost of 25¢ to 50¢ a barrel.  World wide wealth is
maximized if the world uses the cheaper energy supplies, because
it would permit the saved amounts of capital and labor to be used
in other ways.  Also, provided suitable trade and investment
conditions can be worked out, individual countries--both producing
and consuming--will benefit economically by the use of the world's
lowest cost energy.

But it would be politically and diplomatically imprudent for
consuming countries not to accelerate development of domestic
resources.  Particular encouragement is needed for synthetic
fuels development.  Actively developing the potential for greater
domestic energy output through synthetic fuel production would
make it possible to utilize foreign supplies with less risk
because it would be apparent to the producing countries that the
U.S. can produce sizeable amounts of domestic energy if forced to
do so.

Specific programs to implement a policy of accommodation
might include the following:

1.  A conference of consuming and producing nations should
be promoted to work out what the producers want in such areas as
technological assistance, aid in industrialization, and protection for their foreign investments.  Efforts should continue
to help resolve political conflicts in the Middle East.  A
principal aim of such endeavors would be to provide a stable
environment--uncertainties about prices and supplies are greatly
aggravating the current situation.

2.  Greater efforts should be undertaken to develop an
improved international financial and banking system to recycle
OPEC funds back to the west.  This is urgently needed not only
because of the balance of payments problems of individual countries and the strain on the international monetary system but
also because OPEC may be tempted to use financial pressure (such
as movements of funds) as a future bargaining tool.

3. Consuming countries should endeavor to use energy more frugally. Letting the free market price mechanism work would be the most effective way.

4. Consuming countries should push ahead developing domestic energy supplies. In the U.S. there should be greater availability of public lands for resource development. Synthetic fuels technology should be developed to the point of commercial viability. Over the long term, research should be pressed for scientific breakthroughs that could lead to desirable alternative energy technologies.

## CHANGING FUTURE ROLE OF PRIVATE COMPANIES IN INTERNATIONAL OIL

The position of private companies in international oil activities has changed dramatically in the recent upheaval. The companies' control of and influence on production rates and prices have greatly diminished, even disappeared in some cases. No longer are private companies dealing on a more or less equal footing with the producing nations; no longer are consuming country governments taking a passive attitude towards international oil affairs.

While the relations of private companies with producing countries and consuming countries have been altered drastically, Continental Oil Company believes that private companies still have much to contribute in international oil activities. To continue their effective participation in international oil, it will be necessary to develop new arrangements between private companies and producing country governments and new relationships between private companies and consuming country governments.

### Contributions of Private Companies

Private oil companies are expected to perform much the same technical functions as in the past but under different institutional arrangements. Specific contributions will be as follows:

1. Risk-Taking. Private companies will continue to assume the risk-taking function. This is a proper role for profit-oriented companies and is one that is usually difficult for governments to perform.

2. Efficiency. Private companies can organize and operate the complex oil business more effectively than governments.

The profit motive of private companies leads to more efficient operations than more broadly diffused governmental motives such as maximization of employment or subsidization of particular groups in society. The companies already have top flight people with the necessary operating skills.

3. Technology. Generally, private companies are more effective in developing and utilizing technology. This is particularly true in exploration. Companies already employ people with considerable processing and logistical skills.

4. Buffer. Historically, private oil companies have served as an effective buffer between producing and consuming countries. With a few notable exceptions, oil trade has been on a commercial, non-political basis. Companies can still perform this buffer function. Within a policy framework established by governments, private companies can best handle the commercial aspects of getting oil from the wellhead to the consumer. This avoids introducing possibly divisive political considerations into day-to-day petroleum operations.

## Relationship Between Companies and Producing Country Governments

The greatest change in private companies' position in international oil activities has occurred in the exploration-production phase of the business. This relationship is still in a state of flux. One aspect is clear, however. The old type concession arrangements are a thing of the past.

Also, it appears that equity ownership in OPEC countries will be disappearing in the relatively near future. Already government participation or ownership is up to 60% in bell-weather countries such as Saudi Arabia and Kuwait. There is a general belief that participation will go to 100% in short order.

Companies will likely become essentially contractors in well established producing areas. Payment to companies in such cases may be through a fee or preferential supply arrangement.

One of the more vexing problems will be how to facilitate exploration by private companies in new areas where there is no existing production. Obviously, the companies will need an incentive to take this exploratory risk. Separation of the rewards for success in exploration from the return on investment from developing production may be one possibility. But the most promising trend seems to be toward production sharing types of arrangements. Under this approach, private companies typically assume all the risks and expenses for exploration. If oil is found, the country and the company share in the production in some ratio agreed to beforehand. Usually the contract allows a specified recovery of costs by the company in addition to production sharing.

There are several advantages to this approach. One attractive feature of production sharing is that the question of who owns the oil is not an issue. It clearly belongs to the host government. Also, this type of arrangement is flexible. The division of shares can be varied depending on the size of the discovery. It is likely that future exploration arrangements in new areas will follow the production sharing approach.

## Relationship Between Companies and Consuming Country Governments

While not as drastic as the change in relationship with producing nations, significant alteration of the relationship between companies and consuming country governments is also anticipated. While the logistical, processing and marketing functions will likely continue to be performed largely by private companies, consuming country governments will probably closely scrutinize these operations. In general, there will be a trend to greater government intervention. Despite distorting effects, price controls may be utilized in some cases. A close examination of transfer prices from crude production to the ultimate consumer appears likely. The total effect of these actions will tend to put a squeeze on company margins and adversely affect the ability of the industry to raise capital for much needed investments.

## ROLE OF U.S. GOVERNMENT IN INTERNATIONAL OIL

Continental Oil Company believes the U.S. government can make an essential contribution in international oil activities. The proper contributive role of the U.S. government would be (1) to set a favorable environment for the U.S. oil companies to operate abroad and (2) to work with producing country governments and other consuming country governments in establishing policy guidelines. Within these guidelines, commercial operations should be left to the private sector. Governmental participation in the conduct or prior review of industry activities is both unnecessary and counterproductive.

## Favorable Environment for U.S. Oil Companies to Operate Abroad

Actions of the U.S. government have an important influence on the international operations of U.S. oil companies. This is particularly true in the area of taxation. Punitive measures such as elimination of foreign tax credits and repeal of the depletion allowance on foreign oil production could seriously weaken the competitive position of U.S. companies in foreign operations. Continental believes that it is in the best interest of the U.S. to encourage U.S. companies to develop oil overseas. In the first place, the more oil that is discovered in a variety of countries, the less vulnerable is the U.S. (as well as other consuming countries) to actions of a few producing countries. Secondly, if U.S. companies are discouraged from exploring overseas, exploration will be done by foreign companies which in many cases will be state companies or companies with close ties to particular countries.

Considered in a broader context, international operations of U.S. oil companies are compatible with U.S. foreign policy objectives. Both strive to promote world trade and both undertake activities that foster economic growth in less developed nations.

This community of interest between the U.S. government and U.S. oil companies seems to be largely ignored in setting U.S. foreign policies that are affected by oil. Better use could be made of U.S. company expertise in formulating foreign policy options.

However, compatibility of objectives should be distinguished from implementation of U.S. foreign policies. The government should not expect U.S. oil companies to implement U.S. foreign policies. Any attempt to use the companies as instruments of U.S. foreign policy would be ineffective and counterproductive. In relation to foreign governments, it could seriously compromise the apolitical appeal of U.S. companies.

## Cooperation with Producing Country Governments

As mentioned previously, it would be appropriate for the U.S. government, along with other consuming nations, to meet with OPEC countries in an effort to determine what the producing

countries want in the way of technical assistance, industrialization aid, recycling of OPEC funds and protection for their
foreign investments.  Also the U.S. government should continue
its endeavors to reconcile the Arab-Israeli conflict.

## Cooperation with Consuming Country Governments

Coordination of policies among consuming nations is an
effective area for U.S. government involvement in international
oil activities.  Strengthening the international monetary
system, especially to recycle OPEC funds, is a matter of great
urgency.  It lies at the heart of a satisfactory resolution of
the divergent attitudes of the OPEC nations and the consuming
countries and accommodation of the impact introduced by higher
oil prices.  Lack of solid progress in this area could lead
to world depression and possible military adventures.

Coordination of oil policies with other consuming countries
would be another appropriate role for the U.S. government.
Coordination could cover such areas as provisions for emergency storage, agreement to allocate oil supplies among consuming countries in an emergency, and common measures to dampen
demand growth.  Also the U.S. government should promote agreement that (1) trade restraints will not be used to "correct"
balance of payments deficits caused by high energy prices and
(2) individual countries will avoid seeking special advantage
over other importing countries by direct negotiations with
producing nations.

## Undesirable U.S. Government Roles in International Oil Activities

While it is important for the U.S. government to take
an active role in setting broad policy guidelines in areas
affecting international oil, it is also important that the
government refrain from some activities.

1.  Promotion of a consumer cartel to negotiate directly
with OPEC is not recommended.  It would likely lead to confrontation and an impasse on important issues.

2.  Likewise, it would be inappropriate for the U.S.
government to undertake direct bilateral negotiations with

producing countries on such matters as specific prices and specific supply arrangements. National pride in such government-to-government negotiations is likely to worsen present difficulti[

3. Requirements that the U.S. government approve supply agreements between U.S. companies and producing country governments would complicate, if not stall, negotiations and would not result in lower crude prices. The basic factors and relative bargaining strength which have recently set crude oil prices would be unchanged by such a requirement.

4. Direct entry on an equity ownership basis of the U.S. government into international oil operations would not be effective. Present private companies can do operating jobs more efficiently. Furthermore, such direct participation would heighten tensions with producing nations. In fact, some countries prohibit operations by national oil companies of other countries.

ROLE OF THE U.S. GOVERNMENT IN DOMESTIC OIL OPERATIONS

No longer can oil activities be neatly separated into international and domestic components. Especially since the removal of volume controls on oil imports, the two markets have become closely related as oil imports into the U.S. increased sharply.

The U.S. government is instrumental in setting the institutional framework in which the oil industry operates. In this role, government hearings have been a forum for recent criticisms of oil companies and for suggestions to alter the way domestic oil operations are conducted. The government also performs a more positive role in energy affairs by establishing policy guidelines.

Examination of Criticisms of Private Oil Companies

A number of criticisms have been directed against oil company operations. Since policy decisions may be affected by these criticisms, it is important that their validity be carefully examined.

1. <u>Excessive Profits</u>. Oil profits increased sharply in 1973 and 1974. Much of these increases occurred from one-time events--increased value of inventories and changes in the exchange rate of currencies. Two criteria can be used to judge the level of profits. First, how do they compare with profits in other industries? On this basis, rates of return in oil have fairly closely paralleled those in other manufacturing activities. Second, do the profits generate a cash flow that exceeds the need for reinvestments? Again, on this basis oil profits have not been excessive. In fact, they have not been sufficient to generate the funds required for the large outlays needed to expand operations.

2. <u>Contribution to Inflation</u>. Oil prices have increased sharply in the past year. The immediate causes for this increase were events outside the industry, namely the actions of OPEC countries in arbitrarily raising prices and some producing countries in restricting production and imposing an embargo on shipments to the U.S. Fundamentally, there is a strong case for rising oil prices. Higher prices are necessary to bring an equilibrium in supply and demand by dampening demand growth and encouraging the development of new supplies. Also, over time, upward price adjustments are necessary because of the rising cost nature of an extractive industry such as oil.

3. <u>Too Favorable Tax Treatment</u>. Numerous proposals have called for increased taxes on domestic oil operations. Given time, an industry can adjust to a changed tax situation since eventually taxes on businesses are paid for by the consumer. However, at a time the nation needs to expand its energy resources, it would be inappropriate to raise taxes on energy activities. The threat of tax changes creates a further uncertainty and inhibits investment in an already highly risky business.

4. <u>Monopolistic Practices and Excessive Size</u>. Much of the criticism directed at the oil industry is concerned with alleged monopolistic practices and excessive size of the oil industry and individual oil companies.

That the oil industry is monopolistic is a myth that is perpetuated by constant repetition. An examination of market shares of individual oil companies and market performance in oil activities reveals that the oil industry is one of the

most competitive industries among major U.S. industry groups.
The concentration ratio in oil is relatively low.  There are some
10,000 companies engaged in the exploration for and production of
crude oil and natural gas; the largest company accounting for
only 7 percent of U.S. production.  In oil refining there are 131
companies with the largest company owning less than 10 percent of
U.S. refining capacity.  The four largest companies account for
only 32 percent of the domestic shipments of refined petroleum
products; by contrast, over 54 percent of the industries classified as manufacturing industries by the Department of Commerce
have higher concentration ratios.  In petroleum marketing,
according to the American Petroleum Institute, there are some
15,000 industrial wholesalers and jobbers, large and small.  The
top firm markets about 10 percent of the total.

   Freedom of entry into the industry (Tenneco, Occidental and
Amerada Hess have become major companies in the postwar period)
and strong competition at the service station level are other
indications of a vigorous, competitive industry.

   The charge of excessive size of the industry and of individual companies needs to be put into perspective.  Of course,
size is relative.  The oil industry is large because of the
enormous magnitude of demand for petroleum products, which in
turn, is related to (1) the pervasive needs for energy in all
phases of the U.S. economy (2) the importance of the automobile
in American society and (3) the dominant role of oil and gas in
the total energy picture.  The oil industry should also be viewed
within the context of total society--we have big government, big
unions and big industries.

   A second aspect of the "bigness" question relates to the
size of individual oil companies.  Large companies are necessary
to get the job done in providing energy for the U.S. economy.
This fact is illustrated by the size of individual projects in
the energy field.  A winning bonus bid on an attractive offshore
lease often may cost $50 to $75 million dollars (some have gone
as high as $200 million); a new economical size refinery of, say
250,000 barrels daily will cost $600 million dollars; and a coal
gasification facility is estimated to cost $700 million.  Only a
large company (or a group of companies) is able to undertake
investments of this magnitude, particularly when considering the
riskiness of individual exploratory plays; the long lead times
which elapse between the inception of investment in major
energy projects and the first generation of revenues; and the

costly and comprehensive technical support organizations needed
to conduct these operations.

### Alternative Ways to Conduct Domestic Petroleum Operations

Related to recent criticisms of the oil industry have been
suggestions for alternative ways of organizing domestic petroleum
operations other than the private enterprise - free market
system. Continental Oil Company believes that under the latter
system the oil industry has done a good job of serving the
public. The industry has been innovative, as indicated by the
offshore technology developed by private companies and the
increasing quality of gasoline. The industry is efficient
which is illustrated by the effective and complex logistical
system for processing, distributing and marketing products.
Except in emergencies like the recent Arab embargo, the American
public has been adequately supplied with petroleum products at
reasonable prices. (Gasoline prices at the service station,
excluding taxes, were approximately the same in 1921 and 1973.)
It is questionable if any of the alternatives, discussed below,
would be more effective in serving the public.

1. Breakup of Integrated Operations. There have been
proposals that the integrated organization of oil operations
be broken up into two or more segments. One extreme possibility
would be a fourway separation into exploration-production,
pipeline, refining and marketing segments. Such a divorcement
would supposedly protect some independent businesses, which,
according to this thesis, would help foster competition. There
are several fallacies to the divorcement approach: (a) the
oil industry is already competitive (b) because of the need
for close coordination of the flow of oil from the well to
the consumer and the specialized nature of some oil facilities,
logistical efficiency would be lost through divorcement (e.g.,
oil pipelines and service stations are specialized facilities,
limited largely to handling oil) (c) the promotion of small
business units could mean more costly operations because of
losses of economies of scale (e.g., in the 1950's and 1960's,
until recent spurt in inflation, economies of scale along with
other technical innovations were instrumental in holding refinery
processing costs constant).

2. Utility Status for Oil Companies. In order to regulate
closely the operations of oil companies, it has been proposed
that these companies be converted to utilities. A close examination indicates the inappropriateness of this approach.
While utilities are closely regulated, they have other attributes

such as low risk operations, guaranteed market areas, and guaranteed rates of return. These characteristics do not fit the oil industry. Oil companies by nature are risk takers, particularly in exploration. It is difficult to see a utility mounting and sustaining a broad based exploration program. (Some utility companies have made limited exploration investments, frequently by giving support money to other companies' programs.) Petroleum refinery and marketing are clearly not utility-type activities, where guaranteed markets and guaranteed rates of return would be appropriate. Unlike a telephone or electric company, there is no logical reason an oil company should be given a monopoly position in a given area.

3. Federal Oil and Gas Company. Another drastic suggestion is that a federal oil and gas company be established to explore for and produce oil. According to its proponents it would be a useful standard to judge the performance of private companies. Such a company would have a choice of federal offshore lands at little or no cost and would presumably pay no taxes.

This proposal is unwise in a number of respects: (a) its operations would likely be inefficient and subject to political whims (b) it would be unfair competition for private companies and not useful as a standard for judging private company performance because of its preferred status in obtaining leases and in paying taxes (c) it would merely transfer skilled people and operating equipment, both of which are in short supply, from private to government operations and (d) it is not needed because the function of exploring for and producing oil is done efficiently by private companies. This latter point is demonstrated by experience overseas where private companies have tended to be more efficient than state companies.

## Positive Role for U.S. Government

Continental Oil Company believes there is a positive role the U.S. government can perform in domestic energy activities. Performance of this role is hindered by the atmosphere of suspicion between the oil companies and the government which largely grew out of a misinterpretation of events during the oil embargo and energy crisis in the U.S. Unfortunately, many people have felt these developments were contrived by the oil

industry for its own advantage. This has led to several congressional hearings and suits alleging a conspiracy by oil
companies. This attitude probably reflects the public's search
for an easy answer to our problems. The government should aid
business in laying this unfortunate conspiracy theory to rest,
for certainly no policy or progress towards current solutions of
our problems can be made without business being a full partner in
the considerable effort required.

The following are some suggestions of items to be included
in a national policy framework for energy activities, a major
contribution that could be made by government:

1.  The government should promote energy conservation. In
doing so, it should seek to preserve the individual consumer's
choices to the fullest degree, but to influence those choices
towards fuller conservation efforts through the price system.
This is an area in which the United States considerably lags
behind other industrial countries. Through stringent price
controls, domestic oil and gas are sold at well below world
prices.

2.  The government is responsible for working out a balance
between ecological and energy needs. Fortunately, the shrillness
of the early debates on this topic has been somewhat replaced by
a more comparative harmony of dialogues on the appropriate
methods of achieving and financing our environmental programs,
but significant differences still exist and constitute an important barrier to resource development and utilization. As in
the case of conservation, the passage of time will lead to
further gains in environmental quality, through the development
of new technology which will permit the production and use of
energy sources to take place with less environmental impact.

3.  The government can help expand domestic energy supplies
by making public lands available for development of energy
resources. Encouraging steps have been taken to expand offshore
leasing for oil exploration. But additional initiatives are
needed, particularly to convince the energy-short Northeast of
the need to explore off the Atlantic Coast. Opening up the Gulf
of Alaska for exploration and resumption of drilling off the
Pacific Coast would be other important moves toward development
of more domestic energy supplies. Federal western coal lands
should be made available for lease.

4.  The government should encourage research into alternative energy sources.  While the government can appropriately participate directly in pure research, applied research should be done mainly by private companies.  Instead of the government spending massive sums for applied research, the government might designate broad areas of investigation which are eligible for preferred tax treatment.  Individual companies could decide on the specific program to undertake within that field.  For each dollar spent, it might receive, say, a $.30 tax credit.

5.  The government should push ahead in demonstrating the potential for greater domestic energy output by underwriting a prototype commercial plant to produce synthetic fuels.  As mentioned earlier, this would demonstrate the feasibility of such processes to the producing countries. Preferably the prototype facility would be a coal gasification or liquefaction plant, because these processes appear to be the best alternatives for developing synthetic fuels. One approach would be for the government to lend a company a significant portion of the capital required to put in such a plant.  There would be an understanding that if the plant could never compete economically, the loan would not be repaid.  If the plant becomes economic, the loan would be repaid out of profits.  The government loan might provide about 75% of the cost with the company putting up 25%.

6.  The administration should recognize in its antitrust policy that joint ventures are increasingly necessary because of greater risks and the much larger scale of operations necessary for efficiency.  Unfortunately, government policy is moving the opposite way as indicated by plans to restrict joint bids by certain companies in offshore lease sales.  The high cost of building an economical size refinery may be restricting some fairly large companies from undertaking such projects.  Perhaps joint ventures should be allowed in this case.

APPENDIX E

APPENDIX E

[§E.0]  SELECTED DEPARTMENT OF STATE
QUESTIONNAIRE DATA ON PRODUCER
GOVERNMENT ATTITUDES

    The following are comments received from the
Department of State desk officers on Abu Dhabi, Algeria,
Ecuador, Kuwait, Libya, Nigeria, Saudi Arabia and Venezuela
in December 1974 and January 1975 in response to a questionnaire prepared by the Study Contractor.  They are quoted
verbatim without quotation marks following the questions to
which they were addressed.

A.  [§E.1]  Petroleum  Prices and Production

1.  Does the Government believe that consuming countries will
be successful in reducing demand and maintaining conservation
policies?

ABU DHABI

     Although in Abu Dhabi there is considerably more
reason to expect that future discoveries will increase present
reserves, the Government there sees a finite limit to these
new discoveries which is most likely to leave Abu Dhabi in
about the same position as Kuwait in a few years--that is,
hoping for a maintenance of high oil prices and a controlled
world demand that will have the effect of stretching the
saleability of Abu Dhabi's reserves over the longest possible
period.  The Government of Abu Dhabi is not sure of our
ability to conserve, but would prefer that we succeed in our
efforts to do so.

ALGERIA

     GOA has not expressed view on this.  It has, however,
come out in favor of conservation on general principles--reserves
will last longer; developed countries using too much of world
resources, etc.

ECUADOR

     The Government of Ecuador (GOE) has made no public
statement of its views of the possibilities of consuming
countries reducing demand and maintaining conservation policies.

IRAN

     The Government of Iran has been urging conservation
and development of alternative energy sources on the consumers.
Presumably it believes such policies can be successful.

IRAQ

     Iraq has been one of the most vocal states in re-
pudiating the efforts of consuming countries to cooperate
in reducing their oil consumption.  There is no real evidence,
however, that Iraq believes that these efforts will meet with
any success.

## KUWAIT

Given the economic "ups" and "downs" which the consuming countries have faced during the past several years, the
Government of Kuwait possesses no absolute conviction that
these countries will be successful in reducing demand and
"maintaining" - perhaps "introducing" is a more appropriate
word - conservation policies. The Kuwaitis, however, do
respect the West's technological ability and its ability
to get things together at times of real need. They want us
to conserve energy so that their reserves - which are unlikely
to increase through future discoveries - will provide them
with a profitable income over a longer period of time. They
sincerely hope our efforts in this field will succeed.

## LIBYA

The Libyan government has not expressed a clear
view on this.

## NIGERIA

No reports on this question, but FMG probably
believes industrialized countries may reduce growth of
demand, not demand itself.

## SAUDI ARABIA

Saudi Oil Minister Yamani has on numerous occasions
mentioned the need for consumer countries to practice conservation and has welcomed steps in support of conservation
noting this will prolong the life of oil assets of oil exporting countries. At the same time, Yamani and other Saudis
have shown some degree of skepticism whether the U.S. and
other Western countries are prepared to take the disagreeable
steps that this will require. Present conservation measures
may be more a reflection of depressed economic conditions
than really effective steps taken by the governments to hold
down consumption. While the Saudis have high regard for
Western, and especially U.S., technological capabilities and
expect that alternative energy sources will eventually be
developed which will cut down on the need for imported oil,
they also realize that these alternatives will be costly.
Therefore, they expect that if general economic conditions

begin to improve, it will be difficult to maintain oil conservation policies among the major consumers especially if
oil continues to be a relatively cheaper source of energy.

## VENEZUELA

The Government has not expressed itself on this
point but is in general in favor of such measures.

2. Has the Government made any cut-backs in petroleum
production during 1974? If so, how much?

## ABU DHABI

Yes. Throughout most of 1973, Abu Dhabi oil
production was in the neighborhood of 1.9 million barrels
per day. Following the temporary sharp reductions instituted at the time of the October 1973 Middle East hostilities, it recovered to about 1.6 million barrels per
day during spring and summer 1974. However, participation
negotiations in the latter part of 1974, during which the
Government took over 60% of the major concessions operating
in its territory, have created a pro rata production situation based upon 40% equity, 40% buy back, and 20% direct
Government sale and the practical result has been to cut
Abu Dhabi production to a current average of around 1.2
million barrels per day.

## ALGERIA

Not during 1974. But production dropped in '73--
officially because GOA was going along with OAPEC cutback,
but actually because of technical problems in oil fields.
Production has not returned to former "highest levels."

## ECUADOR

The GOE cut back daily production quotas from
250,000 b/d to 210,000 b/d in April 1974, claiming a need
for conservation, the oil companies claim that well-head
restrictions make it impossible to produce more than
190,000 b/d. Ecuadorean petroleum exports demonstrated
a sharp decrease during the period July-November 1974,
falling from an average of 6-7 million barrels per month
in the first six months of 1974 to a low of 2.1 million

barrels for November. The initial cause in July 1974 was a break in the trans-Andean pipeline, which suspended production for approximately two weeks. After the pipeline was repaired, exports recuperated somewhat, but high prices led Texaco and Gulf to reduce liftings and CEPE, the state oil company seemed unable to conclude firm deals for GOE participation crude.

## IRAN

No.

## IRAQ

While Iraq has made some reduction in its export of oil, they have apparently made no production cutbacks. Indeed, all of their plans for the future call for massive increases in production.

## KUWAIT

Yes. Prior to the 1973 Middle East hostilities, the GOK had already instituted "conservation" procedures which limited overall production to about 3.1 million barrels per day. But in that "conservation" and "oil-as-a-weapon" were such popular themes on the domestic political scene, production was forced down to a low of about 1.7 million barrels per day in late 1973. Also, as a result of the oil embargo and subsequent protracted negotiations for the Government's takeover of 60% of the Kuwait Oil Company concession, including the setting of high buy-back prices, this production level was not permitted to rise again until late 1974. Kuwait now permits production of about 2.2 million barrels per day from facilities which could produce 3.8 or 3.9 million barrels per day.

## LIBYA

Libyan crude production declined from 2,030,000 barrels per day in January to 953,000 BPD in November. Although precise details are not available most of the reduction appears to have resulted from Libya's inability to market oil at the high prices it demands and from inefficiencies in production following on nationalizations of foreign owned operations. Libya has, however, followed a deliberate conservation policy since 1970.

NIGERIA

Yes.   Presently producing at 81% capacity.

SAUDI ARABIA

No.   Outside of the period when the oil embargo
was in effect in late 1973 and early 1974, Saudi oil production has remained at a level of 8.8 million bpd rising
to 9 million bpd by the end of 1974.   The only exception
was in August when production dropped to 8.3 million bpd
because of a combination of circumstances - bad weather
and a shortage of tankers.   On the other hand, the Saudis
have not really allowed their production to continue to
rise to a level commensurate with production capacity, as
had occurred prior to the October 1973 war.   Production
capacity is now probably close to 10.5 million bpd.

VENEZUELA

Yes.   As of October, 1974, the monthly average
petroleum production for the current year was 3,014,000 b/d,
an amount below the 1973 monthly average of 3,366,000 b/d.
Venezuelan production peaked at 3.7 millon b/d in 1970.


3.   If the answer to the previous question was affirmative,
have reductions in production created problems for the
Government in balancing its national budget or in realizing
its national plans for development?   If so, how do you expect
the Government to handle this problem?

ABU DHABI

No.   Even at present production levels, Abu
Dhabi income will approach $3.5 billion in 1974 and surpass
programmed budget expenditures by $2 billion.

ALGERIA

No problems--because price increases have counter-
acted drops in production.   If GOA is obliged to cut back
on development budget it will be because price of oil drops
substantially below current level, not because of production
drops.

## ECUADOR

The drop in crude oil exports will require a reduction in GOE expenditure plans and it is expected that the country will finish the CY 1974 with a net budget deficit. Similarly, foreign exchange reserves peaked at $404 million on June 30 and fell to $330 million by October 31, 1974. With respect to both government revenues and foreign exchange availabilities 1974 represents such a significant increase over prior years that the shortfalls in revenue will not be a serious hardship.

Ecuador has experienced some difficulty in marketing its petroleum, however, a new Natural Resources Minister was installed in November 1974. The new minister, Rear Admiral Salazar, has already succeeded in concluding certain modest, advantageous oil sales to ENAPE in Chile (at $12.20) and Derby (at $11.58), which have the effect of supporting high GOE price levels. In the final analysis if Ecuador continues to have marketing difficulties we can expect that they will find a face-saving way to reduce the price.

## IRAN

Not applicable.

## IRAQ

Not applicable.

## KUWAIT

No. Even at reduced production levels, income far exceeds budget and development needs. (Kuwait's FY 74/75 budget expenditures are about $3 billion; 1974 income is estimated at about $7.5 billion.)

## LIBYA

So far there is no evidence of this. In any case the LARG has in excess of $3 billion in foreign exchange reserves upon which to draw. However, if production and prices remain at the present level they will probably have a deficit in 1975.

## NIGERIA

The cutbacks have occurred very recently. There have been no budgetary problems for the governments.

## SAUDI ARABIA

No. Saudi revenues from oil are far beyond the Kingdom's requirements.

## VENEZUELA

No.


4. If the major consuming nations were to substantially restrict increases in their petroleum demand through 1980, such that present levels of petroleum production in the Country could not be significantly expanded, would the Government be sufficiently "pinched" in terms of its budget and national aspirations to either reduce price and increase production or raise price on current production in an attempt to increase petroleum revenues? If so, which would you expect it to do and why?

## ABU DHABI

No. So long as foreign commitments were kept in hand, Abu Dhabi would feel no pinch and could actually get by well on significantly less than current production. If the Rulers proclivities to use his money as an instrument of foreign influence were permitted to grow significantly beyond their current limits (and we doubt they will), Abu Dhabi would put itself in the very unlikely position of having to break ranks with its larger OPEC partners over price and production policies. We do not think it would ever do this on its own.

## ALGERIA

No. There is little prospect of substantial increase of production in next few years anyway. Outlook for new finds rather dim.

ECUADOR

Although petroleum exports have enabled Ecuador to move away from its historical position as a "one-crop" country (bananas), to becoming a "two-crop" country, it remains a highly vulnerable member of the petroleum-producing world. Clearly, as a very small producer, Ecuador is not in a position to set an independent policy and will follow the line set by larger producers.

IRAN

Iran does not now plan to expand production significantly beyond present levels. If, as is predicted, it once again becomes a net importer of capital within the next 3-5 years, that budget pinch may lead it to seek higher prices on current production.

IRAQ

If a major reduction of oil consumption were to occur, it would indeed put a "pinch" in the Iraqi budget, and national development plans, which are based almost entirely on oil revenues and on the expectation of an increase in those revenues. As to recourse, it is doubtful Iraq would face strong external pressures against doing so. It would possibly be willing to lower prices, since it has done so in the past.

KUWAIT

No. Total revenues currently running between $4 and $5 billion per year in excess of a $3 billion budget, which includes in addition to all domestic programs, the most sophisticated and developed foreign aid program of any OPEC state. Kuwait will not be pinched by having to reduce its production. At the same time, it will probably support any OPEC moves to raise prices since it will add to its national wealth and tend to make its oil reserves last longer.

LIBYA

No. However, because Libyan oil is overpriced at present they may be forced to lower prices simply to reverse the current trend toward decreased production.

NIGERIA

A lot would depend on the rate of inflation of its imports. I would expect Nigeria to continue to go along with OPEC price increases. In any event, it does not have sizable excess capacity.

## SAUDI ARABIA

No.  The Saudis would not be pinched if their production remained at its current level even if current prices did not increase.

At current (post December 1974 OPEC prices), Saudi Arabia is producing 7 million bpd in excess of its domestic revenue needs, and almost 8 million bpd in excess of its foreign exchange requirements for the purchase of imports. Even if its present foreign aid commitments are included (which will probably amount to $3.2 billion in FY 75), Saudi production is nearly 7 million bpd in excess of its requirements.  While the Saudi economy can be expected to grow at a rate of at least 20% a year during the next decade, revenue requirements will still fall far short of income received from oil during this period.  Moreover, this oil revenue will be supplemented by rapidly rising revenues received from Saudi foreign exchange assets (foreign treasury bills, investments, etc.).

While the Saudis will probably seek to hold down further price increases because of the adverse impact on the world economy, they are unlikely to break ranks with OPEC if other producers press hard to increase their revenues with further price increases.

## VENEZUELA

No, if the current world petroleum price levels do not significantly drop.  The Government has announced that it, in fact, plans to further reduce production to 2.0 million b/d by 1980, presumably based on the continuance of current prices.

5.  What is the likelihood of the government breaking ranks with OPEC if it believed it could increase its petroleum revenues by lowering price or utilizing non-price variables (such as easier credit terms) to accomplish the same objectives as a price cut?

## ABU DHABI

Extremely unlikely, see answer to question to question #4 above.

## ALGERIA

None.

## ECUADOR

Membership in OPEC became fundamental to Ecuadorean energy policy during the tenure in office of former Minister of Natural Resources Jarrin, who held the post of President of OPEC until his reassignment in November 1974. For reasons of national prestige it is unlikely that Ecuador, as the smallest member of OPEC in terms of petroleum exports would break ranks unless there were some major realignments such as Venezuela quitting the organization.

## IRAN

None.

## IRAQ

The likelihood of Iraq's "breaking ranks" with OPEC is slight. Its membership in OPEC is important to it not only economically but politically. Moreover, there is such a wide range of action possible on most OPEC decisions that a "break" would in most cases probably be unnecessary.

## KUWAIT

None. Kuwait will never break ranks with OPEC (particularly so long as most member states are Arab) in order to increase its oil revenues above their current levels in relation to other members.

## LIBYA

Although it is unlikely to break openly with OPEC the LARG has already shown that it is willing to make under-the-table deals if this is in the Libyan interest.

## NIGERIA

Nigeria is unlikely to get out too far in front of OPEC in any direction. Besides, it has little incentive to offend other OPEC members as long as present revenues are so far in excess of Nigeria's ability to spend them.

## SAUDI ARABIA

Very unlikely. The Saudis have not accepted the argument, despite efforts by Treasury representatives, that lowering prices now might increase their petroleum revenues in the long run. The Saudis have time and time again indicated that they have no desire to break ranks with OPEC. Moreover, there is a growing number of Saudis who are becoming more vocal in support of high prices for economic and conservation measures. Thus, any attempt to take a unilateral role on prices would arouse domestic opposition among many younger educated Saudis who see oil as a national treasure that should be preserved for as many generations as possible.

## VENEZUELA

The likelihood appears remote. A Venezuelan citizen is the principal founder of OPEC and, ever since, the country has based its major petroleum policies on joint, OPEC action. For years, Venezuela urged within OPEC the adoption of a system of production controls for the purpose of price support.

6. If one or more OPEC nations unilaterally reduced petroleum prices, what would be the probable response of the Government?

## ABU DHABI

Abu Dhabi's reaction to a unilateral price reduction by one or more OPEC nations would most probably be precisely the same as Kuwait's. (See Kuwait questionnaire #6)

## ALGERIA

Depends upon market prices and which countries cut prices. Also, Algeria is more likely to follow OAPEC rather than larger OPEC policies. GOA tends to go its own way on everything and will charge what market will bear, counting on exceptionally high quality of its oil and closeness of market to protect price somewhat.

## ECUADOR

If the OPEC nations were to reduce petroleum prices unilaterally, the GOE would be obliged to lower its prices.

## IRAN

That would depend on the share of the market those nations had. If their share was large enough to affect world prices, Iran would probably first try to get other hard-line OPEC members to reduce production to put upward pressure on prices. Failing in that it would probably lower prices as necessary to remain competitive.

## IRAQ

The probable response of the Iraqi Government in such a case would be a strong burst of condemnatory rhetoric against the offending and reactionary culprit.

## KUWAIT

If Saudi Arabia and/or Iran was among those uni-laterally reduced petroleum prices, Kuwait would probably respond by pegging its crude to the new Gulf price struc-ture than would prevail as a result. If OPEC members other than Saudi Arabia and/or Iran broke ranks and reduced prices, Kuwait would rush to join ranks with the remaining members which did not reduce prices.

## LIBYA

This is difficult to predict; but it would probably not affect Libya's own prices which are higher than other OPEC producers at present and reflect a strong go-it-alone attitude. Of course much depends on how the reduction is made and by which countries.

## NIGERIA

It would depend on who did it. Nigeria might follow Saudi Arabia's and/or Iran's lead.

## SAUDI ARABIA

If a major OPEC oil producer such as Iran uni-laterally reduced its prices, the Saudis would probably go along. If it were a small producer, such as Ecuador, be-cause it badly needed extra revenue, the Saudis probably would concert with other OPEC countries and probably would not go along with a price reduction.

VENEZUELA

        The Government would perhaps first attempt to
restore prices by private efforts with the nations involved.  However, if these efforts were unproductive and
if the reduction appeared to threaten world price levels
and/or the integrity of OPEC itself, the Government
would possibly issue a statement of public disapproval
and work diligently within OPEC to counteract the reductions as well as to hold the line against further
defections.


    B.  [§E.2]  Recycling of Surplus Petroleum Revenues

7.  What is the estimated dollar amount of the Country's
petroleum revenues and Net Balance of Payment in 1974,
1975 and through 1980?  (Please state this in terms of
1974 dollars and assume current petroleum prices through
1980.)

ABU DHABI

|                       | Petroleum Revenues | Net Balance of Payments* |
|-----------------------|--------------------|--------------------------|
| 1974                  | $3.5 billion       | $2 billion (+)           |
| 1975                  | $4 billion         | $2 billion (+)           |
| Total through 1980    | $30 billion        | $16 billion (+)          |

*  Current Account

ALGERIA

        This information is available from IMF studies.
Revenues in 1973 from crude oil and related products was
$1,530 million (average price $3.96 per bbl).  Estimated
revenue for 1974 is $4,635 million at average price of
$11.40 per bbl.  (IMF figures).  Algeria is not involved
in recycling problem as it needs maximum oil revenues to
plow into $27.5 billion development plan, and will still
have to borrow from domestic and foreign sources to cover
remainder.

ECUADOR

|      | Petroleum Revenues US$MM | Net Balance of Payments |
|------|--------------------------|-------------------------|
| 1974 | 540                      | 444                     |
| 1975 | 840                      | 293                     |
| 1976 | 1,117                    | 553                     |
| 1977 | 1,316                    | 637                     |
| 1978 | unavailable              | 638                     |
| 1979 | unavailable              | unavailable             |
| 1980 | unavailable              | unavailable             |

(Source:   World Bank, "Current Economic Position and Prospects
           of Ecuador," August 26, 1974)

IRAN

|                    | Petroleum Revenues | Net Balance of Payments |
|--------------------|--------------------|-------------------------|
| 1974               | 20 billion         | 3.8 billion             |
| 1975               | 23 billion         | 2.5 billion             |
| Total through 1980 | 118 billion        | 0                       |

IRAQ

|                       | Petroleum Revenues            | Net Balance of Payments |
|-----------------------|-------------------------------|-------------------------|
| * 1974  (1973/74)     | $1.7 billion est.             | N/A                     |
| * 1975  (1974/75)     | $5.2 billion est.             | N/A                     |
| Total through 1980    | $43 billion (IMF/IBRD figures)| N/A                     |

* Ministry of Finance figures; 1 Dinar = $3.40.
  Iraqi fiscal year begins on April 1.

KUWAIT

|                    | Petroleum Revenues | Net Balance of Payments* |
|--------------------|--------------------|--------------------------|
| 1974               | $7.5 billion       | $4.5 billion (+)         |
| 1975               | $9 billion         | $5 billion (+)           |
| Total through 1980 | $66 billion        | $40 billion (+)          |

*   Current Account

## LIBYA

This information may be available from IMF.
Revenue from the oil sector in 1973 (in SDRs) was 1,613.1
million (IMF figures).

## NIGERIA

|  | Petroleum Revenues | Net Balance of Payments |
|---|---|---|
| 1974 | $7.8 billion | +$7,700,000,000 |
| 1975 | $8-9 billion, growing to $11 billion by 1979-80 |  |
| Total through 1980 |  | Downward trend because development expenditures and imports growing faster than revenue and exports. |

## SAUDI ARABIA

|  | Petroleum Revenues | Net Balance of Payments |
|---|---|---|
| 1974 | $24 billion | $18 billion (+) |
| 1975 | $32 billion | $24 billion (+) |
| Total 1974 through 1980 | $216 billion | $140 billion (+) |

Note: By 1980, Saudi Revenues from foreign holdings
should reach $10 billion a year in addition to oil revenues.

## VENEZUELA

|  | Petroleum Revenues | Net Balance of Payments |
|---|---|---|
| 1974 | $11 billion | $7 billion |
| 1975 | $10 billion | $6 billion |
| Total through 1980 (7 years) | $65 billion | $35 billion |

The above numbers are based on an anticipated annual decline in production rates coupled with a growing import bill.

8. Does the Government believe that there are serious world monetary problems arising from current levels of petroleum prices? If so, what solutions is it considering?

## ABU DHABI

The opinions of the Government of Abu Dhabi regarding the causes of world monetary problems are the same as those of Kuwait. (See Kuwait question #8).

## ALGERIA

Algeria not convinced of seriousness of world monetary problems. Sees it all in light of greedy industrialized states who are trying to maintain their exploitative position vis a vis the have-nots. Claim that balance can only be achieved by reordering structure of world economy. They believe Arab oil producers with surplus revenues should first offer AID to less-favored Arab States, then secondly to other LDC's, and as last priority, invest in developed countries.

## ECUADOR

The GOE reacted in a moderate fashion to the public statements of President Ford and Secretary Kissinger on energy matters in September 1974. President Rodriguez in a speech delivered on September 28, 1974, acknowledged the existence of an inflationary crisis, "apparently sharpened by a reasonable increase in the worldwide price of petroleum," but stated that "it is a vital matter for us to defend our natural resources and the sovereignty that protects them." No Ecuadorean official has offered any public suggestions on how to resolve the crisis.

## IRAN

Iran refuses to acknowledge that oil prices are an important factor in world monetary problems and claims that through its purchases of equipment from the consumer

countries and its extensive foreign assistance loans it is
doing its share in recycling and helping the most affected
states.

## IRAQ

No. Iraq has not indicated that it sees any serious--
or at least unjustifiable--difficulty in the high price levels
of petroleum. It sees these prices as being necessary for the
welfare of the producing countries and apparently is not particularly concerned about the problems which consuming countries
claim they are facing.

## KUWAIT

The Government believes there are serious world
monetary problems resulting from the inability of the major
industrial countries to check a multitude of equally serious
inflationary tendencies that have been growing over the past
decade. Petroleum prices are admitted to be important, but
are far from the only root cause of world monetary problems.
Oil prices and basic industrial prices must be controlled
together if these problems are to be solved, the GOK feels.
The recent rise in oil prices, it maintains, was long over-
due and simply brought the cost of this precious resource
in line with other basic items.

## LIBYA

The LARG has shown no concern for possible world
monetary problems due to high oil prices, which they feel
bring some balance back into the existing unequal distribution
of the world's wealth.

## NIGERIA

It has unofficially proposed indexing petroleum
prices to capital goods prices.

## SAUDI ARABIA

The Saudi Government has become increasingly aware
of the serious monetary problems arising from current petroleum prices, especially the balance of payments position of a
number of petroleum importers. They do not, however, accept
the argument that the rapid rise in oil has been a major
cause of world inflation arguing that serious inflationary
tendencies among the industrialized countries have been underway and gone unchecked long before the price of oil was
increased.

Partially to offset the high price of oil, the Saudis have made a variety of aid commitments (grants and loans) mainly to Islamic countries which will probably amount to at least $2.2 billion in FY 75. Moreover, they have allocated $200 million for the Islamic Bank, $3 billion to a newly established Development Fund which will provide loans on a concessional basis to LDCs, and contributed to a number of other financial institutions such as the Arab Fund for Social and Economic Development, the Arab Fund for Africa, the Arab Bank for African Development, and the Inter-American Development Bank. Outlays for these organizations or loans by the Saudi development fund could well amount to another $1 billion during FY 1975.

The Saudis have also invested some of their surplus funds in the IBRD (purchasing $750 million in IBRD bonds at over 8% in December) and have pledged $1.2 billion at 7% to the IMF Oil Contingency Fund.

For the future, the Saudis have indicated that they would be willing to expand their participation in an enlarged IMF oil contingency fund. They tend to view the recent proposal for an independent special lending facility organized by consumer countries as a confrontation tactic. However, they believe it is likely to fail since the consumer countries would end up having to raise the cash from their own resources and take all the credit risks themselves.

The Saudis are also beginning to look at triangular operations where investments might be made in third countries, where western technology is married to Saudi capital. A good example is growing Saudi interest in the Sudan which has a very large agricultural potential which could be developed with Saudi capital and Western agricultural technology, and thus assure the Saudis' access to a nearby source of food.

Finally, the Saudis have been studying the placement of their reserves in various medium and long term instruments of various oil consumer countries, including the United States, and in making medium term loans to certain European countries with serious balance of payments problems whose weakening economies might cause more radical forces to take political control. The problem, however, is that Saudi Arabia does not yet have well organized financial institutions

to handle its rapidly growing wealth which has tended to
make its aid programs almost entirely politically motivated.

## VENEZUELA

The Government does not appear to view the present
world monetary problems from the same perspective as that
of the industrialized world.  It has, instead placed the
problems in a wider context of the need for a more equitable
distribution of the wealth, just prices for LDC raw commodities, and a greater voice for the Third World in international financial dealings.  The Government proposes that
the industrialized world and developing nations meet to
discuss the problems.


9.  Would the Government be willing to invest a portion of
its surplus revenues in an international fund which would,
in turn, loan the money to economically depressed or developing
countries for petroleum purchases or development projects?
If so, how much would it be willing to invest and under what
conditions would it make such investment?  Would these loans
be concessional, nonconcessional or a mix of the two?  Would
the Government require guarantees of these loans as a pre-
condition to its investing?  If so, to what extent and by
whom must the loans be guaranteed?  How would the Government
react if the United States or other nations were unwilling
to guarantee such loans?

## ABU DHABI

Although like most OPEC states, Abu Dhabi still
much prefers to meet its foreign development aid obligations
bilaterally, it has shown itself willing, if not enthusiastic
to take part in international funds such as the Islamic Fund
for development and the IMF oil contingency fund.  For the
foreseeable future it would be willing to invest just about
as little as it could get away with and stay respectable--
say $50 million a year??  This would be purely political
money and would thus probably be concessional and not requiring guaranties.

## ALGERIA

GOA already has pledged money to Arab Development
fund--does not regard these funds as "surplus" however.
Other questions irrelevant to Algeria or unanswerable.
GOA has been and continues to be recipient, not a giver
of loans, investment, etc.  It gives practically no aid
on bilateral basis.

## ECUADOR

Ecuador is a comparatively new member of the petroleum-exporting fraternity of nations, and it has only begun to plan on the ways in which it may relieve its chronic poverty and underdevelopment. Despite its new "wealth," it is still considered a poor nation. It is unlikely to wish to divert any of its petroleum wealth from its own needs.

## IRAN

Iran is putting a small amount of its foreign exchange surplus into the IBRD and IMF, but has shown a strong preference to use those funds for bilateral loans serving its own political and economic purposes.

## IRAQ

Iraq is not likely to have too much in the way of excess revenues, but will likely absorb the great bulk of its revenues into national development plans. Also, Iraq has not shown any appreciable interest in multilateral aid funding. It has said that Arab money should first of all be spent in Arab countries. This has not prevented it from acting in bilateral agreements, though on a very limited basis. It has, for example, made a sizeable loan to Afghanistan and has sold oil on a concessional basis to India. There are also reports of a major loan to France and oil/loan agreements with Italy and Japan. France, however, has denied such an agreement and firm details on the other two agreements are not available.

## KUWAIT

Although preferring bilateral programs, Kuwait has traditionally shown a willingness far greater than any other OPEC country to commit considerable capital to international development funds. The Arab Fund for Social and Economic Development, the Islamic Fund, the IMF Oil Contingency and even the unsuccessful OPEC Fund all have GOK support. The Kuwaitis are perfectly aware that they cannot hope to survive as an island of wealth in a sea of need; they want very much, in addition to their very extensive bilateral programs, to encourage multilateral aid efforts and could be counted on to match the contributions of far larger OPEC states, if a workable international fund were instituted. Concessional non-guaranteed loans would be forthcoming.

## LIBYA

The LARG has contributed to the Arab Development Fund and has made a number of financial contributions on a bilateral basis but would be unlikely to give more than a nominal sum to less politically oriented enterprises.

## NIGERIA

Nigeria has already offered nonconcessional loans to the IMF oil facility. It might be interested in a concessional-non-concessional mix, but probably would want some form of guarantees.

## SAUDI ARABIA

Although the Saudis have preferred up to now to deal with foreign aid on a bilateral basis, they have indicated a willingness to expand their contribution to the IMF Oil contingency fund, they have recently established a Development Fund (see above) which is available to all LDCs, and they have been prime movers behind the Islamic Fund which would benefit poor Moslem countries.

If a new international fund or a fund under IMF auspices were established with the cooperation of producer and consumer countries, the Saudis might be willing to commit some of their capital. The return on their capital would be a factor since they would expect to receive at least 6 percent on their advances. They would leave the administering of the loans to the Agency but would want that it obtain some kind of guarantees from the recipient governments making use of this facility. If such a fund were established and if the U.S. as the largest oil importer refused to issue any guarantees, the Saudis might well be reluctant to go very far with such an institution. If guarantees were made, the Saudis would probably be willing to see concessional loans made to the LDCs and a mix of concessional and commercial loans for industrialized countries which have friendly relations with the Saudis and which are faced with severe balance of payments problems.

One important factor in any Saudi cooperation would be whether Israel would benefit from such an institution. The Saudis could be expected to insist that Israel not have access to such a fund.

## VENEZUELA

Yes, as it already has done. The Government, until it is in a position to absorb funds internally, could place some $2 billion or more per year abroad. Recent Government loans have been nonconcessional and have been guaranteed, in the case of some loans to countries, by those countries' central banks. The Government has not shown any need for the guarantee of the U.S. or other, third country.

It should, however, be noted that in those instances where Venezuela has made loans to IFI's (IMF, IBRD, IDB) it has retained varying degrees of control of the funds at interest rates of approximately 8%.

10. Is the Government concerned about the possibility of one or more major developed nations facing financial instability or insolvency as a result of higher petroleum prices? Does the Government consider that event to have any adverse effect upon the Country? To what extent would the Government be willing to assist such a developed nation and how?

## ABU DHABI

Not really. Although fearful of general economic instability, Abu Dhabi finds it difficult to imagine that the higher petroleum prices of the past year by themselves might cause instability and insolvency in one or more developed nations. "Assistance" to developed countries will continue to be on straight commercial terms and geared to Abu Dhabi's own self interest.

## ALGERIA

No. And ideologically it believes that the developed countries have it coming to them anyway, as retribution for the way they've treated the LDC's for all these years. It certainly would not offer assistance to get any IDC's out of the hole.

## ECUADOR

The GOE has made no statements on the possibility that one or another of the developed countries risk insolvency as the result of higher petroleum prices.

## IRAN

Iran has provided large loans at commercial rates and advance payments to such countries as the U.K. and France and may do something similar for Italy. The Government has an intellectual understanding of the importance to it of a stable and solvent Western economy, but so far has shown no sign of willingness to sacrifice any part of its oil incomes to assist in shoring up the economy.

## IRAQ

No.

## KUWAIT

Kuwait is aware of and is concerned about the possibility of one or more developed nations facing financial instability as a result of current world economic instability - including oil's contribution thereto (see #8 above). It realizes that its current well-being and future development depend upon cooperation with western industrial nations. Politics being what they are, however, Kuwait assistance to developed nations will for the time being have to be measured in non-concessional terms: commercial loans, equity investment, non-speculation - out of self-interest - at times of currency instability, and, hopefully, stable, but probably continuingly high prices.

## LIBYA

As in 8 above the LARG has shown no evidence of concern for the fortunes of developed nations which they believe have been exploiting the poor nations all along.

## NIGERIA

The FMG has not addressed the problem. It would probably consider that rich developed countries should assist.

## SAUDI ARABIA

Yes. Italy is a good example. The Saudis have not indicated what steps they might take but it is not inconceivable that they might quietly arrange a loan to the Italian Government working through third parties at some stage if they considered that Italian communist party might otherwise take control.

## VENEZUELA

The Government is concerned about the economic difficulties of major developed nations. It is aware that these difficulties are threatening its export market for petroleum and non-petroleum products alike, the profitability and security of its short term investments, its access to essential imports, etc. The Government has not shown itself willing to assist the developed world directly. Instead, it has assigned its highest priorities, first to the country's own, internal development, and then to the development of its sister, Latin America nations.

11. Where does the Government intend to spend its petroleum revenues? Approximately how much would you estimate will be spent for the following items:

      (a)  Purchase of armaments?

      (b)  Purchase of food?

      (c)  Purchase of equipment and technology for diversification in the petroleum industry and related industries (e.g. petrochemicals)?

      (d)  Purchase of other manufactured goods and services from consuming countries?

      (e)  Purchase of foreign assets?

## ABU DHABI

Expressed in estimated percentages of yearly budget:

      (a)  10%.

      (b)  20%.

      (c)  10%.

      (d)  15%

      (e)  Remaining Funds not committed elsewhere.

## ALGERIA

Revenues will be used for general operational needs of Government and to finance development plan.

1973 IMF statistics Central Government Expenditures by Administrative Departments.

(a)  Total defense budget was 541.9 million dinars out of total budget of 6,082.5 million dinars.  4.192 dinars = $1.00.  No figures available on arms expenditures.

(b)  In 1973, 13.6 percent of imports were food. Valued at 1,191 million dinars out of total import bill of 8,724 million dinars.

(c)  Unavailable.  Total imports of investment goods was 35.4 percent of import bill.

(d)  Other semifinished and consumption goods 44 percent of total.

(e)  N.A.  prob. none.

ECUADOR

According to a study made in the Department in February 1974, approximately $625.8 million in petroleum revenues were to accrue to the state in 1974.  The destination of these funds were estimated as follows:

Destination of Estimated 1974
Ecuadorean Petroleum Revenue
(at $13.70 reference price)

|  | $ Million |
|---|---|
| Central Gov't | 285.6 |
| Gen'l Revenue | (159.0) |
| Earmarked |  |
| Military | ( 87.2) |
| Min. Public Health | ( 10.0) |
| Min. Social Welfare | ( 19.9) |
| Min. Agriculture | ( 9.5) |
| Nat'l Dev. Fund | 209.7 |
| Other Earmarked | 130.5 |
| Local Gov'ts | ( 14.2) |
| Universities | ( 12.0) |
| INECEL | ( 82.4) |
| Housing Bank | ( 19.9) |
| Port Authorities | ( .5) |
| CEPE | ( .5) |
| Educ. Credit Instit. | ( .6) |
| Central Bank | ( .4) |
| Total Revenue | 625.8 |

Additional Note:

The Government of Ecuador has established a national development fund which receives funds from all government receipts from petroleum sales beyond $7.80 a barrel. Some of the government receipts are used to subsidize low prices for certain commodities such as wheat, corn and beans. It is the intention of the GOE to invest in the construction of an oil refinery and certain petrochemical plants such as ammonia, LNG, etc., with products derived from natural gas in the Gulf of Guayaquil and from crude oil.

## IRAN

(a)  Purchase of armaments?  25-35% over next 3-5 years

(b)  Purchase of food?  5-10%

(c)  Purchase of equipment and technology for diversification in the petroleum industry and related industries (e.g. petrochemicals)?  3-5%

(d)  Purchase of other manufactured goods and services from consuming countries?  10-15%

(e)  Purchase of foreign assets?  5%

## IRAQ

Based on Ministry of Finance and Ministry of Planning 1974/75 budget estimates.  (millions of Iraqi dinars) *Available categories.

(a)  National defense 308.0

(b)  Agricultural development 190.0

(c) & (d)  Industry, transportation, and communication 345.0

(e)  Construction & social services 175.0

(f) Loans for investment by public organization 40.0

(g) Other investment expenditure 419.0

* NB These expenditures are from a budget that includes non-petroleum revenues; petroleum revenues, however, account
for about 90% of these funds.

## KUWAIT

Expressed in Estimated Percentages of Yearly Budget

(a) 10%

(b) 20%

(c) 10%

(d) 15%

(e) Remaining funds not committed elsewhere

## LIBYA

No reliable figures are available to us; possibly
they could be obtained from IMF. There is no evidence of any
intention to purchase foreign assets.

## NIGERIA

(a) Purchase of armaments? 5%

(b) Purchase of food? 10%

(c) Purchase of equipment and technology for
diversification in the petroleum industry and related      50%
Industries (e.g. petrochemicals)?

(d) Purchase of other manufactured goods and      10%
services from consuming countries?

(e) Purchase of foreign assets? 2%

## SAUDI ARABIA

Saudi Government expenditures outside of what is
earmarked for foreign aid is expected to rise from $4

billion in FY 74 to $16 billion by FY 80.  In this period, the Saudis will probably spend 30% of their budget on armaments (or 25 billion) which would be equal to 10% of estimated oil and non-oil revenues during this period.

    (a)   armaments - 10%

    (b)   food - 5%

    (c)   industrial
           diversification - 8%

    (d)   other manuf. goods - 15%

    (e)   foreign assets (remaining
           funds not committed    - 55%
           elsewhere less foreign aid)

## VENEZUELA

The Government is placing its revenues at home (e.g., expansion of agricultural, petrochemical, metallurgical production, etc.)  and abroad (e.g., international lending institutions, short term investments, bilateral arrangements, etc.).

(a)  Military expenditures - The 1975 budget bill submitted to the Congress calls for a defense budget of about $490 million or about 5% of the total budget.

This budget will probably reflect increased personnel costs rather than totally for equipment.

(b)  Purchase of food?
$125 million;

(c)  Purchase of equipment and technology for diversification in the petroleum industry and related industries (e.g. petrochemicals)?
$1 billion;

(d)  Purchase of other manufactured goods and services from consuming countries?

Venezuela's major trading partner and major consumer is the United States and we can expect that the

bulk of food and machinery purchases will come from the
United States particularly those involved in the upgrading
of the petroleum and petrochemical industries.

> (e)  Purchase of foreign assets?

> Minimal according to Government statements.

### C.  [§E.3]  Bilateral Agreements

12.  With what consuming nations has the Government entered
into long term (5 years or more) bilateral agreements within
the past four years?  What is the quid pro quo, either
implicit or explicit in each?

ABU DHABI

> None.

ALGERIA

> List not available and it would be major research
job to find out.  Does this refer to oil contracts, gas
contracts, or trade treaties in general.  Normally, terms of
treaties not published.  Also, there are contracts with
private Western companies, not governments.  This is a badly
presented question.

ECUADOR

> The GOE has entered into no long-term bilateral
agreements within the past four years.

IRAN

> No long-term agreements.

IRAQ

> Recent agreements with other governments have included
France, Spain, Italy, and Japan.  Unfortunately, confirmed detailed information on these agreements is not generally available.
The primary ingredients seem generally to include some assurance
of petroleum supplies in return for technological goods and services.

KUWAIT

None.

LIBYA

Information not available.

NIGERIA

None known of.

SAUDI ARABIA

Saudi Arabia entered into a three year, 200,000 bpd agreement with France early in 1974 in return for investment in a joint shipping scheme, and possibly a refinery in Saudi Arabia but at a price believed to be close to $11.00 a barrel. The French have been seeking to negotiate a longer term - 20 year deal - for 800,000 bpd but the Saudis so far have not agreed. If any longer term agreement is negotiated, political reasons would probably be important particularly if the Saudis believed the other country could play an important political role supportive of the Arab position in the Middle East.

VENEZUELA

The US, Guyana, Central America among others. These agreements, in the case of the LDC's, involve a combination of assistance for developing nations and return on the Government's excess petroleum revenues which are not placed domestically. There is also an implicit benefit to Venezuela in the form of an outward projection of its political influence.

13. Would the Government consider entering into further petroleum-related bilateral agreements? If so, what would the Government expect to achieve by so doing?

ABU DHABI

Long term petroleum-related bilateral agreements are not preferred at the present time. However, they might be considered should the guaranteed acquisition of arms or technology be considered necessary and probably would become popular if world demand for oil were clearly slackening.

## ALGERIA

Information not available.  If question were directed to GOA you can bet they wouldn't tell us.  It would be giving away trade secrets.

## ECUADOR

It is unlikely that the GOE would consider entering into any petroleum-related bilateral agreements.  It has been fairly successful in maximizing financial returns from its comparatively small petroleum possibilities over its short history as a producer, and it also gains certain political satisfactions in playing a maverick role.

## IRAN

Iran is limited by the existing agreement with the Consortium on the amount of oil it has available for bilateral deals.  It would probably enter such deals in exchange for assured supplies of certain raw materials and commodities, but would almost certainly insist that the bilateral agreement provide that the price of the oil would go up in step with the world market price.

## IRAQ

Probably, with Iraqi goals being primarily either political or the strengthening of its program of national development through the acquisition of greatly needed technological goods and services.

## KUWAIT

The development of national control over oil appears to be producing a GOK sales organ which will be desirous of maintaining a flexible position in the world market.  We do not now see Kuwait desiring to commit any significant portion of its production to long-term bilateral agreements, but this pattern could develop as a way of guaranteeing the availability of needed arms or technology - or if the present sellers market became a buyers one again.

## LIBYA

Possibly, but with basically political goals in mind.

NIGERIA

        Price agreements indexed to the price of capital
equipment necessary for Nigeria's economic development.

SAUDI ARABIA

        As Saudi Arabia gains full control of its oil re-
sources, it might consider bilateral arrangements in return
for certain food supply, hard-to-get technology, and guaranteed
and favorable entry of industrial products manufactured in
Saudi Arabia (such as methanol, petrochemicals).  But in all
likelihood, an important motivation would probably be to
enhance the Kingdom's or the Arab's political position in
the Middle East (see #12).

VENEZUELA

        Yes.  The Government would expect to receive a good
return on its investment and, in those cases in which it is
to receive petroleum produced at some future date, an extension
of its oil reserves now estimated to last some 15 years at
current rates of production.


    D.    [§3.4]  Consumer-Producer Discussions

14.  Does the Government favor commencing multilateral discussions, formal or informal, with consuming nations?  If not,
why?  If yes, when would the Government prefer such talks to
commence?  Which countries would be participants or within
what organizational structure, if any, would the Government
prefer such discussions to take place?  What subjects would
the Government expect to be discussed?

ABU DHABI

        The Government of Abu Dhabi would support multi-
lateral discussions on the same principle as would Kuwait
(see item #4 on Kuwait questionnaire).

ALGERIA

        Yes.  It is active proponent of producer/consumer
and DC/LDC conference to discuss all commodities, not just
hydrocarbons.  This is tied in with their advocacy of Special
UNGA next fall to discuss restructuring of world economy and

fairer share of world's wealth for have-nots. They will buy
French proposal for producer/consumer conference limited to
oil for a starter however. Want it to take place asap --
probably spring 1975. Participants would be those agreed on
within OPEC and between French-U.S. (Martinique talks) and
within International Energy Agency. GOA has not specified
precisely which countries should participate.

## ECUADOR

The Government has not yet pronounced its position on the proposal of the French and American presidents
to hold a meeting between producers and consumers. It is
likely to follow the position of the majority of OPEC members.
The GOE would be likely to approach such a meeting with
considerable caution and even reluctance if it appeared that
a serious confrontation could not be averted. President
Rodriquez has told our Ambassador that producers and consumers should cooperate, but he has not elaborated on what
form this cooperation should take.

## IRAN

Iran has since early 1974 been calling for consumer/
producer conferences to start as soon as possible. Participants and framework have been left vague, as has the agenda.
Indexation of oil prices to prices of other commodities is
almost certainly a main item Iran would want to discuss.

## IRAQ

The Government of Iraq is visibly cool toward the idea
of consumer-producer talks, having repeatedly rejected the concept of "confrontation." There is, however, some indication
that it would go along with the French idea for some form of
such a conference, outside the framework of any established
organizational structure. Primary topics of Iraqi interest
would be the general one of raw materials, the availability
of technology and import of capital goods, and the role of the
LDC's.

## KUWAIT

Yes.  Talks could commence just as soon as the Kuwaitis were convinced the consumer group would sincerely tackle the totality of inflationary problems and not just attempt to "force" lower oil prices and higher production. Kuwait has shown a preference for discussions with industrial countries within the C-20/IMF mechanisms.

## LIBYA

The Libyans have taken no formal position on this issue, but judging from their hardline position they would expect any such discussions to deal with all commodities, including those produced by the oil-consuming countries, which the Libyans feel are overpriced and exploitative.

## NIGERIA

Nigeria would probably favor formal discussions soon, but the government has not spoken of the issue.

## SAUDI ARABIA

Yes.  Oil Minister Yamani has for many months proposed starting with a limited consumer-producer conference composed of 5 consumers (U.S., EC representative, Japan, India, Brazil) and 5 producer countries (Saudi Arabia, Iran, Venezuela, Nigeria, and Algeria) as a prelude to a larger producer-consumer conference.  The Saudis are interested in discussing not only petroleum but other raw materials as well which are subject to depletion.

## VENEZUELA

Yes.  The Government has noted that it is waiting for the industrialized world to agree to such discussions. The Government has suggested that they take place at the UN, that all countries participate, and that the agenda deal with a more equitable distribution of the world's wealth.

15.  If the Government favors the immediate commencing of discussions with consumers, what would you expect to be its reaction to a refusal or failure on the part of consumers to begin discussions?  What action might it take?

## ABU DHABI

This question has been largely overtaken by the Ford -- Giscard d' Estaing meeting in Martinique, which set a March 1975 target for the preparatory consumer/producer meeting. Should a full, substantive conference fail to materialize, however, we would expect the Government of Abu Dhabi to feel little pressure and simply to sit back and wait for future developments between larger producers and consumers.

## ALGERIA

In view of recent developments, consumers will not refuse; therefore question is obsolete.

## ECUADOR

See answer to Question 14.

## IRAN

Primarily verbal, although it might use such a failure as an excuse to join with other OPEC states in a new price rise before next October.

## IRAQ

Not applicable.

## KUWAIT

The Ford-Giscard d'Estaing meetings in Martinique December 14-16 have set a March 1975 target for a preliminary producer/consumer meeting, and thus refusal on the part of consumers to begin discussions now appears unlikely. However, should a full, substantive conference fail to materialize, Kuwait can, we believe, be counted on to support continued efforts to arrange such a conference, subject to the conditions outlined in item 14 above.

## LIBYA

Not applicable.

NIGERIA

Not applicable.

SAUDI ARABIA

This question is somewhat academic in light of the
Martinique communique between Presidents Ford and Giscard
d'Estaing.  The Saudis will be watching to see how quickly
we move.  They would be willing to start discussions as
soon as they felt the consumer group was prepared to discuss the totality of inflationary problems and not just
to talk about bringing down oil prices and increasing production.  The Saudis would be interested in indexation of
oil to other raw materials and would want to see how the
consumer countries would be prepared to approach this subject.
If, despite the Martinique communique, nothing occurs in 1975
in the way of a producer-consumer conference, the Saudis
will simply continue to support joint OPEC action on oil
prices and might also decide to take action to reduce oil
production somewhat.

VENEZUELA

The Government would continue to search for new
ways to encourage discussions.  Actions might include new
calls by the President for discussions, encouragement of
other LDC's to advocate them, and diplomatic endeavors
through OPEC and other international forums to bring them
about.


16.  What is the Government's attitude toward the International
Energy Agency ("IEA"), the International Energy Program ("IEP"),
and the Emergency Allocation Plans recently conceived by the
Energy Coordinating Group?

ABU DHABI

To our knowledge, the Government of Abu Dhabi
has taken no specific, public position with respect to IEA,
IEP, and the Emergency Allocation Plans.  We would, however,
expect its attitude toward these organizations and plans to
be similar to that expressed by Kuwait (see item #16 on
Kuwait questionnaire).

## ALGERIA

GOA has roundly condemned IEA and IEP as instruments of confrontation designed to further exploitation of producers. They regard IEA as cartel of consumers, and nothing we say will change their minds.

## ECUADOR

We are unaware of specific positions on the IEA or other plans.

## IRAN

It claims to favor consumers organizing to conserve oil, but has warned against the use of the IEA to set up a confrontation with producers.

## IRAQ

The Government of Iraq has generally responded very negatively to any suggestion that the consuming nations may be attempting to coordinate their energy policies. Iraq has been very sensitive to any sign of what it sees as the "ganging up" of Western consumer nations against the oil producers.

## KUWAIT

The Government of Kuwait has (1) noted with interest the reaction of these organizations; (2) reiterated its support of increased conservation efforts by consumer states; and (3) stressed that any consumer efforts to "artifically manipulate" the world oil market and force down the price of oil would be considered a hostile policy by OPEC and one doomed to failure.

## LIBYA

Although we have seen no public statment on the IEA or IEP per se, the Libyans view U.S. efforts to coordinate the policies of consuming nations as hostile and threatening.

## NIGERIA

These institutions are semi-confrontational.

## SAUDI ARABIA

The Saudis see the IEA as a hostile act directed against the producer countries. They also consider that if the IEP is used for purposes other than emergency sharing, it would mean confrontation with the producer countries. The Saudis have not been very vocal about the IEA and IEP partly because they believe that sharing agreements are difficult to implement and will be difficult to carry out. However, they have indicated that if the consumer nations choose to use these instruments to try and bring down oil prices, the consumers would come out second best.

## VENEZUELA

The Government has voiced little opinion on the three. It generally favors conversationist practices on the part of the consuming nations, presumably, however, only to the point at which the practices would significantly affect Government revenues. The Government is embarked on a conservationist program of its own, having announced, as noted above, that it plans to reduce petroleum production from today's 3.0 million b/d to 2.0 million b/d in 1980.

17. Does the Government believe that a viable "consumer cartel" is a possibility? Why or why not?

## ABU DHABI

Yes. For the same reasons as do the Kuwaitis (see item #17 on Kuwait questionnaire).

## ALGERIA

See above. For them it already exists. They claim however that producers will not cave in to pressures from IEA.

## ECUADOR

The Embassy has reported that certain members of the GOE believe that the drop in offers for Ecuadorean crude is due to some form of international conspiracy on the part of oil companies or even the U.S. Government to gang up on Ecuador. Although the GOE has not made a public statement concerning its estimates for the possibility of establishing a "Consumer cartel", it would no doubt look upon such an institution with much suspicion.

## IRAN

Not clear.  Probably not, as long as OPEC maintains its solidarity.

## IRAQ

Although it regularly condemns any efforts in this direction, as noted, there has been little indication that Iraq thinks such efforts will really succeed, at least under present conditions.

## KUWAIT

Given the size, strength, and technical know-how of the industrialized states, Kuwait assumes that more effective economic cooperation is achievable between them than has been the case recently.  It definitely believes that a "consumer cartel" built about a nucleus of these states is a possibility.

## LIBYA

The Libyans seem to believe that such a cartel is virtually a reality but this view grows out of their highly emotional view of the problem and is not based upon rational analysis.

## NIGERIA

Yes.  Nigeria believes the major industrial consumers have the power to exert more influence on oil events than has been the case.

## SAUDI ARABIA

The Saudis believe a consumer cartel would be very hard to organize because of the many conflicting interests. They also believe that oil availability could be used as a device to wean away countries heavily dependent on oil from joining such a consumer cartel.

## VENEZUELA

The Government has not expressed itself on the topic but tends in general to urge against confrontation and to argue the need for producer-consumer dialogue.

18.  How would the Government react if the U.S. Government
imposed a ceiling on the maximum FOB price of imported
petroleum and said ceiling were 50¢ below the price of
the Country's participation crude?  How would it react if
the ceiling were $2.00 below?  What would be its reaction
if such action were taken by all consuming nations?

## ABU DHABI

If the U.S. acted alone, the result would be the
removal of approximately 100 thousand barrels/day of Abu
Dhabi crude sold to the U.S. markets.  If all consuming
nations imposed FOB ceilings of anywhere from 50¢ to $2.00
below the current participation sale price, Abu Dhabi would
panic and run to Kuwait and Saudi Arabia for advice on what
should be done.  Since on purely political terms, the
survival of Abu Dhabi as well as of the United Arab Emirates
depends upon good relations with both Saudi Arabia and Iran,
we doubt that Abu Dhabi would bolt the common OPEC position
under these circumstances.

## ALGERIA

Impossible to answer.  We import only about 120,000
barrels a day of crude from Algeria -- about 10 percent
of their production.  If we refused to pay the price they
would shift their sales to Europe where they have well
established and ready markets.

## ECUADOR

Ecuador, as a country which once expounded its
theory of "economic aggression" before several international
gatherings, would be likely to exercise every opportunity
to express its disagreement with any attempt to force prices
down.  It did not participate in the Arab oil boycott of
late 1973 and early 1974.  Because of its small size in
terms of exports, Ecuador would be forced to follow the decision
of the majority of OPEC members in reacting to an action
taken in concert by all consuming nations.

## IRAN

The US market is not sufficiently important to
Iran for such a measure to have much effect.  Furthermore,

Iran does not sell its oil directly to major consumers, but sells through the companies. If all consumers joined in, it is possible, although not certain, that Iran would join in a total OPEC embargo - assuming that the foreign exchange surpluses it has built up are sufficient to keep its economy going for the rather short time it would expect a consumer embargo to last. Again, much would depend on whether OPEC maintained its solidarity.

## IRAQ

Iraq sells very little oil to the U.S. Under these conditions, it would simply sell oil elsewhere.

## KUWAIT

On December 18, 1974, Kuwait apparently eliminated sales of "participation" oil in favor of a "one-price" system, having an initial $10.15 per barrel (31° API) price tag for principal concessionaires. A unilateral US maximum FOB price ceiling at 50¢ or more below this level would simply remove from the US market the quite small amount (about 45 thousand barrels/day) of Kuwaiti petroleum currently reaching it. If, however, all consuming nations took similar steps the fact would be in the fire and Kuwait would stand with its OPEC partners in victory or defeat in the ensuing confrontation.

## LIBYA

Since Libya exports little petroleum to the U.S., and in fact has never lifted its embargo, there would probably be very little reaction to a lowered price ceiling. It is impossible to predict what would result if this action were taken by all consuming nations, although it is a safe bet that the Libyans would put up a stiff fight with whatever means and influence they could mobilize.

## NIGERIA

Nigeria would begin looking for alternative markets for its crude. If all consuming nations tried to drop the ceiling by $2.00, Nigeria would likely join other OPEC countries in restricting production.

## SAUDI ARABIA

If the US Government were to impose a price ceiling 50 cents below the present $10.24 base price, no Saudi oil would move to American markets. The same would be true if the ceiling were $2.00 below the base price. If the US sought to do this, the Saudis might well decide to cut back their production by the amount they formerly furnished to the U.S. (about 700,000 bpd) since they might interpret this as confrontation.

If all consuming nations were to take these measures, the Saudis would not act independently but would probably stand with their OPEC partners since they would definitely see this as confrontation. The Saudis believe that consumer nations, especially the U.S., have for too long felt that OPEC countries were incapable of cooperation and would not be able to continue to do so over an extended period. Since alternative energy sources are too far in the future to help with the present situation and are likely to be very costly once they are developed, any pressure on oil prices will have to come from belt tightening by the consumer nations and through discussions with the producer nations. But since many producer nations, especially Saudi Arabia, can cut back production sharply without hurting their economies, consumer nations will have to make attractive offers to gain producer cooperation.

## VENEZUELA

The Government would react strongly and negatively to such ceilings. It would presumably first work, through OPEC, to find a solution which would tie the price of industrialized country goods to that of the LDC's raw commodities in some type of index. Were this not possible, then the Government might seek a more pragmatic solution involving petroleum prices alone. (We should not forget the other important US interests in Venezuela such as $3 billion of private investment and an annual export market for about $1.5 billion of US goods and services.)

19. What role will foreign petroleum companies be playing in the Country one year from now? Five years from now? If any foreign companies now have equity oil or other

preferential supply arrangements with the Country, for how long do you expect such arrangements to continue?

## ABU DHABI

Abu Dhabi has announced that it will follow the Saudi example and will quickly acquire 100% ownership of oil concessions (i.e. the remaining 40%) operating within its territory. We expect this full nationalization will occur sometime during 1975 and that from then on the companies will find themselves in the position of being combined service contractors/preferred customers.

## ALGERIA

Foreign petroleum companies are in joint exploration ventures with SONATRACH, and number includes five U.S. firms with actual agreements and three under negotiation. Their technology is required for drilling, seismic work, etc., but terms very clearly restrict duration of arrangement; sharing if oil is found and exploited, and control of every aspect is retained by State Oil and Gas Corp., SONATRACH. Under these contracts the foreign companies get preferential share, but not necessarily price; there are some special arrangements with French oil companies but these are supposedly to be ended eventually and all foreigners put on same footing. Excellent description of GOA policy in this regard is to be found in Petroleum Press Service of October 1973, in article entitled "Sonatrach Rewrites its Contracts." Prices in article are outdated but basic info remains. Petroleum Intelligence Weekly of fall 1973 also had good rundown on subject.

## ECUADOR

The GOE took over a 25% participation in the equity of the Texaco-Gulf consortium in June 1974. Following his return from the September meeting of OPEC members in Vienna, former Minister of Natural Resources Jarrin announced to the press that the timetable for taking over a majority share (51%) of the consortium would be advanced from 1980 to "some time in the near future". Although domestic political considerations require that the new Minister of Natural Resources maintain this tough position, it is probable that the GOE will wait until its financial situation is clarified and managerial possibilities are improved. This may take two or three years. Although these same domestic political considerations, the world petroleum situation and OPEC moves will probably be the major factors in forcing a decision to take over, it is almost certain that the GOE will have taken over at least its 51% within five years. At present Texaco-Gulf markets only their own equity oil (75% minus royalty and internal Ecuadorean consumption). If the GOE continues to have difficulty selling its own participation crude a sales contract with T-G is not out of the question.

## IRAN

Foreign oil companies have been involved in Iran primarily as purchasers of crude since 1951 and should continue to be so involved for the foreseeable future -- albeit with steadily waning influence.

## IRAQ

Iraq has nationalized all of its oil production except for part of the Basra Petroleum Company; estimates vary from about 80% to 92% of the oil production now being under government ownership. There have been indications that the government is now thinking about making that figure 100%, although no definite timetable has been given.

## KUWAIT

Although one year from now, Gulf and BP may still share between them nominal control of 40 percent of the Kuwait Oil Company, they have in fact already become little more than preferred (i.e., 30¢/barrel off the established price) customers. Five years from now, full nationalization of the concession is sure to have been accomplished. However, given the traditionally very good relations between the GOK and Gulf and BP, we would expect a special, preferential arrangement to continue to be accorded to the companies.

## LIBYA

The LARG is on record as favoring the "liberation of the oil sector from foreign control and exploitation". Since 1971 the Libyans have totally or partially nationalized all foreign oil companies operating in the country and, while the exact schedule cannot be predicted, the process is expected to continue until all foreign ownership has

been eliminated.  Those companies which were only partially
nationalized retain equity arrangements which will last
until full nationalization.  As part of their settlements
a number of companies have obtained buy-back rights but
these normally do not provide for preferential prices.

## NIGERIA

Several companies say an equity role for them
may continue for only about 10 more years.

## SAUDI ARABIA

A year from now, ARAMCO will probably be fully
owned by the Saudi Government.  By then, ARAMCO's former
owners will probably have accepted in return for 100% participation guaranteed access to a certain percentage of
Saudi crude at the prevailing market price.  The former
owners will, for a fee to be determined, continue to provide
management, operational, and technical services, and undertake exploration activities.  This situation will also probably
prevail five years from now except that ARAMCO will probably
by then have become the prime mover in the Kingdom's
industrialization.

The Saudis want to preserve ARAMCO which they
view as a unique institution which combines managerial and
technical capability.  Not only do they want ARAMCO to
continue to operate the Kingdom's principal oil-producing
facilities but because it is able to undertake major projects,
they will want ARAMCO to expand its operations, especially
LPG production which is scheduled to increase 250% by 1977,
and enter new fields as well.  ARAMCO is likely to take over
responsibility for all electric power production in the
Eastern province and handle all gas gathering and distribution and processing in the province.  Thus, accessibility
to Saudi oil by the former owner companies will be tied
directly or indirectly to the technological transfer and
support for a Saudi-owned but still a largely US staffed-
at-the-technical-level ARAMCO.

## VENEZUELA

Foreign petroleum concessions are expected to
revert to Venezuelan ownership in 1975.  Based on the recent

settlement with US iron ore companies, the Government agreement with foreign petroleum companies could involve Venezuelan management, but service contracts and some sort of continuation of current supply levels to individual companies.  But all of this remains to be worked out.

20.  What would be the effect on the supply and price of the Country's petroleum if all preferential supply arrangements in favor of foreign companies ceased and the Country sold its petroleum to all buyers at a single price?

## ABU DHABI

Supply would probably decrease somewhat as the country's inexperienced marketing organ tried and failed to reach alternative contracts quickly with independent companies.  The former concessionaries would, however, continue to buy a majority of the production they always took -- except at a price anywhere from 30¢ to 50¢ per barrel more.

## ALGERIA

Question non applicable; very small portion of Algeria's oil affected and GOA's total production relatively minor anyway.

## ECUADOR

The marketing and supply situation would become more chaotic than it already is as the GOE sought ineffectively to extract the highest prices possible.  It is likely that output would decline.

## IRAN

None.

## IRAQ

See preceding question.

## KUWAIT

The supply would remain about the same, and the price for the majority of the 2 to 2.5 million barrels daily we expect Kuwait to be producing during 1975 would go up by about 30¢ per barrel.

## LIBYA

This is impossible to say.

## NIGERIA

Unknown.

## SAUDI ARABIA

The supply would probably remain the same assuming that they used ARAMCO as a marketing organ. If PETROMIN were used as the marketing organ, the supply might decline somewhat because of PETROMIN's lack of experience and bureaucratic inability to handle at this time the sale of large quantities of oil. Should this occur, presumably, the cost to the consumer would go up by another 30-50 cents per barrel since the majors would continue to buy a substantial amount of their crude from the Saudis.

## VENEZUELA

The effect would depend upon what that single price would be and upon what actions other major producing nations took vis-a-vis their markets. If the "single price" is at the current price, and if the foreign companies were unable effectively to resist the Government move, then the supply and price of the country's petroleum would not be affected. Some Venezuelans, however, suggest that in the elimination of the private oil companies lie the seeds of a reduction in the price of oil.

21. To what extent is the Government or its national oil company (if any) able to explore for petroleum, develop reserves, refine its production and market its crude or refined products abroad without the assistance of foreign petroleum companies? Will this situation be different five years from now? How?

## ABU DHABI

The Abu Dhabi National Oil Company (ADNOC) engages in none of the activities listed, and could only do so with foreign technical assistance it hopes to acquire from established sources in increasing amounts during the next few years. Five years from now, ADNOC will still be learning the trade and not yet able to engage in independently in the activities listed.

## ALGERIA

It is about 80 percent dependent on foreign technology for exploration for oil; 100 percent dependent for construction of LNG plants and refineries; can operate the LNG and refinery facilities with about 95 percent Algerian personnel but the top 5 percent are foreign; Sonatrach sells to foreign petroleum companies for most part. Estimate GOA will depend on foreigners for top-ranking technological people for 10-15, maybe 20 years yet, even with enormous training programs now planned. Sonatrach contracts direct for much of its foreign personnel and for services; it does not necessarily work through foreign petroleum companies.

## ECUADOR

At the present time, the GOE and CEPE do not have the technical personnel available to explore, develop or refine its production. Its poor marketing record has already been discussed. There is no reason why experience and education will not result in greater Ecuadorean participation in all of these functions within five years, although the result will probably fall considerably short of U.S. efficiency standards.

## IRAN

The national oil company has some experience in these fields and is steadily gaining more. Its experience should continue to develop. Even now, its dependence on foreign companies for advice and technical assistance is small and growing less.

## IRAQ

In June 1974, the GOI cancelled negotiations with foreign oil companies that might have led to special pricing arrangements in return for undertaking exploratory operations. However, the GOI is not now in a position to handle extensive exploration on its own. It is therefore probable that some foreign companies will become involved in this and related work, though it almost certainly will be done on a purely service, not concessionary, basis for the forseeable future.

## KUWAIT

The Kuwait National Oil Company (KNPC) has explored – so far unsuccessfully – for petroleum in a joint venture with Hispanoil, and refines and markets petroleum products abroad on its own hook. It has no developed reserves of its own and with the limited prospects for new finds in Kuwait plus the GOK's now fostering the new Kuwait Oil, Gas, and Energy Company (KOGEC) to run government acquisition from major concessionary companies, it is doubtful whether any reserves will be developed in the future. As a country, however, Kuwait is rapidly developing the requisite experience and expertise to carry out the activities listed on its own; this process should be complete in five years.

## LIBYA

The Libyan National Oil Company explores, develops and markets oil. Libya, however, lacks the skilled manpower to do this on its own and remains highly dependent upon foreign oil companies and foreign nationals hired under contract. The stated goal of 100 percent independence is unrealistic for the foreseeable future.

## NIGERIA

None now. Nigeria expects to have the necessary expertise by the early 1980's.

## SAUDI ARABIA

PETROMIN has relatively little capability. However, the Saudis want to preserve ARAMCO as an institution (see above). ARAMCO would operate the present facilities, do exploration, and probably marketing. The Ras Tanura refinery might operate as a joint venture with ARAMCO's former owner companies with marketing of petroleum products handled separately or through ARAMCO.

It is possible that five years from now, a new national institution will be extablished to market petroleum and petroleum products abroad leaving PETROMIN to handle domestic distribution of petroleum products.  However, much will depend on whether the Saudi Government is able to preserve the ARAMCO organization and the cooperation it gets from other owner companies.  If the Saudis succeed, ARAMCO will probably handle marketing of most crude and refined products abroad.

VENEZUELA

The Government ability to explore and develop reserves without the foreign companies is limited.  Refineries in the country now employ very few foreigners and presumably can operate under Venezuelan management without significant problem.  In five years, the Government will undoubtedly have significantly increased its capability to explore and develop without foreign assistance.  Marketing capability of the state-owned company is today very limited but will probably increase.


22.  In your opinion, have foreign petroleum companies negotiating supply arrangements in the Country been successful in obtaining the lowest possible price?  If not, has it been simply an inability to negotiate a better price (if so, why?) or the existence of other factors (e.g. maintaining access to supply) which has caused the companies to settle for a higher price?  Do you believe a U.S. Government petroleum corporation or a U.S. agency could negotiate a lower price?

ABU DHABI

Response for Abu Dhabi is identical to that for Kuwait item #22.

ALGERIA

No basis on which to reply, except to note that Sonatrach has been obliged to drop from its posted price of over $16 a bbl. in January 1974 to around $12 because of buyer resistance.

## ECUADOR

Texaco-Gulf have a large, unamortized investment in facilities in Ecuador (about $300 million). The field has been in production only about 16 months. After the basic tax formula was negotiated in 1973 T-G have had little control over the price which has been moved up steadily in response to OPEC moves. A U.S. Government corporation could probably negotiate a slightly better price.

## IRAN

As long as they can maintain their profit levels, the companies have no interest in keeping prices low -- in fact, they have an interest in seeing prices go up and provide them with windfall inventory profits. Those considerations should not be important to a US national procurement agency, but such an agency would have other difficulties -- mainly that every decision on foreign sources would be political.

## IRAQ

Not applicable. Considering the state of U.S.-Iraqi relations, the chances of U.S. interests, private or government, getting a lower price are virtually nil.

## KUWAIT

Given the disadvantageous position from which the companies have had to bargain under the growing and insistent adherence by the producer governments to the concept of the "law of changing circumstances", in a time of general inflation of basic prices in other sectors, and in light of the ceaseless whipsawing tactics of the producing countries, we feel the companies have been lucky to negotiate prices and guaranteed supplies at the levels they have over the past three years. The hope of maintaining access to supply has, of course, been one of the key factors in company acceptance of higher prices in Kuwait. Maybe a US agency or US petroleum corporation could have negotiated some what lower prices during this period, but direct USG involvement in crude purchases would at the same time increase the Arab purchasing governments' tendency to use oil as a weapon in the Middle East political context.

## LIBYA

The Libyans do very little negotiating, except on their own terms. A U.S. corporation would be unable to affect this situation and given the Libyan attitude probably would be less able than a private company to negotiate a lower price.

## NIGERIA

Nigeria has followed other OPEC pricing arrangements, so direct negotiations between the companies and the FMG have been relatively unimportant. Doubtful if a U.S. institution could have done better.

## SAUDI ARABIA

Since oil shifted from a buyers to a sellers market in 1970/71, the oil companies have been in an increasingly disadvantageous position in trying to hold down prices. They probably have done as well as might be expected but have been faced with circumstances beyond their control, particularly during the October 1973 war when oil production was cut back thereby giving OPEC countries an opportunity to unilaterally exact a major increase in prices. Since then, the companies have feared that they would lose access to their oil if they tried to force a lower price because they realized that many producers could now easily cut back production without hurting their economies.

While a US government-owned oil corporation could become a single point for purchasing crude, it is unlikely that it would be able to negotiate any significant lower price since the producer governments through their ownership of oil resources now have the power to determine oil production, and hence affect the price of oil. Making purchases through a US oil corporation would probably also put oil supply in an even greater political context than it is now leaving no flexibility for trade-offs and switches (as was possible during the last Middle East war) in the event of another Arab-Israel conflict when an embargo would be reinstituted.

## VENEZUELA

The companies have been unable to withstand Government pressure for higher prices. If a U.S. Government petroleum corporation replaced U.S. private companies, it could possibly negotiate a lower price by including in agreements non-petroleum factors not available to private companies.

23.   Are U.S. companies operating in the Country  generally concerned about their future access to crude?  If so, is the concern centered on a fear of general reduced production or fear of competition from other petroleum companies?  Are the fears justified?

## ABU DHABI

Yes.  The companies' fears are justified ones based upon anticipated competition from other petroleum companies offering ever-higher bids in an effort to entice, more and more direct selling.  Working in the concessionary companies advantage is the current, but temporary, lack of experience by the Government in direct sales to independent companies.

## ALGERIA

Not applicable.  U.S. companies involved in joint ventures have not yet made significant strikes so question of their continued access to their production has not yet come up.

## ECUADOR

T-G obtains relatively so little of its crude from Ecuador that their principal concern is more likely to be to recoup their investment rather than maintain access to crude.

## IRAN

They are worried, primarily because they fear at some time Iran will decide to do all its own marketing and refuse to deal with the companies.

## IRAQ

There are no U.S. oil companies operating in Iraq, although two U.S. companies, Mobil and Exxon, have a residual interest in their expropriated shares of the BPC.  Negotiations have recently reopened to settle the exact status of these companies' interest in BPC operations.

## KUWAIT

Yes. The concern is based upon justified fears of competition from other oil companies plus possibly reduced production as a result either of Kuwait oil conservation policies or its disenchantment with the lack of security and return on the capital investment of oil proceeds.

## LIBYA

The best source for this information would be the companies themselves: Exxon, Mobil, Occidental, Continental, Marathon, Amerada Hess.

## NIGERIA

Not unusually concerned. The companies believe their marketing apparatus will be useful to the Nigerians for some time.

## SAUDI ARABIA

Yes. The ARAMCO owner companies are concerned lest they be replaced by independent American oil companies and especially their European and Japanese competitors. These fears are probably justified. Since the Europeans and Japanese are more dependent on oil from the Saudis than is the U.S., their governments can be expected to give their nationals and oil companies direct support in providing services to Saudi Arabia's oil production operations should ARAMCO be dismantled because the former owner companies decided to walk away and encouraged American employees of ARAMCO to leave.

## VENEZUELA

Yes. The concern relates to probable nationalization of the industry in 1975 and thus is centered on the loss of a major source of petroleum supplies brought about by political factors rather than supply-demand factors. In addition, however, tapering off of production and conservationist-inspired cutback suggest a declining level of supply for everybody.

# PERSONNEL OF NOSSAMAN, WATERS, KRUEGER, MARSH & RIORDAN CONTRIBUTING TO THE STUDY

## Legal Staff

Robert B. Krueger
Harold Marsh, Jr.
Thomas L. Caps
Jeffrey L. DuRocher
Howard D. Coleman
Bruce G. Merritt
Paul R. Alanis
Thomas J. Weiss
Sarah R. Giffen
Janice Stewart

## Word Processing Center Staff

Sandra F. Cobos
Kathleen L. Cooke
Sharron M. Dunford, Supervisor
Michelina E. Durflinger
Maureen E. Evans
Joyce M. Topolse, Supervisor
Bonita L. Taylor
Rosaleen F. Tillman
Joyce M. Wachtman

Forrest P. Dewey - Business
   Manager and Study Security
   Officer

Sylvia Hoffman - Firm Librarian
Charlotte Robison - Xeroxing

## Project Secretaries

Mary Hodkinson
Ronni E. Spickard
Susan K. Yates

## Secretarial Staff

Barbara A. Boots
Dulce M. Conde
Connie Cruz
Randa K. Day
Carolyn E. Fariss
Betty R. Frazier
Sandi J. Goss
Babs A. Hood
Linda M. Ito
Susan G. Kaplan
Cathy M. Lewis
Toni Michalowski
Rae A. Moore
Sharon L. Nicholson
Dolores M. Pinho
Sherry L. Schoetensack
Cecilia E. Thompson
Linda S. Toussaint

## Independent Economic Advisers

Walter J. Mead
Russell O. Jones

## ABOUT THE AUTHOR

ROBERT B. KRUEGER, a senior partner in the Los Angeles law firm of Nossaman, Waters, Krueger, Marsh, and Riordan, has published over a dozen articles on the legal aspects of the use of land, oil, and other natural resources.  In 1968, acting as his firm's Project Director, he supervised the influential Study of the Outer Continental Shelf Lands of the United States for the Public Land Law Review Commission.  From 1970 to 1973 he chaired the California Advisory Commission on Marine and Coastal Resources. He is a member of the National Security Council's Advisory Committee on the Law of the Sea, and since 1973 has served as adviser to the United States delegation to the UN Seabeds Committee and the Third UN Law of the Sea Conference.

Mr. Krueger holds an A.B. degree from the University of Kansas and a law degree from the University of Michigan.

RELATED TITLES
Published by
Praeger Special Studies


THE ENERGY CRISIS AND U.S. FOREIGN POLICY*
                    edited by
                    Joseph S. Szyliowicz and
                    Bard E. O'Neill


ISRAEL AND IRAN:  Bilateral Relationships and
Effect on the Indian Ocean Basin
                    Robert B. Reppa, Sr.


MIDDLE EAST OIL AND U.S. FOREIGN POLICY:
With Special Reference to the U.S. Energy Crisis
                    Soshana Klebanoff


THE MULTINATIONAL CORPORATION AS A FORCE IN
LATIN AMERICAN POLITICS:  A Case Study of the
International Petroleum Company in Peru
                    Adalberto J. Pinelo


THE SOVIET ENERGY BALANCE: Natural Gas, Other
Fossil Fuels, and Alternative Power Sources
                    Iain F. Elliot


STRATEGIC AND LONG-RANGE PLANNING FOR THE
MULTINATIONAL CORPORATION
                    John Snow Schwendiman


*Also available in paperback as a PSS Student Edition